This is a volume in

THE UNIVERSITY OF MICHIGAN HISTORY OF THE MODERN WORLD

Upon completion, the series will consist of the following volumes:

The United States to 1865 *by Michael Kraus*

The United States since 1865 *by Foster Rhea Dulles*

Canada: A Modern History *by John Bartlet Brebner*

Latin America: A Modern History *by J. Fred Rippy*

Great Britain to 1688: A Modern History *by Maurice Ashley*

Great Britain since 1688: A Modern History *by K. B. Smellie*

France: A Modern History *by Albert Guérard*

Germany: A Modern History *by Marshall Dill, Jr.*

Italy: A Modern History *by Denis Mack Smith*

Russia and the Soviet Union: A Modern History *by Warren B. Walsh*

The Near East: A Modern History *by William Yale*

The Far East: A Modern History *by Nathaniel Peffer*

India: A Modern History *by Percival Spear*

The Southwest Pacific to 1900: A Modern History *by C. Hartley Grattan*

The Southwest Pacific since 1900: A Modern History *by C. Hartley Grattan*

Spain: A Modern History *by Rhea Marsh Smith*

Africa to 1875: A Modern History *by Robin Hallett*

Africa since 1875: A Modern History *by Robin Hallett*

Eastern Europe: A Modern History *by John Erickson*

THE UNITED STATES
TO 1865

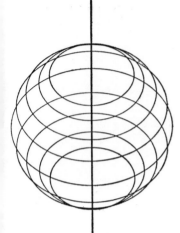

The University of Michigan History of the Modern World

Edited by Allan Nevins and Howard M. Ehrmann

THE
UNITED STATES
TO 1865

BY MICHAEL KRAUS

NEW EDITION
REVISED AND ENLARGED

Ann Arbor: The University of Michigan Press

Preface

The creation of a new society in America is one of the great epics of mankind. It is my hope that I have been able to capture at least a trace of that epic in this historical narrative. Each generation, in its turn, thought to begin the world again. Out of the will of the people, plus generally wise leadership, good fortune, and nature's abundance, a nation was created. Its growth, its trials, its failures, and successes to 1865 are the theme of this volume.

Professor Allan Nevins has given generously of his time and experience in counseling me. My wife, Vera Edelstadt, offered unflagging encouragement.

The new revised edition contains a fresh chapter, "The Gift of the Negro," and added material on Negro participation in America's wars. The "Suggested Readings" have also been updated to include some of the important books published in the past decade.

Stony Point, N.Y., Sept. 1968

Contents

BOOK 1

THE NEW WORLD

THE HISTORY of the settling of America has been an open book. Her origins do not lie in the mist-covered antiquity that veils the beginnings of older nations. From the very days of her discovery by Columbus the story of America, her settlement and growth, was recorded by contemporaries. There were on-the-spot observers, and there were writers in Europe who talked with returned travelers and collected materials of wide variety, ranging from awe-struck reports of exotic flora and fauna to routine commercial statistics.

Columbus wrote a detailed account of his voyage; and later when colonization began, the people who were building a new society and a new life for themselves wrote down their impressions of the vast wilderness as well as the record of their trials and progress, their fears and hopes in the new-found land. The incredible exploits of Spanish conquistadors, the bluster of Elizabethan buccaneers or, as in Bradford's account of the Pilgrims, the quiet gratitude for God's aid in a quest accomplished, all this and more belong to the American story.

Since printing became popular in time to record Columbus's discovery and all the stirring events that followed, the historian has a wealth of material for his purpose. Such abundance leads to a multiplicity of interpretations. To gather from the observations of several witnesses what happened in even a simple occurrence such as, say, an ordinary accident may be difficult enough. How much more difficult to get an accurate picture from the reports, documents, and letters detailing the history of several centuries. And yet in all this seeming chaos of event succeeding event a recognizable pattern does emerge.

American history is nothing if it is not the story of a people linked to their future. No country had ever before been founded by men so conscious of a break with tradition, looking with fresh eyes on their environment and keenly aware of their historic opportunity. For most of them who traversed strange lands and stranger seas to reach America the past was a slough of despond. Endless wars, poverty, and galling class restrictions had been borne for centuries—and suddenly a way of escape appeared on the horizon. America opened a new vista and helped shake vast numbers of people out of their resentful resignation to share in the thrill of shaping a new commonwealth.

Americans, perhaps more than any other people, were at home in the imaginative geographical realm conceived by Oscar Wilde. "A map of the world that does not include Utopia," he said, "is not even worth glancing at, for it leaves out the one country at which Humanity is always landing. Progress is the realization of Utopias."

Yes, America is promises. But the receiver of promises is an exacting creditor. Unlike the European who only hoped that tomorrow would be no worse than today, Americans felt cheated if tomorrow were not better than today. Close watch was kept on American performance. It was as though all the world were observers at a laboratory experiment—an experiment in democracy. The verdict of participants and onlookers has been that its successes have far outweighed its failures.

CHAPTER I

Europe Discovers an Unknown Land

The discovery of America was a by-product of European expansion. The Norse discoveries of Iceland, Greenland, and finally America were part of the larger sweep of the Norse pirates, traders, and settlers eastward through Russia to the Black Sea, and westward into France (Normandy), and around France into Sicily and neighboring regions in the Mediterranean.

Superb seamen that they were, Norse sailors outdid themselves in venturing into waters wholly unknown to Europeans when they cautiously felt their way along the North American coast as early as the tenth century. In the Norse discoveries accident played its part, but design was more important. The discovery of Greenland by Gunnbjörn Ulfsson was accidental, but thanks to his carefully recorded sailing directions, Erik the Red was able to explore much of Greenland's southwest coast. At Brattahlid Erik established a colony of several hundred people migrating from Iceland. The green grass and the native reindeer (caribou) that they found there gave promise of an easy life.

It was Bjarni Herjulfsson who accidentally found the shoreline of Labrador or Newfoundland. His finds prompted the voyage of Leif, son of Erik; Leif sailed southward from Bjarni's landfall and explored the New England coastline; "For a long time he was tossed about upon the ocean, and came upon lands of which he had previously had no knowledge. There were self-sown wheat fields and vines growing there." And the Norsemen found to their great pleasure that the grape of Vinland, as they called the country, "yields the best of wine." Leif's brother, Thorvald, headed an expedition to Vinland that lasted for two years, and his was the first European attempt to establish a colony in the New World continent. Colonization of America has a martyrology of its own, and Thorvald's name is the first recorded; his premature death meant that his bones enriched the soil of the new land before his hands could do their work.

The major effort of the Norse to establish a foothold in America was made by Thorfinn Karlsefni. Under his leadership 160 people in three ships, with cattle and equipment for permanent habitation, set out hopefully for the land to the west in the spring of 1003. To their delight they found fertile soil with grain and berries growing wild. They met with natives (Skraelings) who were friendly and would trade furs for bits of red cloth. The Norse remained through the following winter; "no snow came there, and all of their livestock lived by grazing." It was a promising beginning. In the new land, the wife of Thorfinn bore him a son, named Snorri, who thus became the first born of Europeans in America.

The colony in spite of its auspicious beginning was not to flourish. The original friendliness of the natives changed to sullenness when the Norsemen drove harder bargains, offering smaller bits of cloth for the furs. And then "it so happened that a bull, which belonged to Karlsefni and his people, ran out from the woods, bellowing loudly. This so terrified the Skraelings that they sped out to their canoes, and then rowed away to the southward along the coast." When the natives returned they were in a belligerent mood and a battle ensued. According to the saga, "It now seemed clear to Karlsefni and his people, that although the country thereabouts was attractive, their life would be one of constant dread and turmoil by reason of [the hostility of the] inhabitants of the country. So they forthwith prepared to leave and determined to return to their own country." Thus the unexpected bellowing of a Norse bull, it has been amusingly suggested, delayed the settlement of America for five hundred years.

The history of Norse colonization in America encompasses hardly more than a generation from Bjarni Herjulfsson's first view of the North American continent to the acceptance of defeat by Thorfinn and his associates. Settlement of the New World was seemingly beyond the limited resources available to the European of the eleventh century. It waited on a later day when states were stronger and treasuries larger before the false dawn of American history became the real daybreak with the discovery by Columbus.

★ TO CATHAY

Norse accomplishments were celebrated in native sagas but the imagination of fellow Europeans seemed untouched. These other Europeans of the middle ages lived in a Mediterranean-centered world whose orientation was generally eastward. In that direction lay the fabled wealth of Asia. In the eastern Mediterranean and southward in North Africa resided Christianity's greatest rival, Mohammedanism. Europe was dazzled by the glitter of worldly riches to be won and was absorbed by the prospect of saving souls for Christianity. For centuries cross vied with crescent for political and religious supremacy. At the same time, however, scholars and tradesmen of both faiths found it possible to engage in profitable interchange. Rescue of the Holy Land from the infidel was a prime objective in Christian strategy, but Europeans were also aware of the economic advantages in the Levant. Constantinople, Queen of the Byzantine Empire, overflowing with wealth and bustling activity, was the dynamo that generated economic energy throughout the Mediterranean world, and merchants of Venice, Genoa, and other European cities were envious of her power.

Europe's comparatively simple, monotonous existence was enriched by imports from the East—spices, perfumes, gems, "cloths of silk and gold," and tapestries of brilliant colors to liven somber walls. From the Levantine cities of Constantinople or Alexandria or perhaps Antioch, the products from farther east were transhipped to Europeans who received them in wide-eyed wonder. Travelers of the thirteenth and fourteenth centuries penetrated to remote lands and brought back incredible tales of the marvels they had seen and heard of in Persia, India, China, and the "noble island of Cipangu" [Japan]. Cipangu was "most fertile in gold, pearls, and precious stones, and they cover the temples and the royal residences with solid gold."

The most famous of these travelers was Marco Polo, a Venetian who had gone with his father and uncle to the court of Kublai Khan in Peking. Marco became a favored resident there and a counselor of the Mongol emperor, and in his wide-ranging trips over the empire gathered up a store of experiences which were never to fade in his memory. After a score of years the elder Polo brothers and young Marco returned to Italy to enchant their astonished countrymen with such stories of wealth and grandeur as to excite the whole community. So expansively did Marco talk of the Khan's revenues, estimated to be in the millions of *saggi,* that Italians thereafter spoke of him as Ser Marco Milioni. "At all hours of the day," we are told, Marco "was visited by the noblest gentlemen of the city [Genoa]. Witnessing the general eagerness to hear all about Cathay and the Great Khan, which indeed compelled him daily to repeat his story till he was weary, [he] was advised to put the matter in writing." It was so done in a Genoese prison, where he lay captive after the defeat of Venice in 1296. The fascination of Marco Polo's *Travels* wielded its spell over Europeans for centuries; among the ardent readers was Christopher Columbus.

The vaunted splendor and greatness of a Venice or Genoa or Padua sank to village proportions when measured by the overpowering impressiveness of giant Oriental cities swarming with people and shining with gilded palaces. On a single great river of China it was reported, there was "more wealth and merchandise than on all the rivers and all the seas of Christendom put together." Europeans who prided themselves on their trade with the Levant in the Mediterranean were told that it was a puny business in eastern eyes. And pretentious princes, feudal and merchant, who lorded it over countryside and city in Europe were discomfited by the knowledge that their power was insignificant in the scale of Oriental values. It was there in the East, in truth, that princes possessed "all the great treasures of the world."

Europe had from ancient times been deficient in precious metals with which to support industry and trade. Businessmen were hampered by shortages of a convenient means of exchange. Historians of the Roman Empire tell us that one of the reasons for its decline was the constant drain of gold and silver from the Mediterranean area eastward to pay for expensive imports from Asia. For hundreds of years, after the revival of trade between East and West beginning in the ninth century, this regular export of precious metals eastward was maintained.

Westerners naturally sought to correct this unfavorable balance of trade. Some, more daring, even hoped to control the wealth of Asia at its source. The Arab middleman reaped large profits for his services in bringing Oriental goods to the entrepôts of the eastern Mediterranean. How attractive it seemed to Europeans to eliminate this middleman and accumulate his exorbitant profits for themselves! The Arab was an infidel, and he defiled the Holy Land as well as despoiled Europeans, they thought. To wage holy war upon the Arab and deprive him of his valuable possessions were truly worthy of a Crusader's zeal.

Arabs controlled both land and water routes to the riches of the Orient. To break through the center of the Arab world via the Red Sea to the Indian Ocean and beyond was more quickly achieved by armchair strategists than by practical merchants. Imaginative seamen, however, had conceived what was, in effect, a global end run—a voyage through the Atlantic, around Africa, and then on into the Indian Ocean.

The achievement of so bold a venture remained for the future. But its beginnings were laid in the thirteenth century with the daring, if disastrous, voyage of Genoese seamen who never returned from their pioneer attempt. Neither Genoa nor any other of the Italian cities, wedded as they were to established commercial routine and torn by bitter rivalries, won the glory of opening a direct sea route to the East. The glory and the profitable lands were won by Portugal. The Arab middleman and the Italian merchants who controlled the sale of eastern wares in Europe could both be bypassed.

★ HENRY THE NAVIGATOR

Portugal's leading city, Lisbon, a great and beautiful seaport with easy access to the ocean, was a busy trading center in the fourteenth and fifteenth centuries. It had the quick, nervous energy found in cosmopolitan communities the world over. Its streets and quays were alive with the measured talk of merchants and the boisterous saltiness of seamen, speaking a babel of tongues—Icelandic, Dutch, English, French, and Italian. Its spirit of commercial enterprise drew to it ambitious men, restless with unfulfilled dreams, yet firmly believing all would come true. Fortunately a resourceful personage of great imagination, Prince Henry the Navigator, was at hand to channel this energy to remarkable ends. This prince, the most persistent of men, was "bound to attempt the discovery of things which were hidden from other men, and secret." It was he who succeeded in getting captains to sail their ships ever farther into uncharted seas.

Portuguese expansion southward and then eastward begins with the capture of Ceuta across from Gibraltar in 1415. From captive Moors Prince Henry learned of the treasures on the Guinea coast of Africa. Again religious exaltation and commercial needs combined to spur men on. Crushing the Moor, they thought, would strengthen Christianity and enrich Portugal. But Henry knew it was not to be done easily.

On Cape St. Vincent, southwestern promontory of Portugal, he created a school of oceanography. Improved aids to navigation were now at hand, and a new type of ship, the caravel, better adapted to the ocean than Genoese vessels, was to carry the flag of Portugal to remote seas. In Sagres roadstead close by, mariners from many lands were gathered whom Prince Henry pumped for their hard-earned knowledge. He engaged the most noted seamen of Europe to push their ships ever southward into unknown waters, hoping to round Africa's western bulge. Disheartened navigators returned in discouraged mood only to be propelled forward once more by his driving force. He had to fight skeptics of all sorts; and for years his seemed a battle lost to the elements and superstitious fear of tropic waters, "the green sea of gloom," as the Arabs called it. But at length the waters becoming familiar lost their terrors, and when the land began to yield a rich trade in gold and Negro slaves, doubters were silenced. Caravels inbound from Africa brought each spring elephant tusks, carefully guarded chests filled with gold dust, and shuffling Negroes destined for the slave market. Prince Henry was also in search of a mythical Christian kingdom, Prester John's, hidden in Africa, but the disappointment at not finding this domain with its fabled riches was assuaged by discovering a truly royal road to wealth on the dark continent.

Prince Henry died in 1460, his dream of rounding Africa still unrealized. But by then his ultimate victory was more than half won. The will to believe had been inculcated in a host of followers, and in the generation after the Prince's death his vision found justification in the voyage of Bartholomew Diaz in 1487. It was then that the Portuguese finally learned that Africa really did have a southern terminus, called thereafter the Cape of Good Hope. Just over a decade later Vasco da Gama sailed all the way to India, thus completely vindicating Henry and, in the process, transforming an apparent will-o'-the-wisp into an empire, the envy of all Europe. Arab middlemen in the Indian Ocean were eliminated. Small Portugal, with its 2,000,000 people, lorded it over a vast expanse of land and water, and Europe was obliged to pay tribute to Lisbon's hegemony in the eastern trade. Spain and other rivals of Portugal, frozen out by her monopoly of this trade route, were forced to seek alternate paths to the east.

★ PEPPER, GINGER, PEARLS, AND CINNAMON

The achievement of Vasco da Gama was of spectacular proportions, for with the first cargo brought back from India (1499) the expenses of his entire expedition were paid for many times over. Portuguese prosperity from trade in the Indian Ocean rested on the fact that the products her ships returned were an extremely light, concentrated cargo, cheap at the source, but commanding, usually, high prices in Lisbon and London. These products included pepper and ginger of Malabar, pearls and cinnamon from Ceylon, mace and nutmeg from Amboyna, exotic frankincense and indigo. In the two small islands of Ternate and Tidor was the most valuable plant of all, the clove tree. The Spice Islands were indeed a land of enchantment.

When Portugal was building her maritime empire which stretched from Lisbon to the Indian Ocean, Europe was in a stage of transition from the Middle Ages to modern times. Kings and nobles, it is true, were to occupy their privileged places for long years to come. But seated now close by were princes of a different order, men whose baronies were not feudal estates but vast commercial emporiums and docks and warehouses and numberless ships. They were bankers, too, who held in mortgaged thrall decadent landed nobility. Ownership of land was no longer the sole foundation of power. Business enterprise was a rival power, and its home was in the city. Kings found allies in this newly risen middle class to curb the power of feudal nobles, and in time royal and bourgeois strength combined to create national states in western Europe.

Titans of finance were matched by titans of art, for this was the age of the Renaissance. Rarely has there ever been so great a concentration of genius as in this period. Leonardo da Vinci, Michelangelo, Raphael, Titian, and Benvenuto Cellini were among its artists, and Lorenzo the Magnificent and others had the wit and wealth to foster their amazing productivity. The horizon of man's spirit was vastly extended by their imaginative flights. At this same time man's physical horizon was also greatly enlarged. The crowding boundaries of Europe were suddenly broken, for off in the west was found another world. There millions were at length to build homes and a new society, and ultimately to create a nation whose power came to overshadow that of its parent Europe.

★ CHRISTOPHER COLUMBUS

Even before the voyage of Diaz, young Christopher Columbus had conceived an idea as daring as any sea captain had ever entertained. He believed that by sailing west the trip to the Indies would be shorter than the route, south and eastward, then being taken by the Portuguese. But the navigator from Genoa had underestimated the size of the earth. He found support for his view in Marco Polo's incorrect estimate of Asia's eastward extension, which brought that continent comparatively close to Europe. Many authorities with great prestige, including Cardinal Pierre d'Ailly, whose *Imago Mundi* was a favorite with Columbus, strengthened his conviction that Asia lay not too far west.

Paolo Toscanelli, the noted Florentine geographer, who may have encouraged Columbus in his view, likewise believed that Asia's eastern shore was much nearer to Portugal than fellow scientists imagined, and might more easily be reached by sailing west. Columbus thought that Cathay extended so far eastward as to lie not many days sailing distance from the Azores; for like so many of his contemporaries he believed "nature could not have made so disorderly a composition of the globe as to give the element of water preponderance over the land destined for life and the creation of souls."

A love of sailing was natural to Columbus. His native Genoa, which looked out upon a broad expanse of sea, had for generations bred the finest sailors and mapmakers in the Mediterranean. The glamour and excitement of the beckoning sea made his father's trade of woolen weaver seem too dull a way of life, although as a dutiful son he remained at the family loom until his early twenties. But he must often

THE UNITED STATES TO 1865

have been aboard the ships that plied the coast for, as he wrote in after years, "at a very tender age I entered upon the sea sailing." He was in his mid-twenties when a vessel he had shipped on was wrecked in a fight off Portugal, and he was washed ashore at Lagos.

Columbus was treated hospitably and sent on his way to Lisbon, where he found many fellow countrymen from Genoa. He was a tall, affable young man who endeared himself to all who met him, and he rose quickly in the social circles of Portugal. Three years after being shipwrecked he had gained the confidence of Portugal's leading families and married the daughter of a captain in Prince Henry's service. Columbus was now able to mingle with people of prominence. Within half a dozen years he was pressing the King of Portugal to sponsor his project of finding the Indies by sailing westward (Diaz had not yet rounded Africa), but Columbus suffered a humiliating refusal.

Turning then to Spain, Columbus saw his hopes alternately rise and fall in agonizing frustration. Influential leaders, lay and ecclesiastical, were favorably disposed toward him; the Royal Council, however, disapproved. The Queen was sympathetic, but all eyes at the moment were fixed on the climactic struggle with the age-old Spanish foe, the Moors. Procrastination lengthened the ordinary delays of governmental procedure, and Columbus' whole project seemed threatened when Diaz at length proved that the route around Africa was feasible. Columbus, in fact, was in Lisbon in December, 1488, when the ships of Diaz came home. In a marginal note written in his own copy of Pierre d'Ailly's *Imago Mundi,* Columbus recorded that Diaz had "described his voyage and plotted it league by league on a marine chart in order to place it under the eyes of the . . . king. I was present in all of this."

Fortunately for Columbus the Portuguese were slow to follow to its logical conclusion the lead offered by Diaz. Actually, as we have seen, more than a decade elapsed before Da Gama reached India. By that time Columbus had already succeeded in winning the support of King Ferdinand and Queen Isabella. Once converted to his cause the Queen became his most ardent supporter.

This royal support came with dramatic suddenness. More than six years of petitioning, entreaty, and argument with royal counselors had seemingly ended in a final "no" in January, 1492. In angry disappointment Columbus left the royal presence at Santa Fé. At this moment Luis de Santangel, keeper of the privy purse and friendly to the Great Enterprise of Columbus, interceded at court. He told the Queen that "he was astonished to see that her Highness, who had always shown a resolute spirit in matters of great pith and consequence should lack it now for an enterprise of so little risk, yet which could prove of so great service to God and the exaltation of His Church, not to speak of very great increase and glory for her realms and crown, an enterprise of such nature that if any other prince should undertake [it] . . . it would be a very great damage to her crown, and a grave reproach to her."

Santangel offered to finance the expedition himself, and was no doubt surprised when the Queen, moved by his enthusiasm, offered her jewels to raise the needed funds. A messenger was hurriedly sent to catch up with the disconsolate Columbus, who was astonished at the command to return again for a royal audience. His case was now won.

Excitement mounted as plans were made and funds raised for the momentous voyage. Pawning the crown jewels proved unnecessary as Santangel played the leading part in raising some 2,000,000 maravedis (the equivalent of about $25,000 today according to one calculation) to launch the expedition; the monthly payroll was another 250,000 maravedis.

The Admiral of the Ocean Sea (this was the title bestowed on Columbus by his Spanish sovereigns) set sail from Palos at dawn of a quiet day, a memorable Friday, August 3, 1492. Palos had ships and men accustomed to voyages in the Atlantic and along the coasts of Guinea. Three ships, "Niña" (about sixty tons), "Pinta," and "Santa Maria," well built, skilfully designed, and rigged for their hazardous task, and manned by ninety crew (nearly all Spaniards) set out on this historic voyage. Small by modern steamship standards (Niña was only about seventy feet overall, drawing some six feet), the vessels were nevertheless seaworthy and able to make good time. They went out with the ebb tide and made for the Canaries where they rested for a month, refitting and taking supplies, before pushing directly west on into the unknown sea.

Week after week, through storm and fearsome sailing over "shoreless seas" Columbus urged his men on and on. Hesitant and even mutinous seamen were cajoled and led by as great a captain as ever sailed a ship. Thursday, October 11, the little fleet sped along, making nearly seven knots. Fears at last were quieted by the many signs which indicated land was near—a flower on a green branch, a carved stick, a land plant. Late that night, Columbus thought he saw a light in the distance. But it quickly vanished. Two hours after midnight the lookout on the "Pinta" was the first to see the welcome land.

With supreme skill in navigation, to which modern navigators attest, Columbus, in the early hours of October 12, thirty-three days after leaving the Canaries, brought his ships to safety off the small Bahama island of Guanahaní. The vessels loafed off shore till daybreak.

The dawn revealed a low lying island, and from its cover of lush tropical foliage streamed naked inhabitants gazing in wonder at the strangers "as though we had come from heaven," said Columbus. The Admiral came ashore with the royal standard, and in the name of his sovereigns, Ferdinand and Isabella, took possession of the land which he called San Salvador. "Arrived on shore, they saw trees very green, many streams of water and diverse sorts of fruits."

Columbus' *Journal* then continues, "As I saw that they [the inhabitants] were friendly to us, and perceived that they could be much more easily converted to our holy faith by gentle means than by force, I presented them with some red caps, and strings of beads to wear upon the neck, and many other trifles of small value, wherewith they were much delighted, and became wonderfully attached to us. Afterwards they came swimming to the boats, bringing parrots, balls of cotton thread, javelins and many other things which they exchanged for articles we gave them, such as glass beads, and hawks' bells; . . . But they seemed . . . to be a very poor people. They all go completely naked, even the women . . ." In describing the lands he found Columbus spoke of them as though they were a new Garden of Eden, and thus was born the legend of a Utopia in the west. "I assure your Highnesses" he wrote to his sovereigns, "that . . . there are not under the sun better lands, considering the fertility of the soil, the temperature of the air and the abundance of fine streams of water. . . . Here are to be seen the most beautiful pine trees and the most extensive fields and pastures . . . honey and many kinds of metal," except iron. "The nightingale and countless other birds were singing although it was the month of November when I visited this delightful region"; it was all "wonderfully enchanting."

America's discoverer bore letters for the Grand Khan and was disappointed that that Oriental ruler was not to be found. Columbus sailed from island to island, and discovering Cuba at last, believed it to be the mainland. But vast cities and the splendor of eastern potentates were nowhere to be seen. It was high time, nevertheless, to set sail for home with word of the new-found route to the Orient—for Columbus did not doubt that just beyond the islands barring his way lay the coveted East.

He began the return trip on January 16, 1493, "turning the prow East by North," and sailed through the swishing weeds of the Sargasso Sea spellbound in the moonlight. A gale blew the vessels along at remarkable speed, which for brief periods reached almost eleven knots an hour. But later stages of the homeward voyage were stormy and Columbus was lucky to make port at Lisbon, on March 4. "Niña" was refitted for the triumphant last leg of the voyage, and on the fifteenth of March, "at midday with a flood tide," the great discoverer proudly entered the port of Palos. "Let us rejoice," wrote the Admiral, "for the exaltation of our faith as well as for the augmentation of our temporal prosperity, in which not only Spain but all Christendom shall participate." News of the discovery spread rapidly in the Mediterranean but percolated more slowly into northern Europe.

Though filled with enthusiasm for the lands he had discovered as a domain for an expanding Christendom, Columbus had not brought back a cargo of "gold, pearls and spices," the goal of his enterprise of the Indies. His own royal patrons seemed rather doubtful that he had reached the Orient, while the Portuguese thought Columbus had trespassed in their waters off the South African coast, or perhaps had discovered more islands of the fabled Antilles. Spain's rulers decided to take no chances and sought to protect their claims and warn off intruders by winning from the pope recognition of their sovereign status over the new lands. European custom had recognized papal authority to dispose of lands anywhere in the world not ruled by a Christian prince. Through papal proclamation in establishing the Demarcation Line, 1493, and the following year by the Treaty of Tordessillas with Portugal, the world was divided between the two Iberian powers. A line was drawn 370 leagues west of the Cape Verde Islands, the area to the east of the line was reserved for Portugal, that to the west for Spain. Brazil thus fell within Portugal's sphere.*

The invincible Columbus sailed again to the west, September, 1493, firmly convinced that the resplendent country of Kublai Khan lay ahead, behind the island barriers. This was a large expedition, seventeen ships carrying 1,500 colonists, to establish Spain's foothold in this region. While neither Columbus nor his immediate successor voyagers found the treasures of the glamorous East, he did find a vast, tropical continent (South America) with rivers whose mouths were broad as inland seas. The Florentine merchant, Amerigo Vespucci, was one of those who reached South America and wrote an account of his voyage which attracted much attention. Historians today feel that Vespucci, once belittled by skeptical students, belongs with the giants of the discovery period. Slowly it dawned on the Europeans that this was as Vespucci said, "a new world, since our ancestors had no knowledge of it." That the New World should have been named in honor of Amerigo Vespucci, instead

---

* This treaty had been foreshadowed by an earlier arrangement, the Treaty of Alcacovas in 1479, in which Spain retained the Canaries, and Portugal was given the Azores, Madeiras, and other islands from the Canaries to Guinea.

of Columbus, was due to an obscure professor of geography, who coined the word "America" in his *Introduction to Cosmography,* published in the early years of the sixteenth century.

Perhaps, as Columbus' brother thought, this continental mass was itself a huge peninsula stretching southeastward from Asia. Or possibly a narrow sea separated this obstacle from the rich goal of the Spaniards. It was all a baffling puzzle that was cleared up by the voyage of Ferdinand Magellan.

Magellan, a Portuguese who had been to the Spice Islands in the East Indies (which he believed were well within the region allotted to Spain by the Demarcation Line) was commissioned by King Charles of Spain in 1519 to find a western passage. Commanding five ships he set forth on the most remarkable voyage in history. Sailing far down the eastern coast of South America (much of it already explored), Magellan, hampered by an undependable crew, forced his ships through the dangerous straits which bear his name and out into the exhaustingly broad Pacific. Endless days succeeded countless fearful nights, weeks stretched into months, and the crew wasted away from sickness and starvation. Ship vermin and whatever leather could be found aboard became the daily bread. At long last the Philippine Islands were reached, but here Magellan met his death in a fight with the natives. The expedition continued on with one ship, the "Victoria," which then followed the established route through the Indian Ocean, around the Cape of Good Hope, arriving home in Spain, September 7, 1522. Three long and tortuous years after the pioneering voyage had begun, the first circumnavigation of the earth had been completed. The opening of the ocean route to the East Indies and the discovery of America have been acclaimed as two of the greatest events in the history of mankind.

The "Victoria" brought with her twenty-six tons of cloves from the Moluccas, but she brought, too, the discouraging truth about the vast size of the earth, miscalculated by Columbus. A profitable trade route to the Indies of the East apparently was not to be won by sailing west, but men continued the quest. The interminable Pacific stretched endlessly away, and between it and the increasingly familiar Atlantic lay a giant land mass—the New World of America.

CHAPTER II

The Old World in the New

The claim of Spain to exclusive possession of the western lands did not go unchallenged. Portugal won Brazil after Pedro Álvarez Cabral touched there in 1500. Other nations in search of a western all-water route to the Orient sent expeditions across the Atlantic vainly hoping to find a passage through the Americas or around their northern boundary. They were so certain of its existence that they gave it a name—the Strait of Anian. England's King Henry VII had commissioned John Cabot and his son to search for it. The merchants of Bristol had been sending out expeditions to the west for several years before the Cabots entered the scene. Hints dropped by close-mouthed fishermen from northern and western Europe told of rich yields in distant waters in the North Atlantic. Giovanni Caboto, originally of Genoa, settled in Bristol whose temper intensified his own determination to find the Spice Islands by sailing west. The Cabots failed in their attempt in 1497. But they sailed along the coast from Newfoundland southward and westward and though they found no alluring prospects for trade there, Henry nevertheless claimed the land as England's own. Cabot, like Columbus, thought he had reached Asia's eastern shore. Neither Henry nor anyone else knew the size of the dominion appropriated by him, as he did not occupy it. For a long time it scarcely mattered; almost a century elapsed before Englishmen awoke to the value of their inheritance.

Spanish and Portuguese pretensions to divide the world between them were derided by the cynical French monarch Francis I, who sent Giovanni da Verrazano, a Florentine, westward to seek the coveted passage to the east. Though Verrazano also failed, he was the first European to enter the beautiful harbor of New York which he, like so many later arrivals, found "a very agreeable location." Verrazano's cruise along the coast of North America gave Francis the right to claim a portion of the new land. Within another few years the French ruler sent Jacques

Cartier, a skilled St. Malo navigator, on voyages of exploration. Cartier sailed up the broad St. Lawrence River in 1534, touching at the islands en route, and gave to a small Indian settlement the name Montreal. In the name of his king Cartier laid claim to a vast region drained by the St. Lawrence.

Thus large areas of the North American continent were carved out for future exploitation by Spain, England, and France. But boundaries were very vague, and so conflicting were the claims that for centuries they were cause for disputes which often broke out into war. Meanwhile explorers and *coureurs de bois* ranged over enormous stretches of the continent's interior whose vastness was overwhelming. But the persistent search for the passage to the East Indies continued.

Two centuries after Magellan's historic feat, European and American navigators still sought a western route to the Indies through Panama or some passage running northwestward which led them into forbidding Arctic waters. The time had long since past, however, when America was considered only an impediment to sailing vessels hopeful of finding gaps through which they could pass to the islands of the East. From its earliest settlement America was valued for its own wealth—for the products of its land and waters as well as for its special enrichment of the human spirit.

Spaniards early in the sixteenth century branched out from their original center of Hispaniola to include other West Indian islands in their empire, and thence to the North American mainland. Friar and freebooter, sometimes at odds or in reluctant alliance, combined to expand the boundaries of the Kingdom of God and the kingdom of Spain. Hispaniola had been converted into a stronger colony with the despatch, in 1502, of Nicolas de Ovando's fleet of 32 ships and 2,500 settlers. In less than a decade Puerto Rico, Jamaica, and Cuba were being administered by Spanish officials.

Columbus, though himself a poor administrator, had correctly prophesied that America would be a source of great increase for the royal revenues, and a field for the expansion of Christianity: "And your Highnesses will win these lands which are an Other World, and where Christianity will have so much enjoyment, and our faith in time so great an increase. All this I say with very honest intent, and because I desire that your Highnesses may be the greatest lords in the world, lords of it all I say . . ."

It was to Florida that Juan Ponce de León went for treasure and the elusive Strait of Anian. Other Spaniards explored the eastern coast far to the north and some turned west toward the Gulf of Mexico. It was when they reached the coast of Yucatan and finally learned about the wealth they had long been seeking that the course of Spain in the New World was fixed for generations thereafter. Hernando Cortés fought his way inland toward the heart of the Aztec capital, Tenochtitlán (Mexico City). A Spaniard climbed the almost 18,000 feet to Popocatepetl's top, and his excited description of the fabulous city, forty miles distant, spurred his fellow Four Hundred.

Bernal Díaz del Castillo, companion to Cortés and chronicler of the conquest in 1519, revealed the wonder that was the Aztec capital. "I stood looking at it," he wrote, "and thought that never in the world would there be discovered other lands such as these." "We did not know what to say, or whether what appeared before us was real . . . and some of our soldiers even asked whether the things that we saw were not a dream." Mexico City was a huge walled fortress, set in a lake, with many temple pyramids and towers rising from the water and with several causeways connecting with the shores.

Within a short time the famed conquistadors, the courtly Cortés and the ruthless Francisco Pizarro, had overthrown the great native states of the Aztecs in Mexico and the Incas in Peru. The wealth that had been dreamed of by adventurers to the East was now spread before the eyes of Spanish conquerors. Pizarro in Peru wrung from the Inca a ransom in gold which filled a room seventeen feet by twenty-two feet, nine feet high—a pile estimated to be worth many millions of dollars. No such booty had ever fallen to a conqueror in all history. From vast accumulation of treasure and from mines of silver there flowed to Spain riches the like of which Europe had never seen. Peter Martyr, first historian of the New World, described some of the jewels, textiles, and gold ornaments shipped to Spain from Mexico: "If ever artists of this kind of work have touched genius, then surely these natives are they . . . I have never seen anything, which . . . could more delight the human eye." Thirty lean years of not very profitable exploration now yielded their enormous reward.

Adventurous explorers pushed out from Mexico and Florida to find Cibola, the fabled Seven Cities of the American South West—or perhaps coerce another Montezuma into piling treasure at their feet. Álvar Nuñez Cabeza de Vaca started out from Florida in 1528, and with several companions walked across two-thirds of the continent before finding sanctuary with fellow Spaniards in northern Mexico. Francisco Vásquez de Coronado saw no cities, though he marveled at the Grand Canyon; and Hernando de Soto, once companion of Pizarro of Peru, found no wealth nor passage to the Pacific in his fruitless wanderings between Florida and the Mississippi. He found instead his grave, in the great river. There his body, exhausted by three years of incessant effort,

Early voyages of discovery

SPANISH

——·——·—— Columbus, 1492

— — — — — Columbus, 1493-96

—·—··—··— Columbus, 1498

————————— Columbus, 1502-04

—·——·——·— Vespucci, 1497-98

+—+—+—+—+ Ojeda, 1499

—·|—·|—·|— Pinzon, 1499-1500

+·+·+·+·+ Magellan, 1519-21

—·——·——·— Cabrillo & Ferrelo, 1542-43

PORTUGUESE

—————————— Pedro Alvarez Cabral, 1500

→——→——→ Gaspar Corte Real, 1501

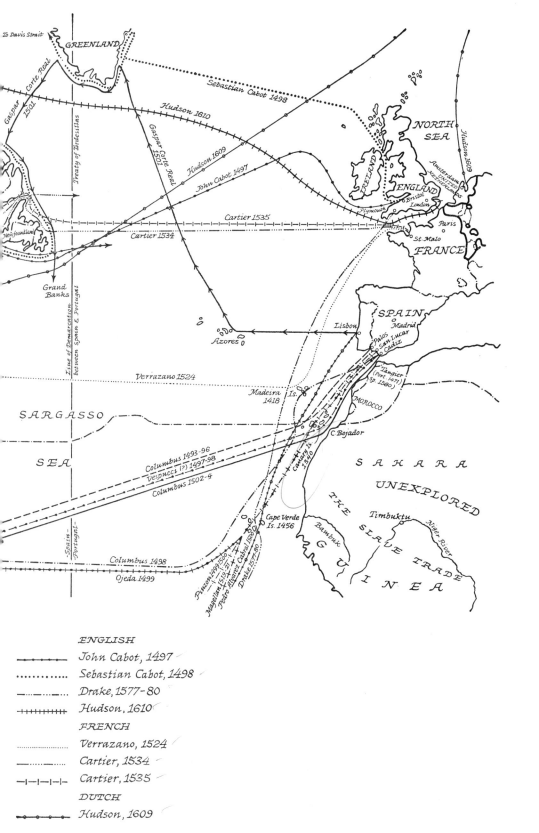

To Davis Strait

GREENLAND

Gaspar Corte Real 1501

Sebastian Cabot 1498

Hudson 1610

Gaspar Corte Real 1501

Hudson 1609

Treaty of Tordesillas

John Cabot 1497

NORTH SEA

Hudson 1609

Newfoundland

IRELAND

ENGLAND

Bristol

Plymouth

London

Cartier 1535

Amsterdam UNITED NETHERLANDS

Cartier 1534

Grand Banks

Line of Demarcation between Spain & Portugal

Paris

St. Malo

FRANCE

Verrazano 1524

Azores

Lisbon

SPAIN

Madrid

Palos

San Lucar

Cadiz

Madeira Is. 1418

Tangier (Port. 1471 Sp. 1580)

SARGASSO

MOROCCO

C. Bojador

SEA

Columbus 1493-96

Vespucci (?) 1497-98

Columbus 1502-4

Canary Is. 1340

SAHARA

UNEXPLORED

THE SLAVE TRADE

Timbuktu

Niger River

Columbus 1498

Ojeda 1499

Pinzon 1499/1500

Magellan 1519-21

Pedro Alvarez Cabral 1500

Drake 1577-80

Cape Verde Is. 1456

Bambuk

G U I N E A

—Spain—

—Portugal—

ENGLISH

—•——•—— John Cabot, 1497

•••••••••• Sebastian Cabot, 1498

—••——••— Drake, 1577-80

++++++++ Hudson, 1610

FRENCH

•••••••••• Verrazano, 1524

—•••——•••— Cartier, 1534

–|–|–|–|– Cartier, 1535

DUTCH

—•——•——•— Hudson, 1609

was laid to rest in the spring of 1542. De Soto's expedition, while barren of immediate gain, had penetrated the mysteries of a large area of the future southern United States. The reports of the surviving half of De Soto's group of 600 expanded the imperial ambitions of Spain and excited the imagination of her rivals.

It was not until almost three quarters of a century after Columbus' voyage, 1565 to be exact, that the Spaniards located at St. Augustine, Florida, their first permanent habitation in the future United States. This fortified position was the Spanish outpost against a threatened French incursion from the region now known as South Carolina. The French threat was eased when her colony of Fort Caroline was wiped out. Florida, under Spain, for three hundred years hardly advanced beyond the status of a northern military outpost protecting the West Indies. Nevertheless, beyond the tiny settlement of St. Augustine to the north and west, the Spaniards laid claim to a vast territory. In their confused image of America's geography they continued to dream of finding an all-water route through the Americas to the East.

In Mexico and South America, Spain created a civilized community with splendid churches and universities years before the first English or French settlements were planted in North America. Spain's imperial energy was, in the main, expended in tropical, rather than in temperate regions. *There* were to be found the products needed by Europeans; hence the Spaniards derided the seeming advantages of a temperate climate which promised an economy similar to Europe's. As Peter Martyr, historian of the New World, expressed it: "What need have we of what is found everywhere in Europe? It is towards the south, not towards the frozen north, that those who seek fortune should bend their way; for everything at the equator is rich."

It should be noted that the Spanish colonies lying off the tip of Florida were the true progenitors of the agricultural economy of our own South. The West Indies were to help set the pattern of Negro slavery in America, and to emphasize the value of such crops as tobacco, indigo, rice, and cotton. As for sugar, the progression ran from the Canaries to Hispaniola, thence elsewhere in America. In later years many Negroes sold to English settlers had Spanish or Portuguese names. These slaves were one of the means through which the agricultural experience of the West Indies was channeled to the North American mainland.

★ SPANISH TREASURE

The treasure laden galleons that sailed in guarded convoy from Spain's possessions in the New World back to the motherland made that country the richest state in Europe, enhancing greatly the prestige of her monarchs. But these imports, creating inflationary pressures, raised prices 200 per cent or more by 1600. The striking results of this inflation effected changes in class relationships, which benefited especially the bourgeoisie.

These were matters of concern to the Spanish sovereign as well as to other rulers, but of greater moment for mankind were the overarching imperial designs of Spain's Philip II. The brooding Philip, as the American historian, Prescott, described him, was the master spirit who secluded himself in the dark recesses of his palace, "himself unseen even by his own subjects," and who watched over the lines of communication which ran out "in every direction to the farthest quarters of the globe."

Philip's far-reaching plans included the reconquest for Catholicism of those areas in Europe which had been won by Protestantism. They provided, too, for the extension of Spanish Habsburg political power in Europe and the enlargement of territorial possessions overseas. It seemed as though this richest sovereign in Europe, gathering revenues from Spain and his Italian possessions as well as from America, had the means to prosecute his plans. The magnitude of his projects bore so heavily upon his revenues, however, that loans were needed from German and Italian bankers. This meant that American gold and silver were often pledged in advance to Spain's creditors.

This in itself was bad enough for the prestige of the Spanish crown. But what made it doubly oppressive was the fact that much of Spain's wealth was finding its way into the hands of the Dutch. Their port of Antwerp was one of the busiest in Europe, and it had become the continent's chief financial center. The Netherlands, although part of Philip's empire, were too independent for that king who would, in truth, be monarch of all he surveyed. Dutch Protestantism, he thought, must be crushed and the commerce of the Netherlands made to yield its returns to the Spanish crown. After long years of stubborn war neither aim had been accomplished. Protestantism had survived in the northern Dutch provinces which, in their prosperous center at Amsterdam, had also taken over much of the trade formerly controlled by the now ruined Antwerp.

The Dutch carried the war to Spain's vulnerable West Indies, because discerning Europeans understood that it was American treasure which shored up Spain's strength. As this treasure was brought home by sea, it meant that Spain was only as strong as her naval power. And her possessions were too widely scattered to be protected by equal strength everywhere. Francis Bacon reflected contemporary sentiment when he wrote that "money is the principal part of the greatness of Spain; for by that they maintain their . . . army. But in this part, of all others, is most to be considered the ticklish and brittle state of the greatness of Spain. Their greatness consisteth in their treasure, their treasure in the Indies, and their Indies . . . are indeed but an accession to such as are masters of the sea." The French joined the Dutch in hit-and-run (sometimes smash-and-hold) attacks on the colonies and ships of Spain. French filibusters and Dutch "sea beggars" were man-made terrors of the deep that scourged the Spanish main. And even more lasting damage than they had done to Spanish power was inflicted by Queen Elizabeth's England.

★ ELIZABETHAN ENGLAND

Sixteenth-century England was one of the emergent national powers which were already overshadowing the medieval political pattern of feudal principalities and city states. Tudor tact, and ruthlessness when needed (and the popular Queen Elizabeth had both these qualities), hammered together a nation that showed as much sense of unity as any other European state could then offer.

England at the close of Elizabeth's reign had a population of nearly 5,000,000, living for the most part in a rural environment whose centers were small villages of about 300 people. London was the only big city at the time, boasting a population of 250,000. It was London and a few smaller port towns which became the leaders in many national activities.

English society of that day may be divided roughly into four groups. The first included the titled nobility, the landed gentry, and the top men among the learned classes; a second was made up of people below the gentry living off the land, such as tenants and wealthier peasants; the third group, the bourgeoisie, comprised merchants (sometimes wealthy), smaller tradesmen, and skilled craftsmen; the last group was made up of unskilled laborers, poorly paid artisans whose work required little skill, and a poor humble peasantry. But considerable social mobility prevailed even at this early date, and from the two extremes among the classes the bourgeoisie was constantly being augmented. Sons of English nobility were readier to engage in trade than most of their continental counterparts. Sons of gentlemen sat alongside children of yeomen, parsons, and mercers in local grammar schools. Throughout England's towns and villages civic functions had long been performed by men of little or no rank, thus providing experience in community organization for future emigrants.

During Elizabeth's reign there seemed to be a veritable fever for building schools. So many were established during these years that few towns of some size were without one, or even two. Even very small towns began to build schools. Though women were excluded until the early years of the seventeenth century, somehow many of them (at least among the upper and middle classes) learned to read and write. Books had begun to play a vital role in the life of the average Englishman. The printed word was giving him a wider perspective of the world around him. Books on self improvement even then were among the best sellers. The English lower classes had already been long enough emancipated from feudalism to show little of that servility then found in most parts of the continent.

Deep-seated social changes in the England of Elizabeth and the early Stuarts (call it an economic revolution) were the forces moving many of its people overseas. The separation of England from the Church of Rome and the confiscation of church wealth created profound divisions among the population and dislocated traditional economic and social relationships. The poor, who in former times used to resort for relief to monasteries, seemed cast adrift. Increased prices, unaccompanied by increased wages, depressed the living standards of workmen. The extension of holdings by wealthier farmers, enclosing for themselves lands hitherto held in common, pushed many of the weaker off the land. This process of enclosure was undertaken to provide more grazing land for the sheep supplying England's most profitable commodity, wool. It meant that farms were bought up for pasturage, and the displaced farmers in their anger said bitterly "the sheep were eating up the men."

Some projects were undertaken to reclaim waste lands in England at this time, but they added comparatively little to the country's arable area. The increasing scarcity of farm land in England made it easy for a promoter to arouse interest among the discontented at home in the unlimited and fertile spaces of America.

Vagrant wayfarers plodded England's country roads and her city streets, everywhere unwanted by the local inhabitants. Frightened communities jailed them, and when their support grew burdensome, handed the poor unfortunates money and food enough to get on to other neighborhoods on which to park their unwelcome selves. America as a more permanent resting place appeared to be the answer to the prayers of harassed Englishmen. And many were glad to go, for it seemed a land where one might not only earn a living, but also escape from the wars that had plagued Europeans for centuries. Emigration "skimmed the milk of bitterness in England," and eventually left society at home less sour.

Acquiring homes for the homeless and for social outcasts was only one phase of England's program of overseas empire. Her merchants, in quest of greater trade, sought "vents" (as they called markets) for their wool and other products. It was the export of woolen cloth which brought England into world commerce in a significant manner. Out of the guilds of medieval cities grew the great companies of adventurers who learned to trade on the farthest seas. Visitors from the continent, accustomed to think of England as a relatively poor country, were surprised to see that this trade had provided large funds for overseas enterprise.

The companies picked up where inspired but frustrated pioneers, Raleigh and the rest, had failed. With the death of Raleigh the heroic age of colonization came to an end. The glamorous visionaries who wrote and acted the prologue to empire left the stage to prosaic accountants and hardheaded businessmen. These at length undertook the arduous task of creating the imperial structure. But in English chartered companies, operating matter-of-fact business enterprises strictly for profit, were men who were also filled with romantic dreams. Freer from governmental supervision than similar business organizations formed by Dutch or French contemporaries, English companies were founders of empires in America and Asia carrying with them the institutions of their homeland. Samuel Daniel's poem, "Musophilus" (1601), fully expressed the current English sentiments:

> And who in time, knows whither we may vent
> The treasure of our tongue? To what strange shores
> This gain our best glory shall be sent
> To enrich unknowing nations with our stores!
> What worlds in the yet unformed Occident
> May come refin'd with the accents that are ours!

The chartered companies provided the impetus for American colonization, but, for the most part, organization of the settlements was the achievement of colonists who expended the toilsome effort to keep them going. The civilization created in the colonies by emigrants was determined by the cultural inheritance carried with them and by the strange, new environment surrounding them. In their adaptation to its challenge the colonists fashioned in America institutions different from those imagined by sedentary statesmen and methodical merchants in England.

★ ELIZABETH AND PHILIP II

The English, who have a deep historical sense, eagerly read the large mass of literature which celebrated their country's greatness and her spreading maritime power. Richard Eden, and more importantly Richard Hakluyt, the younger, informed fellow Englishmen of the new lands east and west which were coming within the ken of venturesome captains. It was Hakluyt's great collection of voyages, the prose epic of England, that made his contemporary readers sharers in spirit of their country's imperial enterprise. Christopher Marlowe caught his country's mood:

> I'll have them fly to India for gold,
> Ransack the ocean for orient pearl,
> And search all corners of the new-found world
> For pleasant fruits and princely delicates
>
> .   .   .   .
>
> From Venice shall they drag huge argosies,
> And from America the golden fleece
> That yearly stuffs old Philip's treasury.

All kinds of people were excited by visions of a bountiful land in the West, and in tavern and market place they exchanged gossip of imagined treasures awaiting them overseas. Raleigh and Drake lifted Englishmen out of their insular world and gave them magic carpets to carry them to regions of enchantment. But with the silver lining there was a cloud—Spain.

Spain was an economic, political, and religious threat to the Protestant England of Elizabeth. This resolute Queen was determined to preserve the religion of her countrymen against the aggression of her Catholic rival, Philip II. She was equally ambitious to make her nation one of the first powers in the world. Experienced statesmen counseled her, and together they made plans for strengthening England's economy, finances, and naval power. Shrewd diplomacy steered England through dangerous zones of international friction. Trade, legitimate and otherwise, became a weapon of English patriotism.

Hostility to Philip II seemed a blessed national crusade. Piracy and privateering were thinly distinguished from each other in those days, and a hero's mantle was draped upon many a captain over whom in a more law-abiding age might have dropped a noose. John Hawkins, one of the most successful of these captains, showed the English how frail were the overseas defenses of Spain (and Portugal as well); and the profits of his exchange of Negro slaves for sugar and hides in the West Indies enticed his countrymen. Hawkins and other Englishmen had been engaged in profitable trade with Spain and the Canary Islands for a number of years. England's ambition was to add the West Indies to this trading area, or, if the Spaniards proved obdurate, raiding area. In one year alone, 1589, over ninety Spanish prizes were brought into England.

Despite the raids of English "sea dogs" on Spanish ships and seaport towns, England and Spain continued to engage in peaceful trade. The fear of Englishmen was that Philip might arbitrarily limit or even destroy it entirely. Trade and imperial expansion were judged essential to English national existence. Englishmen in the sixteenth century did not know the word *lebensraum* but they knew its meaning.

★ "THE BREATH OF GOD HAS SCATTERED THEM"

A far more celebrated captain than Hawkins was Francis Drake. He tormented the Spaniards in both the Atlantic and the Pacific in a famous exploit lasting over three years. The imperious Elizabeth had joined men of business in raising funds for the expedition led by Drake. On an investment of £5,000 the enterprise was ultimately to yield a return of £600,000.

Drake sailed into the Pacific in 1577, plundering unprotected seaports and feebly-armed vessels which believed themselves safe from attack. Sailing northward, accumulating treasure as he went, he reached upper California, anchoring under the white cliffs of Drake's Bay in June, 1579. He claimed it for his country and called it New Albion. Knowing that the return would be full of hazard, with Spaniards hoping to catch him, Drake took the bold course of sailing across the Pacific and then home by way of the Indian Ocean. After Magellan's, Drake's was the next voyage around the globe. But striking as was this feat of navigation to seamen, the masses were more highly excited by the treasure he wrested from Spain and the blows he inflicted upon her. Sober businessmen were even more impressed by the opening up of trade with the Spice Islands. Queen Elizabeth delighted to wear a crown set with five gorgeous stolen emeralds which Drake had given her. The deck of Drake's flagship, the "Golden Hind," was a proud place when the Queen there knighted her glamorous subject. "The Dragon," as fearful Spaniards called this "master thief of the Unknown World," became the undying inspiration of his adoring countrymen.

Spectacular as were the achievements of English sea-dogs, more severe devastation of Spanish maritime power came with the destruction of her Invincible Armada in 1588. To blight Spain's effort before it gained momentum, Drake had already sailed, with insulting effrontery, into the harbor of Cadiz, which was filled with eighty vessels. By fire or cannon he destroyed them all, thousands of tons of shipping along with a great quantity of stores. Off the Azores, Drake took captive a carrack home-bound from the East Indies with goods valued at £114,000. His unorthodox daring utterly confused the Spaniards. Philip II determined to overpower England with as great a show of strength as had ever been massed by a state in Europe. It was an awe-inspiring spectacle of some 130 vessels carrying 22,000 men. In conjunction with soldiers to be ferried across from the Netherlands, the combined veteran forces were expected to defeat with ease the 6,000 regular soldiers available to Queen Elizabeth. But a surge of national power such as England was to know again in later days enabled her to face this historic crisis. Armies were quickly formed, and seamen experienced in many a fight with Spanish ships added their strength to the small royal fleet.

Privateersmen joined with men of the royal navy in harassing the slower moving Spanish galleons which were beaten off before they could effect a landing. Stung, as it were, by a swarm of bees, burned by fire, lashed by storm, the lumbering, stately vessels fell prey to the English fleet. Greater gun power, superior sailing qualities possessed by the English ships, and better tactics defeated Spain. Barely half the vincible Armada limped back to home ports. "The breath of God has scattered them," proclaimed a commemorative medal celebrating the victory. In the wreckage of the Armada were strewn the hopes of Spain to unchallengeable dominion though she still had strength to mount other armadas. She made later attempts to invade England but these also failed. England saved Protestantism, but she did even more. On the freed waters of the Atlantic rode the ships of many peoples—Dutch, French, English, Scandinavian. In European homelands plans were maturing for permanent settlement in the Western Hemisphere.

★ ARCHITECTS OF EMPIRE

Spain's claim to proprietorship of the New World was challenged not only by force of arms but by force of argument as well. To the Spanish assertion that right of discovery had given her priority, England answered that John Cabot had been scarcely behind Columbus in finding America, and had opened North Atlantic regions to prospective English settlement. An even more satisfying principle, particularly attractive to Englishmen eyeing the advantages of southerly territories, was the doctrine of "effective occupation." Ownership, under this principle, thus went to the country that actually occupied the land. (The French at this time were not seriously pressing their claims to New France.)

It is true that Cabot had given Englishmen a claim to America but many years had gone by before they showed much interest in the Western Hemisphere. It was in 1555 that Richard Eden publicized the discoveries in his *Decades of the Newe Worlde or West India,* and thereafter with increasing momentum English interest and activity rose in the western Atlantic. The early adventurers were in search of a northwest passage to the East Indies or seeking to establish settlements near the West Indies to be used as springboards for attacking Spain's colonies. Sir Martin Frobisher and Sir Humphrey Gilbert spent their own fortunes and risked their lives in several unsuccessful attempts to gain these ends. Gilbert's approach to America inclined to the northern route, touching at Newfoundland, but his tragic failure in 1583 strengthened the position of those who advocated a more southerly approach. The sailing route followed by the Spaniards seemed to be the best after all, and lands in the warmer climates gave greater promise of satisfying England's needs.

The two Richard Hakluyts were the architects of empire in the Elizabethan period. In their manuscript notes and published writings are found the blueprints of the future colonies. One of the earliest links in the chain of events which ultimately bound England to America was

Two theories of the relations of America and Asia

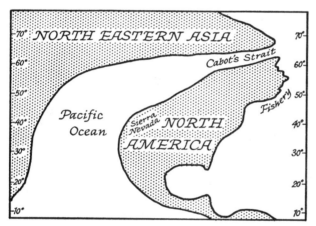

Sebastian Cabot

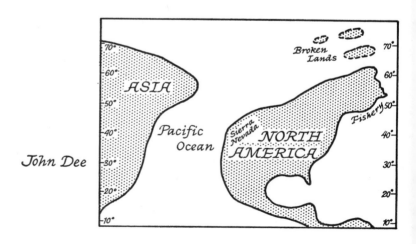

John Dee

Hakluyt's *Divers Voyages Touching the Discovery of America*. The younger and more celebrated imperial chanticleer brought out this small publication in 1582, an important item in the long story of English colonization. His suggestions for choice of site help explain the locations of Roanoke Island and Jamestown: "To plante upon an Ilande in the mouth of some notable river, or upon the poynt of the lande entring into the river, if no such Iland be, were to great ende. For if such river were navigable or portable farre into the lande, then would arise great hope of planting in fertile soyles, and trafficke on the one or thother side of the river, or on both, or the linking in amitie with one or other petie king, contending there for dominion."

But Hakluyt was interested mainly in the problem of finding areas which could produce products for trade with the mother country. He spelled out the details of a mercantilist policy for England, advising that "great observation be taken what every soyle yeeldeth naturally, . . . and what it may be made to yeeld by indevour, . . . that there-uppon we may devise what meanes may be thought of to rayse trades." Ship timber and naval stores should be produced "if great woods be founde," and if the soil should prove favorable "we might so use the matter, as we should not depende upon Spaine for oyles, sacks, resinges, orenges, lemons . . ." Thus might England be freed of dependence upon "doubtfull friends" for her many needs, and at the same time conserve her own wealth.

Hakluyt had no doubt as to England's rightful claim to the land running north of Florida to the Arctic. It was easily accessible from England and defensible at no great cost against possible Spanish op-position. The territory's diversity of climate and soils would "yelde unto us all the commodities of Europe, Affrica and Asia . . . and supply the wantes of all our decayed trades." Colonization would in-vigorate the country's whole economic life, relieving unemployment by expanding industry and commerce. As John Donne later expressed it, overseas settlement would serve not only "as a spleen to drain ill hu-mours of the body, but a liver to breed good blood."

Of even greater significance than the *Divers Voyages* was Hakluyt's "Discourse on the Western Planting," presented in 1584 to Queen Elizabeth in royal audience. This document was sponsored by Sir Walter Raleigh, who was then seeking national support for his Amer-ican venture. The Queen limited herself to approval and good wishes, leaving it to speculating capitalists to risk their funds overseas.

To plant a permanent settlement in a remote region was a complex enterprise, requiring administrative skill, comparatively great financial outlays, and resourceful leadership. It involved thousands of people, moving in entire families and carrying with them their civilization. By comparison looting of Spanish ships and towns by freebooters, while spectacular enough, was a simple undertaking. The latter required small funds and only a few men with a large measure of daring and ruthlessness.

Organizers of "adventures" to America had to compete for available funds with other projects, notably the Levant Company formed in 1592, and the East India Company eight years later. The merchants of London did not view with much enthusiasm American colonizing ventures until after 1606. The superior resources of this business community were then thrown into the successful effort to establish an English colony overseas. Added sources of capital were now tapped by the newer devices of joint-stock companies which spread risks among a larger number of investors, aptly termed "adventurers."

The commercial corporation of this era had many of the characteristics of a self-governing state. It was self-perpetuating (while its charter lasted); it had a constitution and a territorial basis in a grant of land sometimes vaster than European kingdoms. It followed a democratic procedure in the admittance of new members, who would then have a vote in the company; the corporate body acted in a legislative capacity and elected its own officers. It had many of the attributes of sovereignty—coinage of money, regulation of trade, collection of taxes, provision for defense. Here then in the chartered corporation was the prototype of the later governmental structure of the American state.

The reluctance of London merchants to participate in earlier enterprises was no doubt underscored by the pathetic failures of Sir Humphrey Gilbert and his half-brother, Sir Walter Raleigh. Gilbert and Michael Lok, a rich London merchant, another captive of the northwest chimera, backed three voyages (1576, 1577, 1578) led by Martin Frobisher. With incredible courage Frobisher forced his way well into the channels clogged with ice in America's arctic. A decade later (1585–87) John Davis made three voyages into Baffin Bay and the strait that bears his name. In 1610 Henry Hudson, seemingly in continuous search for the way north to the Orient, penetrated the forbidding waters of Hudson Bay and James Bay. Through fog and mists pierced by screams of fluttering sea birds, Hudson pressed on to where the water ran out on the desolate shore. Instead of the Pacific, a continent lay before them which, in time, was to ship to the outside world much of its furs through this frigid corridor.

Gilbert's venture at settlement in Newfoundland in 1583 was quickly doomed, but Raleigh's for a while gave promise of success. Raleigh, the daring soldier and glamorous courtier, was a royal favorite at this time. To him the Queen gave a patent to all the lands he could colonize, asking in return 20 per cent of the profits derived from mining any precious metals that might be discovered there.

★ "I SHALL YET LIVE TO SEE IT AN ENGLISH NATION"

In April, 1584, Raleigh sent out a small advance party to search for a prospective site for settlement. Piloted by a Portuguese navigator, the English ship sailed by way of the Canaries to the West Indies. It was carried northward by the Gulf Stream toward the coast of what was later called North Carolina. Raleigh named this new-found land Virginia, though he gave it no very definite boundaries—vaguely it stretched northward from Florida the entire length of the coast, and westward through wilderness to the "south sea." Among the islands and sand bars a spot was chosen for his colony.

Roanoke Island, sixteen miles long and not quite so wide, seemed to fulfill all the requirements laid down by Hakluyt for pioneer settlement. Roanoke and its neighboring islands formed what was in effect a protected sea running two hundred miles in a north-south direction and varying from ten to fifty miles from east to west. The rivers that flowed into it gave ingress to the mainland. The scouting party returned to England and reported the soil fertile, the seas running with fish, and an equable climate like that of southern Europe—a land "the most plentiful, sweet, fruitful and wholesome of all the world."

In April, 1585, the expedition to settle Roanoke set out from Plymouth under command of Sir Richard Grenville. In addition to a carpenter, sailmaker, and other necessary skilled craftsmen, there were on board several scientists, including Thomas Hariot, and a painter named John White, who went along to record the nature of the land, its inhabitants, its fauna and flora. Unfortunately the small group landed too late in the year to grow food for themselves. The gales of winter revealed unsuspected dangers for their exposed settlement, which lacked a satisfactory harbor. Then, aggravating a bad situation, the once friendly Indians became hostile. With food dwindling and men dispirited, and no sign of Grenville, who had gone back to England promising to return with additional supplies, the Raleigh colony was abandoned. Sir Francis Drake, who was at his enjoyable task of singeing the Spaniard's beard, had just sacked St. Augustine and called at Roanoke. His offer to take the disconsolate settlers home was eagerly accepted. Two weeks after the crude shelters of these first English colonists had been deserted the long delayed Grenville arrived at the ghostly settlement.

Another group of colonists was sent out a second time by Raleigh and his associates in 1587. This group of sixty-eight men, seventeen women (two of them expectant mothers), and nine children intended to land at Chesapeake Bay, but a series of misadventures brought them to Roanoke, the scene of the earlier failure. John White was governor of the colony, which included his daughter and his newborn granddaughter, Virginia Dare. White did not remain long in the colony. He left for home expecting to return shortly with additional settlers and sorely needed supplies. But he had come back to an England feverish with preparations for the war with Spain. It was difficult to find support for the little far-off American colony. When White finally did get back, in 1591, the group had disappeared traceless. The vanished settlement became in the fullness of time the lost colony of sorrowful legend.

The legacy of Raleigh's abortive settlements was, however, richer than the disappointed promoter knew. It gave us Thomas Hariot's *Briefe and True Report of the New Found Land of Virginia* (1588), one of the rarest treasures in any collection of Americana. From the colonizing enterprise came also John White's fascinating water colors of Indian society and of American plants and animals, which were the first English visual representations of the American scene. Hariot's report and White's paintings, published by Theodore De Bry in 1590, became very popular. This publication, with its pictures of Indians and American scenes, fed the curiosity of large numbers of readers anxious to learn about the exotic lands to the west. Though Roanoke failed as a colony, its plan of procedure was still a useful guide to the next generation that successfully founded Jamestown. Despite setbacks Raleigh was doomed to experience in America, his faith long persisted. His prophetic words, "I shall yet live to see it an English nation," had the ring of vitality denied to his ill-fated colonies.

★ THE NEW ENVIRONMENT

The waters of the Atlantic gradually became familiar to Europeans in the century after the voyages of Columbus and Cabot. French, English, and Portuguese fishermen all came to the Grand Banks off the coast of Newfoundland where the sea swarmed with incredible numbers of fish. To America's attraction as a region of superb fishing grounds was added another when its great supplies of fur were revealed. It was pursuit of furs, and yet more furs, that eventually drew Frenchmen, Englishmen, and Dutchmen into America's interior. A few hardy traders had landed on the coast to exchange trifles for precious furs. These pathfinders brought back stories of the little known western land, which were eagerly caught up. But the tales inadequately described America for those who had more than idle curiosity about it; emigrants planning permanent settlement found the venture surrounded with awesome anticipation.

For the emigrants the sea was filled with marvels and dread terrors. Most colonists were landsmen—farmers, servants, craftsmen, clerks—who had had no experience with "blue water." Though captains felt confidence in their ships, landlubbers boarded the craft with misgivings, knowing the violence of seas they would have to face. One fearful Puritan described the nightmare of a storm when the "wind blew mightily, the rayne fell vehemently, and the sea roared . . . and the waves powred themselves over the ship." In the pitch-black darkness the anxiety of passengers was deepened by the tenseness and fears of the crew "running here and there, lowd crying one to another to pull at this and that rope." But landsmen soon learned to console themselves with the knowledge that storms were ordinary at sea, and, as one traveler concluded, "it seldom falls out that a ship perisheth at them if it have sea-roome." From a ship which took the northern route the passengers "saw a mountayne of ice shining as white as snow like to a great rocke or clift on shoare." Icebergs were an astonishing spectacle; equally strange but more amusing were "divers kyndes of fishes sporting in the great waters, great grampuses and huge whales going by companes and puffing up water streams."

The travelers did not have many amusements to look forward to on the long voyage. They were resigned to weeks of seasickness and were thankful if no more serious "maledictions" laid them low. There were, on occasion, terrible afflictions aboard. Epidemics such as small pox, yellow fever, and the plague might race through the ship, and survivors had the sad task of lowering the bodies of victims into the sea.

When finally vessels came within sight of the shore excited passengers could see immense forests broken by clearings of Indian villages. Along the southern reaches of the Atlantic coast were "palms, laurels, cypresses, and other varieties, unknown in Europe; . . . the highest and reddest cedars in the world." The offshore wind carried with it the fragrance of exotic trees and flowers. Northward maples and oaks covered the land, and the pines came down to the shore. The Puritans sailing along the coast near Cape Ann on their approach to America could see "every hill and dale and every island full of gay woods and high trees." What with "greene trees by land and . . . yellow flowers paynting the sea," said the Rev. Francis Higginson, "it made us all desirous to see our new paradise of New England."

The vast forests spelled great wealth to a people coming from an England which was fast being stripped of its trees to supply charcoal for the manufacture of iron and for the building of merchantmen and warships. In these forests newcomers saw huge supplies of lumber for their houses, timber, pitch, and tar for their ships, and towering masts for the royal navy.

The Maine coast with its "high craggy Cliffy Rocks and stony Iles," said Captain John Smith, "was a Country rather to affright, than delight one." But despite the appearance of barrenness "good woods, springs, fruits . . . and fowle" suggested that the interior might well be "verie fertile." Below that region along the coast were broad bays which offered calm after an ocean crossing. Smith found Massachusetts "the Paradise of all those parts," for it had a wealth of corn, Indian gardens, groves, mulberries "and good harbors." Cape Cod was "only a headland of high hills of sand, overgrowne with shrubbie pines, hurts [blueberries], and such trash, but an excellent harbor for all weathers." From the bays there led inland the many rivers offering easy access to the rich interior. But for many years to come homes in America were confined close to the coastal region.

The coast line was actually much longer than the distance measured as the crow flies; the deep indentations multiplied at least three times the frontage of land on the sea. The many fine harbors were open to shipping at all seasons.

Europeans found the American climate strange, and at first hard to adjust to. From the earliest days of discovery it was observed that the extremes of heat and cold were much greater in America than in Europe. The colonies were in the belt of the prevailing westerly winds; and as America lay "to the westward of the Atlantic ocean," wrote one observer, "we therefore feel less of the warming effect of the sea air in winter, as well as less of its cooling effects in summer." Englishmen, accustomed to the damp winds blowing across their island, were surprised at the dryness of American air which they found invigorating. The transition from one season to another in northerly regions was often sharp. Autumn came with a dramatic show of color, making the woods seem all aflame. In the southerly regions of the Carolinas the settlers learned that seasons faded more imperceptibly into one another, and an inviting languor hung in the air.

Even before the first colonists set foot in America they had learned something about its natives. Some of these exotic beings had been exhibited in Europe. Pictures had been made of them in their native habitat, and books had been written about them; the legend of the "noble savage" had already been created. The captain of Raleigh's settlement at Roanoke found the natives hospitable, "most gentle, loving, and faithfull, voide of all guile and treason, and such as live after the manner of the golden age." The Indians had been described as tall, straight-limbed, their complexion "swarthy and tawny," with long black hair; they "bedaube them with oyle, and colours" and "weare feathers of Peacocks and such like."

The "noble savage" had, however, a terrifying aspect also; stories were told of how he attacked in the dead of night with blood-curdling yells, how he set houses afire with flaming arrows, and how he scalped the fleeing inhabitants. There were horrifying narratives, too, of cannibalism told with all the grisly details. The earliest settlers, leaving the comparative safety of their ships, were understandably fearful about the reception that awaited them.

While the Indian was sometimes hostile, he often proved a veritable lifesaver to the whites. When the earliest settlers faced starvation, hospitable Indians brought them fish and maize. The Plymouth colony and the Jamestown settlement were rescued from disaster by supplies from the natives, who not only brought them food but taught them how to grow Indian corn, which matured rapidly; May planting yielded good sized ears to be eaten fresh in July. As grain it provided a supply beyond that of any crop known to Europe. Corn also gave fodder for cattle and husk beds for the colonists. It was the Indians who taught the settlers how to scratch the soil with a pointed stick to plant the kernels in the seed hill.

Through all the years when forests covered the land, and whites built crude homes, hunted, fished, or fought in these primitive surroundings, it was the Indians who taught the Europeans how best to live in the new environment. Whites learned how to travel light in the country, living off the land. Indians taught them how to blaze a trail in the trackless woods, to build fires and signal with columns of smoke. The natives taught the colonists how to hunt deer and bear, to trap the beaver and the fox, and taught them, too, how to dress the skins. Indians showed the settlers how to make maple sugar, and native medicine men revealed many secrets of the healing power of herbs and roots.

It was a sere, brown leaf that most intrigued the colonists. Natives had offered the dry leaves as tokens of friendship to Columbus, and he had marveled at the way men and women drew smoke from the rolled and twisted plant. Within a few decades the fame of the tobacco plant had spread all over Europe, for it had won a universal reputation as a remedy for small pox and nearly all other human ills. People having no need of it as medicine were quick to appreciate its real virtues. Tributes were written to "the bewitching vegetable"; Hawkins and Drake popularized the weed in England, and the ingratiating Raleigh made it acceptable at Queen Elizabeth's court. King James I, however, found it "lothsome to the eye, hatefull to the Nose, harmful to the braine, daungerous to the lungs," but his English subjects relished this "precious stink." They learned from the Indians how to grow it, cure it, and then use it to chew, snuff, or smoke.

Indians taught the colonists how to make and use the canoe on the rivers, which were the only highways to inland America. The lightness and ease of handling the craft made it the ideal means of transport into the interior, from which regions were brought great quantities of valuable furs. The fur trade was most important, and it accounted for the successful settlement of some of the colonies. Indians exterminated one another to control lines of communication in the fur trade. The demand of white men for furs seemed insatiable. Indians tanned buckskins and collected buffalo hides and buffalo wool for the European market. (On the other hand, Indians themselves became, by the end of the seventeenth century, an important market for European goods.) An old New England peddler was an enthusiastic witness to benefits bestowed by the Indians; "A mocacin's the best cover a man ever had for his feet in the woods," he said, "the easiest to get stuff for, the easiest to make, the easiest to wear. And a birch-bark canoe's the best boat a man can have on the river. It's the easiest to get stuff for, easiest to carry, the fastest to paddle."

White settlers were to learn from bitter experience that the Indian could be a cruel foe as well as a helpful friend. Often Indian belligerency was roused by the "fire water" sold to the natives by white traders. Just as King James railed against the tobacco of the Indians, so an Indian sachem indicted the alcohol of the white man. In piteous language an Indian chieftain said that "strong liquor was first sold to us by the Dutch; and they were blind . . . they did not see it was for our hurt; . . . if people will sell it to us, we are so in love with it that we cannot forbear it; when we drink it, it makes us mad, we do not know what we do, we then abuse one another, we throw each other into the fire." This same sachem urging peace between his people and the colonists said, "We are your brothers, and intend to live like brothers with you; we have no mind to have war for when we have war, we are only skin and bones . . . We have not the benefit of the sun to shine on us, we hide us in holes and corners."

Though some Indians found they could live in peace with their white neighbors, others fought to hold their lands against the encroaching colonist. Differences between Indians and whites over conflicting conceptions of land ownership (the natives understood only clan, not individual possession) led to ruptured relations between the two cultures. Sudden attacks on isolated frontier settlements by small bands, or large-scale warfare involving hundreds on both sides marked the tragic course of Indian-white relations. But the increasing strength of whites ultimately overpowered the natives whose weakness was accentuated by warfare among themselves. Had the Indians been able to combine their forces European settlement of America would have been long delayed.

CHAPTER III

Founding the Settlements

★ VIRGINIA

The disinclination of the state to be the chief instrument of empire meant that Britain's early imperial ventures were the creations of private enterprise. Chartered companies (following established custom for doing business in Europe) were organized for the pursuit of private gain in Asia and America. But desire for individual profit was co-ordinated with a vision of a prosperous national community, so eloquently proclaimed by Hakluyt. While the state officially abstained from committing its financial resources, it threw its prestige and approbation, and its diplomacy when necessary, behind colonial enterprise.

Permanent English settlement in America begins with Jamestown in 1607. Large expenditures and intensive efforts were made there for several years. Then in 1612 attention was diverted to Bermuda. From 1618 to 1623 Virginia was again the focus of large-scale colonial activity. After that date the emphasis was for awhile once more on the West Indies. On the mainland, New England in the 1630's was the most important achievement in settlement, with the Chesapeake area playing a secondary role.

The famous charter granted to the Virginia Company in 1606 acknowledged two groups; one from London, generally referred to as the London Company, which included "Knights, gentlemen, merchants" planning to settle in the southern part of that vast territory they called "Virginia"; the other group, known as the Plymouth Company, contained adventurers from the ports of Plymouth, Bristol, and Exeter interested in settling its northerly region. A royal council of thirteen was to be the supreme governmental authority, under the crown, over both colonies.

Just over a hundred men left London toward the end of 1606 bound for Virginia in three ships. Following the established route to the West Indies via the Canaries, where they stopped on the way, the ships arrived at Chesapeake Bay in April, 1607. In accordance with instructions to find a defensible site, suitable for trade and for searching out the resources of the interior, the colonists moved some thirty miles up a river (the James) emptying into the Bay. There, on a swampy peninsula affording good anchorage and seeming protection from land and sea, the choice was made. The settlement was called Jamestown after King James. "Now Falleth every man to work," said Captain John Smith, "the council contrive the fort, the rest cut down trees to make place to pitch their tents, some provide clapboard to relade the ships, some make gardens, some nets, &c." Even before settlers could build proper homes they felled trees for lumber to be marketed in London. The increasing scarcity of wood in England made this a valuable cargo.

The colony progressed with painful slowness. Men on the ground had a different view from those in comfortable London. They knew from sad experience what it cost in human terms to plant a colony in the wilderness. "Our drink was water," wrote Thomas Studley wryly, and "our lodgings castles in the air." Their food was a small portion of wheat and barley which, "having fried some 26 weeks in the ship's hold contained as many worms as grains. . . . With this lodging and diet, our extreme toil in bearing and planting palisadoes so strained and bruised us, and our continual labor in the extremity of the heat had so weakened us as were cause sufficient to have made us . . . miserable . . ." In the few months from May to September, says Studley, "fifty . . . we buried." When their plight seemed most dark "all our provision spent" and "each hour expecting the fury of the savages," God "the patron of all good endeavours, in that desperate extremity, so changed the hearts of the savages that they brought such plenty of their fruits and provision that no man wanted." Studley was unwilling to throw all the blame for the troubles endured by the settlers on the Company: "First, the fault of our going was our own. What could be thought fitting or necessary we had, but what we should find, what we should want, where we should be we were all ignorant, and supposing to make our passage in two months, with victual to live and the advantage of the spring to work, we were at sea five months, where we both spent our victual and lost the opportunity of the time and season to plant."

But the unbroken spirit of men like Thomas Studley portended eventual success for English colonization; "Such actions have ever since the world's beginning been subject to such accidents," he wrote, "and everything of worth is found full of difficulties but nothing so difficult as to establish a commonwealth so far remote from men and means."

As did most early colonists these made a search for gold—which did not exist. But while it lasted the hunt was feverish; as Captain Smith reported, "no talke, no hope, nor worke, but dig gold, wash gold, refine gold, load gold," that turned out not to be the precious metal. The settlers soon outgrew their dreams of sudden wealth, and Virginia gold became a subject for ribald laughter on the London stage. The colonists were expected to forget the gold and to plant certain products suitable, it was believed, to that climate. These included sugar, prunes, grapes, olives, cotton, and tobacco.

To create a settlement required leadership; to tame a wilderness hard manual labor; and to deal with natives tact and resourcefulness. Added to the difficulties were temperamental differences among the leaders in Jamestown which led to friction and bitterness. William Byrd, a sophisticated chronicler of his native colony, was to write at a later date that the original settlement consisted of "about an Hundred men, most of them Reprobates of good Familys."

The enterprise was handicapped by the quality of the first settlers, most of them unused to hard work, undisciplined, unadaptable. Smith wrote that "a hundred good workmen were worth a thousand such gallants." Another handicap was the original pooling of the produce of labor into a common stock, to be the property of the company backing the Virginia settlement. The idler was thus allowed to live upon the industrious. "When our people were fed out of the common store and laboured jointly together," said Smith, "glad was he could slip from his labour, or slumber over his taske . . ." But when private ownership was later established, he said, people did in a day what had formerly taken them a week; "wee reaped not so much corne from the labours of thirtie, as now three or four doe provide for themselves." Only when Smith took charge of the bickering group toward the end of 1608 did promise of success attend the Jamestown experiment. With the threat of banishment to the wilderness he forced the drones to do their share of work.

Smith was a typical soldier of fortune, supremely self-confident, but with justification, for time and recent research have vindicated the claims he made about his own achievements. Perhaps it isn't true that he was rescued by Pocahontas, the attractive Indian princess who, in her youth played the tomboy, naked, in the streets of Jamestown. But as he told it, it made a first-rate story.

In England more funds were sought by the London Company, then being reorganized under a new charter and invigorated under the leadership of Sir Thomas Smith, the country's greatest merchant. The company was given a grant of land extending "from sea to sea" (for hopes persisted of finding a westward passage), and from Point Comfort as the center, 200 miles north and a similar distance south. All the machinery of propaganda was called into play to tempt investors. A ballad advertising a lottery for the colony appealed to every sentiment:

> Let no man thinke that he shall loose,
>   Though he no Prize possesse;
> His substaunce to *Virginia* goes,
>   Which God, no doubt will blesse,
> And in short time send from that land,
>   much rich commoditie;
> So shall we thinke all well bestowd
>   upon this Lotterie.

The old familiar voice of Hakluyt also joined in the siren song.

The irresistible appeal in behalf of patriotism, religion, and profit yielded a most gratifying public response. Nobles and merchants, along with 282 "citizens" invested generously, and as the Spanish ambassador reported, "there is no poor, little man, nor woman, who is not willing to subscribe something for this enterprise."

In June, 1609, 600 people, 500 of them men, the remainder women and children, were sent out to Virginia on nine ships. A thousand more were to follow in August. The essential tools for clearing the land and building homes, churches, and fortifications were all aboard. So too, were the chests filled with clothing, linens, and all the familiar items of household use: needles and thread, scissors, wooden dishes and bowls, kettles, frying pans, soap, candles, drugs, etc. These things, which to established societies seem so commonplace, are to pioneer communities veritable treasures. Food was carried overseas until the first harvest of grains and vegetables (for which seeds were carried along) should bring its fruits. A few precious animals were taken on the crowded ships for breeding stock in the new land.

The people who went in this migration "on adventure" received a specified number of shares in the expected profits of the company. The colonist with superior technical competence or performing official functions was given a larger number of shares than the investor who stayed at home and risked only his money. Here was an acknowledgment of the settlers' vital role in the undertaking, and it was designed to refute the rumor that the migrants to Virginia were helpless and exploited. The planters (the name given to those planting a colony) had thus gained at the outset not only equal rights in all dividends, but a certain dignity of standing which satisfied a basic human need.

The governor of the colony, advised by a council, was given great power. The strongest bulwark against arbitrary action lay in the promises to the colonists that they would possess "all Liberties, Franchizes, and Immunities" commonly enjoyed by Englishmen. But the colonists were to find by bitter experience that a long fight lay ahead to translate these promises into realities. Eventually they won far more than was promised.

The settlers bit by bit created the structure of representative government. While resting upon the valuable English foundation, colonial institutions in time came to diverge from those of the mother country. Much more than their countrymen in England, who had no written constitution, the colonists placed a high value upon written documents as safeguards of their liberties. This firm belief in a body of written, fundamental law has been of deep significance throughout American history.

The inherited formula of government underwent a sea change, and in the fullness of years an increasing proportion of the population won political power. This power was to be used to curb the authority of governors and to enlarge the area of human freedom—in creating opportunities for earning a livelihood, in religion, in education, and in the social relations of man to man. What had once been thought a goal worthy of achievement in itself, the recreation of English institutions overseas, was to be found inadequate. The sights were set higher, and a colonial people was ultimately transformed into an American society freed from the fetters of Old World constrictions.

★ THE PRECARIOUS COLONY

It was one thing to erect safeguards against the behavior of arbitrary officials, it was another to create an orderly society. The winter of 1609–10 in Virginia was a severe testing time for the infant colony. After long weeks at sea, physically weakened, colonists were easy prey to disease in an unaccustomed climate. Their late arrival in the colony in 1609 prevented much of a crop from being harvested. Undisciplined settlers behaved anarchically; "no man would acknowledge a superior," it was complained, "nor could from this headless and unbridled multitude, be anything expected but disorder and riot." Untenanted houses were made into firewood; animals brought over with great difficulty for the breeding of needed herds were eaten; hostile Indians killed the unwary; and there were dark rumors of cannibalism. When spring came after the "starving time" of that winter, less than seventy planters were alive.

The survivors were ready to abandon this scene of desolation in June, 1610. They were already on shipboard, moving down the James River, when the providential arrival of three ships with 150 men gave new spirit to the colony. By so slim a margin was the settlement preserved—

for future trials. Again new funds were raised in the homeland, £18,000 by the early part of 1611, and more supplies and men were sent to Virginia.

Under the leadership of Sir Thomas Dale, who instituted rigorous discipline, the colony was reorganized. Emphasis was now placed on exploiting the agricultural and trading possibilities of the area of settlement, rather than on vain expectations of striking it rich through commerce with the South Seas or on discovering a gold mine.

In 1611 the colony had about seven hundred people, only thirty of whom were women, and everyone living under an almost military routine. The planters lived in "two fair rowes of houses of Framed timber" in a community with market place, church, and a wharf which handled the cargoes of ocean-going ships. But Jamestown, despite various agricultural experiments, including the culture of grapes and silkworms, was still without a satisfactory marketable product. Absence of anticipated riches diminished the enthusiasm of promoters in England, who fixed their eyes more hopefully on the Bermudas.

This did not mean abandonment of Virginia, however, but rather a linking of the two colonies together with priority favoring the Bermudas. The latter fell under control of the Virginia company by the terms of a new charter granted in 1612. A significant feature of this charter was the democratization of the Virginia council which was the chief governing authority of the colony in America. It now had the very important function of drafting "Laws and Ordinances, for the Good and Welfare" of the overseas settlement. With the establishment later of a general assembly of the Virginia colonists, the planters in America had, in effect, duplicated the existing pattern of government created by the adventurers at home. Virginia remained under control of a typical English commercial company until the colony came under the direct authority of the crown in 1624.

Though many shiploads of people had gone to Virginia since 1607, it numbered only 350 in 1616. One token of the company's recognition that it was establishing a commonwealth, and not a trading post, was its decision to send out groups of women, most of whom were certified to be "young, handsome, and well recommended." They were so eagerly welcomed that others quickly followed. The planters paid ardent courtship to the girls, and as each was won, her betrothed husband paid the passage money in tobacco. Supplying wives for the restless males would, it was hoped, make them "more settled and less moveable." As Edward Eggleston says: "When there were house mothers in the cabins, and children born in the country, the settlers no longer dreamed of returning to England: and there was soon a young generation that knew no other skies than those that spanned the rivers, fields and vast primeval forests of their native Virginia, which now for the first time became a home."

To increase interest in the plantation, it was proposed to distribute among individual owners a good share of acreage so dearly bought from the tenacious wilderness. The general feeling was apparently one of dissatisfaction at working for a company in England not always sympathetic to the planters' problems. The company therefore decided to award more land to the colonists, under the headright system, by which a planter would get an additional fifty acres for every person transported at his expense to the colony. For those suffering from land hunger, and nearly everybody was, Virginia's large expanse offered opportunities vastly greater than the Bermudas' restricted area.

After a dozen years the infant Jamestown settlement showed definite signs of emerging from its swaddling clothes. The profitable cultivation of tobacco was, in the end, to guarantee long life to the colony. It was in 1612 that John Rolfe planted West Indian seed that produced the superior tobacco leaf which, at length, brought wealth beyond the measure of Aztec gold or Peruvian mines. In a few short years so valuable was tobacco that Virginians were planting it everywhere, even in the streets of Jamestown. As early as 1630 exports from the colony were at the rate of a half-million pounds a year.

Relations with the Indians were eased. The marriage between Rolfe and Pocahontas was in the nature of a "dynastic match," bringing peace (for a time) between the English colony and Powhatan, father of the bride and subtle "emperor" of the local Indians.

The sense of increasing security was reflected in a new code of laws drawn up by the company under pressure from the colonists. The latter, objecting to the martial law they had been forced to endure, insisted that civilian authority take precedence over the military in accordance with English tradition. In the provision for a representative assembly in the colony there was promise of greater authority for the planters in Virginia. "The generall Assemblie" was made up of two bodies: one, a council of state comprising the governor and other appointees of the company; the other, the House of Burgesses, included two representatives chosen by the inhabitants of each community. This assembly, holding its first historic session in July, 1619, met to hear petitions, legislate, exercise judicial power and, in time, won the right also of taxation. The governor still had the right of veto, as did the company in London. But the latter promised that greater stability in Virginia would win for the colonial assembly a status equal to that of the company. None of its orders would then bind the colony "unless they bee ratified in like manner in ther generall Assembly."

The improved economic position of the planters and the recognition of their political aspirations would, it was hoped, overcome the hesitation of Englishmen to venture to a settlement seeming ill-starred. Granted that these concessions were made under pressure, and in hopes of profit, the fact remains that a commercial organization extended overseas the familiar pattern of a civilized society, with its precious guarantees, so laboriously built up through the centuries in England.

★ VIRGINIA BECOMES A ROYAL PROVINCE

The failure of the Virginia Company to return anticipated profits and suspicions of mismanagement resulted in 1619 in a new group taking over its direction. This group was led by Sir Edwin Sandys, who for years had been associated with adventures to America. At home he was a leader in the parliamentary effort to curb Stuart despotism. Sandys was a gifted promoter, and in a few years reinvigorated the Company. Within three years of his election nearly 3600 people emigrated to Virginia.

Sandys made a remarkable attempt to fulfill the economic program that Hakluyt had sketched for a colony. In the effort to establish an iron industry in Virginia £5,000 were spent. Polish experts were sent over to guide the colonists in producing pitch, tar, and potash; Germans were brought from Hamburg to aid in cutting timber; a Frenchman was summoned to help produce salt for the fisheries. Even the manufacture, under Italian guidance, of glass beads for trade with the Indians was projected. Such grandiose plans needed funds larger than were available to the Company. Besides, the run of ill luck had not yet ceased for Virginia.

A great blow fell in March, 1622, with a wholesale massacre by the Indians. The attack came, with startling suddenness, on the unsuspecting colony which had been lulled by several years of peace and the belief that the Indians could be converted to Christianity. The colony was less compact than formerly, leaving it open to devastating raids. About 350 whites were killed and the settlement was demoralized. Because crops were neglected in the desperate struggle with the natives, food ran short and the "starving time" of earlier memory was repeated. In the year after the massacre 500 more of the colonists died. The colony had shrunk to less than 1,300 although 4,000 had come to the settlement since 1618. In a five-year period the death rate had reached the catastrophic figure of three out of four. From so great a disaster the Virginia Company could not recover.

Internal dissension among the London adventurers added to the Company's woes. There were individuals close to King James, hostile to Sandys, who wished to destroy the Company. An investigation revealed its bankruptcy as well as the straitened circumstances of the colony. It was estimated that more than £100,000 had been expended on it; if the colony were to be shouldered with the Company's debts its growth would be impeded for many years. To save the colony it was decided to wipe away the corporation's obligations, which was done by dissolving the Virginia Company in 1624. Virginia now became a royal province, and entered on a new stage in her already turbulent history.

★ NEW ENGLAND BEFORE 1620

The charter given in 1606 for colonization in America, it will be remembered, provided for a Plymouth Company to settle the area to the north of that pre-empted by the London Company. The Plymouth group vainly attempted to plant a colony at Sagadahoc, Maine, in the summer of 1607, but after a few months conceded victory to the climate, disease, and Indians. The colony, said one of its backers, was pursued with "the malice of the Divell." This part of America had been first explored in some detail by Bartholomew Gosnold, George Weymouth, and others. Weymouth took back to England a cargo of timber, fur, and "five savages, two canoas with all their bows and arrows." The naked Indians, struggling to escape, could only be dragged on board "by their long hair." Here was a prize to be exhibited before Englishmen fascinated by everything relating to the fantastic New World.

Published reports of voyages stimulated the interest of Ferdinando Gorges, and his associates, in the northerly region. A number of trading and exploring expeditions were dispatched to it in the decade after the failure at Sagadahoc, on the Kennebec River. Captain John Smith made a map of this part of "Virginia," to which he gave the name New England, described it with care, and brought back to England fish and furs valued at £1,500. No permanent settlement, however, was made there by the English as a result of these efforts, which lacked the sustained drive of the London Company in their part of "Virginia." Meanwhile the French and Dutch were also in the northern region laying claims to various portions of it.

Gorges and forty associates in 1620 reorganized the old Plymouth Company into a new group called the New England Council or Corporation for New England. The charter of this corporation gave it the right to award title to land and to establish colonies in an area between 40° and 48° North Latitude. The New England Council, inadequately supported, did little on its own in its fifteen years of existence to take advantage of its privileges, but it did sublease its land to others. It made many grants, often overlapping, which occasioned long-drawn out disputes in the future. Four grants were the bases of permanent colonies: the area at Plymouth to the Pilgrims in 1621; seven years later the land between the Merrimac and the Charles Rivers to the Company of Massachusetts Bay; two grants in 1629 between the Merrimac and the Kennebec which were the foundations for New Hampshire and Maine.

Some of the leaders in colonizing enterprises in America were at the same time promoting colonization in Ireland. Protestant Scots in large number were sent over to Ireland to settle lands taken from the Roman Catholic natives. English imperial policy counted on the Scots to make Ireland safe against future Spanish attacks based on this territory. The reasons advanced for American colonization were the same put forth for settlement in Ireland: relief for excess population, markets for goods, and land for the land-hungry. Between 1609 and 1625 thousands of Scots went to Ulster, surpassing in number the emigrants to Virginia. But in the long run America was to prove more attractive than Ireland to prospective settlers.

★ PURITANISM

Land and trade, of themselves, were insufficient to bind Englishmen to New England. Firmer bond was found in the fixative quality of religion. The Protestant Reformation in Europe had resulted in the creation of a number of churches independent of the authority of Rome. Among them was the Church of England which, though differing in theology, had retained much of the structure and practice of Catholicism. The Puritans, originally in the Church of England, which many of them were reluctant to leave, sought to purify the established church of any vestiges of "popery," preferring a church organization of councils (Presbyterianism) or a federation of independent churches (Congregationalism). Queen Elizabeth scoffed at Puritan proposals. "Those kinds of platforms and devices which they speak of are absurd." "I see many," she told Parliament, "overbold with God Almighty, making too many subtle scannings of His blessed will, as lawyers do with human testaments."

Puritans wanted the good life on this earth, just as others did, but their deep, religious convictions demanded it be lived under the discipline of a Holy Commonwealth. This was to be built in accord with standards laid down in that supreme authority, the Bible. The image of such a commonwealth was to a Puritan all too obviously wanting in Elizabethan and Stuart England.

It is difficult to speak with accuracy about Puritanism (the word itself first came into use in 1567), for there were many kinds of Puritans whose beliefs changed with the changing scene. But there were some fundamental tenets to which they generally adhered. Central to Puritanism was an experience of conversion which marked off the believer from the mass of men. "The root of the matter is always a new birth," writes Alan Simpson, "which brings with it a conviction of salvation and a dedication to warfare against sin." Long before John Bunyan popularized the image, Puritans spoke of a daily walk with God during which man's mind was filled with thoughts of the spiritual life. Puritans deplored the loose behavior of English society, whose refusal to take religion seriously scandalized them. They had an intense feeling about civic freedom, a deep moral earnestness and a horror of carefree gaiety. Puritan intolerance was not always to blame for the ban on pleasure. Local statutes occasionally forbade dice and cards in the ale-house, as well as excessive drinking. Professor Wallace Notestein, in his recent book, *The English People on the Eve of Colonization 1603–1630,* has suggested that Puritans were becoming more ascetic in their outlook at just about the time when they were embarking for Massachusetts. It was a stricter type of Puritanism that was carried overseas. It may well be that New England Puritans, at least in their earlier years, cut off as they were from the main currents of English life, were more fanatical than their brethren in the old country.

Calvinism (which in many respects seemed synonymous with Puritanism) had a strong appeal to the middle class. For all his otherworldliness the Puritan seemed to be equally at home on both sides of the Jordan. Though the emphasis of Puritanism was on salvation and morality it also was much concerned with industry and thrift. As one Puritan preacher expressed it, those who will not sweat on earth shall sweat in hell.

Puritanism appealed not only to businessmen, but also to farmers in some rural areas like East Anglia; and among university men, particularly in Cambridge, it found some of its most able supporters. From these circles came the most distinguished leaders of the Puritan migration to New England. Originally Puritanism was probably a movement of the intelligentsia, who were strongly supported by middle-class elements—merchants, lawyers, and small landholders. Puritanism had influential voices in the press, parliament, and among many of the country gentry. Certainly the emphasis on education was a permanent characteristic of Puritanism. Literacy was a minimum requirement, for Puritans insisted that all should be able to read the Bible for themselves.

Their "zeal" (so the Puritans themselves spoke of it) was their hallmark, and their intellectual toughness a byword. Long after the Puritans ceased to be politically important, the well-known Puritan conscience lived on, for good and ill, to affect profoundly the American character. Unselfishness, and humble immersion in a cause that transcended the life of any one individual, were not uncommon among Puritans. It was an expression of their ability to maintain, for the most part, excellent balance between individualism and the requirements of the social order. Puritans, like practically all of their contemporaries, believed in the union of Church and State, and emphasized especially that "the moral leaders of a people should have political power." Though Puritans were a minority they had impressive religious, political, and economic strength in England, which they exerted to the discomfiture of royalty.

The Puritans had virtues enough without our imputing to them imaginary ones. And they also had their shortcomings. They were, for example, close to their own generation in such an important matter as intolerance. Only in their time of trial did they even consider the idea of religious toleration. In common with all tightly knit communities Puritans frowned on any important divergence of opinion. In politics their flirtation with democratic ideas had no conviction; if the crown had been willing to aid them the Puritans seemed ready to accept the theory of divine-right monarchy.

The Puritans indeed wished to be thought of as the most law-abiding of subjects, abjuring, for the most part, the right of revolution. A Puritan in Elizabeth's England found guilty of writing a seditious pamphlet lost his right hand to the executioner, but raised his hat with his left hand, crying "God save the Queen!" They did insist, however, that whatever social restrictions were imposed by authority must be satisfactorily explained to the community, which was not to accept them on blind faith. The average Puritan, in the running of his ecclesiastical organization, played a more important part than did the Catholic in his. (One of the bitter legacies of Puritanism, it should be recorded, was its unyielding anti-Catholicism.) Though in outward practice the ideals of Puritanism were often subverted, the inner emphasis tended to be on the play of the free mind. Therein lay the seed of future rebellions against its own leadership.

★ "PLIMOTH PLANTATION"

In England the Pilgrims were a group more radical than their fellow Puritans, and "seeing they could not have the word freely preached, and the sacraments administered without idolatrous gear . . . concluded to break off from the public churches and separate in private houses." This movement became known as Separatism, and was severely prosecuted by the crown. To preserve their religious community a small group left Nottinghamshire for Holland where at Leyden in 1609 they established a Congregational Church. They lived there for twelve years, but desire for economic improvement and the yearning to preserve their English heritage forced them to consider moving again. Like millions of later emigrants, consideration for their offspring was uppermost in their minds: "For many of their children, that were of best dispositions and gracious inclinations, having lernde to bear the yoake in their youth . . . were, oftentimes, so oppressed with their hevie labours, that though their minds were free and willing, yet their bodies bowed under the weight of the same, and became decreped in their early youth, the vigor of nature consumed in the very budd as it were."

But where to go? And the answer given in that incomparable chronicle of the Pilgrims by William Bradford was "some of those vast & unpeopled countries of America, which are fruitful & fitt for habitation" and which were "devoyd of all civill inhabitants." To the faint in heart who objected to removal thither where famine, disease, and scalping Indians awaited them, Bradford made brave answer: "that all great & honourable actions are accompanied with great difficulties, and must be both enterprised and overcome with answerable courages. It was granted the dangers were great, but not desperate; the difficulties were many, but not invincible."

The Virginia Company, at the prompting of Sir Edwin Sandys, gave the Leyden group a grant of land, while London merchants and the Pilgrims subscribed £7,000 to finance the plantation in the usual manner of a joint stock enterprise. After many aggravating delays the "Mayflower," crowded with 101 passengers, left in September, 1620. Cramped by tight quarters, weary of dirty weather and a monotonous diet of cheese, dried fish, and hard tack, with only an occasional drink of beer to cheer them, they arrived nine weeks later at Cape Cod harbor, "where they ridd in saftie." Before debarking they entered into a compact among themselves (the famous Mayflower Compact) to "submit to such government and governours, as we should by common consent agree to make and choose . . ." "After our landing," wrote one of the Pilgrims, "we came to a conclusion to . . . set on the main land, . . . on an high ground. . . . So there we made our randevous, and a place for some of our people, resolving in the morning to come ashore and to build houses."

The time of their arrival was unfortunate. "It was winter," Bradford recalled, "and they that know the winters of that country know them to be sharp and violent, and subject to cruel and fierce storms, dangerous to travel to known places, much more to search an unknown coast. Besides, what could they see but a hideous and desolate wilderness, full of wild beasts and wild men?" And Bradford remembering their great loneliness said, "If they looked behind them, there was the mighty ocean which they had passed, and was now as a main bar and gulf to separate them from all the civil parts of the world."

The tragedy of that first winter is starkly revealed in Bradford's report that only half of the colonists survived it. Two friendly Indians, Samoset and Squanto, eased their trials by teaching them how to grow corn and catch fish. In the fall of November, 1621, their first Thanksgiving was celebrated, for a harvest had been reaped, huge turkeys and venison were abundant, and a supply ship had returned from England. But crops were not to be counted on too regularly, and within a year or so the dependence of Massachusetts on the ocean was made manifest when Bradford wrote, "God fedd them out of the sea for the most part . . ."

From the plentiful supply of timber at hand the Pilgrims built the boats needed for fishing. Captain John Smith, who knew the New England waters, had suggested that "the main staple" for trade be fish. He conceded that though fish "may seem a mean and base commodity," it was the source from which the Hollanders gained their great wealth; "Never could the Spaniard with all his mines of gold and silver pay his debts, his friends, and army half so truly as the Hollanders still have done by this contemptible trade of fish."

The Pilgrim settlement, in its first days, like the earlier one at Jamestown, suffered from its decision to pool the property of the community. The whole accumulation was to be the possession of the London corporation which fitted out the emigrants, and at the end of seven years it was to be divided, every settler and every shareholder in England who paid ten pounds sharing equally. This was an unfavorable bargain for the colonists. They had to enter into partnership with stay-at-home shareholders or "adventurers" and see the latter profit by their exertions; while they had to share in the colony itself on a perfectly equal basis, so that the idle and incompetent fared as well as the most industrious and efficient settlers. The Pilgrims were an unusually thrifty and homogeneous set of men, bound together by a strong religious enthusiasm, yet the experiment was a failure with them as with the Virginians. For a time the colony underwent dissensions and quarrels, some of the members were rankly insubordinate, and idleness and wastefulness limited the means of all.

After two years, however, the settlement was placed on a more satisfactory basis. The sagacious William Bradford, who became governor, divided the land among the various families, and made each the owner of its farm. Every household, it was decreed, must look out for its own wants, or suffer the consequences. Bradford was able to write a few years afterward: "Any general want or suffering hath not been among them to this day." Though the company in England disliked this division, it was the only way to give the colony vigor. Ultimately, the English partners sold out their interest for £1,800, and the whole joint-stock principle was abandoned. Each family in the colony was confirmed in the title to its own farm, and the movable property was likewise divided.

With great tenacity and ably led by Bradford and Elder William Brewster, the Pilgrims worked to make a success of their settlement; after ten years their colony numbered 300. By fishing and trading for furs with the Indians they assembled cargoes for commerce with other American communities and with Europe. Supplying the new Puritan settlements nearby with food and livestock proved profitable. They were thus able to pay off their debt to their London backers and establish an independent community. In after years offshoots were founded close by, but the Plymouth colony never grew to sizable proportions.

The bequest of the Pilgrims to America cannot be measured by any quantitative scale. In an age of intolerance they practiced at least some toleration. Where other Puritans insisted on harsh justice they were inclined to preach charity. They reduced the large number of capital offenses in England's criminal code to seven, and actually demanded the sentence of death in but two, sodomy and murder. Not wealthy in this world's goods, they left a remembrance of high courage, which is one of this country's richest legacies.

★ MASSACHUSETTS BAY COLONY

While the Plymouth colony was winning its fight to survive, several small trading and fishing settlements to the north were struggling to maintain themselves. One of these, on Cape Ann, had been acquired by a group of Puritans. In 1628 John Endicott and a few others arrived as advance guard for the large migration expected to follow. The next year, under a charter granted by Charles I, the Massachusetts Bay Company was formed under such leaders as John Winthrop and Thomas Dudley. In the spring of 1630, on Easter Monday, near a thousand men and women left England on seventeen ships to begin their lives anew in Massachusetts Bay Colony. One of their leaders had urged them on with the reminder that "those that love their owne chimney corner and dare not go farre beyond their owne townes end shall never have the honour to see the wonderfull workes of Almighty God."

The great Puritan migration which thus began was closely related to political and religious change in England, for it coincided with a period of depression and apprehension if not of actual persecution. When the first seventeen ships came over, the Protestant cause seemed darkly beset in Europe. Germany was in the throes of the Thirty Years' War, and Wallenstein had won important victories over the Protestant forces; in France, Richelieu had crushed a Protestant revolt and reduced their cities to submission. In England the new king, Charles I, and his principal clerical adviser, Bishop Laud, were committed to a restoration of high-church ceremonies in the Church of England, and to the vindication of episcopal authority. They insisted on genuflection, the proper intonation of services, and obedience to the church heads appointed by the crown. Puritans resented this intensely, for many feared that Charles and Laud would finally bring the Church of England back into the Catholic fold and thus undo the results of the Reformation.

More moderate Puritans might have swallowed Laud, but it was harder to swallow the political humiliations they suffered. In 1629 the quarrel between Charles and Parliament became so bitter that it burst all bounds. The King dissolved Parliament, imprisoned his opponents, and for ten years got on without any Parliament at all. It was a decade in which the Crown, Laud, and the Earl of Strafford seemed bent on subverting the liberties of all Englishmen; and many believed that the best course was to quit English soil, and build up in America a new commonwealth, with a purified church and full political freedom. The result was the great migration which, using no fewer than 1,200 vessels, brought over so many people—with cattle, household goods, and other property—that whole towns in north-central and northeastern England were left half depopulated. Their new settlements included doctors, ministers, lawyers, schoolteachers, businessmen, artisans, craftsmen, and writers.

Among these settlers were ancestors of a number of Presidents: the two Adamses, Abraham Lincoln, Theodore Roosevelt, Calvin Coolidge, and Franklin D. Roosevelt. Boston had become a thriving city with links southward to the Caribbean and eastward to the Mediterranean and to the ports of the mother country. The New England which thus arose across the Atlantic was a microcosm of Old England, and had within it the seeds of vigorous growth in a hundred different fields.

The Puritans who left in the spring of 1630 had a stormy voyage with rain and breaking North Atlantic seas soaking the quarters below. Having endured intense cold and grown quarrelsome from close confinement they went ashore at Cape Ann in relief, and were delighted to come upon "a store of fine strawberries." But like the settlers in Virginia and at Plymouth, who experienced terrible decimation the first winter, those at Massachusetts were also quickly cut down. Within a few months two hundred had died, and among the anguished remainder some were forced to spend a pitiless New England winter in tents. Only because the clearness of the air gave the sun surprising warmth was it possible to endure the "north-west wind which . . . comes over the cold frozen land." Wolves skulking close to the new settlements preyed on the few heads of live-stock that had not been lost at sea. Many settlers suffered severely from scurvy, until a newly arrived ship brought lemon juice to cure them. Scurvy was not the most serious of their ills; deadlier ailments kept their mortality rate high.

The colonists buried their dead, built homes for the living, and took heart in the knowledge they were creating a new society. They began to cultivate "land which . . . never had been Ploughed since the Creation." Here they grew good crops of Indian corn whose virtues they quickly learned to appreciate. It was an abundant and nourishing crop which could be eaten in various forms. One of its great advantages was that it could be grown together with beans and pumpkins. The corn maturing first served as bean poles, while the pumpkin vines spread along the ground to ripen in the fall. From the sea were harvested great quantities of cod, haddock, herring, mackerel, and "lobsters very great."

Returning weary from their labor in the fields or on the sea the men welcomed the crude comfort of their primitive homes. These were made of boards fixed vertically in the ground like a fence, which formed the walls. The roof, sloped front and back, was thatched, and through the peak came the chimney which was made of tightly interlaced branches, daubed with clay. The fireplace was the center of family life. Here food was cooked and eaten. Here the men whittled, and the women did their spinning, and here too, the family gathered to read the word of God.

★ THE BIBLE COMMONWEALTH

Community life centered in the meetinghouse, which was both church and town hall. The political development of Massachusetts was to offer some striking contrasts to Virginia. The Puritans had purchased the stock of the Bay Company, and now as complete owners of the corpora-tion had carried their charter with them to New England. This act transformed the conventional trading company, managed by resident English stockholders, into a self-governing community almost independ-ent of the mother country. The New England spirit of independent-mindedness, which so frequently proved troublesome to the homeland, thus had a legal justification.

Massachusetts at the very beginning was by its charter an oligarchy, headed by Governor John Winthrop and ruled by less than a dozen magistrates. The charter of the Bay Colony vested authority in a legis-lative body (general court) made up of shareholders or "freemen," along with a governor, deputy governor, and a council of "assistants" chosen by the freemen. But fewer than 1 per cent of the colony's population were freemen in its first days. Almost immediately the demand was raised that a larger number of people be granted the right to participate in political decisions. When a tax levy was imposed in 1632, one community, Watertown, protested "that it was not safe to pay moneys after that sort, for fear of bringing themselves and posterity into bondage." Soon the slow process of enlarging the area of political freedom was begun. The governor and his assistants, who were voted upon each year, were now to be joined by two representatives (deputies) from each town in the levying of taxes. By 1634 deputies had also won the right to participate with the governor and the assistants not only in taxing but in making all other laws and extending the vote to more members of the community. Nonfreemen voted on local matters and could hold local offices. The electorate in Massachusetts, it is worth noting, was proportionally larger than in England.

Certain precedents in Massachusetts practice were the foundations of American political traditions. The set date for annual election of governmental officials and representatives became, with modifications, an established feature of American life. It fixed in the public imagination the responsibility of authority to the will of the community. And the ever-present insistence on written documents was once again manifested. Winthrop revealed this development in his *Journal,* under date of 1635: "The deputies having conceived great danger to our state, in regard that our magistrates, for want of positive laws, . . . might proceed according to their [own] discretions, it was agreed that some men should be appointed to frame a body of grounds of laws, in resemblance to a Magna Charta, which . . . should be received for fundamental laws." As a result of the steady pressure for broadening the base of government, the famous "Body of Liberties" was adopted in 1641. It expressed hostility to feudal restrictions on land and to monopolistic practices in business. It safeguarded traditional English liberties of trial by jury and due process of law. Its list of capital crimes was a small fraction of the fifty for which death was demanded in England.

Though the new arrangements seemed to have changed the oligarchical character of the Puritan colony, the power of the elite minority was little diminished. Their idea of good government has been described as "government of the people, by and for the saints." John Cotton summed it up: "If people be governors, who shall be governed?" In New England the clergy were not overshadowed by lords of the manor as were ministers in old England. Though the clergy did not hold civil office their influence was great in community life, and more than once it was used to enlarge the liberties of freemen. Yet the number of freemen remained small, and nonchurch members were rigidly excluded from the franchise. Even those with the right to vote habitually returned to their positions the same men year after year, so that a professional office-holding class seemed to have been created. These latter were, in the words of a sharp critic, the "unmitred popes of a pope-hating commonwealth."

Among the best of them was Winthrop, whose sense of duty was that of an aristocratic servant of his people. The remembrance of his contribution was kept alive in later generations, which recalled that he "had done good in Israel, having spent not only his whole estate . . . but his bodily strength and life, in the service of the country; not sparing, but always as the burning torch, spending . . ."

Religion was central to New England society for their desire was to create a Holy Commonwealth. As a contemporary Puritan historian phrased it, it was as "unnatural for a right N. E. man to live without an able ministery, as for a Smith to work his iron without a fire." While only the religious leaders of the community were expected to be deeply learned in theology, it was assumed that everyone should actively participate in the town's religious life.

The best of the ministers of the first generation wrote of sin, of death, and of divine love with passionate intensity. But they were careful to speak a language that would have meaning for farmers, sailors, fishermen, craftsmen, and shopkeepers as well as for the gentlemen sitting in preferred pews in the congregations. The call to faith was made in homely terms: "Here's infinite, eternall, present sweetness, goodnesse, grace, glory, and mercy to be found in this God. Why post you from mountain to hill, why spend you your money, your *thoughts, time, endeavors,* on things that satisfie not? . . . Thy cloathes may warm thee, but they cannot feed thee; thy meat may feed thee, but cannot heal thee; thy Physick may heal thee, but cannot maintain thee; thy money may maintain thee, but cannot comfort thee when distresses of conscience and anguish of heart come upon thee. This God is joy in sadness, light in darknesse, life in death . . ."

Though the Bible was the main source of a Puritan's reading, John Foxe's *Book of Martyrs* was almost equally familiar and it left a deep impression on the New England imagination. The heroic age of Protestantism in the previous century came to life in its pages, and from the deeds of martyred dead the Puritans and their children drew increased devotion to their cause.

In this community, as in the Geneva of John Calvin, close watch was kept on the manners and morals of citizens. For example, strict observance of the Sabbath was demanded of everyone. Walking idly on the street or visiting ships anchored in the harbor were forbidden on Sunday. No work of any kind was permitted on the Lord's Day. In New England, as elsewhere in America and Europe, the whipping post, the stocks or the gallows were used in public as helpful reminders of what awaited sinners in this world. A servant convicted "of most foul scandalous invectives against our churches and government, was censured to be whipped, lose his ears, and be banished the plantation . . ." Severe as this punishment seems, the penal code of Massachusetts was generally milder than England's. Governor Winthrop, more moderate than other Puritan leaders, was warned that he was too lenient toward lawbreakers. He was reminded that "strict discipline . . . was more needful in plantations than in a settled state, as tending to the honor and safety of the gospel."

It was easy then, and more so later, to point to the divergence between practice and the finest ideals of Puritan society, but there was no denying the enduring strength of these ideals. Despite the conformity exacted by the ministry, Puritanism bred so deep a devotion to a life lived in accord with moral convictions that there were many, like Roger Williams, who were forced by this ideal to nonconformity. As the later Rev. Solomon Stoddard put it: "If the practices of our Fathers in any particulars were mistakes, it is fit they should be rejected, if they be not, they will bear Examination; If we be forbidden to examine their practices, that will cut off all hopes of Reformation." There is, he said with emphasis, "a necessity of vindicating the Truth, yet we cannot do it without making some disturbance."

In the case of Williams the choice led away from the Holy Commonwealth of Massachusetts Bay to travel a lone, hard road. Speaking of the Puritan, the nineteenth-century historian, Moses Coit Tyler, said: "Though his prayers were often a snuffle, his hymns a dolorous whine . . . the idea [of God] that filled and thrilled his soul was one in every way sublime, immense, imaginative, poetic . . ."

★ "TO EXCEL IN HOLINESS"

The tide of English emigration which, in the beginning, had been directed to the West Indies and Virginia now included a very heavy proportion bound for New England. About 20,000 people, brought over in many ships (totaling nearly 200 voyages), were in the colony when emigration was shut off in the mother country with the outbreak of civil war. They were mostly from lower middle-class elements, and they came from East Anglia, London, and other areas where Puritanism was especially strong. They journeyed in family and community groups, often under the leadership of a popular preacher. And to those w waited at home for word from the emigrants a letter was "Venerated as a Sacred Script, or as the writing of some Holy Prophet"; people came from miles around to read it.

The settlers had early begun to spread out from the original area at Salem and Boston; in 1633 the governor's son, John Winthrop, Jr., went with twelve others "to begin a plantation at Agawam, after called Ipswich." In a little more than ten years fifty new settlements were made. As has always been true among immigrant groups in America, people who had known each other in the old country kept close together in the new. Thus Hingham, in Massachusetts, was settled by people from Hingham in England.

As each new settlement was founded a familiar pattern was followed in laying out the town. A village green was marked out around which was built the meetinghouse and the homes of leading citizens; to each inhabitant lots were assigned for homesteads. In town meeting local problems were ordinarily settled in democratic fashion. Here taxes were apportioned, poor relief allotted, school questions discussed, funds voted for laying out new roads and repairing the old, prices were regulated, and inducements held out to bring new enterprises to the community.

New Englanders were accustomed to penetrate new regions by co-operative effort. Small groups struck out over Indian paths for some new promised land. Tired bodies wrestled with entangling branches, while trap-like roots snared the footsore with almost human malignance. For their first shelters in a new community settlers burrowed like animals into a hillside. Their unprotected sheep and swine fell prey to wolves. But they faced their trials with wonted courage, challenging the woods with their psalms, resolving "to excel in holiness."

For economic and religious reasons, as well as from military necessity (mainly defense against Indians), they preferred to settle not too far removed from the older areas. Land was granted free by the legislature to groups of qualified men anxious to form a new settlement. A town site would then be chosen, measuring some six miles square. The original founders were for all practical purposes owners of the land and could dispose of it by sale or gift. Tracts were commonly set aside for ~ls and churches. People with varied skills were enticed to settle ·~· for example, Stephen Daye of Cambridge, the first s, was given 300 acres of land. Another town with offered land as a gift to a midwife "to answer the hich at present is great."

land distribution made for a compact society but it content among poorer farmers. They were disgruntled because they found that the best lands were usually taken by a few proprietors. Cheaper lands on some adjacent frontier, however, often stilled agrarian grievance.

Agriculture in New England's reluctant soil did not generally make for wealth, although in fertile Connecticut Valley crops were large and cattle flourished. It was a life of hard work, and the land was tilled with homemade, crude wooden tools and a heavy ox-drawn plow. Ingenious Yankees early learned to make and improve the domestic necessities which lifted life above the level of brute existence.

The primitive shelters of the earliest days of settlement gave way to more durable homes. Edward Johnson (in his *Wonder Working Providence*) remarked that by mid-century "The Lord hath been pleased to turn all the wigwams, huts and hovels the English dwelt in at their first crossing into orderly, fair and well-built houses." Extra rooms were added, but the fireplace room, larger than the others, retained its central position. In time houses were built with a second story, and when the large families grew larger a "leanter" (lean-to) was added at the rear. The back roof extended to cover the lean-to and gave the whole structure the appearance of a salt box.

Fire, which was a major hazard from earliest days, continued to cause grievous losses. Regulations were passed to eliminate wattle and daub chimneys, which caught on fire when the clay fell out and left the flammable wood exposed. Chimneys were to be built of brick or stone, and thatched roofs were prohibited. Force of habit was so strong, however, that house builders persisted in using thatch for many years, though better roofing materials were at hand. While loss of life from fire was not common, the loss of houses, furniture, clothing, and other possessions built up by slow, painstaking accumulation was disastrous.

Every member of the family contributed his share in producing the things needed for simple living. Women did the spinning, walking back and forth many miles a day in winding the yarn. Boys whittled spools and reels, while girls prepared dyes made from hickory bark or sassafras, pokeberry, goldenrod, or iris. Women made the candles and churned the butter. Unending toil was, however, lightened by occasional "frolicks" and singing and dancing. "Dancing (yea though mixt) I would not simply condemn," said John Cotton; "Only lascivious dancing to wanton ditties, and in amourous gestures and wanton dalliances, especially after great feasts, I would bear witness against . . ."

New Englanders were as much attached to the sea as they were to their land. A hardy breed of Yankee seamen was early developed, and they soon ranged far to fish and trade. Larger ships were built for distant voyages and to hold their spread of sail great white pine masts were cut from the forests of New Hampshire. Salem launched "a prodigious ship of 300 tons" in 1641, more than one and a half times the size of the "Mayflower." It wasn't long before a large fraction, one-third of the total tonnage of Great Britain, was being built in the colonies. The cost of ship-building in America was less than half that in Europe. The average vessel engaged in trading to the West Indies and to England in earlier years was smaller than Salem's monster, some 140 tons. Vessels plying American waters measured less than 80 tons, with a crew of eight or nine, sometimes even fewer. New England ships, often backed by London capital in the seventeenth century, carried their exports near and far, offering salt, lumber, tobacco, horses, rum, furs, and beaver skins. Fish was a major item. Much of it was salted, and the best sent to Spain and Portugal, while the worst went to the West Indies to be fed to Negro slaves.

In early years Massachusetts authorities tried to establish maximum wages for artisans, whose services were in so great demand that they could ask (and get) payments far beyond the prevailing rates in England. Maximum wages for carpenters, bricklayers and other skilled workmen were set at two shillings a day in the colony, eight pence more than they were paid in the old country. Restrictions were evaded by collusion between employer and workman, or the latter might merely refuse to labor at his craft, becoming a farmer instead. The monetary rewards for artisans were apparently considerable, for many of them became citizens of substance and standing in the community.

The Puritans were not only soldiers of Christ in New England, as they liked to call themselves, they were soldiers of the secular community. For defense, mainly against hostile Indians, every male eighteen years and older underwent military training. Most youngsters, long before their obligatory training, however, knew how to handle firearms. New Englanders were reputed to be among the most military-minded in America. Their long, exposed border vulnerable to attack forced them to be watchful and prepared.

Despite the fact that life was real and life was earnest, there was always concern for the preservation of cultural values. New England's clergy were generally better educated than the run of ministers in rural parishes of the mother country. The Puritan emphasis on education required as a minimum the ability to read, which was taught at home or in a village school. "To the end that learning may not be buried in the graves of our forefathers," it was commanded in New England "that every township, after the Lord hath increased them to the number of fifty householders, shall appoint one to teach all the children to write and read; and where every town shall increase to the number of one hundred families, they shall set up a grammar school; the masters thereof being able to instruct youth so far as they may be fitted for the university." Though the educational system in practice was less comprehensive than that enjoined upon the separate towns it was a remarkable achievement for so young a society.

Some of the larger towns had secondary schools, publicly supported, where Latin and Greek were the main, and generally the only, staples of the curriculum. From these schools the young men at the age of fourteen or fifteen might go on to Harvard College, founded in 1636. Every family under the jurisdiction of Massachusetts Bay taxed itself in kind or coin to support the college. The curriculum was bravely intended to provide an education similar to that of European universities, but the expectation was that from the college would come "a school of prophets" to guide the Bible Commonwealth. At Harvard students might prepare for the ministry (half of the earlier graduates did) but they also became merchants, farmers, doctors, government officials. Although not many of them became career officials in government, nearly all Harvard alumni performed some kind of public service and they left an indelible imprint on early America. Whatever their vocation their superior education usually gave them positions of prestige in the community.

It was the four fundamental institutions—town, congregation, school, and militia—which fashioned the education of New Englanders.

★ EXPANSION OF NEW ENGLAND—
RHODE ISLAND AND CONNECTICUT

The Massachusetts Bay Colony was, within a few years, probably the most powerful settlement of Englishmen overseas. Her influence tended to spread over all New England. She annexed New Hampshire for forty years, and also added Maine to her territory in 1652. Puritan settlements were made in the Connecticut Valley to the west and on Long Island Sound to the south. New colonies, which in time were established, exhibited the same degree of independence that animated the mother community.

The same factors which had prompted migration of Puritans from England—desire for freedom from religious constraints, the urge for economic and social betterment—were likewise operative in the minds of people moving out of Massachusetts Bay. Robert Child expressed the discontent that many people had toward the authorities in that colony. "There are many thousands in these plantations," he said, ". . . freeborne, quiett and peaceable men, righteous in their dealings, forward with hand, heart and purse, to advance the publick good . . .

who are debarred from all civil imployments (without any just cause that we know) not being permitted to bear the least office . . . no not so much as to have any vote in choosing magistrates, captains or other civill and military officers; notwithstanding they have here expended their youth, borne the burthen of the day . . . paid all assessments, taxes, rates . . ." But the Holy Commonwealth would not contain heresy, political or religious, and heretics were forced to leave. Roger Williams was the chief of these.

Williams, then just past thirty years of age, was pastor of the Salem church in 1631. To his congregation and to anyone who would listen he preached doctrines which make him more akin to our own times than most of his contemporaries. Civil government, he claimed, had no power over men's religious beliefs; sanctity of conscience was inviolable. Under his doctrine of "soul liberty" churches orthodox or heterodox would be granted equal liberty. So novel a doctrine would blot out hatreds kept virulent by persecution, for they would be erased in a society based on the acceptance of religious differences. Contrary to the practice of men throughout Christendom, including Winthrop and the other Puritan leaders, Williams believed in separation of Church and State. "Forced worship stincks in Gods nostrils," he asserted with his usual vigor, and "there is no other prudent, christian way of preserving peace in the world but by permission of differing consciences."

It was these deviations of Williams from orthodoxy that struck the imagination of later generations who found his ideas congenial to their own thought. But it should be remembered that on many matters Williams was at one with the rulers of Massachusetts Bay. He did believe in predestination and he did think that salvation was man's only real concern. He, too, accepted scripture as the supreme authority, and he had no genuine desire to establish a democratic society. His fundamental quarrel was with the pattern of religious leadership in Massachusetts which he felt perverted God's design for mankind.

He asserted, too, that whites had wrongfully expropriated land from the natives, and could only gain valid land title from the true owners of the soil, the Indians, by outright purchase. Clearly Williams was a revolutionary influence in Massachusetts and, in the view of its rulers, dangerous to its continued existence. Called upon to disavow his beliefs, Williams refused, declaring himself "ready to be bound and banished and even to die in New England." The authorities decreed he be exiled from Massachusetts Bay. (It was Artemus Ward who said that Puritans came to this country "to worship God according to their own consciences and to keep people from worshippin' Him accordin' to theirn.")

Soon after the banishment of Williams another controversial figure,

Anne Hutchinson, arose to challenge orthodoxy. She was, as Winthrop admitted, "a woman of a ready wit and bold spirit." Soon she attracted a considerable following who listened to her comments on the sermons of established ministers. She taught that men could communicate directly with God and needed no clerical intercession. One of her unlettered admirers said she preached "better gospel than any of [the] black-coats at the Ninniversity." Very quickly what started as a dispute over theological interpretations became an issue with dangerous political potentialities. Cotton Mather, in his history of New England, was to speak of her as "the prime seducer of the whole faction which now began to threaten the country." Her doctrinal differences were judged heretical, and she, too, was banished from the community. The decree was justified in the age-old sentiment of orthodoxy; all who differed from the Puritans on fundamental matters "shall have free liberty to keepe away from us."

Governor Winthrop, less implacable than his colleagues toward Williams, had privately advised him to steer a course for Narragansett Bay, outside the jurisdiction of Massachusetts. "I took his prudent motion," said the outcast, "as an hint and voice from God." Leaving Salem "in winter snow which I feel yet" (he wrote in retrospect thirty-five years after the event), he struck out for the safety of a place without a government, without even a name. "For fourteen weeks," he recalled, he "was sorely tost in a bitter season, not knowing what bread or bed did mean." Often alone, against the freezing night, he wandered through the woods, unwarmed and unfed. The worst of his trials came to an end when he found sanctuary among the Indians who remembered him as their champion.

Williams and a few companions at length found a place to make their settlement. This nameless site he called Providence, in gratitude for God's mercy. "I desired," he said, "it might be a shelter for persons distressed for conscience." Putting his beliefs into practice Williams bought the land from the Indians and established his government on democratic principles. It was a settlement as independent of royal authority as was Plymouth or Massachusetts Bay. Additional exiles from Massachusetts, including Anne Hutchinson, founded three other settlements by 1643. All four were soon after brought together in the federated community of Rhode Island.

The path to mutual forbearance was not easy in Rhode Island either. The individualism that stamped its founders bordered close to eccentricity in some, and none was yoked in comfort with another. But they were in agreement that no church establishment should be maintained, that no religious tests should be imposed on voters or officeholders, and that Indians should be treated as fellow human beings. Rhode Island had many idealistic inhabitants with "the root of the matter" in them, as had Roger Williams, and the fruit of the vigorous tree which grew therefrom has been tasted by Americans and found good.

★ CONNECTICUT, LAND OF "FRUITFULNESS AND COMMODIOUSNESS"

In the dispersion of the Puritans, Connecticut's attractiveness exerted a magnetic pull, for, as Winthrop observed, it was a land of "fruitfulness and commodiousness." It was argued that Massachusetts Bay Colony was overcrowded, "that towns were set so near each to other" there was "want of accommodation for their cattle." Massachusetts was reluctant to lose good colonists, as it still felt itself "weak and in danger to be assailed." She complained that a new colony "would not only draw many from us, but also divert other friends that would come to us."

Small groups had left for the Connecticut Valley in the fall and winter of 1635. In late spring of the following year the historic migration led by the Reverend Thomas Hooker began. His colony numbered about a hundred, and driving their herds before them, they "fed of their milk by the way." Traveling about ten miles a day the migrants moved through unknown woods, and crossed uncharted hills and streams before reaching the valley of their hearts' desire.

A wish for better land and dissatisfaction with Massachusetts political and religious practices, as well as "the strong bent of their spirits," had caused them to move westward. Here in one of the most fertile valleys in New England three townships were set up the same year. Cattle flourished on the meadows of the valley; and on a terrace, called the "meadow hill," settlers built their houses to be safe from spring floods which regularly swept through the region.

Within a short time (1639) the towns announced themselves a commonwealth, with a constitution, the famous "Fundamental Orders." The government was composed of a governor and six assistants, elected each year by the freemen and representatives from the towns. Each town sent four deputies to a general assembly. All persons who had been accepted by majority vote of any township had the right to vote and exercise other civic functions, but orthodox Puritans retained control.

Another settlement in Connecticut was made at New Haven in 1638 by Theophilus Eaton, a merchant from London, and the Rev. John Davenport. Here was a "fit place to erect a Towne, which they built in very little time, with very faire houses, and compleat streets." The settlement gradually spread out to include the opposite shore of Long Island and thus gave to that region a distinctive New England quality.

In the New Haven colony another, stricter, "Bible Commonwealth" was created by the "Brahmins of New England Puritanism." They had a franchise restricted to church members, and a government almost militant in the assertion of its independence. The New Haven settlement and the towns up the river valley joined in 1662 to form the colony of Connecticut.

The dispersal of colonies, while satisfying certain social needs, was also fraught with danger. Their weakness exposed them to the guns of the French and the tomahawks of Indians, while the Dutch maintained pressure on the western flank. Uncertainty prevailed also in the colonies with respect to the intentions of the crown then confronted by rebellious Puritans in England. In view of these circumstances four of the New England colonies (they disdained association with Rhode Island), in 1643 entered into "a firme and perpetual league of friendship and amity for offence and defence, mutual advice and succor." The governing body was a board of two commissioners from each of the members—Massachusetts, Connecticut, Plymouth, and New Haven. They could judge disputes among the colonies, return escaped servants and prisoners, and determine policy toward the Indians. None of the participating colonies could engage in war without approval by six or more of the commissioners. Money and men were levied in proportion to a colony's resources, which meant that comparatively rich and populous Massachusetts bore the largest share. Despite friction among its members, the league performed useful services and endured for forty years. Its most valuable contribution was its example of co-operation, which was not lost on a later generation in the Revolutionary era. They were to remember it when faced with the problem of building a more perfect union.

Thus within a quarter of a century of the planting of Plymouth colony, New England had settlements stretching from the rugged coast of Maine to the terraced hills of the Connecticut Valley. These communities recognized a formal allegiance to England but in practice seemed independent alike of the mother country and of each other, though acknowledging mutual obligations. Theirs was the burden of defense, of dealing with Indians, developing and regulating trade and evolving needed institutions. Theirs was the reward of creating a new society.

★ NEW NETHERLAND

The southern part of that region loosely called "Virginia," and the northern part known as "New England," were settled by Englishmen whose imprint in these areas has never worn off. Between these colonies the Dutch founded a settlement in New Netherland that lasted for fifty years but whose traces wore thin as the past receded. Names such as Haerlem and Breukkelen recall the villages of the original Dutch settlers immortalized in Washington Irving's satiric *History of New York*. The dwindling number of Dutch family names in New York and the Hudson Valley records the gradual disappearance or absorption of a stock once important in the early American scene.

The settlement of New Netherland was a small part of the worldwide program of empire on which the Dutch had embarked. They had long been active in the trade of Lisbon, and their own commercial centers in the Netherlands were among the most flourishing in Europe. The war of Dutch independence against Spain closed the port of Lisbon to them after 1580, at which time Philip II, the Spanish king, assumed the Portuguese crown as well. The Dutch thereupon invaded the preserves of the Portuguese in the East Indies, and their aggressive trading communities soon won control of the valuable Spice Islands. Branching out from there, the Dutch discovered Australia and New Zealand, established trading posts to the north with China and Japan, and extended their conquests in the Indian Ocean to include Ceylon. Dutch success gave to their shrewd merchants and their profitable ships a position of leadership, long the envy of other Europeans.

The Dutch joined in the search for a northeast or northwest passage to India. Their powerful East India Company engaged the English captain, Henry Hudson, to look for both passages. He found neither, but his historic ship, the "Half Moon," carried him south from Nova Scotia in the summer of 1609 to Chesapeake Bay. While engaged in retracing his route he rounded a low "sandy hook" and moored his ship in the waters of "The Great North River of New Netherland."

Still in search of the elusive westward route he sailed in early fall up the broad river which bears his name. The Hudson Valley's autumnal magic delighted the eyes of sailors weary of blue water, white caps, and far, gray horizons. The hills were ablaze with brilliant foliage, the sheer wall of the western shore astonished the seamen. On they went past stretches where the river broadened into bays and then narrowed between towering hills. At length the expedition reached the present site of Albany where the trail ended. The wealth of India was still inaccessible by this route, but a rich treasure right at hand was revealed to the Dutch in the fur trade of this region. The Indians along the river had "Bevers skinnes, and Otters skinnes, which we bought for Beades, Knives, and Hatchets." Other Dutch explorers then came to give their countrymen claims to territory covering the whole area between New England and Virginia.

Merchants with a nose for spices, who had employed Henry Hudson, were not the men to appreciate the wealth that lay before them. It was another group, the Dutch West India Company, founded in 1621, which ultimately exploited the promising fur trade. Originally this company thought an easy way to wealth was to relieve the Spaniards in the West Indies of theirs. They did a spectacular job of it once when Admiral Piet Hein rounded up a whole Spanish treasure fleet.

Dutch strength at sea indirectly helped assure the safety of the struggling English colonies from Spanish attack. And their power made possible settlements of their own, as well as those of the French and English, in the Caribbean. The Dutch West India Company was able to conquer and hold on to Brazil for a number of years, although eventually she lost it to its earlier rulers, the Portuguese. While Dutch captains were freeing the sea lanes to the western hemisphere, Dutch scientists and artists, using materials they had gathered in America, were stimulating Europe's interest in the New World.

Like their rivals, the French *coureurs de bois,* Dutch *boschlopers* followed wherever the trail took them to fur. It took them into the Mohawk Valley stretching west from the Hudson; it took them, as early as 1614, up the Connecticut River where they eventually ran afoul of competing traders from Massachusetts. Not until 1623 was a permanent settlement made by the Dutch in New Netherland. That year one colony was located at Fort Orange (Albany) with eighteen families; and another smaller one was established at Fort Nassau, on the Delaware River near present Camden, New Jersey. Three years later Peter Minuit, Director General of the company, made his famous purchase of Manhattan Island from the Indians, and at its tip established New Amsterdam. The Dutch trading depot on the Connecticut River, near Hartford, was on land claimed by the Pilgrims. Though warned that they had trespassed, they were permitted to remain.

The slow growth of New Netherland (it had about 350 in 1629) caused the company to adopt measures similar to those used by the Virginia Company to spur emigration—particularly the issuance of extensive land grants. Under a charter of privileges, patroonships were created which were vast holdings along the Hudson, given to any one settling at his own expense a colony of fifty adults. The patroon held this land under feudal tenure as lord of the manor.

To no one's surprise the directors of the company quickly pre-empted the choicest lands in New Netherland, taking hundreds of thousands of acres. One of the directors, Kiliaen Van Rensselaer, became the most noted patroon with a vast estate near Albany running many miles inland from the river. It long remained in the family as a feudal principality. Thus by encouraging monopoly of land and commerce, and vesting authority in a small ruling class, the Dutch made their settlements less inviting to Europeans than were other American colonies.

The legendary, fat, easygoing governors of New Netherland, chosen by weight, said Irving, in his inimitable portrayal, were not characteristic of the efficient Dutch leaders building up the empire elsewhere. Those in America were singularly inept in dealing with the Indians, and their autocratic behavior to their own people provoked intense dissatisfaction. In between his caricaturing, Irving could describe Dutch governors with unflattering truthfulness: "they were in a manner absolute despots in their little domains, lording it over both law and gospel, and accountable to none but the mother country; which it is well known is astonishingly deaf to all complaints against its governors, provided they discharge the main duty of their station—squeezing out a good revenue."

One-legged Peter Stuyvesant in blunderbuss fashion tried to straighten out the disorganized community, and though he succeeded in initiating some needed reforms he ignored more fundamental needs. A convention in 1653, meeting in New Amsterdam, complained of arbitrary government and ordinances "without the knowledge or consent of the people . . . odious to every free born man and especially so those whom God has placed under a free state in newly settled lands." Stuyvesant's practice of ignoring such complaints merited the bitterly derisive appellation by which he was known, the "great Muscovy Duke."

This arbitrariness was again exhibited when the Dutch annexed the Swedish colony of Fort Christina (Wilmington) on the Delaware. The Swedish settlement there, which had only two hundred people after fifteen years, was too weak to resist Dutch pressure. The brief Swedish experiment at colonization, though quickly eclipsed and leaving apparently no trace, exerted the greatest influence on homebuilding by frontiersmen. It was from Swedish colonists that other settlers learned to build the log cabins that we think of as typically American.

Success against the Swedes in 1655 scarcely balanced failures in rivalry with the English. The Dutch retreated in Connecticut and from eastern Long Island. Maryland was ordering them to leave Delaware Bay. The big blow came when Holland and England, at odds over commercial questions, fell out and engaged in war. Inevitably the colonies were drawn in. Charles II granted the land inhabited by the Dutch to his brother, the Duke of York, who then sent over a fleet to claim possession. The New Netherland colony, disrupted by internal feuds and neglected by its bankrupt parent company, was in no condition to defy the English demand for surrender.

New Netherland became an English colony August, 1664, and as New York it long preserved much of its original Dutch character. The Dutch landed aristocracy, who retained their property rights, intermarried with the English merchants and landowners who prospered in New York. In alliance the two exercised great political power in the colony. The Van Rensselaers, Cortlandts, Livingstons, Schuylers, and other dominant families, living on their great estates or doing business in New York, were the nearest approximation the English colonies offered to Old World feudal society.

Gradually the Dutch flavor of New Netherland (which had only 7,000 people at the surrender) was transformed by the cultures of numerous immigrants of other stocks. The eighteen languages heard on the wharfs and streets of New Amsterdam, now New York, were an early promise of the city's cosmopolitanism. Into the nineteenth century, despite the disappearing evidences of former Dutch rule, the Dutch language was still heard in sleepy villages along the upper Hudson, and the names Van Buren and Roosevelt reveal the impress of Holland's influence on American history.

★ MARYLAND AND THE CHESAPEAKE REGION

Dutch settlement in the middle Atlantic region was regarded by the English as an impudent intrusion. Dutch traders appearing in increasing numbers in Virginia tobacco marts were threats to mercantilist practice which sought to confine this commerce to the British Empire. One of the means devised to contain and then coerce the Dutch was to grant adjacent lands to Englishmen, who were expected to establish settlements and then squeeze out the Dutch. The Maryland grant in 1632 on the upper Chesapeake, making it a buffer between Virginia and New Netherland, reflected strongly this strategy. But, as in other settlements, mixed motives explain the Maryland colony. There, too, religion and economics account for the original migration.

Sir George Calvert, the first Lord Baltimore, had been a member of the Virginia Company and of the New England Council, and had vainly attempted a settlement in Newfoundland before turning to the Chesapeake region. The colony founded in Maryland took its name from the Catholic Queen of England's ruler, Charles I. Calvert, who had been converted to Catholicism, finding Virginia inhospitable, desired a refuge for fellow members of his church who faced severe restrictions in England. But he wanted, also, as Lord Proprietor, to carve out a feudal domain in America which might guarantee that his descendants would "be to the manor born." Following a plan similar to one conceived in earlier years by Sir Humphrey Gilbert, colonization was to partake of a huge land speculation with the reproduction, in the New World, of the ancient landlordism of the Old.

Calvert did not live to see the settlement undertaken. His son Cecilius inherited the royal grant and made preparations to send out the first group of colonists. After much delay some three hundred of them, in two ships, aptly named the "Ark" and the "Dove," under command of Leonard Calvert, brother of the Lord Proprietor, arrived in Chesapeake Bay late in February, 1634. After careful consideration the leaders of the proprietary colony chose a site near the mouth of the Potomac, and called it St. Mary's.

One of the most interesting members of this original group was a Jesuit priest, Father Andrew White, who wrote an attractive account of the first Maryland settlement. It was he who reported that "we bought from the [Indians] thirty miles of that land, delivering in exchange axes, hatchets, rakes, and several yards of cloth." Father White found the region to have an idyllic climate, for it was in the same latitude as Jerusalem "and the best parts of Arabia Felix" and China; on the east lay the ocean, on the west "an infinite continent." In addition "it hath two goodly bays, both rich bosoms of fish."

Despite the expressed intent of the Calvert family to make the colony a haven for Catholics, Protestants from the start outnumbered them. To get Protestants to go (since so few Catholics appeared interested), toleration had to be guaranteed them. Maryland was thus, in effect, founded on the principle that men could have freedom of Christian worship. To protect Catholics against a feared growing Protestant majority, the noted Toleration Act was passed by the colonial assembly in 1649. It granted freedom of worship to believers in the divinity of Jesus, but the law made it a capital crime to deny the Trinity.

The Maryland colonists had learned from the numbing experiences of Virginia and New England how to prepare for the first months of settlement. It was their good fortune also to have the now well-established Virginia colony close by. In their very first season the new settlers had a surplus of corn which they exchanged for New England's salt codfish. But the problems of settlement, as always, were many and expenses were high. Lord Baltimore, as proprietor, bore practically all the costs, which in two years reached an estimated £40,000.

By the charter granted him, Lord Baltimore won a royal principality, and was given the right to rule it like an independent prince. But he was an English prince, and at this date in English history princes had learned to rule under limitations. The Maryland proprietor had "free, full and absolute power" to enact laws but he was required to have the advice, assent, and approbation of the freemen of the colony. The governor of the colony, Leonard Calvert (who held the office to his death in 1647), and other important officials were appointed by the Lord Proprietor.

The proprietor generally attempted to ignore the wishes of the assembly chosen by the freemen but the latter gradually strengthened their position winning, for example, the right to initiate laws. Prior to this their function was to approve, amend, or reject measures laid before them by the proprietor.

At a time when parliament at home was engaged in a struggle with the king to maintain its authority, colonial assemblies were likewise conscious of their English political inheritance. In Maryland the assembly modeled its procedure after the mother of parliaments, demanding also the familiar parliamentary privileges. The members learned how to draft legislation with increasing skill. At the same time colonial assemblies practiced the valuable conventions that regulated self-governing bodies. There was great respect for the political tradition they had inherited, though the place of meeting be a ramshackle room, the clothes of members stained with mud, and their speech still unpolished. The dignity of the house was no mere rhetorical phrase when a member was reminded that he had breached it. About the middle of the seventeenth century both Virginia and Maryland created a bicameral legislature.

Maryland reveals, perhaps more clearly than any other community, the gap between the theory of settlement as constructed in England and the actual settlement as evolved in America. Baltimore had dreamed of English lords ruling in baronial splendor in Maryland, but the hard facts of colonial experience made mockery of such expectations. The sixteen gentlemen-adventurers who went out in the "Ark" and the "Dove" no doubt found it difficult to recreate a feudal atmosphere in the American wilderness for their fellow passengers—yeomen, laborers, craftsmen, and servants. It must be remembered that in England itself the practices of feudalism were rapidly vanishing even though its form and spirit still lived on. Land was comparatively easy to secure in America, and many servants at the end of their term of service seem to have become tenants. Tenant farmers often worked their land under advantageous leases. Quitrents (rents which made the tenants "quit" or free of further obligations) were paid to the Baltimore family. The manorial courts scarcely functioned in the colony and the vision of lords living in ample manor houses holding sway over numerous tenants remained sheer romance.

★ THE PLANTER AND PLANTATION

The words planter and plantation, which in the later history of the South connoted social leadership and wealth, had no such meaning in the early years of settlement. Then these terms simply referred to any free colonist and his farm. The typical economic unit in Virginia and Maryland was a farm of less than 400 acres, worked by the owner, his family, and perhaps a few white indentured servants. More than half of those who came over worked out the cost of their passage through a period of service to a planter.

It has been estimated that in any one year, in the seventeenth century, something over 6000 indentured servants were at work in the Chesapeake region. In Governor Berkeley's time 13 per cent of the inhabitants were under indenture, 5 per cent were slaves, while the remaining 82 per cent were free. All told, about 100,000 servants lived to complete their indentures in the tobacco colonies in the seventeenth century. Many of them rose to positions of dignity in the community. One-third of the House of Burgesses in Virginia in 1663, for example, had begun their American life as servants.

When settlements were new it was an achievement just to live. One official, writing in 1671, estimated that in new communities four out of five unseasoned hands died in their first year; "All new plantations are, for an age or two, unhealthy 'till they are thoroughly cleared of wood." When colonies matured the mortality rate of newcomers dropped rapidly; "there is not often . . . that [they] die now," reported the same official.

Negro slaves were not so numerous in this early period. Both slave and servant were regulated by a disciplinary code, sometimes severely enforced, which was especially concerned with the problem of dependents running away from their masters. In this early period legal distinctions between Negroes and white servants were not sharp, indeed Negroes were spoken of as servants. Some, like their white contemporaries, served out their terms of indenture. Between 1660 and 1670, however, the line between whites and blacks was sharply drawn. Negro slaves were thereafter to remain in that status for life. The white servant rather than the Negro slave was the chief form of labor so long as the small farm remained the dominant economic unit.

By the middle of the century some of the colonists had already accumulated sizable land holdings. But it was one thing to be the owner of much acreage and another to cultivate it, for both labor and capital were scarce in the early years. Though William Fitzhugh of Virginia owned 24,000 acres, only 300 were cultivated. The income of a planter depended less on the size of his acreage than it did on the number and efficiency of his working force.

As the seventeenth century advanced there was a marked tendency toward smaller holdings, a development brought about by customs of inheritance more democratic than those prevailing in England, as well as by the pressure of a growing population. In these years the pattern of the English village, surrounded by farm lands, was followed rather than the isolated farmhouse of nineteenth-century America.

In Maryland, as elsewhere in America, land was the chief economic inducement to the prospective settler. For the "first adventurers" that went out, the manorial grant was 2000 acres for any one individual who at his own expense took five adult males with him. The grants handed out in payment for transporting colonists gradually dwindled until they reached the prevailing standard of 50 acres. The quitrent charged (though not always collected) was two shillings for each 100 acres. In both particulars—the size of the headright allotment and rental—Maryland had adopted Virginia practice.

As in Virginia, tobacco was the money crop, and such was the neglect of some farmers to grow food that laws in both colonies were passed to enforce the planting of corn. From the Indians the whites learned to eat succotash, roasting ears, and other dishes which became traditional on the southern menu. Wheat also was raised. Orchards were laid out as much for the ciders they provided as for their pleasant, raw fruit. Peaches came to be the favorite. They ripened in the summer months and flourished so abundantly that every one, man and beast, had enough to gorge himself on. From unworked fields came blackberries, wild strawberries, and wild plums. In the forest were squirrels, wild turkeys weighing forty pounds or more, deer, and bear. In the streams and marshes were fish and geese, while great numbers of wild ducks blackened the waters, and along the coast shrimp, crabs, and oysters were plentiful.

Farms were near tidewater, where stone was scarce, hence fences were of split rails, laid zigzag, "pig-tight, horse-high and bull-strong" to enclose the cultivated fields. The wealth of a farmer was counted, as in customary pastoral societies, in the number of cattle he owned. Horses were scarce until after the middle of the century (as late as the 1670's they were the mark of a rich man), but oxen for plowing were more readily available.

The home of the yeomanry in the Chesapeake area was a dwelling a-story-and-a-half high, with fireplaces for winter warmth. Shutters took the place of glass for windows. Houses were small (about sixteen by twenty feet), and modestly furnished with brass, iron, or pewter utensils, some carpenter's tools, a gun, and a Bible. Beds and bolsters were valuable household furnishings. The few larger plantations that did exist at this time were conspicuous precisely because of their rarity. The house of a wealthy man might contain eight rooms or more and be relatively luxurious in its furnishings. But the expansive, aristocratic living of the plantation elite is more truly associated with a later era.

The man who lived in a home larger than his neighbors' probably ran a general store. In it he sold goods imported from England in the tobacco ships which sailed regularly back and forth across the ocean. The farms of this period all had comparatively easy access to the rivers emptying into the Chesapeake; "every planter," it was said, "has a river at his door." In a land of dense forests there was great attraction in a splendid, natural system of waterways, which offered easy transportation for passengers and freight.

Men traveling over land met unbridged rivers and fallen trees. They had to swim their horses across rivers when there was neither ford nor ferry. The bay country was a low-lying region made up of tongues of land between tidal rivers. At their edges, and even in remoter interiors, swamps were everywhere. Their tangled growths of oak and pine, cypress and gum, made them almost impenetrable. The swamps were home to many varieties of wild animals, birds, and reptiles. In the woods a surprised traveler might even come upon so strange a sight as a buffalo, whose "portly figure," wrote a Virginia wit, was "disgraced by a shabby little tail . . ."

In the Chesapeake region the ease of water communication allowed the colonists to disperse to readily accessible, fresher, more profitable lands as soon as the old were worn out by the exhausting tobacco plant. The American habit of wastefulness in using material resources, which were so prodigiously rich that they inhibited economy, was passed on by early settlers to their descendants.

★ CHANGING INSTITUTIONS

The role of religion in Virginia while less prominent than in New England was nevertheless noteworthy. Settlers in Virginia like those in the Puritan colonies felt that ministers were as much political as they were spiritual leaders. The worldly Hakluyt had counseled the organizers of the Virginia Company that preachers be taken along to settlements "that God may be honoured, the people instructed, mutinies the better avoided and obedience the better used." Virginia's clergy were good Church of England men and their voice in public affairs was second only to that of larger plantation owners.

The established church in Virginia was Anglican but the colony's spirit, as revealed in its codes, was Puritan in its first years. It may be that the enforcement of punishments for Sabbath-breaking, idleness, or drunkenness was less vigorous in the Chesapeake area than in New England, but the word of the law at least was equally severe in both places. The Bible was as devoutly read in Virginia as it was in New England.

The beneficent American practice of setting aside land for public purposes, particularly for education, had its origins in the earliest settlements. Ten thousand acres were to be set aside for a college at Henrico, Virginia, but the school barely got beyond the blueprint stage. Like other dreams of the first settlers this hope of enlarging educational opportunities was bequeathed to descendants whose task it was to realize it. Under difficult conditions Virginians established elementary schools, which (along with private tutoring) kept the literacy rate of the colony fairly high; this despite Governor Berkeley's rejoicing that Virginia had no free schools. The crusty Governor thanked God that Virginia had *"no free schools* nor *printing,* and I hope," he added, "we shall not have these hundred years; for *learning* has brought disobedience, and heresy, and sects into the world, and *printing* has divulged them . . . God keep us from both!"

Colonists brought with them an appreciation of the advantages of English local administration, with its peculiar virtue of central authority and local representation. In Virginia as in England royal authority was represented by local officials who were well known to the people.

Proud as they were of their English heritage, the colonists early began to deviate from institutional practices in the homeland. There was much of course in their cultural inheritance that they shared in common. But even when the colonists asserted they were following English institutional usage they subtly transformed the institution or even abandoned it entirely.

The church in Virginia, for example, was different from the parent structure in England. The dispersal of population, which came in time, and the large size of the Virginia parish itself, prevented the same tight community life from developing which characterized the English parish. The colonial parish was spread over an area too large to be crossed in a day's travel, so that church attendance even once a week was difficult. More isolated families, discouraged by blocked forest trails, rarely visited their log church set in some lonely clearing. The colony had no Anglican bishop, neither did it have the old ecclesiastical courts with their traditional jurisdiction of such items as wills, marriages, and the enforcement of orthodoxy. The very absence of these courts meant that laymen had freer range for extension of their influence in church affairs. This was clearly reflected in the greater control over the ministry exercised by the colonists who, in many church matters, were left pretty much to their own devices.

In the Chesapeake region as in New England, by the middle of the seventeenth century, transplanted Englishmen had already established secure homes in lands just yesterday wild. The hard "starving times" of the lamentable early days had long passed for dwellers on the Atlantic shore. Though the English spirit still remained deeply rooted in American institutions, the patterns of life in the colonies were beginning to change from those in the motherland. People were slowly beginning to think of themselves as evolving a society differing from Europe's, and in their growing self-consciousness they were soon to call themselves Americans.

CHAPTER IV

The Colonies Spread While England Tightens Controls

The evolution of the colonies proceeded without serious interference by the mother country after the dissolution of the Virginia Company in 1624. Englishmen found the rich field of India more rewarding; and even when they did turn their attention to the New World the West Indies retained a favored position. The latter fitted with frictionless ease into English mercantilism, supplying the motherland with non-competing products, and at the same time consuming England's manu-factured articles. The amazing fertility of the West Indies brought such returns as could not then be matched by agriculture on the North American mainland. The crop of sugar cane was enormously profitable, its cultivation being carried on by Negro slaves who had been imported in vast numbers to supplant white laborers.

The French were successful rivals of the English sugar growers. Wealth that flowed from France's West Indian cornucopia was dis-played with ostentation before envious Parisians by visiting colonials. So alluring were the charms of these tropical islands that alien pres-sure was continuously exerted on Spain's possessions there. Jamaica fell to the English in Oliver Cromwell's time, while other Spanish is-lands were occupied by the French, Dutch, and Danish forces.

The English Civil War and its aftermath (1642–60), while guar-anteeing little interference with the colonies, presented them with trouble-some questions. Did they owe allegiance to the Stuarts, whose Charles I had been deposed and then decapitated? Or should their loyalty go instead to a triumphant parliament, in which Puritanism ruled supreme and might therefore be presumed to be sympathetic to colonial interests? Colonials anticipating an easy relationship with parliament were soon disabused. When the colonies in the south were aggressive in their assertions of quasi-independence, they were quickly brought to heel by that same parliament. In Maryland, where Puritans gained temporary control, a small scale conflict reflected the passions exploding in England, but skilful handling brought eventual victory to the Catholic Lord Baltimore.

As for New England, local rejoicing at the victory over the oppressive Charles I and Archbishop Laud was tempered by the economic and political uncertainties that followed. Depression set in with the decline of immigration. Winthrop reported in his *Journal* that the "sudden fall of land and cattle, and the scarcity of foreign commodities, and money, etc., with the thin access of people from England, put many into an unsettled frame of spirit, so as they concluded there would be no subsisting here, and accordingly they began to hasten away, some to the West Indies, others to the Dutch, at Long Island . . . and others back for England."

The southern colonies were likewise affected adversely by the Civil War in England. The tobacco trade fell off between Virginia and London, with serious consequences for the South whose economy was largely based on this one commodity. It affected nearly every phase of southern life. Travelers carried a pouch of tobacco to pay for their expenses on the road; clergymen were regularly paid in tobacco and as regularly complained when its quality was poor or its price had fallen. Later, certificates representing tobacco stored in warehouses were used as money.

Practically all of Virginia's trade was based on tobacco as the medium of exchange. To hold up tobacco prices, destruction of part of the crop was proposed to her planters, who were also asked to restrict acreage devoted to it. (Present-day Americans who favor regulation of crop production and the stabilization of prices thus have an old precedent in colonial Virginia.) American tobacco growers, already facing a glutted market, were confronted, down to the middle of the seventeenth century, with the competition of tobacco grown in England. Some Virginians, in their extremity, even toyed with the idea of closer ties with the Dutch empire, but dropped it when England's parliament exercised parental coercion in the 1650's.

Despite such an occasional display of parliamentary authority Virginia, at this time, was practically a self-governing commonwealth. Increasing authority was being wielded by the House of Burgesses. The heightened sense of importance possessed by the Burgesses reflected the English parliamentary struggle then under way to establish the supremacy of the legislature over the crown.

The needs of Virginia dictated that she once again establish amity with the homeland. From the latter could come the capital and population required for expansion. The small independent farmer with greater ambitions for his children, the physician and lawyer eager for land and the title of gentleman, younger sons of the rural gentry cramped by lack of funds—all these Englishmen saw in the tobacco leaf of the overseas colony a passport to social eminence. England, now forbidden by parliament to grow tobacco in competition with the colonies, provided a well-established market where "the weed" could be exchanged for goods demanded in colonial homes. The allurement of Dutch trade was not enough to overbalance the advantages of continued association with the mother country.

Re-establishment of royal authority in Virginia followed the restoration of the Stuarts in England in 1660. Governor William Berkeley ruled in the name of Charles II, and public officials in the colony made haste to dissociate themselves from remembrance of times past when a throneless England had been governed by a revolutionary parliament.

During the trying two decades in Virginia (1640–60) political control in the colony remained rather steadily in the hands of the same men. Through the enlarged jurisdiction of the county court they administered a rapidly expanding community, whose population reached 40,000 by 1662. The county courts were the base on which rested the political power of the South's ruling class, headed by a small number of the wealthier planters. They rotated among themselves the honorific, as well as lucrative, positions of magistrate, clerk, and sheriff. Comfortably seated in power, Virginia's local leadership worked out an easy relationship with the representatives of the crown. An aristocracy was being born which, with all its limitations of pride and prejudice, was one day to supply America with famed orators and incomparable statesmen.

In Maryland the Calverts, proprietors of the colony, found security in alliance with the more prosperous planters. The upper house of the Maryland assembly was the closest colonial imitation of the English House of Lords. The Calverts, despite their outward friendliness to the planters, were continually engaged in a political tug-of-war with Maryland assemblies jealous of their rights. The colony, like her neighboring province, Virginia, grew rapidly in this period. Native growth was augmented by immigrants from England and Ireland so that Maryland's estimated population of 11,000 in 1660 about doubled in the next twenty years.

In the Chesapeake area there developed a fundamental institution known as the county court. It was an administrative authority, not to be confused with the court of today. The county commissioners who composed this court were responsible for all the cares of local government, which included the recording of vital statistics, the maintenance of standard weights and measures, the regulation of taverns, and the enforcement of price regulations established by the colonial assembly. The county court carefully recorded wills, manumissions, and the documents relating to the service of indentured servants. Perhaps the most important of the records inscribed by the clerks under the watchful eyes of the county commissioners were those detailing land titles.

In Virginia and in Maryland a coveted office was that of sheriff with its attractive financial perquisites. As elsewhere in the colonies the practice in administering justice was to avoid lengthy litigation. A suspicion of lawyers and their devices of delay was to remain with Americans for many years.

★ THE LURE OF CAROLINA

Virginia's dependence upon a single crop economy led many to fear disaster and to think seriously about diversifying crops. The fears of planters were valid; tobacco had been known to drop from three shillings a pound to threepence. Some plantation owners remembered the earlier imperial program of Hariot and Hakluyt which recommended the cultivation of rice, silk, and other products.

One of the more interesting of the personalities in Virginia who experimented with crop diversification was a Scotsman, the Reverend Alexander Moray. Silk, barley, rice, and even the coffee bean were among the products Moray sought to raise. He rejoiced in his surroundings, which he spoke of as a "wilderness of milk and honey." None could know the sweetness of it, said Moray, "but he that tasts it: one ocular inspection, one aromatik smel of our woods, one hearing of the consert of our birds in those woods would affect more than a 1000 reported stories let the authors be never so readible." Moray, speaking of Scotsmen who had gone to Virginia in a condition of servitude, said they were now "living better than ever their forfathers," some of them having become "great masters of many servants themselfs."

The cheerful minister, though delighted with Virginia, thought better prospects for his fellow Scots lay ahead in Carolina. Friction between Scots and the more numerous English in Virginia embittered the former who labored under a sense of discrimination. Moray therefore joined with others in reconnoitering the territory to the south. There, in Carolina, they believed they had found "the hopefullest place in the world."

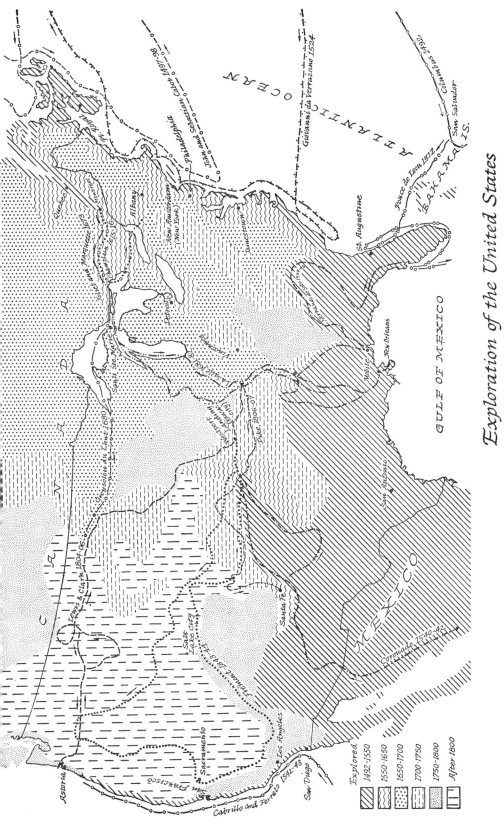

Exploration of the United States

ATLANTIC OCEAN

GULF OF MEXICO

MEXICO

C A N A D A

BAHAMA IS.

Columbus 1492
San Salvador
Ponce de León 1512
Giovanni da Verrazzano 1524
John and Sebastian Cabot 1497-98

Quebec
Joliet and Marquette 1673?
Montreal
Sault Ste. Marie
Detroit
La Salle 1681-82
Albany
New Amsterdam (New York)
Philadelphia
Jamestown
St. Augustine
Mobile
New Orleans
San Antonio
Santa Fe
Salt Lake City
Los Angeles
San Diego
San Francisco
Sacramento
Astoria

Lewis & Clark 1804-06
Pike 1806-07
Coronado 1540-42
Frémont 1843-45
Cabrillo and Ferrelo 1542-43
De Soto 1539-41
Convention Line 1818

Explored
1492-1550
1550-1650
1650-1700
1700-1750
1750-1800
After 1800

★ THE FOUNDING OF CAROLINA

Settlers who had come from Virginia and from New England were in the Carolina region when Charles II granted the area to eight proprietors in 1663. A German physician, John Lederer, had been granted permission in 1669 and 1670 by Governor Berkeley to explore the region to the south and west. His report delighted Carolina's proprietors, who were told that "The Apalataean Mountains (though . . . they deny Virginia passage into the West Continent) stoop to Carolina," and "lay open a prospect into unlimited Empires." The proprietors were men associated with the agencies directing England's empire and were skilled in the ways of court manipulation. Title to this vast region, which reached from Virginia to Florida, was given for a small annual payment.

In the Restoration era Englishmen were spreading the bounds of their fast-growing empire in eastern and western seas. Charles II was informed that his colonies in America were "beginning to grow into commodities of great value and Esteeme," which pay "more custome to his Majestie than the East Indies four times over." Directors of large enterprises had great influence with Charles II, who had an easy way in distributing largess, which diminished neither the royal purse nor its owner's popularity. Seekers of favors moved in a royal atmosphere of frank bargaining.

While the struggle for personal and company advantage proceeded, the administration of the empire was made more orderly and detailed. The Navigation Acts adopted by Cromwell in 1650 and 1651 to combat Dutch competition were re-enforced ten years later. Colonial trade was to be carried in English ships, which meant colonial vessels, as well; "enumerated" commodities sent abroad (sugar, tobacco, indigo etc.) were reserved for export exclusively to the mother country or other portions of the empire; trade with foreign countries had to be carried on through the intermediacy of England. The planting of tobacco was to be a colonial monopoly (it had formerly been grown in England) and the mother country was not to import it from alien lands. Later Navigation Acts (1663 and 1673) were thought by the colonials to discriminate against them, and they began to evade the laws by engaging in direct trade with the European continent, bypassing England.

Thus were the principles of mercantilism effected in England's empire. Self-sufficiency was the objective sought by all states accenting nationalism. To achieve it the economy of an empire was to produce so great a diversity of commodities as to make it independent of the world outside. Into this program of prosperous self-containment it was hoped that Carolina would fit. There, in a climate warmer than that of any other English continental possession, experiments were made with silk, indigo, flax, wine, olives, cotton, and rice. In the last of these, spectacular success was achieved at an early date.

The new colony had an assembly with powers similar to those possessed by the other colonial legislatures. The proprietors promised that no taxes except those imposed by the colonists themselves would be levied upon them. To attract settlers the proprietors followed the familiar headright system and welcomed diverse religious denominations. This liberal religious policy was accompanied by the usual grant to colonists of the customary privileges enjoyed by Englishmen at home. Thus once again, as in the earlier days of Virginia's settlement, promoters of empire, ordinarily conservative at home, found it expedient abroad to expand the area of freedom.

It was in the southerly portion of the new settlement that progress was relatively rapid, but for some years the whole colony presented a somewhat anemic appearance. The northern part was split off to form a separate colony, North Carolina (1691). The proprietors who had counted on large returns for their slight investment (it amounted to only £75 each over a period of three years) thereupon subscribed additional sums to found a settlement at Port Royal. It was hoped that experienced colonists in the older settlements would lend a hand as well as furnish supplies.

A noted document associated with the colony's early years was the "Fundamental Constitutions of Carolina." It was an attempt to realize in the New World the theories of imaginative political scientists of the Old. As such it was one of many social experiments which were carried on in some part of America from the seventeenth century to the twentieth.

The authors of the Fundamental Constitutions, probably the Earl of Shaftesbury and John Locke, created an imaginary society of freeholders and hereditary nobility; the former were to hold three-fifths of the land in the colony, while the few aristocrats (along with the proprietors) were to hold the other two-fifths. The intention was to secure a balance of classes in the foundling colony for, as James Harrington cautioned: "A nobility of gentry overbalancing a popular government is the utter bane and destruction of it, as a nobility or gentry in a popular government not overbalancing it, is the very life and soul of it." To a later generation it seemed an utter futility to recreate in a wilderness setting the pattern of feudal relationships which had evolved in European communities over the centuries.

And yet Shaftesbury and Locke were not harebrained theorists; their objectives were strictly modern—to bait men possessing resources, as well as resourceful men, with large tracts of land. These men, playing the part of minor proconsuls in their own sizable domains, would undertake the hard task of supplying local guidance to the new community. The land policies of these early years were not without significance in the later creation of a Carolina aristocracy whose spirit, if not its form, reflected the ideas of seventeenth-century proprietors. Feudal titles and practices lapsed unregretted, but land-hungry men from the West Indies, from northern colonies, and from western Europe took up their claims under the familiar headright system.

The chief center of the colony was located on the harbor formed by the confluence of the Ashley and Cooper rivers. "Charles Town Bay," wrote an official familiar with the Atlantic seaboard, "is the safest port for all Vessels coming thro' the gulf of Florida in distress, bound from the West Indies to the Northern Plantations; if they miss this place they may perish at sea for want of relief, and having beat upon the coast of New England, New York, or Virginia by a North West Wind in the Winter, be forced to go to Barbadoes if they miss this Bay." The waterways which created Charleston harbor also provided easy access to the interior. Here a low-lying region was covered with forests of the stately long leaf pine tree draped with the soft gray moss called "Spanish Beard."

In the port of Charles Town (it became Charleston in 1783) a thriving community quickly developed. It drew to itself migrants from New England, the West Indies, and French Protestants from Europe. The latter, Huguenots fleeing from Louis XIV's persecution, early gave to Carolina's capital a cosmopolitan flavor. The pattern of American urban streets, straight and at right angles to each other, was first laid down there. The town, said a contemporary booster, "is regularly laid out into large and capacious streets, which to Buildings is a great Ornament and Beauty. In it they have reserved convenient places for Building of a Church, Town-House and other Publick Structures, an Artillery Ground for the Exercise of their Militia, and Wharfs for the Convenience of their Trade and Shipping." On these wharfs were assembled the commodities sent out in profitable commerce—pork sold to other colonies, pelts (deer skins by the thousands), and soon large quantities of rice, bartered for goods from the mother country.

★ BACON'S REBELLION

In the story of colonization there was, too often, the note of discord between homeland officials and colonists charged with carrying out imperial orders. Distance alone might account for colonial disregard of London edicts; these regulations, however, were often unworkable and revealed a blissful ignorance of American realities. Antipathy existed within the colonies themselves between administrators living in the comfortable, settled parts of the provinces and frontiersmen made angry by the alleged neglect of their economic, political, and military problems. Relations with the Indians also complicated local and imperial politics; the Indian may have been a "noble savage" to the man of letters, but to the white wayfarer in the wilderness he was just a savage—and expendable, unless docile and of service.

A quarrel over Indian policy lay at the root of Bacon's Rebellion in Virginia. Mutual suspicions made difficult any easy association between the two races. The Indians, who had once threatened the very existence of Virginia's settlement, had been reduced to a dependent status, many of them had even been enslaved. There was more of contempt than of fear in the attitude of local white men toward them. But often the Indian was looked upon as an envied owner of desirable land. Enterprising Virginians, notably the progenitor of the distinguished Byrd family, pushed westward and opened new lands to trade and future settlement. Pioneer traders with the Indians had already found the paths to Kentucky and Tennessee. Sales of guns by Virginia's traders to Indians increased social tensions.

Wrathful men gathered in the quiet of the forest and pledged support to each other. Their grievances were mainly against high taxes which bore down disproportionately on smaller landowners. Frustrated planters worried over low prices for their tobacco. They made bitter, perhaps unfair, comments about Governor Berkeley's avarice. Their angry explosiveness matched the governor's quick temper. Beneath all the discontent lay a smoldering resentment against domination of the colony by a greedy governor and a grasping aristocracy.

Early in 1676 long-suppressed passions of white and red men flared into vengeful fighting in frontier areas. Governor Berkeley's indecisiveness in dealing with the conflict fanned suspicions that he was less interested in the health of white men than he was in the wealth from Indian trade. The impetuousness of Nathaniel Bacon aggravated a situation already tense. His cry echoed the common grievance: "these traders at the head of the rivers buy and sell our blood." The governor's apparent disregard of popular demand to fight the Indians strengthened the conviction of many Virginians that their government had hardened into an irresponsible, corrupt oligarchy. It was easy for Virginians so to convince themselves.

Taxes had been increasing, and a small group controlled the chief positions of authority in Church and State. Bacon observed "that all the power and sway is got into the hands of the rich who by extortious advantages, having the common people in their debt, have always curbed and oppressed them in all manner of wayes." How could they expect redress when appeal must be made "to the very persons our complaints do accuse."

Bacon, himself a member of Virginia's select ruling class, but "popularly inclined," led a punitive expedition against Indians considered friendly to the government. Governor Berkeley then denounced Bacon as a rebel. After an interlude in which peace was temporarily patched up (and during which the government adopted several social and political reforms pressed by Bacon), the latter's insistence on carrying the war to the Indians found him a second time proclaimed a rebel. The nature of the conflict had shifted from whites versus Indians to a direct rebellion against Berkeley's government.

"It vexes me to the heart," Bacon said bitterly, "that while I am hunting the wolves and tigers that destroy our lambs, I should myself be pursued as a savage. Shall persons wholly devoted to their king and country—men hazarding their lives against the public enemy—deserve the appellation of rebels and traitors? The whole country is witness to our peaceable behavior. But those in authority, how have they obtained their estates? Have they not devoured the common treasure?" And remembering Berkeley's hostility to education in the colony, Bacon asked scornfully, "what arts, what sciences, what schools of learning have they promoted? I appeal to the king and parliament, where the cause of the people will be heard impartially."

Berkeley was able to assemble new forces to march against Bacon. To prevent the governor from possessing Jamestown, where his troops could find shelter, Bacon's men destroyed the community; one of his prominent lieutenants, William Drummond, set fire to his own house. Initial successes against Berkeley were soon nullified by the increasing strength of the governor, whose aristocratic supporters ridiculed Bacon's men as "rag, tag and bobtayle."

These harassed men pinned their hopes on Bacon, but fever and the strain of battle wore him down, and death came suddenly. "Who is there now to plead our cause," cried his followers in agony. "His name must bleed for a season; but when time shall bring to Virginia truth crowned with freedom, and safe against danger, posterity shall sound his praises."

Now leaderless, the rebellion dragged to a dreary end, the survivors running for "shelter amongst the Woods and Swomps." Then the vindictive old governor harried and hung all the leaders who could be tracked down. Twenty-three were hanged, but the governor's unslaked blood-lust thirsted for more. At length the assembly voted an address that the Governor "spill no more blood"; "had we let him alone, he would have hanged half the country," said one of its members. Posterity did sing Bacon's praises, for his tragic story became part of the folklore of the American people.

★ NEW JERSEY AND THE "HOLY EXPERIMENT" IN PENNSYLVANIA

At the time when England's American empire was stretching southward into Carolina, it was also filling out in the center, in the middle Atlantic area. There, as a result of the defeat of the Dutch, a large region had fallen to the Duke of York. His possessions now ran from the Connecticut River to the Delaware, and included also Long Island, Nantucket, and Martha's Vineyard as well as eastern Maine. Finding it impossible to manage so great an area profitably, the Duke shortly granted to favored friends large segments of it. To Lord John Berkeley and Sir George Carteret he gave the territory of New Jersey, which lay between the Hudson and the Delaware.

In their bid for colonists they, like other proprietors, promised ease of acquiring land, as well as liberty of conscience and an elective assembly. Puritans from New England had already settled in the New Jersey area to which they brought their distinctive political and religious institutions. Here their towns had large powers of self-government and their town meetings functioned much as they did in Massachusetts. Lord Berkeley, who had a half share in New Jersey, sold it to some Quakers, including William Penn, who took that portion known as West New Jersey. The area of East New Jersey remained in the Carteret family which disposed of it in 1682 for £3,400. Twenty years later (1702) both areas of New Jersey having been reunited, the colony was made a royal province.

The English settlements were born of hunger—hunger of the body and of the spirit. They were born of acquisitiveness—that pushed forward gold seekers, real estate speculators, and farmers, and traders. The settlements were also born out of the great humanity of men gifted with a vision of the future. Pennsylvania's origin was singular in its debt to a distinguished founder who dared to believe in his fellow men. Puritans of New England in Penn's time were not believers in man's fundamental goodness. Penn, on the contrary, had so optimistic a faith in mankind as to make his colony a beacon to utopians everywhere.

William Penn had become interested in Quaker ideas while still a student at Oxford. In the years of his childhood a great ferment had taken place among Englishmen who were engaged in a re-examination of their social, political, and religious institutions. The principles of monarchy were called into question, class distinctions were challenged, and conventional religious establishments defied. Few went so far as did the Society of Friends under George Fox, who seemed to be undercutting the foundations of existing society. The Friends, generally known as Quakers, believed in obedience to the "inner light." This was God's direct discourse to His followers, who needed therefore neither the familiar church nor priesthood. All were capable of being inspired by this "inner light" and were expected to give expression to it in "meeting." Penn joined the Quakers formally in 1667, at the cost of being cut off by his indignant father. He was not without funds, however, as he had the support of his mother.

Penn's association with George Fox and other religious enthusiasts filled him with plans for a "Holy Experiment." In his projected colony, as in the "Holy Commonwealth" of Massachusetts, man could make a new start in this world. Penn had already been interested in West New Jersey, but that setting was too restricted for his grandiose dreams. He had visions of a large colony, with himself as proprietor, free to establish a regime of political and religious liberty to which the outcasts of the world could repair. He differed from proprietors with an authoritarian bent. On one occasion he urged people "not to give away anything of Liberty and Property that at present they do . . . enjoy . . . and understand that it is easy to part with or give great privileges, but hard to be gained if once lost."

Penn's father, wealthy Admiral Sir William Penn, conqueror of Jamaica, royal creditor and friend to influential people at court, was finally reconciled to his son and bequeathed him a fortune; gifts from other sources also came to him. In consideration of debts due the Penn family the king gave to William Penn a large portion of the land which had earlier been granted to the Duke of York. "After many waitings, watching, soliciting, and disputes in council," wrote Penn, "my country was confirmed to me under the great seal of England. God will bless and make it the seed of a nation." To this territory was given the name Pennsylvania (1681). The next year the three "Lower counties," comprising the future Delaware, were added to Pennsylvania. Some two decades later (1704) they were detached from Penn's province to form the separate colony of Delaware.

A number of settlers, mainly Dutch and Swedish, had been in the newly named territory of Pennsylvania for some years. They helped ease the path of new arrivals. Penn, who was a skilful organizer, anxious to quickly populate his lands, set about publicizing the advantages of his colony to Englishmen, Dutchmen, Frenchmen, and Germans. The news was rapidly circulated that the new land had opened "an asylum to the good and the oppressed of every nation." Political and religious liberty were promised. "I purpose," said Penn, "to leave myself and successors no power of doeing mischief; that the will of one man may not hinder the good of a whole country." Land was more easily acquired there than anywhere else in the colonies; 50 acres headright free; 5,000 acres could be secured for £100; tenants could get 200-acre farms at a rental of a penny an acre.

In late October, 1682, Penn arrived to inspect his dominion, whose capital he founded between the Delaware and Schuylkill rivers. Thereby, he said, "it hath two fronts upon the water, each a mile, and two from river to river." Its situation, said Penn (who had visited the illustrious cities of Europe), was unsurpassed by any "among all the many places [he] had seen in the world." The plan he laid out for the chief town of his colony remained the guide for future generations. He named it Philadelphia, "with the pious wish and desire, that its inhabitants might dwell together in brotherly love and unity."

Penn had already issued a *Frame of Government* for his "Holy Experiment." It provided for a governor and deputy-governor, and a council of seventy-two elected by the freemen. The latter were landowners or taxpayers, and they were also empowered to choose an assembly to act on laws initiated by the council which was to be composed of elite citizens. A striking feature of Pennsylvania's code of laws was the mildness of its penal legislation. Most of the other American colonies were also less severe than the mother country in the punishment of criminals, but it remained for Pennsylvania to reduce the many crimes for which capital punishment was exacted to only one, murder. Unhappily, after some forty years of experience, conservative influences brought about a hardening of this humane code. Not until the American Revolutionary era did Pennsylvania again march in the van of progressive penology.

Soon after the original *Frame of Government* went into effect, modifications were made in it looking toward wider participation of the citizens in their government. The executive and judiciary were dependent on the people; the pacifist character of the settlement was underscored by the failure to provide for any armed forces. Penn urged his colonists to be humane in dealing with the Indians; "do not abuse them," he counseled, "but let them have justice, and you win them."

In response to his professions of friendship (the "Great Treaty" was signed with them in 1683), the Indians replied, "We will live in love with William Penn and his children, as long as the moon and the sun shall endure." Each remembered his pledge to the other during the next seventy-five years for neither the Indians nor Quakers drew blood from each other, and this when in other colonies vengeful acts drained life away from red men and white men together.

In this land of widest religious freedom (at least for all Protestant sects) there was no established church. In his colony, said Penn, every person "shall have and enjoy the free possession of his or her faith and exercise of worship towards God, in such way and manner as every person shall in conscience believe is most acceptable to God." And thus from its earliest days Pennsylvania had the greatest variety of religious sects to be found in America.

Penn left his colony to return to England in 1684, and thereafter the settlement underwent severe strain. There was constant bickering between assembly and council, for the former wanted an ever larger share in legislation. Penn, the proprietor, misplaced his trust in deputy-governors and other officials who alienated the people. But the province flourished despite the aches of colonials and the pains of proprietors. No colony grew so rapidly. Penn's confident statement, made less than three years after the founding of his settlement, was surely justified; "I have led the greatest colony into America that ever any man did upon a private credit, and the most prosperous beginnings that ever were in it, are to be found among us."

At that time (1685) Pennsylvania had nearly 9,000 people, with Philadelphia, its largest town, having over 350 houses, some of them of brick construction. Its streets, plotted in checkerboard fashion, took their names from local trees—walnut, beech, ash, chestnut, etc. Quakers from Wales settled Radnor and Haverford; English Quakers promoted manufacturing enterprises; Francis D. Pastorius, the learned German clergyman with religious ideas similar to Quaker doctrine, led a Mennonite flock to establish Germantown. Pastorius was overwhelmed by the endless forests, and he vainly longed for some "stalwart Tyrolians, to throw down these gigantic oak and other forest trees."

From the beginning Pennsylvania has always had a large non-British element in its population. But during its earliest years and for a long time thereafter, it was the English Quakers who gave the community its distinctive quality. They supplied the colony with a lively cultured class. Pennsylvania was especially marked by the variety of its humanitarian institutions. Intellectual alertness and energetic business activity were noteworthy features of the life of Philadelphia to which ambitious youths, such as Ben Franklin, were soon to be drawn. It was there that they were to find the widest scope for their talents.

★ KING PHILIP'S WAR

By the 1680's the English had peopled the Atlantic seaboard from Maine to South Carolina. Rival powers—Spain, Holland, France—had been brushed aside in this coastal area, but in the region beyond the Appalachian barrier control was still to be contested. White enemies and red Indians were on the borders, and the Appalachians fenced in the colonists. Another factor holding the settlers to the seaboard was the salt vital for the preservation of meat. Trade and social ties gave to the early colonists an orientation southward to the West Indies and eastward to the homeland. But despite the hold that the Atlantic region maintained on the early settlers, the frontier exerted a powerful pull.

Indian traders had already found routes through the mountains, carrying on their pack horses goods in barter for furs. Close-mouthed Englishmen threaded their way inland into the Mississippi Valley, where they met competing secretive Spanish, French, and Dutch traders, most of whose names are lost to history. It was these unknown explorers who unfolded America's map.

The area of English settlement gradually moved up the river courses, which led inland to the "fall line," where tumbling waters marked the end of easy navigation. The whites were pressing hard upon the Indians on the frontier and, in settled areas, hemmed them in ghetto-like settlements, breaking their spirits. In New England despairing red men were rallied by their King Philip (1675) to make a concerted stand against the advancing invader.

For a year the Indians terrorized the countryside. Whites were slain in ambush or, while at work in the field, fell victim to the sudden bullet of a tree-hidden marksman. The little stream, Bloody Brook, commemorated the horror of the massacre at Deerfield. In Mary Rowlandson's house at Lancaster many townsmen sought shelter. Indians attacked and set it afire. "Quickly, it was the dolefulest day that ever mine eyes saw," she wrote. "Now the dreadful hour is come. Some in our house were fighting for their lives; others wallowing in blood; the house on fire over our heads, and the bloody heathen ready to knock us on the head, if we stirred out. I took my children to go forth; but the Indians shot so thick, that the bullets rattled against the house, as if one had thrown a handful of stones." Made captive, Mrs. Rowlandson told of being taken away, "our bodies wounded and bleeding, and our hearts no less than our bodies . . . Oh the roaring, and singing, and dancing, and yelling of those black creatures in the night, which made the place a lively remembrance of hell . . . All was gone, my Husband gone . . . my Children gone, my Relations and Friends gone . . . There remained nothing to me but one poor wounded Babe . . ."

White ruthlessness matched Indian cruelty. The Indians were surprised in their winter quarters, their wigwams set afire, their food destroyed, and their old people and infants left among the flames. The young warriors who escaped sought cover in icy swamps; they lived on the nuts and acorns dug from under the snow. Through cold and famine they wasted away, but the whites gave them no respite. Philip was deserted by allies anxious for peace. Unyielding to the last he was slain by a fellow red man. The power of the Indians in southern New England was destroyed, but victory came to the whites at great cost. They suffered tragic losses in property and men. One in ten men of military age had been killed by the Indians, and hundreds of homes burned, every eleventh family was homeless. New Englanders abandoned many settlements and it took a generation to regain the lost ground. "So costly was the inheritance which our fathers have transmitted to us," wrote a schoolboys' history 150 years after these sorrowful events.

★ COLONIALS BECOME AMERICANS

Serious as such local setbacks were, the overall picture of growth in the colonies was impressive. Before the end of the seventeenth century the colonies had some 220,000 inhabitants, with the largest number, 95,000, in the southern colonies, 80,000 in New England, and in the middle colonies the smallest number, 45,000. The great majority of these people had been born in the colonies or had come over in their youth. Their origin had been mainly from the middle and lower classes in the British Isles and from similar groups in scattered areas on the continent. Like the "Mayflower" passengers they came from the cottages and not the castles. Extremes of wealth and poverty and of class distinctions were not so great in America as in the Old World. While there were classes, there were no castes. Rank and power rested less on birth or title than on native ingenuity.

The distinctions that did exist among colonial classes were well defined, though blurred at the edges where each touched the other. There was a mixed aristocracy of rank, wealth, and religion. Forty years after the settlement of Massachusetts Bay, Boston was said to have thirty merchants worth from ten to thirty thousand pounds. The leading clerical families intermarried among themselves as did the mercantile aristocracy. The gentleman brought his status with him from the Old World; the large landowner and well-to-do merchant directed local economic and political affairs; the eminent clergy had great moral as well as social prestige. In the next order of importance were skilled craftsmen and small farmers. This group was especially prominent in New England, where many of them voted and served as town officials. "Goodman" or "Goodwife" were titles proudly carried by men and women of this class. Next on the social ladder was the unskilled, free workingman, deferring to his superiors, who addressed him by his first name. Indentured servants formed a fourth class, and beneath them were the slaves. Members of the three lowest classes had no recognized political power, but in social disturbances, such as Bacon's Rebellion, they could add their pressure to other acts of discontent.

A gentleman was permitted sartorial splendor forbidden to the goodman; the latter could dress with more elegance than the laborer. Punishments were meted out to those who dressed above their station. Illegal aping of their "betters"—"wearing silk," growing long hair, "and other extravagancies"—brought many young men and women before the magistrates. Church pews were assigned in accordance with social rank. Punishments were scaled to a person's class. The wealthy miscreant might pay more in fines than the poor, but would be exempted from the more degrading forms of punishment, such as the pillory or the whipping post. In all these arrangements the colonies were following precedents long established in Europe. These class distinctions faded faster from the American scene than elsewhere, and more rapidly in New England than in the South.

In the colonies a stable economic order had been created, based on agriculture, commerce, and to a lesser extent manufactures. Shipbuilding and fishing were important enterprises in the North where a free labor economy had generally been established. In the South the labor force of indentured servants was now being rapidly augmented by Negro slaves. In all the colonies there was unconcealed discontent over land distribution; the favored of fortune had marked out for themselves huge tracts in hopes of speculative profits.

"Land! Land! hath been the Idol of many in New England," wailed Increase Mather. A disillusioned Roger Williams wrote in his later years to John Winthrop Jr.: "Sir, when we that have been the eldest and are rotting [in our graves] a generation will act, I fear, far unlike the first Winthrops . . . I fear that the common trinity of the world—Profit, Preferment, Pleasure—will be here the *tria omnia,* as in all the world . . . and that God Land will be as great a God with us English as God Gold was with the Spaniard."

The migrants who had come from England had arrived with a fund of political experience which enabled them to launch new societies with singular success. In the new environment their political education was furthered, and it is perhaps not too much to say that nowhere in the world at that time was there so large a proportion of the population comprising the active civic community. Colonial assemblies were, even as early as the seventeenth century, conscious of their rights, which prompted them to challenge royal authority.

Massachusetts, in particular, was militant in its jealous protection of her liberties against the mother country. Agents of the crown were rarely present to exercise any influence on colonial acts. There was indeed so little restraint on New England in the administration of local government, including taxation, that she may be said to have achieved an almost independent status. All the powers which go with that status were to be found in the chartered colonies—separate executive and legislative bodies, officials, courts, tax systems, ecclesiastical structures, locally formulated policies relating to frontier expansion and the Indians. The Puritan colonies acted as though English statutes simply did not apply to them.

Even in the proprietary colonies blueprints of monarchical regimes somehow took on different outlines when put to the test in America. Invariably colonists were able to win an ever larger share of power from the reluctant hands of proprietors. Although proprietary colonies were closer in spirit and form of government to England than were chartered colonies, the former were also very lightly bound to the mother country. The English king was a very shadowy figure in the consciousness of most Americans.

Imperial administration was lax, navigation laws were unenforced, and smuggling a local pastime. The remoteness of the colonies from London permitted them to handle their own business in their own way. When that business was of a weighty nature, of large imperial concern, it might come before administrative bodies in England or before parliament itself; but such occasions were rare in this period of American history. In fact no statutes passed in parliament bore vitally on the colonies until after the middle of the seventeenth century. Indeed throughout most of the seventeenth century legislation affecting the colonies was restricted to a few measures regulating trade.

The welcome indifference toward the colonies, of parliamentary and royal authority, changed with dramatic suddenness in the 1680's under the crown's initiative. The restored Stuart dynasty, had it had its way, would have created a centralized government of all the colonies subservient to the crown, much after the fashion of the French. The charter of Massachusetts was recalled; New Hampshire became a royal province, and so, too, did New York. Plymouth's identity as a separate colony was ended. The charters of Rhode Island and Connecticut were suspended. An administrative reorganization (1684–88) set up a dominion of New England, headed by the inflexible Sir Edmund Andros, to which New York and New Jersey were temporarily annexed.

This administrative reorganization had a twofold aim—to recover for the crown powers that had earlier been granted away, and secondly, to mesh the colonies more securely into the fabric of the growing empire. The interests of the colonies were now to be subordinated to the demands of the larger imperial needs. The northern colonies were expected to shift their economy from commerce and manufacturing to the production of naval stores and raw materials to be processed by the mother country. This policy was fraught with danger, for it ran counter to many colonial habits.

Fortunately for the colonies the policies of James II also ran counter to English traditions. The lesson of the years 1640–60, when parliament had overthrown an earlier Stuart, had been lost on him. England's second revolution within a century, the "Glorious Revolution," started a new chapter in modern history. It established beyond question the supremacy of parliament in the British scheme of government, and founded on firmer foundation the liberties of Englishmen which were proudly claimed by colonists as well. In the colonies small scale uprisings undid the administrative reorganization which had recently been achieved. The old colonial boundaries were re-established and suspended assemblies restored. But when the air cleared, one could discern a growing tendency for imperial administrators to favor the royal province as against the proprietary and chartered colony. The latter was too independent for the tastes of king or parliament. Crown authority was increased by converting several colonies to royal provinces, with a governor appointed by the king. The new charter given Massachusetts provided for this changed relationship; New Hampshire and New York had royal governors. As time passed Pennsylvania, Delaware, and Maryland remained as proprietary colonies. Connecticut and Rhode Island continued to be governed by their corporate charters while the other provinces were crown colonies.

The hard decades since Jamestown and Plymouth had thus seen the growth of a new society. In some respects that society had gained added stature in its greater humanity and in enlarging the concept of the civic community. But there were losses too. While the white man conquered the frontier, it is important to note that in many ways it vanquished him. In making his adjustment to primitive surroundings he was forced to leave behind him much of the substance of civilization. In the wilderness he shed his European clothes, tools, and intellectual habits. He wore moccasins and a hunting shirt, fought and took scalps like the aborigines, and even looked like an Indian. In fact the white born in America was sometimes spoken of as a "Tame Indian."

The refinements of cultivation in science, arts, and education had been dulled by neglect while more pressing matters claimed attention. Clearing the land, building homes, laboring from "day-break to back-break," were exhausting tasks which left little energy for cultural pursuits. In "Unfurnisht America," wrote a contemporary, the sparseness of her cultural milieu prevented the growth of mind and spirit. The clergy, notably in New England, exercising great influence but handicapped by lack of books, struggled to keep alight the lamp of learning. Much of their influence, a century after Boston's founding, seemed to be thrown to the support of property rather than the heavenly city of the founders.

Communications were difficult, and in the absence of newspapers and postal service each community tended to lead an ingrown existence. Roads were still hardly more than trails worn by Indian footsteps. They took the easiest grades and wound in and out among boulders and the giant trees of the forest. Slowly white settlers, by hatchet and ax, widened the eighteen-inch trails to permit travel on horseback. Even more effort was required before paths could be made usable for carts. Many a wheel and axle were broken against rocks and roots, or surviving these disasters, carts foundered in mudholes and washouts in vanishing roadbeds. Rain and melting snows carried dirt from hilly paths leaving them a series of steps on a staircase of stone.

For years to come travel by land over any considerable distance took courage. Bridges for the crossing of rivers were rare and of uncertain construction, and snakes and wild animals were everywhere. Madame Sarah Knight, in a trip from Boston to New York, risked drowning, unseating by a stumbling horse, and the terrors of forest darkness. At Norwalk this courageous traveler "crept over a timber of broken Bridge about 30 foot long and perhaps 50 foot to the water"; and at Stamford she crossed over another rickety structure, "exceeding high and very tottering and of vast length." Conditions gradually improved in America's physical and cultural environment, but at least half a century passed before there were a sufficient number of congenial spirits to raise in significant measure the level of culture in America.

At the end of the seventeenth century the colonies were still in many respects outposts of Europe. Americans in their traditions were transplanted Europeans. But the very fact of transplantation to a distant land with a new environment had wrought its changes. Characteristics of equality and uniformity in American society were already apparent, especially in New England. American institutions in their main outlines were fashioned in this period. A valuable English political inheritance, as well as conditions in America, predisposed the colonists in favor of self-government. In this confident temper they faced the future.

BOOK 2

THE COLONIES IN THE EIGHTEENTH CENTURY

THE EIGHTEENTH CENTURY opened with bright prospects for the American colonists. Queen Anne's War (known to Europeans as the War of the Spanish Succession) clouded these expectations, but with its close in 1713, the future seemed clear. Political stability had been achieved in the mother country, and she was prospering in commerce and manufactures. Along with other lands she was offering continually expanding markets for colonial products. Steadily the volume of shipping inbound and outbound from colonial ports increased, and the reputation of Yankee seamen and their vessels won the respect of the entire Western world.

While American ships sailed the seas, both near and far, landsmen were moving westward away from the coast line. As yet there was no great momentum in this drive to the west. It was fitful; there were plenty of empty spaces to be filled close to the older settled regions though these were fast rising in cost. The pressure of population became greater after mid-century.

Larger accumulations of capital available for speculative investment found opportunities for profit in the west. But men of wealth generally were not those who actually went to the frontier region. The settlers of this area were usually men without money, bent on inheriting the earth, and not, it should be said, through meekness. Rather they were tough and aggressive, perhaps with something of a grievance against the world, but with no excess of sourness. Like their fellow colonials in the towns, they leaned to the brighter side of life. After all, they had survived the stagnation of life in Europe, the perils of an ocean crossing, and the trek to the frontier.

With so much of an unloved past behind them, small wonder that Americans fell in love with their future! Their reaction was inspired by emotion as well as practical considerations. Friendly travelers caught the contagion of this hopefulness and wrote glowing accounts of the New World. The speed of growth in the colonies, their exuberant self-confidence and their faith in their mission to rejuvenate mankind deeply impressed the sympathetic observer. The latter prophesied a future for Americans as wondrous as even the most hopeful of colonials could foresee. Sir Thomas Browne spoke of the time:

> When the New World shall the Old invade
> Nor count them their lords, but their fellows in trade.

It remained for the colonial almanac-maker, Nathaniel Ames, to prophesy his country's future in most extravagant language:

"The Curious have observ'd, that the Progress of Humane Literature (like the Sun) is from the East to the West; thus has it travell'd thro Asia and Europe, and now is arrived at the Eastern Shore of America. Arts and Sciences will change the Face of Nature in their Tour from Hence over the Appalachian Mountains to the Western Ocean; and as they march . . . the Residence of Wild Beasts will be broken up . . . and the inestimable Treasures of Gold & Silver [will] be broken up. Huge Mountains of Iron Ore are already discovered; and vast Stores are reserved for future Generations; this metal more useful than Gold and Silver, will imploy Millions of Hands, not only to form the martial Sword and peaceful share . . . but an Infinity of Utensils improved in the Exercise of Art and Handicraft amongst Men. Stone from the vast quarries will be piled into great Cities. O! Ye unborn Inhabitants of America," Ames concluded dramatically, "When your Eyes behold the Sun after he has rolled the Seasons round for two or three Centuries more, you will know that we dream'd of your Times."

CHAPTER V

Beginning the World Again

The English possessions in America at the beginning of the eighteenth century stretched from French Canada to the Barbados in the Caribbean. The people of those communities which would one day form the United States totaled about a quarter of a million, with Virginia and Massachusetts the strongest and most populous of the colonies. Tobacco had created an upper class in the Chesapeake area; trade had done likewise in New England; land and trade together were doing the same for the middle colonies. Family dynasties were already to be found in most of the provinces, pulling the strings of power or sitting in the seats of authority themselves.

The expansion of population came partly from immigration but mainly from native increase (a high birth rate was the chief factor). The rate of growth far outstripped that of Europe's population (itself now fast increasing), and was a topic of excited comment throughout the Western world. Peter Kalm, the Swedish traveler, himself influenced by American enthusiasm, said "the English colonies in this part of the world have increased so much in their numbers of inhabitants, and in their riches, that they almost vie with Old England."

Colonial towns were growing rapidly; Boston with near 7,000 was the largest. Philadelphia, less than twenty years old, now had over 4,000, as did New York, which was "a pleasant well compacted place," said Sarah Knight. Newport and Charleston were lesser communities but very important, nevertheless, as economic and cultural centers for a large surrounding area.

The people who lived in these urban and rural communities were, for the most part, of English stock. This was especially true of New Englanders, who were spoken of as "a very home-bred people" and "exceeding wedded to their own way." Although England furnished the overwhelming mass of emigrants in the first century of colonization,

Englishmen did not migrate in such large proportions in the eighteenth century. Protestant dissenters were less oppressed in these years in England, which meant that religious discontent was a lesser factor than formerly in spurring emigration. Many hands once thought surplus were now being absorbed by the Industrial Revolution. A steady flow of workmen, merchants, professional men and younger sons of landed gentry, however, continued to increase the numbers in the population belonging to the original colonial stock.

To the American towns went craftsmen whose skills were to make the New World self-sufficient—stocking weavers from Nottingham, clothiers from Gloucestershire, and watchmakers from London. High wages and cheap land weaned workers from English fields and factories. Curbs on emigration were vain. British officials even went so far as to offer to pay return passage, but the emigrants would not come back.

More and more immigrants were then arriving whose origins were Scottish or German or French. As the vast majority of them were seekers of land they were forced into the back country, for the best lands near the coast were either occupied or too expensive. One visitor in the early years of the eighteenth century wrote that close to Philadelphia "the uncultivated ground, which is not grubb'd, sells for ten times the Value it did at first; though there is none of that sort within ten Miles round the City: And that within the Neighbourhood that was sold for ten Pound at first, will fetch above three hundred now."

Immigrants came from those regions of northern and western Europe where people were already experiencing greater mobility. Developments in agriculture and industry uprooted people from age-long residence in their communities, and lifted their eyes to far horizons. Commerce and wars, too, stimulated interest in overseas regions. Newspapers, magazines, and improved postal facilities made America a favorite topic of conversation. "The knowledge of distant countries is now become general," wrote a contributor to an Edinburgh magazine. "Those who in the last wars had occasion to see the continent of America, and other parts, have diffused this knowledge among their countrymen. Ships of merchandise frequently pass and repass by the western parts of Scotland and frequent commerce with these inspires the inhabitants with a romantic turn for voyages."

While governmental authorities in the Old World sometimes encouraged departure, particularly of religious nonconformists, they also raised barriers against it. Men were needed to work the land and make their countries strong by serving in their industries and their armies.

★ THE HUGUENOTS

Those anxious to leave Europe to "begin the world again," somehow managed their departure. Those who left of their own free will either paid for their own passage or had it advanced for them. The debt (and half of those who came to America before 1776 were such debtors) was paid in the form of service to the creditor. The person obligating himself to bound labor was known as an indentured servant or re-demptioner. The indentured servant ordinarily had signed his contract with a shipowner before embarkation. The "redemptioner" on arrival in America sought a purchaser who would assume the costs of ocean passage in exchange for the immigrant's labor. When his term of service (four years or longer) was at an end he was given clothing, a little money, perhaps a gun, and generally land. His status now was that of other free workers of the community; he could remain in the area and become a laborer working for pay or he could leave and take up remoter lands for himself.

In addition to those who entered more or less freely into indentured servitude, thousands of men and women who had been in British jails (often for very slight offenses) were sent to America as bound work-men. To the number of immigrants who came to America under duress should be added the largest group of all, those who came in chains—the Negro slaves. It has been estimated that about 250,000 of them were in the colonies by the middle of the eighteenth century.

The eagerness of colonial officials and land speculators to populate the provinces more rapidly and promote their economy led to a relaxa-tion of restrictions against people formerly unwelcome. Thus the Hu-guenots, harried by persecution in France, were permitted to settle in all the colonies before the beginning of the eighteenth century. Because they were Protestant, prejudice against them was less than that held against other "foreigners." Their experience in growing grapes and in manufacturing silk was expected to add to American wealth. But their lot was hard in many communities, though not in South Carolina. There they founded distinguished families and helped to make Charleston one of the most interesting towns on the Atlantic coast. They settled in New York (particularly in Westchester County), and in Virginia; a few went to Massachusetts. Never very numerous, the Huguenots made a large contribution to American life, for among them were people with great gifts of leadership. The roll call includes the names of Legaré in South Carolina, Maury in Virginia, Jay and DeLancey in New York, and versatile Paul Revere.

Like most other "foreign" groups the French in time lost most of their distinctive characteristics and became indistinguishable from their neighbors. Many of them transferred their religious allegiance to the Anglican church; they Anglicized their names (Blondpied became Blumpey and Whitefoot, Rivoire became Revere), their children went to the same schools as their playmates and later intermarried with them.

★ THE GERMANS

The Palatine Germans were a large group who added their numbers to the non-English stock in America. Their lands in southwest Germany had been desolated during a long period of warfare. To this evil was added religious persecution of Mennonites and other Protestant sects by Catholic princes. The cruelest winter in a hundred years set in, early in October, 1708, to deepen the blackness of the blighted region. Wine froze solidly, birds on the wing suddenly fell dead. Swift flowing rivers turned to ice. The most astonishing spectacle of all, never seen before, was the sight of heavy carts moving over the frozen sea along the coast.

Many of the inhabitants fled to England. In three months over 11,000 of them, alien in customs and speech, flooded into London, a city already overcrowded. Although English authorities extended relief to them there, it was felt that a more permanent solution to their problem was to send them to the unpopulated lands of America. Overseas they could be useful in preparing timber and other supplies for the royal navy.

It was hoped that the Germans, besides strengthening the economy of the empire would, by settling on the New York frontier, be a bulwark against French military power. The Palatines first headed for New York (1709), staying for a few years along the Hudson and in the Mohawk Valley. A resourceful leader, Conrad Weiser, told of their clearing in fifteen days a fifteen mile pathway through the woods to make a settlement in the Schoharie area. Promises given to them by New York officials were broken, but despite the inhospitable treatment the Germans remained for a time in the area, continuing "to manure & sew the Land that they might not be starved for want of Corn & food." Wild potatoes and strawberries, recommended by Indians, filled out their larder.

Aggrieved at their mistreatment (they were told they had no legal title to the land they had laboriously cleared and improved), many left the region (1723) to trek over the hills to the more inviting province of Pennsylvania. They cut a path from Schoharie, then made canoes and moved down the Susquehanna. Those who had preferred to remain behind in New York formed communities which attracted kin among later comers. But the bulk of the migrants found their Garden of Eden in Pennsylvania.

Word of this wonderland quickly spread abroad, and a flood of Germans anxious to take ship for the New World streamed to the North Sea ports, especially Rotterdam. To reach these ports the Palatines journeyed down the Rhine for a month or longer. On the way people questioned them eagerly and enviously about their future life in America. Many pamphlets and other publications were widely circulated in Germany urging emigration to Pennsylvania. Her advantages were recited in a language that would bring praise from the most facile of modern real estate promoters. Pennsylvania became the best publicized province in America, William Penn and his agents using the press as skilfully as present-day publicity men. Their technique was so effective it led a modern wit to rephrase a famous slogan: "no colonization without misrepresentation."

Christopher Sauer, a prominent leader among the newcomers in Pennsylvania, said he had written to his friends and acquaintances in Germany about the colony's civil and religious liberties. "My letters were printed and reprinted," he said, "whereby thousands were provoked to come to the province, and they desired their friends to come." Ship captains and land promoters also combined to recruit the emigrants. Most of them left from Germany as redemptioners, since few of them had resources enough to pay their passage and still have sufficient left over to begin life in America.

The same ships engaged in so many of these trips that they seemed a transatlantic ferry. In the first quarter of the eighteenth century about 50,000 Germans embarked for America. They were followed by many more (5,000 a year between 1749 and 1754), so that by the middle of the century 100,000 were living in the colonies, 70 per cent of them in Pennsylvania.

Conditions aboard ship were discouraging. The boats were small, 200 tons or less, and sleeping quarters were a very tight fit. Food was poor. Foul odors and vermin made the passage miserable, especially in dirty weather when passengers were confined below. Many of the younger children died. Typhus ravaged some of the ships, and the disease became so closely associated with these immigrants that it was known as "Palatine fever." Generally ships had a passenger list of one person per ton, but many vessels carried even heavier loads. In later years colonial legislatures enacted laws against the worst of shipping evils, especially overcrowding, but it was difficult to enforce this legislation.

Penn's prospectus to travelers informed them that fare was five pounds for each adult, fifty shillings for children, "Sucking Children Nothing," forty shillings per ton of freight, though each passenger was allowed one chest of belongings free. "The Goods fit to take with them for use or sale are all Utensils for Husbandry and Building, and Household Stuff; Also all sorts of things for Apparel, as Cloath, Stuffes, Linnen &c."

While some Atlantic crossings were made in about four weeks, the voyages were usually a good deal longer. Individuals who started these arduous journeys malnourished were among the first victims of contagious diseases, which sometimes swept a closely packed ship with horrifying results. It should be remembered, however, that disease took its dread toll on land as well. As for the slowness of travel, in the eighteenth century people had a different concept of time and had more patience than modern travelers. But under any circumstances the sight of the western shore was always welcome to the voyager of the Atlantic sea.

The Germans in these years usually entered America by way of Philadelphia. Ports to the southward, in the Carolinas and Georgia, were lesser gateways to the American interior. Germans were brought to develop iron mines in Virginia; the Virginian William Byrd offered special inducements to bring immigrants to his lands. He sponsored a bill in his colony's legislature "to make all foreigners that shall seat upon our frontiers, free from taxes for seven years." In North Carolina Germans founded the town of Newbern. German-speaking Swiss immigrants (12,000 between 1734 and 1744) settled southern communities, notably in South Carolina. From the port towns the Germans moved into the back country, mingling with pioneers of Scotch and English stock.

German and Swiss craftsmen brought with them their special skills in making shoes, textiles, and home furnishings. Their iron stove conserved the heat which the English open-hearth wasted, their Conestoga wagon was a sturdy carrier, and their long rifle became the frontiersman's prized possession. In a short time Germans had the reputation of being the best farmers in America, carefully tending their healthy livestock in their oversized barns. These farmers nursed the land's fertility, rather than violated it as was the habit of more spendthrift neighbors.

★ THE SCOTS BREAK GROUND "ON BARE CREATION"

The Scotch-Irish, together with the Germans, made up the largest group of immigrants in this period. Scots had been living in Ulster, Northern Ireland, for a century or more. They were staunch Presbyterians, generally living apart from the Catholic Irish on lands confiscated from the natives. It was from this group that many left for overseas. In the case of the Ulster Scots the causes for migration lay in discrimination by

England against their agricultural products and their textile industry. Tenants whose leases had expired were forced by their landlords to pay higher rents. They were also excluded from all political and military offices, and at the same time were obligated to pay tithes for the support of the Anglican church.

Crop failures in 1716–17 hurried the exodus from Ulster. Jonathan Swift, the famous author of *Gulliver's Travels,* bitterly described conditions in Ireland, where the old and sick lay "dying and rotting, by cold and famine . . . And as to the younger labourers they cannot get work and consequently pine away for want of nourishment . . . if at any time they are accidently hired to common labour, they have not the strength to perform it." Refugees who fled from Ireland to America carried in their hearts a deep hatred for England, which was passed on from one generation to another. A tombstone inscription in the Shenandoah Valley of Virginia told the story: "Here lies the remains of John Lewis, who slew the Irish lord, settled Augusta County, located the town of Staunton, and furnished five sons to fight the battles of the American Revolution."

The Scotch-Irish scattered throughout the colonies. Reports of success by earlier migrants, said one British official, "raised a spirit of Emigration amongst others of the like station in this Country next to Madnes." In a period of six years (1714–20) fifty-four vessels from Ireland brought immigrants to Boston. They founded settlements in western Massachusetts, New Hampshire, and Maine. Scotch-Irish located in New York, where the appropriately named Ulster and Orange counties reflect the point of origin of the early settlers. "The humour of going to America still continues," read one report in Ireland, "and the scarcity of provisions certainly makes many quit us; . . . and if we knew how to stop them, as most of them can get neither victuals nor work at home, it would be cruel to do it."

Thousands of them (more than of any other nationality) went to Pennsylvania where they became the most experienced of frontiersmen. "It looks as if Ireland is to send all its inhabitants hither," wrote an unfriendly Pennsylvania official (1729); "last week not less than six ships arrived, and every day, two or three arrive also. The common fear is that if they continue to come, they will make themselves proprietors of the province." Like the Germans many of the Scotch-Irish moved down the valleys from Pennsylvania to settle in the western portions of colonies to the southward, again and again breaking ground "on bare creation."

Vessels which carried flaxseed from Philadelphia and from Newcastle, Delaware, to Irish ports brought back immigrants as their human cargo. These newcomers found their way to Maryland and New Jersey where advantages seemed as promising as in Pennsylvania.

Another stream of Scots came from their own Highlands to America. The Highlanders who were rebels against the crown, had been defeated in 1715, and thought it wiser to migrate. They had economic grievances as well, for they found it increasingly difficult to pay rents to their landlords. The call of free land to the west was irresistible. These Highlanders, smaller in number than the Scotch-Irish, established communities in the southern colonies. The total number of Scots and Irish who had come to America reached some 100,000 by the middle of the century. This figure was to grow rapidly in the next twenty-five years.

Scottish emigrants to the colonies totaled some 25,000 in the period 1763–75. Young and old joined the exodus. Thirty families arranged to meet at Killin in Perthshire in May, 1775. After spending a night in barns they were brought together in the morning to the sound of bagpipes. "Dressed in their best attire and some of them armed in the Highland Fashion in spite of the law, they settled the order of march, bade farewell to their friends and relatives, and set off down the road." By foot and by boat they arrived at Greenock where they took ships for the New World. Another group of 200 about this time were also marching off to Greenock. Among them was a woman of 83, on foot, her son preceded her playing "Tullochgorum" on his bagpipes. Some of the emigrants took along children a month old, who were carried in baskets on their fathers' backs.*

Smaller numbers of Scandinavians and Jews (the latter settling in coastal towns) added to the diversity of American population. These, like other immigrants, in time became indistinguishable from the rest of the community. English became their tongue and they learned to think and act like their neighbors. The Germans in Pennsylvania (ancestors of the "Pennsylvania Dutch") were more isolated than others from the main stream of the English cultural tradition which was dominant in the colonies. They retained, much longer than fellow immigrants, the characteristics that set them apart from other groups. All immigrant stocks by their own distinctive skills, whether in business enterprise, agriculture, or art, made their special contribution to the sum total of American civilization.

★ CONDITIONS OF WORK

Of the many thousands of immigrants to the colonies the vast majority were peasants or workingmen, those who labored with their hands.

---

* I. C. C. Graham, *Colonists from Scotland, Emigration to North America, 1707–1783* (Ithaca, N.Y.: Cornell University Press, 1956), p. 75.

Upper class people were infrequent arrivals but merchants, teachers, clergymen, newspapermen, and traveling artists were not uncommon. The immigrants went either to the growing towns or to the back country, where they did manual labor for someone else or for themselves on frontier lands.

As the colonies grew older free immigrant labor constituted a larger fraction of the working force, but as already remarked, for most of the period down past the middle of the eighteenth century the dependable supply of white workers came over as indentured servants or redemptioners. There was generally a large profit to the merchant or captain who assembled the prospective emigrants. To procure a servant, equip him, and transport him to the colonies might require an outlay ranging from four to ten pounds. In America he could be "sold" to an employer for anywhere between six and thirty pounds. A skilled worker naturally brought the highest figure.

Since many prospective employers had little cash, ship captains exchanged servants for colonial products which could be sold abroad profitably. The *New York Gazette* (1728) advertised the arrival of indentured servants: "On Wednesday last arrived here the ship George, John Anthony Adamson, Commander, from Ireland, who has on board several Irish men, women and Boys, Servants, among whome there is several Trades Men, as Carpenters, Weavers, Taylors, Blacksmiths, etc." Their "time" was offered for sale to prospective purchasers who could pay "either Flower or Wheat."

In England people sometimes mysteriously disappeared, kidnapped to add to the American labor supply. In Germany "Newlanders," recruiting agents, went through the land assembling emigrants for the colonies. Exaggerated, as well as true, reports spurred the movement to the New World.

It was eagerness of people on both sides of the ocean that explains this migration: desire on many counts to leave Europe, and the need of America for labor, preferably cheap. Employers in the colonies were always complaining about the high rates of wages. When labor in England was paid a shilling a day the rate demanded by free workmen in America was two or three times that. "There is hardly any Trade in England but the same may be met with in Philadelphia," wrote one visitor; "and every Mechanick has better Wages; a Journeyman Taylor has twelve Shillings a Week, besides his Board, and every other Trade in Proportion has the same Advantage." Colonial governors were unable to attract young men to the fighting services with their low pay; the colonists, explained one official, "live so plentifully at home and have so great wages besides."

Bound workmen, temporary or permanent (slave), seemed an answer to labor scarcity. Franklin observed that the labor of the colonies was "performed chiefly by indentured servants brought from Great Britain, Ireland, and Germany, because the high price it bears cannot be performed in any other way." Despite these importations labor was never plentiful in the colonies, and wages in America have always been higher than elsewhere.

In New England, where farms were small, fifty to two hundred acres, a father and his sons, with an occasional "hired man," supplied the necessary labor force. A larger supply of apprentices and skilled workmen was to be found in that region than in other colonies. Growing urbanization, fishing, trade, and manufactures required their services. But New England had a large proportion of bound labor, too, and from the late years of the seventeenth century indentured servants and Negro slaves increased in that area.

In the middle colonies the number of indentured servants was larger, in New York workmen often labored alongside Negro slaves who had now become numerous there. By the middle of the eighteenth century Negroes comprised about one-seventh of the population of that province. New Yorkers became fearful of them, particularly after slave "revolts" in the first half of the century.

Everywhere in the world of that day the lot of unfree workmen was hard. Even in America, where life was easier than elsewhere, their burdens were heavy. There was scarcely any limitation on the tasks assigned to them; food and clothing supplied to them might often be inadequate. Servants needed the consent of masters to marry. Discontent sometimes caused servants to run away, although if caught they were punished severely and their term of service lengthened. Colonial legislatures attempted to throw a protective screen around the servants by giving them the right to bring court action against employers who violated provisions of indenture contracts. Servants on southern plantations seemed to be more harshly treated than in other communities, and the mother country instructed governors there and elsewhere to back laws to check brutality against these working people.

★ NEGRO SLAVE LABOR

In the colonies of Virginia and Maryland at the beginning of the eighteenth century about 2000 indentured servants were being imported annually. They performed the same tasks there as fellow servants did in the North, and many of the Scotch-Irish served as tutors to the children on plantations. When the youngsters acquired the "burr" of their teachers parents sought other instructors.

After 1700 Negro slave labor became far more important than indentured servitude. By the middle of the century Virginia had near 120,000 slaves, while the white population was about 170,000. In South Carolina Negroes already far outnumbered the whites. Several reasons explain the shift from white servants to slaves. The latter were servants for life, the whites for a relatively short period. The offspring of slaves were unfree and were added to the labor force. Negroes cost less, in food and clothing, and were usually more manageable than white servants.

Negro slaves ordinarily were divided into three groups—field hands, domestics or house servants, and craftsmen. The first group was made up of the "Guinea" Negroes, recently arrived from Africa's west coast, and therefore newest to white man's civilization. Their tasks were the hardest on the plantation, clearing fields and forever bending weary backs over the crops. Their death rate was high in the malaria infested rice swamps of Carolina. Relations between "Guinea" Negroes and their white masters were likely to be more strained than those between whites and other slaves. The second and third groups, domestics and craftsmen, came from "country born" Negroes who had grown up from childhood in contact with whites. Because the adjustment between them was easier, the whites considered them more intelligent, and trained them for skilled work.

Many of the Negroes were quick to learn, becoming carpenters, masons, smiths or wheelwrights. Negro mechanics were often hired out, and thus brought additional income to their masters. So great a value was set upon the skills of the most expert among them that one master in South Carolina refused over £500 for three of his slaves. Colored people, while themselves acquiring the culture pattern of the whites, in turn left a mark upon their masters. "They that are born there," said a traveler in Virginia, "talk good English, and affect our language, habits and customs."

Codes for the regulation of Negroes became more complex as their numbers and value increased. They were regarded normally as property, and as such had no legal or political rights. They had no claim to a jury trial nor could they appear as witnesses against whites. They could not move freely about without proper documents; they could not gather together with other Negroes for fear of plots against their masters. Like indentured servants, many of them ran away, and newspapers printed announcements offering rewards for their recapture. Thus the *Pennsylvania Journal* (June 8, 1749): "Run away from Nicholas Bearcraft of Hunterdon County, a Black Wench, named Hecatissa alias Savina, Country born, about 27 Years of Age, short Stature, gloomy down

Look, often troubl'd with Cholick, it is thought she may be gone towards Maryland. Whoever takes up and secures said wench . . . shall have Twenty Shillings Reward . . ."

It is worth observing that out of care for valuable property alone, as well as considerations of humanity, slaves were often treated like the human beings they were. This seems especially true of Virginia whose attitude toward slaves was less harsh than that of more southerly colonies. One visitor to Virginia observed that the apparent profitableness of Negro slaves obliged owners "to keep them well, and not overwork, starve, or famish them . . . which is done in a great degree, to such especially that are laborious, careful and honest, though indeed some masters, careless of their own interest or reputation, are too cruel and negligent." One close observer even believed that in Maryland Negroes were better off than white servants; the former, he said, "being a property for life, the death of slaves, in the prime of youth or strength, is a material loss to the proprietor; they are, therefore, almost in every instance under more comfortable circumstances than the miserable European, over whom the rigid planter exercises an inflexible severity."

★ COLONIAL COMMERCE

Traffic in white servants and black slaves was big business in the colonies, and was the source of much of the wealth enjoyed by merchants and ship captains. Shipping men in Old England and in New England were especially prominent in the slave trade.

In the seventeenth century New England traders had already worked out the pattern of their familiar triangular traffic between their home ports, the African coast, and the West Indies. Freighted with rum, ships plied the Guinea coast, exchanging their cargo for slaves. These were then taken to the West Indies where they were profitably disposed of. The ships then loaded sugar and molasses for the last leg of the journey back to home ports in New England. The molasses was distilled into rum in New England towns (Newport alone had twenty-two distilleries by 1762), and then the triangle started over again. With the increasing demand for slaves in the southern colonies captains reserved some of their Negroes for American plantations, where they were exchanged for rice and tobacco. Busy Newport, by the middle of the eighteenth century, had 120 ships engaged in oceanic commerce, many of them in the triangular trade.

New England ships also carried less doleful cargo than slaves. They brought home food supplies from the bread colonies, New York and Pennsylvania. They caught and transported fish throughout the Atlantic world and into the Mediterranean Sea. Before the eighteenth century was half gone Massachusetts had 400 vessels and 6000 men in the fisheries. Profit and adventure were irresistible lures to the young Americans who manned the vessels laden with goods and people from strange lands. When not yet twenty some of them commanded their own ships. This was an exciting road to wealth and to social distinction, much to be preferred to the slight returns from the struggle with New England's stony ground.

No other New World activity had the glamour of whaling. At first whales were caught off shore. Candles were made from whale oil, and they proved to be a large item in New England exports. Nantucketers soon found that the sperm whales gave a better oil and began to hunt them in deep water. Daring captains pushed their ships into remoter seas as the spouting mammals became scarcer off New England. Before the middle of the eighteenth century, whalers had been constructed to boil and stow the oil while at sea thus permitting ships to stay out a longer time.

The skill and fearlessness of these audacious New Englanders captured the imagination of men everywhere. It won them a dramatic tribute by Edmund Burke, who used them as an object lesson in cautioning England not to rein in too tightly so high-spirited a people: "Look at the manner in which the people of New England have of late carried on the whale fishery. Whilst we follow them among the tumbling mountains of ice, and behold them penetrating into the deepest frozen recesses of Hudson's Bay and Davis's Straits, whilst we are looking for them beneath the Arctic circle, we hear that they have pierced into the opposite region of polar cold, that they are at the antipodes. . . . Nor is the equinoctial heat more discouraging to them, than the accumulated winter of both the poles.

"We know that whilst some of them draw the line and strike the harpoon on the coast of Africa, others . . . pursue their gigantic game along the coast of Brazil. No sea but what is vexed by their fisheries. No climate that is not witness to their toils. Neither the perseverance of Holland, nor the activity of France, nor the dexterous and firm sagacity of English enterprise, ever carried this most perilous mode of hard industry to the extent to which it has been pushed by this recent people; a people who are still, as it were, but in the gristle, and not yet hardened into the bone of manhood." The fame of these seamen hunting whales became one of the most cherished possessions of Americans.

The ships the Yankees sailed were built in their own yards. So many vessels were launched in the colonies that English shipbuilders complained of the competition. Americans were constantly experimenting with new types of craft to develop superior sailing qualities. Shipbuilding required the services of a specialized group of craftsmen—sailmakers, rope makers, ship carpenters, etc.—and in this enterprise was to be found an early example of the division of labor in American industry.

New Englanders had to be careful about the lumber selected for the mast of their vessels lest they trespass on the king's preserves. The crown officials marked with a broad arrow choice trees for use by the royal navy. But squatters and "loggers" had scant respect for His Majesty's arrows, and the woods resounded with the crash of these giant trees felled by contemptuous axmen.

New Englanders provided themselves not only with their own ships; they had also learned how to make their own clothes. A letter to imperial officials in London (1708) complained that "country people and planters are entered so far into making their own woollens, that not one in forty but wears his own carding, spinning, etc. If the growing trade of woollens be no way prevented in its growth, England must loose the woollen export to all this part of America." Parliament, already fearful of colonial competition, had passed the Wool Act, 1699, forbidding Americans to engage in intercolonial or foreign trade in woolen products.

Scotch-Irish immigrants brought with them to New England their superior knowledge in the making of linen. Thereafter this industry experienced a rapid expansion. Enthusiasts for home production (impelled also by sentiments of philanthropy) formed the Boston Society for Promoting Industry and Frugality just before the middle of the century. On its fourth anniversary, during the "Spinning Craze," 300 young female spinsters put on an exhibition, working at their wheels on Boston Common.

Less important than fishing, shipbuilding, or the making of textiles were other enterprises in New England—glassmaking, paper mills, and shoe manufactures in Lynn, Massachusetts. Americans were supplying themselves with all the nails they required; they were making many of their own tools; their axes in particular were sufficient for their needs and superior in quality to imports. But New England, along with other American colonies, could not produce all its desired manufactures, and her imports of these commodities left the community a heavy debtor to English merchants. Cadwallader Colden, of New York, described the situation ruefully: "Whatever advantages we have by the West India trade," he said, "we are so hard put to it [to] make even with England, that the money imported [from] the West Indies seldom continued six months in the province, before it is remitted for England."

★ WEST INDIAN TRADE

The place of domestic manufactures in New England, important as it may have seemed to contemporaries, was far less significant than her trade. Central to her economy was her trade with the West Indies. From her profits in that commerce, she was enabled to settle (at least temporarily) adverse trade balances with the mother country, and accumulate capital for further economic expansion. Connecticut reported that its vessels "go to the French and Dutch plantations [in the West Indies] carrying horses, cattle, sheep, hogs, provisions and lumber, for which are received molasses, cocoa, cotton and some sugar, and from the Dutch plantation, bills of exchange . . ." The needs of West Indian planters were greatest in fish, lumber, and provisions. West Indian economy and American economy became so interwoven that each became almost indispensable to the other.

Partnerships between colonists and West Indians were not uncommon. Over eighty vessels, most of them built at Philadelphia, were registered there in the years before the Revolution as owned jointly by Pennsylvanians and West Indians. It must not be supposed that every transaction was profitable. It was easy to glut a market in the West Indies with colonial exports, and captains were then forced to peddle their cargoes from island to island. On the other hand a hurricane immediately increased the demand for North American lumber to repair buildings.

All the continental colonies participated in the West Indian trade. At the middle of the eighteenth century Boston, Newport, New York, and Philadelphia were the leading ports, with Providence gaining in importance on the eve of the Revolution. Vessels from northern colonies picked up produce from the southern colonies which they exchanged for West Indian molasses. Colonial vessels engaged in a profitable carrying trade between the West Indies and Great Britain, but British shipowners complained about the competition.

Nearly all the large mercantile fortunes in colonial America owed something to the West India trade, which was the chief lubricant of the Atlantic economy in the eighteenth century. As the latest and most careful student of this subject, Professor Richard Pares, puts it, "More North American shipping was employed in this trade than in any other, . . . every North American port and nearly every North American merchant had something to do with it." *

* Richard Pares, *Yankees and Creoles, The Trade Between North America and the West Indies Before the American Revolution* (Cambridge, Mass.: Harvard University Press, 1956), p. 163.

New England's share in this trade exceeded that of her rivals. Boston's leadership was especially notable in the distilling of West Indian molasses into rum, although New Yorkers and Philadelphians looked down their red noses when discussing New England's "inferior" brand. Besides carrying their own products they also handled a large fraction of the commodities for their sister colonies. Another source of revenue for New England shipping were the returns from commerce within the area of the West Indies themselves. Seamen from Yankee ports were equally at home in Nevis, Antigua, Barbados or a dozen other islands in the "Carribees." Captain Penmure of the "Charming Polly" took a cargo of goods out of Newport, Rhode Island. He was instructed to take his ship to St. Vincent's in the Danish West Indies to dispose of the cargo, "if he can. If not to proceed to Dominico [Spanish] and there sell what he can and proceed from thence to St. Eustatius [Dutch] and dispose of any part of the cargo he may have left . . . and when the whole is converted into money to proceed with all possible dispatch to the island of Hispaniola [Spanish] . . . and there invest the neat [net] proceeds of his cargoe in good molasses, best muscovado sugars and Indigoe." The Dutch islands of St. Eustatius and Curaçao were popular with American colonials. They were the best market places in the Caribbean, making it easier to assemble return cargoes there.

To prevent the diversion of business from themselves to alien ports, where specie might more readily be secured, British West Indian planters backed a bill in parliament (Molasses Act, 1733) which charged a heavy duty on foreign sugar and molasses imported by the colonists. But the act, while an irritant, did not diminish trade with the non-British West Indies.

★ SMUGGLING AND CAPTAIN KIDD

To the profits from legal trade must be added the rewards from illegal transactions, especially smuggling. Smuggling goods across frontiers to avoid payment of duties had been anciently practiced in Europe. Americans proved adept pupils. While it may be true that the volume of smuggling in the colonies has been exaggerated, there can be no doubt that it loomed large in the pleased eyes of colonials, as well as in the glare of frustrated government officials.

The Atlantic coast line might almost have been designed by smugglers. Its many bays, rivers, and even creeks provided sanctuary for the relatively shallow boats of that day. The number of officials administering the navigation acts was small, and bribes weakened their civic virtue. Among the colonists themselves it became a matter for self-congratulation to evade the navigation laws, much as their descendants did in the era of prohibition. The tightening of regulatory measures (for example, trying accused smugglers in vice-admiralty courts) only incensed colonials the more, for they thought the navigation acts were unjust to begin with.

Officials, thinking at first that their assignments would prove lucrative, were soon disillusioned. John Townshend was a customs house officer at Oyster Bay, Long Island Sound, New York. He was given a salary of £30 and one-third of the seized goods of smugglers. It looked like a comfortable, remunerative job, but within a month the post that Townshend had accepted with alacrity he now begged to be relieved of. Though Oyster Bay was filled with his relatives, said Townshend, "yet he was threatened by them to be knocked on the head, and he already suffered many abuses, insomuch as he was in fear of his life."

Rhode Islanders, as well as others, bought merchandise in Dutch and French West Indian ports, which by the navigation laws they should have secured only in England. The smuggling into New England of these goods, which were usually cheaper, cut down the sales of English merchants and offended official sensibilities. These illegal practices, said one angry official, "will never be put an End to till Rhode Island is reduced to the subjection of the British Empire; of which at present it is no more a part than the Bahama Islands were when they were invaded by the Bucanneers." Staid Quakers were accused of abetting smugglers, as were the soberest of New Englanders, described by an unfriendly critic as people with "great dexterity at palliating a perjury as well as to leave no taste of it in their mouth."

If smuggling was almost conventional, privateering and piracy were adventurous and dangerous. In time of war between England and rival powers colonial governments authorized private ship captains to capture enemy ships and their cargoes on the high seas. Captain and crew shared the spoils, saving a portion perhaps for a merchant who may have financed the privateering expedition. Rewards were great and excitement high. "Brave living with our people," wrote Captain Benjamin Norton, bound for the Spanish West Indies in 1741: "Punch every day, which makes them dream strange things which foretells Great Success in our Cruize. They dream of nothing but mad Bulls, Spaniards and bagg of Gold."

Piracy was a short step from privateering which had, at least, a cloak of legality. There was nothing stealthy about the pirates who paraded their flamboyance before admiring colonials. Captain Bartholomew Roberts wore a "rich crimson Damask Wastcoate, and Breeches, a red Feather in his hat, and a Gold Chain ten times around his Neck."

Colonial merchants and even officials were suspected, often cor-

rectly, of dealing with pirates to their mutual advantage. Rhode Island
and New York apparently flourished from this association. Governor
Fletcher of the latter province sold protection to the pirates at the rate
of 100 dollars per head "besides what private presents report saith were
made to his Lady and daughter." The most notorious of the pirates
was Captain Kidd, whose fascination has never died for the young of
all ages. It was reported from New York that "many flockt to him from
all parts men of desperate fortunes and necessitous in expectation of
getting vast treasure." Sent out to squelch piracy he turned pirate himself, finally to hang on Execution Dock in London. Captain Bartholomew Roberts and his crew vowed that before they met the fate of
Captain Kidd they would rather "put fire with one of their Pistols to
their Powder and go all merrily to Hell together."

★ THE BREAD COLONIES

New Yorkers and Pennsylvanians, though benefiting from illegal trade
practices, probably rested their economy more on legitimate commerce.
The exports of the middle colonies were chiefly agricultural, giving to
these provinces the reputation of being the bread basket of America.
Colden, in New York, reported that "several of our neighbors upon the
continent cannot well subsist without our assistance as to provisions
for we yearly send wheat and flour to Boston and Rhode Island as well
as to South Carolina . . ." Port authorities, jealous of the reputation
of their colony's flour and anxious to please the customers, insisted on
the maintenance of high standards in exporting this commodity.

The export of breadstuffs required the making of barrels, and the
cooper's occupation was well rewarded. Many barrels were shipped
empty to be filled in Ireland with butter and salt provisions, or to the
West Indies where they were packed with sugar and molasses. Other
lumber products, shingles, boards, etc., much of which was exported,
were made in large quantities by craftsmen and by farmers in their
spare time.

New Yorkers had a favorable balance of trade with the West Indies
which supplied them with credit and Spanish dollars. But they found
themselves in debt regularly to Madeira as their insatiable thirst for
her wine was more than could be paid for by goods shipped from their
colony.

Pennsylvania was noted for the vigor of her shipbuilding industry
in colonial days. To transport the thousands of immigrants entering the
province, and to carry her bulky exports, required many ships. Her leading citizens, including William Penn himself, therefore encouraged the
establishment of local shipyards. Four generations of the Penrose family

in Philadelphia built ships, large and small, over a period of one hundred and fifty years. Ships, and always more ships—this was the cry of merchants, imperial officials, or just plain emigrants awaiting their turn to cross the ocean.

Inhabitants of the middle colonies made their own clothes and, as elsewhere, Scotch-Irish settlers promoted the linen industry. The governor of New York reported that nearly every family made its own "coarse Cloths (Linsey Woolseys) . . . everywhere swarms of children are set to work as soon as they are able to spin and card, and as every family is furnished with a loom, the itinerant weavers put the finishing hand to the work."

The iron industry in the colonies had progressed so far by the middle of the century as to arouse the fears of nervous manufacturers in England. They sought to prevent its growth by restrictive legislation but failed. The Iron Act of 1750 prohibited the colonies from building mills, furnaces, and forges, though it encouraged the export from America of pig and bar iron. The latter was to be made into finished products in Great Britain. Colonials were not to make finished products which competed with those of the mother country. The Swedish traveler, Acrelius, who was in the colonies in 1750, reported that in Lancaster county, Pennsylvania, the ironworks consisted of a "furnace which makes twenty-five tons of iron a week and keeps six forges regularly at work." The casting of plates for Franklin stoves was done locally and it proved a profitable enterprise.

One of the most valuable articles of commerce in colonial New York was the trade in furs. "There is not a place in all the British Colonies, the Hudson Bay Settlements excepted," said Peter Kalm, "where such quantities of furs and skins are bought of the Indians as at Albany." Merchants in that town, paddling their canoes down navigable streams and carrying them across country to the next portage, made contact with the Iroquois Indians at Oswego on Lake Ontario. There they spent the summer exchanging goods and liquor for the valuable beaver and other skins. Beaver fur was especially suited for making felt, but colonials were not encouraged to make their own hats out of it. London feltmakers brought pressure on parliament to pass the Hat Act (1732) forbidding intercolonial trade in hats and restricting the training of apprentices in the trade.

★ PLANTATION ECONOMY

The trade in furs was a factor of significance in the economy of southern colonies. It was an adventurous commerce, for relations with the Indians were unpredictable. A tough crew, mainly Scots, were hired by

Charleston merchants to deal with the Indians. In the spring they loaded their pack horses or dugouts with stocks of goods to carry to the back country in exchange for deerskins or even Indian captives to be sold as slaves.

The Indian traders gradually built a network of trails or "paths" which covered much of the back country. Dr. Henry Woodward (1670), an adventurer knowledgeable in Carolina's back country and an experienced trader, cultivated the natives to encourage their hostility against Spain. He and other traders made use of the Indian trails which linked the Catawbas, the Cherokees, and the Creeks. Some of these Indians had been offended by the Spaniards and were ready to be courted by the English.

Constant hunting depleted the nearer supply of skins so that traders were forced ever farther into the region beyond the southern Appalachians. The way west was easier from Charleston than from Virginia; from the former a pack train could travel directly west to the Mississippi and meet no land barrier higher than foothills. In the southwestern area of colonial America British traders and imperial officials confronted the equally aggressive rivalry of the Spaniards and the French. The English offered cheaper and better goods to the Indians than did the Spaniards, whose power consequently declined in the region.

The wealth that Charleston merchants won from trade was ploughed back into newly acquired plantations, for the prestige of land ownership was greatly coveted. The Indian trade was overshadowed in the south by the importance of her staple crops, rice and tobacco. Millions of pounds of each commodity were raised for colonial and foreign markets. Another important crop was indigo, which had recently been introduced into South Carolina (1742), and its cultivation sprouted an indigo aristocracy. In mid-eighteenth century South Carolina may have had a larger concentration of wealth than any other colony.

It is a common mistake to suppose that southern life was entirely wrapped up in the production of these staples. The rapid rise in local population, white and black, required larger food supplies. Domestic needs and export markets (in the West Indies) encouraged the planting of corn and wheat and the raising of live stock. Pigs were everywhere. South Carolina was described as swarming with swine "which multiply infinitely and are kept with very little charge because they find almost all the year acorns, walnuts, chestnuts, herbs, roots, in the woods, so that you give them ever so little at home and they become fat, after which you may salt and send great quantities to the Isles of Barbados, St. Christophers, Jamaica, etc., which produce very good return in money or merchandise." Imperial bounties rewarded the production of forest products, thus encouraging South Carolina to ship more pitch and tar than all the other colonies together. In North Carolina the lumber industry stood close to the top in colonial America.

Decreasing returns from worn-out tobacco lands stimulated diversification of crops. It caused some southerners to promote various industrial enterprises, including the making of textiles and the manufacture of shoes. A Virginia resident reported that he and his neighbors were well able to get along without many of the things formerly imported: "I now wear a good suit of cloth of my son's wool, manufactured, as well as my shirts, in Albemarle, my shoes, hose, buckles, wig, hat, etc. of our own country and in these we improve every year in quantity and quality."

The southern plantation was in process of becoming the self-sufficient community so much more familiar to the nineteenth century. It was more than a society resting exclusively on a single crop. The integration of the varied resources of land and forests in the creation of a distinctive way of life was the ideal sought by the southern planter.

The ideal, as usual, fell short of the reality. Too many plantations clung to the one crop economy, depleting the soil disastrously. Productivity per acre was declining, "break even points" were rising, and fluctuating prices added to the problems of planters. The latter charged that marketing costs—commissions, warehouse rent, cartage, etc.—levied by English merchants were exorbitant. Finally mercantilist regulations prevented American tobacco from being sent directly to the continent of Europe; it had first to go to England whence four-fifths of it was re-exported by her merchants.

The planter was encouraged in his extravagant way of life by British merchants who were usually ready to extend credit, often charging excessive prices for inferior merchandise shipped in exchange for tobacco. Debts were transmitted from one generation to another, and they were looked upon as almost a normal part of life. But normal or not it was resented. Few Virginians were rich, said her historian, Robert Beverley, with sarcasm; their estates were "regulated by the Merchants in England, who it seems know best what is Profit enough for them in the Sale of their Tobacco, and other Trade." With the passing of time anger was to mount against the elegant servitude of the south's aristocracy to the merchants of England.

The people of America underwent great changes during the first half of the eighteenth century. They took on the character of a mixed society which distinguishes them to this day. Their origins were diverse, but their destiny was one. Some catalytic agent, compounded of hope, a feeling of common grievance against imperial regulations, and a swelling sense of their own grandeur, was at work in the colonies to generate a reaction that could prove ominous to the structure of empire.

The English cultural inheritance—religion, law, letters, speech, politics —although not understood in exactly the same way in all the colonies, had a basic unity everywhere. This provided the language of common understanding. Chief among his possessions the provincial prized his political legacy from seventeenth-century England, and it was to be a potent weapon in colonial hands.

CHAPTER VI

Striving for Greater Freedom

The seventeenth century had strengthened the place of legislatures in the scheme of government throughout the British realm. Executive authority, whether it be kingly in England or gubernatorial in the colonies, was on the defensive and aggressive assemblies in America were pushing their advantage. The colonists who had once defied kings now faced distrusted governors who were backed by the power of parliament.

England's interest lay in compressing the colonies into an imperial mold, not necessarily harmful to them, but intended primarily to be beneficial to her. She attempted to do this by steadily enlarging the scope of mercantilist legislation and expanding the area of administrative and judicial authority. But much of it remained on paper, unenforced and unburdensome to its intended subjects. Indeed colonial shipping, as well as agriculture and industry, benefited from bounties and premiums paid by the mother country. By a policy which Edmund Burke called "salutary neglect" the mother country and her colonies flourished together, despite the misgivings of merchants in Britain and the groaning of the resentful in America.

The local ruling classes in the colonies—the merchants in the north, the landlord-merchants in the middle colonies, and the plantation aristocracy in the south—all had in common an angry contempt for the laws of trade and commerce laid down by parliament. But they had also in common a problem nearer home—how to maintain themselves securely in their positions of pre-eminence against the democratizing pressures of the unprivileged. Thus the task of the domestic rulers of the colonies was twofold—on the one hand to evade or to block the authority of parliament, and on the other to deny to "inferiors" a share in the government run by and for their "betters."

In noting the conflicts which punctuated relations between governors and assemblies it should not be inferred that colonials from the beginning aimed at independence from the mother country. Rather it should be assumed, as it was then, that the mutually dependent relationship between the colonies and England would continue indefinitely. What was at issue was the distribution of power within the empire. And on that rock the imperial ship of state ultimately foundered.

★ THE POWER OF COLONIAL ASSEMBLIES

In each colony, with the exceptions of Rhode Island and Connecticut where the chief official was elected, or in Pennsylvania and Maryland where he was named by the proprietor, the governor, and generally the council as well, were royal appointees. While executive and administrative power resided in the hands of the governor and his council (the latter thought of itself as a House of Lords), legislative authority for the most part lay with elective assemblies. This arrangement was the one preferred by the crown; nor was it too distasteful to men of wealth in the colonies, for they sat on the provincial councils by virtue of their prestige and, through a suffrage resting on property, they won seats in the assembly by right of their wealth.

Colonials almost from their earliest days self-consciously created for themselves an image of England's political structure. Massachusetts Bay Colony was only two years old when Winthrop wrote "this government was . . . in the nature of a parliament." Elsewhere, in Virginia and Maryland, to name but two, assertive assemblies long before the eighteenth century were narrowing the limits of a governor's authority. While Americans adopted the political structure of the mother country, in this as in other institutions, change was as important as similarity. For example, Americans, unlike Englishmen, became accustomed to the practice of sending to the legislature only representatives who lived in the districts they represented.

The victory of parliament over the crown in 1689 encouraged disrespect by colonial assemblies of the governors set over them. The political philosophy of John Milton, Algernon Sidney, James Harrington, and above all John Locke seemed to warrant legislative aggressiveness against executive power by the colonies which felt under no necessity to explain themselves.

The history of the English parliament's struggle with the crown was kept fresh in colonial memories, and legislators in these provincial assemblies followed the maternal example by gradually whittling away royal supremacy. A crown official reported from Virginia (1703) that the Assembly of that province "conclude themselves entitled to all the rights and privileges of an English Parliament, and begin to search into the records of the honourable house for precedents to govern themselves by."

In Massachusetts, the Reverend John Wise, finding himself originally engaged in a dispute over a proposed ecclesiastical organization which threatened the autonomy of the independent congregation, broadened the whole question to embrace political issues. His writings, *The Churches' Quarrel Espoused* (1710), and *The Vindication of the Government of the New England Churches* (1717), had the quality to fire men's imaginations generations after, which they did in the Revolutionary era. Independently of Locke, Wise with equal vigor talked the language of social compact, natural rights, and the right of revolution. Englishmen, meaning colonials too, "hate an Arbitrary Power . . . as they hate the Devil," he said. "Government was never Established by God or Nature, to give one Man a Prerogative to insult over another." All this, he said, "is as plain as day light."

Colonists were quick to see that the administrative officers in England failed to reinforce with overt action royal instructions given to the crown's representatives in America. In the course of the eighteenth century assemblies were less and less willing to be hindered by the governor's instructions.

The crown was meeting its match in the assemblies in matters of legislation and administration in the generation that preceded 1776, and the balance of power was clearly shifting from the governor to the legislature. Victory after victory was won by the assemblies over the governor. William Smith, the historian of New York and long time member of its council, said that the colonies for half a century before independence had outgrown the constrictions of their government; an American assembly, he said, found it easy to believe "that themselves were the substance, and the Governor and Board of Council were shadows in their political Frame." In South Carolina the Anglican churches were even instructed to pray for the legislature rather than for the governor!

As a rule those who won appointments as governors were capable men, and were typical of the contemporary British governing classes, possessing both their virtues and their vices. (Lesser administrative posts in the colonies were often occupied by inferior men.) If a governor felt obliged to be literal in obeying royal instructions he was bound to run into trouble with colonial assemblies; if he attempted to apply his instructions discreetly he was suspected of being weak, and the home officials became critical. The instructions repeated to each successive governor revealed no change in the policy that the colonies existed primarily for Great Britain's benefit, and when the interests of the two conflicted it was the British that were first to be protected.

But a governor who left for overseas convinced that it was his duty to uphold such a theory suffered many bruises when he ran up against the hard facts of colonial experience.

The growing self-consciousness of the Americans could not accept the theory that they existed as a "means to a British end." The spirit of the constitution on both sides of the Atlantic made royal interference with legislation in either place an anachronism. Royal authority was particularly weak in those colonies which played an important part in the intercolonial wars. Through local control over the necessary military appropriations governors were forced into many compromises of their executive position. By the end of the period of intercolonial conflict (1763), with the French defeated, provincial assemblies had won almost as complete a control of local finance as the House of Commons possessed in England. In this controversy the assemblies possessed a ready weapon, for some of the governors were dependent on the provincial legislatures for their salaries. When parliament after 1763 attempted to win the control that the crown had lost, colonial opposition was predestined. The rigidity of the imperial political mind, in a period which demanded flexibility, spelled crisis for the empire.

★ GOVERNOR VERSUS ASSEMBLY

The importance of the conflict between governor and legislature may be seen in the annals of New York, where political parties were well organized and won significant victories against the crown's representatives. It was that colony's misfortune to have some of the poorest governors sent over to rule in America. Of them all the worst seems to have been Lord Cornbury who held office from 1702–8. A Restoration rake and an embezzler of public funds, he did as much as any other single individual to bring English authority into disrepute among the colonists.

Money that the assembly had voted to fortify the Narrows was taken for Cornbury's own use. To prevent any further diversion of funds the New York Assembly appointed a treasurer, responsible to itself, in whose hands all incoming and outgoing moneys should rest. The colony's assertion of financial autonomy drew the frowns of parliament which proposed to tax New York directly (1711). But the proposal was never enacted into law, and instead of being intimidated the assembly extended its control over finances, denying to the council the privilege of amending money bills.

The council claimed that the crown had granted it this right. The assembly, basing its power on "inherent right," retorted that the share the "Council have (if any) in the Legislation [comes] only from the meer Pleasure of the Prince . . . On the contrary, the inherent Right the Assembly have to dispose of the money of the Freemen of this Colony, does not proceed from any Commission, Letters Patent or other Grant from the Crown, but from the free Choice and Election of the People: who ought not to be divested of their Property (nor justly can) without their consent." This was doctrine that Americans were to hear more of half a century later when James Otis and Patrick Henry were to make their great speeches in behalf of colonial rights.

★ ZENGER "NOT GUILTY"

While the struggle over control of finances was the key constitutional issue in the colonies, contests over other points revealed how the political power of local assemblies was steadily strengthened. In the case of North Carolina the royal government declared its right to determine the number of representatives in that colony's assembly. But the crown failed to uphold its contention and was forced to permit the Carolinians to arrange for their own apportionment of representation.

Elsewhere the story was the same, monotonous defeat for the crown, heady success for the colonists, particularly as the eighteenth century wore on to the midpoint. Governor Morris of New Jersey in 1739 said, complainingly, that there was a strong "inclination . . . in the meanest of people (who are the majority and whose votes make the Assembly) to have the sole direction of all the affairs of the Government." Six years later London complained that the New York Assembly "had taken to themselves not only the management and disposal of the public money, but have also wrested from your Majesty's governor the nomination of all officers of government, the custody and direction of all military stores, the mustering and regulating of troops raised for Your Majesty's service, and in short almost every other executive part of the government."

Colonial assemblies were very self-conscious of their role as champions of the people's rights, and in these institutions were trained the men who took leadership in the Revolutionary era. The art of government was by then no mystery to them, and the experience they had received in provincial assemblies helped to make them the artists they became in the crises of later times. It was almost natural for them in the days of independence to direct the affairs of a larger America, for they had served a long apprenticeship on smaller stages in all the colonies.

Americans were kept informed of the discussions in their legislatures. In some of the colonies journals of the assemblies were published; the proceedings were also reported in their newspapers. When constitutional questions reached the crucial stage in the 1760's it was in the press that some of the most influential discussions took place. The freedom of speech that newspapers enjoyed was in large measure made possible by the outcome of the famous Zenger case in 1735.

The *New York Weekly Journal,* published by John Peter Zenger, and supported by politicians opposed to the government, printed severe criticisms of Governor William Cosby. The latter thereupon had the printer arrested and charged with criminal libel. To defend Zenger, Andrew Hamilton, one of the ablest lawyers in America, was secretly brought to New York from Philadelphia. A contemporary historian described him as having "art, eloquence, vivacity, and humour . . ." and possessing "a confidence which no terrors could awe." Then almost eighty years of age, Hamilton was far stronger in mind than in body. The words he spoke in behalf of freedom of the press still ring eloquent.

The prosecution asserted that publication of itself was libelous, its truth or untruth being irrelevant. Hamilton maintained that the right to criticize officials was a natural right, a right claimed by all free men. In a dramatic appeal to the jury he urged it to consider the facts in the case and render a verdict which would secure to posterity "that to which Nature and the Laws of our Country have given us a Right—the Liberty —both of exposing and opposing arbitrary Power . . . by speaking and writing Truth." "The Question before you," Hamilton said to the jury, "is not of small nor private concern, it is not the cause of a poor Printer, nor of New York alone . . . ; it is the best Cause. It is the Cause of Liberty." To the cheers of a crowded courtroom Zenger was declared "not guilty," while a mixture "of amazment, terror and wrath appeared [on] the bench." Hamilton was feted by the whole community which gratefully granted him the freedom of the city.

The aged lawyer's address to the jury became a classic in America and in Great Britain, and on both sides of the Atlantic the proceedings of the trial were reprinted a number of times during the rest of the century. Englishmen showed great interest in the Zenger trial, and in similar cases on later occasions successfully invoked it to uphold freedom of the press as a check against despotic power. Gouverneur Morris, a keen student of politics, looking back from the era of the American Revolution asserted that the trial of Zenger was "the morning star of that liberty which subsequently revolutionized America."

★ WEALTH VERSUS NUMBERS

Although colonial assemblies professed to speak for American rights these legislative bodies were themselves not entirely representative of local sentiment. The allotment of seats in the legislature often favored seaboard areas over the interior. They favored wealth as against numbers. Suffrage and office-holding were based on property, personal or real. Ordinarily, to exercise the suffrage a voter had to possess about fifty acres or a personal property of at least £40. Considerable numbers of the urban male population were thus unable to vote—laborers, small shopkeepers, clerks, artisans, and most fishermen (women were not supposed to vote in the eighteenth century). Negroes, slave or free, Indians, and indentured servants were also without the suffrage. Religious qualifications generally existed also as a condition for voting, and these operated to disfranchise Catholics and Jews.

Property qualifications for holding office were higher than for the right to vote. In New Jersey an assemblyman had to own 100 acres; in South Carolina a legislator was required to possess 500 acres or own real and personal property worth £1,000. Men of wealth and prestige in the colonies, while often critical of governors and other English officials, had no intention of sharing power with the mass of people in their own communities. For the most part they and their supporters were conservative in local politics and in social outlook.

Restrictions on voting and office-holding curbed the political power of small farmers, particularly on the frontier where squatters had no legal possession of the land they worked and thus were ineligible to vote. On the other hand recent research has indicated that in some colonies the suffrage was more widely enjoyed than was formerly supposed. In New Jersey and Massachusetts by mid-eighteenth century most adult males were eligible. It was not too difficult for rural residents, in legitimate possession of their land, to qualify for the suffrage. In Pennsylvania the vote was granted to Christian males who had lived there for two years, owned 50 acres (12 cleared), or possessed property worth £50. This last qualification was probably beyond the means of many town dwellers. In southern colonies franchise requirements were stiffer than in the north. Though the suffrage was thus relatively extensive, it was not always used. In fact, according to some estimates, generally not more than a tenth of the people went to the polls. Narrow as this base of government seems, it was far wider than that in England.

But the misrepresented and the unrepresented in the colonies were hardly concerned with conditions in England. In fact England troubled them far less than did the local ruling class which in most of the colonies were returned to office with punctual regularity. In part this was due to the deference usually shown to traditional leadership. "We were accustomed to look upon what were called *gentle folks* as being of a superior order," wrote Devereaux Jarrett, who grew up to become a noted minister in Virginia.

A relatively small group in nearly every colony dominated political life through membership in the council and in the assembly. In Virginia for a hundred years before the Revolution nearly two-thirds of the men in the council came from twenty-three families, and almost all of the councilors were bound by ties of kinship. In New York the heads of great families, especially landowners, sat on the governor's council and, by controlling elections, placed their relatives and supporters in the assembly. In the quarter century before the Revolution 80 per cent of the important officeholders in New York were large landowners. Difficulty of travel limited the number of voters, and even when they reached the polls, lack of a secret ballot made heterodoxy dangerous. The ruling elements in the colonies everywhere were knit together by blood and marriage, as well as by common social and economic interests. On occasion they quarreled among themselves but to the rest of the world they displayed unity.

Even in the New England colonies, where the dominance of family dynasties was supposedly less than elsewhere, the same names constantly reappear in political office. The concentration of political power in the hands of a tiny minority seemed as great in Connecticut as in Virginia though it is not likely that in New England the small group had comparable social and economic power.

Connecticut may have looked like the land of steady habits to some of its own proud inhabitants, but to the wealthy landowner in the neighboring province of New York emigrants from New England were "fierce republicans" and "levellers." They insisted on acquiring outright ownership of the land with no tenant obligations. One New York aristocrat described them as squatters "who came in without knocking; sat down without invitation; and lighted their pipe without ceremony; then talked of buying land; and finally, began a discourse on politics" which would have done honor to the most extreme radicals of seventeenth-century England during the Puritan Revolution.

Despite grumbling by many of the inhabitants, conservative men usually had the reins of power secure in their hands. Rhode Island alone seemed to be the exception to the rule of general political conservatism in the colonies. Governor Hutchinson of Massachusetts, in a noted interview with King George, said Rhode Island was "the nearest to a democracy of any of your colonies. Once a year all power returns to the people and all their officers are new elected. By this means the governor has no judgment of his own and must comply with every popular prejudice." Rhode Island's lone equalitarianism stood out in striking contrast to the conservative tendencies in her sister colonies.

★ AGRARIAN DISCONTENT

The resentment that frontier communities felt because of under-representation in their assemblies was strengthened on other counts. Small landholders, as well as the landless, watched in sullen anger as huge areas were added to already swollen estates. While the average size of all plantations grew, the estates of large landowners increased disproportionately. By 1750, for example, while the average holding in Virginia was about 750 acres, a select group of individuals owned 50,000 or even 100,000 acres each.

In New York the size of individual or family holdings was even larger. Governor Colden, writing soon after the middle of the century, said that three estates embraced over a million acres each. There were others over 200,000 acres in size. These grants, said Colden, "contain a great part of the province" and were given away at scarcely any cost to the grantees. One huge grant of over 300,000 acres was taxed with the slight rent of twenty shillings a year, and even these small charges were almost always in arrears. The greater part of the large grants, said Colden, remained uncultivated and were without any benefit to the community. They were a "discouragement to the settling & improving the lands in the neighborhood of them, for from the uncertainty of their boundaries, the Patentees of these great Tracts are daily enlarging their pretensions, and by tedious & most expensive Law suits, distress and ruin poor families who have taken out grants near them." Lawyers were accused of prolonging suits to increase costs of litigation. One person who sought lands among Indian and rival white claimants vividly expressed a common feeling when he said, "the one would take your Scalp, the other your Estate in Law Suits."

Loose phraseology allowed limited grants to be inflated enormously; one of 300 acres in New York became a 60,000-acre claim. Colden himself, though not taking very large grants in his own name, did profit greatly from the accumulation of fees he was careful to collect from grants to others.

It was observed that young men left New York for other provinces where land was easier to own outright. Great landholders were reminded that "People will not become their Vassals or Tenants," for many of them had left Europe especially "to avoid the dependence on landlords, and to enjoy in fee to descend to their posterity that their children may reap the benefit of their labor and industry."

John Wise, who had won fame in opposing arbitrary ecclesiastical power, was remembered too as a pioneer spokesman for the agrarian interest. He was the spiritual ancestor of nineteenth-century Populists pleading for cheap money. The people, said Wise, "are fully Resolved not to be Hectored or wheedled into unsolvable Penury and Vassalage, for want of a Plentiful Medium [when] it is in their own Power to Remove those who stand in their way, and supply themselves." The language of Wise implied revolution.*

Everywhere in the colonies by the middle of the eighteenth century social tensions had risen because of agrarian discontent. It did not always take the same form in each of the colonies. Sometimes it was an antirent riot; on another occasion it was a contest for more secure tenure; yet again it was anger against seaboard-dominated governments for their laxity in providing frontier defense. Antirent riots were not uncommon in New York and New Jersey, but the fury of small landholders in North Carolina's back country was even greater. There farmers over a period of eighteen years (1734–52) refused to pay quitrents. In Pennsylvania frontiersmen, the "Paxton Boys," enraged at alleged eastern indifference to Indian attack, marched toward Philadelphia killing and threatening peaceful Indians befriended by whites. Benjamin Franklin's tact and courage calmed this threat of civil war. The Penn proprietors had long refused to allow their lands to be taxed even for defense funds. When the Penns finally yielded the colonial assembly joined in voting the required sums.

The more extreme expression of dissatisfaction was that associated with the "levellers" (a term borrowed from the radicals of the seventeenth-century Puritan Revolution in England); they sought the break-up of vast holdings for distribution of lands among poor tenants. Squatters took over vacant lands and challenged authorities to dislodge them. They said they had been urged to come to America (for example into Pennsylvania by the proprietor); they answered they had come and now they must live. The Scotch-Irish took thousands of acres of the best land in Pennsylvania proclaiming "it was against the laws of God and Nature, that so much land should be idle, while so many Christians wanted it to labor on and to raise their bread." New Jersey "levellers" argued that "No man is naturally intitled to a greater Proportion of the Earth, than another."

★ CURRENCY AND POLITICS

In the agricultural society of eighteenth-century America great landowners dominated the political machinery of their respective provinces.

* Perry Miller, *The New England Mind: From Colony to Province* (Cambridge, Mass.: Harvard University Press, 1953), pp. 317, 322.

But in those colonies where commercial interests were a power, wealthy merchants had a strong grasp on the reins of government. Working in alliance with some other group they were generally able to control local politics. The best example was to be seen in Philadelphia where well-to-do Quaker merchants dominated the city. It was not too difficult a task, as only one in ten of the male population of Philadelphia probably went to the polls. In combination with fellow Quaker farmers and conservative Germans in the eastern part of the province, the merchants also ruled the colonial assembly, engaging in a running fight with supporters of the Penn proprietors. Following familiar practice in the colonies, seats in the Pennsylvania assembly were allotted in such a way that the eastern part of the colony could not be outvoted by the western settlements.

In all the colonies one of the chief concerns of conservatives was the maintenance of a stable currency. Merchants had mixed feelings about this crucial question, for the problem was how to secure an enlarged volume of currency without inflation. From the earliest days of settlement it had been a troublesome issue. Various commodities had served as legal tender—tobacco, corn, wheat, cattle, and Indian wampum. The gold and silver coin in circulation was never adequate for business needs. When pirates came ashore, however, scattering it lavishly, colonials blinked their eyes and winked at the crime.

Very little English coin ever found its way to the colonies owing to the generally unfavorable balance of trade that existed between them and the mother country. Parliament in fact refused to allow English coin to be exported to the colonies or even to permit the Americans in the eighteenth century to mint their own coinage from the bullion that did come their way. Colonials, nevertheless, followed English practice in applying the words "pounds," "shillings," "pence" to the Spanish and Portuguese coins which were the source of their hard currency. In America, however, a "pound" was not worth the same as an English pound sterling, and the values varied from one colony to another. The Spanish-milled dollar, the famous "piece of eight," was the one most commonly known to Americans, who used it as the basis of their monetary system (in 1786 Congress adopted it as the standard for the coinage of the United States). Milling the coin was to prevent its being clipped, thus reducing its metallic content. The gold coin in the colonies ordinarily was the Portuguese "johannes" or "joe," equal to sixteen Spanish-milled dollars.

Since colonials had no banks in which to deposit their money they often had it made up into beautiful silverware which could be used in the home. The pitchers, teapots, spoons, and saltcellars provided a sense of financial security. The possessor of silverware was also comforted by the thought that if it were lost or stolen it was more readily identifiable than coin. Businessmen were severely handicapped by the complexity of colonial financial systems; they needed money for their operations, not silverware.

Paper money seemed a way out of their currency problem. Promissory notes issued by a colonial assembly and tobacco-warehouse receipts had long been in use as money in the colonies. But the first approximation to the type of paper money familiar to latter-day Americans came in Massachusetts in 1690. In that year Sir William Phips undertook to capture Quebec from the French. In anticipation of loot from the expedition Massachusetts gave to the participating soldiers and sailors paper notes; this paper currency was to be acceptable as legal tender for taxes. Although it quickly depreciated, the action of the government in receiving it at face value gave it relative stability. This official paper money was the first in the English-speaking world, and in fact almost the earliest in the modern world, being preceded only by a similar currency in Sweden. Other American colonies soon followed the lead of Massachusetts in issuing these "bills of credit" (the source of our expression a dollar "bill"). This paper currency was based on the expectation that future prosperity would provide the taxes to redeem it.

In colonies like Pennsylvania, which followed a cautious policy in printing paper money and where it was readily redeemable, little depreciation occurred. Not all were so conservative as the Quaker colony. In a comparatively short time larger volumes of money were being issued to pay for increased outlays necessitated by successive wars and other emergencies. Currency inflation was welcomed by the debt-ridden farmer, for it raised the price of his produce and made it easier to pay off his obligations. Creditors were less happy to receive depreciated money. In Rhode Island, where farmers had great influence in the government, so much of this currency was put into circulation that prices in terms of paper money rose more than thirty fold.

Another financial device that pleased debtors and infuriated creditors was the expedient called the Land Bank, the most noted being the one established in Massachusetts in 1740. Land banks were more generous than private lenders in such matters as interest rates and holding borrowers to fixed dates for repayment. Under the Land Bank arrangement the colony issued bills with land as collateral; this currency was declared legal tender for all purposes. Farmers who found it difficult to pay debts brought pressure on assemblies to pass laws to "stay" collection (that is, enact a moratorium on debts). The Land

Bank, angrily condemned by creditors, touched off one of the bitterest controversies in colonial history; farmers, in alliance with town workers, even proposed direct action against Boston obstructionists. Merchants then appealed for support in England, and parliament responded by declaring the Land Bank illegal. The collapse of the scheme ruined many in Massachusetts, including the father of Samuel Adams. (The radicalism of the son was due in no small measure to the bitterness of this defeat.)

England never did satisfy the demands of the American colonists for plans of a workable currency. Fear of depreciated currencies led parliament to pass the Currency Act of 1751, prohibiting formation of land banks in New England, and laying down stronger guarantees for the safety of new issues. Down to the Revolution the lack of satisfactory money inconvenienced colonial businessmen, while the struggle to supply it sharply divided Americans, from each other and from the mother country, leaving permanent scars on the body politic.

★ THE WORSHIP OF GOD

The unprivileged in the colonies were embittered by their grievances over political representation, land, and currency. But a fourth issue, probably more corrosive in its effects, was the discrimination against nonconformists in religion. In the world of the eighteenth century, established churches were the rule. Even where people were allowed to practice a faith different from that established by the government, such permission was usually carefully qualified. It never meant complete religious liberty but only toleration, which was granted and could be revoked at the will of authority. England was freer than most countries in tolerating nonconformity but in her colonies demands were made for widening further the boundaries of religious freedom.

In America the established churches were the Congregational in New England and the Anglican in some of the other colonies. Dissenters were expected to support establishments by taxes, in addition to contributions to their own churches. Residence in some colonies, citizenship, voting, or office-holding were all conditioned by religious tests. The building of houses of worship by dissenters and the preaching of doctrines different from the established theology met official disfavor. Quakers, Catholics, and Jews suffered the greatest discrimination; Baptists and Presbyterians, who were especially numerous in frontier areas in the southern and middle colonies, also experienced much intolerance. Itinerant ministers preaching to outdoor gatherings were forced to secure licenses. It should be mentioned that the mother country sometimes exhibited a more liberal spirit than the colonies and on occasion stepped in to moderate their harshness to religious minorities. In Massachusetts, Baptists and Quakers were excused from taxes to support the Congregational church after 1734, and Anglicans were also relieved of similar taxes.

The Anglican church, because it was the established faith in England, had a favored position in the colonies. Royal officials were Anglican and they acted as a cultural bridge between the mother country and the provinces. Anglican ministers lent their influential weight to the support of the status quo by preaching the doctrine of nonresistance to established power. They frowned upon variation from familiar routine. One Anglican criticism of the great religious revival in the mid-eighteenth century said that the eloquent Presbyterian preacher, Samuel Davies, was "holding forth on working days to great numbers of poor people, who generally are his only followers." Their absence from work, it was complained, harmed business enterprise. The Congregational clergy, in upholding the established order in New England, preached the necessity of everyone keeping to the station God had ordained for him.

Besides exercising religious discipline Anglican clergy attempted to mold proper political and social attitudes. When political controversy got warmer in the Revolutionary era a South Carolina minister said that "mechanics and country clowns had no right to dispute about politics, or what kings, lords, and commons had done." This indiscretion brought him dismissal from his congregation and a rebuke from a Rhode Island newspaper which declared that "all such divines should be taught that mechanics and country clowns . . . are the real and absolute masters of kings, lords, commons, and priests."

Dissenters were the most politically minded people of their day. They were the foremost challengers to conservative views in the colonies, and their pressure was constant to broaden the area of freedom. But they could be intolerant toward others and even among themselves; their cultural horizon was generally more limited than that of Congregationalists or Anglicans. Through the shared experience of wresting privilege from a common adversary dissenters were leagued together.

Their sense of community was vitalized by the conviction that their own faiths had more genuine spiritual strength than older, established creeds which had become formalized and almost perfunctory in religious observance. In the eighteenth century old religious organizations in Europe and America seemed to have hardened into institutions devoid of spiritual power. Into these drained shells fervent believers poured their own religious strength in an effort to reinvigorate them. Or fail-

ing to change them they, like the Methodists, formed their own organizations. The rise of evangelicalism and Methodism was part of a
larger social movement which demanded more democracy in politics
and a more humane attitude by the rulers of society towards their fellow
men.

It was the movement known as the Great Awakening, a vast religious
revival sweeping across the Atlantic world in the 1730's and 1740's,
which caught up the hungry in spirit and released their energies for
personal and social reconstruction. Pietists in Germany, Moravians in
Europe and America, John Wesley in England, Jonathan Edwards in
New England, Gilbert Tennent in the middle colonies, and George
Whitefield seemingly everywhere influenced one another in the common
task. John Wesley, on his way to Georgia in 1735, experienced a spiritual rebirth from his meeting with Moravians aboard ship. He was so
moved by the simplicity of their church organization that it made him
almost forget, said Wesley, "the seventeen hundred years between, and
imagine myself in one of those assemblies where form and state were
not, but Paul the tent-maker or Peter the fisherman presided . . ."

The revival stirred up intense religious differences throughout America, and because of the intimate relationship between politics and religion, political alignments followed those in religion. The conservative
faction known as the "Old Lights," which disapproved of the revival,
ordinarily came from well-to-do families and higher governmental authorities. They spoke with scorn of the "unlearned, common, labouring
men" (the "New Lights") who participated by the thousands in revival meetings. They ridiculed and yet were startled by the "screechings,
faintings, convulsions [and] visions" brought on by the hypnotic power
of evangelical preaching. Benjamin Franklin, testifying to the effect of
Whitefield's preaching, said that "from being thoughtless or indifferent
about religion, it seemed as if all the world were growing religious, so
that one could not walk thro' the town in an evening without hearing
psalms sung in different families of every street."

Those anxious about the established order were frightened at the
"fierce and wrathful" New Lights criticizing their "rulers and teachers."
It was an unpleasant experience for the rulers of society to hear "Mur-
murers and Complainers . . . despising Government." In some colonial communities, Connecticut for example, New Lights were charged
with subverting the government and were thrown into jail; students
joining in revivals were expelled from college; public officials who were
sympathetic to New Light principles were relieved of their duties. Elections in some towns for a number of years centered upon the religious

affiliations of the candidates. One careful observer believed that the growing political strength of New Lights in Connecticut was due to their intense concern with civil affairs and their consciousness of solidarity.

It was the magnetic George Whitefield whose preaching gave universality to the great revival in America. His voice was loud and clear, his diction so perfect that Franklin estimated he could be heard by 30,000 listeners. His trips through the colonies and his vigorous ministration to all sects bound them together in a joint religious purpose. "If I see a man who loves the Lord Jesus in sincerity," he said, "I am not very solicitous to what outward communion he belongs." No doubt sectarian tendencies were strengthened by the Great Awakening, but in the fervor of the revival Americans awoke to the consciousness of a common spiritual life. The singing of psalms, once dull and lifeless, took on a vitality which joined revivalists in a deep emotional experience. The stir in the religious world had affected the young, wrote one preacher; "It looks like a fresh Spring a coming on by those budds, Sprouts & Blossoms in so many places & forms."

In the organization of their churches more power was shared with the rank and file than among Congregationalists or Anglicans. Ministers in the older churches spoke with aloof authority. Evangelists exhorted not from the pulpit of a church—the "preacher's throne," but on the listeners' level, in barns, open fields, or humble homes. It was not so much the leader and the led as it was a democratic fraternity of believers. Dissenting sects gained members who fell away from established churches.

In a reaction against the doctrine of salvation by faith alone, people were inspired to participate in good works which lifted them to new levels of community life. Humanitarianism expressed itself in agitation against the slave trade and against the institution of slavery itself. Though revivalists were occasionally identified with anti-intellectualism, progress in education was indebted to the Great Awakening. Its impetus helped establish new colleges in the colonies, promoting at the same time a more liberal tone in some of them. Presbyterians were responsible for founding the College of New Jersey (Princeton); Baptists, the College of Rhode Island (Brown); the Dutch Reformed, Queens (Rutgers). The acceptance of religious liberty was hastened by the evangelical movement. Those who were not members of the established churches were bound together in opposing privileges resulting from the union of Church and State.

The Great Awakening was the religious manifestation of a larger indignation against aristocratic indifference to the dreams of the un-privileged. In politics and economics the right of all to walk like men was heard with a rumbling insistence. In lonely frontier settlements, in populous eastern communities, the religious revival brought a sense of unity to thousands of people whose democratic tendencies prefigured an American future different from the image of the established order of the eighteenth century.

CHAPTER VII

Pushing Westward—
The Struggle for Inland America

The image of the future America was fashioned in towns and villages, on large plantations and small farms, little sanctuaries in a primeval forest. But a special cast was given to it by people living courageously on the edges of white man's civilization—the frontiersmen. The sense of difference from Europeans, the belief in a great destiny, the deep concern for equalitarianism were to mark all Americans, but frontiersmen most of all. When the westward moving pioneers reached the "fall line," they had to abandon their boats. They left forever the life of tidewater bay or the towns and farms along the rivers emptying into the Atlantic. A forest curtain fell behind them. In their minds the Old World took on a faraway quality, and even the eastern coast of America seemed a strangely distant place. Their eyes were now turned ever westward where the land was without boundaries and the soil without masters. There, in clearings they cut for themselves and shadowed by giant trees, or in the valley meadows shielded by rolling hills and towering mountains, an American way of life was to be created different from an Old World pattern.

Americans awoke to the grandeur of their scenery, their rivers and their mountains which dwarfed England's streams and hills. The rattlesnake and hummingbird, the flocks of wild turkeys and the countless pigeons like racing clouds darkening the sky—all was extraordinary in the new wilderness. The expansiveness of the dreams of pioneers matched the generous setting provided by nature. The promise was vast but the beginnings were small and unpretentious.

★ SETTLING THE OLD WEST

Beyond the narrow zone of coastal settlement, and stretching westward to the Appalachians, was the region of the Old West. In the south, the

Piedmont sloped slowly upward to the mountains. Among the hills and well-watered lowlands were the farm sites to satisfy the longing of the land-hungry. Pathfinders, many of them unknown to history, found gaps in the walls of the Appalachian Mountains through which the rivers rushed to the sea. These gaps were the gates through which the pioneers passed to reach the Great Valley of the Appalachians, an area of rich fertility. Beyond the western rim of the valley rose another mountain barrier, the high wall of the Alleghany Front, where openings were few and difficult to pierce.

In the Great Valley the line of communications ran roughly from southwest to northeast, reaching across Pennsylvania and into New York. Along the Delaware, the Susquehanna, the Juniata, and the Mohawk or the upper Connecticut, settlers in the middle and northern colonies built their cabins either on their legal grants or their "tomahawk claims." The latter were possessed by right of an "improvement" consisting of deadening trees near the head of a spring and marking them with the initials of the claimant. As the valleys filled, newcomers were obliged to go farther and climb the bordering highlands. The movement west was slowed by a forbidding stone barrier which formed the White Mountains in New Hampshire and became the Alleghany Front in Pennsylvania. In the Great Valley of the Appalachians, remote from the seaboard, a sense of community was created which tied together the pioneers of the Old West.

Indian traders had penetrated into the southern part of this region during the seventeenth century. Leaving with their trains of pack horses from the last outposts of white civilization they pushed on for hundreds of miles into Indian villages to trade for furs. The traders disclosed the westward trails which were soon trod by the determined step of the pioneer farmers. Governor Spotswood of Virginia led his fellow "Knights of the Golden Horseshoe" (as they playfully called themselves) on a gay exploring expedition through the James River gap into the Shenandoah Valley in 1716. The explorers killed bear and deer, turkeys and rattlesnakes; they axed their way to the top of the mountain to find the "very head spring of James River, where it runs no bigger than a man's arm, from under a large stone." The light-hearted cavalcade claimed the region in the king's name and drank a round of toasts to the royal family; the "King's health in champagne . . . the Princess' health in burgundy . . . and all the rest of the royal family in claret." And when they ran low on these preferred liquids they fell back on Virginia red and white wine, brandy, rum, punch, cider—and water.

Governor Spotswood and his "Knights" granted themselves vast areas of the interior for speculative purposes, in portions of ten to forty thousand acres. Within a generation after the governor's expedition, the whole of the Virginia (as well as the Carolina) Piedmont had been signed away for trifling considerations, mainly to tidewater planters. The latter, in order to populate their lands, brought over settlers directly from Europe or from the eastern parts of their provinces. But poorer settlers often found it difficult to acquire lands for themselves, as the larger owners sometimes preferred to rent tracts, expecting them to rise in value. Similarly in the north speculators who had the necessary political influence took the finest lands in New York's richest river valleys, crowding German and Scotch-Irish pioneers into a small number of settlements. Despite the obstacles that speculators threw in the path of settlement, people continued to march to the frontier.

In Pennsylvania it had become more difficult to acquire cheap land because the colony's proprietors were now asking £10 or more for 100 acres. Maryland and Virginia drew off prospective Pennsylvania settlers by cutting the price in half. By the middle 1720's German immigrants were treking down the Great Valley of the Appalachians. Within the next thirty years they occupied much of the Piedmont in Virginia, and advanced south along the west side of the Blue Ridge in the Shenandoah Valley, moving on into the western hills of the Carolinas. From the Carolinas to New York, Germans pioneered a vast area which pushed the settled region ever farther from the Atlantic coast.

★ LIFE ON THE FRONTIER

Frontier life was never easy, and in its first stages was particularly hard. Conrad Weiser, a noted Indian trader, told of Germans from frontier New York starting before dawn for Schenectady to buy a bushel or two of flour. It took all day to make the trip and, quickly expediting their business, they started back. They traveled throughout the night to reach home the next morning while hungry families anxiously awaited them. Farming implements were often crude—a shovel made from the end of a log hollowed out with painstaking care, a fork for haying made from a tree branch, a maul from a heavy knot of wood at the end of a branch which was used as the handle.

Furniture was equally primitive. A table was a split log in which were set four sturdy sticks for legs. Stools were made in the same way. The first huts among the Germans apparently were without fireplaces, cooking being done in stone ovens outdoors. When more permanent homes were built, fireplaces were made by adding a stone chimney to the outside wall, with a small hearth and stone sides for protection against fire. A bar across the fireplace, hung with chains for cooking utensils, made for the hard-worked women a home out of a wilderness cabin. As time passed, better furnishings were built, even the prized rocking chair appeared in a proud family's possessions. Clothing was fashioned from the skins of deer and beaver; shoes, if they were not moccasins, were made of heavy leather, the soles hobnailed for protection against rough wear.

Families were large in frontier communities, where girls married young. Since ministers were not readily available, custom sanctioned the practice of couples living together and having children until a clergyman might eventually arrive to sanctify the necessary irregularity. Marriage was reckoned in many of the settlements a civil contract; "a country justice," said the sophisticated William Byrd, "can tie the fatal knot as fast as an archbishop"; "so it was," he remarked during a surveying expedition into Carolina, "that though our chaplain christened above a hundred, he did not marry so much as one couple."

Scotch-Irish settlers followed the Germans to frontier regions and took up areas even more exposed to Indian unfriendliness. Their process of settlement was less communal than that of the Germans, many of whom stayed close together preserving more of the substance of white man's civilization. The Scotch-Irish, in their isolated cabins, accustomed themselves more quickly to the forest environment which demanded adaptability as the price of survival. Their clothes, said a visitor, "consist of deer skins, their food of Johnnycakes, deer and bear meat. A kind of white people are found here who live like savages. Hunting is their chief occupation." Tea and coffee, said a backwoodsman, were "only slops," good enough for "people of quality" who did no manual work. Such liquids, he complained, "did not stick by the ribs." These tough frontiersmen matched the Indians in meeting the challenge of wilderness life. They hated the natives and land speculators alike. Devout Presbyterians, the "buckskins," according to one acid writer, kept the Sabbath and "everything else they could lay their hands on."

The frontier stimulated individualism though the kind of men who went to exposed settlements were the very people who had often been nonconformists in older communities. Their boldness, their aggressiveness, and their lawlessness had freer range in an environment not yet laced by a crisscross of social disciplines. Above all, said a close observer of the frontiersman, "he revolts against the operation of laws. He cannot bear to surrender up a single natural right for all the benefits of government." But the much vaunted individualism of frontiersmen should not be exaggerated. They co-operated in the purchase of a horse; they cleared land together; built homes by joint enterprise; exchanged farm implements; and planned for defense against Indians by communal effort. In America, said a French traveler, "a man is never alone, never an isolated being." Neighbors made it a point of hospitality to aid the new farmer, especially in building his log cabin; "A cask of cyder drank in common, and with gaiety, or a gallon of rum, are the only recompense for these services."

In New England the former practice of orthodox believers of setting up compact, new townsites alongside older communities was abandoned. "The newcomers do not fix near their neighbors," complained an older settler; they "take spots that please them best though twenty or thirty miles beyond any others." Some of those who moved to distant areas were Scotch Presbyterians who wanted to be freed of Congregationalist domination. The growing population in Massachusetts and Connecticut forced homeseekers to spread out over the Berkshires in the west and northward into Vermont, New Hampshire, and Maine. In these regions, as in areas to the southward, land was quickly gobbled up by influential speculators. Absentee ownership became a particularly obnoxious feature of frontier life, for landlords in distant Boston, Philadelphia, or Charleston had little concern with the problems of remote settlers. During the whole of the Revolutionary era westerners were bitter in their denunciation of eastern land policy.

Settlers grumbled over excessive prices for land or quitrents for their holdings. Many of them found a simple solution to their grievance— they became squatters and ignored landholders. Squatters were too numerous to be ejected. Of 670,000 acres occupied in the Shenandoah Valley between 1732 and 1740, 400,000 were taken without title. The proprietors of Pennsylvania were obliged to permit squatters to pre-empt their holdings with the promise to pay for them later. But James Logan, a Pennsylvania official, had little faith in their promises; they "pretend that they will buy," he remarked, "but not one in twenty has anything to pay with." He was especially annoyed with the Scotch-Irish; "the settlement of five families from Ireland," he said, "gives me more trouble than fifty of any other people."

Clearing the land was the first task of the settler, once he had built his cabin. The "Yankee Method" was to cut down the trees and, with the aid of neighbors, roll them into heaps for burning. Another method was to kill the trees by cutting a circle around them about three feet from the ground and letting them rot. The ground around the trees was then ploughed and seeded with corn.

Corn was planted toward the end of May and in three months or so green, unripe roasting ears were ready. During the summer the frontiersman's family fed on the small quantity of grain carried with them, and the abundant fish and game of the forest. Improvident settlers some-

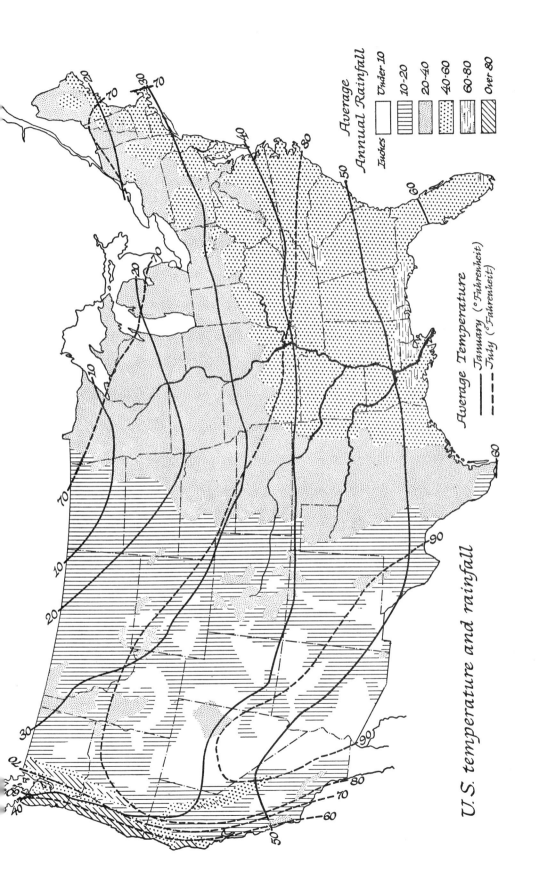

U.S. temperature and rainfall

Average Annual Rainfall
Inches
Under 10
10–20
20–40
40–60
60–80
Over 80

Average Temperature
January (°Fahrenheit)
July (°Fahrenheit)

times exhausted their supply of Indian meal before the new corn was ready, so that as one pioneer recalled "for that length of time we had to live without bread. The lean venison and the breast of wild turkies, we were taught to call bread. The flesh of the bear was denominated meat. This artifice," he remarked, "did not succeed very well . . . the stomach seemed to be always empty, and tormented with a sense of hunger. I remember how narrowly the children watched the growth of the potato tops, pumpkin and squash vines, hoping from day to day to get something to answer in the place of bread. How delicious was the taste of the young potatoes when we got them! What a jubilee when we were permitted to pull the young corn for roasting ears. Still more so when it had acquired sufficient hardness to be made into johnny cakes by the aid of a tin grater. We then became healthy, vigorous, and contented with our situation, poor as it was." Settlers eventually raised a surplus of grain, which was carried to market in Conestoga trucks, the famous "covered wagons."

There were two indispensable tools for living on the frontier—the long-handled ax and the rifle. Probably no one anywhere ever used an ax more skilfully than the American frontiersman. He made his home, his farm implements, his furniture and wooden kitchen ware with the ax. He was self-sufficient except for iron and salt. The rifle guaranteed that the crude civilization built with the ax would be secure. Skilled gunsmiths modified the European weapon for quicker and quieter loading, transforming it into the deadly long-barreled "Kentucky Rifle," the treasured companion of the pioneer in the fringed hunting shirt.

By the middle of the eighteenth century English-speaking traders were in the Ohio Valley in force. Many were as wild as the Indians with whom they traded and joined in rum-guzzling debauch. Pathfinders had already located the Cumberland Gap, through which thousands of settlers were to pour westward in later years. Speculators were feasting their eyes on the anticipated returns from the fat western lands. Farther south, Indian traders had long since pierced the mountain barrier, and were competing for furs with traders from another land and speaking another tongue—French. British traders brought a quarter of a million deerskins, as well as other furs, into Charleston in one year alone, 1731. The steady pressure of traders from the coast was an ominous threat to the French hold on the western lands. Control of the great valleys beyond the Appalachians was long in doubt. It was not resolved until 1763.

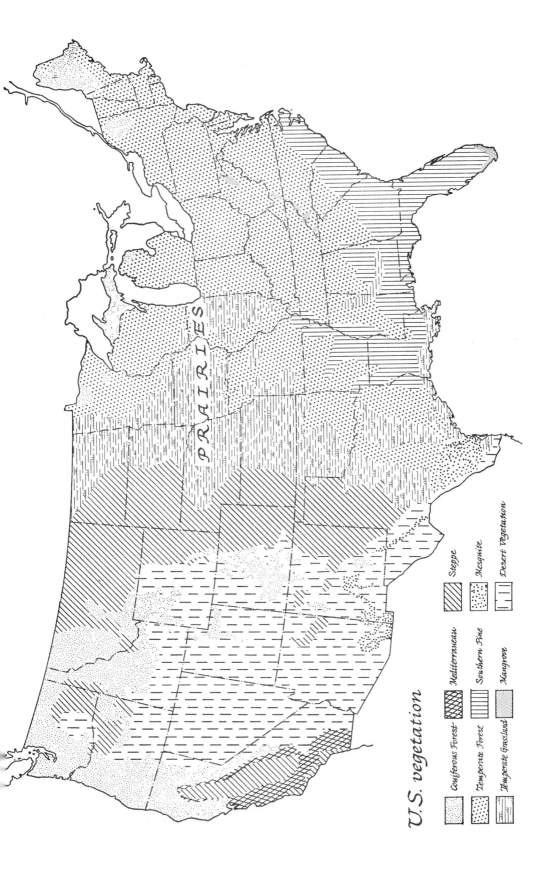

U.S. vegetation

PRAIRIES

Coniferous Forest	Mediterranean
Temperate Forest	Southern Pine
Temperate Grassland	Mangrove

Steppe	
Mesquite	
Desert Vegetation	

★ THE FRENCH IN THE INTERIOR

The French had ranged over the vast interior of America from the time they first established a settlement at Quebec, in 1608. Samuel de Champlain, founder of Quebec, had made himself, by study and two-year residence in the West Indies (1599–1601), an expert in geography and in colonial matters. As royal geographer to Henry IV, he hoped to enlarge men's knowledge of the world, increase the French realm, and win fame for himself. He was successful in all three aims. It was Champlain, says J. B. Brebner,* "who invented, as it were, the *coureurs de bois* and the *voyageurs* who carried French influence from the St. Lawrence to the Rockies and from Hudson Bay to the Gulf of Mexico." He encouraged young men to live among the Indians and to explore the rivers whose torrential rapids awed even the experienced Champlain. Young adventurers, forgotten to history, made known to whites trails hitherto familiar only to Indians. It was these young men who first established lines of communication between the Great Lakes and the St. Lawrence. The lakes were no longer mistaken for the Pacific, and the water on which canoes of the Hurons rode was truly named the Sweetwater Sea.

Chivalrous explorers, keen businessmen, and fearless friars unveiled the secrets of forest and expansive lakes, whose limits lay beyond the straining eye. "We were Cesars," wrote one adventurer (Pierre Radisson), prizing his lonely dominion, "being nobody to contradict us." In their light birchbark canoes, able to carry a dozen men and drawing only six inches fully loaded, they moved easily from stream to stream bearing their burdens of merchandise. From the French the Indians eagerly sought knives, which "they love better than we serve God."

The French searched for furs, "the best manna of the countrey," and at the same time they sought a great empire. They hoped also to win souls for Christianity. These aims took them up the St. Lawrence through the Great Lakes, down the rivers of America's heartland to the Gulf of Mexico. Pitted against Dutch and English opposition, French-men secured a large share of America's fur trade, and in the process mapped much of North America. Young Etienne Brulé, befriended by Champlain, when still in his 'teens ventured where whites had never been. He was, Professor Brebner tells us, "first up the Ottawa, first at Lake Huron, first at Lake Ontario . . . first to find the Susquehanna route from the Great Lakes to the sea."

The resolute, melancholic La Salle had penetrated the mystery of the

* *The Explorers of North America, 1492–1806* (Garden City, N.Y.: Double-day, 1955), p. 131.

Mississippi, arriving at its lower reaches in the beginning of April, 1682. As he "drifted down the turbid current, between the low and marshy shores," wrote Francis Parkman, "the brackish water changed to brine, and the breeze grew fresh with the salt breath of the sea." At the mouth of the Father of Waters he set up the banner of St. Louis, and called the region Louisiana. "After we had chanted the hymn of the church 'Vexilla Regis' and the 'Te Deum,' the Sieur de la Salle, in the name of his Majesty, took possession of that river, of all rivers that enter it and of all the country watered by them." "By means of this River and the Lakes," wrote a contemporary, "there is open to the [Frenchman's] view such a Scene of inland Navigation as cannot be parallel'd in any other Part of the World."

La Salle was more than the romantic explorer he seemed. He, too, was a fur trader with grandiose visions of winning for France a monopoly of the business. But the French, he hoped, would also colonize the interior, blocking off the English east of the Alleghanies and the Spaniards in the Southwest. The French were driving a wedge down through the Mississippi Valley, and the colonies of England and Spain felt the pressure. French bases on the Gulf of Mexico (Biloxi, Mobile, New Orleans) were clearly better situated for trade with the Mississippi region than was distant Charleston.

Military posts were located on the important waterways of the interior. These posts were a compound of soldier, merchant, and missionary—the soldier as a symbol of royal authority, the merchant to trade with the Indian, the black-robed Jesuit to convert the heathen savage to Catholicism. Canada, it has been said, was little more than "a musket, a rosary, and a pack of beaver skins." It was an attempt of feudalism, monarchy, and Rome to subdue a continent. Even commerce, wrote the distinguished historian Francis Parkman, "wore the sword, decked itself with the badges of nobility, aspired to forest seignories and hordes of savage retainers." France in the New World was not to be built on a broad foundation of independent farm owners. The English, Protestant in spirit, were building a society in America whose traders and farmers moved with elemental force across the mountains that walled them from the open lands of the West.

★ THE CONTEST FOR THE INTERIOR

The French in New France were few in number but, in alliance with friendly Indians, they kept the borders of the English colonies intermittently ablaze. Indian tribes who had fought each other for hunting grounds during countless moons now found they were courted by white men who killed one another for land, or furs, or king, or God. Indian skirmishes eventually became transformed into a hundred-years' war in which the English fought the French and the Spaniards for the great prize—North America.

From 1643 the Iroquois, seeking a monopoly as middlemen in the fur trade, waged a twenty-years' war against the French and their Indian supporters. The fearsome Iroquois, said a Jesuit, approaching "like foxes," fighting "like lions" and flying "away like birds," terrified their opponents who sought safety westward toward Lake Superior and eastward in French forts. Even French colonists were ambushed and scalped within sight of their fortifications, whose safety could not muffle the chanted taunts of victorious Iroquois. The latter, armed by the Dutch, cut deeply into the slender French population (about 3,000 in 1660), so that Canada was almost lost by France. The French counter-attack, 1666–67, in the Mohawk Valley wrought such destruction among the Iroquois that the Indians asked for peace. Fresh leadership gave New France the vigor to survive. Severe trials, however, lay ahead of the colony.

The English won the Iroquois to their side. Under the prodding of Governor Thomas Dongan of New York, the Indians attacked the French and their allied tribes in 1684. This was the beginning of a long story of attack and counterattack which was to continue through four wars to New France's collapse. These struggles were in reality world wars, fought not only on ancient battlegrounds in Europe, but in hot, remote corners of Africa and India, in placid Caribbean waters, and in the green stillness of American woods. Americans knew these con-flicts by these names—King William's War, Queen Anne's War, King George's War, and the French and Indian War. People who had fled Europe and its age-old dynastic conflicts which forced them to shed their blood in battle found themselves, even in the New World, still harnessed to the ambitions of rival kings.

After the setbacks of the 1680's the French were rallied by the vig-orous leadership of an old warrior, Count Frontenac, reputed to be the most remarkable man who ever represented the crown of France in the New World. With great imagination he prepared a plan to envelop and hold in check the expanding populations of the English colonies. He won over to his side hesitant Indian allies, generally by cajolery and blandishment, but once by holding aloft a tomahawk and leading them in a blood-curdling war dance.

The New York frontier, where traders trespassed on each other's preserves and where rival imperial ambitions were in closest contact, was always a dark and bloody ground in Anglo-French warfare. There, on a freezing February night in 1690, over snow so deep it was believed no enemy could approach, a force of French and war-whooping Indians surprised the sleeping Schenectady settlement. They massacred over sixty, carrying another twenty-seven into captivity, and leaving the village in ashes. The whole back country from New York to Maine was set afire. King William's War continued, with its sickening brutalities, for seven years, ending in 1697 with no important change in territory for either side. It was hardly more than the clanging of the gong marking the end of round one in a battle to be continued.

Violence flared again five years later, with the start of Queen Anne's War, and lasted until 1713. It was on a broader scale than the earlier struggle, being fought in the south on the debated ground between the Carolinas, Florida, and Louisiana, and in the north in the forbidding wilderness that lay between the colonies and Canada. In the south Spaniards, who had been in Florida and along the Gulf since the sixteenth century, were allied with the French. The Indians, allies of the French, were detached by the British with gifts and goods cheaply sold. Despite favorable opportunities, however, England failed to wrest this region from her enemies. In the north, after many raids and reprisals on frontier communities, New Englanders carried the war direct to New France by launching a seaborne attack on Port Royal, in Acadia. The strong French outpost, which had long shielded sorties against New England shipping, was overpowered by superior numbers and surrendered.

British arms were also successful elsewhere, and this round in a world-wide battle ended with decisive advantages for victorious England. By the Treaty of Utrecht, Spain gave up Gibraltar; France signed away to the English Newfoundland, as well as Acadia (renamed Nova Scotia), and the Hudson Bay region. In the latter area British traders, by diverting Indian trappers from French Montreal, had built a flourishing fur trade. The interior of the continent was still claimed by France; territory close to the Gulf of Mexico was still in doubt, and the rival courtship of potential Indian allies still pursued its unromantic way.

For a period of thirty years, officially, neither war nor peace prevailed, although for the French in Louisiana, harassed by Indians allied to the British, it was martial enough. Behind a screen of Indians the British expanded their boundaries south and west. In 1732 they founded a new colony, Georgia, in large measure to bulwark the English colonies against the looming threat of Spanish and French attack. James Edward Oglethorpe, the main spirit in establishing the thirteenth colony, was a distinguished English humanitarian anxious to relieve the lot of poor debtors by settling them in America; his philanthropic vision embraced aid to others defeated by social and religious discrimination. But he was also a military man, and was aware that Georgia had a role to play in imperial strategy. He therefore looked carefully to the new colony's defenses, and brought the Creeks, Cherokee, and Chickasaw Indians to the side of the British.

War broke out between England and Spain in 1739 (the War of Jenkins' Ear it was called) when English captains violated the Spanish mercantile monopoly in the Caribbean. Spanish officials decided to discourage British economic competition by drastic action; and that was how Jenkins, a dubious character trading on the Spanish Main, said he lost his ears. In the colonies attacks were launched from Georgia on Florida. These were successful in subduing the Spanish settlements there, with the exception of the strongly held fort at St. Augustine. A large Spanish expedition in turn sought to conquer Georgia, but General Oglethorpe, leading Highland Scots who had recently arrived, proved more than a match for the Spaniards.

The Anglo-Spanish conflict was a lesser episode in the larger struggle between Britain and France. Anglo-French borders were bristling again by 1744. Each side was carefully choosing strategic posts in the Lake Champlain region; and at both ends of the long border in Maine and in Georgia undeclared war was under way. The conflict, when it became official, was known in America as King George's War, and in Europe as the War of the Austrian Succession.

In the colonies hostilities centered largely in the New England region. To protect the English bastion in Acadia an attack against Louisbourg on Cape Breton Island was planned in the spring of 1745 by Governor William Shirley of Massachusetts, one of the ablest officials the colonies ever had. It was an audacious expedition for untrained fighters—fishermen, mechanics, lumbermen and farmers—to sail against one of the strongest fortresses in America. In sight of Louisbourg, they let down their whale boats and "flew to shore, like eagles to the quarry." The undisciplined Americans had long since revealed behavior in warfare unconventional to disciplined European soldiers. They laid siege to the "impregnable" fortress, and after seven weeks the French commander of America's Gibraltar surrendered. At the war's end, which came in 1748 with the treaty of Aix-la-Chapelle, Louisbourg, to the chagrin of New Englanders, was restored to the French, who yielded Madras, in India, to the British. The third round, providing for the return to the *status quo ante,* was a draw. Fishermen went back to their nets, mechanics to their tools, lumbermen to their trees, and farmers to their fields. In those days of spring and summer fighting, enlistments for offensive attacks involving extended campaigns ran for a few months, but frontier communities had to be prepared for hostilities at any time of the year.

Each side made preparations for the next round which, it turned out, was to be the last. In the six years that intervened until the beginning of the new war, energetic French officials built new forts in the interior and successfully wooed Indians angered by British niggardliness. In the South, too, in the region between Georgia and Louisiana, French confidence soared as Indians abandoned the British.

It was in the Ohio Valley that the French believed themselves most seriously threatened by the English. The latter had been in the region for some years trading rum and guns and cheap goods for the Indians' furs. Along the valley's navigable rivers and trails coursed the ubiquitous trader, living in lonely cabins or carousing in Indian villages, indistinguishable from the native red men. Traders and interpreters skilled in the ways and tongues of the natives—men like George Croghan and Conrad Weiser—extended the influence of Pennsylvania merchants from the Alleghanies to the Wabash River. Equally adept at diplomacy, Croghan and Weiser won the Indians to the British side. The fact that British goods excelled the French in quality and were priced lower influenced Indian attachment. On occasion the French even encouraged their native allies to trade with the British for woolen cloth; the French then bought it for use in trade with tribes far removed from the scene of white rivalry. Outdistanced in economic competition, France delayed her imperial eclipse by the skill of her military leadership. The French were further agitated by widely publicized plans for large-scale land settlement in the Ohio Valley by Anglo-American companies. The English had so firmly planted themselves in the region before 1750 that the French were forced to act before this threat to their inland empire overwhelmed them.

★ THE FALL OF NEW FRANCE

The odds against New France look imposing. Her population was less than 80,000 as against 1,250,000 English colonists. There were rivalries between Jesuits anxious about Indian souls and traders anxious only for furs. The government of Louis XV, whose energies were enmeshed in European politics, extended little support to its American possession, remote from the pomp and glitter of Versailles.

But France in America was less weak than she seemed. A centralized administration permitted an energetic governor to move quickly and decisively. The French who had roamed through the American interior for over a century were more intimately acquainted with the spacious, inland valleys than the English colonists. And finally, at critical moments, they won Indians over to their side who had been neutral or even friendly to the English. The latter neglected their Indian allies, whose respect was reserved for strength. An Indian chief rebuked the English: "the French are men," he said; "they are fortifying everywhere. But you are like women, bare and open, without fortifications." There was no likelihood of the French being powerful enough, even if they so desired, to erase English settlements east of the mountains. But there was a strong French expectation that they and their Indian allies might wreak such havoc among the English west of the Appalachians as to slow up indefinitely their westward advance.

French hopes were not wholly unreal. Their English opponents, despite numerical superiority, were far from united. True, plans for colonial union and imperial defense were discussed in Albany and London but they remained on paper. Benjamin Franklin, as well as other imperial-minded leaders in the colonies, realized the necessity for joint action. Under Franklin's prodding the Albany Congress adopted his plan for intercolonial union, providing for a government transcending provincial boundaries. It was to be a Grand Council on which would sit representatives from each colony, apportioned according to population and wealth. The Grand Council was to advise the executive comprised of a treasurer and president-general (a royal appointee) having the right of veto. Indian affairs, control of distant frontier areas, disposal of western lands, the power to levy taxes for colonial military needs were all to be functions of the Grand Council. For various reasons, jealousy of their respective sovereignties chiefly, both London and the separate colonies ignored this farsighted proposal, which was thus relegated to the might-have-beens of history. Meanwhile the empire floundered.

The flanks of the English colonies, Massachusetts and South Carolina–Georgia, were belligerent enough, but in general each colony was concerned with the French danger only when its own immediate interest was threatened. Proposals for even the smallest expenditures or raising troops resulted in lengthy debate in colonial assemblies, usually ending in recriminations between governors and legislatures. It is very likely that had the mother country along with the colonies joined in aggressive, intelligent action rivaling that of the French, the latter would have lost their American empire a half century before Wolfe's victory at Quebec. An obvious weakness of the English was their practice of trading with the enemy during hostilities. Another serious handicap to the English were the flabby military preparations of one of their most populous and vitally situated colonies, Pennsylvania. Her Quakers and the German rulers of east Pennsylvania were, by conscience or by calculation, slow to expend funds on the military. The burden was largely borne by the angered Scotch-Irish and Germans in the western part of the province.

In 1753 and 1754 the Marquis Duquesne, who had determined to protect France's claim to the Ohio country by building a series of log forts from Lake Erie to the forks of the Ohio, reached the site of Pittsburgh. To forestall the French, Virginia's governor, Robert Dinwiddie (himself involved in trading and land ventures) sent youthful George Washington, versed in the ways of the forest, into the region. The French, however, had arrived first and constructed the strong Fort Duquesne. Washington's inferior forces were badly beaten on a soggy July day, and the French ruled triumphant in the Ohio country. The small skirmish at Fort Necessity, in the western woods far from the chancelleries of Europe, was the spark that set ablaze battle fields in the Old World, in India, and all over North America.

The war for some time went badly for the British in North America. General Edward Braddock, a capable commander though ignoring warnings of Indian ambush, set out in 1755 from Virginia to reduce Ft. Duquesne. His force of redcoats and Virginia militia under Washington, as well as Indian scouts, when near the fort were cut to pieces by the French and their whooping native allies; the survivors were sent reeling back toward Virginia. Western settlements were naked to French and Indian raids. In the North, to protect their insecure hold on Nova Scotia, the English expelled the local Acadians, distributing the pathetic refugees through all the colonies. Elsewhere along the northern frontier the English suffered setbacks in their attempts to take Fort Niagara and Crown Point on Lake Champlain. The lone success that year was won by William Johnson on Lake George.

Johnson, who lived among the Indians in the Mohawk Valley, was remarkably adroit in dealing with the natives, and it was his ability that offset French skill in such negotiations. He understood Indians as few whites ever did; he decorated his face with war paint and joined in the Indian war dances. Johnson had entered the Mohawk Valley nearly twenty years before to develop the real estate holdings of a rich uncle. The young man became one of the great traders in the region, extending his influence far beyond the valley. His prestige with the Iroquois was immense, and in this crisis Johnson was named Superintendent of Indian Affairs.

Colonial wars, as fought by provincial troops, had an informal quality that drove British regulars to distraction. Johnson assembled about 3,000 troops near Albany in July for the push northward. His soldiers were farmers, or their sons, from New England and New York, who had volunteered for the summer campaign. Occasionally one would have a makeshift uniform, but most of them wore their everyday clothes. Their blankets had been supplied to them, but they had brought their own guns. In place of bayonets they carried hatchets in their belts; powder-horns were slung at their sides.

Over a newly made road, where stumps and roots jolted his wagon train, Johnson started for Lake George. He was a jovial, informal commander, sharing food and drink with his men. "Stopped about noon and dined with General Johnson by a small brook under a tree," wrote a New England soldier; "ate a good dinner of cold boiled and roast venison; drank good fresh lemmon-punch and wine." Although Johnson beat the French and Indian troops of General Dieskau he failed to exploit his success by driving further north, and the results of his victory were strictly limited.

In 1756–57 British arms suffered disaster in many corners of the globe. In America the French devastated the New York frontier, forcing settlers to flee to the safety of Albany. In the winter of 1757 the cause of Britain looked grave. In this crisis England turned from blue-blooded political leaders to William Pitt, a man without "the parade of birth and title." "I know," said Pitt, "that I can save England, and that nobody else can."

With driving energy he harnessed a giant war machine. Prussia, with English subsidies, was to fight the common enemy on the continent of Europe; the English navy was to prevent France from reinforcing her overseas colonies. America was now thrust forward as a primary, rather than secondary, theatre of war. In Pitt's grand strategy the conquest of Canada and the west would add an enormous field for imperial expansion. Young, imaginative men like Wolfe were elevated to the highest commands in the field. Pitt ordered that the military ranking of colonial officers, fighting in the imperial forces, should follow the same procedure as for the regular British army. The pessimism of the colonists was quickly transformed into an offensive spirit.

The tide did not turn at once. The French had in Montcalm a commander the equal of England's best. In the spring of 1758 he blasted an English force attempting to storm Ft. Ticonderoga by frontal assault. British troops were caught in a web of felled trees with sharpened entangling branches. In the face of a withering fire 2,000 of General Abercromby's best troops were lost in the brave, but rash, action.

The odds against the French were, however, fast mounting. They lost Ft. Frontenac on Lake Ontario to the British in a surprise attack. The loss of the fort, with all of its supplies for the French posts to the south, cut the line of communications between Canada and the Ohio

Before and after the French and Indian War

Valley. Indian allies fell away from the French and transferred their uncertain affections to the English. The French had too few men to guard the vital approaches. The drain on their manpower left only the very old and the women and children to gather the harvest. Ft. Duquesne, the gateway of the West, was taken by the English, strongly supported by Washington, and renamed Pittsburgh after the inspiring war leader. Louisbourg was also captured. In India and Africa, too, the fortunes of war favored England. In Europe, England's Prussian ally was successful in beating off French, Russian, and Austrian enemies.

The successes of 1758, topped by the remarkable victories of 1759— in Europe, the West Indies, and finally the great achievement in capturing Quebec—filled England's cup of happiness full. The lanky, red-haired James Wolfe led a massive convoy up the St. Lawrence, while Amherst struck overland, capturing Crown Point and Ticonderoga. But Amherst was blocked at the head of Lake Champlain, leaving Wolfe to carry the burden of the final assault alone. Wolfe was only thirty-two years old at the time, but his military genius was unrivaled. To take the formidable fortress at Quebec shielded on the north by 300-foot high rock walls required all the daring and ingenuity Wolfe possessed.

In his first attempts to take the fortress he was turned back. He then devised a ruse which enabled him in the predawn darkness to scale, undetected, the rocky heights above the city where he placed his 4,500 men. There, on the Plains of Abraham on the misty morning of September 13, Wolfe's men awaited the attack of the surprised Montcalm. The French came on, and, when they were within forty yards, the rigidly disciplined British opened a heavy, concentrated fire. A single volley determined the historic battle. The two great commanders fell in that brief encounter, Montcalm's life ebbing away with the death of New France. Wolfe, in death, gave his countrymen an imperial realm. With the surrender of Montreal the next year North America was free of French power.

Elsewhere, however, the war dragged on. Spain entered the conflict only to feel the force of English naval superiority. She lost to the British the best of her possessions in the West Indies, as well as Manila in the Philippines. The new King George III, anxious for peace, was ready to negotiate with his defeated enemies. After complicated diplomatic maneuvers the Peace of Paris (1763) gave to Britain all of French Canada (minus two tiny islands in the St. Lawrence), the territory east of the Mississippi (except New Orleans), and the Spanish Floridas; Spain's hurt was eased when she received from France the vast territory of Louisiana west of the Mississippi. The enfeebled Spanish empire also retained Cuba and the Philippines.

Britain's empire was at the height of its glory: India won, Canada hers, almost all land east of the Mississippi in English hands, her flag flying over choice West Indian islands, and her navy triumphant on every sea. The fame of Pitt and Wolfe became the heritage of every Englishman. A happy unity knit the empire in a pleasant glow of self-congratulation. Britain's happiness was marred only by the knowledge it could not last. The costs of war had to be reckoned, and a host of domestic problems within the empire awaited solution.

France was forever removed as an American rival, but suddenly a haunting thought troubled the sleep of imperial statesmen. Did the expulsion of the French remove England's strongest disciplinary rod over her American colonists? More than a dozen years before the Peace of Paris, Peter Kalm had written: "I have been told that the English colonies . . . in the space of thirty or fifty years would be able to form a state by themselves, entirely independent [of] Old England. But, as the whole country which lies along the sea shore is unguarded, and on the [frontier] is harassed by the French . . . these dangerous neighbors are sufficient to prevent the connection of the colonies with their mother country from being quite broken off. The English government has therefore sufficient reason to consider the French . . . as the best means of keeping the colonies in their due submission."

CHAPTER VIII

A Native Culture Emerges

The American colonists by the middle of the eighteenth century had matured greatly in their economic and political life. They were producing goods for their own needs in larger measure than before, and their political institutions were successfully meeting the challenge of administering an orderly society. They were a rural people, hardly 5 per cent living in the towns. There was, as yet, no very sharp division between town and country. Squealing pigs ran through tree-lined streets, and open fields were not far away. Towns were relatively small, covering a few square miles. At the water's edge, where the ships were berthed, a forest of masts towered over the town's tallest buildings. In the vicinity of the docks were centered mercantile activities that helped to differentiate town and country. Urban communities were not only commercial centers; they were gathering places for intellectual and social life. They had an importance in the American scene wholly out of proportion to the number of their inhabitants.

Paralleling developments in economics and politics, but moving more slowly and at a respectful distance behind, were the achievements in the life of the spirit. In the rawness of a wilderness setting, to which migrants must make their hard adjustment, the standard of value was the usefulness of an idea or an object; beauty was apparently a luxury the frontiersman could do without. Almost a century after the founding of Massachusetts, New Englanders were reminded that usefulness was still the first consideration: "It's more noble to be employed in serving and supplying the necessities of others, than merely in pleasing the fancy of any. The Plow-Man that raiseth Grain, is more serviceable to Mankind than the Painter who draws only to please the Eye. The Carpenter who builds a good House to defend us from Wind and Weather, is more serviceable than the curious Carver, who employs his Art to please the Fancy."

Nevertheless while the emphasis was on the useful, the simple taste of carpenters, silversmiths, and cabinet makers resulted often in the creation of objects with genuine beauty. It was when colonists had more wealth and more leisure that the attempts "to please the Fancy" with ornate decoration spoiled the simpler beauty of earlier houses, furniture, and silverware.

★ ALONG THE COLONIAL HIGHWAY

Emigrant Europeans brought with them their folk culture; the Englishmen their songs and dances, the pious Germans their music and their sturdy furniture, the French their delicate wrought-iron work. The homes of people in older established areas were more comfortable than in former times, but they still seemed crowded because of the many children. In the ordinary home the busy kitchen was the living room and also the sleeping room. The space for living was even smaller in a tradesman's house, for generally a room fronting on the street was set aside for his shop where he made his silver or his chairs, or sold the latest silks brought from London. From the house of a silversmith came the smell of burning charcoal for melting down old silver to make the teapots, pitchers, and tableware that increasing numbers of well-to-do people were demanding. Benjamin Franklin's father, hanging his sign of a Blue Ball in front of his Boston door, sold soap and candles in his small but prosperous shop. Apprentices, wearing their leather aprons, worked long hours under the direction of masters to learn the skills that produced good printing, fine cabinet work, and lovely silver.

Craftsmen, like the young journeyman printer, Ben Franklin, went from town to town where there was work to be had. Travel along the coast was being made easier by better communications. As the eighteenth century advanced, ships passed more frequently between the colonies, and even transportation by land was improved. Roads between the larger towns, particularly in the northern colonies, were much better than the blazed trails through the forest of earlier years. An English traveler in Boston, 1740, thought the roads were "exceeding good in summer," and, remembering conditions at home, he was grateful for the "safe travelling night or day, for they have no highway robbers to interrupt them."

The rapid settlement of the coastal region north of Philadelphia to Boston required better highways. A traveler from Boston to New York a few years before the Revolution noted that "you scarcely lose sight of an house." Almanacs printed the routes between the larger towns, and before the middle of the eighteenth century the first American guide book had appeared. It indicated the road running from Boston, through

Providence, New London, New York, Philadelphia, on through Virginia to Charleston. Thus over hundreds of miles of direct and connecting roads colonials could travel for pleasure and business, although at any considerable distance from a town the roads could still hardly be called pleasurable. Even for relatively short trips many people still preferred to go by water. St. Paul's Chapel in New York had its main entrance facing the Hudson, and parishioners could come to church by boat, leaving their craft at the river's edge and then taking the pleasant walk up the slow green rise to the church.

Most people traveling by land rode on horseback, but carriages were being used by an increasing number. Near the middle of the eighteenth century Massachusetts had about seven pleasure carriages to every thousand persons; New York's proportion seemed to be larger. At the popular racing grounds on Hempstead Plains, Long Island, over seventy chaises and chairs were counted, while about a thousand horses brought the humbler spectators. Regular stage routes between the larger cities were in operation. The first through stage, advertised as the "flying machine," ran between New York and Philadelphia (1764) taking two days for the trip. The New York–Boston stage took four days or longer. Sloops and schooners attempted to maintain a fairly regular service between the busy Atlantic ports. Navigation guides, lighthouses, and improved docks, all were proof of increasing sea travel and commerce.

In an earlier day, when nearly impassable roads discouraged travel, inns were very rare. The sorely tried travelers depended on the hospitality of an occasional inhabitant along the way, or on some unlikely and untidy inn where they were badly fed, and men and women lodged together in the same room for the night. As more travelers moved through the colonies, inns were improved, and some of them, like Fraunces' Tavern in New York and the Raleigh Tavern in Williamsburg, Virginia, became famous meeting places for political leaders in the Revolutionary era.

Communications were speeded up by the improvements in the postal service instituted by Franklin when he was named postmaster-general in 1753. Between New York and Philadelphia a letter could be sent and a reply received within two days because the mails now traveled day and night; between Boston and Philadelphia in six days instead of the former three weeks, though the schedule was not regularly maintained. Franklin lowered the rates, which were graduated according to distance and weight. Weekly newspapers were a regular part of a postman's load, and enterprising postmasters (like Franklin himself) were also publishers of papers, having an obvious advantage in delivering their own periodicals and in gathering the news.

The small four-page newspapers were printed with no headlines. The first with any degree of permanence was the *Boston News Letter,* in 1704, and from then on through the rest of the century towns, large and small, had their local papers. They printed advertisements and chronicled fires and drownings, arrivals and departures of ships, and local political affairs, but they also took notice of happenings in other colonies. More than any other institution newspapers gave the people a sense of belonging to a society larger than their own colony. Americans have always been newspaper hungry, and in the eighteenth century the weeklies were a significant educative force in the community, with their reprinting of English literature and the publication of native prose and poetry. It was the newspapers, almanacs, and magazines (imported and domestic), which played an important part in promoting common cultural interests throughout the colonies and popularizing the ideas of leaders of thought in Europe and America.

★ "NATURE" THE TEACHER

The history of colonization indicates that it is easier to transplant political and economic institutions than the more fragile things of the spirit. Even when a moderate success in transplantation to the American colonies had been achieved, the pattern of creation overseas was often nothing more than a pale imitation of the original. "Cultural colonialism" was a stamp of inferiority which stigmatized New France, New Spain, and New England. The creation of art is one of life's many unsolved mysteries; the fact remains that New France produced no Molière, New Spain no Cervantes, New England no Milton. Nevertheless the judgment of Professor Kenneth Murdock * seems sound: "The more this work [the literary accomplishments of the colonists] is examined in the light of the handicaps the colonists faced and the standards they set for themselves, the more impressive it becomes. In seventy years they made Boston second only to London in the English-speaking world as a center for the publishing and marketing of books, and they produced a body of writing greater in quantity and quality than that of any other colonial community in modern history."

Under adverse circumstances individuals scattered through the American colonies developed their creative talents and found a market for their work. "After the first Cares for the Necessaries of Life are over,

---

* *Literature and Theology in Colonial New England* (Cambridge, Mass.: Harvard University Press, 1949), p. 31.

we shall come to think of the Embellishments," wrote Franklin; "Already some of our young Geniuses begin to lisp Attempts at Painting, Poetry and Musick."

Practicing artists in the colonies often fell prey to the comfort of self-pity. In a defensive spirit, the Boston artist, John Singleton Copley, when ordering materials, wrote to a Swiss painter: "You may be surprised that so remote a corner of the Globe as New England should have any demand for the necessary eutensils for practicing the fine Arts, but I assure You Sir however feeble our efforts may be, it is not for want of inclination that they are not better, but the want of oppertunity to improve ourselves. However America which has been the seat of war and desolation, I would fain hope will one Day become the School of fine Arts . . ."

One of the circumstances Copley regretted—the lack of a stimulating group of intellectuals and artists—was not entirely a handicap. Americans learning much by themselves, escaped the reins fashioned by schools of thought in Europe which regimented youthful imaginations. Thus, in medicine, while only a small number of American practitioners held degrees in the middle of the eighteenth century, the practical instruction they had received as apprentices in the sick room made them the equal of average European doctors whose study had mainly been in theoretical medicine. Similarly in painting, Benjamin West extolled the lessons learned from nature: "had I come to Europe sooner in Life I should have known nothing but the Receipts of Masters." American portrait painters in the eighteenth century, though greatly influenced by British example, were better when they followed their own instincts. Robert Feke and Copley (in his earlier phase) had developed an excellent native style capable of a more intimate revelation of a sitter's personality than the artist trained conventionally abroad. For consistent, superior accomplishment in the arts and sciences, however, teachers better than "Nature" were required and ultimately the colonists found them.

★ WITCHCRAFT

Copley was able to become the artist he craved to be partly because the very "oppertunity" whose absence he had deplored was now at hand. The growth of wealth and the secularization of life made the patronage of artists more common than in earlier decades. The presence in the colonies of itinerant teachers acted as a stimulus to the native neophyte. These teachers, some of whom stayed in the colonies permanently, brought to America knowledge of a broader, cosmopolitan culture and art standards higher than those customarily found in a provincial society.

Communication is a fundamental key to the creative experience, and by this period of American life intellectuals and artists more frequently than in earlier years enjoyed the stimulus that came from an exchange of ideas. Contact with Europe was closer than in the seventeenth century because of more frequent sailings and better postal facilities. Libraries, colleges, scientific societies and their periodicals, bookstores with their latest importations—were all available to Americans by the middle of the eighteenth century. The colonists, too, shared in the emancipation of the Enlightenment that started in Europe and spread over the Atlantic world.

Even before the end of the seventeenth century the Americans, to a limited extent, participated in the scientific revolution then under way. The Royal Society of England was the center of scientific studies and Americans like John Winthrop, Jr. (interested in chemistry), Paul Dudley (writing on whales and earthquakes), Thomas Brattle (on astronomy), and Cotton Mather (on medicine and natural history) added to the stores of knowledge in the Society's *Philosophical Transactions*. The Mathers, father Increase and son Cotton, who had a genuine scientific curiosity, were also deeply absorbed in cataloguing the activities of "Spectres or Agents in the invisible World." In the seventeenth century and for many years thereafter science was to a large extent still wrapped in a smothering cocoon of old wives' tales and hobbling superstition.

One of the worst of the superstitions was the age-old belief in witchcraft. Tens of thousands had been killed in Europe over the centuries because of men's belief in the power of sorcery. It seemed perfectly plausible for some of the best minds of Europe and America to share the universal belief in witchcraft and yet practice the scientific method in chemistry or medicine or astronomy at one and the same time. At the very moment that Salem Village did to death its witches, Harvard students had manuals of science which indoctrinated them with an observant, experimental attitude toward the world in which they lived. It was the failure on the part of educated leaders to disentangle witchcraft from science, plus widespread hysteria, which brought on the tragic episode of the judicial murder of the Salem witches.

The nerves of people in Massachusetts had been drawn taut by the revolution of 1689, the swift political changes, and Indian attacks during King William's War. In this overwrought state, the hysteria of a few young girls, bewitched, they said, by a Negro slave, easily communicated itself to nearly the whole population. Within a few months in 1692 accused people, to escape hanging, were charging others with witchcraft. Mass suggestion resulted in confession of broomstick rides, consorting with the devil, and "putting the evil eye" on animals. It was dangerous for anyone to speak up rationally and ridicule the popular frenzy. In a short time a hundred alleged witches were in jail waiting to be tried. Before the fever ran its course nineteen were hanged and one, Giles Corey, was pressed to death by the weight of rocks upon his chest. The doomed included a grandmother, too deaf to hear the judges' questions, a straightforward farmer, a pipe-smoking slut, an old lame man speaking salty language through toothless gums, the Rev. George Burrows repeating the Lord's Prayer just before hanging—these were among the witches and wizards whose lives were forfeit on Gallows Hill.

Puritanism has been blamed for this terrible case of social pathology. Emerson spoke of his tough-minded ancestors as "great grim earnest men," while other critics have commented on the absence of humor among them. The Puritan, says Professor Simpson, "was obsessed by his sense of sin. Taught to expect it everywhere, and to magnify it where he found it, he easily fell into the habit of inventing it." But long after influential Puritans had admitted that a grievous miscarriage of justice had been done in Salem and had made amends, witches were still sentenced to death in non-Puritan lands in Europe.

The witchcraft episode in Massachusetts was a sad setback to the growth of rationalism in the colonies, but fear of the devil eventually diminished. Half a century after the lamentable events in Salem Village, Nathaniel Ames's almanac, widely circulated among the same kind of people who had once cried death to witches, could safely ridicule belief in witchcraft; "If there be an old woman . . . prodigious ugly . . . she is a witch forsooth; but the handsome young Girls are never suspected; as tho' Satan took a Delight in the Dry Sticks of Human Nature, and would select the most neglected Creature in the human Species to be his Privy Counsellor."

★ THE ENLIGHTENMENT

In Europe there were vast stirrings in political and scientific speculation, suggested by Bacon, Descartes, Hobbes, Locke, Boyle, and Newton. Jethro Tull and others were advocating revolutionary changes in agriculture. Orthodox religion was being challenged by the advance of skepticism and deism and the growth of secularism. All these are features of the cultural scene which were reflected in America. Even before the seventeenth century was out the intellectual solidarity of New England had given place to deep cleavages of opinion. "A shedding of the religious conception of the Universe" became apparent, writes Perry Miller,* "a turning to a way of life in which the secular state . . . has become central." Scientific ideas acceptable to leading European intellectuals quickly found a welcome in America. Along with Europeans, Americans deferred to the genius of Newton; he was, said Cotton Mather, "the perpetual Dictator of the learned World." Like Newton, Cotton and his father, Increase Mather, hailed the approaching eighteenth century as "the most wonderful Age that ever was since the World began." To which Cotton added, "America is Legible in these Promises."

Bacon suggested a questioning spirit. Sir Edward Coke, antagonist of the first two Stuarts, was a great lawyer whose words in the seedtime of English constitutional liberties were to be echoed in America a century and a half later; said Coke against the attempt of Charles I to collect forced loans, "The King cannot tax any by way of loans"; said the Massachusetts Assembly of the Stamp Act, "against Magna Charta and the natural rights of Englishmen, and therefore, according to the Lord Coke, null and void." Locke's political treatises spoke of government arising originally from a compact among people to protect their lives and property, and the English philosopher maintained that the oppressed had the right to revolt against despotism. Newton explained that the universe ran in accordance with "natural laws," and thus denied the old beliefs of God's capricious interference in the operations of the earth and the heavenly bodies. Deists accepted Newton's "natural laws," believing that God had created the universe to function in accord with these laws; orthodox religion had a new challenge to face.

In time the colonists were to learn about Voltaire's histories and Montesquieu's *Spirit of the Laws* and Rousseau's *Social Contract.* From these Frenchmen, and from Locke, Americans were to gain confirmation of beliefs they already held about the doctrine of natural rights—that all people, unprivileged as well as privileged, were entitled to the rights of life, liberty, property, and the pursuit of happiness. Voltaire preached the idea of progress, which fitted in with the actual experience of Americans who found it easy to believe that advance in the arts, the sciences, and individual well-being was the great destiny of man.

The process by which a young man's intellect was broadened and deepened may be seen in the case of Samuel Johnson, who grew up to become the first president of King's College (Columbia). He enrolled at Yale, where his prescribed studies introduced him to a medieval scholastic atmosphere. He was satisfied with his progress, he said, until

* *The New England Mind: From Colony to Province,* p. 171.

"accidentally lighting on Lord Bacon's . . . Advancement of Learning . . . he immediately bought it, and greedily fell to studying it." At about the same time (1714) a princely gift of books reached Yale. Johnson now had access to the best English poets, philosophers, and theologians. "All this," he said, "was like a flood of day to his low state of mind." Jonathan Edwards, also a Yale student, to become in time the greatest theologian in America, read John Locke's *Essay on Human Understanding* in this new collection of books. He had "more satisfaction and pleasure in studying it," he said, "than the most greedy miser in gathering up handfuls of silver and gold from some new discovered treasure." Edwards was drawn to speculate on matters different from those of the worldly-wise Franklin. His concern was with man's fading passion with God's transcendent power, and his life work was to remind neglectful men of divine omnipotence.

Edwards, however, seemed to express less the temper of the intellectuals than did the rationalists of the school of Franklin. The run-away Boston printer's apprentice had become the American minister of the Enlightenment. Americans interested in science and medicine made several efforts to form a society of their own for discussion of these subjects, but it was the group organized by Franklin in Philadelphia, the American Philosophical Society, 1743, which became the most important in the New World. "The first drudgery of settling new colonies," said Franklin, "which confines the attention of people to mere necessaries, is now pretty well over; and there are many in every province in circumstances that set them at ease and afford leisure to cultivate the finer arts and improve the common stock of knowledge."

With halting steps colonials, scattered through the dispersed provinces, added their small contributions to science. They produced no scientists of the first rank except Franklin, whose work in electricity made him peer of Europe's best. But Americans like botanist John Bartram furnished some of the data on which the grateful Linnaeus built his classification of plant life. Linnaeus paid tribute to the simple Bartram as "the greatest natural botanist in the world." Jared Eliot, of Connecticut, wrote essays on agriculture because the English books hitherto in use were inapplicable to the different conditions in America. Patient individuals, like Dr. John Lining of Charleston, made careful meteorological observations to trace a relationship between weather and disease.

Many of the Americans interested in science were doctors by profession. They had studied medicine as apprentices in colonial offices or had gone to Europe (particularly Edinburgh) for their training. Medical practice in Europe and America was, in many respects, still primitive.

The doctor was physician and apothecary at the same time, preparing his many "potions," "elixirs," and "infusions." Patients were liberally dosed with wormwood, nitre, antimony, sulphur, and calomel. On southern plantations the planter's wife doctored her own family, the servants, and slaves. Many homes had their herb gardens where the housewife had her home-grown remedies. Indians, from their knowledge of medicinal plants, supplied many cures to colonists. Traditional and nauseating formulas were also used to "cure" disease—crushed toads, dried snake-skin, and for bruises a mixture of butter, black snails, cow dung, hen dung, and frankincense, the last no doubt to make the rest bearable. The bleeding of patients was standard practice for many ailments which the sick might have survived if let alone. The whole level of medical training and practice in the colonies experienced a remarkable improvement in the Revolutionary era with the establishment of medical schools and hospitals in the larger towns.

In at least one field of medicine, the treatment of smallpox, the colonists made contributions significant enough to be praised through-out Europe. Doctors, clergymen, and laymen, on both sides of the Atlantic, joined together to make a fight in common against the dread scourge. The method used, inoculating a healthy person with a mild case of smallpox to immunize him in case of an epidemic, succeeded in greatly reducing the mortality rate. In this transatlantic co-operation be-tween doctors a specific group of colonial scientists for the first time were accepted on equal terms by their European colleagues.

Cotton Mather and other clergymen in New England had played im-portant roles in winning acceptance of inoculation. Opposition on re-ligious grounds had to be overcome on both sides of the Atlantic and Mather ridiculed those who enlisted God in their behalf. "It is *cavilled* . . . that this *New Way* comes to us from the *Heathen.*" Well, asked Mather, was not Hippocrates a heathen? And did not the whites learn some of their "very Good Medicines from our Indians? . . . And, Gentlemen Smoakers, I pray, whom did you learn to Smoke of?" Con-trary to conventional belief, the proportion of scientifically-minded men among ministers seemed to be unusually high in the eighteenth century. A close student of intellectual life in the colonies, Dr. C. K. Shipton, maintains that "no scientific idea that won general acceptance with the leaders of European thought failed of quick adoption in New England parsonages."

There were of course, many clerics who clung to the old, just as there were numerous laymen who engaged their opponents in angry de-bate. The contest between rationalism and supernaturalism was clearly defined in the controversy following an earthquake in New England in

1755. Professor John Winthrop of Harvard, Newton's leading disciple in America, delivered a scientific lecture on earthquakes which drew the fire of the historian, the Reverend Thomas Prince. The latter, opposing natural explanations as being detrimental to religion, argued that catastrophes were manifestations of God's displeasure. Winthrop replied, defending philosophical discussion from "imputations of impiety or irreverence." Rationalists elsewhere in America rallied to Winthrop's side, one of them writing that "Mr. Winthrop has laid Mr. Prince flat on his back." The ground of controversy was widened to include the advocacy of free inquiry, not only in science but also in religion and in politics.

Franklin, annoyed by the same kind of opposition which confronted Winthrop, wrote to a correspondent: "Surely the Thunder of Heaven is no more supernatural than the Rain Hail or Sunshine of Heaven, against the Inconveniences of which we guard by Roofs and Shades without Scruple." The way to scientific progress was lined with road blocks of ancient bias. When Winthrop proposed to erect lightning rods on a Harvard building he had to face stubborn disapproval. No wonder he complained to Franklin, "How astonishing is the force of prejudice even in an age of so much knowledge and free inquiry!" To which the worldly-wise Franklin replied that it was not unusual for even learned people to oppose innovations.

Skeptics found comfort in each other's unbelief. Franklin wrote to Dr. Cadwallader Colden in New York: "It is well we are not, as poor Galileo was, subject to the Inquisition for Philosophical Heresy. My whispers against the orthodox doctrine, in private letters, would be dangerous, but your writing and printing would be highly criminal. As it is, you must expect some censure, but one Heretic will surely excuse another."

Deism and free thinking had apparently made rapid strides in Virginia, even before the middle of the eighteenth century. "The church & clergy have many Enemies in this country," wrote Governor William Gooch, "free thinkers multiply very fast having an eminent Layman for their Leader, and the Current runs in some places almost without opposition."

Behind Franklin's jesting with Colden was a sober reminder of the risk in being openly known as heterodox in religion. In the early years of the eighteenth century the young graduates of Yale were warned against the new philosophy (associated with the names of Boyle, Locke, and Newton) "that of late was all in vogue." It threatened to bring in "a new Divinity and Corrupt the pure Religion of the Country." A correspondent in Northampton, Massachusetts, ordering unorthodox books from Boston, asked that they be packed carefully "intirely concealed," lest neighbors pry into his reading.

Most of the intellectual leadership in America proclaimed its devotion to rationalism. They were one with Immanuel Kant who declared that the motto of the Enlightenment was "Dare to use your own understanding." Man needed not the aid of miracles to understand the world; his own mind was itself the transcendent miracle which could fathom all others. "Everything is full of miracles," said Leibniz, "but miracles of reason."

★ THE PROFESSIONS

Before the era of the Revolution many doctors had already won a distinguished position in American life. They were social and political leaders as well as intellectual lights. Another group that gained a notable place for themselves, despite much hostility, were the lawyers. Many young men who, in former days, might have become clergymen were turning to the law. The standards of an earlier time, when ministers and merchants acted as attorneys, and men without legal training were named as judges, were slowly improving. Not, however, until higher standards prevailed, as the result of study in London and self-regulation by the local bar, did lawyers begin to play a significant part in community life.

All told there were only a few hundred in the colonies in the middle of the eighteenth century; but the growth of trade, and numerous opportunities arising in connection with transfers of land, gave lawyers a place of real importance. In some of the colonies it was said that lawyers were making large fortunes within ten years, often by land speculation. In New York they were ranked socially almost on a par with the great landowners of the colony, with whom they were in fact related by kinship and commercial ties. Acting together with merchants and large landowners lawyers were to be a powerful factor in molding political opinion in the Revolutionary era.

★ "THE DRUDGERY IS PRETTY WELL OVER"

The long French and Indian war through which the colonists had passed impoverished some and enriched others. Those living in the relative safety of coastal towns and tidewater plantations were generally the lucky ones. Colden said that many merchants in New York "have rose suddenly from the lowest Rank of the people to considerable Fortunes, & chiefly by illicit Trade in the last War." In the rapidly growing ports of Charleston, Philadelphia, New York, and Boston, and on spacious southern plantations, a sophisticated society lived a life far removed from the crudeness of early days.

Europeans who visited America found in these communities cosmopolitan men and women whose intelligent conversation made the time pass agreeably. Visitors often praised the physical surroundings of these urban centers; one observer remarked that Philadelphia needed only the streets to be paved "to make it appear to advantage, for there is few towns if any in England that are better Illumin'd with Lamps, & those of the best Sort, nor their watch better regulated." New York and Boston houses were said to compare favorably with London's; and in after years Jefferson, who was an excellent judge, thought Philadelphia handsomer than Paris or London.

The homes of wealthy colonials, larger than in former times, were designed in accord with the latest architectural patterns copied from English books. These emphasized the classical balance that all Europe had taken from Andrea Palladio in Italy. Palladio conceived of the house as a complete unit from the start; no additions were to be made later to mar its original perfect exterior symmetry. The American houses, though differing in detail from each other, had a general similarity in the Georgian style. In the absence of professional architects colonists became skilled amateurs, often with remarkable results. Some of their best houses still stand and are justly treasured.

Architecture in New England was, perhaps, more original than elsewhere. Here buildings were constructed mostly of wood. In colonies to the southward brick or stone were used more frequently, although stone houses were common only in Pennsylvania. While the exterior of homes often looked alike, the interiors might reveal individual preferences; for example, there was no regularity in the layout of the four rooms which went to make up the usual floor plan. Large homes in the South, with a wide hall allowing the breeze to blow through, were well adapted to the warmer climate. On the best designed of the plantations the outbuildings were placed with relationship to the main house so as to give an impression of perfect symmetry.

Many of the planters, seeking to escape the monotony of their rural life, had town houses in Charleston or Williamsburg or Annapolis, where the gathering families could enjoy a season of dinners, dancing, theater, and horse racing. Gay Charleston had in its St. Cecilia Society the best musical organization in the colonies.

Americans were quick to follow the fashions of England. "I am almost inclined to believe," wrote an English visitor to Maryland, "that a new fashion is adopted earlier by the polished and affluent Americans, than by many opulent persons in the great metropolis [London]." Merchants and their wives, adorned with jewels, were richly and fashionably dressed. In the South families, yeomen in origin or even begun by indentured servants, had learned, with the accumulation of wealth, to model themselves on the way of life of the English aristocracy. In many of the colonies, south and north, family wealth was kept intact by primogeniture and entail, and often enlarged through judicious marriages; daughters and widows "well placed" were eagerly sought by business-like suitors.

The mansions of merchants and landlords revealed a discriminating sense of luxury in their interiors. Beautiful staircases were a central feature of distinguished houses; fine wainscoting and paneling made by skilled, nameless craftsmen added warmth and distinction to formal interiors. Fine cabinetmakers, or "joyners," usually borrowing English styles—Chippendale, Hepplewhite, or Sheraton—fashioned the furniture which graced luxurious homes. Gone was the time when a home had only one chair, and that reserved for the head of the house. In a day of lessened austerity the other members of the household, who once sat on stools, now also had graceful chairs designed for comfort.

★ A DEMOCRATIC CULTURE

While the rich in the colonies were modeling themselves after the English aristocracy, the spirit of American life was fundamentally opposed to aristocratic pretensions. The flexibility of the American class structure, where people moved up, and even down, with relative rapidity, made such pretentiousness a little ridiculous. Colonials laughed at the returned traveler from England bringing back exaggerated habits of speech and behavior; the "elegant expressions, Split me Madam; By Gad; Dam me," seemed artificial and out of place to earthy Yankees.

There was never, in the colonies, the same aristocratic indifference to the well-being of the unprivileged as in Europe. In England itself, by the beginning of the eighteenth century, that lordly callousness had been strongly tempered, as evidenced by the many humanitarian organizations which were set up in those years. Religious groups such as the Anglican Society for the Propagation of the Gospel promoted education as well as orthodoxy in the colonies.

On both sides of the ocean many of the leading participants in these movements in education, prison reform, antislavery, came from the middle classes who were strongly influenced by the Enlightenment. The secularization of thought fostered greater concern with humanitarianism, less obsession with sin and an exacting divinity. As Jefferson wrote to John Adams, Calvin's God "is not the God whom you and I acknowledge and adore, the creator and benevolent Governor of the world."

In the whole English-speaking world it was often the initiative of Quakers which brought about social advance. They were the conscience of the eighteenth century, troubling a smug society with persistent questioning. Philadelphia, a Quaker stronghold, was praised as excelling all other American cities in making "useful improvements . . . particularly in the science of humanity." The saintly John Woolman preaching against slavery, or the philanthropic Anthony Benezet planning to cure his fellow men of such evils as intemperance, dueling, and lack of education, were two of the lesser-known names in America's calendar of heroes.

Colonials like Franklin, born of the "middling people," though successful in rising above the handicaps of their class, did not feel superior to it. Intellectually at home with the greatest men of their century—Newton, Montesquieu, Voltaire, Beccaria, David Hume—the concern of Franklin and his Philadelphia friends was often with the problems of everyday life: keeping homes warm with a new type of stove, protecting them from dangers by means of a voluntary fire company, a town police, or a lightning rod. They paved the city streets and gave them lights; they founded a hospital, a college, and a library.

The pressure was steady to broaden the opportunities for the mass of men. While their formal schooling was often restricted to a brief period in youth, supplementary education was offered in day and night classes for men and women. Foreign languages, arithmetic, and bookkeeping were taught, as well as surveying and navigation—appropriate subjects in a period much of whose activity was connected with the buying and selling of land, or sailing the ocean. Geography and history were also taught in these classes. Publicly supported schools in New England were said to be superior to those in Europe; and the knowledge of reading in the northern colonies seems to have been general. Throughout the colonies youngsters studied the *New England Primer,* which in its long history "taught millions to read and not one to sin." The chief purpose of Puritan education, at least in its earlier years, says Professor E. S. Morgan, "was to prepare children for conversion." *

Americans were not less advanced than Rousseau in urging new ideas in pedagogy. Samuel Johnson, president of King's College, who preferred to spare the rod in education, wrote that children should be thought of as much more important "than we usually apprehend them to be," and he urged greater candor and patience in teaching them. A schoolmaster, transplanted from Germany to teach his fellow Mennon-

* *The Puritan Family* (Boston: Trustees of the Public Library, 1944), p. 47.

ites in the colonies, observed that because of the broader humanitarian sentiments in America teachers could not be as strict with children as they were in the Old World.

Culture for the masses was already an American ideal. In addition to libraries, which were to be found in many towns large and small, numerous public lectures, newspapers, and almanacs probably made Americans the best-informed people in the eighteenth-century world. In New England one family in four subscribed for a weekly newspaper which they shared with their neighbors. As for the paperbound, pocket-sized almanacs, Franklin's "Poor Richard" sold more than 10,000 copies a year, while Ames was said to dispose of the incredible number of 60,000 copies annually. It is not surprising that a British author should have told his readers that in New England learning was "more generally diffused among all ranks of the people than in any other part of the globe."

Americans were thought to be indifferent to formal learning, but they were credited with a good natural intelligence. They revealed, said one German traveler, "a better expression of their understanding than people of the same rank in Europe." They talked with as much assurance as their religious and political leaders about abstruse theological doctrines and practical political problems. Religion and politics were inextricably mixed, and as the eighteenth century advanced, ministers were concerned with the solution of political problems of their flocks as much as with the salvation of their souls. Politics was a popular subject of conversation. A patriotic American said there were not five men in all Europe "who understand the nature of liberty and theory of government as well as they are understood by five hundred men in America."

Observers who were familiar with Europe and America remarked that the word *people* in the New World had a different meaning than it had in the Old World. In the Old it meant really only the classes who ruled society; in the New it meant the whole community and included every human creature. In America, noted Crèvecoeur, an immigrant Frenchman, the poor "are become men"; "everything tends to regenerate them; new laws, a new mode of living, a new social system." The newcomer, who in Europe had not lived but only vegetated, "now feels himself a man, because he is treated as such."

Formerly, said Crèvecoeur, the ordinary folk of Europe "were not numbered in any civil lists of their country, except in those of the poor; here they rank as citizens. By what invisible power has this surprising metamorphosis been performed? By that of the laws and that of their industry. The laws . . . protect them as they arrive, stamping on them the symbol of adoption; they receive ample rewards for their labours;

[they procure lands;] those lands confer on them the title of freemen, and to that title every benefit is affixed which men can possible require. This is the great operation daily performed by our laws. From whence proceed these laws? From our government. Whence the government? It is derived from the original genius and strong desire of the people ratified and confirmed by the crown. This is the great chain which links us all, this is the picture which every province exhibits." The American is a new man on the earth, in whom flows the blood of many nations. He "acts upon new principles; he must therefore entertain new ideas, and form new opinions."

Thomas Pownall, an English official who had governed in Massachusetts, probably understood better than others the difference between European and American liberty. "The liberty of the People of America," he said, "is not merely that share of Power, which an Aristocracy permits the people to amuse themselves with and which they are taught to call Liberty." Neither, said Pownall, was it a crumb thrown by a monarch to the people to win their aid in contests with the aristocracy. "The genuine Liberty on which America is founded is totally and intirely a New System of Things and men. . . ." Every inhabitant of America, he continued with some exaggeration, was "equal in his essential inseparable rights of the individual to any other individual"; he was "in these rights, independent of any power that any other can assume over him, over his labour or his property; this is a Principle in act and deed, and not a mere Speculative Theorem."

Taxes in America were negligible. New Jersey's residents, spoken of as "the most Easie and happy people of any collony in North America," had an annual per capita tax burden (1774) of three shillings, equivalent to one day's pay. Pennsylvania, in 1767, was almost entirely free of taxes. Thus America gave greater substance to the concepts of political and religious freedom, economic opportunity, and humanitarian ideals; and her example hurried the peoples of the world to their fuller realization. Even this early in their history Americans thought of themselves as belonging almost to a distinct race of mankind.

★ THE RISE OF AMERICAN NATIONALISM

These men of the New World certainly had long been thinking of themselves as different from Englishmen. They had spoken of themselves as Americans before the eighteenth century began. With the passing years their accent on being American became sharper. The wars in which colonists fought besides Britons actually seemed to widen the gulf between them. They found each other peculiar; the disciplined redcoat regulars, accustomed to tactics of warfare in Europe, thought

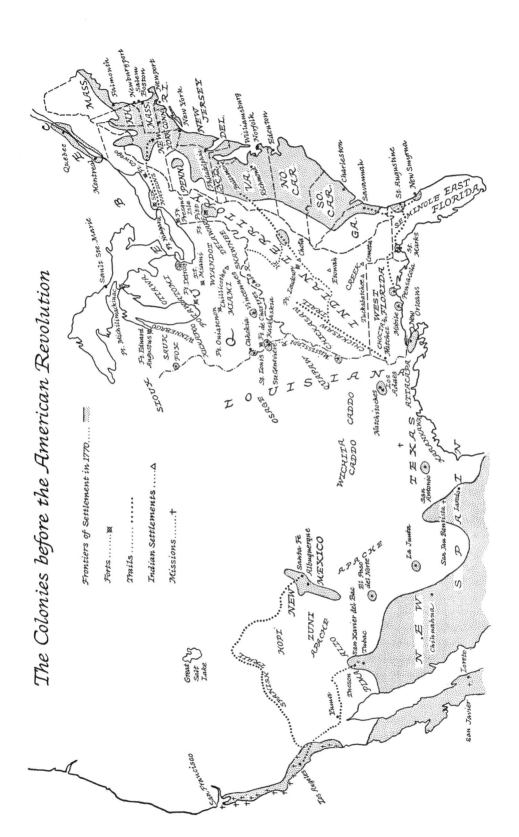

The Colonies before the American Revolution

the Americans poor soldiers, while the Americans resented the superior airs of British officers, as well as discrimination in military and political appointments.

The American tradition of mechanical ingenuity and "natural genius" was already fixed. One correspondent of Ezra Stiles, president of Yale, wrote exultantly, "I am convinced that America abounds in Natural Genius as hardly a town but has its Genius." In the first years of the eighteenth century Cotton Mather had written with annoyance about old-fashioned people who ridiculed "well projected Inventions for the good of the World"; had they encouraged them instead, "we should before now have seen the World in much better circumstances than it is." Mather told the Royal Society in England that ingenious Americans were planning all sorts of inventions "to render the Wind as well as the Water Serviceable to us." Lord Sheffield said that American axes had so high a reputation that British manufacturers found it easier to sell their own product by labeling them made in New England.

The growth of a national consciousness was to be seen, about the middle of the century, in the increasing output of historical works relating to the colonies. Newspapers, magazines, and almanacs all began to reflect a rising interest in history. Ames, in one of his almanacs, urged that a vast citizenry be prepared for participation in politics to the end that popular control might be insured. The study of history and geography was recommended, and like a true nationalist Ames said, "it is proper to begin with the history of your own nation." In encouraging a fellow colonial to finish his history of Massachusetts, Stiles said a European writer could not do justice to American history. Colonials were conscious of the need to correct English misconceptions of America, and in their writing they revealed a pride in their past and a strong confidence in their future.

The embryonic nationalism of this period was expressed in the gradual emergence of the new American-English language. The appearance of an "American dialect" was already recognized, with familiar words taking on different meanings, such as "fall" for "autumn." The American language borrowed from the Indian, the Dutch, and the French. From the Indian it took *skunk, hickory, terrapin,* and many others; from the Dutch, *cruller, stoop, scow, cookey;* from the French, *bureau, portage, prairie.* The colonists coined many fresh words which sprang almost spontaneously out of their new environment: *bullfrog, popcorn, coldsnap, snowplow.* Picturesque adjectives, such as *handy, kinky, chunky* were already part of American everyday speech. Most Englishmen disliked colonial changes in the common tongue that began to divide them, but one British scientist thought that Americans had improved the language by introducing vigorous and concise words and phrases in place of roundabout wording. In an earlier generation John Wise, the vigorous clerical defender of democratic ideas, used vivid, earthy language. He spoke of "swapping Governments" and denounced certain proposals as a "cruel Dose." Benjamin Franklin's pungency in language owed much to his New England boyhood. The growing self-consciousness of the colonies resulted in a proposal for an "American Society of Language," with members in all the colleges. One of the words which seemed to intrigue everybody was "Yankee," which sprang to popularity on the eve of the Revolution.

The colonial colleges themselves, though relatively small, promoted the feeling of expansiveness and self-sufficiency. Young, native-born graduates were counted upon as future political leaders who might better represent their communities than royal officials and their appointed favorites. At each college were some students from various colonies; Princeton in particular had many students from outside the home colony —New Jersey. This mingling re-enforced a sense of fraternity in civic affairs, especially the southern colonies where a strong sense of loyalty to the college and its liberal principles had already been created.

All kinds of ties were binding the colonies closer together: business and social contacts, religious organizations, improved postal and travel communications, education, and the press. Though the circulation of individual newspapers was not large (one publisher claimed over 3,000), these weeklies stimulated a growing self-consciousness among the colonies. In the political controversies of the Revolutionary era they played a most important part. News spread fast. In the growing crisis of the early 1770's, when every one was on the alert, word that British troops were on the move was circulated in a few days to a million widely scattered people.

In great crises colonial papers showed a united front. Appealing for concerted action against the French in 1754, the newspapers rallied behind the Albany Congress by printing the design of a snake in many parts, with the slogan, "Join, or Die." Franklin had first published it, and since he knew nearly all the colonial printers, some of whom he had put in business, they were quick to follow his lead. The cartoon, apparently the earliest in America, was reprinted again, at the time of the Stamp Act, against which the newspapers were unanimously opposed. It appeared once more in 1774 when a New York paper, which was the mouthpiece of the radical "Sons of Liberty," published it.

In the years just prior to the Revolution representatives from the colonies had met on important occasions to consider their various difficulties—the Albany Congress, the Stamp Act Congress, and the Continental Congress. These meetings of men from widely separated colonies made clear to all that they had many problems in common. Eyes were lifted above local boundaries to some larger unity. With an oratorical flourish Christopher Gadsden, of South Carolina, swept away colonial boundaries at the Stamp Act Congress: "There ought to be no New England man; no New York, known on the Continent; but all of us Americans."

Had English statesmen been more imaginative they might have welcomed such a combination of American colonies and embraced it within the larger imperial structure. This was a solution adopted many years later in the British Commonwealth of Nations with the grant of dominion status to Canada, Australia, and other portions of the empire. But in the eighteenth century many of the statesmen in power in Britain were noted for minds inflexibly set against democratizing tendencies in their own country and wholly unfamiliar with the deep-lying changes which had occurred in America. In the New World any remaining feudal elements in society were fast disappearing, while the colonial assemblies had been transformed into powerful legislative bodies as self-conscious of their power as was the House of Commons in England. The colonies were far more advanced politically and socially than the ruling classes of England imagined. The Americans could not longer be held in leading strings. "What a disjointed Empire is this!" wrote a New Yorker in 1767. "I am afraid it is too complex for so vast an Extent. At all Events America must rise." Tom Paine was soon to sum it up with his usual directness: "To know whether it be the interest of this continent to be Independent, we need only ask this easy simple question: Is it the interest of a man to be a boy all his life?"

European travelers in the colonies caught the contagion of this American effervescence. A recent arrival in New York, the Reverend Archibald Laidlie, wrote to his brother in Scotland that North America "bids fair for being one day the greatest Empire in the world." Prophets foretold that the center of gravity in the Atlantic community would shift to the New World. One of these seers asked archly, "What is to be the name of the city that will then give laws to Europe—New York or Philadelphia?"

These were the daydreams of the eighteenth century to be abundantly realized in a distant future. For the present, it was still London, however, that gave the laws to New York, Philadelphia, and all the other towns and villages and farms through the length and breadth of America.

BOOK 3

A NEW NATION IS BORN

THE LAST QUARTER of the eighteenth century was one of the great turning points in human history. Two world-shaking revolutions, the American and the French, announced the appearance of new democratic forces in the affairs of men. "The decree has gone forth and cannot now be recalled," said John Adams, "that a more equal liberty than has prevailed in other parts of the earth, must be established in America." The rattle of bullets, the rumble of men marching, and New World voices declaring that "all men are created equal" echoed in the streets and market places of the Old World.

The American Revolution undermined reactionary strength first in Britain. Eventually Ireland, France, Belgium, Italy, the German states, the Netherlands, Scandinavia, and ultimately South America felt the winds of revolution which blew from the far away forests and towns of America. A complete history of the American Revolution, said Adams, would be "a history of mankind during that epoch." And in his old age Adams, one of the chief architects of the Revolution, spoke of its continuing, unspent force: "Its effects and consequences have already been awful over a great part of the Globe; And when and where are they to cease?"

CHAPTER IX

The Gathering Storm

★ THE COSTS OF EMPIRE

The British Empire in 1763 was, in many ways, the greatest the world had yet seen. Self-sufficient, prosperous, it was far more enlightened in its handling of colonial relationships than its rival empires, French, Spanish, and Portuguese. Colonial autonomy in political and religious affairs was more widely enjoyed in Britain's empire than anywhere else. The promise of imperial harmony never seemed brighter, yet within a few years the empire dissolved in discord. For the moment its splendor was dazzling.

The celebrations greeting the close of the French and Indian War were over, but the bookkeepers of the empire, in London, had already been at work calculating its cost. The yearly bill for the British civil and military establishments in America was up from the prewar figure of £70,000 to £350,000. Great Britain's national debt after the war was £130,000,000 having more than doubled during the struggle. It seemed reasonable to expect that in the support of the vast empire, which had fallen to Britain, the American colonies would contribute their share to its upkeep and to the common defense.

That the administration of the colonies needed overhauling was obvious to London officials. A customs service which yearly collected £2,000, but which cost £7,000 to maintain, and whose officials connived at all sorts of illegal trade, was an expensive luxury. In America itself royal officials, like Governor Bernard of Massachusetts, were advising that the whole imperial administrative organization be completely renovated.

The war had shown the incapacity of the colonies to arrange for a satisfactory defense of the frontier; and the need for closer control of Indian trade was emphasized by intercolonial rivalries and threats of

Indian uprisings against further white encroachment. The smoke of settlers' clearings drifted over the contracting hunting grounds of the natives. Red men listened eagerly to the plans of Pontiac, chief of the Ottawa tribe, to turn back the whites. The threats of Indian uprisings became an ugly reality in Pontiac's conspiracy which brought fire and death to the Ohio Valley in 1763. From Niagara to Virginia the frontier felt the fury of savage assault, and all the western forts, except Detroit and Pittsburgh, fell to Pontiac. At length the Indians were beaten, but by British soldiers, not by Americans. Once again the inability of the colonies to co-operate satisfactorily in war strengthened the case for more rigorous imperial control.

That control, however, was to have a striking innovation. The navigation acts of earlier years were designed to regulate trade, the new measures were to raise revenue. The whole program for tighter colonial control had larger objectives than raising a revenue and providing for joint defense. It included the reassertion of the mercantilist principle that the colonies were to be the suppliers of raw materials for the homeland and the consumers of her profitable manufactured goods. It was all right for colonials to mine ore to be turned into iron, but they were not to make tools or weapons out of it. Restrictions were vain. America's iron industry had grown to such proportions by 1750 that English manufacturers were fearful of losing the colonial market. The average Englishman took it for granted that colonies existed to provide him with sugar and rice, tobacco and indigo, lumber and naval stores, and at the same time pay a good price for Britain's exports.

Britain's growing interest in the colonies as markets sharpened fear of colonial rivalry in manufacturing finished goods. The statistics of England's trade from the close of the seventeenth century pointed up Franklin's observation on the value to Britain's economy of an increasing population in America. In 1698, only one-eighth of England's colonial trade was with the middle colonies, New England and points north, the rest with the southern colonies and the West Indies; by 1767, provinces north of Maryland were taking two-thirds of England's colonial exports. American manufacturing and commerce were to be fitted into a pattern beneficial to the whole empire, but it was expected that the greater advantage would fall to England. It was assumed that British capitalists should be given preference in the grant of western lands and in the fur trade. To govern the colonies required many officials, and the British ruling class was ready to supply them. The whole attitude of the British official and commercial world was that America was to remain permanently inferior to England.

The new legislation designed to put in effect the ideas of mercantilism would involve an increasing number of officials. More ominously, British soldiers were, if necessary, to be quartered in the colonies, to see that the laws were enforced. The prospect of a military establishment in peace time was foreign to the English heritage, and British sympathizers of the colonists expressed alarm, fearing that the precedent in America might be extended in time to Britain herself. Dr. John Erskine, a Scottish minister with many American friends, said that "Nothing can so much tend to prevent the establishment of despotism in the British empire, as every part of that empire considering it as at once their interest and duty, to guard against encroachments on the right of every other part."

Erskine's apprehension at the possible subversion of traditional British liberties was felt even more strongly by Americans. The controversy over writs of assistance in 1761, in which James Otis won his place in the pantheon of Revolutionary heroes, sharpened these fears. Writs of this type were general search warrants (not naming specific places) authorizing examination of premises suspected of containing goods imported illegally. Otis argued in behalf of his Massachusetts merchant-clients that such writs (which had long been used in British official procedure) invaded privacy and did violence to the fundamental rights of Britons. In the courtroom "Otis was a flame of fire. . . . Every man of an immense crowded audience appeared . . . to go away, as I did," wrote the entranced John Adams, "ready to take arms against writs of Assistance. . . . Then and there, was the first scene of the first act of opposition to the arbitrary claims of Great Britain. Then and there, the child Independence was born."

Though Otis lost his plea against the legality of writs of assistance his appeal to the doctrine of natural rights and denial of parliament's competence to enforce its authority in the colonies focussed attention on the fundamental question: to what extent could parliament exercise sovereign powers within the whole empire?

As Otis in Massachusetts rested his argument on natural rights, so did Patrick Henry in Virginia two years later, in 1763. The Virginia assembly had passed a measure, the Two-Penny Act, relating to parson's salaries. The clergy, believing themselves victimized by the law, appealed successfully to the Privy Council in London for its veto. Against the right of the Council to exercise such veto, the sharp-featured intense orator made his dramatic address. It immediately lifted him from the ranks of county lawyers to a position as a leading spokesman for Virginia.

The King, said Henry, "by annulling or disallowing Acts of so salutary a nature, from being the Father of his people degenerated into a Tyrant, and forfeits all right to his subjects' obedience." Scorning cries of "Treason, Treason!" Henry went on to assert that people forbidden to make their own laws lived in bondage; and as for the clergy those "rapacious harpies would . . . snatch from the hearth of their honest parishioner his last hoe-cake, from the widow and her orphan children their last milch cow! the last bed, nay, the last blanket from the lying-in woman!" Inflamed by his oratory his hearers carried him triumphantly out of the courtroom.

The evolution of the British system of government in the eighteenth century was toward greater centralization of authority in the hands of parliament and the crown agencies subordinated to it. It was now using this authority in a maladroit effort to regulate imperial relations. The resolution of the British government to draw the reins tighter came at the very moment that the colonies were least willing to be disciplined. Proudly, in their colonial assemblies, they had developed conceptions of parliamentary privilege which, in the crisis of the 1760's, led them to claim full local legislative autonomy. In nearly every phase of their lives—economic activity, intellectual vigor, and political thinking—they had reached a maturity too far advanced to be bound by parliamentary coercion. Americans flexed their muscles as they counted their remarkable rate of growth, their population doubling every twenty-five years, while Old England had not doubled once in a century. True, England had 6,500,000 against 2,250,000 in the colonies, but the Americans with their eyes on the future felt that at no very distant date their land would be the center of empire.

The fact of the matter was that the colonial economy had grown too big to be handled in outworn mercantilist relationships. On the eve of the Revolution the colonies were operating more furnaces and forges than were England and Wales, and their production of pig and bar iron was larger than all of Great Britain's. American iron and steel manufactures were not behind in quality either. In shipping, too, America's activity was impressive. By 1775, just under a third of the ships used in the commerce of the mother country were built in the colonies where construction costs were half those in Britain. At the same time 75 per cent of all the commerce of the colonies was transported in their own ships, leaving to Great Britain little in the New World outside of the West Indies. England feared that the thousand fishing vessels that swarmed out of New England (1771) would drive Britain's fishermen from the Banks of Newfoundland. American competition was felt, too, in the production of pottery, stoneware, and glassware. Carolina's rice was so superior to the Mediterranean product that Europeans paid premium prices for it. Other crops from American fields, plantations and forests had long since made their deep impress on the Atlantic economy.

American interests in many respects directly opposed those of Britain. Colonial manufacturers and merchants wished to be eased of restrictions in order to develop their own enterprises and to trade freely with the world outside Great Britain; the navigation acts confined their trade to the motherland. Colonial big business competed for the western lands with British bigger business. Political plums which went to British favorites looked as juicy to hopeful colonials. And, as for contributing revenue for the upkeep of empire, Americans maintained they were already sharing that responsibility to the limit of their ability. They pointed to direct support in money and men, but even more emphatically to indirect contributions in port duties collected in England and the latter's monopoly of American trade. Pitt said that the profit to Great Britain from her trade with the colonies was £2,000,000 annually; "this," he admonished his fellow Englishmen, "is the fund that carried you triumphantly through the last war."

At the time that George Grenville, Chancellor of the Exchequer, was introducing into parliament the measures to raise a colonial revenue, a French traveler in the colonies reported that America "Can not be long subject to great Britain, nor indeed to any Distant power; its Extent is so great the Daily Encrease of its Inhabitants so Considerable, and haveing every thing necessary within themselves for . . . their own Defence, that no Nation whatsoever seems beter Calculated for Independency."

★ THE STAMP ACT IS "AGAINST MAGNA CHARTA"

Even if Grenville could have known about the Frenchman's observations he would not likely have been deterred by them. He was described as one of the ablest men in Britain, though with a legalistic, pedantic mind. He knew the rules, saw the financial requirements, and proceeded logically to apply his knowledge. He was recognized to be the most capable man of business in the House of Commons. In March, 1764, he introduced a measure (the Sugar Act) to tax certain colonial imports coming from places outside Great Britain—coffee, wine, silks—while the tax on sugar was raised. The duty on molasses was reduced by half to discourage smuggling from the French West Indies. As the colonial merchants were paying in bribes a penny and a half per gallon, surely, it was argued by the too shrewd Grenville, they could well pay threepence honestly. Country squires and merchants in parliament smiled approvingly at the reading of a budget aimed at relieving the former of taxes and increasing the profits of the latter.

The Massachusetts assembly expressed restrained opposition to the measure but New York's was vigorous. The assembly there claimed total exemption from taxation by parliament, both internal and external: "An Exemption from the Burthen of ungranted, involuntary Taxes must be the grand Principle of every free State." All impositions, it affirmed, "whether they be internal Taxes, or duties paid, for what we consume, equally diminish the Estates upon which they are charged. . . ." Otis, in a pamphlet which won wide support, warned Englishmen against the belief that an "external" tax on trade would be more acceptable to America than an "internal" direct tax.

The provisions of the Sugar Act were less disconcerting to the colonists than Grenville's expressed intention that, unlike former years, the taxes now would be collected. To make more certain of the act's enforcement, jurisdiction over cases involving customs revenue, formerly handled by colonial courts reluctant to convict, was now given to the admiralty courts. If the act were rigidly enforced the distilling trade in New England, which smuggled most of its molasses from the French and Spanish West Indies, would be severely hit. The British sugar islands could not supply all of New England's needs. It was the favorable balance of trade with these West Indian islands which supplied the American colonists with specie to pay off their debts owed to Britain. No wonder that John Adams in retrospect said that "rum was an essential ingredient in the American Revolution."

As if the imposition of new duties were not enough to disrupt business in America, parliament added to the injury by passing another measure the same year, the Currency Act, forbidding the colonists to issue paper money. This measure, designed to protect creditors against forcible acceptance of inflated currency, aroused less antagonism than the Sugar Act, but because it deprived the colonists of a needed medium of exchange its ultimate effects on trade and industry were equally severe. Business bankruptcies mounted in New England; church collections showed more copper than silver; and a great decline occurred in the number of ships clearing for the West Indies.

The discontent of the colonists in 1764 was mild compared with their anger the next year when the Stamp Act was passed. England herself had long been used to stamp taxes, and there seemed to be nothing unusual in extending them to the colonies. There was no intimation in parliament, that February day in 1765, of the uproar which would soon follow. Horace Walpole recorded of parliamentary proceedings, "Nothing of note, except one slight day on the American taxes." A little flurry in the House of Commons was created by an exchange between Charles Townshend and Colonel Isaac Barré, who had fought at Wolfe's side at Quebec. Townshend asked testily whether "these American children, planted by our care, nourished up by our indulgence . . . and protected by our arms" would be so ungrateful as not to contribute their small share to imperial revenues? Colonel Barré sprang to his feet to defend the colonists whom he praised as "Sons of Liberty." *"They* planted by *your* care! No your oppression planted them in America," he threw back at Townshend. "They fled from your tyranny to a then uncultivated, inhospitable country, where they exposed themselves to almost all the hardships to which human nature is liable. *They* nourished up by *your* indulgence! They grew by your neglect of them. . . . *They* protected by *your* arms! They have nobly taken up arms in your defense; have exerted a valor amidst their constant and laborious industry, for the defense of a country whose frontier was drenched in blood, while its interior parts yielded all its little savings to your emolument."

While parliament was only momentarily stirred from its drowsiness by Barré's speech, Americans long remembered it. But while grateful for his words of praise, the colonists needed little instruction in the defense of their liberties. And they felt that parliament had invaded the rights of free-born Englishmen—which they considered themselves to be even though they resided in the colonies. "British subjects, by removing to America," said Franklin, "do not thereby lose their native rights." In Boston town meetings, under the direction of Samuel Adams, challenging questions were raised: "If our trade may be taxed, why not our lands? Why not the produce of our lands, and everything we possess or make use of? This we apprehend annihilates our charter right to govern and tax ourselves." Americans did not sit in parliament, and, if taxes were laid upon them without any representation there, were they "not reduced from the character of free subjects to the miserable state of tributary slaves?"

While Sam Adams and others were concerned about constitutional questions most influential people (including Franklin at first), assumed that the new laws would take effect, and they were hardly prepared for the storm which soon broke over their heads. Patrick Henry, a young member from the back country of Virginia, loosed his oratorical lightning in the House of Burgesses, meeting in Williamsburg in May, 1765. Introducing several resolutions, he declared that Virginians were not bound to obey any laws designed to impose taxation upon them, other than acts of their own legislature. Taxation without representation was dangerous and threatened American liberties. Virginia's lead electrified the colonies, though there were misgivings as to its treasonable nature. Newspapers in the northern towns printed the Virginia resolutions (not quite as inflammatory as Henry's phrases), and out of the mounting excitement came a Massachusetts proposal to hold a Congress in New York in October. The Stamp Act was scheduled to go into force in November.

The stamp tax was to be imposed on newspapers, advertisements, almanacs, legal documents, bills of lading, notes and bonds; in short it fell most heavily upon the very people who were most articulate in the community—merchants, lawyers, and publishers. (Governor Colden of New York wrote angrily, "Associations of lawyers are the most dangerous of any next to the military.") In the summer of 1765 these men, hardly firebrands, organized to resist the tax. They resolved to import no goods from Great Britain, not even the black clothes for mourning; and they joined Sons of Liberty organizations.

The movement which started as a comparatively orderly repudiation of parliamentary legislation quickly became a violent mob action destroying the property of crown officials and threatening their lives. A Boston mob, many of whom were suffering from unemployment attributed to British revenue measures, marched through the town's narrow twisted streets until it reached the beautiful home of Lieutenant-Governor Thomas Hutchinson. They sacked it, plundered its furnishings, drank its wine, and scattered through the streets the books and manuscripts on American history that Hutchinson had been collecting for thirty years. Through all the colonies orators denounced the Stamp Act as "against Magna Charta," while mobs destroyed the stamps and forced stamp agents to resign. Popular leaders of Sons of Liberty, like Isaac Sears and John Lamb of New York and "Captain" Ebenezer Mackintosh and William Molineaux of Boston, arose to lead street demonstrations against the Stamp Act. Andrew Oliver, the Boston agent and brother-in-law of Hutchinson, was brought before the Sons of Liberty meeting, under the famed elm, the Liberty Tree. With 2,000 people listening he gave his promise, under oath, never to sell a stamp.

Delegates from nine colonies, twenty-seven men in all, assembled in New York in the fall of 1765. They included men who had already gained fame in the controversy with Britain, notably James Otis of Massachusetts, and others whose names were soon to be known through all America, among them Gadsden of South Carolina and John Dickinson of Pennsylvania. These men were no street rioters; their language was even more moderate than that of the Virginia resolutions. But while they spoke of their loyalty to the king and the government of Great Britain they continued to affirm that the Stamp Act subverted "the rights and liberties of the colonies." The colonists, they repeated, should not be taxed except by their own legislatures. To parliament was conceded the right to legislate but not to tax.

A cloud of misunderstanding about the proper relationship of the colonies to Britain was darkening men's minds. "All the political evils in America arise from the want of ascertaining the relation between Great Britain and the American colonies," wrote Governor Francis Bernard of Massachusetts, in November, 1765. "Hence it is that ideas of that relation are formed in Britain and America, so very repugnant and contradictory to each other. In Britain the American Governments are considered as Corporations empowered to make by-laws, existing only during the pleasure of Parliament . . . and hath at any time a power to dissolve them. . . . In America they claim . . . to be perfect states, no otherwise dependent upon Great Britain than by having the same King; which having compleat legislatures within themselves, are no ways subject to that of Great Britain; which in such instances as it has heretofore exercised a legislative power over them has usurped it. In a difference so very wide who shall determine?"

The debate raged in America; Liberty Boys rallied one another from Boston to Charleston, while business in Britain, already suffering from a postwar recession, languished as a result of the American boycott of English goods. A merchant in Bristol trading to America, moaned that "The Avenues of Trade are all shut up. . . . We have no Remittances, and are at our Witts End for Want of Money." The debts of £4,000,000 "owing to British merchants on the part of colonials were now wielded as a club with telling force." *

Before the end of 1765 Americans were reported to have canceled £700,000 in orders, while other commissions were to be completed only on repeal of the Stamp Act. Through the long, gloomy winter manufacturers all over England waited for the orders that did not come. Dejected iron workers in Birmingham and Sheffield shambled along the streets in idleness. Over the waterfront of once busy ports like Bristol, where American ships were wont to dock, hung an empty stillness. Bankruptcy stared British businessmen in the face, and the unemployed muttered threateningly in the streets. Petitions for relief poured in on parliament from the whole country.

Pitt rejoiced that America had resisted: "Three millions of people, so dead to all feelings of liberty, as voluntarily to submit to be slaves, would have been fit instruments to make slaves of the rest. . . ." The Stamp Act, he urged, should be repealed immediately. Its defenders,

* L. H. Gipson, *The Coming of the Revolution,* 1763–1775 (New York: Harper and Brothers, 1954), p. 107.

very conscious of the tax load they were carrying in Britain, claimed that it was not burdensome on colonials, one shilling per capita annually, that is, one-third of a day's income of an American worker. But such arguments missed the point completely. Colonials did not plead inability to pay; they claimed the constitutional right *not* to pay.

To stave off the mounting chaos parliament repealed the Stamp Act early in March, 1766, to the cheers of British traders who waited through the long night to watch the vote. Parliament maintained in a Declaratory Act, however, its right to "make laws and statutes of sufficient force and validity to bind the colonies in all cases whatsoever."

Americans generally ignored the Declaratory Act and greeted with noisy celebration the repeal of the Stamp Act, drinking unending toasts to Pitt and Barré, British friends of the colonies, all the while declaring fervently their loyalty to King George III. In Boston, John Hancock's wine flowed freely for gentry and "commonalty" alike. Hundreds of men, women, and children converged on the famed Liberty Tree with their lighted lanterns which they hung like fluttering fireflies from its branches. In England factories were reopened, bells were rung in seaport towns, and captains readied their ships for the rush to America with eagerly awaited goods. A deceptive calm settled briefly over the Anglo-American world.

★ "NO REPRESENTATION, NO LEGISLATION"

After a series of quick changes in the British ministry Charles Townshend, witty and indiscreet, tricky and generally loose-tongued from too much drink, became Chancellor of the Exchequer in 1767. He practically ran the ministry in the absence of his ailing superior, William Pitt. Although he was among those who had voted for repeal of the Stamp Act he did not believe that Grenville's policy should be dropped. Townshend was convinced that the success of his program would be more easily achieved by having the salaries of governors and judges paid by England from revenues raised in America. These officials would thus be freed of dependence upon colonial assemblies, whose control of the purse had long been a whip over governors.

Despite Otis' warning that external as well as internal taxes were unacceptable, Townshend, misled by Franklin into believing that taxes on imports might be more palatable, proposed only external duties: on paint, lead, glass, paper, and tea. To insure the collection of duties and to tighten up the whole customs service, Townshend provided for the establishment in Massachusetts of a Board of Customs Commissioners, a fundamental reform in colonial administration. The commissioners were to earn their salaries from the duties they were to collect, clearly an open invitation to "customs racketeering." In the judgment of Professor O. M. Dickerson,* the measure creating the Customs Commissioners was "England's most fateful decision," for from it may be traced the sequence of events which thrust Americans toward independence. The colonists disliked the Townshend Acts almost as heartily as they did the Stamp Act.

In New York the assembly was dissolved for refusing to provide food and shelter for troops in accord with the Quartering Act (colonials thought it an indirect tax), while not long after, the legislatures of Massachusetts and Virginia were also dissolved for their opposition to the revenue measures of Townshend. Voices in the colonies which had been shouting "No Representation, No Taxation" were beginning to cry "No Representation, No Legislation."

Moderate gentlemen, like John Dickinson, the lawyer from Philadelphia, did not go so far—yet. In his *Letters from a Farmer* he sought to justify American opposition to the Townshend Acts by drawing a subtle distinction between duties for regulation of trade which were permissible, and duties for revenue, which were not. The former, Dickinson conceded, had long been the right of parliament in administering the colonies, but the imposition of duties for revenue were taxes, and hence "unconstitutional." Americans, said Dickinson, ought "firmly to believe . . . that unless the most watchful attention be exerted, a new servitude may be slipped upon us under the sanction of usual and respectable terms." Apart from Pitt, parliament was in no mood to have boundaries set to its authority.

Dickinson's *Letters from a Farmer* were published in newspapers and read throughout the colonies where they won strong support from businessmen. But lawyers, arguing the fine points of constitutional procedure, were carrying most of the colonists beyond their depth. Even Franklin confessed, "I am not yet master of the idea these . . . writers have of the relation between Britain and her colonies." Then with his usual directness he said, "The more I have thought and read on the subject, the more I find myself confirmed in opinion, that no middle ground can be well maintained, I mean not clearly with intelligible arguments. Something might be made of either of the extremes; that Parliament has a power to make *all laws* for us, or that it has a power to make *no laws* for us; and I think the arguments for the latter more numerous and weighty, than those for the former."

While publicists were discussing the extent of parliamentary authority, merchants hostile to the Townshend acts once again banded together

* *The Navigation Acts and the American Revolution* (Philadelphia: University of Pennsylvania Press, 1951), pp. 198, 298–99.

to boycott English goods. Colonials wore homespun, and an unpainted house was a sign of patriotism. A strong impetus was given to native manufactures as a result of nonimportation agreements. Though the latter were not observed with equal firmness everywhere, imports fell off as much as 80 per cent. New York's imports, worth £482,000 in 1767–68, fell to £74,000, in the next year. The rioting and violence connected with the Stamp Act three years earlier were generally absent, except in New England.

In Boston a group of middle-class people, comprising merchants like John Hancock, lawyers of John Adams' type, journalists like Benjamin Edes, and prosperous artisans like Paul Revere, met regularly to talk politics and keep the fires of controversy alight. Sam Adams, then in his forties, was the most prominent of the leaders. His father had been ruined by the failure of the Land Bank scheme more than a score of years before, and the younger Adams could never recoup the family's modest wealth. Sam Adams was not interested in business; his passion was politics. His genius lay in formulating plans of political action and in manipulating the men whose task it was to carry them out, either in legislative chambers or in demonstrations on Boston streets. Boston in the decade after 1765 seemed almost to be governed by mob rule, but as one observer noted, it was "a trained mob." Many men of wealth and standing in the community were so incensed at British interference with their trade that they lent support to organized mob rule.

Customs officials were intimidated, mobs breaking their windows and hanging them in effigy from the Liberty Tree. A large scale riot broke out when the customs commissioners, in a systematic campaign of harassment against Hancock, seized his sloop "Liberty" on a technical violation of the law. For the protection of officials and to make sure that the laws were carried out, Governor Bernard asked that British troops be sent to Boston. "On Friday, Sept. 30, 1768," wrote Paul Revere, "the ships of war came up the harbour and anchored round the Town; their cannons loaded . . . as for a regular siege." On Saturday the soldiers debarked "and marched with insolent parade drums beatting, fifes playing, up King Street each soldeir having recived six-teen rounds of powder and ball." Sam Adams and other Sons of Liberty decided for the time being against a policy of violence, but made it plain to the British redcoats that they were very unwelcome. A town meeting in Boston had already gone on record with the declaration that main-taining a standing army amongst them "without their consent . . . would be an infringement of their natural, constitutional and charter Rights; and the employing of such Army for the enforcing of Laws made without the consent of the People, in Person, or by their Representatives would be a Grievance."

On the other hand the presence of the soldiers reassured government officials and the more conservative people of the community, who were fearful that the rioting aimed at British representatives might be extended to their own persons and property as well. Apparently in other communities, too, as the months passed, conservatism was strengthened with the stricter enforcement of the customs regulations and the declining enthusiasm of many merchants for nonimportation. The support that the American cause had received a few years earlier from British merchants was, at this time, less in evidence. Englishmen had found new outlets for their goods in Europe and Asia, and were therefore less pinched than formerly by the American boycott. The trade of Britain was, however, sufficiently hurt to cause her merchants to apply for relief to parliament. In response the Townshend Acts were repealed, all except the duty of threepence per pound on tea, and this was retained to remind the colonists that parliament still had the authority to tax them. This action of parliament came on March 5, 1770. By coincidence the same date marks a grim day in Boston's history.

★ "BOSTON MASSACRE"

British troops in Boston, though encouraging to officialdom, were annoying to most of the people. By their presence alone they suggested compulsion and were an affront to civil liberty. Friction between soldier and civilian was constant. The people, wrote a highly placed contemporary, "had been used to answer to the call of the town watch in the night, yet they did not like to answer to the frequent calls of the sentinels posted at the barracks . . . and either a refusal to answer or an answer accompanied with irritating language, endangered the peace of the town." It appeared to Puritan Boston, accustomed to a quiet Sunday, that the soldiers took particular delight in making noise with fife and drum on the sabbath. Another source of bad feeling was the practice of the soldiers to work for little pay at odd jobs for civilian employers, thus angering workmen of the town. Tavern brawls were common and running fights between civilians and soldier workmen added to the mounting tension. Little boys shouted insults at the redcoats, calling them "bloody backs" and yelling "Lobsters for sale." By March 5, the nerves of soldiers and townsmen were getting rawer by the hour.

Angry civilians were baiting hot-tempered soldiers. Boys threw snowballs at sentries. That night a larger crowd than usual was out to taunt the soldiers. Rumors flew through the streets that the soldiers were slashing the people. Sailors and longshoremen joined the throng in the square before the customhouse. They now began to press against a lone sentry standing guard. He called for help and a small group of soldiers rushed to his rescue. The mob was momentarily quiet and then pressed forward again. Suddenly out of the darkness came the order to fire; four Bostonians (some say three) were killed outright, a fifth died a few hours later. Among the fallen was a seaman, Crispus Attucks, tall, powerful, and black, in whose veins flowed Indian blood. Attucks, conceded an unfriendly John Adams, was "the hero of the night," attacking the British soldiers with reckless courage. The dead were buried in a common grave after a procession through the town. Thousands walked in solemn silence behind the hearses while church bells tolled in Boston and neighboring towns. Though the British soldiers were acquitted of the charge of murder after an able defense by John Adams and Josiah Quincy, the community was horror-struck at the "Boston Massacre," and for years thereafter commemorated the bitter day.

★ THE "PROCLAMATION LINE"

While merchants and workingmen in the East had been engaged in defying British trade regulations, settlers in the West were also undermining the authority of parliament. An important part of the program of reorganizing the empire included the pacification and development of the region beyond the Alleghanies which had been won in the French and Indian War. The Indians, as Pontiac's conspiracy showed, were a grave threat to the English settlements. Other troublesome problems were arising; one was the regulation of trade with the Indians; another was the conflicting claims of the separate colonies to the western lands; and finally, and perhaps most important, was the question of who should exploit the western region. The latter problem was complicated by the rivalries of land companies formed in America and England. Parliament decided to freeze the existing situation until a detailed plan could be elaborated to deal with these various difficulties. It did so in the Royal Proclamation of 1763, which drew a line on a map running along the top of the Alleghanies, and forbade the colonists to settle in the region west of the boundary. The crown assumed sole right to dispose of the western lands. The proclamation made provision also for setting up the provinces of East and West Florida, and for Quebec, in Canada.

Though the English ministry may have planned the Proclamation Line as a temporary measure, the Americans saw in it a deliberate attempt to stem the westward movement and to benefit English land speculators and fur traders. British officers at Fort Pitt were ordered to keep white hunters and squatters out of the Indian reserve. Settlers saw in the line a barrier to the land-hungry whose appetites had been whetted by the glowing reports brought back by Indian traders. The latter were angry at a provision in the proclamation requiring them to be licensed by royal officials. American speculators, busy in forming companies to take up huge grants of western land, were afraid they would be shut out by British companies with greater influence at court. Pioneers, traders, merchants, and owners of large tracts of land eager for more—all were convinced that Britain had deliberately set out to curb the liberty of Americans to do what they wished on the frontier. It was, in effect, a revolutionary departure in their lives to be excluded from almost any lands they desired and no decrees were likely to dam the westward-moving flood.

Royal officials in the colonies were better informed about the spirit of Americans than line-drawing ministers in London. Thus Governor Dunmore wrote from Virginia in 1772: "I have learnt from experience that the established Authority of any government in America, and the policy of Government at home, are both insufficient to restrain the Americans; and they do and will remove as their avidity and restlessness incite them . . . In this Colony," continued Dunmore, "Proclamations have been published from time to time to restrain them. But impressed from their earliest infancy with Sentiments and habits, very different from those acquired by persons of a Similar condition in England, they do not conceive that Government has any right to forbid their taking possession of a Vast tract of Country" (either uninhabited or occupied by a small number of Indians whom the colonists despise).

Dunmore knew what he was talking about. The trek west, which the French and Indian War interrupted, was now gaining momentum. Daniel Boone, agent of the energetic promoter, Judge Richard Henderson of North Carolina, had been hunting in the choicest regions of Kentucky. He spent the better part of a year roaming the forest, living off the country, and dodging Indians on the warpath. In these months he ranged over much of the bluegrass country and learned more about the region than any of his white contemporaries. He and his companions, known as "Long Hunters" (because of their prolonged trips), were the most skilful of white men in the forest. They read its message in footprints and broken twigs; its wild game and fish fed them; its animal hides furnished them with coonskin caps, leather hunting-shirts, and buckskin leggings. In their belts they carried a hatchet and hunting knife. With their long rifle and well supplied with powder and lead, they were lords of the woods. Their tales of the wonders of "Kaintuck" filled the minds of prospective settlers back east. And when the settlers came to the end of their trip over the Wilderness Road, which spilled them into the bluegrass country, they too felt the singing heart of the "Long Hunters." "Perhaps no Adventureor Since the days of donquicksotte," wrote one pioneer, "ever felt So Cheerful & Ilated in prospect, every heart abounded with Joy & excitement."

Settlers from Virginia followed the streams into northeastern Tennessee. From Pennsylvania and New Jersey the pioneers went overland to the upper Ohio, whence they boarded flatboats for the downstream journey. The westward tide rose fast. George Croghan, the famous Indian trader, said that during 1769 over 4,000 families settled beyond the mountains, while through the spring and summer months the next year roads were lined with wagons moving to the Ohio. By 1771 it was estimated that 10,000 families had settled along the Ohio and its tributary streams. Back in Connecticut where Ezra Stiles kept proud watch over America's growth he wrote in his diary: "The Wilderness of America is all alive with the Travels of Settlers." The Proclamation Line of 1763 had vanished in the derisive hoots of pioneers.

★ CONSERVATIVES VERSUS RADICALS

Thus the disregard for British regulations, in both eastern and western sections of America, promoted a general contempt for authority. Herein, however, lay the very reason for the growing caution of normally conservative men, who reasoned that contempt for authority was contagious —and might spread to contempt for themselves. Moreover wealthy colonials even risked losing the support of crown officials in dealing with local lower-class discontent. When antirent riots broke out against great landlords in New York, right after the Stamp Act disturbances, General Gage looked upon them as a just retribution visited upon the "Rich and Most Powerfull People" in the colony. "They certainly deserve any Losses they may sustain, for it is the work of their own Hands," Gage wrote. "They first Sowed the Seeds of Sedition amongst the People and taught them to rise in opposition to the Laws. What now happens is a Consequence that might be easily foreseen after the Tumults about the Stamp Act, and I could wish that this uneasiness amongst the People had happened just at that Time."

Elsewhere in the colonies conservative elements were threatened by many dangers. The old discontent of back country against eastern town and tidewater was further inflamed by the added grievances of thousands of westward-moving pioneers. In Pennsylvania the hostility of frontiersmen against the east for failure to provide adequate defense almost lead to civil war; in North Carolina war between east and west did break out.

In North Carolina the western areas, settled by Scotch-Irish Presbyterians, were bitter over unequal taxation, eastern land speculators, the expense of litigation, and discrimination against religious dissenters. The rebellious people were ranchers, farmers, rugged individualists all. These men, called "Regulators" (vigilance committees originally formed to combat local crime), demanded more paper money to raise the prices of their crops, debt cases to be tried by a jury with no lawyers participating, and voting to be by a ballot rather than by show of hands. Large-scale hostilities occurred in May, 1771, at the "Battle of the Alamance," when 2,000 of the Regulators were defeated by Governor William Tryon and the provincial militia. Though beaten, and then granted amnesty, the back countrymen continued to nurse their grievances; when a few years later the east took up arms against Great Britain, many of the frontiersmen remained loyal to the crown almost, it seemed, in order to wreak vengeance upon the victors in the civil war. Many of the defeated Regulators sought sanctuary in what is now Tennessee.

Judge Henderson, who had been threatened by the Regulators, spoke of their "total subversion of the Constitution." In his own Transylvania settlement in Kentucky, a few years later, frontiersmen mocked his efforts to transfer to that region an outmoded proprietary form of government, with annual quitrents payable to him and his associates.

In South Carolina civil conflict was narrowly averted when the easterners satisfied the demands of the west for more satisfactory law enforcement. Horses and cattle thieves and other lawless elements kept the region turbulent. Westerners, who had to travel long distances to courts, were mollified by the establishment of additional courts in their region. The pleasant life of aristocratic Charleston was given a serious jolt when the mechanics and tradesmen forced the local merchants to join the nonimportation agreement against the Townshend Acts.

What was happening in South Carolina was duplicated in northern provinces as well. Small traders, clerks, craftsmen, sailors, and laborers, who made up the group identified as "mechanics and tradesmen," were participating more aggressively in public affairs either through the suffrage, which some of them had, or in mass meetings. In New England the conservatives, fearing sedition, disapproved of town meetings where "the lowest Mechanics discussed the most important points of government with the utmost freedom." A hostile official in Massachusetts wrote that "the lower part of the people" now had "such a sense of their importance that a gentleman does not meet with what used to be common civility, and we are sinking into perfect barbarism." New York had an old tradition of political mass meetings, and in this period of social disturbance mechanics' candidates were presented to the public gatherings. In Pennsylvania a letter to a newspaper credited the "laborious Farmer and Tradesman" with supporting liberty, and complained that the ruling class did not wish them to "intermeddle in State affairs." A more frightening prospect faced conservatives, notably in Pennsylvania, of a combination of farmers and urban workers against landlord-merchant domination.

Under the middle-class leadership of Sam Adams, Gadsden, and the New Yorkers Lamb, Sears, and Alexander McDougall, the unprivileged, however, did "intermeddle in State affairs." The controversy with Great Britain over legislation and taxation was thus paralleled by an internal conflict within the colonies between democratic and conservative forces. Men of wealth in America led the movement for home rule, taking it for granted that they would be the rulers, but other Americans were challenging this easy assumption.

★ A CALM INTERLUDE

Conservatives, seeking an orderly accommodation with the mother country, were gaining the upper hand in 1770. Business prosperity returned, customs were being collected, smuggling was restrained. Merchants were even paying taxes on imported tea and molasses. "The people," wrote an American official, "appear to be weary of their altercations with the mother country"; and he added that discretion on both sides would restore harmony between the colonies and Great Britain. Rioting had ceased and the Sons of Liberty became less conspicuous. Lawyers were less unified than in the Stamp Act controversy, and conservative opinion in newspapers was more boldly expressed. Even in Massachusetts, the hotbed of agitation, tempers cooled after the Boston Massacre. Thomas Hutchinson was now governor and, for the moment, not unpopular. He noted that a small group was still "sour enough, yet when they seek matter for protests, remonstrances, they are puzzled where to charge the grievances which they look for." Hutchinson observed that "Hancock and most of the party are quiet, and all of them, except Adams, abate of their violence. Adams would push the Continent into a rebellion tomorrow, if it was in his power."

But Samuel Adams' power was not yet strong enough. In fact his influence waned, though he kept alive the bitter animosity between himself and Governor Hutchinson. The latter, though a man of honor, courage, and learning, was without tact, and his blood was too ostentatiously blue for most of his fellow citizens. And the governor, instead of ignoring the attacks of Adams, was drawn into damaging disputes over the power of parliament to legislate for the colonies. Adams, through mass meetings, resolutions, and newspaper articles, kept the political pot boiling. But for the mass of people controversies over constitutional issues were arid; their emotions could not easily be roused except by events involving direct, physical action.

One such event occurred in June, 1772, when a customs vessel, the "Gaspee," pursuing a suspect ran aground near Providence, Rhode Island. The commander and crew of the small warship had earned, by their petty exactions and thievery, an evil name among local inhabitants. During the night she was boarded and burned by dozens of colonials, including the prominent merchant, John Brown. A court of inquiry, walled off by silent Rhode Islanders, could never discover the names of any of the many men who had participated. The "Gaspee" incident was very limited in its repercussions, and there was no strong exploitation of it by radical leaders. After all, the alleged symbol of "despotism," the "Gaspee," had been destroyed, and people could not be frightened by beaten "tyranny."

More damaging to amicable relations between Great Britain and the colonies was Governor Hutchinson's announcement to the Massachusetts assembly that he no longer would accept his salary from them; in the future the customs revenues would supply it. The king would, in effect, be responsible for the governor's salary. Soon after, it was disclosed that judges of the Superior Court would also be paid by the crown. Freeing the governor and judges from financial dependence on the legislature was a direct blow to the power it had long enjoyed; its response could have been predicted. It feared, said the assembly, "a despotic administration of government." Radicals who had been biding their time now formed in Boston committees of correspondence which soon spread to other colonies, and waited for something more to turn up. It did. First, private letters of Hutchinson to London denouncing the behavior of Massachusetts as seditious were published. Second, the British government, in 1773, gave the English East India Company a monopoly on the sale of tea to the colonies.

★ THE BOSTON TEA PARTY

The East India Company, which had built an empire in Asia and had great influence in Britain, was having serious financial difficulties. Its warehouses were bulging with tea, 17,000,000 pounds of it. By reason of tax concessions by the government the company was able to price it below the usual cost, and made arrangements to sell the tea in the American colonies through its own agents, bypassing the regular merchants, who would thus be frozen out of a profitable business. Immediately the cry of monopoly was raised, forecasts of other destructive commercial monopolies filled the press, and colonial merchants in their anger found themselves once again linked arm in arm with political radicals who kept the mails busy through their committees of correspondence.

Like ancient Puritans whose obsession was sin, committed or anticipated, their descendants were obsessed with thoughts of tyranny, real and fancied. The East India Company, it was said, had drained Asia of its wealth; they now "cast their eyes on America . . . to exercise their talents of rapine, oppression, and cruelty. The monopoly of tea, is . . . but a small part of the plan they have formed to strip us of our property." A patriot thanked God Americans were not degraded natives of Asia, "but British subjects, who are born to liberty, who know its worth, and who prize it high."

When the tea arrived in the colonies (the shipments were small) radicals were awaiting its coming. In Charleston it was landed but promptly placed in a warehouse to remain unsold until it was eventually auctioned off for the benefit of the government during the Revolution. At Philadelphia and New York the tea was not even put ashore, but was returned to England. In Boston a livelier reception awaited the unwelcome tea. Placards announcing its arrival were posted over the town declaring "The Detestable Tea" to be "the worst of Plagues"; Bostonians were warned the "Hour of Destruction . . . Stares you in the Face."

The consignees in Boston, among whom were Governor Hutchinson's sons, insisted on unloading the tea, but the townspeople kept watch night and day to see that none of it got ashore. After fruitless negotiation with Hutchinson, a band of men with blackened faces and disguised as Indians boarded the three tea ships and threw the tea into the harbor. Boston radicals were exultant; the next day John Adams wrote in his diary: "This Destruction of the Tea is so bold, so daring, so firm, intrepid & inflexible, and it must have so important Consequences, and so lasting, that I cannot but consider it as an epocha in History."

England felt differently. Even such friends of the colonies as Pitt and Barré deplored the violence, while King George III and his Prime Minister Lord North were bent on punishing Boston. Parliament passed a series of measures, the Coercive Acts: the Boston Port Act closed the harbor until the town should pay for the destroyed tea; changes were introduced into the government of Massachusetts which concentrated more power in the hands of the governor; officials indicted for a capital offense could be tried in England to avoid judgment by a local jury; and troops were to be quartered on the inhabitants. These "Intolerable Acts," particularly closing the port, meant the destruction of Boston, for she lived by and from the sea. Boston was to be cut off from the rest of

America and put, so to speak, in solitary confinement. General Gage, besides being chief of the military forces, now became head of the civil government as well. Governor Hutchinson left for England, to die there, an unhappy, homesick exile.

Boston appealed for support to the other colonies, and it came swiftly. It came in the form of sympathetic resolutions; and it came in thousands of bushels of wheat and corn from Virginia, cargoes of rice from Charleston, and flour from the middle colonies. The radicals now had the whip hand in the colonies, for by universal support of Boston, nearly everyone seemed committed to sanctioning violence. In Britain moderates urging conciliation were shunted aside, and stubborn men, disregarding warnings that the Americans were on the verge of rebellion, determined to follow through a policy of repression.

The act closing the port of Boston was to go into effect on June 1, 1774. A few days before, on May 27, the call had gone out from Virginia for a colonial congress. The colonies agreed to send delegates to meet in Philadelphia on September 5 in the first Continental Congress to consult upon their "present unhappy State."

CHAPTER X

Independence

Three days after the call had gone out on May 27, 1774, for a Continental Congress, Nicholas Cresswell, a Tory who was traveling in Virginia, wrote in his journal: "Dined at Colonel Harrison's. Nothing talked of but the blockade of Boston Harbour. The people seem much exasperated at the proceedings of the Ministry and talk as if they were determined to dispute the matter with the sword." Ten weeks later, when John Adams left Boston for Philadelphia, he was able to report that everywhere along the way people were "very firm" in their support of Massachusetts against the government of Great Britain. The agitation against offensive legislation had come to a head in a gathering which, for the first time in American history, could be spoken of as a truly national meeting. It was outside the bounds of constitutional procedure, and was therefore truly revolutionary in nature. All the colonies, except Georgia, whose governor prevented the naming of delegates, sent representatives, fifty-five in all, to the Congress scheduled to meet in September at Philadelphia.

While Adams found that sentiment was "very firm" against Britain, he also learned that opinions differed as to the steps to be taken to surmount the crisis. On his stopover in New York he heard that merchants were reluctant to enter a new nonimportation agreement, and were fearful of civil war. Another group, he was told, were "intimidated lest the leveling spirit of the New England colonies should propagate itself into New York." He made every effort to study the men who were to play important roles. The representatives from New York to the Congress included John Jay, an able lawyer, and Isaac Low, who it was said, "will profess attachment to the cause of liberty, but his sincerity is doubted." Of other New York leaders, Adams thought James Duane had a "sly, surveying eye . . . and very artful," while Philip Livingston was "a downright, straightforward man." It did not take Adams long to discover that in all the colonies there were seekers of government favors "exactly like the tribe in . . . Massachusetts, of Hutchinsonian Addressers." To his disgust some of these men had been named as delegates to the Congress.

In Philadelphia Adams was greatly cheered by the quality of Virginia's delegation, the "most spirited and consistent" of them all. George Washington and Patrick Henry, the Demosthenes of America, were among them, and so was Richard Henry Lee, a "masterly man," and ready for strong measures. Gadsden, as always, seemed most violent, willing to attack General Gage in Boston at once. From the middle colonies came some of the most cautious of the delegates, who were wary of being pushed too fast and too far by the men from Massachusetts. In a terse summary of opinion at Philadelphia, Adams said it was "one third Whig; another Tory; the rest mongrel."

Even Whig sentiment, however, was far from united. The much admired Lee of Virginia, it appeared, was prepared for vigorous measures only because he was sure that "the same ship which carries hence the resolutions will bring back the redress." He and most others at the Congress were not yet ready, Nicholas Cresswell thought, "to dispute the matter with the sword."

★ THE "RADICAL CHANGE" IN COLONIAL OPINION

Though they were not yet ready to take up the sword, the time for speaking and passing resolutions was rapidly running out. The "war of the quill" was soon to be ended in a blaze of gunfire on Lexington common. But the fighting itself was not considered to be the Revolution. John Adams, in his old age, said that the Revolution "was in the minds and hearts of the people, and in the union of the colonies; both of which were substantially effected before hostilities commenced." The real American Revolution, he maintained, was "the radical change in the principles, opinions, sentiments and affections of the people" toward Great Britain.

What had caused this "radical change" in the feelings of people toward the mother country? It came from a combination of many factors—economic, social, political, religious, psychological. Merchants and manufacturers had been annoyed, then irritated and finally infuriated, by parliament's measures to tax commerce and prohibit production. "A colonist cannot make a button, a horseshoe, nor a hobnail, but some sooty ironmonger or respectable button maker of Britain shall bawl and squall that his honor's worship is most egregiously maltreated, injured, cheated and robbed by the rascally American republicans."

While Americans were resentful of political and economic restrictions, they objected even more strongly to any reminders of immaturity. Captain Evelyn, a British officer serving in Boston, wrote to his father in February, 1775, noting that the true cause of the Revolution was to be found "in the nature of mankind . . . I think that it proceeds from a new nation, feeling itself wealthy, populous, and strong; and that they being impatient of restraint, are struggling to throw off that dependency which is so irksome to them." * Though the fact was hidden from British officialdom, America had attained her majority.

In the South, aristocratic plantation owners, though well-versed in the ancient battles against Greek and Roman tyranny, might hardly be expected to lead a revolution. But they, too, had grievances against British merchants who allegedly underpriced the tobacco, rice, and other products sent from the colonies, and overpriced the articles shipped to America in exchange. Planters, living comfortably, even lavishly, fell easily into debt, and Jefferson expressed Virginia's bitterness when he wrote, "planters were a species of property, annexed to certain mercantile houses in London." Virginia's debt owing to British merchants, in 1775, was estimated at more than £2,000,000, which was over twenty times the amount of money in circulation in that colony. A war might well cancel that load of debt.

Parliament's prohibition against the issuance of paper money in the colonies, and its attempt to restrict settlement of the west, affected all levels of the colonial population. While Americans had often argued heatedly about these issues among themselves, now they focussed their combined antagonisms against England. The grievance arising from obstacles to westward expansion planted by Britain was further accented by the ill-timed Quebec Act.

Parliament's passage of the Act, in 1774, though not necessarily connected with the punitive measures of that year, were so linked in American minds. From the viewpoint of imperial administrators, sitting in London, it was merely the natural outcome of the conquest of Canada and the pressing need to organize the new colony. It gave the French Catholic colonists in Canada religious freedom, but it also enlarged the area of Quebec southward to the Ohio River and westward to the Mississippi, a region which included some French-speaking settlements. British officials may have been thinking of ease of administration in drawing these boundaries, but to Americans it was the old Proclamation Line of 1763 all over again, intended to confine the colonists east of the Alleghanies.

What added to American dislike of the Quebec Act was its alleged

* Eric Robson, *The American Revolution in Its Political and Military Aspects 1763–1783* (New York: Oxford University Press, 1955), p. 27.

favoring of Catholicism. It was denounced as a threat to Protestantism, and political radicals on the eve of the Revolution exploited anti-Catholic sentiment. Quebec's Catholic institutions would presumably have a privileged position not only in Canada, but also in the area north of the Ohio, and this favor was charged to Anglican friendliness for Catholicism. New England Puritans, with their heritage of anti-Catholicism and anti-Anglicanism, lumped together "Popery" and "Prelacy," lampooning the latter as a half-way house to Rome.

In the colonies south of New England, the Anglican Church was either the established church or, as in New York and Pennsylvania, favored in many ways by royal benevolence. The Anglican clergyman had his salary paid by taxes, could collect certain fees, and had given to him his parsonage and the property attached to it. Wherever the Anglican was the established church all had to pay taxes in support of it, even Dissenters, who were thus faced with the necessity of supporting Anglican ministers as well as their own. The fact that members of the Anglican Church were in the minority in all the colonies made their preferred position all the more odious. Dissenters in America were leagued with coreligionists in England to ease their common lot against discrimination. English Dissenters were openly sympathetic to Americans even after the outbreak of military hostilities; New England, it was said, was "more the country of their hearts than the England wherein they were born and bred."

Dislike of Anglicanism was strengthened by exaggerated fears that it was pressing for the establishment of a bishop in America. Memories of what Anglican bishops had done to Puritan ancestors in the seventeenth century made "anti-episcopacy" an effective rallying cry. The frank support by Anglican ministers of conservative, and eventually of Tory sentiments did not endear them to the mass of Americans. When John Adams reached Philadelphia for the first Continental Congress he was warned against the Anglican minister, Dr. William Smith, provost of the local college and a stimulating cultural influence in the community. Smith, it was said, was a "soft, polite man," "who is looking up to Government for an American Episcopate and a pair of lawn sleeves." In New York the conservative element was known as the "Church" party, and radicals the "Presbyterian." While Anglican did not always equal conservative (especially among Virginia planters), nor Dissenter equal radical, the correlation was fairly close in many of the colonies.

In the dozen years that followed the French and Indian War, the signs were many that Americans and Englishmen had drifted farther and farther apart in their social and political ideas. Americans felt that their people were infinitely better off than Englishmen (or other Europeans for that matter). Even Tory Americans, when at length they chose exile in England, were astonished to find how alien the homeland had become. England, at this time, seemed to be heading in the direction of reaction, but America was moving toward democracy. While an English writer was saying that a fundamental condition for a prosperous state was "a large and solid basis of the lower classes of mankind" at the bottom of the social pyramid, a Yankee editor urged his readers "to prevent the execution of that detestable maxim of *European* policy amonst us, *viz.:* That the common people, who are three quarters of the world, must be kept in ignorance, that they may be slaves to the other quarter who live in magnificence."

Americans, proud of their English heritage, were thinking of Magna Charta and the Petition of Right, the England of Drake when England was building an empire, the England of the seventeenth century when the great traditions of political liberty were most soundly laid. From the writings of Milton, Sidney, Harrington, and especially John Locke's *Two Treatises on Government,* the colonists drew moral support in their disputes with the homeland in the Revolutionary era. Locke had spoken of man's natural rights and of the duty of people to abolish or alter their government when it violates these rights. "The true remedy of force without authority is to oppose force to it," Locke had written. The ruling classes of England in the eighteenth century, while remembering Locke in the abstract, preferred to ignore his challenging words. Americans did not forget them.

Colonials spoke easily and confidently of natural law and natural rights, while Englishmen based the powers of parliament upon the foundation of positive law. The staid British cited legal precedent, the Americans appealed to the rights of man. Language which was clear as crystal to the colonials, and which to them expressed the simple truths of politics, seemed to British conservatives nothing more than American sophistry to justify rebellion.

British policy toward America was not tyrannical; it was uncertain, fumbling, not ill-intentioned, but ill thought out. It was confused, as one British official revealed in a letter to another (1767): "There is the most urgent reason to do what is right, and immediately; but what is that right, and who is to do it?" As Eric Robson put it, "The actual steps taken were a series of advances and retreats, cajolings and menaces." *

The men who led the Empire were unequal to the heavy new tasks placed on them. George III was a snuffy, well-meaning, shortsighted man

* *Ibid.,* p. 33.

with many private virtues and little public strength. He was temperate—
he had seen his uncle the Duke of Cumberland die of dissipation at 44—
and preferred barley water to wine. He rode to court on horseback in
all weathers, and sometimes hunted from eight in the morning till night-
fall. He was a model of industry; he would labor at his desk all day, have
some tea, bread, and butter, and toil on till eleven at night. Punctual,
patient, greedy for details, he was conscientious and indefatigable. He
was a shrewd politician, who knew how to manage elections by adroit
use of patronage, and had the names of political leaders and figures of
local contests clear in his memory. But of statesmanship he understood
little.

England's King George was not the monster of American historical
legend. He was really a virtuous (too virtuous for his looser contemporaries), well-read monarch, forever battling with disdainful politicians
to maintain the proper constitutional place of the king in the British
system of government. His were the actions of the bull in the china
shop: "I know I am doing my duty and therefore can never wish to
retract"; "It has ever been a certain position with me that firmness is
the characteristick of an Englishman." Professor Richard Pares * puts
it concisely: "His idea of firmness was extremely simple: flat refusal
to make any political concessions to anybody." The prototype of
Colonel Blimp, his courage was admirable, but his rigidity, unbreak-
able, helped break the empire. Unimaginative as he was, he was no
worse, some say better, than most members of parliament whose vision
rarely ranged beyond their own localities. England's empire may have
been built in a spell of absent-mindedness; it was being lost in a display
of tantrums.

Among King George's ministers there was no towering statesman like
Lord Chatham. The King was surrounded by a crew of little power-
hunting men. Of one leader of the time, Sir Francis Dashwood, who
became finance minister, the radical John Wilkes declared: "From
puzzling all his life at tavern bills, he was called by Lord Bute to administer the finances of a kingdom above one hundred millions in debt."
The Prime Minister, Lord North, had brains, but he put them and his
conscience without reservation in the hands of the sovereign. He submitted in the palace to King George, and in the House of Commons
bought every borough seat that he could reach.

Such men did not have sufficient flexibility and insight to meet the
problems of the expanded empire. The colonists acknowledged the
sovereignty of the crown, and professed allegiance to it. But they denied

* *King George III and the Politicans* (Oxford, England: Clarendon Press,
1953), p. 67.

that the two houses in Westminster, sitting without any colonial representatives, could vote laws which the colonies had to obey, or impose taxes which must in all instances be paid. Various men made proposals for colonial representation. Franklin, for example, suggested that the colonies be given a hundred members in the house and some among the peerage. This was essentially impracticable; the interests of Britain and America were too diverse for a single legislature. The question whether Parliament really did have constitutional power to tax the colonies in all instances was debatable, with forcible legal arguments on each side. But this was not the important question. The important fact was that it was highly inexpedient to do so; that expediency counseled leaving the power of taxation, in general, to the colonial assemblies.

Englishmen and Americans were obviously not well informed about each other. General Gage had told King George that Boston would be very meek "if we take the resolute part." With four regiments, he said, he could tame Boston. He got his regiments and warships, too, but found the Americans untameable. They refused to build barracks for the soldiers; they burned the straw intended for soldiers' beds; they withheld food from them. When the names of the new councilors (provided for under the reorganization of the government of Massachusetts) were published, the harassed officials were hounded by the people and forced to seek shelter under Gage's protection. The General, in fact, found that his troops instead of overawing the people were themselves quarantined. Within a few months the disillusioned Gage was writing to England, urging that the "Intolerable Acts" be suspended until a larger force of troops could be sent to America.

The colonists, on the other hand, were possibly misled into thinking that support for their cause in Great Britain, by religious Dissenters and political radicals, was strong enough to influence official policy. Americans were cheered by the support of John Wilkes, the English political gadfly; he and the colonists muttered about combined action against military authority. Granville Sharp, collaborator with Americans in many important humanitarian activities, feared that parliament's departure from valued ancient precedent might lead to imperial disaster. Horne Tooke defended the American colonists in a speech to fellow Englishmen: "The Security of their Freedom and their Rights is essential to the enjoyment of our own. We should never for a moment forget this important truth, that when the people of America are enslaved, we cannot be free; and they can never be enslaved whilst we continue free. We are stones of one arch, and must stand or fall together."

But significant as these voices were in the press and streets of Britain, they were rarely more than a whisper in the houses of parliament.

There even Burke and the other friends of America, though still pleading for conciliation, went along with the king and Lord North in voting for a policy of coercion. The colonists had now gathered in national congress to face this policy.

★ THE CONTINENTAL CONGRESS

In Philadelphia the delegates argued about the measures to be adopted. Moderates favored dignified protest and continued negotiation. However the "Suffolk Resolves" from Massachusetts pushed the moderates into favoring a policy of commercial nonintercourse with Great Britain. The Resolves, originally adopted in Suffolk County, Massachusetts, maintained that no obedience was owing to the "Intolerable Acts," and that no funds should be voted for the colony's treasury until the reestablishment of the old government. The endorsement of the Resolves practically meant that Congress had sanctioned rebellion in Massachusetts. In his diary, under the date of September 17, John Adams wrote, "This was one of the happiest days of my life. In Congress we had generous noble sentiments, and manly eloquence. This day convinced me that America will support Massachusetts or perish with her."

The delegates, however, wishing to disclaim any desires for independence, drew up a moderate "Declaration of Rights," which recapitulated all the grievances against king and parliament. Conservatives, attempting to arrest the radical tide of the Congress, backed a plan introduced by Joseph Galloway of Pennsylvania for an imperial parliament. He proposed a separate American government, with a president general appointed by the crown and a legislature made up of representatives from the respective colonies. The legislature was to regulate all intercolonial affairs, with the right to veto parliamentary legislation relating to the colonies. On the other hand parliament was to have the right to veto laws of the American legislative body. Englishmen and Americans were impressed by this intimation of the future relationship within the British Commonwealth, and it failed of adoption by only one vote. While Americans had proclaimed to the world their grievances, they were not exerting much pressure on Britain. Such pressure was to be achieved by throttling her American trade. Imports from Great Britain practically ceased but the effect on her was less than expected as she had greatly expanded her markets on the continent and in the East Indies.

The measure (called the "Association") to paralyze British commerce by complete suspension of trade with her was to be enforced by local committees in every town and county throughout the colonies. These committees were to expose all who failed to live up to the Association "to the end that all such foes of the rights of British-America may be publicly known and universally condemned as the enemies of American liberty." To impress people with the solemnity of the step Congress had taken, all kinds of "extravagance and dissipation," particularly horse racing and other sports but including as well plays and even private dances, came under the ban of the Association. Offenders were tarred and feathered, and their property destroyed. Radicals called the tune: were you with them or against them? Noncompliance with the Association stamped one as a Tory. The division between patriots and loyalists grew greater. The latter preferred the authority of parliament to the snooping of local vigilance committees. Samuel Seabury, an Episcopal clergyman from New York, though critical of recent parliamentary measures towards the colonies, accused these committees of conducting an inquisition into everyone's private affairs. "Will you submit to them?" he asked, noting that they were often "chosen by the weak, foolish, turbulent part of the . . . people. I will not. If I must be enslaved, let it be by a King at least, and not by a parcel of upstart, lawless committeemen." Seabury came from Westchester County; there he had many supporters, but in another part of New York, Ulster, his writings were ordered burned, and the author was denounced as an enemy to his country.

While the mass of people were taking things into their own hands, their intellectual leaders had finally arrived at the conclusion that the colonies, unrepresented in parliament, were beyond its jurisdiction. This position was upheld by Thomas Jefferson in *A Summary View of the Rights of British America;* by James Wilson, of Pennsylvania, a brilliant student of the law, in his *Considerations on the Authority of Parliament;* and by John Adams in the *Novanglus* papers. Wilson maintained that the various portions of the British Empire were self-governing units, independent of one another, and bound together only by the authority of the crown. Jefferson now maintained that *all* regulations of parliament, including the old navigation acts, were measures "of arbitrary power . . . over these States." He asked if there was any reason why 160,000 electors in Great Britain should make the laws for millions of Americans. And he then pleaded with King George to stop "sacrificing the rights of one part of the empire to the inordinate desires of an other; but deal out to all equal and impartial right."

Pleas were in vain. The king and his minister still failed to see that rebellion was continent-wide and not restricted to New England. At the Continental Congress Patrick Henry had said, "The distinctions between Virginians, Pennsylvanians, New Yorkers, and New Englanders, are no more. I am not a Virginian, but an American." In November,

1774, the king told his minister Lord North that "the New England governments are in a state of rebellion, blows must decide whether they are to be subject to this country or independent." The blows were not long in coming.

★ LEXINGTON AND CONCORD

General Gage, in command at Boston, was a kindly man, seemingly friendly to Americans, for he had lived among them a long time and had taken one as his wife. He was, however, a soldier, and his job was to carry out the acts of parliament. Every now and then, tipped off by Tories, he would send out some soldiers to seize arms and powder, or to protect some hapless loyalists. In April, 1775, he learned that considerable supplies had been stored at Concord. His plan was to leave Boston on April 18 to seize the stores, but the time and objective were kept a close secret. The radicals, however, knew from spies, redcoat deserters, and their own careful observation practically all the supposed secrets of the British military. Hancock and Sam Adams, then at Lexington, were warned to hide. The people in Concord, also forewarned, concealed their cannon and military stores. "Minutemen" were alerted for miles around to keep their weapons close and be ready for instant action.

Paul Revere, who had often served as courier for the Sons of Liberty, hoped to be able to ride out and spread the alarm when the British troops should start to move. Fearing that he might be prevented from doing so, he arranged that Sons of Liberty in Charlestown should keep watch for the signal which would be flashed to them from the easily visible Boston church steeples. "If the British went out by water we would show two lanterns in the North Church steeple—and if by land one as a signal . . ."

In the bright, cold moonlight of April 18, Revere and William Dawes rode out to warn the countryside that British troops had started to march to Concord. When the troops, some 800 of them, reached Lexington in the early morning of the 19th, they saw about fifty Minutemen lined up on the common. For a moment there was uncertainty, then suddenly the first shot was fired—from which side nobody knows. Firing on both sides left eight Americans dead, the rest dispersed; the British then continued on to Concord. There, after destroying small quantities of unhidden stores, they began their homeward march to Boston.

By this time the warnings of far-clanging bells had brought hundreds of alerted farmers to the scene of the battle. Young men dropped their saws and hammers; ministers laid aside their Bibles to shoulder their muskets. Americans crouched behind stone walls and barns, rocks and hill-tops, and picked off the bright-uniformed soldiers marching doggedly along on the dusty road. Meanwhile General Gage had dispatched a relief force of 1,500 men in support of the first column, which it joined near Lexington. From there the enlarged force once again was under attack all the way until they reached the safety of Boston. When they counted their casualties they found they had lost 273 men in killed, wounded, and missing. The light-hearted expedition to seize Yankee stores had ended in ghastly failure.

The news of Lexington and Concord was carried throughout the country by special messengers, and the response was immediate. Minutemen poured into Cambridge; Boston became a city under siege. In South Carolina two regiments of infantry were recruited; in the north Ethan Allen and the Green Mountain boys were preparing to take Fort Ticonderoga and Crown Point, where they seized much needed guns and other military supplies.

While the whole country was learning about the momentous events in Massachusetts, delegates were arriving in Philadelphia for the second Continental Congress, to begin on May 10, 1775. This group was more radical than the first, but their temper was still averse to immediate secession from Great Britain and to the creation of an independent state. Nevertheless they were determined to resist British arms. In a spirited "Declaration setting forth the Causes and Necessity of their taking up Arms," written by Jefferson and Dickinson, the delegates said, "We are reduced to the alternative of chusing an unconditional Submission to the tyranny of irritated Ministers, or resistance by Force. The latter is our choice . . . We cannot endure the infamy and guilt of resigning succeeding generations to that wretchedness which inevitably awaits them, if we basely entail hereditary Bondage upon them." The Declaration went on: "Our cause is just. Our union is perfect. Our internal Resources are great, and if necessary foreign Assistance is undoubtedly attainable . . . The Arms we have been compelled by our Enemies to assume, we will . . . employ for the preservation of our Liberties; being with one Mind resolved to die Freemen rather than to live Slaves." While it was true that feeling was not yet strong enough to call for independence, the hint was contained in the Declaration: "We mean not to dissolve that union which has so long and so happily subsisted between us. Necessity has not yet driven us into that desperate measure, or induced us to excite any other nation against them. We have not raised Armies with ambitious Designs of separating from Great Britain, and establishing Independent States."

It is true that at first the colonists had thought only of redress, not severance of the imperial tie. Washington wrote in October, 1774: "I am well satisfied that no such thing as independence is desired by any thinking man in North America; on the contrary, that it is the ardent wish of the warmest advocates of liberty that peace and tranquility on constitutional grounds will be restored, and the horrors of civil discord prevented." John Adams said in March, 1775, of the people of Massachusetts: "that there are any that hunt after independence is the greatest slander on the province," and Massachusetts, in an address to the king, spoke of the popular devotion to the crown. As late as the early months of 1776 Thomas Paine's pamphlet advocating independence, which circulated everywhere, filled members of the South Carolina legislature with consternation.

★ INDEPENDENCE ROLLS IN "LIKE A TORRENT"

While the Continental Congress was still hopeful of staying in the empire, the links that joined the colonies to Britain were snapping fast. The old forms of government were breaking down in many parts of America. In Massachusetts, for some months now, the real authority was the Provincial Congress and its committees. It had taken over many of the duties of governing, including the collection of taxes and the raising of troops. Elsewhere similar developments were under way. Committees organized to carry out the Association agreement practically took over the functions of government. A "constitutional post," organized by William Goddard, an enterprising journalist, was operating alongside the royal postal system, and the latter soon came to an end. By the outbreak of military hostilities royal and proprietary governors were exercising only nominal authority.

The battles of Lexington and Concord were closing the door to conciliation with Britain. George Washington was appointed by the Congress commander-in-chief of the armed forces. Washington was a wealthy Virginia planter whose military reputation, gained in the French and Indian War, was known throughout America. He was already recognized as a superb leader of men. His remarkable qualities of character were soon to be severely tested. In New England the numerous militia blockading Boston were incorporated into the continental army. That army was enormously elated by the Battle of Bunker Hill in June, 1775, when untrained troops stood their ground under fierce British assault. Although the Americans, with 400 casualties, retreated in the end, they left over 1,000 British killed and wounded on the field of battle. "I wish we could sell them another hill at the same price," said Nathanael Greene.

Tactics suitable for European battlefields were found ill-adapted against colonials. "Never had the British Army so ungenerous an enemy to oppose," read one report of the battle. The Americans "send their riflemen five or six at a time who conceal themselves behind trees etc till an opportunity presents itself of taking a shot at our advance sentries, which done they immediately retreat. What an unfair method of carrying on a war!" The contempt of professional soldiers for colonial militia was quickly changed to respect. The intensity with which Americans were preparing strongly impressed a British observer; "they are all determined to die or to free [;] it is not the low idle fellow that fight only for pay but men of great property are common soldiers who say they are fighting for themselves and posterity."

The Continental Congress was meanwhile trying to run a war and govern a country which was neither in nor quite out of the British Empire. Still seeking a peaceful solution, the Congress addressed a final petition to George III (the Olive Branch Petition) in hopes that he might restrain a misguided parliament and venal ministry. Independence was still hard for many Americans to swallow. As late as the winter of 1775–76 the provinces of Pennsylvania, New York, New Jersey, and Maryland instructed their delegates in Congress not to vote for independence. Yet the vital move could not long be postponed. The American economic position was weakened with the cessation of trade which had been ordered by the first Continental Congress. The suppression of trade was more harmful to the Americans than to the British; besides war supplies were urgently needed. Americans, therefore, gladly opened their ports to the world on April 6, 1776. But as Richard Henry Lee remarked: "no state will treat or trade with us so long as we consider ourselves subjects of Great Britain." The Americans could not count on foreign aid, meaning France, until they declared themselves an independent nation.

King George, contemptuous of the Olive Branch Petition, made their decision easier by proclaiming the colonies in a state of rebellion; parliament followed in December, 1775, with an act forbidding all trade and intercourse with the colonies. John Adams hailed the act as "a complete dismemberment of the British Empire. It throws thirteen colonies out of the royal protection, and makes us independent in spite of supplications and entreaties."

Apparently, however, it needed more than King and parliament to force the Americans out of the British Empire. An overwhelming mass sentiment, still wanting, was required to force Congress to take the fateful step. That sentiment was roused by Thomas Paine's little pamphlet, *Common Sense,* issued in January, 1776.

Paine, a journalist who had been introduced to America by Franklin, did not write profound political treatises in the style of John Locke. His writing was devoid of subtleties and the temperate language of loyalty and obedience in which petitions to the crown had been phrased. He understood that revolutions, as later Lord Byron expressed it, were not "to be made with rosewater." Paine's words were intended for mass appeal. *Common Sense* came at the psychological moment, and its trumpet call to independence shook the waverers and forced them into line.

With a sure instinct Paine touched the deepest emotions of Americans by appealing to them to turn their backs on the outworn institutions of the Old World and to create in America a new society. He ridiculed sentimental attachment to Britain and he was sarcastic about the supposed excellences of the British constitution. How kings "came into the world so exalted above the rest, and distinguished like some new species, is worth inquiring into," said Paine; are they "the means of happiness or of misery to mankind?" He answered his own question by saying that only misery was the fruit of royalty. Monarchy, he maintained, tended naturally to despotism; one honest man was worth "all the crowned ruffians that ever lived." The colonists should abandon any notions that they had secured great benefits from Great Britain; the progress America had already achieved "is but childhood, compared with what she would be capable of arriving at, had she, as she ought to have, the legislative powers in her own hands."

"We have it in our power to begin the world over again," wrote the eloquent Paine. "The birth day of a new world is at hand, and a race of men, perhaps as numerous as all Europe contains, are to receive their portion of freedom. . . . Independence is the only Bond that can tye and keep us together. . . . Let the names of Whig and Tory be extinct," Paine exhorted, "and let none other be heard among us, than those of a good citizen, an open and resolute friend, and a virtuous supporter of the rights of mankind and of the free and independent states of America." "The cause of America," he told his willing listeners, "is in a great measure the cause of all mankind."

Paine's pamphlet was one of the most influential writings in American history. Soon 100,000 copies were circulating through towns and villages and remote settlements. Leaders and the led were carried away by it. "Sound doctrine and unanswerable," said Washington. And John Adams told his wife that soon the doctrines of Paine would be "the common faith"; "Every post and every day rolls in upon us Independence like a torrent." In several of the colonies independent governments had been set up, and everywhere radicals were ousting conservatives from positions of power. In the important province of Pennsylvania a more democratic government was installed, which quickly instructed its delegates to the Continental Congress to vote for independence. North Carolina had already told her delegates that they could vote for independence; Virginia soon followed with stronger instructions to her own delegation to *propose* independence.

In Virginia itself, the local governing body, the convention, went forward with plans for a reconstitution of her government. The Bill of Rights and the state constitution which were adopted became famous documents in American history, and inspired liberal sentiments in France and England. Virginia was too impatient to wait for action by the slow moving Continental Congress. She declared her own independence of Great Britain.

In the Congress in Philadelphia on June 7, Richard Henry Lee, speaking for the Virginia delegation, moved that "these United Colonies are, and of right ought to be, free and independent States." The debate was hard and long, with the delegates from the middle colonies hesitant (they "were not yet ripe," they said, "for bidding adieu to the British connection"), but on July 2 Lee's motion was carried. Caesar Rodney, representing Delaware, but absent from Congress on July 1, disregarded thunder and rain of a summer storm to ride his horse through the night to be in Philadelphia in time to vote his state on the side of independence. The final decision had already been anticipated with the appointment (June 11) of a committee to prepare a formal declaration setting forth the reasons "which impelled us to this mighty resolution." The committee consisted of Jefferson, Adams, Franklin, Roger Sherman, and Robert R. Livingston. After agreeing upon the main points to be covered, Jefferson, whose eloquent writing was well known to his colleagues, was assigned the task of clothing the statements "in proper dress." The Declaration of Independence, his great handiwork, was ordered printed on July 4, 1776.

In imperishable language the Declaration took its stand on the broad ground of the natural and inherent rights of man: "We hold these truths to be self-evident; that all men are created equal; that they are endowed by their Creator with certain unalienable Rights, that among them, are Life, Liberty, and the pursuit of happiness. That to secure these rights, Governments are instituted among Men, deriving their just Powers from the consent of the governed. That, whenever any form of Government becomes destructive of these ends, it is the Right of the People to alter or to abolish it, and to institute new Government, laying its foundation on such Principles and organizing its Powers in such form, as to them shall seem most likely to effect their Safety and Happiness."

Nowhere in John Locke's writings, from which so much of the Declaration's philosophy was derived, can be found the glow of Jefferson's language. Where Locke spoke to the brain, Jefferson spoke to the heart; where Locke spoke of the rights of life, liberty and property, Jefferson, with a surer understanding of the human spirit, substituted for "property" the words "pursuit of happiness."

The indictment of King George, with which the Declaration continued, summarizing the long list of American grievances that thrust the colonists into Revolution, is not what the world remembered of the famous state paper. In after years, wherever and whenever men craved freedom and the good life—in the United States, Europe, Asia, South America, and in other regions unknown to Jefferson—they turned for inspiration to the immortal words of the Declaration. Jefferson had so willed it in 1776, and fifty years later, just before his death, he again bequeathed the Declaration and July 4 to posterity. "May it be to the world, what I believe it will be (to some parts sooner, to others later but finally to all), the signal of arousing men to burst [their] chains . . . and to assume the blessings and security of self-government. That form which we have substituted, restores the free right to the unbounded exercise of reason and freedom of opinion. All eyes are opened, or opening to the rights of man. . . . There are grounds of hope for others. For ourselves, let the annual return of this day forever refresh our recollections of these rights and an undiminished devotion to them."

Yes, there were "grounds of hope for others." Three years before Jefferson's death, Lord Byron, who had always been aware of the impact of the American Revolution on the world, had gone to help the Greeks in their war for independence. He began his journal in Greece with these lines:

> The dead have been awakened—shall I sleep?
>   The World's at war with tyrants—shall I crouch?
> The harvest's ripe—and shall I pause to reap?
>   I slumber not: the thorn is in my couch;
> Each day a trumpet soundeth in mine ear,
>   Its echo in my heart—

★ PATRIOTS VERSUS LOYALISTS

The Declaration of Independence put an end to doubt. Patriots (Whigs) took an oath of loyalty to the new nation; Tories, loyal to England, were now traitors. There was still time for the hesitant to declare themselves. In the end many professed attachment to the new nation, but large numbers became Tories opposed to independence. So strongly were they opposed that over 50,000 of them at one time or another fought against their fellow Americans during the Revolution. Families were divided in the crisis, and in the test of arms kin faced each other on the field of battle. In the final choice, it was estimated, about a third of the population was strongly Whig, perhaps another third was Loyalist (mostly passive), and the last third, concealing its sentiments, did not contribute strength to either side. Most revolutions, including the American, have been engineered by a militant minority.

The Loyalists were among the most eminent people in America. Holders of high offices and the Anglican clergy generally supported the established order; officials of a lower rank often chose the side of revolution. Men of wealth were inclined to the Loyalist side (though not in Maryland and Virginia); probably a majority of the more prosperous businessmen opposed independence. The ultimate division was not necessarily along economic lines. Merchants and lawyers who had once worked together to oppose disliked revenue measures of parliament were now split into Tory and Whig camps. Large landowners in the north were usually Tory, but some of the wealthiest in New York joined the patriots. In the latter colony, however, the Loyalists were stronger than in any other northern community. Small farmers were preponderantly patriots. Many mechanics and small tradesmen were found among the Loyalists, but the great mass of them were on the side of the radicals. The latter were able to sway many of the moderates in all classes to their side, for these reluctant rebels had been too deeply committed by ten years of agitation and petitioning in co-operation with radicals to withdraw their support at the last moment.

Throughout the colonies the radicals were generally successful despite the strength of the opposition. In the end, masterly propaganda, good organization, and a positive program won the support of enough people to insure success for the Revolution. As for the Loyalists who, often with anguished heart, preferred continued association with the empire, success of the Revolution meant disaster. They suffered expulsion from the community and confiscation of their property. Over 70,000 of them left America for England, Canada, and the West Indies. Their departure, though welcomed by the patriots, left serious gaps in the American scene, for among the Loyalists were many able minds and cultivated spirits who had done much to raise the whole level of colonial culture. The significance of this loss was a matter for comment by later, detached historians. At the moment of independence there were no regrets.

Copies of the Declaration were sent to the farthest corners of the thirteen states, now sovereign and independent. In town and tiny village, guns and bells, bonfires and parades celebrated the reading of the Declaration. John Adams had prophesied that Independence Day would be "celebrated by succeeding generations as the great anniversary Festival . . . It ought to be solemnized with pomp and parade," he said, "with shows, games, sports, guns, bells, bonfires, and illuminations, from one end of the continent to the other, from this time forward, forevermore."

Abigail Adams, wife of John, described the reading of the Declaration from the balcony of the State House in Boston. "Great attention was given to every word," and when the reading was ended, she said, three cheers "rent the air," and the cry went up "God save our American States . . . After dinner, the King's Arms were taken down from the State House, and every vestige of him from every place in which it appeared, and burnt in King Street. Thus ends royal authority in this State," wrote Mrs. Adams triumphantly. "And all the people shall say Amen."

★ "IMPOSSIBLE TO CONQUER A MAP"

Royal authority in America did not end, however, with cheers and the reading of the Declaration. It really ended only after six long years, during which heartbreaking disappointment, defeat, and disillusionment almost undid the resoluteness of Washington and those who stood with him in the times that tried men's souls.

Summer soldiers and sunshine patriots were not the stuff from which Washington could fashion armies. Politicians interfered frequently in running the war. Military officers (although themselves generally civilians and not professional soldiers) angrily complained about meddling by civilian officials. Even those with a will to fight took poorly to discipline. Militiamen had been accustomed to elect their own officers, and spoke their minds freely to military superiors. Men usually enlisted for short periods, and when they felt like going home to harvest the crops, or for any other reason, they just went. They were reluctant to fight far from their homes. After a number of defeats in 1776, Washington's army, when it moved into winter quarters that year, had dwindled to less than 5,000 men fit for duty. While it was difficult for Baron Steuben and others to remold American troops in the image of the European mechanical military formation, the Americans, fighting in their own frontier fashion, often won important engagements like that at King's Mountain, in western Carolina. Their chief qualification, wrote a baffled British officer, was their "agility in running from fence to fence and thence keeping up an irregular, but galling fire on troops who advance with the same pace as at their exercises."

Americans, in their nondescript appearance, looked very unsoldierly to Europeans accustomed to the color and shine of troops in the Old

World. But an officer in Burgoyne's army said that the Americans were "never contemptible in the eye of a soldier," for they fought with "great courage and obstinacy." And a German officer said the Americans "stood like soldiers"; he thought "the whole nation had much natural talent for war and military life." It was noted that farmers in America were much more suited to war than were peasants in the Old World. They were familiar with arms from childhood and used them expertly. Frontiersmen traveled light and fast in the wilderness and were unexcelled marksmen.

To bolster America's fighting strength, Negroes formerly unwelcome in the armed forces, were gradually added to the military in the various states. It has been estimated that 5,000 blacks served in the integrated patriot forces. Peter Salem fought at Lexington and Concord and at Bunker Hill, where he won renown shooting down the valorous British Major Pitcairn. In this same battle, Salem Poor, another black, won special commendation for bravery.

By 1778 the Continental army, especially in New England, had a noticeable infusion of blacks. Most slave soldiers, writes Professor Quarles, "received their freedom with their flintlocks." During the entire Revolution Negroes participated in nearly every battle from Lexington and Concord to Yorktown. "They helped to gain our liberty and independence," wrote an admiring white veteran. Late in the war, a European observer watching the Continental army passing in review, noted that a Rhode Island regiment consisted mainly of Negroes. He praised the unit as "the most neatly dressed, the best under arms, and the most precise in its maneuvers."

Many Negroes, long accustomed to the sea, served on naval vessels. They made an especially valuable contribution as pilots in Virginia waters. The most famous was Caesar, a slave, set free by a grateful state legislature. Some Negroes were spies, notably a slave, James, who served with Lafayette. The glamorous Frenchman urged the Virginia assembly to emancipate James, who now called himself James Lafayette.

While thousands of Negroes, free and slave, aided the patriot cause, other thousands gained freedom in service to Britain. Most were in labor units (as were the majority of Negroes on the patriot side) but the British also used them as shock troops, guides, and spies. With Britain's defeat some 20,000 blacks left the independent United States along with the vanquished whites.

Despite the problems General Steuben faced, he was ultimately able to whip American soldiers into a force which equalled the skill and discipline of Britain's best. A people little used to restraint must be led, remarked Washington, "they will not be drove, even those who are ingaged for the war, must be disciplin'd by degrees." Steuben had been on the Prussian general staff, and his contribution to American military efficiency was very great. Some Europeans were more of a hindrance than an asset, but men like Lafayette, Kosciusko, Pulaski, and De Kalb left an indelible imprint on the imaginations of Americans with whom they fought in the common cause.

Raising troops for the war was hard enough; raising money to finance it seemed even more difficult. Congress had to get funds from the separate states, and as they were reluctant to tax themselves they contributed very little; domestic loans and foreign loans (mainly from France) brought additional sums to Congress. But taxes and loans were not enough to supply the needed funds; the money was found simply by printing it. Paper money came from the presses in a steady stream, and while it helped at first to get needed supplies, it rapidly depreciated. Over $200,000,000 had been issued by Congress by 1779, and the individual states had printed nearly as much. By the next year $40 in continental currency were equal to a dollar in specie. Before the end of the war continental currency was so nearly worthless it was used for wallpaper. Washington complained that it took a wagon load of paper money to buy a wagon load of supplies. The British added to currency chaos by flooding the rebellious colonies with counterfeit money. "Not worth a continental" came to express the feelings of Americans toward anything useless. The collapse of the currency disrupted economic activity and led to widespread indulgence in questionable practices that undermined moral values. Much of the hardship American soldiers endured was caused by monetary inflation. Only toward the very end of the war, through the administrative abilities of Robert Morris, were the finances of the country put on a sounder basis.

Jealousies among the colonies added to their handicaps. Fear of a centralized authority left the Continental Congress with very limited power. Congress debated interminably: "We murder time, and chat it away in idle impertinent talk," said Charles Carroll of Carrollton; "However, I hope the urgency of affairs will teach even that Body a little discretion." Despite its limitations, however, and its scurrying from place to place with its records carried in wagons just ahead of the pursuing British, Congress nevertheless kept an army in the field, negotiated with foreign powers, and kept the flame of revolution alight in the blackness of defeat.

The Continental Congress kept the country together, and by strengthening the loose ties of national feeling it laid the foundation for the later strong Constitution. In its deliberations and in its legislative achievements the Congress established precedents of great value for American government in the future. But to contemporaries, in 1775, the Congress, hobbled by many weaknesses, seemed often a frail reed.

While Americans faced many difficulties they were also aided by certain advantages. England had her weaknesses, too. There was no great enthusiasm in England for the war. To get the needed soldiers German mercenaries, many from the principality of Hesse, were hired. Influential liberal Englishmen all during the war expressed sympathy for the American cause, which they likened to their own fight against royal reaction. The British conduct of the war was flabby, since hope still persisted of conciliation. A determined policy might have isolated the chief areas of disaffection, and their subjection might have ended the struggle before France's entry.

More than one military expert in England thought that the conquest of the colonies was an insuperable task. Pitt had said it was impossible to conquer a *map*. The Americans fought on ground of their own, to which Britain had to transport troops and supplies from distant bases. Supply lines from Britain, at least in the war's early period, were uncertain; during the winter of 1775–76 only eight out of forty transports reached Boston. British strategy was conditioned by ease of communication, which meant her troops had to stay near rivers close to the coast. Americans could move more quickly than their heavily encumbered opponents. British troop training was not for the American terrain. To subdue this vast wooded land, inhabited by an inflamed people, was an almost insurmountable task, wrote a British officer in November, 1775. The whole country, said another, noting its mountains, its creeks, its swamps, was seemingly designed by nature to aid the defensive. Lord George Germain, Secretary of State for the American Department, pointed up the problem: "the manner of opposing an enemy that avoids facing you in the open field is totally different from what young officers learn from the common discipline of the army." The Americans could lose in one place, but hold in another; the task of the British was to win in all places.

Washington generally grasped the proper tactics. "We should on all occasions avoid a general action," he told Congress, "and never be drawn into a necessity to put anything to the risk." Constant harassment of the enemy, depriving them of food and supplies, was his prescription. A distinct American advantage lay in the mediocre quality of British leadership under Howe, Clinton, and Burgoyne. After Bunker Hill, they usually husbanded men and supplies, for neither were plentiful. More than once, in New York or Philadelphia, the British allowed victory to pass them by. Lord North remarked that while he did not know whether the British generals would frighten the enemy, they certainly frightened him whenever he thought of them.

With their command of the sea (which they did not use to advantage) the British presumably should have been able to reduce American supplies to a thin trickle. Yet there were many harbors, the coast line was long, and Americans had hundreds of ships ready to run through blockades. In fact American privateers, taking the offensive, seized British ships on many seas, enriching their owners and at the same time doing great damage to British trade. During the course of the war over 2,000 American privateers roamed the seas in search of their prey. Even in home waters off the British Isles American vessels, sailing close in shore, fluttered their flags in contemptuous disregard of England's naval power. John Paul Jones challenged that power in spectacular fashion in the famous battle between the "Bonhomme Richard" and the "Serapis," which enhanced America's reputation, but in the long run did little to advance her military cause.

The greatest asset America possessed was the leadership of General Washington. His greatness, as his contemporaries insisted and as posterity has adjudged, lay in the wonderful balance of a group of qualities. Taken singly not one was brilliant, but in combination they presented an almost matchless array of virtues. His soundness of judgment, never showy or merely clever, impressed every associate. When Patrick Henry was asked who was the greatest man in the Continental Congress, he replied: "If you speak of eloquence, Mr. Rutledge of South Carolina is by far the greatest orator; but if you speak of solid information and sound judgment, Colonel Washington is unquestionably the greatest man on that floor." He was wise not merely as to his immediate problems, but in foresight. The consummate illustration of that foresight was his masterly plan of campaign in 1781, which culminated in the capture of Cornwallis and ended the Revolution.

As prominent as his calm wisdom, and almost as important, were his traits of decision and firmness. It was Washington's decision which gave force to his memorable speech to the Virginia provincial convention in the summer of 1774, when he declared: "I will raise one thousand men, subsist them at my own expense, and march myself at their head for the relief of Boston." It was decision which brought him to the Continental Congress in September, 1774, punctual there as always, to sit in full uniform. The moment he took command of the Continental Army, he showed characteristic decision and energy in organizing the raw volunteers, collecting provisions and munitions, and inspiring Congress and the several State governments to come to his support. These qualities of firm decision made him a stern disciplinarian. He had no patience with cowardly, dishonest, or inefficient subordinates, and during the siege of Boston boasted that he had "made a pretty good sort of slam among such officers." He gave harsh sentences of flogging, and once erected a gallows forty feet high, writing: "I am determined if I can be justified in the proceeding, to hang two or three on it, as an example to others."

It is the Washington firm in adversity, rather than the Washington of victory, who chiefly compels our admiration. His unfaltering determination to cling to his strong lines at Valley Forge, enduring without complaint the criticism of the public, the murmurs of his soldiers, and the quarrelsome interferences of the Continental Congress remains unforgettable. This was the same Washington, more experienced and mature, who had been a model of calmness, unresting energy, and resourcefulness in the dark hours just after Braddock's defeat.

Washington was no military genius; critics have pointed to his many mistakes and his defeats. But he supplied what Americans then needed most, an almost elemental force around which men could rally and draw strength when their own had ebbed. He supplied faith when others were depressed; he could be decisive when others were uncertain; he had enough courage to invigorate an army. His reserve and rigid self-discipline seemed to set him apart from ordinary men, but his angry temper could boil over in scathing condemnation of offending soldiers. Such scenes were rare, however, and his men remembered rather his devotion, his integrity, his fairness. In after years men elsewhere in the world were to remember the character of Washington, for when Belgians or Greeks or other people in revolution wanted to praise their own heroes they pictured them in the image of the American commander-in-chief.

★ DEFEAT—AND SARATOGA

Washington needed his great fortitude, as there were more dark than bright days during the long drawn out hostilities. The American attempt to win Canada by assault on Quebec during a driving snowstorm on New Year's eve, 1775, had failed. Richard Montgomery, one of the American commanders, had been killed. The other, Benedict Arnold, was wounded, and was eventually forced to lead his men back in a fighting retreat. The following few months were more cheerful for the Americans. The Carolina Loyalists had been beaten at Moore's Creek Bridge at the end of February, 1776. In June, a large-scale attempt by the British under Lord Cornwallis and Sir Henry Clinton to establish a base at Charleston, South Carolina, was beaten off when the ships failed to get by Fort Moultrie. In the north, Washington had achieved a signal success in forcing Sir William Howe to evacuate besieged Boston on St. Patrick's Day, 1776.

The successes of these months were to be followed by discouraging setbacks. Washington had left Boston for New York, anticipating that it would be the next British objective. Washington's presence in New York gave a great lift to patriot sentiment there but he could not hold the city against the superior weight of Sir William Howe's troops and the fleet commanded by his brother, Admiral Lord Howe. The American troops lost the battle of Long Island (August 27, 1776), and abandoned Brooklyn Heights. Two days later they escaped entrapment by a retreat to the Manhattan shore in a dense fog that shrouded their movements from Howe. Washington continued the retreat to Harlem Heights, fighting rear-guard actions, while the British took command of New York City, where they stayed for the duration of the war.

Washington's position was steadily getting weaker: many of his troops were vanishing, while those who remained trudged along discouraged. The grim commander ferried his troops over the Hudson, retreating across New Jersey to the south side of the Delaware River, keeping just ahead of Howe's slow-moving soldiers. The latter took nineteen days to cover seventy-four miles; bad roads, destroyed bridges, and rain contributed to delay them. Washington's difficulties were aggravated by

Central military campaigns of 1776

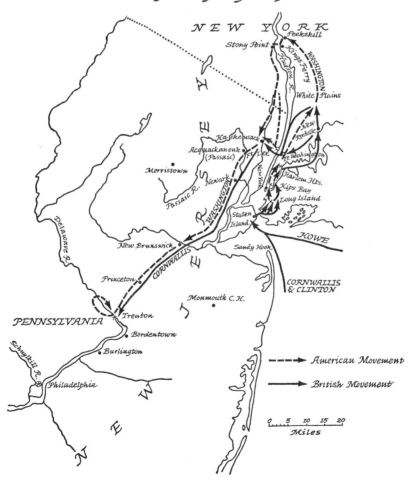

the temperamental behavior of Charles Lee, a rival for chief command.

Washington at this time wrote to his brother, Augustine, that "the game is pretty near up," and he placed the blame chiefly on "the accursed policy of short enlistments" and "too great a dependence on the militia." "You can form no idea of the perplexity of my situation," said Washington. "No man, I believe, ever had a greater choice of difficulties, and less means to extricate himself from them. However, under a full persuasion of the justice of our cause, I cannot entertain an Idea that it will finally sink, tho' it may remain for some time under a cloud."

The gloom of a depressing winter for the Americans was lifted for a time by Washington's spectacular recrossing of the ice-choked Delaware to attack the Hessians at Trenton. In the sleet and snow of Christmas night, 1776, the Americans took by surprise the Hessians, carousing on this festive evening, and captured a thousand of them. The victors herded these prisoners back to their own lines, and the sight of so many captives greatly heartened the American troops. A British force of 8,000, led by Cornwallis, was unable to catch Washington who, after beating some of the enemy troops at Princeton, retreated to a favorable defensive position in northern New Jersey, near Morristown. Washington's successes in these few days gave great hope to the American cause and won new recruits for his forces. But it was hard for him to keep an army together during the winter months; in March of 1777 his force numbered scarcely 4,000.

In that year the British planned a co-ordinated movement, by way of the Hudson River and Lake Champlain, to cut off New England from the rest of America. Colonel Barry St. Leger was to march from Oswego through the valley of the Mohawk to Albany; Burgoyne was to move south from Canada to Albany to meet the troops coming up the Hudson. Howe himself was to take Philadelphia, the chief town in America, and thus the "United Colonies" would be broken in several pieces. Though Howe took Philadelphia, defeating Washington at the Battle of Brandywine Creek, the British plans in the Hudson Valley went awry from lack of co-ordination and from failure to take into account the hardships of campaigning in the wilderness of upper New York.

The Americans, wrote a British officer, were extremely cunning; they showed great industry in cutting down trees, creating road blocks (they were compared to a family of beavers); and they improvised more quickly than their opponents. The rank and file in the British army carried full European equipment, weighing sixty pounds, over the roughest kind of terrain. The mountains were so steep, wrote a British ensign with Burgoyne, "we were obliged to pull ourselves up, and let ourselves down, by the branches of trees"; the road "running round the bottom of steep rocks was so very crooked that we seldom saw 300 yards before us."

"Gentleman Johnny" Burgoyne, a bon vivant, commanded the 10,000 British troops moving down from Canada in the summer of 1777. Transporting supplies (including Burgoyne's champagne), and the portage of boats first to Lake George and from there to the Hudson slowed the army's progress, all the time depleting the commissary. A British officer remarked that for every hour Burgoyne spent in planning to fight, he had to allot twenty in calculating how to feed his troops. To replenish his supplies Burgoyne sent a foraging expedition to Vermont. But the troops gathered no food; the countryside in a true people's war rose against them, and the Green Mountain Boys, led by Colonel John Stark, destroyed the British force of 800 men at Bennington. To add to Burgoyne's woes he also learned that St. Leger had

Central military campaigns of 1777

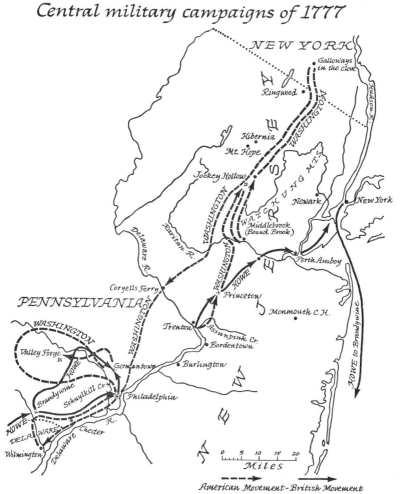

American Movement - British Movement

been unable to get through the Mohawk.

Burgoyne himself was losing sizable fractions of his army through desertion and losses in small battles against the Americans now pressing him on all sides. They hovered about his flanks and, wrote Burgoyne, "were very expert in securing themselves and in shifting their ground . . . many placed themselves in high trees in the rear of their own line [at Bemis Heights], and there was seldom a minute's interval of smoke, in any part of our line, without officers being taken off by a single shot." The Americans, increasing their forces daily until they reached 20,000 in October, now far outnumbered Burgoyne's 5,000. At Saratoga, finding himself surrounded and with food supplies running low, he surrendered his whole army to General Horatio Gates. Burgoyne's surrender, October 17, 1777, marked the end of one of the decisive battles of history, for it brought a hesitant France openly to the side of the Americans, which meant eventual victory.

★ FRANCE JOINS THE AMERICAN REVOLUTION

The Americans had been angling for French assistance ever since the Revolution began. It was logical to turn to France, for she had been waiting for just such an opportunity to undo the disastrous results of the Seven Years War. The Comte de Vergennes, directing French foreign affairs, saw the American war as a means of upsetting British predominance and restoring to France the leadership in international affairs she had formerly enjoyed. Frenchmen were psychologically prepared to lend assistance to the American cause. For years French writers, notably Voltaire, had idealized America and had spoken of the New World as a utopia under whose beneficent guidance the Old World would find a better way of life.

Frenchmen thought of Americans as a simple, homespun people, possessing the virtues of "natural men," freed of the artificialities which surrounded the sophisticated society of Europe. France was, therefore, ready to receive with open arms so characteristic an American as Benjamin Franklin. His lack of affectation, his simple dignity, and his great fame as a scientist opened all doors to him. Franklin was, of course, less simple than his French admirers imagined. He played the part of the rustic philosopher to perfection, and was lionized by the elite and the masses alike. He was the greatest ambassador the New World has ever sent to the Old, and he won for the United States enormous prestige in political and intellectual circles everywhere in Europe.

The Continental Congress had dispatched commissioners (chief of whom was Franklin) to solicit French support, which had already been granted privately. Even at this early stage secret French aid in money

Northern military campaigns of 1777

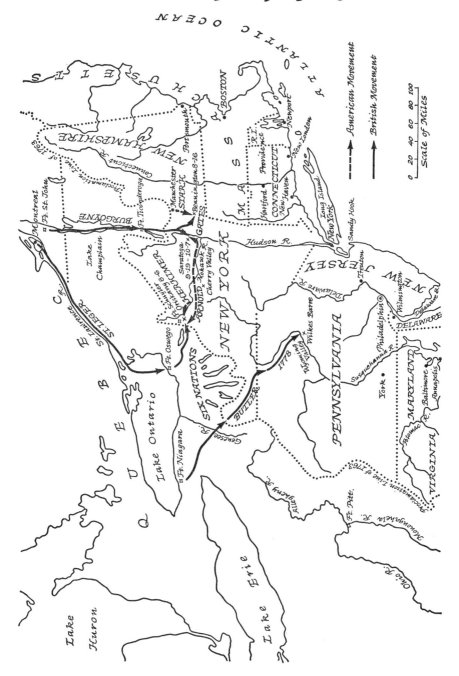

and supplies, particularly munitions, was invaluable. The commissioners were successful in getting additional supplies and recruiting enthusiastic Frenchmen to fight for the American cause. Officially, however, France held back from open participation until the news of Saratoga arrived. Paris learned of Burgoyne's defeat in the first days of December. The wheels were immediately set in motion to effect an alliance between the United States and France, and on December 12 the American commissioners met secretly with Vergennes. The possibility of peace between England and America, which would frustrate French plans to humble Britain, may well have spurred Vergennes to hurry the signing of the alliance, on February 6, 1778. Britain, in fact, then was ready to concede almost complete autonomy to her former colonies, who were asked in exchange only to acknowledge the sovereignty of the king.

David Hartley, Franklin's friend, expressed at this time the views of many Englishmen sympathetic to America. He proposed to "cement the two countries together by a mutual nationalization in all rights and franchises to the fullest extent. We are derived from the same stock;

Central military campaigns of 1778

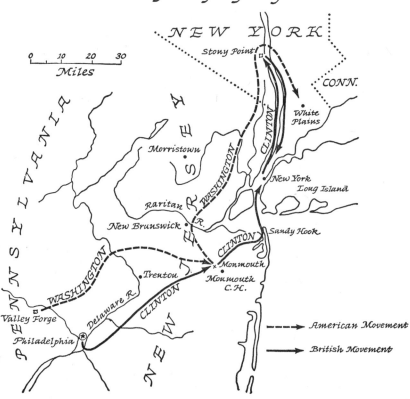

we have the same religion, the same manners, the same language, the same temper, the same love of liberty and of independence, and if we must be seemingly divided, let there be at least an union in that partition." It was Edward Gibbon, the famous historian, who remarked that the two greatest nations in Europe were "running a race for the favour of America." France won—but America won much more.

French espousal of the American cause made the Revolution a world war. Spain joined in it as an ally of France in 1779, hoping to wrest Gibraltar from Britain; Holland, as well as Spain, lent encouragement to Americans, sheltering their ships and exchanging manufactured goods for their cargoes. All through the war the Dutch West Indian island of St. Eustatius had been furnishing Americans with military supplies. Catherine II of Russia headed a League of Armed Neutrality, which deterred British interference with neutral, but unfriendly, traders. Britain's strength could not be concentrated exclusively in the American theater, but she had sufficient to keep the issue in doubt till the French navy, winning control of the sea at a crucial moment, gave the Americans the extra margin needed for victory.

★ YORKTOWN AND INDEPENDENCE

At the time when France was allying herself with America the latter's will to fight seemed at its lowest ebb. Washington was with his shivering, hungry troops at Valley Forge, while General Howe and the British soldiers were enjoying the warmth and hospitality of Philadelphia's Loyalists. Mutterings of discontent with Washington's leadership were spread by jealous officers, but there was no one to supplant him. The common soldier's fortitude won the praise of professional military men. Praising the morale of American soldiers facing cruel want, De Kalb thought no army in Europe would have borne such hardships so stoically. British spirit weakened under less arduous conditions. "It takes citizens to support hunger, nakedness, toil, and the total want of pay," wrote Lafayette proudly. He believed the American soldiers to be "the hardiest and most patient that are to be found in the world."

In June of 1778 the British in Philadelphia, now under command of Sir Henry Clinton, left for New York. They reached their objective despite an attempt by Washington to intercept them in the battle of Monmouth, New Jersey, on June 28, 1778. Washington's forces were too weak to attack Clinton in New York. The American commander camped with his army at White Plains, and strengthened some posts to prevent the British from moving up the Hudson. Clinton's troops did move up the river, occupying Stony Point in the spring of 1779. Americans led by General Anthony Wayne captured this post on July 16 of that year in a well-planned attack which overcame swamps and strongly fortified hill positions. It changed hands again, however, in the next few months. Shortly thereafter Benedict Arnold was negotiating with the British for the surrender of West Point, and he fled from the American lines when the plot was discovered. He brought to the British side his expert knowledge of fighting under American conditions. With his boldness and daring in Virginia in 1781 he overshadowed his new colleagues. The war in the North was practically at an end by 1780.

In the West American settlers huddled together in compact fortified areas to weather attacks by Indians stirred up by the British. The defensive policy of the Americans left them at the mercy of marauding Indians and Tory Rangers. The Americans, in a change of tactics, decided on offensive action in the belief that capture of the British posts north of the Ohio would end the British attacks. George Rogers Clark led an expedition in the summer of 1778 which, in a short time, won control of the Illinois country. The British, however, recaptured Vincennes that winter. Clark, then at Kaskaskia, determined to retake the post 180 miles away. In the dead of winter, with 127 men, he started for it, marching through mud, cold rain, and freezing streams. The unsuspecting British, thinking themselves secure for the winter, were startled by the firing of the Americans who had slipped quietly into Vincennes in the early twilight of February 23, 1779. After an all night battle the British surrendered the next morning, thus restoring to American control an important link in the fortifications of the northwest area. But the British and their Indian allies, in the following two years, regained control of most of the area, only to lose it ultimately with the signing of the treaty of peace.

Along the seaboard British strategy having failed in the North, the base of operations was shifted to the South where the presence of many Tories seemed to promise quick success. From the Carolinas it was expected that the tide of British victory would roll northward. The pace of war in the South, however, was very leisurely. First Savannah was captured, in the last days of 1778, then Charleston was taken (May 1780), along with an American force of 5,000 men under General Benjamin Lincoln. In the Carolinas vindictive fighting between patriots and Tories (each supported by regulars) gave the war a particularly sanguinary character. General Nathanael Greene described the country as "ravaged and plundered by both friends and enemies." A British observer of the scene, after the fall of Charleston, spoke of the "fund of hatred and animosity in the hearts of people, as time only can extinguish. The men being prisoners do not dare to speak out, but the women make full amends for their silence, they amuse themselves by teaching their children the principles of rebellion, and seem to take care that the rising generation should be as troublesome as themselves."

In August, 1780, the Americans were again beaten, at Camden. They did, however, turn the tables on a thousand Loyalists at King's Mountain in October, 1780, killing or capturing nearly every one of them.

More important for the Americans than this victory was the appointment of Nathanael Greene to command in the South. Greene, who had learned much of the art of war from military manuals, had insufficient troops to launch a sustained offensive. However, in the battles he fought (Guilford Court House, for example, in March, 1780), this able commander inflicted heavy casualties on the British. Partisan leaders, notably Sumter and Marion, constantly harried the British forces. "As for this damned swamp fox [Marion], the devil himself could not catch him," muttered a frustrated enemy officer. The battered Cornwallis moved on into Virginia to make contact with the American traitor Benedict Arnold, then leading another British force. Toward the end of

Southern military campaigns of 1780-81

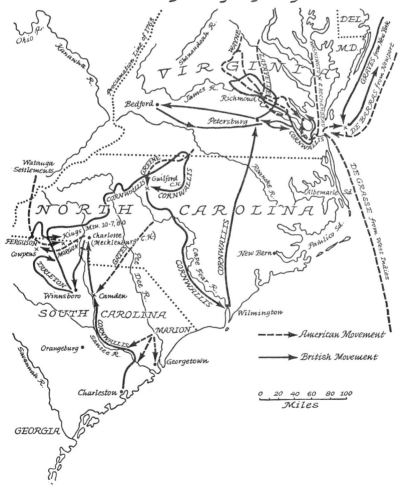

summer, in 1781, Cornwallis, thinking himself secure with the help of British sea power, prepared to fortify Yorktown.

As it turned out, he was far from secure. Now the French alliance was to bear rich fruit. Admiral De Grasse sent word from the West Indies that his fleet would co-operate with land forces in an attack on Cornwallis. Two armies moved south, Washington's and Rochambeau's, and by a master stroke of timing and good luck, land and sea forces arrived about the same time in the Chesapeake area. The French fleet defeated British naval forces and gained control of the sea, thus blocking any escape over water by Cornwallis. On the last day of September the combined French and American armies of 15,000 men (twice the size of the British) began the siege of Cornwallis' well-fortified position. Washington, Rochambeau, and Lafayette headed the allied troops, whose task was made easier by French knowledge of siege operations. British troops were worn out, sick and disheartened, and Cornwallis himself had no great will left to fight. On October 19, 1781, he surrendered his troops, and they marched out between the French and American lines to the tune of "The World Turned Upside Down." "It is all over!," cried Lord North in England, when he learned of the defeat at Yorktown.

By this time the war had become very unpopular in England. Even the conservative landowners, who had formerly been the strongest supporters of coercive measures against the colonies, now were tired of a struggle which promised nothing except higher taxes. Englishmen were confronted with the fact, as one of them put it, that "we were to be taxed and stamped ourselves, instead of inflicting taxes and stamps on others." The king was still obstinate, but his remaining garrisons in Savannah, Charleston, and New York could no longer take the initiative. The southern ports were abandoned in 1782, and the next year the British troops were evacuated from New York, along with thousands of Loyalists. Britain preferred to concentrate her power against France and Spain.

Peace negotiations had been under way for some time. Franklin, John Adams, and John Jay, paying little attention to their French ally with whom they were supposed to negotiate jointly, were very successful in winning liberal terms in the Peace of Paris. The first thing the Americans won was the acknowledgment of their country's independence. Other provisions in the treaty promised British creditors an opportunity to collect their American debts; Americans were to have their customary fishing rights in northern waters; Spain acquired Florida. For the new American Republic the most important provision of the treaty, after independence, was the recognition of its enlarged territory, a rich wooded prairie country, running westward from the Alleghanies to the Mississippi and northward to the Great Lakes. Lord Shelburne, who understood the Americans better than most Englishmen and who was gifted with a prevision of future Anglo-American relationships, had favored the extension of American territory westward, rather than allow the contested region to be the source of continual friction. "The deed is done," he wrote, "and a strong foundation laid for eternal amity between England and America."

★ WASHINGTON BIDS FAREWELL TO HIS MEN

Washington, meanwhile, had established his headquarters at Newburgh, on the Hudson River. Here, in a modest house overlooking the river and the distant highlands, Washington's main task seemed to be keeping his restless, unpaid army under control. Some of his officers, thinking in Old World terms, hinted at the establishment of an American monarchy, with the commander as king. Washington sternly rebuked the suggestion: "No occurrence in the course of the war has given me more painful sensations," he wrote. "I am much at a loss to conceive what part of my conduct could have given encouragement to an address, which to me seems big with the greatest mischiefs, that can befall my country."

At length the long awaited word of the end of hostilities came, and on April 19, 1783, eight years to a day from the war's beginning, the armistice was proclaimed to the American army. On December 4, Washington bade farewell to his officers in Fraunce's Tavern, New York. Lifting a glass of wine, he spoke feelingly: "With a heart full of love and gratitude I now take leave of you, most devoutly wishing that your latter days may be as prosperous and happy as your former ones have been glorious and honorable." He took affectionate leave of the men with whom he had waged the good fight, and Washington then went on to Annapolis, where Congress was sitting, to resign his post as commander-in-chief.

His resignation was an impressive ceremony, "a solemn and affecting spectacle," wrote a member of Congress; "such an one as history does not present. The spectators all wept, and there was hardly a member of Congress who did not drop tears. The General's hand, which held the address shook as he read it." General Washington recovered his composure, and concluded his remarks: "Having now finished the work assigned me, I retire from the great theatre of action, and bidding an affectionate farewell to this august body, under whose orders I have so long acted, I here offer my commission, and take my leave of all the employments of public life." On December 24, 1783, he rode away to his cherished Mount Vernon, the most illustrious citizen of his beloved republic.

CHAPTER XI

The Revolution Completed

★ DEMOCRATIC REFORM

"The American war is over," said Dr. Benjamin Rush in 1783, "but this is far from being the case with the American Revolution." Rush, Jefferson, and Madison were men who believed that winning independence from Great Britain was only one phase of a broader revolution which should transform the character of American political, social, and intellectual life. Jefferson looked forward to the time when the "plebeian interest" would prevail over "the old aristocratical interest." Royall Tyler, a youthful veteran of the Revolution, in the prologue to his play, "The Contrast," produced in New York in 1787, spoke the democratic language:

> Exult each patriot heart!—this night is shewn
> A piece, which we may fairly call our own;
> Where the proud titles of "My Lord! Your Grace!"
> To humble Mr. and plain Sir give place.

Patriots had not waited until 1787 to exult. During the war years they had gone far to overturn the "aristocratical interest." The departure of Loyalists, and the discrediting of conservatives, made it possible to speed up reforms which had long been agitated. In America great social changes were made within a few years which, in the Old World, took generations to accomplish.

While British power was crumbling, the colonies (through their provincial congresses) transformed themselves into states and drew up blueprints for self government. Rhode Island and Connecticut continued to operate under their old colonial charters. The new state constitutions varied in their political coloration from fairly advanced democracy to a moderate conservatism. They generally had a bill of rights naming liberties of the people free from government invasion; standing armies and general warrants were prohibited. Trial by jury, habeas corpus, freedom of the press, the right to petition were among the guarantees provided for in these constitutions. The precedent established by Massachusetts, in 1780, in calling a special convention to draw up a constitution suggested the similar procedure for the federal government seven years later. To European observers, looking at the American scene from a broad perspective, the Americans had taken a long step forward toward equalitarian democracy.

The new governments were formed by men favoring the Revolution, but among them were influential leaders like Edmund Pendleton in Virginia, James Duane and John Jay in New York, and John Rutledge in South Carolina, who opposed drastic innovations in their own states. In some communities the same men governed who had done so before the Revolution. Despite the persistence of conservative strength, however, such proposals as extended white male suffrage (it was not quite universal) and the secret ballot, and limited imprisonment for debt were incorporated into the new constitutions. Distrust of the executive branch of government led to restrictions in the governor's authority; he was generally forbidden the veto. Remembering the key role played by colonial assemblies in contests with the crown in pre-Revolutionary years, the legislatures (all bicameral, except Pennsylvania's) were granted the greater strength in the new governments. Discrimination against western communities in the allotment of legislative representation was still practiced in some states, notably in South Carolina.

The most important of the political changes, apart from the destruction of the authority of the crown, were those which broadened the suffrage and made representation in the legislatures more equitable. In Pennsylvania, for example, there arose in 1775–76 a strong demand for two democratic reforms; one to abolish the property qualifications and the naturalization requirements which had restricted the suffrage, and the other to give the western counties full representation in the assembly. Both reforms were promptly won. In March, 1776, the legislature admitted seventeen additional members, most of them from the western counties. At a slightly later date the right to vote was broadened, per-mitting many Scotch-Irish and German farmers, and many poor Philadelphia artisans and laborers, to vote for the first time. In a number of States gross inequalities in county representation still existed; at the beginning of the Civil War the grievances of that part of Virginia beyond the Blue Ridge had much to do with the creation of West Virginia, while New York City still complains of under-representation at Albany. A number of States also retained property qualifications, such as fifty acres of land, for the ballot. But when the Revolution ended any male adult taxpayer in Pennsylvania, Delaware, North Carolina, Georgia, and Vermont might vote. One conservative grumbled that the tendency was to give sovereign rights to "every biped of the forest."

Everywhere aristocracy was on the defensive and, though it raised a barrier here and a dam there, the surging democratic tide flowed around and over many of the obstacles. Richard Price, a warmhearted friend of America, wrote to Franklin that European liberals were hoping "that, whereas the kingdoms of Europe have traveled to tranquility through seas of blood, the United States are travelling to a degree of tranquility and liberty that will make them an example to the world, only through seas of blunders."

The economic basis on which a privileged land owning aristocracy had rested was altered. Crown limitations on the settlement of vacant lands were wiped out; huge holdings once belonging to the king were now transferred to the states. Quitrents amounting to $100,000 annually, paid to the king and the proprietary families, the Penns and Baltimores, were swept away. Loyalists' estates, some of them vast possessions like Sir William Pepperell's property running for thirty miles along the Maine coast, or the Phillipse's holdings of some 300 square miles in New York, were confiscated and ultimately partitioned for sale to thousands of small farmers. (Sometimes, however, new groups of speculators again built up large concentrations of property.)

The dispersion of the loyalists, good sturdy Americans who preferred the old order to a republic, changed the texture of American life; in some ways for the better, in some for the worse. By scores of thousands, from Boston, New York, and Charleston, they sailed away in whole fleets, their destination "Hell, Hull, or Halifax." More than 40,000 fled to Canada alone, giving that colony a new vigor. Thousands went to the West Indies, and so many found refuge in the mother country that one of them wrote: "There will scarcely be a village in England without some American dust in it by the time we are all at rest." The country could well dispense with the aristocratic contempt many of them had shown for the common people—for those whom Dorothy Hutchinson of Massachusetts called "the dirty mob." Their departure gave the plain middle-class farmers and villagers who constituted the vast majority of the population a free field to create a civilization after their own hearts. But the loyalists had possessed a great part of the culture of America. After they left the social graces counted for less, and energy and rude self-assertiveness counted for more. The young nation could ill spare many of these men. Among them were Thomas Hutchinson, whose family had come to Massachusetts in 1634, and who as judge, collector of books and manuscripts, and historian, gained high distinction; John Singleton Copley, of an equally old Boston family, who became one of the first painters of his time; and Benjamin Thompson (Count Rumford), distinguished scientist and philanthropist.

Other contributions to democracy appeared in the decreased attention to English political precedent, and the rise of the American common law. Until independence was won Americans naturally appealed to Magna Charta, the Petition of Right, and other great English instruments bulwarking political and civil liberties. Now they began to formulate their own political philosophy, founded in great part on a distinctively American set of ideas. American law and American judicial decisions separated themselves from the English statute and common law, and as they did so, they nurtured a democratic spirit.

The character of American society was changed, too, by the abolition of primogeniture and of entails (which had preserved intact the family estate). These vestiges of an outworn society had already become outmoded in America. Jefferson carried the spirit of the Declaration of Independence into Virginia politics and fought successfully in the legislature of that state for the abolition of entail. In a few years nearly all the other states had done likewise with entails and, as for primogeniture, it was abolished everywhere. Great family estates, long held intact, were now broken up. These radical changes in the laws, said Jefferson, would result in a legal system freed of any taint of aristocracy, "and a foundation laid for a government truly republican." The confiscation of Tory estates and their resale in smaller lots, and the breakup of other holdings, made it easier for relatively obscure men to move into the seats of power. The Revolution helped transform the economic climate; in an atmosphere tending toward a laissez-faire economy freer rein was allowed to enterprising entrepreneurs.

The American Revolution was a dissolvent of religious, as well as economic privilege. In 1776, only Pennsylvania and Rhode Island were without an established church. Anglicanism, the established faith in several colonies, had been identified with loyalism in the popular mind. It was therefore more vulnerable to assault than the other established faith, Congregationalism, in New England, which had thrown in its lot with the Revolution. The Anglican church did not give up its privileges without a fight, notably in Virginia. There the struggle was drawn out over a tempestuous ten years before Jefferson's bill establishing freedom was passed by the legislature. Jefferson, in France when the bill was enacted, wrote triumphantly to Madison, who had spearheaded the fight in its later stages: it "has been received with infinite approbation in Europe, and propagated with enthusiasm. I do not mean by the governments, but by the individuals who compose them"; "it is comfortable to see the standard of reason at length erected, after so many ages, during which the human mind has been held in vassalage . . ." And Jefferson concluded proudly: "it is honorable for us to have produced the first legislature who had the courage to declare, that the reason of man may be trusted with the formation of his own opinions."

Richard Price had unbounded enthusiasm for the Virginia measure; "It is the first of the kind that was ever pass'd," he said, and it was a "happy omen of the benefit to mankind that may arise from the American Revolution." English radicals, hostile to the established church in their own land, quoted the American example to prove that "government can do better without an established church than with it."

The enactment of 1786, declaring that the government must not interfere in church affairs or matters of conscience, and that no citizen should suffer any disabilities for his religious opinions, was one of the landmarks of modern history. It became the cornerstone of religious freedom not only in Virginia but in many another State, and some foreign lands. To people in countries where intolerance still prevails it shines as a beacon of reform for it has been translated into all important languages. Jefferson declared that he wished the inscription on his tomb to recall that he had been author of the statute for religious freedom, of the Declaration of Independence, and of the University of Virginia.

In this connection another democratizing influence may be noted: the rise of the Methodist Church. The followers of John Wesley had only a slight foothold in America when the Revolution began, and their sect fell under some suspicion for loyalist leanings. But in 1784 Francis Asbury and Thomas Coke, as joint heads, organized a separate American church on the authority of Wesley, who sent over a prayer book, liturgy, and discipline which they followed. Asbury shrewdly appealed to the dominant middle class in the older colonies, and sent circuit-riding preachers and missionaries to the farthest reaches of the frontier. These men put a democratic fervor into their gospel. Asbury's own energy and devotion were heroic. He was said to have traveled 300,000 miles in his long career as minister and administrator; and we can believe this when we read in his *Journal* that his horse was growing stiff because "I have ridden him upon an average of 5,000 miles a year for five years successively." The Methodists were the first religious body to give formal greeting to the new government under Washington.

Almost another half century passed before the Congregational church was deprived of its privileged status in New England, but even during the Revolutionary era the stringency of laws affecting Dissenters in that region was relaxed. Calvinist theology had been gradually modified by emergent Unitarianism, or more deeply eroded by the spread of deism.

The altered religious temper of the period benefited Catholics, too, for there was a noticeable decline in the traditionally hostile feeling toward them.

Steadily the Americans were justifying their heritage by enlarging the area of human freedom. The common law, brought from the English homeland, was criticized by Americans because of its severe punishments and its bias against debtors. The harshness of penal codes was relaxed, notably in Pennsylvania, whose humanitarianism was a challenge not only to other American states but also to European countries.

The U.S. at the end of the American Revolution

The position of debtors in prisons was eased, largely as a result of Quaker pressure. A strong fight was waged, on both sides of the Atlantic, against slavery and the slave trade. In Massachusetts and New Hampshire slavery was declared illegal in 1783; the next year Rhode Island and Connecticut adopted legislation providing for gradual emancipation. Pennsylvania had already initiated its program of gradual emancipation. Maryland, Virginia, and North Carolina put an end to the slave trade. Under a law permitting manumission, Virginians voluntarily freed 10,000 slaves between 1782 and 1790. At this time the practice of indenturing white servants was vigorously criticized as inconsistent with the principles of a democratic society.

The first effects of the Revolution on education were unfortunate. The marches of the armies, the confusion, and the financial strain caused a real retrogression. Yale for a time closed its doors, and the students scattered far and wide. In 1797 the president of William and Mary was teaching a group of barefoot youths, and in 1800 the Harvard faculty consisted only of the president, three professors, and four tutors. Even in New England reading and learning declined. The first school law in Massachusetts after the war registered a shocking retreat. It cut the length of the school term in half, and changed the law which had required towns of 100 families to keep a grammar school—only towns of 200 families had to meet that stipulation.

Nevertheless, the Revolution strengthened the prevailing impulse to democracy in education. John Adams, though fairly conservative now in his political views, was extremely liberal in urging a comprehensive educational program. "Every class and rank of people, down to the lowest and poorest," he said, should have an education. Community schools, he believed, "would draw together the sons of the rich and the poor." Jefferson argued similarly that, as the people were the "only safe depositories of political power," free elementary education, for a few years at least, should be supplied by the state. The abler students should then be selected for higher education at state expense. "Preach a crusade against ignorance," Jefferson urged his fellow Virginian, George Wythe.

Benjamin Rush and Noah Webster were also vigorous promoters of broad educational programs. Rush proposed the creation of a national university which should indoctrinate students with a devotion to democratic ideals. To be long lived, republics must invest in popular education, said Rush, for he believed that little could be done by American public bodies until they carried the people along with them. Webster published texts for children (including the famous *American Spelling Book*) which were flavored with a strong Americanism. The increase in other institutions of a democratic culture—newspapers, libraries, public lectures—all testified to the strength of the popular desire for self-improvement. The Land Ordinance, a measure with great significance for the future of American culture, was adopted by the Confederation in 1785, and it eventually made available millions of acres of land for the support of public education.

The war released the energies of vast numbers of people hampered by the discipline of a hierarchical society. They participated more freely in political discussion, and constantly brought pressure on their state legislatures to increase the influence of the mass of men in governmental affairs. A contemporary historian of the war years said "the science of government has been more generally diffused among the Americans by means of the revolution. The policy of Great Britain, in throwing them out of her protection, induced a necessity of establishing independent constitutions. This led to reading and reasoning on the subject." During the Revolution leaders of many communities were banished, and into their vacant posts stepped men unknown to fame. "It seemed as if the war not only required, but created talents," wrote a contemporary historian who marveled at the way inexperienced men measured up to their opportunities. "Men whose minds were warmed with the love of liberty, and whose abilities were improved by daily exercise, and sharpened with a laudable ambition to serve their distressed country, spoke, wrote, and acted, with an energy far surpassing all expectations which could be reasonably founded on their previous acquirements."

★ ARTICLES OF CONFEDERATION

While the separate states were adopting their constitutions, the body carrying on the war—the Continental Congress—was also planning a form of government to embrace all thirteen commonwealths. Dealing with a continent was more complex than managing a colony which had been the extent of their experience thus far. Local jealousies were not dead, agreement was difficult in the apportionment of voting and expenses. Central authority, even if now American, was as suspect as when it was British. In the midst of constant war emergencies the Congress hammered out a plan, the Articles of Confederation, which was then submitted to the states for adoption. Slowly, between 1777 and 1781, the states got around to ratifying the Articles, and finally Maryland remained the lone holdout. She, along with other states which had no western land claims insisted first that Virginia and other states cede to the United States their western grants which could then be held in trust for the people of all the states.

Maryland and New Jersey were fearful that a state possessing western lands, Virginia for example, might sell them and thus, without any local taxation at all, have sufficient income for her needs. People from nearby states would then move to Virginia to enjoy exemption from taxes, thus increasing the burden of those citizens remaining in their former homes and threatening poorer states with bankruptcy and depopulation. Rival speculators had an important stake in the decision naming the supervisory authority of western lands. Virginia speculators naturally wanted their state to retain control; speculators from other states (and they were especially influential in Maryland) believed that validation for their cloudy titles to purchases in the Ohio Valley made before the Revolution stood a better chance with Congress. Virginia finally yielded her western lands but she laid down conditions: the new states to be carved out of this vast Northwest territory were to be between 100 and 150 miles square, and when ready to enter the union, were to be admitted with the same "rights of sovereignty, freedom, and independence as the other States." Virginia's statesmanship thus guaranteed that Americans moving west would not be inferior "colonists," stigmatized by second-class citizenship.

Maryland won her point, but she herself, still in the grasp of speculators, was subject to pressure to sign the Articles from a totally unexpected quarter. Maryland had appealed to the French for aid in warding off British sea power in the Chesapeake. The French, anxious that their American alliance be made as strong as possible, thereupon urged Maryland to ratify the Articles of Confederation and thus solidify the American union. Maryland did so, and on March 1, 1781, the final ratification of the Confederation of the United States of America was proclaimed. Cannons boomed, bells rang, fireworks were shot off and toasts drunk to "The United States of America." The *Pennsylvania Gazette* hailed the union, "begun by necessity, cemented by oppression and common danger, and now finally consolidated into a perpetual confederacy of these new and rising States."

Even before the Articles were finally ratified critical observers saw their inadequacy, but with all its faults this frame of government went beyond previous experiments in federal organization in European countries. Stubborn regard for local considerations was overcome in the Articles, and it required much courage and strength of will for the representatives of the separate states to subordinate their attachment to their own communities in behalf of some larger, ill-defined unity.

Under the Articles the individual American states asserted their sovereignty, but delegated exclusive jurisdiction to Congress over foreign affairs and interstate disputes. Congress was charged with the responsibility for national defense. It also had power over coinage, the postal system, and the handling of Indian affairs. It could borrow and request men and money from the states, but Congress lacked power to enforce its requisitions. An important feature of the Articles, one which strengthened the sentiment of nationalism, was the provision that guaranteed to citizens moving from one state to another the privilege of citizenship in the new community. Under the Articles a permanent staff of government employees was built up which was invaluable to the government established in 1789.

In three noted ordinances between 1784 and 1787 Congress established the basic policies guiding American expansion for a century thereafter. In the ordinance of 1784, drawn mainly by Jefferson, the Northwest Territory was cut up into seven districts, each with the right of entry into the union as a state equal in powers with the original thirteen when its population was as large as that of the smallest of the older states. In the interim autonomous territorial governments were to be set up, which were not to interfere with provisions made for the sale of public lands by Congress. The latter made such arrangements in an ordinance the next year, 1785; public lands were to be sold in townships six miles square, to be divided equally into thirty-six lots (each lot was a mile square, or 640 acres); the minimum price was one dollar an acre.

New England speculators, forming the Ohio Company, evaded this stipulation by a deal with corrupt congressmen. The group acquired 1,500,000 acres at about nine cents (hard money) an acre. Squatters were taking over large tracts for nothing at all and then challenging Congress to dispossess them. To protect the nation's rights in this domain, sale of which was to pay the country's debts, Congress decided to tighten up the organization of government in the Northwest Territory.

It did so in a third ordinance, 1787, which, by revising earlier arrangements, curtailed the autonomy of territories by providing for a governor and judges appointed by Congress. When the territory had 5,000 adult males it could elect a general assembly, but the appointive governor had the right of veto. Suffrage was given to those owning fifty acres. From three to five states were to be carved out of the region, each to enter the union on terms of equality with older states when its population reached 60,000. The same civil liberties enjoyed in the East were to be incorporated into constitutions of the new states as well as freedom of religion. Slavery was forever outlawed.

The region of the Southwest (south of the Ohio and west of the mountains) was also bedeviled by rival speculators. Settlers in North Carolina's western lands organized a new state, Franklin, in 1784, and sought admission to the union. North Carolina still claimed sovereignty over the area, which was also being wooed by Spain. Eventually (1790) the territory was ceded to the United States, to become six years later the state of Tennessee. The region just south of the Ohio went through similar travail until it became the state of Kentucky in 1792. In the north, in the Vermont region disputed between New York and New Hampshire, the Allen brothers, Ethan, Ira, and Levi, had taken large portions. Yorkers and Yankees snarled at each other, but out of it all came the fourteenth state, Vermont, in 1791.

Handling of interstate disputes by Congress gave Americans cause for pride and prophecy. Rival western land claims by Connecticut and Pennsylvania were amicably settled, and Robert R. Livingston, in 1783, wrote joyfully to Lafayette: "It is a singular event. There are few instances of independent states submitting their cause to a court of justice. The day will come when all disputes in the great republic of Europe will be tried in the same way, and America be quoted to exemplify the wisdom of the measure."

There were solid achievements in the Confederation, but its defects oppressed the spirits of thoughtful men. They pointed to the absence of taxing power in Congress. In the last stages of its life its total revenues could not even cover the interest on the foreign debt. Congress had no real authority to regulate foreign or interstate commerce, though obstacles to the latter were being eased. It was vested with executive as well as legislative authority, which meant weak government by committee. There was no federal judiciary, and in its absence Congress was dependent on the state courts for carrying out its laws. The individual citizen was thus beyond the direct exercise of national power.

Congress itself was in the nature of a gathering of ambassadors from sovereign states, any one of which could veto a proposed change in the Articles. When Congress was in desperate need of funds, it sought an amendment to the Articles of Confederation granting it the right to impose a 5 per cent duty on foreign imports. On two separate occasions unanimity was blocked, first by Rhode Island and at a later time by New York. Each state in the Confederation was equal to every other state in voting strength; each state voted as a unit. The approval of nine states was required for the adopting of important measures, and as it often happened that not more than nine or ten states were in attendance in Congress, it meant that in practice unanimous acceptance was demanded. Impotent government has been almost as abhorrent to men as tyranny.

The scrapping of the Articles of Confederation was eventually brought about by several factors—the needs of commerce were hampered by restrictions imposed by the several states; there was fear on the part of conservatives lest the democratizing process go too far; and finally the commanding leadership of a small group of imaginative men, led by Alexander Hamilton, James Madison, Robert Morris, George Washington, skilfully capitalized on nationalistic sentiments. In place of the Confederation was erected the enduring structure of the federal Constitution. But the struggle to create it was hard, with the result in doubt until the climactic days of 1788, when the required number of states adopted the new instrument of government.

★ NATIONALISM AND SHAYS' REBELLION

The half dozen years after 1781, when the Articles of Confederation were in effect, have traditionally been spoken of as the "critical period." Actually they were not critical in the former use of the term, which maintained that the country had been rescued from social anarchy by the framers of the Constitution. This period was critical, however, in that Americans at a great crisis in their history surmounted it by choosing a form of government which promised greater stability. These were years of important social, economic, and cultural reconstruction, in which democratic energies released by the Revolutionary War found further fulfillment.

Gradually American business enterprise surmounted the postwar depression, promoting local manufactures and sending ships to trade in familiar European ports or new harbors in distant Asia. Quietly, vindictiveness died away, the less vociferous Loyalists who did not emigrate were reabsorbed by their fellows, and they endured no permanent stigma. In fact, some of them soon became prominent again in their old communities.

The 1780's have been described as years during which state rivalries and class jealousies threatened disruption to the frail union. State antagonisms were indeed prominent (resulting in tariff wars between them), and class hostilities were deep (as Shays' Rebellion revealed), but the forces promoting nationalism were strong enough to permit founding a new federal government. In truth co-operation between the states, on matters of trade, boundaries, and navigation, was more in evidence than antagonism. David Ramsay of South Carolina, who had been a member of Congress in these years, testified to the influences cementing Americans together. "A continental army, and Congress composed of men from all the States, by freely mixing together," he said, "were assimilated into one mass. Individuals of both, mingling with the citizens, disseminated principles of union among them. Local prejudices abated. By frequent collisions asperities were worn off, and a foundation was laid for the establishment of a nation, out of discordant materials. Intermarriages, between men and women of different States, were much more common than before the war. These became an additional bond to the union. Unreasonable jealousies had existed between the inhabitants of the eastern and of the southern States; but when they became better acquainted with each other, these in a great measure subsided. A wiser policy prevailed," said Ramsay. "Men of liberal minds led the way in discouraging local distinctions, and the great body of the people, as soon as reason got the better of prejudice, found their best interests would be most effectually promoted by such practices and sentiments as were favorable to union."

Improved communications by land and water, more frequent mails, and reduced postage were additional factors promoting bonds of nationalism. Interest in American history and the success of school books appealing to American nationalism, written by Noah Webster and Jedidiah Morse, gave fresh proof of the pervasiveness of this sentiment. In the America of that day the feeling of nationalism was bolstered by self-congratulation that this country was superior to decaying Europe. The more the New World differed from the Old the better for her youthful civilization. "This country must, at some future time," said Webster, "be as distinguished by the superiority of her literary improvement as she is already by the liberality of her civil and ecclesiastical institutions. Europe is grown old in folly, corruption, and tyranny—in that country laws are perverted, manners are licentious, literature is declining, and human nature is debased. For America in her infancy to adopt the present maxims of the old world would be to stamp the wrinkle of decrepit age upon the bloom of youth, and to plant the seed of decay in a vigorous constitution."

Thomas Paine, with his usual sure instinct, stirred deep emotions with his appeal to national pride. "Our great national character depends on Union of the States," he wrote in *The American Crisis*. It is only through union, he insisted "that we are, or can be nationally known in the world; it is the flag of the United States which renders our ships and commerce safe on the seas, or in a foreign port." Distinctions between residents of different states ceased when Americans went abroad. "We have no other national sovereignty than the United States," wrote Paine. "Our great title is AMERICANS."

Distinguished men in public life added their powerful voices to the call for a strong national state. "In speaking of national matters," said Washington, "I look to the federal government, which in my opinion it is the interest of every state to support; and to do this, as there are a variety of interests in the Union, there must be a yielding of the parts to coalesce the whole." Jefferson had written in similar language to Monroe, that in every way possible the people should be encouraged to "look up to Congress as their head." In the year before the Convention met to frame a new federal constitution, John Jay wrote to John Adams that it was one of his greatest hopes "to see the people of America become one nation in every respect." Their state legislatures should bear the same relationship to the Confederation that counties had to the state of which they were parts, "merely as districts to facilitate the purposes of domestic order and good government."

Without a foundation of national feeling it would have been impossible to raise the structure of the Constitution. But more than wishes and proclamations of devotion to a national ideal were required for this historic accomplishment. It required adroit management by men of great imagination to convince the people to adopt the new government. There was a natural reluctance on the part of Americans to accept a fundamental change in their way of life, for inbred in their bones was dislike of "strong government."

Conservatives feared the strengthening of the democratic element in American life and the threat it posed to their domination. A French observer of the American scene remarked that while the country had no nobles, it had "a class of men denominated 'gentlemen' who, by reason of their wealth, their talents, their education, their families, or the offices they hold, aspire to a pre-eminence which the people refuse to grant them. . . . Almost all of them dread the efforts of the people to despoil them of their possessions, and, moreover, they are creditors and therefore interested in strengthening the government, and watching over the laws."

Massachusetts revealed elements of the conflict between debtors and creditors more sharply than elsewhere. In that state conservative merchants and lawyers had written a constitution, in 1780, designed for "quarter deck efficiency in government, and the protection of property against democratic pirates." The constitution of Massachusetts favored mercantile interests through a disproportionate representation of their districts in the state legislature. In that body this class repealed legislation aimed to relieve debtors, raised taxes, and adopted a hard-money policy. Farmers complained that taxes took a third of their income. Even when corn and wheat were plentiful, deflation brought such low prices that the harvest might as well have been bushels of stones for all the money it yielded. Rural grievances included the high cost of litigation, scarcity of money, and the harsh treatment of debtors who faced prison for nonpayment of debts and loss of family homesteads. In Worcester County, Massachusetts, in one year alone, 1784, there were more than 2,000 suits for debts. Revolutionary War veterans, whose pay had been in depreciated paper, threatened to hold back their taxes.

Law-abiding citizens in Massachusetts, early in the 1780's, were reported "on the point of turning to the Mobb," before which sheriffs and their deputies would be "like Stubble before devouring fire." An arrested ringleader of a riot was released by his followers who broke open the town jail in Springfield. The discontented were saying that their present rulers were more expensive than "the Great Men under George 3d."

Elsewhere in New England the distress of debtors was equally great. Resentment flared into the open at local gatherings and in the state legislature. To the consternation of creditors Rhode Island made its depreciated paper currency legal tender. Demands for paper money and relief for debtors became more insistent. A convention in Hampshire County, Massachusetts, in 1786 resolved that taxation bore unequally on the farmers, and that holders of government securities were unduly favored. The angriest of the malcontents in the state urged the abolition of the courts of common pleas and general sessions.

A force of 1,500 men, including war veterans, seized the courthouse in Northampton in August, 1786, and prevented the court from functioning. Other counties in the central and western portions of Massachusetts, Worcester in particular, were soon aflame with discontent. Barns of government officials were burned and haystacks set ablaze by angry farmers. For a few months the state authorities had inadequate strength to subdue the rioters. In the winter of 1786–87 a vigorous campaign, led by General Benjamin Lincoln and supported by the contributions of prosperous conservatives, was launched against Daniel Shays and his followers. In below-zero weather many of these hunted men, hungry and exhausted from plodding through heavy snows, collapsed in the snow-covered fields.

On a February morning in 1787, during a violent storm, Lincoln caught up with Shays and his disheartened men in Worcester county, and with scarce any bloodshed took most of them captive. Shays' Rebellion was ended, but it had struck fear in the hearts of conservatives. In their terror they demanded death for the insurgent leaders, but at length passions cooled and pardons were granted the condemned men. Washington, with characteristic magnanimity, reminded his friends of the danger "of entirely alienating the affections of a people from their government."

Shays' Rebellion was turned to advantage by well-to-do conservatives who now claimed that only a strong national government could protect society against subversion. Some of the more militant conservatives seemed to welcome the agrarian outbreaks as object lessons to frighten the undecided into supporting the program for a powerful central government. One conservative, fearing the spread of radicalism, expressed a sentiment common to his group when he said that the "ambition of the poor, and the avarice of the rich demagogue can never be restrained upon the narrow scale of a state government." When the constitutional convention met in Philadelphia, General Henry Knox said that "it would clip the wings of a mad democracy." Discouraged men talked of setting up a monarchy in America, and there were dark hints of military dictatorship to rescue the country from its despair.

Fear alone was not enough to sway the mass of Americans to positive action. Before undertaking a positive program they had to be convinced that a strong government would solve monetary ills and commercial difficulties with foreign states, and that it would also win respect for America from its own citizens as well as those of alien lands. A strong government would encourage native manufactures and protect American shippers in foreign waters. A central government, with power, would curb the Indians whose threat to frontier areas slowed the settlement of western lands.

The pressure for a stronger national government mounted. There seemed to be a race between those who would achieve that strength by amending the Articles of Confederation and those who would find it by scrapping the Articles and creating a new government. Virginia, which was having difficulties with Maryland over navigation of the Potomac, sent out a call for a convention to meet in September, 1786, to discuss problems of commerce and taxation. The Annapolis Convention drew delegates from only five states, and the sparse turnout left them dispirited. In the gathering, however, as delegate from New York, was the leading champion of strong, national government, the brilliant Alexander Hamilton. It was rumored that the Annapolis meeting "was only intended to propound a question much more important than that of commerce," and Madison's correspondence with intimate friends proved the rumor to be correct. He had previously written Jefferson, "Gentlemen both within and without Congress wish to make this meeting subservient to a plenipotentiary convention for amending the Confederation." Under the leadership of Hamilton, and Madison representing Virginia, the delegates passed a resolution asking Congress to call a convention with a larger membership, whose task it would be to amend the Articles of Confederation. Congress agreed and summoned the states to send delegates to Philadelphia and report "such alterations . . . as shall render the Federal Constitution adequate to the exigencies of government and the preservation of the union." All complied, save Rhode Island, and the historic assembly gathered in May, 1787, to frame a stronger government for the United States.

★ THE CONSTITUTIONAL CONVENTION

The fundamental problem that the noted gathering was called upon to solve was to write a constitution which would preserve the identity and dignity of the states, and at the same time maintain a fair distribution of authority between the national center and the component parts. It was the most difficult of all problems in political organization. More than one imperial structure (including the British Empire in 1776) had foundered from failure to solve it. Could America find the solution, she would make one of the greatest contributions of any people to the art of government. The delegates were aware of their responsibility to posterity. "The whole human race," said Gouverneur Morris, "will be affected by the proceedings of this Convention."

The leaders in this assembly at once resolved to go far beyond its allotted powers. The Continental Congress had called it "for the sole and express purpose of revising the Articles of Confederation"; it determined to scrap them and adopt a new instrument. Hamilton called this a "revolutionary" step; Martin Van Buren later described it as "an heroic but lawless act"; a more recent authority, John W. Burgess of Columbia, wrote that if Napoleon had done anything of the kind, it would have been pronounced a *coup d'état*. The plan for a wholly new Constitution could not have been broached in advance. As Richard Henry Lee said: "Had the idea of a total change been started, probably no State would have appointed members of the Convention." Elbridge Gerry of Massachusetts took the same view: not one legislature, in choosing delegates, had a real idea "that they would without any warrant from their constituents presume on so bold and daring a step," or would have agreed to such a course. But necessity ruled. The larger States had special reason to be discontented with the old government. The ablest and most influential men in the body saw clearly that a completely new system was imperatively needed. James Madison did; James Wilson of Pennsylvania did. So above all did Washington, who said: "my wish is that the convention adopt no temporizing expedients, but probe the defects of the constitution to the bottom, and provide a radical cure. . . ."

Fortunately for the United States many of the men who met in the State House at Philadelphia were greatly skilled in the theory and practice of government. From Virginia came an especially notable delegation, including Washington; James Madison, able politician and profound scholar; George Wythe, a great lawyer and teacher; George Mason, who gave a strong stamp of liberalism to his state's constitution; and Governor Edmund Randolph, an able debater. Pennsylvania's delegation was equally distinguished, headed by the mentally lively, patriarchal

Franklin. At his side were Robert Morris the "pecuniary dictator," who in a dark hour had raised funds for the Revolution, and the sophisticated Gouverneur Morris, a skilled debater. A crippled arm and the loss of a leg could not dampen his wit nor dull his language. The most valuable member of the Pennsylvania group was James Wilson, born and educated in Scotland. His learning in political science was vast, and his services were the most useful of any (with the exception of Madison's) in bringing the work of the convention to a successful end.

South Carolina sent to the convention General Charles C. Pinckney, along with his youthful cousin Charles Pinckney, and also Pierce Butler, proudly aristocratic, and John Rutledge, a noted orator. The Massachusetts delegation included two very able men, the eloquent Rufus King and Elbridge Gerry, the latter especially trained to deal with questions of commerce and finance. New York's most distinguished representative was Alexander Hamilton who, though in his early thirties, had already won a great reputation for his fertile mind and his ardent nationalism. New Jersey sent its perennial governor, William Livingston, as well as William Paterson, who distinguished himself as a champion of the interests of small states. Paterson was ably supported in his position by Maryland's representative, the long-winded Luther Martin.

All told, the number of delegates at the convention were fifty-five, most of whom had seen service in Congress or in high office in their own states. Their average age was forty-two years, but some of them were old enough to have served in the Stamp Act Congress, and eight had signed the Declaration of Independence. Most of the delegates were experienced in affairs that transcended state considerations, and they were predisposed to think in national terms. They included men of wealth who were accustomed to leadership. For the most part they were planters, merchants, and lawyers, with the last especially numerous. The temper of the delegates was generally conservative and inhospitable to the doctrinaire. Patrick Henry, the flaming orator of the Revolution, was among the missing, as was Sam Adams. Henry had been elected to the Virginia delegation, but refused to go to Philadelphia, saying that he "smelt a rat." Jefferson and John Adams were abroad, but their ideas had able spokesmen in Madison and Gouverneur Morris.

The convention, which met from May to September, 1787, named Washington chairman by unanimous vote. Washington sat on a raised platform in a large high-backed chair, from which, with great dignity, he exercised a powerful influence on the deliberations of the Convention. May 25, when the convention was organized, was a stormy day and only twenty-nine members had shown up. They met behind closed doors, pledging secrecy to each other. Notes were kept of the debates, however, particularly by Madison, after whose death nearly half a century later they were given to the world.

It is clear from the records we have of these secret debates that while the convention wrangled long and bitterly over various matters, its members were in agreement on a number of fundamental questions. Because of the large area of agreement on which the majority of delegates could stand, the convention had remarkable success. Moved by the desire to protect economic interests, animated by altruism and principle, always conscious of the fearful consequences of failure, this body of men achieved greatly. Their reading of ancient history, in which they were proficient, reminded them that the alternative to strong union was a multitude of commonwealths, sapping one another's strength in jealous economic strife or outright war, all ultimately to fall prey to an alien conqueror.

Former example suggested, however, the seeming impossibility of a large-scale republic. But this Revolutionary generation was not dismayed. "Is it not the glory of the people of America," asked Madison, "that, while they have paid a decent regard to the opinions of former times and other nations, they have not suffered a blind veneration for antiquity, for custom or for names, to overrule the suggestions of their good sense and knowledge of their own situations, and the lessons of their own experience?" Their experience made this generation the most fertile in political thought of any in modern history. Only England during the period of the Commonwealth matched its vigorous imagination.

On the second day of the convention Randolph, a gifted speaker, presented to the members, in a long and vigorous address, a picture of the inadequacies of the Articles of Confederation. He urged the delegates to join together in creating a strong government. The chief danger facing the country, this conservative Virginian said, "arises from the democratic parts of our [state] constitutions." Randolph then unrolled a manuscript he had been holding and read a lengthy series of resolutions drawn up by his colleague, James Madison. They called for a national executive, a national judiciary, and a two-house legislature, the lower chosen by popular vote; in both houses representation was to be based on population or wealth. The resolves, which came to be known as the Virginia plan, were intended to guide the convention in framing a powerful national government in which the role of the states would be greatly diminished. Thus at the very start of the sessions the convention had ignored its original authorization, which was to draft amendments to the Articles of Confederation.

As the debates proceeded it was clear that a majority of the delegates were in agreement that the Articles of Confederation should be discarded and replaced by a new Constitution. It was understood, too, that in the new government there was to be a division of power among three departments—the legislative, executive, and judicial. It was assumed that the new Congress would have legislative power covering matters affecting the entire nation, such as the common defense, the regulation of interstate and foreign commerce, and the coinage. Congress was to have the power to tax and spend national funds for the general welfare. A majority of the convention's delegates also agreed that the powers of state governments were to be strongly curbed.

While the delegates were agreed as to the main objectives of the new constitution, controversy arose as to the means to achieve them. In the Virginia plan, which called for a bicameral legislature, proportional representation would have given the large states overwhelming domination in the proposed new government. The proposal was challenged by a New Jersey plan, which would have preserved the powers of the small states on a basis of equality with their larger neighbors. In the debates on the issue of representation in the legislature the heat of the argument matched the temperature outside. Fortunately for frayed tempers, at a critical moment the weather turned cool. In a calmer atmosphere a compromise (the "great compromise") was adopted, providing for proportional representation in the lower legislative house and an equal vote for the states in the upper house. Thus, in effect, there was to be equality for men in the House of Representatives and equality for States in the Senate.

While the main division of interest or economic outlook, as Madison remarked, was between the planting states of the South and the commercial states of the North, the main division of political outlook was between the small and large States. The lines were not always hard and fast. Thus Madison of Virginia and Rutledge of South Carolina made speeches on the Northern side of the question of the regulation of commerce, and this side prevailed. But the small states of Connecticut, New Jersey, Maryland, Delaware, and (sometimes) North Carolina stood as a compact unit behind the contention that the states have equal representation in Congress, as under the old Confederation. Long afterward, in 1847, John C. Calhoun paid them tribute. "It is owing mainly to the States of Connecticut and New Jersey," he said, "that we have a Federal instead of a national [that is, unitary] government—the best government instead of the worst and most intolerable on earth. Who are the men of these States to whom we are indebted for this excellent form of government? I will name them. Their names ought to be written on brass, and live forever. They were Chief Justice Ellsworth and Roger Sherman of Connecticut, and Judge [William] Paterson of New Jersey. The other States farther south were blind; they did not see the future."

A second compromise, "the three-fifths compromise," provided that three whites were to be counted equivalent to five Negroes in matters involving direct taxes and representation in the House of Representatives. Another threatening issue, slavery, was surmounted by a provision that Congress was not to forbid imports of slaves before 1808, though it might lay a tax up to ten dollars a head on those brought in.

Delegates from the large states believed they had suffered a grave defeat on the question of representation, and they even contemplated breaking up the convention. But on second thought they decided to carry on with the proceedings. As for the delegates from the small states they were all smiles, and they were now more co-operative in strengthening the central government. More discussion revealed agreement about the general principles on which the new government should be based. To reduce these ideas to coherent form a committee of five was named, with Rutledge as chairman, to frame a constitution. The convention then adjourned, on July 26, for ten days.

In the ten-day period Rutledge and his associates worked with great intensity, drawing on various sources to produce a document which the final Constitution closely resembled. The convention resumed its sessions on August 6 and spent many wearisome hours in the next five weeks going over the document submitted by Rutledge's committee, line by line, phrase by phrase. But the spirit of the convention was now one of compromise, and in a more relaxed atmosphere the members were prepared to yield to one another.

In the new Constitution the weaknesses of Congress under the Articles of Confederation were remedied. The new legislative body was granted specific powers to tax, to regulate commerce, and "to call forth the aid of the militia, in order to execute the laws of the Union, enforce treaties, suppress insurrections, and repel invasions." In a broad phrase, capable of covering much in later generations, Congress was given power to provide for the "general welfare of the United States." To make sure Congress could enforce its authority it was given the right "to make all laws which shall be necessary and proper for carrying into execution the foregoing powers." The unanimity which had been required for amending the Articles of Confederation was changed to the provision that, once passed by Congress, a proposed amendment would be added to the Constitution after ratification by three-fourths of the states.

The experience of the colonists themselves, as well as the history of Great Britain, had made Americans cautious about endowing with too much power any one branch of government. The idea of "checks and balances" was uppermost in the minds of the constitution makers. The power of Congress was limited by the grant of a veto to the president, who could be overridden, however, by a two-thirds vote in both legislative chambers. As a result of Southern pressure the Senate was required to have a two-thirds vote to ratify treaties. Congress was forbidden to impose export taxes, and other prohibitions were also placed upon it.

The judiciary, which in after years attained a place of great importance in American government, was not conspicuously emphasized in the Constitution. A federal Supreme Court with appellate jurisdiction was to be created, and Congress could establish inferior courts. There is nothing in the document itself about the power later assumed by the judiciary to upset Congressional laws said to contravene the Constitution ("judicial review"). And yet the leaders in the constitutional convention believed that the courts would exercise the power of judicial review, even though such authority was not expressly granted to them. Article VI, section 2, however, indicated that measures of states trespassing on the powers of Congress were to be declared unconstitutional. The Constitution and the federal laws were to "be the supreme law of the land . . . anything in the constitution or laws of any state to the contrary notwithstanding." This article enabled the federal government to go over the heads of state authorities and exercise compulsion upon individuals directly by its own coercive agencies.

The states, however, retained much strength, for they possessed many powers in running local government. Most of the contacts of people were with their own states, which controlled schools, local communities, and the police. The states established qualifications for the franchise and incorporated business enterprises. The Tenth Amendment (operative after 1791) reserved to the states all powers not granted specifically to the federal government.

It was difficult for the convention members to agree on the nature of the executive to be established although it was relatively easy to decide that a single, rather than plural, executive should be created. Still eighteenth-century minds found it not easy to think of heads of states in other than monarchical terms. In fact many members of the convention thought that in setting up the presidency they were creating an office somewhat like that of a monarch, though severely limited in power. John Adams thought that a satisfactory title for the president was "His High Mightiness, the President of the United States and Protector of their Liberties." Apparently Americans outside of the convention shared the impression that they were getting a quasi monarchy.

When the convention had finished its sessions Franklin was asked by a lady: "Well, Doctor, what have we got, a republic or a monarchy?" "A republic," replied the venerable sage, "if you can keep it."

The delegates to the convention engaged in lengthy discussion about the process of electing the chief executive, and about his term of office, before they finally agreed on the system of the electoral college and a four years' term with no restriction upon re-election. The power of the presidency was enhanced by the grant of authority to appoint ambassadors and judges (with the advice and consent of the Senate), and to negotiate treaties, subject to ratification by two-thirds of the attending Senators. The only point about the presidency seemingly free of controversy was the name of the man to fill the post. By common consent George Washington was to be the first executive of the new state.

The members of the convention, having sat in session throughout the summer, were now anxious to finish their task. A committee was appointed to "revise the stile of and arrange the articles which had been agreed to by the House." Gouverneur Morris, whose gift of expression was great, was named to the committee, which made its report on September 12. Again the convention went over the document line by line, and then on Saturday, September 15, ordered the Constitution to be engrossed. Two days later, September 17, the convention met for the last time, and thirty-nine delegates from twelve states signed the Constitution. A few of the delegates, including Edmund Randolph, who disliked the document refused to sign.

As the last signatures were being added, Franklin glanced at Washington's chair on whose back was painted a blazing sun, and remarked to some fellow members in the convention that painters often found it difficult to make the rising sun appear different from a setting sun. Franklin then said that "often and often, in the course of the Session, and the vicissitudes of my hopes and fears as to its issue [he] looked at that [sun] behind the President without being able to tell whether it was rising or setting. But now, at length, I have the happiness to know that it is a rising and not a setting Sun." Probably not a single delegate was completely satisfied with what the convention had done. Yet, as some members said, they believed that the Constitution was "the best they could ever agree upon, and that it was infinitely better to have such a one than break up without fixing on some form of government."

★ RATIFICATION

A formidable hurdle had still to be taken before the advocates of a strong central government could call their victory complete. The Constitution they had adopted could go into force only after ratification by conventions in nine of the states. This meant in effect that the people were to pass judgment on the work of the men in Philadelphia.

There was no certainty that the required number of states would accept the new government. Those behind it were known as Federalists, while its opponents were anti-Federalists. The former were comprised of the judiciary, lawyers, large landowners, many of the leading clergy, merchants, and capitalists. The anti-Federalists, who scorned their opponents as "the well-born," found the mass of their own supporters among smaller landowners. Yet many of them, including former followers of David Shays, voted for ratification. Leaders of the anti-Federalists were often men of political and social distinction who were opposed to the increased concentration of power in the central government. Creditors who believed strong central government would sustain public and private credit favored the new Constitution; debtors who found that state legislatures were willing to adopt laws easing their financial difficulties denounced the Constitution. Each side was also moved by contrasting political theories as to the kind of government most suitable to American conditions.

There was genuine fear on the part of "states firsters," that republican government could not survive in a large land. Madison argued to the contrary that, because of the greater ease of creating coalitions to form a majority in a small republic, more danger threatened the minority there than in a large one. Opponents of the Constitution argued that the proposed House of Representatives would be too small (55 men) to adequately represent numerous divergent views. In fact, the wealthy, they said, would dominate both houses of Congress. An old Massachusetts farmer, Amos Singletary, who had been in the local legislature, uttered a common cry against the new government: "These lawyers, and men of learning, and moneyed men that talk so finely, and gloss over matters so smoothly, to make us poor illiterate people swallow down the pill, expect to get into Congress themselves; they expect to be the managers of this Constitution, and get all the power and all the money into their own hands, and then they will swallow up all us little folks." *

Within a few months several of the states, Pennsylvania being the only large one, voted to adopt the Constitution. There, by strong-arm tactics, the Federalists forcibly gathered obstructive delegates to form a necessary quorum. They bought up the newspapers to present their side alone. The votes of Massachusetts and Virginia, because of their size, and New York because of its geographical position, were crucial,

* E. S. Morgan, *The Birth of the Republic* (Chicago: University of Chicago Press, 1956), p. 149.

and the outcome in those states was watched with mounting anxiety. The debate in Massachusetts was long and hard. From its western region, whose men had marched with Shays, came delegates hostile to the Constitution. The weather-beaten face and calloused hands generally identified an anti-Federalist. The majority in the Massachusetts convention seemed against ratification, though the division was close. Opponents were reminded that the Constitution was a cure for such disorders as Shays' Rebellion. Two hesitant, key figures, Hancock (before whom a large carrot of political advancement was dangled) and Samuel Adams, finally threw their support to the Constitution, which was ratified by a slight majority, 187 to 168. The price of ratification demanded by many reluctant supporters was the future addition to the Constitution of a bill of rights. Jefferson encouraged those who held out for a bill of rights, as he indicated in a letter to Madison: "I wish with all my soul that the nine first conventions may accept the new Constitution, to secure to us the good it contains; but I equally wish that the four latest, whichever they may be, may refuse to accede to it till a declaration of rights be annexed."

In Maryland supporters of the Constitution won an easy victory, and in South Carolina the vote ran two to one in its favor. In New Hampshire the division was comparatively close, 57 favoring and 46 opposing the new Constitution. It had now (June, 1788) been ratified by the required nine states, enough to permit it to go into operation. Two of the most important states, however, Virginia and New York, had not yet acted, and a national government without them was inconceivable. Virginia had supplied some of the chief architects of the Constitution, and in the debates that raged over ratification within the state men like Washington, Madison ("father of the Constitution"), George Wythe, and Edmund Pendleton threw their powerful weight into the fight. John Marshall first achieved prominence in this struggle. Randolph, who had refused to sign the Constitution, now decided to favor ratification. Against them were arrayed leaders with great influence, Patrick Henry and George Mason. Fence-sitters indicated willingness to vote for the Constitution provided certain amendments were added prior to ratification.

At length, four days after ratification by New Hampshire, Virginia on June 25, by 89 to 79 voted to ratify, "under the conviction that whatsoever imperfections may exist in the Constitution ought rather to be examined in the mode prescribed therein, than to bring the Union into danger by delay, with a hope of obtaining amendments previous to the ratification." The criticisms of anti-Federalists did result in the addition of the first ten amendments to the Constitution, which were in the nature of a Bill of Rights.

In New York the struggle over ratification was intense. When that state's convention met in June, probably two-thirds of the delegates were anti-Federalist. To create a majority in favor of the Constitution out of a group initially hostile was a political achievement of great magnitude. It was accomplished by the familiar give and take of most political gatherings, the influence of Virginia's example, and by the eloquence and directness of Alexander Hamilton, who argued with great clarity against the opposition. A campaign of popular education was undertaken in the press to expound the Constitution so that its value would be made clear to the average citizen. Hamilton enlisted the aid of Madison and Jay in the enterprise, and from their pens came eighty-five contributions signed "Publius." These most authoritative commentaries on the Constitution, known ever since as *The Federalist,* deservedly rank as one of the greatest political treatises in history. It cannot be determined how many supporters were won over to the Constitution by *The Federalist,* but it made a deep impression on contemporary minds and on subsequent generations. When finally the vote was taken in the New York convention, thirty favored and twenty-seven opposed the new Constitution.

There was great rejoicing in the country over the end of the long drawn out debate, which had been a remarkable demonstration of a people engaged peacefully, albeit energetically, in weighing the virtues of one form of government as against another. Two states, North Carolina and Rhode Island, held out for some months longer, but under threat of economic pressure they also came under "the new roof." Jefferson was proud of his countrymen: "The example," he said, "of changing a constitution by assembling the wise men of the state, instead of assembling armies, will be worth as much to the world as the former examples we have given them."

Meanwhile provision had already been made by the dying Congress of the old Confederation to pass the torch on to its successor. Washington, as was universally expected, had been chosen the first president of the new government. From his beloved home on the Potomac he set out in the spring of 1789 for New York to head the government he had done so much to make possible. It was a triumphal procession, with grateful citizens along the way paying their respects to the general in roars of acclaim. He was rowed across New York harbor in a gaily decorated barge manned by white uniformed men, and his approach to the city was heralded by the booming of thirteen guns. The upper bay was filled with boats of every size, colorful in flags and bunting. During the night bonfires lit up the sky and revelers thronged the streets and coffee houses. Boats brought people from towns along the Hudson and from distant communities in New England and the middle states. Overland from remote villages farmers came on horseback or in wagons to be on hand for the great event.

Cheering crowds filled the city for the historic inauguration on April 30. On that day Washington stood on the balcony of newly renovated Federal Hall in Wall Street, where the oath of office was administered by the Chancellor of New York. In a clear voice, while the crowd stood hushed, Washington spoke the now familiar words: "I do solemnly swear that I will faithfully execute the office of the President of the United States, and will, to the best of my ability, preserve, protect and defend the Constitution of the United States." And in a tone of deep emotion, he added, "So help me God." After tendering the oath the Chancellor turned to the great multitude, and cried out "Long live George Washington, President of the United States," and the words came back in answering shouts from the hearts of his fellow citizens.

LAUNCHING the new government was recognized as an event of great importance for America and, potentially, of enormous significance to the world. The Americans, said Joseph Priestley, the English scientist and friend of Franklin, had gone far beyond the Glorious Revolution of 1689 in his own country. That revolution had overthrown the Stuart dynasty but replaced it by another. America, said Priestley, had "formed a *completely New Government* on the principles of equal liberty and the rights of man—without Nobles, without Bishops and without a King." Another Englishman praised the American constitution as "the most free one we know of; the Government of the New World is stronger, because juster, than any we witness in the Old." Washington was the hero of people everywhere: "No man in his sober senses," said an English radical, "will compare the character of any of the kings of Europe with that of General Washington."

An American orator proudly listed the lessons his country had taught the world:

1. A large country could be ruled by a republican form of government without monarchy or an aristocracy.
2. Religious worship needed no legal establishment: "To allow all to think freely for themselves in matters of religion, and to worship God according to the dictates of their own Consciences is the best policy."
3. Church and State could subsist without alliance.
4. Milder punishment for crimes tends to prevent them.
5. People are happier and more contented under a "mild and equitable government," which is far stronger than arbitrary governments and in less danger of being overturned.

6. America had also shown the world "that to admit the Jews to all the privileges of natural born subjects, is far from being a dangerous experiment, as has been generally supposed."

The orator hoped that the time would come soon "when all the world shall learn and practice these lessons in a still more perfect manner than they are yet practiced in America itself."

European liberals wistfully envied Americans, who were said to possess the benefits, without the corruptions, of civilized society. Those who wished America well gleefully looked to the day, not far off, when the new state "would rank on a footing of equality with the first Empires in the world." The United States, it was expected, would have a great impact on Europe; one prophet foresaw the time when America would "change the face of the commercial world and the face of empires." "Who knows," he asked, "if America will but then avenge the outrages she has received and if our old Europe, placed in the rank of a subaltern power, will not become a colony of the New World." With remarkable clairvoyance a German student of the New World said that America would be a vast cornucopia whose horn of plenty would spill its largess over Europe's poverty.

Europeans, unwilling to endure their continent's penury, had been sailing to the west again after the interruption of the Revolutionary War. Real wages in America were reckoned at 30 to 100 per cent more than wages in England. Workmen in America, who had accumulated some money, often abandoned their jobs to become independent landowners. The opportunity of acquiring land, and owning it outright, was to many Europeans more of an attraction than America's higher wages.

It was estimated that the best lands in America cost a third of what the poorest sold for in Germany. German immigrants were described as having been rescued from "a state of vassalage in their own country, mere hewers of wood and drawers of water." In America they found themselves "entitled to all the rights of citizenship in a free country, and with a small pittance enabled to purchase a freehold estate for themselves and family."

In commenting on the beneficent laws in America, an English clergyman praised the practice of parents buying land for their children so that all might share equally, for a parent would "shudder at the thought of making 5 children slaves or beggars for the sake of making the sixth a gentleman."

Newcomers were warned that America was no place for the "lazy good-for-nothing"; it was no East Indies or Peru where wealth might easily be gathered, "but . . . a very beautiful country" which guaranteed "to the industrious and ambitious worker a peaceful existence, a comfortable income and an independent prosperity." Because of the absence of poverty, people on the lower economic levels were free of that abject cringing which marked the poor of Europe.

Instead of cringing, Americans, however poor, placed great emphasis on equalitarianism. They did not like the use of the word "servant," preferring "hired man" or "hired girl," and it was noted by travelers that native men would not act as domestics. If a servant were asked if his master were home, he might reply: "Master! I have no master; do you want Mr. Such-a-one?" Upper-class travelers from Europe were startled to see the coachman eat at the same table with the passengers riding his stage.

The American environment changed more than just class relationships; in every respect it was said to be most favorable to humankind. People apparently lived more contented lives in this New World utopia; and their lives, it seemed, were also longer. American and European statisticians at the close of the eighteenth century agreed that life expectancy was higher in the United States than in the Old World. The normal death rate was far lower in American towns and villages; and because labor was relatively well paid, marriage was easier and therefore more common, and it occurred at an earlier age than in Europe. An American student of population, proud of his land's rapid growth, said that therein lay a lasting source of his country's national vigor and greatness.

Americans thus counted their blessings in the infancy of their nationhood, and Europeans confirmed them in their belief that they were the hope of the world. The new republic, in the eyes of its own citizens, was already a great state tipping the balance of world affairs by its youthful virility. As always in their history the future had become merged with the present. The present had problems whose magnitude would have frightened any except a youthful optimist. It was America's good fortune to have, along with the hopefulness of youth, the sagacity of adult experience which had come from piloting the country through the Revolutionary era. The daring imagination of Hamilton, the patriotism of Washington, the sobriety of Adams, and the idealism of Jefferson gave a firm foundation and strong walls to "the new roof."

CHAPTER XII

The New Roof

The United States, when Washington was first inaugurated, was a land of imperial dimensions. Stretching from the Atlantic Ocean to the Mississippi River, and from the Great Lakes to the Spanish-held Floridas, the Americans had a domain of 1,000,000 square miles, almost equal to all of western Europe plus the British Isles. The 4,000,000 inhabitants, including 700,000 slaves, were not yet spread deep into the interior. Settlers from western North Carolina and western Virginia had spilled over into Tennessee, Kentucky, and Ohio. They had been joined by people coming from New England and the middle Atlantic states, who were now moving down the Ohio from Pittsburgh.

Kentucky, which had a handful of people on the eve of the Revolution, in 1790 claimed a population of over 73,000. Settlers, following the paths of earlier years, poured down the mountain valleys into the back country of Virginia, the Carolinas, and Georgia. Virginia's population of 400,000 when the Revolution broke out had jumped to nearly 750,000 when Washington became president.

In the back country of the South small farmers usually worked their own land, as they generally had no slaves. Their cultural horizon was limited, and they were inclined to be intensely sectarian. Their emotional response was quick and fervent to the excited preaching of Methodist circuit riders or itinerant Baptists and Presbyterians. From southeastern Pennsylvania to the uplands of Georgia the guttural speech of the "Pennsylvania Dutch" mingled its accents with the varied English of Ulstermen and Highland Scots.

New England was well populated, except for Maine, where settlement stayed near the coast. The New England states had a homogeneous population—the original English stock had altered little since colonial days. New York had large empty spaces in her central and western regions, but they were already attracting New Englanders who had discovered the superior virtues of this fertile expanse over their own small, hilly farm lands. From Albany, soon after the Revolution, came a report that the roads were filled with migrant peoples; the "rage for land here exceeds all conception and the influx of people from the East is so great, that this kind of speculation is the object of every person who has the means to embark on it." Travelers spoke of America as the land of speculation; the hurrying American shortened the word to "spec," and in this form it was the staple of most conversation. During the decade of the 1780's an estimated 100,000 people, spreading out in all directions, had moved out of the older states of New England, seeking better lands and lower taxes.

Americans were an agricultural people, nine out of ten living in a rural environment. At this time, however, urban population began to increase. While many people were heading for new farms, others were heading for the towns. The percentage of Americans living in sizable communities was yet small (under 4 per cent), but these centers of commerce and small industry were growing. Philadelphia with over 40,000 (including its suburbs), and New York (recovering from the ravages of the war) with some 33,000, had grown by a third in fifteen years. Baltimore, with more than 13,000, had doubled its population in the same period. Baltimore was the country's boom town at this time, and it was reported that her brick houses were "building away . . . in every corner of the town as fast [as] possible." The old port of Boston, hard hit by the Revolution, had 18,000, while Charleston, the most flavorful city in America, had over 16,000.

★ ALONG THE HIGHWAY

Communications, though somewhat improved over colonial days, were not greatly changed. Travelers preferred to journey by sea, stream, and lake when possible rather than face the hazards of travel by land. But travel by water, even on sheltered rivers, was uncertain. When the winds were favorable, three days sufficed to make the Hudson trip from New York to Albany; but contrary winds delayed many a traveler a week or longer. On land, beyond the environs of larger towns, traffic picked its wary way over poorly built roads. A fitful light pierced the overhanging branches of giant trees which still bordered long stretches of roads near the coast. A young traveler, fresh from London, found American roads depressing: "To travel day after day, among trees a hundred feet high, is oppressive to a degree which those cannot conceive who had not experienced it." In the Northern states, however, the scene was less gloomy. There the way ran through cultivated farm land, bounded by zigzag rail fences or walls made from large stones cleared from the fields.

By stagecoach or wagon, on horseback or on foot, men slowly covered the unending miles of America's vastness. To reach the remoter settlements men loaded their wares on horseback. Sometimes there were twenty horses in a train, each animal bearing as much as 200 pounds in the balanced baskets that hung at his sides. Furs and hides were carried to town; hardware and some small luxuries were taken back through the forest paths. New England peddlers, smooth in manner, often won the dislike of bilked customers, thereafter suspicious of slick Yankees.

Glib-tongued peddlers had to make way on the road for the leather-lunged wagoner, who guided a team of four or six horses pulling a large wagon painted a bright blue and red. This striking vehicle was shaped like a deep dory, high in front and back to keep the load from sliding on the downgrade or the uphill pull, and it was so constructed that for river crossings the wagon bed could be taken off the wheels and used as a boat. The wagon was protected against the weather by a tunnel tent of hemp or linen stretched on bows of hickory. A skilled driver in such a wagon could take fourteen barrels of flour over the steep ridges of the Alleghanies. These wagons and the powerful draft horses that drew them were given the name "Conestoga." The tough Conestoga wagoner seems to have been the first to adopt the habit of keeping to the right in traffic; the English custom was to drive to the left.

Cattle driven to market raised clouds of dust on the roads leading to the growing towns. Increasing demand for meat forced drovers to tap supplies from regions farther and farther away from urban centers. Americans were scolded for eating too much meat and not enough vegetables, but they did not change their habits. Foreigners also remarked that Americans ate too fast and gulped their food almost unchewed. The practice, however, seemed to have no ill effects.

Traffic of all kinds was increasing at a rapid rate and required better highways. Europeans, notably Telford and Macadam in England, were setting the pace in improved road building. Often the best of these new roads, called turnpikes, were built both in Europe and America by private corporations who were granted the right to collect tolls. Three years after Washington's inauguration a company was chartered to build a sixty-two mile highway from Philadelphia to Lancaster. The road, which was soon built, was acclaimed as a "masterpiece of its kind . . . paved with stone the whole way and overlaid with gravel, so that it is never obstructed during the most severe season." Elsewhere, notably in New England, similar enterprises were begun, but for many years communications lagged far behind the needs of American traffic.

Postal service was improving but it was expensive; it cost thirty-four cents to send a letter from New York to the southern end of the postal route in Savannah. In 1790 the main route, extending from Maine to Georgia, served fifty offices, while additional offices were reached by lateral branches. Pittsburgh was the post office farthest west at this time. To promote traffic, which it was recognized would knit the country more closely, rates were reduced in 1792, the range extending from six to twenty-five cents, according to the distance. In the wilderness the post office might be a settler's cabin, but even in older regions in the East the postmaster generally gave out the mail from a nook in his general store or tavern.

Americans, spread over a great land mass, held together by frail communications and uncertain ties of national sentiment, faced the problem of welding individualistic states into a lasting federal republic. The experiment had never before been made on so impressive a scale. Many observers, European and even American, doubted it could be done. The lessons of history seemed to promise failure. It has been one of America's virtues, however, not to be frightened by the past but boldly to make its future.

★ THE FEDERALISTS

The new government started with certain advantages which have generally been denied to other states in similar circumstances. No rival leader to Washington existed on the American scene around whom dangerous malcontents might rally. The elimination of most of the Tories from American life, though grievous in many respects, did have the effect of removing the one possibility of forming a base on which could rest a counterthrust against the new federal government. It is true that a counterrevolutionary spirit was present among some commercial elements, and it was vocal enough to give concern to critical observers. James Sullivan, of Maine, who had traveled through the country in the early months of 1789, was deeply worried over the number of "anti-revolutionists" who were becoming active in politics. He was certain they despised democracy, and he suspected them of monarchical tendencies.

Actually, however, the great majority of Americans were committed to the Constitution. Even the most conservative of Americans had political and social views astonishing to Europeans. There was no organized, irreconcilable group whose malignancy could destroy the state. The men who had opposed the adoption of the Constitution accepted the decision of the majority, believing that the law of the land should be improved in a legal manner. "I will be a peaceable citizen," said Patrick Henry, after his defeat in the ratifying convention in Virginia. "My head, my hand and my heart shall be at liberty to retrieve the loss of liberty, and remove the defects of that system in a constitutional way." The prompt addition of the promised bill of rights to the Constitution was important in quieting the fears of many, and thus strengthened their attachment to the new government. Acceptance of the federal Constitution did not mean the quieting of differences. The honeymoon was soon over, and when the administration of Washington disclosed its policies there arose again the shrill voices of partisanship.

The weaknesses of the federal government were more obvious than its impalpable strength. The new government was without funds, though faced with a large debt, and no tax collecting machinery was in operation. A tariff bill was, however, soon enacted by Congress. The armed forces were negligible, no navy and an army of less than 700. Foreign empires, England and Spain, were pressing their claims to lands belonging to the United States. Dissident settlers west of the Appalachians joined with alien Spanish conspirators in plans to harass the fledgling state by threats to set up independent governments.

After the end of the Revolution, Spain closed the port of New Orleans, hoping that this pressure on westerners would separate Kentucky and Tennessee from the weak United States. If these western communities seceded from the union they would be granted the use of the lower Mississippi, with the right of free deposit at New Orleans. Shortly before the new government was launched there had been strong sentiment in Congress to agree to a treaty to surrender for twenty-five years American claims to use the Mississippi through Spain's territory. In exchange merchants along the eastern coast were to be granted attractive commercial privileges in Spain. Many conservative easterners were quite willing to see cantankerous frontiersmen join the Spanish Empire. Nothing came of the proposed treaty except anger at the East for its apparent willingness to sacrifice the interests of the West. The Indians were encouraged by British officials to go on the warpath once more against the frontiersmen.

The unease which disturbed American officials was reflected in Washington's note to a friend when he prepared to take charge of the government in 1789: "My movement to the chair of government," he said, "will be accompanied by feelings not unlike those of a culprit, who is going to the place of his execution . . ." In characteristic language he offered "integrity and firmness" in guiding the new ship of state.

Out of a difficult set of circumstances, in the first ten years of the nation's life, the Federalist party fashioned a stable government. They took over the few officials of the Confederation and established the needful machinery of government; they created the federal judiciary; they encouraged commerce and manufactures; they established a sound national credit; they settled frontier differences with Britain and Spain; rebellious farmers in Pennsylvania were made to feel the weight of the national government's power; Indians were thrust farther westward; a land policy was laid down which, though altered later in important details, set the pattern for westward expansion. In the swirl of international complications touched off by the French Revolution the steady hands of Washington and John Adams kept the new ship of state sailing on a straight and peaceful course. To be sure the Federalists were not solely responsible for this impressive total of achievement. The opposition lent support in some of these accomplishments, but the initiative came from the Federalists, and theirs was the larger share in the national and international successes won by the young nation.

★ HAMILTON'S PROGRAM

New states often have the problem of finding men of suitable experience to take over important posts in government. The United States had a limited number of men available for administrative positions in 1789, and as Washington naturally preferred to appoint only those who had the strongest attachment to the new government his range of choice was all the more narrowed. Washington had wanted Robert Morris for his Secretary of the Treasury. Morris declined but recommended strongly the choice of Hamilton, and as Washington was very favorably disposed towards him, the New York lawyer was invited and accepted the appointment. Edmund Randolph was the Attorney General; Henry Knox, the former bookseller of Boston, and general in the Revolution, became Secretary of War. These were men who had been among the most vigorous advocates of the new government. For Secretary of State Washington named Jefferson who, though less ardent than his colleagues in espousing the federal Constitution, was nevertheless firmly attached to it. Jay, who had guided the department of foreign affairs under the Articles of Confederation, held on to this post until 1790 when Jefferson took over. At that time Jay was named to head the Supreme Court as Chief Justice. A determining factor in Jefferson's appointment was his experience gained as minister to France, where he had served as successor to Franklin. Perhaps the inclusion of Jefferson in the official family might help create an impression of a nonpartisan administration.

The illusion of nonpartisanship was soon shattered. Seemingly so slight an issue as the title by which the chief executive should be known stirred discord. Lovers of pomp wanted him called "His Highness, the President of the United States of America and Protector of their Liberties." Rabid republicans, like William Maclay, laughed at aristocratic affectation, and in the end the matter was settled by referring to the head of the government as "Mr. President." Federalist society, with its ostentation, was dubbed the "Republican Court"; its provincial imitation of European aristocratic customs and fashions aroused sarcastic comment among American democrats. The latter were quarantined, socially, by the Federalist aristocracy.

But these were small matters compared with the storm which arose over the government's economic policies. When the proposed customs tariff was introduced to raise needed revenue, first its enactment was delayed, and then it was rendered inoperative for a few weeks until the northern merchants had received, duty free, the goods they had ordered from abroad. The circumstances attending the adoption of this act were suspect; it was the first in a series of measures in which the government seemed to have turned in favor of the moneyed class.

These suspicions were well founded, for the animating spirit formulating the government's economic program was the Secretary of the Treasury, Alexander Hamilton. Hamilton at this time was approaching his middle thirties, a brisk, compact man. He was about five feet seven, handsome, with fair complexion and dark eyes. Women enjoyed his company, beguiled by his charm, but men were more conscious of his driving will. It was familiar knowledge that he distrusted the common man, for he believed that the mass of men were incapable of self-government. Hamilton had observed, in the debates at the federal convention, that "all communities divide themselves into the few and the many. The first are the rich and well-born, the other the mass of the people . . . The people are turbulent and changing; they seldom judge or determine right. Give, therefore to the first class a distinct, permanent share in the government. They will check the unsteadiness of the second, and, as they cannot receive any advantage by a change, they therefore will ever maintain good government."

It is fair to note that on another occasion he did say that "the true principle of a republic is that the people should choose whom they please to govern them. Representation is imperfect in proportion as the current of popular favor is checked. This great source of free government, popular elections, should be perfectly pure, and the most unbounded liberty allowed." But his instinct and his actions belied his words, for he had no faith in the mass of men.

Hamilton believed that men were moved by self-interest, and his admiration was reserved for the self-made man. He cared little for money, his passion was rather for power and influence. Born an illegitimate child in the West Indies, he had gone as a young man to New York where he rose to a position of distinction at the bar and in politics. He had always stressed the need to make the central government strong. While real power should rest in a few hands the government could be made more stable by winning for it a favorable public opinion. An appeal to self-interest (and this, Hamilton believed, revealed itself most clearly in money matters) would bring to the side of the government the valued support of moneyed men. Their success was to be tied to the success of the government, so that the latter's stability would ever be the concern of the prosperous citizen.

The more citizens there were with a material stake in their country the larger its body of loyal supporters. The kind of stake Hamilton was thinking of was not the small farm, but rather government bonds or a business dependent upon a tariff. Hamilton's concern, therefore, was to increase the number of moneyed men in American society, and thus enlarge the base of governmental power. National wealth, power, law, and order—these comprised the circle of his ideas.

Hamilton's power rested to a large extent on Washington's support. He had more influence over the first president than any one in the country. With probable exaggeration Vice-President John Adams said that he was only viceroy under Washington and the latter was viceroy under Hamilton. With the towering reputation of the president as a shield Hamilton was enabled to carry out his program, for critics hesitated to launch an attack against him lest their shafts hit the venerated general.

Hamilton presided over secret caucuses of Federalists, to whom he laid down the party line. Step by step he unfolded his comprehensive, audacious plan. It included an excise tax as well as the creation of a United States Bank, which stabilized the currency and made business operations throughout the country easier. The most controversial item in Hamilton's program related to the national debt. The total public debt, including federal and state obligations, stood at $74,500,000 * in December, 1789. Hamilton proposed that the new government take over the whole debt and fund it at face value. This was the foundation of his whole program. There were two aspects to his plan, first a Funding Bill, in which the new government would shoulder claims against the Confederacy, and second, assumption of state debts by the federal administration. The temper of the country seemed favorable for submission of such a program for, at the moment, the sense of unity was strong and people were suffused with a general desire to make the new

* Authorities differ over these figures.

government work. The foreign debt, $12,000,000, to be repaid through sale of a new bond issue, occasioned not much debate. The recommendation relating to federal obligations, $40,000,000, and the state debts of about $22,500,000 had hard sledding.

Most of the securities representing the public debt had fallen greatly in value as a result of arrears in payment of interest. Holders of federal and state bonds, from disgust or need, had sold them, often at discounts as high as 80 or 90 per cent. Many of these bargain purchases had come into the hands of speculators, hopeful of a rise in their value. Jefferson described the scramble of speculators to buy up securities: "Couriers and relay horses by land, and swift sailing pilot boats by sea, were flying in all directions. Active partners and agents were associated and employed in every state, town and country neighborhood, and this paper was bought up at [great discounts] before the holder knew that Congress had already provided for its assumption at par. Immense sums were thus filched from the poor and ignorant, and fortunes accumulated by those who had themselves been poor enough before." One of the leading speculators of the time, Andrew Craigie of Boston, admitted that "the greater part of the public debt is held by rich people."

Sectionalism played a great part in the contest. John Marshall later wrote in his life of Washington: "As an inevitable effect of the state of society, the public debt had greatly accumulated in the middle and northern States, whose inhabitants had derived from its rapid appreciation a proportional augmentation of their wealth." Government paper of all sorts, state and national, had naturally accumulated where the capitalist groups resided, in Charleston, Philadelphia, New York, and Boston. This would have happened even had speculators operating from these cities not encouraged the process. This was not a period in which statistics were plentiful. Still, we do have records of what the national government paid on the public debt in 1795, after assumption had been effected. They show that four New England states received $440,000 out of a total of about $880,000 thus expended. Massachusetts alone received in interest one-third more than all the Southern states, including Maryland. Spokesmen for the people of the South naturally thought Hamilton's measures a scheme to enrich Northern nabobs at the expense of the poor, hard-working farmer and mechanic—a scheme, said Senator James Jackson of Georgia, that would have made Warren Hastings blush.

It is clear that a number of Congressmen, taking advantage of their positions, speculated in government securities in 1789 and 1790. Craigie was in New York during the period when the first Congress was in session and he stayed in a boarding house there with six New England Congressmen who were among the staunchest followers of Hamilton. Large speculators such as Craigie and William Duer were familiar with the closest secrets of Congress and the Treasury. It should be remembered, however, that many representatives supported Hamilton's measures with no thought of personal profit but rather their country's good.

Immediately the storm broke. Senator Maclay charged that Hamilton was at the head of the speculators. These, along with the "courtiers" of the administration, said Maclay, "are on one side. These I call the party who are actuated by interest. The opposition are governed by principle." But the Senator concluded gloomily that "interest will outweigh principle." Another critic prophesied that Hamilton's proposal "will occasion discord, and generate rancor against the Union." On the other hand supporters of Hamilton rallied to his side with the argument that his measures would firmly establish the public credit.

The real fight was not over funding the debt but over the following issue: whether in redeeming the existing securities, a distinction should be drawn between original holders of the bonds (often purchased at full value) and speculators who had bought their holdings at a fraction of their face value. The debates in and out of Congress were sharp and loaded with bitter recrimination. Madison, up to this moment close to Hamilton, now argued that a distinction should be drawn between speculators and original purchasers, often soldiers and their relatives or creditors who had granted supplies and money when the American cause looked dark. The southern states and Pennsylvania were particularly strong in their opposition. In the latter state it was said that few of its leading citizens held any of the paper to be redeemed. Pennsylvanians were especially irked at the assertion that it was impossible to work out a plan which would discriminate fairly between original and present holders; that was precisely what they had done with their own state debt. The farmers, said the Pennsylvania Gazette, "never were in half the danger of being ruined by the British Government that they now are by their own."

Joel Barlow, a prominent Republican spokesman, pointed out in after years the international consequences of Hamilton's plan of debt funding. "It has had," he said, "a pernicious influence on the policy of our government with foreign powers. The payment of the interest was made to depend in a great measure on the duties to be levied on imported merchandise, which were by law appropriated for fifteen years to this object. This made every stock-holder a partizan of commercial connections with that country [England] whose commerce with us was supposed principally to secure this revenue; however injurious those connections might become to the general interest of the United States."

The fight was especially bitter over assumption of state debts. Communities that were paying off their debts, Virginia and Pennsylvania, believed themselves penalized to benefit speculators in New York and Massachusetts. Only South Carolina among the southern states stood to gain by assumption, and without her support the plan would have failed. It is important to note that the strongest criticism of assumption came from men who had been most ardent in support of adopting the Constitution.*

Hamilton finally secured a needed majority in the federal legislature. To win the extra votes needed (several House members switched sides), Hamilton was eventually supported by Jefferson. The latter, though suspicious of the projected financial program, feared that if it were not effected "our credit will burst and vanish and the States separate to take care everyone of itself." Jefferson played host at a dinner to which Hamilton and Madison were invited. There an agreement was made to bring to Hamilton's aid the required votes in exchange for his support of the location of the permanent federal capital at a site on the Potomac River. The national capital was to remain for ten years at Philadelphia (where it had moved from New York soon after Washington's inauguration), and then it was to be transferred to the new location.

Hamilton's financial program smashed the semblance of harmony with which the federal government began its life. In the Congressional votes a noticeable sectional division was shown, a division which portended the emergence of national parties. The northern states voted twenty-four in favor, nine against assumption; in the South, ten were for it, eighteen against. But South Carolina, which supported assumption, could not be counted on to back other Federalist proposals. The vote to establish a bank showed only one from the North in opposition (33 to 1); in the South it was six for, nineteen against. Even in New England where Hamilton found much of his support there was glum head-shaking about his fast pace. But skeptical Federalists continued to be loyal to him for they felt that his program seemed to guarantee conservative control of American life. John Adams, though suspicious of Hamilton and his measures, supported them, at first, as necessary to the successful launching of the government.

However, Hamilton's alienation of several influential men, Rush and Madison among them, was permanent, leaving profound effects on party politics. Political affiliations in this first decade of the nation's history were unstable, and shifting of loyalties was common.

* Joseph Charles, *The Origins of the American Party System* (Williamsburg, Va.: Institute of Early American Culture, 1956), p. 21.

Hamilton's political generalship excelled that of his opponents, his financial measures won Congressional assent, and their effects were of immediate benefit. American credit was on a sound footing at home and abroad, and a great lift was given to American business enterprise. Hamilton's imagination saw the future of America as a country transformed from an agrarian to an industrial society. Filled with a vision of America's ultimate greatness as an industrial nation he sent to Congress in December, 1791, his noted Report on Manufactures. Industry would guarantee the country's future, but to promote it subsidies and protective tariffs would be necessary. In the agrarian and commercial society of that day it was hard to win support for such a program, and it languished for many years. Other aspects of Hamilton's blueprint for the American economy had better success. He supplied flesh and blood to the skeleton of the Constitution. But his hardness and lack of generous impulse limited his vision to the material structure alone. Without Jefferson the new nation might have lost its soul.

★ THE JUDICIARY

The establishment of the good name of the new nation in the commercial and financial marketplaces of the world was now accomplished. Congress voted bounties to further develop American fisheries, and it encouraged American shipping by special favors. The comprehensiveness of Washington's nationalism may be measured by additional recommendations he made to Congress to pass laws promoting agriculture, science, and education. He also favored the creation of a national university where young men might be trained for public service.

The machinery of government established by Congress included a federal judiciary. In addition to the Supreme Court (provided for by the Constitution) federal district courts were established. To the newly created judicial posts Washington named men known for their strong Federalist sentiments. The highest office in the judiciary, Chief Justice of the United States, went to John Jay of New York, one of the top Federalists.

The tenure of federal judges was for life, subject to impeachment. Thus while presidents and legislators came and went, federal judges stayed on. Their opinions strengthened the influence of the central government in the lives of Americans, notably the great decisions of John Marshall, appointed by a later Federalist President, John Adams.

★ THE UNITED STATES AND THE FRENCH REVOLUTION

The infant nation, like the legendary Hercules, was forced to overcome perils that might well have strangled it. The greatest danger appeared in the international complications ultimately arising from the French Revolution. In its first phases Americans greeted with delight the social convulsion which seemed to be guided by the same principles which inspired their own Revolution. John Adams and his fellow Americans were proud of the impulse to revolutionary action their own deeds had communicated to the French. The French Revolution, said Jefferson, was "but the first chapter of the history of European liberty." Throughout the western world the French Revolution was hailed for its constitutional destruction of princely privilege and its assertion of "The Rights of Man." The thrill of participating with massed humanity in society's redemption ran through men's veins. "We ardently wish," said an English radical, "the triple alliance (not of crowns but) of the *people* of America, France and Great Britain to give freedom to Europe and peace to the whole world."

The hopes of Americans for European progress, kindled by the bright, controlled flame of 1789, were consumed by the roaring blaze the French Revolution became after 1792. A new, more radical government seized power; the King and Queen were put to death and a "Reign of Terror" spread through France. European monarchs joined to crush the Revolution lest they, too, be swept away in the holocaust. War broke out, with France arrayed against a vast coalition in which England eventually played the dominant part.

As soon as France and England were at war in 1793, the United States faced a crisis. Any conflict in which England was involved spelled difficulties for American commerce, because Britain's naval power would be used to cut off neutral trade with her antagonist. What made matters worse France also had a navy which could harass American ships though she was reluctant to press the United States too hard as she needed food from America. To add to the dilemma of the United States, the French had a claim on American support in time of war, which rested on the provisions of the Franco-American treaty of alliance of 1778, when France had assisted the colonists during their Revolution. Despite the moderation of enthusiasm for the French Revolution, the sympathies of many Americans still inclined to the French. Democratic societies which had been formed in many communities to express support of revolutionary France still functioned, celebrating Bastille day and drinking toasts to the principles of her Revolution. Francophiles charged the administration with gross ingratitude for its failure to rally immediately to the side of the French.

President Washington moved cautiously. To fulfill apparent obligations to France would invite crushing retaliation from England. The newly established federal government might easily collapse under the strain. Washington consulted his advisers, among them Hamilton and Jefferson, and the president then proclaimed the neutrality of the United States.

Opinion was divided in the country. Federalists applauded, while anti-Federalists reproved the proclamation of neutrality. Americans were divided into British parties and French parties. In these years events connected with our foreign relations had a profound impact on the evolution of American parties. The hostile sentiment encouraged the French minister to the United States, "citizen" Edmond Genêt, to appeal directly to the American people to disregard their government's policy, and bring pressure on it to uphold the alliance of 1778. The romantic, eloquent, impulsive Genêt had captivated many Americans, and the shouts of multitudes wearing liberty caps and waving French flags misled him into thinking he could, singlehanded, fashion the foreign policy of America. The minister, against the orders of the United States government, outfitted privateers in American ports to ravage British shipping. He encouraged frontiersmen in the Mississippi Valley to plan the wresting from Spain of her possessions in Florida and Louisiana. Genêt's behavior indicated such contempt for the American government and ignorance of the people's national spirit that a strong reaction set in, even among the friends of France. In the revulsion Britain benefited.

It needed a vigorous American reaction against France to effect at this time an easing of relations between the United States and England. Those relations, strained in the years following the Revolution, became tense when England informed the Americans that, despite the Treaty of 1783, she would not give up the frontier posts in the Northwest Territory. The British sought to protect their fur-trading interests in the region. The Governor-General of Canada inflamed the Indians to dream of revenge against the American settlers on the frontier.

Behind all the British policy of harassment lay the hope that the new nation would not endure, and reoccupation of the Northwest would then be possible. If Britain sought justification for failing to live up to the treaty, she supplied it in American actions. British creditors found it difficult to collect pre-Revolutionary debts, and not until 1802 was the matter settled. Also, contrary to the spirit of the treaty, confiscated property of Loyalists was being retained by various states. Ultimately £3,300,000 was granted by Britain herself to satisfy some 5,000 Loyalist claims. Americans, for the most part, were in no mood after the war to be told to pay debts to former enemies or compensate hated Loyalists.

Added grievances piled up when England as a war measure in 1793 forbade the flourishing neutral trade with the French West Indies, and confiscated in those waters American ships and their cargoes of provisions. Britain invoked the "rule of the War of 1756," which maintained that trade forbidden to a nation in time of peace could not be enjoyed in time of war. Three hundred American vessels were seized, passengers abused, and many sailors impressed into the British navy. Belligerent talk against England raced through the United States, even among Federalists inclined to be friendly to the old mother country. Congress authorized the president to lay a temporary embargo on American shipping, and a Nonintercourse Bill was narrowly beaten. Fortunately at this moment England, not anxious for war with the United States, promised to cease harassing American vessels trading in the West Indies. Washington thereupon immediately determined to work out a solution of Anglo-American differences, and he dispatched a trusted adviser, John Jay, to London in April, 1794, to negotiate a settlement.

Jay had had considerable diplomatic experience, but his pronounced aristocratic bias made him suspect to the Jeffersonians. His appearance was friendly enough, his dark eyes accenting the pallor of his kindly face. Vanity was his undoing, and the British knew of this weakness. Jay was too warm a friend of Great Britain to drive a hard bargain with her, a collaborator almost, instead of a negotiator. Whatever bargaining power Jay had was cut from under him by Hamilton's assurance to Hammond, British minister in New York, that the United States would not make war on Britain regardless of the outcome of the negotiations. The treaty he agreed to in November, 1794, did win British agreement to evacuate the Northwest posts, when American ratification was accomplished, though Britain could still carry on her fur trade in the region. On other points Britain conceded very little; nothing on impressment of American seamen was mentioned. In particular on the very sensitive issue of British interference with American trade Jay gained nothing. In the treaty Britain placed such onerous restrictions on America's lucrative trade with her West Indies that the Senate struck out that portion of it before ratification.

Jay's treaty was denounced throughout the country as an abject surrender of American rights, a blow at America's sovereignty, and fury against England rose to such a pitch as to endanger Anglo-American relations. Jeffersonians led the fight on the treaty which, they said, was being foisted on a people deliberately frightened by intimations of war if it were not accepted. It was pointed out that England had too many troubles and too many enemies to take on another at that moment. The flames of Jay burning in effigy lit the sky, while copies of the despised treaty crackled in numerous bonfires. Many Federalists found it difficult to stomach the treaty. Every gathering place—tavern, barroom, cross-roads store—was a forum where men met to communicate anger to each other.

Washington, though he, too, disliked the treaty, rode the storm, playing for the time his nation so desperately needed to grow to maturity. "If this country is preserved in tranquillity twenty years longer," he wrote, "it may bid defiance in a just cause to any power whatever; such in that time will be its population, wealth and resources." After much wrangling in the Senate, envenomed by party strife, the treaty just squeezed through, and Washington signed it in the closing days of June, 1795. It was his prestige alone that had won it ratification; on his assurance that it was for the best interests of the country opponents swallowed their doubts.

An interesting constitutional question was raised by the fact that, as Jefferson remarked, the Administration had lost its control of the House while keeping that of the Senate. After the ratification of Jay's treaty the House in the winter of 1795–96 tried to take a hand in the situation. By a vote of nearly two to one, it demanded that President Washington send it all the papers relating to the negotiation. The treaty, it argued, could not be made effective without a House appropriation, and this fact gave the more popular chamber a right to inquire into all the circumstances. Here was a difficult question of principle on which men still disagree. Washington, however, never hesitated in saying "No," and his whole Cabinet sustained him. He declared that the Constitution vested the treaty-making power exclusively in him and in the Senate; he had been in the Convention, and he knew that this was its intention. He flatly refused, because of "the necessity of maintaining the boundaries fixed by the Constitution between the different departments," to send the House the materials it wanted. Finally, after hearing a powerful speech by Fisher Ames of Massachusetts in support of Washington, the House backed down.

The relaxation of tensions between Britain and the United States stirred Spanish fears of an Atlantic alliance between the Anglo-American powers to carve up Spain's empire. Englishmen had already been urging joint action with Americans to open up South America to the world's commerce. The French, too, were promoting intrigues with American collaborators to despoil Spain of her possessions in the New World. To forestall such an eventuality Spain thought to placate the United States, and prevent aggression against Florida, by making important concessions to the Americans. The Treaty of San Lorenzo, October, 1795 (Pinckney's Treaty, after Thomas Pinckney, minister to Spain), established the northern boundary of Florida at the thirty-first parallel, but more significantly, permitted to Americans navigation of the whole Mississippi. They were also given the right to deposit at New Orleans, free of duty, merchandise for export. This "right of deposit" was to run for three years, with a promise of renewal by Spain.

Thus, by the proclamation of neutrality in 1793, Jay's Treaty the next year, and Pinckney's Treaty in 1795, the United States won a respite from possible war. While she was successfully avoiding the dangers which threatened from abroad, the United States at the same time was being faced internally with threats to her stability. The menace came from disgruntled farmers in Pennsylvania and from Indians in the Northwest Territory.

★ FIREWATER AND INDIANS

Western farmers, especially in Pennsylvania, resented Hamilton's excise law of 1791 which taxed their whiskey. Whiskey was a basic element in their economy. Surplus corn, their money crop, was generally too difficult to haul to market, and was therefore distilled into whiskey. Besides, whiskey was currency in the moneyless frontier region. Hostility to this phase of Hamilton's financial policy was encouraged by Jefferson who warned the president that the excise law was "of odious character . . . committing the authority of the government in parts where resistance is most probable and coercion least practicable." The sectional division precipitated by the debate over funding the debt was further accented in the dispute over the excise. It bore heavily only on considerable portions of the South and western Pennsylvania. Its provisions seemed almost deliberately designed to irritate the frontiersmen.

Tough Scotch-Irishmen, brooding over their wrongs, vowed never to pay the hated tax. By the summer of 1794 revenue agents were being tarred and feathered and run out of various communities by angry inhabitants. Local officials seemed helpless to enforce federal laws, and inflamed mobs ranged over the countryside destroying the property of the government and those who sided with it. Farmers in western Pennsylvania had reached the stage of insurrection.

"The Government," said President Washington, "could no longer remain a passive spectator of the contempt with which the laws were treated." Hamilton strongly supported the president with the plea that a powerful force be thrown into the field to overawe the rebellious frontiersmen. "Without rigor everywhere," said Hamilton, "our tranquillity will be of very short duration." In the fall of 1794, through woods splotched with autumn's brilliant colors, militia from four states converged upon the disaffected region. The "Whiskey Rebellion" promptly evaporated. The hand of the federal government had thus stretched out to make its force felt in remote reaches of the land; but western mountaineers retained resentful memories of needlessly harsh coercion.

In another frontier area, in the Ohio region, the federal government added to its prestige by crushing the Indians, thus opening new lands for the westward moving settlers. The American government had need to re-establish its prestige in the region for it had suffered a grave defeat in 1791, when Indians ambushed General St. Clair and his troops, killing over 600 of them. The Indians had been elated with their victory, and dreamed of finally driving the "long knives" back across the Ohio River. They were encouraged in these dreams by British officials in Canada, who supplied them with provisions and weapons to take the warpath. The British had plans for the establishment of an Indian buffer state to contain the Americans.

The United States countered by sending out an expedition under General Anthony Wayne in command of troops wise in the ways of forest warfare. The Indians waited for Wayne's soldiers behind a barrier of fallen trees. In the famous "Battle of Fallen Timbers," in August, 1794, the American army routed the red men. Discouraged by their defeat, the Indians' spirit was utterly broken when expected British assistance was withheld. Chieftains of the beaten Indians were gathered together at Fort Greenville the following summer, in 1795, to accept the conditions of peace laid down by General Wayne. There, in a forest clearing haunted by spirits long since departed for happier hunting grounds, the vanquished Indian warriors surrendered their claims to much of the Northwest Territory. The long struggle between the whites and the natives for the region had ended. The humbled Indians retreated to remoter lands, and a strange peace settled over the great expanse of territory. The "long knives" were sheathed in unreal quiet.

★ WASHINGTON'S FAREWELL ADDRESS

While the frontier was suddenly still, in Philadelphia the clamor of party politics filled the air. The fight over Jay's treaty deepened party divisions previously accented by the economic policies of Hamilton. Washington himself, once thought to be above the party battle, became the victim of partisan spite. In truth, as time passed, he had become more staunchly Federalist. Hamilton and others fostered the public veneration of Washington to exalt him above criticism. Madison had remarked as early as 1790, "that the satellites & sycophants which surrounded him had wound up the Ceremonials of government to a pitch of stateliness which nothing but his personal character could have supported, & which no character after him could ever maintain."

In the early period of his presidency Washington had tapped a wide variety of sources to gauge public sentiment, but after 1794 his circle of advisers included only those strongly supporting the policy of his administration. This was, perhaps, to be expected, as part of the process of party formation, but he failed to see that he himself had become a strong Federalist. He made his own party synonymous with the government, while opposing political ideas were denounced as hostile to American society. Like many other men of his generation, Washington deplored the rise of parties in the mistaken belief that they were not necessary in our type of political society. Wild charges of embezzling public funds were made against Washington, and he was ridiculed as "the Step-Father of his country." The president, stung by his countrymen's ingratitude, looked forward with relief to the end of his administration; and few could blame him for refusing to run for a third term.

Washington, however, always had been able to think beyond the passions of the moment, and in his famous Farewell Address he bade his fellow countrymen do likewise. Washington warned against the "baneful effects of the Spirit of Party." He urged Americans to "cultivate peace and harmony" with all nations, and to avoid "permanent, inveterate antipathies" against some nations and "passionate attachments" for others. "The Nation which indulges towards another an habitual hatred or an habitual fondness is in some degree a slave." "The great rule of conduct for us in regard to foreign nations is, in extending our commercial relations to have with them as little *political* connection as possible . . ." American isolationism, which has roots older than the Farewell Address, was given classic expression in Washington's caution: " 'Tis our true policy to steer clear of permanent alliances with any portion of the foreign world . . . Taking care always to keep ourselves, by suitable establishments, on a respectable defensive posture, we may safely trust to temporary alliances for extraordinary emergencies."

It has been argued, and with much justice, that the Farewell Address, largely written by Hamilton, was really a piece of Federalist propaganda to influence voting in the coming 1796 election. When Washington asked Hamilton what would be the best time to publish his farewell, Hamilton replied, *"Two months before the time for the meeting of the [presidential] Electors."* The condemnation of parties was really directed at the Jeffersonians. French officials, especially the minister to the United States, Pierre Auguste Adet, interfered brazenly in American politics, notably in the election of 1796, seeking the victory of the Republican party. Their actions boomeranged. British behavior was more subtle, for Hamilton's revelations of confidential information to

English officials relieved them of the need to be too openly involved in America's internal affairs. Destruction of the alliance with France was the aim of Hamilton. Most people were not aware of the immediate political import of the Farewell Address. Its warning against "permanent alliances" with foreign powers made a deep impression on later generations, but in 1796 Washington's words were unheard in the howling winds of partisan doctrine.

Parties had definitely arrived on the scene before the end of Washington's second term. Though Jefferson spoke of the Republican party as early as 1792, there seems to have been no such formal group as yet. It was mainly composed of Virginia representatives who welcomed support from other delegations. Until the election of 1796 it was Madison whom Federalists believed their most aggressive adversary. The open break between Hamilton and Jefferson came in the spring of 1792, but even for some time after that the latter used his influence largely to persuade Washington that men in opposition were not anti-Federalists, Jacobins, or subversives, as frequently alleged. With Jefferson's departure from the cabinet, at the end of 1793, the tone of his followers changed. In the next months they took the offensive. Under Madison's leadership they even sought to detach Federalists in New England by reminding them of England's discriminatory commercial policies against the United States. Great Britain alone, of all the countries with whom America had significant trade, refused to make a commercial treaty.

To some extent the Jay Treaty was initiated as a counterattack by the Federalists to thwart Republican strategy. Jefferson so interpreted it, in a letter to Madison, September, 1795: "A bolder party-stroke was never struck. For it certainly is an attempt of a party, which finds they have lost their majority in one branch of the legislature [House] to make a law by the aid of the other branch [Senate] & of the executive, under color of a treaty which shall bind up the hands of the adverse branch from ever restraining the commerce of their patron-nation." The division on Jay's Treaty definitely signalized the emergence of the two-party system in the United States, with the since familiar picture of organized pressure being exerted on representatives of each side. Jefferson shortly became the leader of his party, and attached to himself many prominent men in the South, formerly Federalists. The administration's handling of the Whiskey Rebellion, Washington's violent denunciation of the Democratic societies, and the Jay Treaty all combined to cause Jefferson to come out openly as formal head of a popular party. The party was not his creation, in a sense it was there looking for a head.

★ PRESIDENT JOHN ADAMS

Washington's refusal to stand again for the presidency left the field open, and it was taken for granted among prominent Federalists, especially in New England, that John Adams should be his successor. Hamilton worked silently to have Adams defeated by Thomas Pinckney, originally intended for the vice-presidency. The electoral system which was in force until 1804, when it was changed by the Twelfth Amendment, made possible the election of men from opposed parties to the two highest posts in the land. Thus in 1796, Adams on the Federalist ticket was named president, while the next highest candidate was Jefferson of the Republicans who won the vice-presidency. Jefferson had indicated in advance he would yield to Adams in case of a tie. Their views on some matters were similar, and extreme Federalists feared a coalition between them. Hamilton sought, unsuccessfully, to exercise the same influence in Adams' administration that he had during that of Washington.

Adams had been one of the noted leaders during the Revolutionary era, serving at home and abroad in the front rank of American statesmen. As a political theorist he was unsurpassed in his time. Adams was a dignified man, a little too fat for his medium height (an unfriendly wag dubbed him "His Rotundity"). In his later years no great faith in democracy stirred within him, though his love of country was unmatched by any one in his generation. His moral courage was unsurpassed, as he showed in his defense of the British Captain Preston involved in the Boston Massacre, and as he was to prove again in averting war between the United States and France. He had not the arts of political address which endeared inferior men to the public. He was irascible; he was too sure of himself; his sense of discipline was too strong for the mass of men who were repelled by his want of warmth. But he and his distinguished wife, Abigail Adams, established a line whose contributions to their country are probably superior to those of any other family in American history.

The chief task of John Adams was to carry on the foreign policy in accord with the principles laid down in Washington's administration. At that time pressure from both England and France jeopardized the peace of the United States. Now, however, the danger to American neutrality came largely from France. She regarded the Jay Treaty as a hostile move against herself, and as a violation of the old Franco-American treaty of alliance. The French professed to believe that American trade was favoring England, and in retaliation they seized and confiscated vessels and cargo belonging to citizens of the United States. The American envoy Charles C. Pinckney, an ardent Federalist who had replaced Monroe (the latter was thought to be too sympathetic to France), was harshly treated by the French. Resentment against the insulting treatment of an American minister added to Federalist belligerency, already mounting dangerously.

By 1797 diplomatic relations between France and the United States had been suspended. The extremism of the French Revolution, whose leaders were alleged to be conspiring against the safety of other countries, roused the fears of conservatives. War fever was rising in America and France; the Americans increased their naval armament and adopted other measures of defense.

Meanwhile Adams sought to arrive at a peaceful understanding with France. He sent a special commission, Charles C. Pinckney, John Marshall, and Elbridge Gerry to the French Directory, and the report of the Americans about their experiences has come down in history as the XYZ dispatches; XYZ represented three subordinate officials with whom the Americans dealt. Talleyrand, then Minister of Foreign Affairs, informed the American commissioners that the Directory could be induced to be friendly to the United States in exchange for a gift of near one quarter of a million dollars. Pinckney and Marshall apparently were willing to bargain, but the asking price for merely reestablishing diplomatic relations was too high. The report of the envoys reached America in 1798, and in embroidered form was widely published. The accent was on French demands for a bribe. In the American press, and in countless stump speeches, the defiant words were hurled back: "Millions for defense; not one cent for tribute."

Friends of France, and that meant Jeffersonian Republicans, quailed before the storm. A wave of patriotic sentiment flooded the land; Adams was showered with loyal addresses, and he glowed in the unfamiliar adulation. A new national song, "Hail Columbia," was cheered in the theaters and sung all over the country. Increased military and naval forces were authorized by Congress.

In the winter of 1798–99, the American navy fought engagements with French vessels in the West Indies, carrying off the honors each time. Americans joined with British forces in operations against French privateers. Hostilities in this undeclared war lasted over a period of two and a half years, during which the United States captured eighty-five armed French vessels, most of them privateers which had been preying on American commerce. Hamilton pressed for the creation of a large army, himself at the head, and a declaration of war against France. Such a conflict might insure continued Federalist power in the United States. His fertile, adventurous mind also hatched a plan of joint operations with the British against the Spanish and French possessions in America. In the campaign Hamilton expected to win personal glory and, at the same time, cement more tightly the various sections in the Union. "That man," said Abigail Adams, would "become a second Buonaparty if he was posessed of equal power." Adams, hard pressed by Hamilton and his confreres in the cabinet and Senate, raised a warning cry of the need to safeguard the position of the presidency in the American scheme of government. In the judgment of a careful student, Joseph Charles, "he was perhaps the one important man of his time who did rise above party on a crucial issue." *

Adams felt there was something of the buccaneer about Hamilton, and the President wanted no part of his piracy. Though intent on upholding his country's rights, he sought peace rather than war. Adams said of himself, "I have always cried, Ships! Ships! Hamilton's hobby horse was Troops! Troops! With all the vanity and timidity of Cicero, all the debauchery of Marc Anthony and all the ambition of Julius Caesar, his object was the command of fifty thousand men. My object was the defense of my country, and that alone, which I knew could be effected only by a navy."

Adams was a wiser politician than the Hamiltonians. His policy alienated him from bellicose Federalists (Hamilton denounced him in a famous pamphlet), but Adams cut the ground from under their feet by reopening diplomatic negotiations with the French who had turned conciliatory. In the early fall of 1800 America reestablished normal relations with the French government, of which Napoleon Bonaparte was now First Consul. President Adams, in pursuing his policy of peace, saved his country from great perils. But concern over the nation's security against alleged internal enemies led his administration to adopt laws which dangerously compromised beneficent American principles.

★ THE ALIEN AND SEDITION LAWS—
ELECTION OF JEFFERSON

The French Revolution, in its later phases, strengthened conservatism in the United States as well as in other countries. Conservatives in England, who disparaged the new nation overseas, now found themselves on common ground with Americans who despised Revolutionary France. Gentlemen farmers in Britain were reminded that "as the danger of commotions increases in Europe the eyes of mankind will necessarily be turned to the [United States] where *Property* remains respected." In England and America aggressive conservatives harried the critics of government.

* *Ibid.,* p. 73.

Many of these critics in the United States had recently come as political refugees from France or from Ireland, and they naturally gravitated to Jefferson's party. They thus became a shining target for fearful Federalists who now used their control of government to impale the opposition. Federalists wrapped themselves in the mantle of Americanism; they stigmatized Republicans as foreign anarchists. In 1798 Congress adopted a series of measures known as the Alien and Sedition laws. The first of these extended from five to fourteen years the period of required residence before an alien could attain citizenship. Other acts empowered the President to send out of the country aliens judged dangerous to the nation; jail terms were prescribed for those refusing to go and for those coming back. A final measure made it a crime to write or publish "any false, scandalous, and malicious" statements about the president or Congress, to bring them "into contempt or disrepute" or to "stir up sedition within the United States."

On their face the Alien and Sedition Acts look so much like madness that they are difficult to comprehend. To understand them we have to realize the passion, and the very real fear of the time, and recall some modern parallels. In 1917–18 Congress passed the Espionage Act and Sedition Act. They were products of the intense popular hatred of Imperial Germany, and the hysterical fear of alien-born enemies, of disloyal pro-German elements, in our midst. These statutes went much too far; Eugene V. Debs was jailed because he attacked the war as a capitalist war. At a later date Senator Joseph McCarthy carried on a campaign of terrorism fed by a hysterical fear of the Communist peril within the United States. Though he made a shambles of traditional American liberties he obtained the willing support of multitudes. In 1798 much the same excitement, prejudice, and overwrought apprehension possessed large bodies of citizens. The nation was apparently going to war with France; troops were to be raised, frigates and privateers were going to sea with guns already loaded, and crowds were singing the new patriotic ballad "Hail, Columbia." The pro-French party was regarded with as much hatred and panic, by many, as the pro-Germans in 1917, or the extreme "leftists" in McCarthy's day.

For there was a vociferous and extravagant French party, which had gone further than leaders like Jefferson approved, and had misled some Frenchmen into believing that the United States had a divided people. Even Washington wished some sharp check imposed. But the intolerant measures taken actually weakened the country.

Jeffersonian editors were jailed or fined, but the Republicans were not intimidated by the intolerant measures of rabid Federalists. The bitterness of party strife scarcely abated, though Jeffersonians had need of caution. Even the outbreak, once again, of an epidemic of yellow fever in the summer of 1798 hardly moderated political warfare. Theaters, taverns, and barrooms were shut, while hundreds of homes where death had struck stood in grim black. The only sounds a traveler heard in stricken Philadelphia were the moans of the dying, the wails of the living, the hammers of the casket makers, and the anguished howls of dogs without masters. Papers printed the lists of citizens who were victims of the raging fever. But the journals saved space for reporting the feverish party battles, scarcely less virulent than nature's own catastrophe.

The Republicans rallied their strength against the Federalist reign of terror. Matthew Lyon, a Vermont Republican and Congressman, was jailed and fined $1,000 under the Sedition Law. His fine was paid by a group of leading Republicans, including Jefferson, Madison, and Gallatin. His aroused constituents re-elected him to Congress, and Lyon's return trip to Philadelphia became a triumphant procession. Uncowed, people throughout the country defied the Sedition Law, while Jefferson and Madison framed arguments against the new legislation on constitutional grounds.

Jefferson drafted the Kentucky resolution, which his friend, George Nicholas, introduced in the legislature of that state; Madison drafted the Virginia resolutions, which were adopted a month later. Both set forth the theory that the Constitution was a compact among the States; both declared the Alien and Sedition Acts unconstitutional. But the Virginia resolutions simply announced that when the national government used unconstitutional measures, the States were in duty bound to *interpose*—just how, was not stated. The Kentucky resolutions went further. They asserted that whenever the general government exceeded its powers and took unconstitutional steps, then its acts were "unauthoritative, void, and are of no force." They also declared that Kentucky would never submit to undelegated and hence unlimited powers; and called upon the "Co-States" to act concurrently on the question whether the Alien and Sedition Acts were allowable under the Federal Compact.

Little real doubt exists that Jefferson intended his Kentucky resolution to assert the doctrine of nullification; he believed a state had the right to pronounce an act of Congress null and void, and prevent its execution. Thirty years later South Carolina, in bringing out its nullification doctrine, appealed to Jefferson's precedent. Madison then denied that he or Jefferson had intended this. He had the right to speak for himself, but not for

Jefferson. In fact, Jefferson in his original draft actually declared that "a nullification of the act is the rightful remedy." The whole issue, however, now went into the election of 1800.

This was the first national campaign in which a well-planned and fairly well-systematized procedure for the nomination of candidates appeared. The Congressional caucus as the instrument of nomination made its bow. In 1796 the two parties had seemed automatically to designate Adams and Jefferson as the rival candidates for the presidency. But no formal agreement was ever made, and the electors actually cast ballots for thirteen persons, giving Samuel Adams, Oliver Ellsworth, and George Clinton respectable votes. But this time only four men received electoral ballots; Adams and Jefferson, Pinckney and Aaron Burr. The precise method by which the two tickets were formed is unknown, but there is no doubt that the Republican and Federalist caucuses in Congress had a great deal to do with it. Federalist members held a meeting early in the year to crystallize party sentiment about Adams. Republican members then held one a few weeks later, not so much to rally everyone behind Jefferson, who was unanimously regarded as the proper candidate for President, as to place the party as a unit behind Aaron Burr as the Vice-Presidential nominee.

The campaign had a modern character in the intensity with which political leaders mobilized all their forces to carry the most critical areas. New York was seen at the outset to be the pivotal State. It had 24 electoral votes out of 138; it had given its electoral votes to Adams in 1796, and might do so again. Actually, if it had repeated its decision, Adams would have won with 16 more electoral votes than Jefferson. But Burr and others strained every sinew in the contest, and the movement of the hour was with them. New York politics had long been dominated by a number of great families, who had almost all been Federalists; but now the families had begun to quarrel and split apart. The Livingston family in particular had gone over to the Republicans on the issue presented by the Jay Treaty, and Chancellor Robert R. Livingston, its most influential member, had spoken against the treaty from the same platform as Burr; while the Alien and Sedition Acts confirmed their feeling—one of the Livingstons said they "would have disgraced the age of Gothic barbarism." One arrest under these laws, that of Jedediah Peck, who was taken two hundred miles from Cooperstown to New York for trial, created widespread resentment. It was said at the time that it did more than two hundred missionaries could have done for the Republican party.

The tide of public opinion, in legislatures, in market places, and in the press, rose relentlessly against the Federalists. Jefferson had done much to form that opinion, through correspondence and conversation. He marshaled his political forces with the instinct of genius. He was certain that a wrathful people would drive the Federalists from power and thus preserve democracy.

As the campaign drew to its close, Jefferson and his aides saw to it that the Republican Congressmen, legislators, journalists, and stump speakers united in a mighty appeal to the people. They declared that Hamilton's fiscal system had tended to enrich a corrupt oligarchy: the cost of the federal government nearly doubled during the Adams administration. No more speculation and corruption, they vociferated; no more interference with freedom of speech and the press, no great standing armies and costly navy; instead, peace, harmony, and state rights. The Federalists countered these attacks by denouncing Jefferson as an atheist, circulating slanders on his private life, and protesting against financial irresponsibility and French influences. It was said that in New England some old ladies, alarmed for religion, hung their Bibles in the well in the butter-cooler to keep them safe. Most potent of all, however, was the skillful campaign strategy of Burr in New York. He had a state ticket of the greatest possible strength chosen, with George Clinton at its head. Under Burr's management, local managers made lists of voters, canvassed wards by streets, and held effective rallies.

In the end the Republican ticket won with 73 electoral votes against 65 for John Adams, Virginia and New York giving Jefferson and Burr their full strength. But even when the party had triumphed, doubt remained as to the next president. The electoral college gave precisely equal votes to Jefferson and Burr, for it failed to recognize the possibly disastrous results of such a course. The election then went into the House of Representatives; and not until this body had taken thirty-six ballots did Jefferson win.

For a time it actually appeared that Burr, who as one astute leader said was "a profligate without character and without property," might win the presidency, in direct opposition to the will of the voters. Many Federalists, distrusting Jefferson, voted for him in the House. More would have done so had Burr given explicit promises that he would administer the government as a Federalist. At this crucial moment some Hamiltonian Federalists became aware of the dangers to the country in choosing the unprincipled Burr over the wrongheaded Jefferson. Burr, said Hamilton, was "a complete Catiline." Ballot after ballot was taken in the House, meeting in the new capitol in Washington on a snowy February morning in 1801. For several days the voting continued without a decision. Finally, after much maneuvering, several Federalists, overcoming their party bias, made possible Jefferson's election.

Jefferson long continued to speak of "the Revolution of 1800" which brought him into power, meaning that in his name the plain people triumphed. Undoubtedly the frontiersmen of the West stood with him. Kentucky, Tennessee, North Carolina, and Georgia were all in his column. In New York City and the adjoining towns he and the Republican party were strengthened by an inflow of poor immigrants. The mechanics and laborers of other commercial towns were on his side. With fervent rejoicing, Republicans hailed an end to the "reign of terror" under Adams, and sang a song bidding Columbia's sons to exult:

> To tyrants never bend the knee,
> But join with heart, and soul, and voice,
> For Jefferson and Liberty.

Thus, as the seat of government was transferred from Philadelphia to Washington, the Federalists lost the presidency and both houses of Congress. But they still had the right, to the end of Adams' administration, to make appointments. They used that right, under the provisions of the Judiciary Act of 1801, to fill vacancies with Federalists. First among them was John Marshall, named Chief Justice of the United States. He presided over the court for more than a third of a century, strengthening and steadily enlarging "the new roof" his party had done so much to construct.

The days of uncertainty for the young American government had ended. Even the conservatives of Europe, who had counted its life as short, were now ready to concede that the merits in the American government were sufficient to guarantee it an enduring life. Liberals in England hailed the election of Jefferson: "the now confirmed government of America," one of them said, "will be, perhaps, to the framers of constitutions, henceforward, a normal school, a model for statesmen to work by." In their own country Americans left workbenches, clerks laid aside their papers, and farmers trooped from their fields to gather together in celebration of the victory of their idol, Thomas Jefferson.

CHAPTER XIII

Jefferson Guides the Republic

★ JEFFERSON

John Adams' coach rattled off on the inaugural morning of March 4, 1801, the defeated president not waiting for his successor to be installed. Jefferson came down for breakfast in Conrad's boarding house on Capitol Hill, where he had been living for some time, and took his familiar seat at the lower end of the table. From Conrad's an observer could see much of the crude town of Washington with its dusty roads and scattered unattractive houses. Two large structures, spaced a mile apart, attracted attention, the unfinished Capitol and the president's mansion. Pennsylvania Avenue ran between miasmic swamps. A half dozen brick houses near the president's house, and a few others more pretentious out toward Georgetown, distinguished the drear landscape. The beautiful city that was to be was still mostly in blueprint. Gouverneur Morris, newly elected to the Senate, wrote to a friend, "this is the best city in the world to live in—in the future."

The new president was nearly fifty-eight years old, tall (six feet two-and-a-half, when he didn't slouch), spare, and loose-jointed. "His dress and manners were very plain," wrote a friendly contemporary; "he is grave, or rather sedate, but without tincture of pomp, ostentation, or pride." While his dress was plain, observers noted that it was of the finest material. And so it was with his tastes in general, never showy, but always sensitive to the best, whether it was architecture, literature, or food and drink. His table was a delight to invited Federalists who might squirm at his political opinions. "I wish," said one of them, that "his French politics were as good as his French wines."

Federalists could not control their hatred of Jefferson, and their bile poisoned the pens which darkened the pages of the press with grim forebodings of America's future. Anarchy, destruction of churches, violation of American womanhood, all these and more would happen to the United States, wrote Federalists hypnotized by self-created fears. But Jefferson tossed off their attacks. He believed, unalterably, in the freedom of the press, even when he was the target of scurrility and personal abuse. To Alexander von Humboldt, who was visiting him in the White House, and who asked why a particularly irresponsible journal was not suppressed, Jefferson replied easily: "Put that paper in your pocket, Baron, and should you hear the reality of our liberty, the freedom of the press questioned, show them this paper—and tell them where you found it."

Jefferson's faith in democracy and his open embrace of the aspirations of common humanity were to become his prime bequests to posterity. His trust in his fellow men did not waver despite Federalist vituperation and disappointment in the course of the French Revolution. Like the eighteenth-century *philosophe* that he was, he believed that the capabilities of all men should have the widest range for self-expression, and that this could be achieved by transforming the conditions under which men lived. Every type of problem, he believed, would yield to reason, and to cultivate that quality he gladly spent much of a life-time in the study of science. Education should be available to all, for this was the chief instrument of social progress. Men should be their own masters, and that condition, he believed, was more readily achieved in an agrarian society than in an industrialized state. Government was not to be imposed on the many by the well-born few, however wise and good, but it should be kept as closely as possible under the control of the mass of the citizenry.

One of the main reasons for his opposition to Hamilton's policies was his fear that they would create in America the rigid class distinctions common to Europe where every man was "either hammer or anvil." In the last letter he wrote (June 24, 1826) Jefferson clung to the beliefs he had long proclaimed: "All eyes are opened, or opening, to the rights of man. The general spread of the light of science has already laid open to every view the palpable truth, that the mass of mankind has not been born with saddles on their backs, nor a favored few booted and spurred, ready to ride them legitimately, by the grace of God."

Jefferson spoke the American language of hostility to restraint by any form of authority, secular or religious, on freedom of inquiry. He was in closest harmony with his fellow Americans in their common tendency to live in the future. In the year of his presidential victory, he wrote to Joseph Priestley: the idea "that we are to look backwards instead of forwards for the improvement of the human mind, and to recur to the annals of our ancestors for what is most perfect in government, in religion & in learning, is worthy of those bigots in religion & government, by whom it has been recommended, & whose purposes it would answer. But it is not an idea which this country will endure; and the moment of their showing it is fast ripening."

On his inauguration day Jefferson may well have thought of these lines written to Priestley a few months before. The moment had ripened for affirmative belief in the future, and those who believed with the new president saw it unclouded, with fair sailing for the ship of state. "The tough sides of our Argosie have been thoroughly tried," said Jefferson. Her strength, he declared, had stood the waves into which she was steered with a view to sink her. "We shall put her on her Republican tack, and she will now show by the beauty of her motion the skill of her builders."

★ ON A REPUBLICAN TACK

Jefferson's inaugural address, which he read in a low, almost inaudible voice to the crowded Senate chamber, promised no startling changes in American life. It was restrained enough in its declaration of political faith to have been uttered by any of his Federalist foes. He asked that political intolerance cease. His principles were "equal and exact justice to all men," "absolute acquiescence in the decisions of the majority" (though the will of the majority should be reasonable), "the supremacy of the civil over the military authority," freedom of religion and of the press, "the honest payments of our debts." Though he had spoken of his election as a revolution, he extended an olive branch; "We have called by different names brethren of the same principle. We are all Republicans—we are all Federalists." And returning to his most cherished sentiment, this government, he said, was "the world's best hope."

In assembling his cabinet Jefferson turned to his long-time collaborator Madison, who became Secretary of State. For Secretary of the Treasury, the president called on Albert Gallatin, a man of Swiss birth who had risen to prominence in Pennsylvania politics. Though Gallatin's speech had an alien accent, his devotion to his new home was deep and filled with understanding. His special fitness as adviser on public finance, and in general his statesmanlike judgment, gave needed stability to a president prone to theorize excessively. Other trusted men were part of the president's official family, but none were closer than Madison and Gallatin who shared with Jefferson for the next eight years the cares of governing the country.

Though Jefferson had spoken of the apparent identity of interests between Republicans and Federalists, his followers had no wish to press the likeness too far. After all he and his party (and his opponents, too, for that matter) believed that his election augured a striking change in American life. The people, it was argued, asked for new faces among appointive, as well as elective, officials. Republicans, hungry for jobs, overwhelmed Jefferson with demands that Federalists, who monopolized the offices, be removed. The latter did not resign and seldom died. Bowing to pressure (and in fact believing his party had justifiable claims to office), Jefferson did remove a number of Federalists. In filling vacant posts he chose almost entirely from his own followers.

The new administration soon erased the despised Alien and Sedition Acts. Those who had been jailed were freed, fines were returned, and the fourteen-year residence requirement was removed to make way for the original five-year stipulation. In many other respects Jefferson's administration departed from Federalist practice. Jeffersonians distrusted incurring a national debt. Keep the finances so simple, the President urged Gallatin, "that every member of the Congress and every man of any mind in the Union should be able to comprehend them." In the simple agrarian society which the Republicans idealized, it seemed logical that each generation, like each individual, should pay its own way and not shoulder on to succeeding generations burdensome costs. Gallatin worked out a financial program by which he believed the debt could be paid off in sixteen years. Repayment would not be made through new taxes (in fact the existing unpopular excise was to be abandoned), but rather by rigid economies. In two years the debt was reduced by $5,000,000. The ax fell mainly on the war and navy departments, as well as on many offices created by the Federalists but now thought superfluous.

★ TO THE SHORES OF TRIPOLI

Jefferson had comforted himself and his countrymen with the belief that "a wide ocean" separated them "from the exterminating havoc" of Europe. Jefferson was, of course, delighted to share in the cultural heritage of Europe, but he was content that in politics his country and the Old World should move in two separate orbits. Fate decreed otherwise, for the most significant matters to be decided by him arose out of the complexities of Europe. A president who liked nothing better than cultivating his own garden and the domestic concerns of his country was diverted to problems of war and diplomacy.

Americans had faced such problems before in their dealings with countries of Europe, notably England, France, and Spain. In the Mediterranean area, where American ships had long traded, commercial and diplomatic relations had a special character. There the pirates of the

Barbary coast, operating from North African bases, levied tribute on the great and lesser powers trading in Mediterranean waters. To pay seemed cheaper than waging incessant war. The United States in its first decade paid near $2,000,000 to assorted Pashas and Deys who headed the Barbary Powers.

Jefferson, though disliking war, concluded that the pirates should be tamed. He sent a small naval force to chastise the Pasha of Tripoli who had increased his demands. The American force was inadequate to crush the corsairs but it could inflict enough punishment upon them to teach them to shy away from United States merchant vessels. The Tripolitan War dragged on for several years, concluding in 1805 with a treaty which still provided for a financial settlement. Nevertheless the Americans gained better terms than European powers, and their flag won increasing respect in North African waters. From the exploits of these years new names, Preble, Decatur, Somers, were added to the roll of American naval heroes, while the navy itself learned lessons of value to all its fighting men.

★ LOUISIANA

Before Jefferson could make peace with Tripoli he was confronted with a far more dangerous opponent, Napoleon Bonaparte, then ruler of France. In Bonaparte's scheme of things America played a minor role; his impact on her history was nevertheless enormous. Through the vagaries of international politics it was he who transferred to the United States the vast region of the Louisiana Purchase which carried the nation's western boundary to the Rocky Mountains.

Acquisition of this great region was in the nature of an accident, though Jefferson himself in earlier years had cast an expansionist eye upon it. He had encouraged exploration of the far west, and was as expansive in his imperial dreams as the most ardent later exponents of "manifest destiny." "However our present interests may restrain us within our own limits," he said in 1801, "it is impossible not to look forward to distant times, when our rapid multiplication will expand itself beyond those limits and cover the whole northern, if not the southern, continent with a people speaking the same language, governed in similar forms and by similar laws."

American interest originally was confined to New Orleans and free navigation of the lower Mississippi as an outlet for the men of the western waters. Frontiersmen and their families had moved into the western regions in great numbers. Kentucky had entered the Union as a state in 1792, to be followed four years later by Tennessee. Ohio became a formal member of the United States in 1803, while Indiana was organized as a Territory. To the south, the Territory of Mississippi had already been set up in 1798.

In admitting Ohio to the Union Congress established two precedents of great significance for after years. In keeping with the provision of the Ordinance of 1785 each state formed out of the Northwest Territory was to be granted one section (640 acres) out of every township to aid education. Also a sum was set aside from the sale of federal lands in Ohio to pay for roads within the state. National aid to education and to road building was to become a more familiar fact to Americans of a later generation.

Pressure for easier conditions of public land purchase forced revisions in the laws. The minimum purchase of 640 acres, required by the act of 1796, had been reduced in 1800 to 320 acres. The same price of two dollars per acre was maintained, but the minimum down payment was cut in half, from 50 to 25 per cent, with the balance to be paid in four years, instead of in one, as formerly. In Jefferson's administration a new Land Act was passed (1804); the minimum purchase was reduced still further, from 320 to 160 acres, with eighty dollars as the down payment.

Settlers who poured into the new states and territories, and transferred from place to place with comparative ease, rarely attempted substantial housebuilding. Most of the homes, even in areas well settled, were log cabins. The men of the community joined together in constructing the familiar cabin with such speed that in one day the simple structure could be finished and the new owner move in before sundown.

Everywhere in these western regions, both north and south, the settler lived by his ax and rifle, though in Mississippi he was already raising cotton. Kentucky even so early, however, boasted a class of large estate owners living in comfortable houses. The settler throughout the West was ordinarily a small farmer living with his wife and numerous children on a large tract of wooded land, 300 acres or so in extent. Only eight or ten acres of his holding were cleared, and these not completely. The birds and animals of the forest, bear, deer, and turkey furnished a steady diet; the most common of the domestic animals were long-legged hogs roaming half-wild through the woods.

The westerners of these years were largely men from the eastern regions of the South. Northerners for the most part were still filling up empty spaces in New England, in central and western New York, Pennsylvania, and northern Ohio. Some 400,000 people were living in the West in 1800, only a small number of them in towns. Lexington was a flourishing community of over 2,000, while Louisville and Nashville were each about 500. Natchez, almost as large as Lexington, was

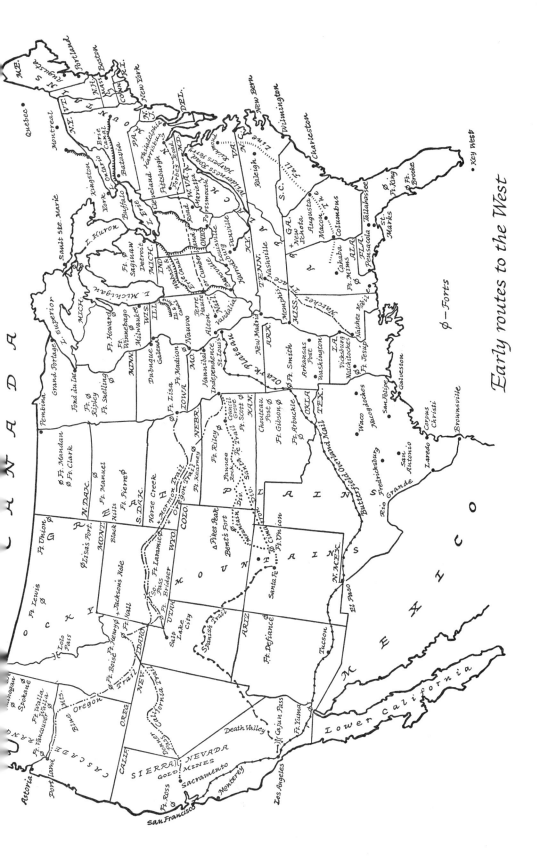

Early routes to the West

ø — Forts

a busy town, drawing its livelihood from the Mississippi River traffic. The boatmen all stopped there, mooring their crowded craft to the bank, while they went ashore for rowdy relaxation and the pleasures of female company.

The rivers of the West swarmed with rafts and boats, carrying men and goods through the vast interior of the United States. On the upper Ohio, at Pittsburgh, and elsewhere along the river, seagoing vessels were built and then sent down the Ohio to the Mississippi, out to the Gulf of Mexico, and thence across the ocean to foreign ports. Americans were scattering over the Louisiana possessions of Spain whose colonial officials were greatly worried over the alien influx. Americans settled in St. Louis and other towns, and joined with French traders who went up the Missouri and the Mississippi to barter beads, powder, paint, and blankets for the furs offered by distant Indians. The pressure of the restless, pushing Americans was building up at an accelerated rate, defiantly penetrating Spanish regions forbidden to foreigners.

Americans had long coveted picturesque New Orleans. Here was a city unlike their own familiar towns. Its varied population included Spaniards, French, their descendants (Creoles), and Negroes, both free and slave. Its thousand dwellings showed no uniform architecture; they were built of adobe, brick, or stucco, some brightly colored, others in softer pastel shades. Beautiful wrought-iron balconies, gateways, and gratings on windows distinguished the homes from the cabins of Kentucky boatmen, or the simple frame houses of Lexington and Nashville.

Soon the spreading ambition of Americans covered a goal larger than New Orleans; it embraced the hinterland as well. The men who lived along the western rivers marked Spain as their natural enemy, for it was she who controlled the lower reaches and mouth of the Mississippi. Through alien hands American products of the western valleys—tobacco, flour, hemp—must find their way to the outside world.

Spain had been persuaded by Napoleon's pressure to give back to France the immense Louisiana province in a secret treaty, in October, 1800. Napoleon had dreams of recreating the French empire in the New World. This empire had once given great wealth and prestige to the France of the Old Regime, and imperial planners in Napoleon's circle sought again this fount of national strength. Prosperous plantations of Santo Domingo had supplied much of Europe with sugar, coffee, and cotton. Creole families, living in Paris, brightened its streets and homes with their ostentatious luxury. But Santo Domingo, though still nominally under French control, was now in the grip of its Negro master, Toussaint L'Ouverture, who had risen to power after a great slave insurrection touched off by the French Revolution.

Napoleon's road to Louisiana was barred by Santo Domingo, and he determined to destroy the power of Toussaint. Command of a large expedition was given to General Leclerc, whose task it was to re-establish the authority of France in the West Indian island. From the reconquered island the revitalized empire of France would spread its power westward to Louisiana and northward up the valley of the Mississippi. Success for the French dictator, who was far stronger than any Spanish ruler, spelled danger to the democracy of America.

Leclerc's expedition left Brest on November 22, 1801, with an army of 10,000 men, and arrived in West Indian waters off Santo Domingo near the end of January, 1802. They went ashore with great confidence, but the Negroes fought with skill under Toussaint and imperiled the French army, whose losses were severe. Toussaint, however, was betrayed by his generals and taken captive by the French, who carried him to their homeland where he died, an isolated prisoner in a desolate Jura Mountain fortress.

Jefferson had already learned of Bonaparte's intentions to add Louisiana to his growing dominion. The president reacted quickly and with unusual militancy. Though the United States had always looked to France as her "natural friend," he said, neither she nor any one else could be permitted perpetual possession of New Orleans. "There is on the globe one single spot," said Jefferson, "the possessor of which is our natural and habitual enemy; it is New Orleans." "The day that France takes possession of New Orleans," he added, "we must marry ourselves to the British fleet and nation." Perhaps nothing since the Revolution, said Jefferson, "has produced more uneasy sensations through the body of the nation."

American anxiety increased when that same year, toward the close of 1802, Spanish officials in New Orleans (who had not yet turned over their posts to the French) suspended the right of deposit for American goods. This right to deposit goods (valued at $1,000,000 a year) duty free, and transship them to larger vessels, had been granted to Americans for three years by treaty with Spain in 1795. Without official agreement the arrangement had continued after 1798, but now it was suddenly canceled. Westerners were furious at this economic blockade, and Jefferson, completely in sympathy with them, sought a solution by quiet negotiation.

In March, 1803, James Monroe was sent to France as envoy extraordinary to join with the regular minister, Robert R. Livingston, in offering to purchase New Orleans and some, or all, of the left bank of the Mississippi, including the Floridas. If Bonaparte were unwilling to sell, then the Americans were instructed to get at least permanent rights of navigation and deposit. If France refused to make these concessions, deemed minimum by Americans, Jefferson was prepared to ally the United States with Great Britain.

Negotiations with Bonaparte dragged at first. But they soon were hurried when his rickety colonial empire showed signs of collapsing. Santo Domingo remained unyielding; 35,000 of the troops had been killed by Negroes or consumed by yellow fever. Deprived of Santo Domingo, Louisiana looked less attractive to Napoleon. The English navy might take Louisiana at any time should the existing armistice between France and England be broken. Besides, Napoleon knew that even if the French could hold Louisiana it would be a precarious control at best. Thousands of American frontiersmen might sweep down river at any time and rob France of her colony.

One day in April, 1803, when Livingston once again pressed Talleyrand, Minister of Foreign Affairs, to sell New Orleans, the American was startled by the question, "What will you give for the *whole* of Louisiana?" Livingston, a little hard of hearing, finally managed to answer twenty million francs. A short period of bargaining followed, and on the last day of the month France signed away her rights to Louisiana for sixty million francs ($12,000,000). Another $3,000,000 in debts owed by France to American citizens was also to be assumed by the United States. Livingston, who bore the main burden of negotiating for the American side, knew the great meaning of what had been done. In a triumphant tone he turned to Monroe exclaiming, "this is the noblest work of our lives."

Jefferson hesitated, momentarily, thinking a constitutional amendment was required to permit the purchase, but he overcame his scruples when warned to make a quick decision. Before the year was out the treaty had been ratified, and the vast territory handed over to the United States. There are few bargains in history comparable to this purchase. The Americans, however, were not quite certain what they had bought. The limits of Louisiana were vague, and in after years boundary disputes bedeviled United States relations with Spain in the Floridas, Mexico to the southwest, and Britain to the northwest. The impressive fact remained that at trifling financial cost an enormous area, 1,000,000 square miles, had been added to the country, doubling the nation's territory. The policy of "containing" the United States, followed by European powers since the American Revolution, had been given a stunning blow.

It remained for the Americans by sweat and blood to possess, in decades to come, their magnificent western heritage.

★ AARON BURR

Thus far Jefferson's stay in the presidency had been singularly successful. The country was prosperous, the debt was being paid off, party passions were moderated, and the purchase of Louisiana met with general enthusiasm. A crystal-gazer foretelling trouble might well have remembered, however, the scene of Jefferson's inauguration. There two of the people who were to vex him most were at his side, Chief Justice Marshall and Vice-President Aaron Burr. It was commonly known that Marshall and Jefferson differed sharply in their political ideas; as for Burr, Republican boss of New York, the president distrusted his conspiratorial mind. Jefferson, himself, like all successful men in political life, could be devious when necessary, but his goals were obvious and openly declared. Burr's goals were questionable and dangerous, and his methods were those of the cynical leader of men with contempt in his heart for the led.

Jefferson disregarded Burr in the distribution of patronage and completely alienated him by entering an alliance with Burr's rivals, the Clintons and Livingstons in New York. Burr sought to rehabilitate himself by linking his fortunes with New England Federalists. The more extreme among them hoped to secede from the Union and establish a northern confederacy of which New York might be a part. Burr ran for governor of New York in the spring of 1804, making vague commitments to New Englanders in the event of his election. He was defeated, however, and having now proven useless to the Federalists, and banished by the Republicans, he was a disgraced politician. He blamed Hamilton for his misfortunes as the latter had advised his followers against supporting Burr. The disappointed Burr demanded that Hamilton retract damaging remarks made about him. When Hamilton refused, Burr challenged him to a duel. Though dueling had already been condemned, most gentlemen still recognized it as part of their code. Hamilton accepted the challenge, thinking the duel would end in a harmless pistol shot, with everyone's honor upheld.

Early on a brilliant summer morning in July, 1804, the duelists crossed the Hudson to the Jersey shore at Weehawken, under the Palisades. Seconds prepared the ground and Hamilton and Burr made ready. At the signal Hamilton withheld his fire; but Burr meaning to kill, took deliberate aim and fired the fatal shot. Hamilton died the next day, a needless victim of a spurious code of conduct. A powerful public revulsion against dueling occurred in the North, where Burr was counted an outlaw. In the South and West, where judgment was less harsh on dueling, Burr faced no special ostracism. It was to the Southwest that Burr next turned to rehabilitate himself.

He had now the desperation of the gambler taking his last fling. He had lost his post as vice-president when the Republicans passed him by and named George Clinton to run with Jefferson for the latter's second term. Jefferson had won overwhelmingly in 1804. Thus Burr was deprived of power in national councils as well as in his own state of New York, where the distribution of patronage was assigned to Clinton. Shunned by many whose society he formerly esteemed, he apparently had nothing left to lose. He now threw in his lot with characters even more dubious than his own.

★ JEFFERSON AND THE FEDERALISTS

In the Southwest were many men who spent their days dreaming of sudden fortune and political power. Buccaneers in spirit, they planned forays into Spanish borderlands or more grandiose projects to detach from Spain's empire large provinces where they could build themselves dependencies. Perhaps even part of America, west of the Alleghanies, could be separated from the Union to form a new independent state.

Burr traveled in leisurely fashion through this western region in 1805, talking with soldiers of fortune and stirring the muddy, conspiratorial waters. He passed the time with an old crony, General James Wilkinson, then commander of the army in the West. Wilkinson for years had been secretly in the pay of Spain to halt the western advance of his country, and now he appeared ready to betray it again in company with Burr. He was truly skilled only in treachery. Burr enlisted Major General Andrew Jackson of Tennessee in his scheme to make war on Spanish possessions, for which the General was always ready. Burr met up with a visionary, Harman Blennerhassett, living in eccentric splendor on an island in the Ohio. After being dazzled with promises of lordly wealth, he pledged his fortune in support of the project to conquer Mexico. In New Orleans Burr found malcontents ever ready for filibustering expeditions. To each listener Burr told little or much of his plans, depending on his shrewd estimate of his confidant's naïveté or his capacity for duplicity.

In 1806 Burr, having failed to secure extensive support for his cloudy projects, determined to move anyway. Just what he planned to do with his few dozen men floating down the Ohio nobody really knows. He had awakened suspicions, however, among westerners strongly loyal to their country, who warned Jefferson. The president, after some hesitation, ordered Burr arrested. In the early weeks of 1807 Burr's enterprise came to an inglorious end with his capture by forces of the American army.

The former vice-president was brought to Richmond and, in a courtroom baked in August heat, tried for treason, with Chief Justice Marshall presiding. The Federalists, who shortly before had execrated Burr for killing Hamilton, were now making a hero out of him, mainly to discomfit Jefferson. "The fact is," the president wrote, "the Federalists make Burr's cause their own, and exert their whole influence to protect him from punishment." Jefferson was very anxious for conviction, but Marshall insisted that the evidence would have to show the commission of treason as defined by the constitution, levying war against the United States, "or in adhering to their enemies." Furthermore, no person could be convicted of treason "unless on the testimony of two witnesses to the same overt act." Burr was acquitted in a trial that shortly became a contest of wills between Jefferson and Marshall. The latter's handling of the case, biased in Burr's favor as it was, deepened Jefferson's dislike of the Federalist judiciary.

That dislike had boiled up before when in the famous case of *Marbury* v. *Madison* (1803) Marshall, flaunting his banner of nationalism, asserted the right of the Supreme Court to review laws passed by Congress or state legislatures. William Marbury had been one of Adams' "midnight appointments" in the closing hours of his administration. Named justice of the peace in the District of Columbia, his commission was not delivered before Jefferson's term of office began. Madison, as Secretary of State, whose responsibility it was, refused to deliver it. Marbury then appealed to the Supreme Court to issue a mandamus ordering Madison to deliver the commission. Though the Court had the authority to do so, by virtue of the Judiciary Act of 1789, Marshall refused to grant Marbury's request.

The Chief Justice had a larger objective in view than an immediate humbling of the Jeffersonian administration. He decided that the portion of the Judiciary Act permitting the Supreme Court to issue the type of writ Marbury had requested was unconstitutional; Congress had no right to grant such authority to the court, which had been given original jurisdiction by the Constitution only in "cases affecting ambassadors, other public ministers and consuls, and those in which a state shall be a party." Thus Marshall espoused what was later known as the "doctrine of judicial review," a doctrine familiar to Americans in the colonial period. This case was significant for its announcement of the court's right to overrule Congress. A far more important instance of the court's action in declaring an act of Congress unconstitutional occurred more than half a century later in the Dred Scott case.

While the failure of Marbury to gain a commission was a nominal victory for Jefferson, the president knew that Marshall was the true victor. Jefferson would have liked to remove from the bench Federalist judges who had treated harshly his own followers, but Marshall's decision deprived the president of the justification he needed. The chief Justice avoided saying that Marbury was improperly appointed; to have admitted that would have played into Jefferson's hands. Instead, Marshall stated that Marbury had both a legal and moral claim to his commission, that Madison and Jefferson were acting illegally in denying him the commission; but the Supreme Court could not intervene because the act under which Marbury sued was unconstitutional.

In another episode, involving Supreme Court Justice Samuel Chase, Jefferson again was worsted. Chase, a Federalist judge, had been an especially objectionable thorn in Republican sides. He was a large, coarse man given to bullying tactics. Like other Federalist judges he participated openly in politics and used his position to vilify political opponents. The Justice was placed on trial in the Senate in 1805, but despite the long list of acts of misconduct with which he was charged, he escaped impeachment. The judiciary had become the last defense of the Federalists, and under Marshall's leadership it waved a banner upholding nationalism and protecting property rights. Jefferson might win elections but Federalists seemed to be winning judicial decisions.

Jefferson was having trouble even in politics. His once dependable lieutenant in the House of Representatives, John Randolph of Roanoke, had turned all his powers of eloquent vituperation against him. This long-legged, youthful looking man, with a clear, penetrating voice which became shrill with excitement, was a dangerous opponent.

He was troublesome to the administration on two issues. One related to a complicated transaction in which corruption was charged to Georgia legislators (1795) in disposing of the state's western lands, near the Yazoo River in present Mississippi. Millions of acres had been granted to the Yazoo Land Companies for one and a half cents an acre, much of which was then disposed of through public sale. When the cry of fraud was raised, Georgia's legislature nullified the original contract with the Yazoo companies. Stockholders in the latter, as well as many innocent purchasers of the tainted property, refused to accept the decision that their titles were invalid. When Jefferson became president an agreement was made that Georgia cede its lands to the federal government, and the Yazoo land claimants would be compensated through the sale of 5,000,000 acres. As part of the agreement, the national government wiped out Indian claims to territory within Georgia; the western lands ceded to the Union were to become a state.

The final settlement of the whole problem was delayed when Randolph objected on the ground that it mainly benefited northern speculators, and was an affront to the sovereign state of Georgia. His states-rights doctrine won enough supporters (they were called "Quids") to postpone for some years Congressional ratification of the agreement. In 1810 the Supreme Court ruled, in the case of *Fletcher* v. *Peck,* that Georgia had no right to nullify the original contract with the Yazoo companies. Four years later, 1814, when Randolph was out of Congress, the latter awarded the Yazoo land claimants $8,000,000.

On another issue, the Florida question, Randolph's break with the administration was counted more serious by Jefferson. The president had convinced himself that the boundaries of the Louisiana Purchase embraced West Florida. The acquisition of this region, which included the good harbor of Mobile Bay, became a cardinal point in Jefferson's foreign policy. The tortuous diplomacy involved in these negotiations, including the presidential request (1805) for a secret fund to acquire the coveted territory, angered Randolph and other Virginia Republicans. Secretary of State Madison was accused of seeking the money to bribe France to bring pressure on Spain to cede West Florida. Randolph, who was chairman of the Ways and Means Committee, angrily declared that he would not sponsor a proposal to deliver "the public purse to the first cut-throat that demanded it." Though Randolph was eventually outvoted, his obstructive tactics held up Jefferson's negotiations. In the meantime, changes in the European scene had diminished Napoleon's interest in the project, and the opportunity of acquiring Florida was then lost to this administration.

★ THE EMBARGO

Thus far Jefferson's setbacks, though serious, were offset by his major accomplishments. The credit of the young nation never stood higher in the world's financial centers. Politically Jefferson had won so many converts, even in New England, that there only Connecticut still looked down her Federalist bluenose. The younger generation was deserting parental political allegiance to enlist under the banner of Jefferson. Guided by his example, Republicans in New England began the long fight for separation of Church and State, which ultimately ended in victory.

At this same time, however, Jefferson was caught in the whirlwind set off by Napoleon's drive for European conquest. America was on the edge of the storm, and though she escaped the vortex she was lashed by the violent winds. In the exhausting struggle that raged in these years between England and France, American rights at sea received scant consideration.

British captains were ever on the search for personnel to man their growing fleet. The search was insistent because wholesale desertions left warships undermanned. Press gangs had long scoured prisons for men to sail the ships. Sailors were hauled off merchantmen, both British and alien, to fill out the crew of ships of the Royal Navy. Many deserting British sailors had found more comfortable berths on American ships where pay was higher and treatment better. English captains disregarded United States complaints about infractions of neutral rights and continued to seize cargo and crewmen, many of whom were Britishers with forged American citizenship papers. Even when the papers were legitimate they were rarely treated seriously by the British who, at that time, did not recognize the right of expatriation.

It was not only men and cargo that were being forcibly taken. American ships as well, especially those engaged in trade between Europe and the West Indies, were being seized and condemned in British admiralty courts. England's resort to commercial warfare was to weaken Napoleon's European empire by throttling trade between it and the rest of the world. British warships lay off American harbors harrying United States vessels by shots and insulting search. Anti-British feeling, easily stirred up in these years, flared in the press and public assembly. England, it was charged, was ever the enemy of neutral shipping. "Never will neutrals be perfectly safe," said a paper in the busy port of Salem, "till free goods make free ships or till England loses two or three great naval battles."

Strong Federalists, normally hostile to Jefferson, were inclining to his view on this issue. Several years before, one of them had written that it appeared strange to him "that the British ministry have never thought it their interest to try and conciliate this country. . . . A very considerable portion of the commerce of this country is carried on with their manufacturers, and the payment for these insures them no small proportions of our exports. . . . They never miss an opportunity of circumscribing our happiness." With a forecast of embargo, he went on to say, "if the British restrict our trade, let us meet them with restrictions on our part, and if we cannot find employment for our capital in commerce, let us enjoy it in either agriculture or manufactures."

The Americans who attempted to conform to British regulations governing trade on the high seas soon found themselves beset by the French. Napoleon decreed that American ships which allowed British search or whose voyage included a stop at a British port were subject to seizure by the French. Thus Americans were caught between two fires; if they traded with that part of Europe under French control the British intervened; if they traded with Britain they ran the risk of seizure by France.

Diplomatic negotiations between the United States and Britain to ease restrictions on American commerce failed. To make matters worse, increasing arrogance of British commanders impressing men from United States ships in American waters further embittered relations between the two countries. An especially flagrant incident was the assault by the British vessel "Leopard" on the American frigate "Chesapeake" while searching for deserters from the Royal Navy. American opinion of all shades was greatly inflamed, and it needed only a nod from Jefferson to touch off war with Britain. "The affair of the 'Chesapeake' put war into my hand," wrote Jefferson in retrospect. "I had only to open it and let havoc loose."

But the president, though adding to the nation's naval strength, hated war, and he hoped economic pressure would force Britain to yield. American commerce, thought Jefferson, was so valuable to Europeans, including the British, that "they will be glad to purchase it when the only price we ask is to do us justice." "Peaceable coercion" would make them bend.

That pressure took the form of the Embargo Act which, under Jefferson's leadership Congress passed in December, 1807. By a step unique in world history, the government withdrew the whole American merchant marine from foreign commerce. This was done under the clause of the Constitution authorizing Congress to regulate trade. John Randolph protested that it really was a measure to destroy commerce, not regulate it; but it passed the Senate by a vote of four to one, and the House two to one. The act remained in force during the entire last year of Jefferson's presidency, 1808, which might be called the Embargo Year. It was a compromise between peace and war, recalling the nonimportation agreements just before the Revolution. Jefferson hoped that, with far less cost in money, lives, and suffering than would result from open hostilities, it would bring the British and French to terms from economic necessity. He also hoped that it would tend to make the United States more self-sufficient.

"The ocean . . . is arbitrarily wrested from us," he wrote, "and maxims consecrated by time, by usage, and by an universal sense of right, are trampled on by superior force: to give time for this demoralizing tempest to pass over, one measure only remained which might cover our beloved country from its overwhelming fury. . . . There can be no question in a mind truly American whether it is best to send our citizens and property into certain captivity, or to keep them at home, and to turn seriously to that policy which plants the manufacturer and husbandman side by side, and so establish at the door of everyone that exchange of mutual labors and comforts which we have hitherto sought in distant regions, and under perpetual risk of broils. . . ."

New England reeled under the immediate impact of the blow. The nation was now the world's greatest maritime carrier except Britain, and New England owned more than half of its million tons of shipping. This now lay idle and deteriorating at Yankee wharves. Shipbuilding dropped off to an alarming extent, farm prices declined heavily, the prices of foreign wares advanced, and both the labor market and the investment market underwent severe dislocations. America's annual exports were reduced from $108,000,000 to $22,000,000. Moreover, the enforcement of the law caused New Englanders a great deal of vexation. The prying tactics of the government officers who now appeared on all the harbor fronts were resented; and a great deal of smuggling began across the Canadian border. Many American shippers, though facing serious risk, had been reaping large profits in transporting goods and food to forbidden ports. Many New Englanders, seeing that the Embargo hurt Britain, but France hardly at all, doubted Jefferson's sincerity. He was France's secret ally, they grumbled.

But while the immediate losses to New England were great, the permanent loss was slight. The Embargo gave the section an inducement to march with greater vigor on the road to its true future, manufacturing. Strong stimulus was given to the shoe industry, in Massachusetts, and to the textile industry in all of New England. The economic future of the region lay with its factories, and not with its merchant shipping.

In the South, on the other hand, the Embargo did little superficial and immediate injury, but its deeper and more permanent effects were disastrous. This was because the South depended quite as much as the other sections on the export trade in its staples, while it lacked the resources of New England, New York, and Pennsylvania for manufacturing. It followed Jefferson blindly and gladly in supporting the measure, while the North abused it for its complacent attitude. Yankee newspapers pictured Nathaniel Macon of North Carolina, for instance, as living a life of perfect ease, his slaves growing all the corn, rice, and tobacco he wanted, and a brisk walk in the woods with a gun giving him a wild turkey or deer to eat. Yet actually the long-term sufferings of the Southerners were deplorable. The price of farm products went down to appalling levels. Thus in Charlottesville, Jefferson's home, quotations of flour fell at once from $5.50 a barrel to $2.50; tar in North Carolina slipped from $2.00 a barrel to 45 cents; and in parts of the South horses sold for $2.50 apiece and hogs were almost given away. Land values fell with equal rapidity. Throughout the South payment of debts became so difficult that the courts would meet and at once adjourn so that creditors could not take legal action to foreclose on property.

The results of the Embargo in the Middle States were mixed. The latter turned more vigorously toward manufacturing, and Philadelphia, as the chief manufacturing city of the Union, experienced a real boom. But in New York the large shipping business was very hard hit, and other ports were full of vessels dismantled and laid up. Not a box or barrel was to be seen on the wide wharves, and most of the exporters' offices and counting rooms were shut up. The coffee house and shorefront grogshops were almost empty. Business failures were so common, that New Yorkers clogged the city's jail as ruined debtors.

On the whole, the Embargo proved a failure. Great as was the hardship caused in Britain, the pressure was far too weak to effect Jefferson's object of bringing that country to terms. For one reason, a violent Spanish rebellion against Napoleon began in 1808; and this resulted in throwing many Spanish and South American ports open to British traders. British exports to the United States during 1808 declined by about $33,000,000 from the 1807 figure; but British exports to the rest of the world, with Spain, South America, and Canada in the lead, gained almost $31,000,-000. For another reason, a great deal of the old British export trade to the United States had really been a re-export trade to the West Indies, and this now went out by direct channels; Britain did not lose it at all. Moreover, Napoleon's Berlin and Milan decrees must in any event have reduced greatly the purchasing power of America. Henry Adams estimates that the real value of the British trade stopped by the Embargo was only $25,000,000, and that not more than $5,000,000 of this was profits. The loss of five millions a year was not going to injure severely so rich and powerful a nation as Great Britain.

Inevitably, political discontent weakened Jefferson's hold on the country. The Federalist party revived in New England, winning local elections, and it rallied sentiment to nullify the despised Embargo Act. It was evaded by many mariners; and contemptuous Federalists, speaking seditious language, were assuring the British that they stood ready to sabotage the embargo. Jefferson and his fellow Republicans were charged with truckling to Napoleon. Despite this threat to Jefferson's national leadership, he was in command when time came for the presidential election. The Federalists were really strong only in New England, and they were unable to challenge successfully Jefferson's candidate, James Madison. The president himself refused to run again as he was opposed to a third term.

Madison's victory over C. C. Pinckney, the Federalist candidate, did nothing to lessen the angry talk in northern ports and on western farms. The embargo lost friends for the administration, and influenced neither England nor France. "Here," wrote the American minister in Paris, "it is not felt and in England . . . it is forgotten." This was inaccurate for there were bankers and merchants in England who denounced their own country's repressive measures, and even toasted Jefferson.

In Jefferson's own country, however, after fourteen months of futility the rising fury of denunciation finally shook his faith in the embargo policy. A bill to repeal it was speeded through Congress and was signed by Jefferson on March 1, 1809. "This embargo act," he ruefully admitted, "is certainly the most embarrassing we ever had to execute. I did not expect a crop of so sudden and rank growth of fraud and open opposition by force could have grown up in the United States." The disappointed president, his administration at an end, left for his beloved Monticello to reflect on the vicissitudes of politics, and to share with his countrymen a great store of wisdom accumulated in a long, magnificent life.

★ MADISON

James Madison, successor in the "Virginia dynasty," had lived for years in the shadow of the more noted Jefferson. Madison was sufficiently distinguished in his own right, but while he possessed talent in politics Jefferson was gifted with genius. Madison's abilities lay rather in scholarly study, especially of political science, or in framing sober acts of legislation. He did not shine as an administrator or as spokesman for the tongueless mass. He was a short, unimpressive man physically, and on his inauguration day pale and nervous. He delivered his inaugural address in almost inaudible tones, asserting again the principles of Jefferson, urging recourse to diplomacy rather than to war to settle differences between nations.

While the president appeared dispirited, his wife, the famous Dolley Madison, brought a note of grace and beauty to the White House. Zestful and gay, she added color to an administration destined to more than its share of gloom.

★ ANGLO-AMERICAN FRICTION

Madison strove desperately to reach an understanding with Britain. At the time the Embargo Act was repealed Congress had re-enacted a Nonintercourse Act, forbidding England and France from trading with America, though authorizing the president to reopen commercial relations with them if they changed their policies. Madison negotiated an understanding with David Erskine, the friendly British minister in Washington, which promised to place Anglo-American relations on a more amicable footing. American shippers, relieved that the impasse had been broken, loaded their vessels with long-stored cargoes, and sent them out to sea. For three months ships sailed unmolested, until suddenly a new blow fell.

England's foreign minister, George Canning, scuttled the Erskine agreement, charging the minister with exceeding his instructions. This action further alienated the Americans whose smoldering anger was ready to burst into flame. Nonintercourse was once again in effect with Britain, as well as France. Almost as if to show his contempt for America, Canning sent to Washington Francis James Jackson as minister to replace the recalled Erskine. Jackson's anti-Americanism was notorious, and there could be no contact between him and Madison. Although a frigid silence quickly developed between the two countries, the buzz of hot war talk could be heard on the streets.

The president, however, still sought to avoid war. In May, 1810, Congress passed a measure known as "Macon's Bill No. 2." It re-established normal commercial relations with everyone, but it also attempted to play off England and France against each other. It proposed to either that if she recognized American neutral rights, the United States would not trade with her enemy. Madison was led to believe that Napoleon had suspended the restrictive decrees against American ships. The president, in February, 1811, then issued an order forbidding trade with Great Britain.

Tension mounted between the United States and England. British warships renewed their practice of halting American vessels off east coast harbors to search them for deserters. In May, 1811, an American frigate, the "President," worsted the weaker "Little Belt" in this undeclared conflict. The Jefferson-Madison policy of peaceful coercion was being overtaken by martial acts. And new men, uncompromising and scornful of Madison's pacific measures, were now in seats of power.

★ THE WARHAWKS

The elections of 1810–11 had brought the "warhawks" to Congress. Among them was the youthful Henry Clay from Kentucky, charming, witty, and eloquent, ready to begin his long, distinguished public career. Led by the aggressive "warhawks," Congress elected Clay Speaker of the House. As Speaker, Clay named to the important committees—naval affairs, military affairs, and foreign relations—militant men impatient with the slow processes of diplomacy.

Many of the newer figures in public life had come from regions bordering the alien lands of the Spaniards in the South and the British in the North and Northwest. Congressmen like John Sevier and Felix Grundy of Tennessee knew the war whoops of Indians. These men from west of the Alleghanies were less concerned with protecting America's maritime interests than they were with acquiring land from Spain in Florida, the Indians in the West, and the British in Canada.

Upper Canada was sparsely populated and its fertile lands looked inviting to nearby Americans. Western New York in 1812, with its 200,000 people, already seemed overcrowded to many of its inhabitants. In the Southwest, Americans moving in wagons and river craft continued to fill up the back country. They drifted down the Ohio on clumsy flatboats, with a few cattle eating their hay at the prow while the children scampered everywhere. The boats provided easy, cheap transportation (they cost about $40), and at journey's end they were broken up to make the settler's home.

Land in the West was now easier to acquire. Modifications of earlier national land acts, with more lenient credit facilities, had stimulated settlement. By 1812 over 250,000 people lived in Ohio, transforming the region into a community of permanent inhabitants, with cultivated fields, better roads, neat villages, and bustling towns. Settlers in greater numbers were spilling over into Indiana, Illinois, and even Michigan. By 1812 Indiana had a population of 25,000, while Illinois had 13,000 scattered over its territory and living for the most part under primitive frontier conditions.

Far to the south, along the Spanish Borderland, Americans were finding their way into West Florida in such numbers as to give them, along the Mississippi, a majority of the population. Jefferson and Madison had been insistent in their claims that this strip of coastal territory, stretching from the Perdido River to the Mississippi, had always been part of the Louisiana Purchase.

The region was ripe for plucking, for the whole Spanish empire was disintegrating as the result of Napoleon's invasion of the Spanish homeland. The Floridas, said Americans, were home to runaway slaves, a nest for pirates, and a springboard for hostile Indians. A group of American revolutionists overthrew the local Spanish government at Baton Rouge, in 1810, and Madison proclaimed the area part of the United States. Success in this venture inspired a similar movement to acquire East Florida, but that province still eluded the American grasp. In a challenging speech, Henry Clay hoped to see "ere long, the *new* United States . . . embracing, not only the old Thirteen States, but the entire country east of the Mississippi, including East Florida, and some of the territories of the north of us also."

Canada was not just a land to be conquered. It was a base from which rival fur traders must be expelled in order to give Americans a monopoly of the Northwest Territory. "Is it nothing to acquire the entire fur-trade connected with that country?" asked Clay. From Canada, too, came support for the Indians of the Northwest, who began to yield their lands too slowly to suit the covetous American frontiersmen. The Indians in this region, forced by threats, seduced by bribes, and befuddled by liquor, had already signed away title to millions of acres under constant pressure of William Henry Harrison, Governor of Indiana Territory. In the decade before 1809 nearly 110,000,000 acres had been taken from the redmen. But the Indians in the Great Lakes area were being hemmed in on the west by the powerful Sioux and Chippewa tribes. The Indians of the Great Lakes had thus to stand and fight for their remaining lands. Their resolve to do so was strengthened by the leadership offered by Tecumseh, a Shawnee chieftain, and his brother, The Prophet, credited by his followers with supernatural powers.

Tecumseh traveled from tribe to tribe preaching unity and abstention from drink to withstand the white man, and thus preserve dwindling hunting grounds. He decided to challenge Harrison's grasp of additional land, and in the spring of 1810 Indians began attacking isolated white settlements. The next year fighting spread over a larger area. An important engagement took place on the Wabash River, on November 7, 1811. In the dawn of a cold, rainy day the Indians attacked the white encampment, but were driven off by Harrison's men, who set fire to the Indian village, Prophetstown, close by Tippecanoe Creek. The "Battle of Tippecanoe" was a hard-won victory, but the defeated Indians were not crushed. They roamed through remoter white settlements spreading death and destruction with fire and tomahawk.

All westerners believed that the red men were being supplied and encouraged by the British redcoats in Canada. Felix Grundy, who had seen three brothers killed by Indians, spoke heatedly of that power which took every opportunity to intrigue with the natives and urge on "the ruthless savages to tomahawk our women and children." "War," he shouted, "is not to commence by sea or land, it is already begun, and some of the richest blood of our country has been shed." Another soaring "warhawk," John C. Calhoun, believed "a single victory over the enemy by sea or land" preferable "to all the good we shall ever derive from the continuation of the nonimportation act."

The martial spirit was rising, but there was confusion in the land. Madison hesitated, still hopeful that peaceful coercion might yet win. Then, too, many Americans were as angry with France as they were with England. Napoleon's deception was clear now to everyone, for American vessels and cargoes were being seized by his officials despite his bland assurance that French restrictive decrees on neutral trade had been suspended. The sins of France, however, were counted venial; those of Britain, venomous.

The British offended America's pride most deeply by impressing her sailors on the high seas and belligerently intercepting vessels even in United States waters. French indignities were imposed in distant waters and were less publicized. The French committed no outrages that burned so deeply as the attack on the "Chesapeake." And it was not the French who conspired with the Indians to halt the westward advance of American settlement. Americans were not allowed to forget British incitement to Indian outrage. Aging men told again to wide-eyed listeners tales of terror-filled nights when redskins were allied with redcoats to scourge the land and its defenseless people during the American Revolution.

Thus the grievances accumulated. And it was easier for Americans to rationalize their dubious ambitions to expand by pointing to the real injustices committed by Britain. Curtailment of commerce accented agricultural depression in the South and West. Inland as well as coast land was whipped by the lash of eloquent tongues. "The true question," said a western Congressman in 1812, "is the right of exporting the productions of our soil and industry to foreign markets." It looked as though East and West, on the basis of a common commercial grievance, were linked in anger against Great Britain.

In Britain itself, closing of the American market helped depress industry and commerce. The winter of 1811–12 was harsh, and it was made more bitter by crop failure and prohibitive food prices. Receipts of American food crops, which had been furnishing 20 per cent or more of England's agricultural imports, had dropped to a trickle. Poor rates soared, jobless men rioted, while merchants and factory owners petitioned parliament to repeal the Orders in Council so that trade with America might be reopened. Government officials in areas torn by riots believed that disturbances might have been averted had trade been free with America. A slow-moving government finally yielded to the many pressures, and on June 16, 1812, it announced that the Orders in Council were suspended. No telegraph or radio existed to flash the news to America. Had rapid communication been available history might have had a different page to record, a page vindicating the Jefferson-Madison policy of peaceful coercion.

Fate willed otherwise. It may be that war momentum had gone too far to be arrested in any event. England still insisted on the right of impressment, and America boiled over with a long list of accumulated grievances. "We are going to fight for the re-establishment of our national character," wrote Andrew Jackson a few months before the conflict began. America would fight, too, against impressment, for neutral rights at sea, and "an open market for the productions of our soil now perishing on our hands because the *mistress of the ocean* has forbid us to carry them to any foreign nation. . . ." The United States would "seek some indemnity for past injuries, some security against future aggression, by the conquest of all the British dominions upon the continent of North America."

While parliament temporized, Congress was preparing to declare war. The declaration came on June 18, but it was a divided America that took up arms. The House vote was 79 in favor to 49 opposed; in the Senate it was 19 to 13. A sizable minority of Republicans, opposed to the arrogant "warhawks" in their party, abstained from voting at all. The West voted for war; the coastal area, though split, had strong sentiment for peace. Federalists inclined to the belief that Napoleon was the real danger and had done more damage to American commerce than Britain. The division in the country was ominous.

★ WAR OF 1812

The Americans were woefully unprepared for war on land; for naval conflict they were in better shape. The regular army, less than 7,000 and poorly officered, could hardly count for additional support on the fighting qualities of the undisciplined militia. Enlistments in the regular army lagged almost everywhere. Of an authorized increase of 50,000 voted in 1812, scarce one-tenth that number joined up after six months had elapsed. The "warhawks" mistakenly anticipated an easy march into Canada, with victory to be followed by a dictated peace.

The general supposition of many Americans, in this war as in some others, was that it would be short and easy. Henry Clay had expressed this view. "It is said," he declared in Congressional debate, "that no object is attainable by war with Great Britain. In its fortunes, we are to estimate not only the benefit to be derived to ourselves, but the injury to be done the enemy. The conquest of Canada is in your power. I trust that I shall not be deemed presumptuous when I state that I verily believe that the militia of Kentucky are alone competent to place Montreal and Upper Canada at your feet. Is it nothing to the British nation; is it nothing to the pride of her monarch, to have the last of the immense North American possessions held by him at the commencement of his reign wrested from his dominion?" But this dream of a swift conquest by the Kentucky militia alone was soon to seem a dream indeed.

The attempts to invade Canada all ended in failure in 1812. Insufficient troops, poor leadership, and poorer planning contributed to the debacle. General William Hull, the inept American commander, surrendered Detroit without fighting to the able Canadian leader, General Isaac Brock, in August, 1812. On the Niagara frontier the militia hampered what might have been a successful invasion. When the militia, predisposed to think in defensive terms, found they were called upon to wage offensive war, they refused to leave New York, abandoning the burden to an inadequate number of regulars.

On water, both lake and ocean, the Americans won balm for land defeats. The Americans were greatly skilled in ship design, and their war vessels were often superior in strength and speed to foreign ships of their class. The victories of the "Constitution" over the "Guerrière," the "United States" over the "Macedonian," and the "Wasp" over the "Frolic" filled America's cup of rejoicing. The fighting strength of the "Constitution" won her the affectionate name of "Old Ironsides." From Lake Erie Captain Oliver H. Perry delighted the country with his famous dispatch. "We have met the enemy, and they are ours." Perry praised the Negroes in his crew, "they seemed absolutely insensible to danger." Blacks made up about 10 per cent of the crews on the Upper Lakes. On salt water some 500 American privateers bore down on British shipping, capturing over 1,300 vessels during the course of the war.

Even on land things seemed to go better for the Americans in 1813. Incursions into Canada were more successful than the year before, with temporary captures of strategic centers. Unfortunately these forays were sometimes marked by burning of Canadian villages and the parliament buildings at York (Toronto); and these were met by retaliation across the border. Canadian counterattacks cleared the Americans out of the country, but possession of Detroit and control of Lake Erie secured the United States against invasion from the northwest. Indians under Tecumseh were decisively beaten, and they then fell away from their former British allies.

The over-all picture for the American cause, however, was not promising. State militia refused to respond to calls for troops by the national government. The government itself was threatened with bankruptcy. Despite Gallatin's urgent appeal Congress was reluctant to vote taxes to raise needed funds. When finally authorized, evasion was common. Subscriptions to new loans dragged, for most moneyed men did not favor the war.

The political situation gave clear sign of friction in the nation. In the 1812 election Madison had vigorous opposition in De Witt Clinton of New York. Clinton was supported by Federalists and peace Republicans. New England, except Vermont, gave all its electoral votes to Clinton, who also led Madison in the middle states. The South and West voted solidly for Madison. The sectional division was depressing to the administration.

In New England, Federalist hostility to the war increased as the conflict wore on. Extreme Federalists wanted no part of "Mr. Madison's War" and, in fact, were prepared to leave the Union, form a New England confederacy, and make a separate peace with Britain. Trading with the enemy by New Englanders was a common occurrence during all the war. They furnished so much meat to the British forces in Canada that at the close of 1813 the British commander there wrote that two-thirds of his troops were eating beef supplied by Yankee contractors. Large droves were coming daily across the boundary. British fleets off the New England coast received provisions from the shore. Meanwhile, New England refused to give financial support to the unpopular war. Of the $11,000,000 loan floated in the spring of 1812, the section took less than $1,000,000, and of the 1813 loan of $16,000,000, Boston took less than $75,000. During the whole conflict the total of Yankee subscriptions to national loans was less than $3,000,000, while the Middle States subscribed for almost $35,000,000. Many New Englanders felt that it was a sectional war—a Southern and Western war; many felt that when England was in a life-and-death struggle with Napoleonic tyranny, the United States was on the wrong side. Some New Yorkers, including the distinguished Gouverneur Morris, took the same attitude.

The New England opposition came to a head in the famous Hartford Convention, which met in December, 1814, amid loud execrations from the Democratic newspapers. The movement for this convention had originated in Western Massachusetts, where the pinch of war was felt specially by a farming population which could not sell its products. Federalists in Northampton suggested a gathering of all the northern and commercial States to discuss means of security "from the future exercise of powers injurious to their commercial interests." Noah Webster in Amherst supported the demand; and the Massachusetts legislature appointed twelve delegates of high character, including George Cabot and Harrison Gray Otis. The Connecticut and Rhode Island legislatures also named delegates, while local gatherings in New Hampshire and Vermont chose unofficial representatives. In all, 26 men met in Hartford. Madison, who had been half prostrated by the nation's military reverses, feared the worst; a visitor reported that "his mind is full of the New England sedition."

Fortunately, the Hartford Convention was controlled by moderate men. They discarded the proposals of extremists, and after twenty days of deliberation, brought in a calm report. They declared against any rupture of the Union, especially in time of war, and pointed out that hasty attempts to change the Constitution were to be deplored. But they did criticize the Administration and the war in harsh terms, and they proposed several amendments to the Constitution, including one to base representation on free population alone.

The lack of unity augured ill for America's prospects in 1814. That same year the success of the coalition against Napoleon left Britain free to prosecute the war against the United States with more energy. Large-scale plans were made; men and ships deployed to invade the United States by way of Lake Champlain in the north, and from New Orleans in the south. The east coast was to be blockaded by British men-of-war. Thus by land and sea America was to be hammered into submission.

The British plan of offensive operations had success only at sea and along the coast. The American navy, so often victorious in the early stages of the war, now found it difficult to break through the British blockade. The enemy craft ranged at will along the coast and, on occasion, sent invading columns ashore. One such column marched on Washington in August, 1814, and, overcoming unheroic resistance, captured the capital. After setting fire to the public buildings the British troops marched back to their vessels. This expedition had less success in its next move, an attempted attack on Baltimore. Fort McHenry stood up to the British bombardment, and a proud American, Francis Scott Key, was inspired to write "The Star Spangled Banner," to commemorate the glory.

Americans covered themselves with shame, as well as glory, in this conflict. They revealed want of discipline and refusal to obey commands in the field. For Hull's ignominious surrender of Detroit no valid excuse can be offered. But one factor in the capitulation was that two companies of Michigan militia, in the face of the enemy, deserted; and their desertion threatened to leave the town exposed to Indian fury. General Stephen Van Rensselaer, commanding on the Niagara frontier, wrote the governor of New York in condemnation of his raw soldiers: "Alarm pervades the country and distrust among the troops. They are incessantly pressing for furloughs under every possible pretence. Many are without shoes; all clamorous for pay; many are sick." And sometimes indiscipline became flagrant cowardice. General Jacob Brown, commanding at Sackets' Harbor in 1813, defended it at the end of May against an advance by the enemy. He later wrote: "My orders were that the troops were to lie close and reserve their fire until the enemy had approached so near that every shot might hit its object. It is, however, impossible to execute such orders with raw troops, unaccustomed to subordination. My orders were, in this case, disobeyed; the whole line fired, and not without effect; but in the moment when I was contemplating this, to my utter astonishment they rose from their cover and fled." His statement was much like that which General Winder made after the battle of Bladensburg: "To my utter astonishment and mortification, when I regained my position I found the whole of these regiments flying in the utmost precipitation and disorder."

There was, however, a heroic side to American participation in the war. The exploits of American tars, sons of the sea-frontier, in single-ship actions amply proved this fact. And so did some of the achievements of American arms in the final stages of the war. While British forces were moving on Washington and taking it, in the Lake Champlain area a veteran British army was thrusting forward, accompanied by a fleet of small vessels, to gain control of that lake and Lake George. Naval possession of Champlain was essential to continuance of the land advance, it was the key to victory. The British were denied that key in a spectacular naval battle at Plattsburg, where the American fleet, under young Commodore Thomas MacDonough, triumphed. The American victory forced the British to retreat to Canada.

At New Orleans the British failure was disastrous. The city was defended by frontiersmen, led by General Andrew Jackson who had won great renown as an Indian fighter. Jackson's sharp-shooting riflemen took up positions protected by a ditch and earthworks to await the British attack. Waiting with Jackson were over 400 Negro soldiers who had built the cotton-bag defenses against the expected onslaught. Jackson had already praised their ardor in preliminary campaigns. In this new test Jackson found his faith justified in the black man's fighting ability. On the morning of January 8, 1815, the redcoats under Sir Edward Pakenham, contemptuous of militia, moved up in massed frontal assault. A wind blew the fog away and Jackson's men saw the solid red line marching stolidly forward. The slaughter was frightful. The British suffered over 2,000 casualties, including Pakenham and other general officers; the entrenched Americans lost thirteen killed. The surviving British then withdrew to their ships. Jackson was now the hero of America. The victory at New Orleans blotted out the memory of past defeats in the war and left Americans with an enormous pride in their military prowess.

The Battle of New Orleans had no effect on the outcome of the war, for the treaty of peace ending the struggle had already been signed at Ghent, on December 24, 1814, though it was not ratified until February, 1815. Negotiations between British and American commissioners had been in progress for several months. Gallatin, one of the American commissioners, played a very important part in reaching the final settlement. His colleague, John Quincy Adams, praised him for his contribution: "Mr. Gallatin keeps and increases his influence over us all. It would have been an irreparable loss if our country had been deprived of the benefit of his talents in this negotiation."

Both sides were finally anxious to end a war which was costly to each and promised little of importance to either. Probably an influential factor in Britain's determination to make peace was the decision of the Duke of Wellington against taking the proffered command in America. "That which appears to me to be wanting in America is not a General," he said, "but a naval superiority on the Lakes."

In the treaty that was finally signed nothing was said about violation of neutral rights and impressment, the reasons given by Madison for the American declaration of war. Each side agreed to a restoration of the *status quo ante bellum*. The treaty provided for the creation of commissions to settle boundary controversies between the United States and Canada (the Rush-Bagot Agreement, 1817, provided for a minimum armament on the Great Lakes; the Convention of 1818 accepted the forty-ninth parallel westward to the "Stony" mountains as the northern boundary of the United States); other disputes, over trade discriminations and fisheries, were to be settled by diplomatic negotiation. Thus ended a needless war, which many even then thought avoidable. The whole conflict occurred under an unlucky star; its declaration came when peace was possible and its final, terrible battle was fought after peace was signed.

On Christmas Day, 1814, the two peace delegations sat down together to dinner. The band played "God Save the King" and "Yankee Doodle." "It was a scene to be remembered," said Gallatin's son, "God grant there may be always peace between the two nations." Through the years that followed it was not always easy to keep that peace, but it is a fact of great significance in world history that young Gallatin's prayer has been answered to our time.

CHAPTER XIV

End of an Era

The men who had been the leaders in the Revolution, who with great vision had guided the new nation through its early perilous years, were passing from the scene. Madison, it is true, still represented the Revolutionary generation, but he came to the end of his second term on March 4, 1817. His successor, James Monroe, continued the "Virginia dynasty," and proved a not unworthy representative of that line. With him the line ended. Though he had won no honors in his diplomatic missions to France and Spain, though he had not the glamour of Jefferson nor the acumen of Madison, Monroe was a self-confident, proud man with a capacity for growth, and his fair-mindedness and magnanimity were acknowledged even by his opponents.

Monroe presided over a country whose spirit had subtly changed. It is, perhaps, symbolic that he was the last president to dress in the eighteenth-century fashion, with silk stockings, silver buckles, and a queue. He and older contemporaries had made their political calculations in the shadow of European maneuvers to extend their rivalries to the soil of the New World. The ruling elements among European powers had not yet convinced themselves that the United States was here to stay. In the process of dispelling that doubt presidents, from Washington to Madison, found themselves, against their will, enmeshed in an incomprehensible pattern of conflicting European imperial ambitions.

The shadows and pitfalls seem to have vanished with the war's end in 1815. America's continuance as an independent power was assured, and the promise of its future greatness was made more manifest. England's pre-eminence in the world, and the establishment of a *Pax Brittannica,* seemed to guarantee quiet growth for America, uninterrupted by European imperial ventures. England's governing class had, at length, accepted the fact of America's permanence.

That acceptance, however, only meant that the United States was a junior member in the family of nations. And its junior status was emphasized when its callowness was made the butt of ridicule by European critics who found the United States wanting in the refinements of their own age-old cultures.

As for the Americans themselves, the generation that had fought to free itself from the toils of foreign intrigue had been closer in spirit to Europe than was the generation after 1815. The men of former years were cosmopolitan in outlook and, though vigorous enough in their assertion of American nationality, had an appreciation of Europe's superior cultural achievements. The newer generation was aggressive in its prideful assertion of political independence, and contemptuous in allusions to European decadence. Its leading men spoke with disdain of European culture, and boasted (though sometimes with inner uncertainty) of the accomplishments of American artists and writers.

The wish of most Americans was to be allowed to develop their vast country in peace, and to create a distinctive civilization of their own. They believed themselves a different breed of men from their European ancestors; the unwanted of Europe had become the chosen of America. The European emigrant tide, which had been interrupted by twenty-five years of war, began to rise again and was soon to affect profoundly every aspect of American life.

Americans exulted in their new found strength which built large cities and extended ever westward the edge of cultivation. The Atlantic Ocean and the lands that bordered it seemed to recede in their imaginations to make room for the endless woods and plains of western river valleys. The Old World seemed dimly distant—and unregretted. It was Henry Clay, a new man of this period, who spoke its spirit: "We should become the center of a system," he said, "which would constitute the rallying point of human freedom against the despotism of the Old World . . . Our institutions now make us free; but how long shall we continue so, if we mold our opinions on those of Europe? Let us break these commercial and political fetters; let us no longer watch the nod of any European politician; let us become real and true Americans, and place ourselves at the head of the American system."

The picture of America severing its ties with Europe and setting its face to the West in this period is only partly true; while its feet pointed westward, America still looked over its shoulder at the Atlantic Ocean and the nations that rimmed it. The ties that had chafed still bound Americans to Europe, although many people then, and more since those years, were unaware of the strength of these bonds. Economic ties were close with Europe; the immigrants might shake the dust of Europe from their feet, but their minds and hearts could less easily discard a cultural inheritance; men with intellectual interests sought stimulation and comfort in the approbation of Old World leaders.

Americans did not merely wait on European judgment. They were confident they had something original to contribute to the content of western civilization—in literature, in democratic education, in humanitarian reforms, in political and social democracy. And they believed that the state of the nation in 1815 promised success for these ends.

★ THE NATIONALISM OF 1815–25

There was good reason for optimism at this time. The Union was never more unified. The loud talk of New England secessionists had been silenced, and in this "Era of Good Feelings" political antagonisms (on the national level) were subdued. The two-party system went into temporary eclipse, though locally, within the states, political rivalries were intense. Monroe had won the presidency in 1816 by a wide margin over Rufus King, standard bearer of the humbled Federalists, who labored under the stigma of treason. The sting of ostracism suffered by New England was soothed with the naming of John Quincy Adams as Secretary of State. Adams was one of America's most skilful diplomats, with a nationalist ardor exceeded by none of his contemporaries.

North, South, and West, spokesmen of a vigorous nationalism held the stage. "The war," said Gallatin, "has renewed and reinstated the national feelings and character which the Revolution had given, and which were daily lessened. The people have now more general objects of attachment with which their pride and political opinions are connected. They are more Americans; they feel and act more as a nation."

National feeling was quickened by the popularity of "Yankee Doodle," which had practically become the country's anthem during the war years. A folk symbol, one destined to evoke strong feelings of pride and loyalty, had been created in the figure of "Uncle Sam." Fourth of July orators, patriotic clergymen, and journalists throughout the country whipped up a sentiment that scarce needed stimulation. "The national vanity of the United States," said an English traveler, "surpasses that of any country, not even excepting France. It blazes out everywhere, and on all occasions—in their conversation, newspapers, pamphlets, speeches, and books."

Surviving fathers of the Revolution—Jefferson, John Adams, Madison, and others—contributed recollections of their heroic age to younger men, who celebrated in biography and history the deeds of the Argonauts. One of the younger men was William Tudor who, as editor of the newly established *North American Review,* fostered historical studies and in general stirred the sluggish stream of intellectual life in the nation. Jared Sparks and George Bancroft, who soon appeared on the scene, satisfied the intense longing of Americans for national historians, and they were well rewarded by a grateful country. Bancroft wrote that Americans had a history worth knowing, and he believed that "a vein of public feeling, of democratic independence, of popular liberty, ought to be infused into our literature." Bancroft's writing appealed to a relatively high level in the population. A writer for the masses was Mason Locke Weems (Parson Weems), whose biographies of Washington, Franklin, and other Revolutionary heroes fixed in the popular mind an indelible impression of heroes already grown legendary. It was he who invented the story of Washington and the cherry tree.

The native voice in literature was heard in the poetry of William Cullen Bryant and especially in the prose of Washington Irving and James Fenimore Cooper. Cooper's novel of the Revolutionary era, *The Spy,* was followed by his *Leatherstocking Tales,* which celebrated the deeds of the picturesque frontiersmen. Cooper wrote in the vein of Sir Walter Scott, whose works powerfully stimulated sentiments of romantic nationalism. (Scott's popularity in America, as elsewhere, was astounding; it has been estimated that 5,000,000 copies of his novels came off the American presses in the decade after 1813). The treatment by Cooper, as well as other writers, of the fundamental facts in the American experience—the Revolution and the frontier—stimulated the growth of nationalism.

That sentiment was largely responsible for the economic policies adopted by the federal government. In 1816 the second Bank of the United States was chartered. That same year when the tariff was under debate, Calhoun, who was at this time an ardent nationalist, defended its protective features. He argued that he was not so much interested in aiding the manufacturer as he was in strengthening the defense of the nation by creating economic self-sufficiency.

Whatever Calhoun's motives were in encouraging native economic enterprise, the fact is that American manufactures were making rapid progress. During the period of the embargo, the years of commercial nonintercourse, and the war, manufacturers had supplied many of the needs formerly met by imports. Cotton spindles increased from 80,000 to 500,000 in the period 1810–14. It is true that in the postwar period many American manufacturers were unable to meet European competition. English merchants dumped exports at bargain rates deliberately intending, as a member of parliament expressed it, to "stifle in the cradle those rising manufactures in the United States, which the war has forced into existence."

Rising to meet the challenge Americans, with characteristic resourcefulness and mechanical ingenuity, achieved striking advances in technology and production. Francis Cabot Lowell, a merchant of Boston, and Paul Moody, a mechanic, perfected the power loom. They established at Waltham, Massachusetts, the first cotton mill which could perform every operation required to transform raw fiber into finished cloth. Within a few years American factories were supplying about half of the cottons, woolens, and linens used in the eastern regions of the United States. The swift-running streams of New England and the middle Atlantic states were dotted with scores of modest textile mills, ironworks, and machine shops. Factories were beginning to cast their shadows over domestic craftsmen.

The nationalism that found expression in politics, in literature, and in economics, was nowhere more vigorously asserted than in the judicial opinions of Chief Justice Marshall. Ably supported by Justice Story, Marshall announced a series of decisions which gave form and solidity to the structure of nationalism. He had the gift, said a contemporary, for "putting his own ideas into the minds of others, unconsciously to them." But it is also important to remember that the arguments of distinguished counsel before the court, in particular Daniel Webster, made so deep an impression upon it that its decisions reflected their reasoning and conclusions.

Marshall's background was the Virginia planter society whose finest Federal symbol had been George Washington. Although Marshall was conservative in his ideas of government, he had an easy, democratic air in his personal contacts. Tall, ungainly, and carelessly dressed, he was a familiar sight as he strolled along with his arms full of purchases from the market place. Marshall's environment was agrarian, but he was the chief instrument by which the political and economic ideas of Alexander Hamilton were triumphantly affirmed.

In a number of cases between 1810 and 1824 the Supreme Court announced the supremacy of the federal government over the states. As mentioned before, in *Fletcher* v. *Peck* (1810) the Georgia legislature's invalidation of a contract was declared unconstitutional by the Supreme Court. In the case of *Martin* v. *Hunter's Lessee* (Story's opinion), the supremacy of the Supreme Court was asserted over state courts where the Constitution, laws, and treaties were involved.

February and March, 1819, were memorable in American history. In those months Marshall delivered some of his greatest opinions. In *McCulloch* v. *Maryland,* Marshall invoked the "implied powers" clause of the Constitution to uphold the right of Congress to establish the Bank of the United States, and to deny the right of the separate states to tax the Bank. Maryland's tax of the Baltimore branch of the Bank was said to be confiscatory. The basic issue in the case was the supremacy of the federal government as against the individual states. Marshall, in his decision, included a Hamiltonian survey of the nature of the Constitution which, he said, "bound the state sovereignties." The national government, he declared, was "emphatically and truly, a government of the people. In form and in substance it emanates from them. Its powers are granted by them, and are to be exercised directly on them, and for their benefit." Marshall was interested in more than the announcement of a constitutional principle; he wished, by supporting a sound financial structure, to counter the fraud and lax bankruptcy laws which plagued American economic life.

In another case, *Dartmouth College* v. *Woodward,* Marshall held that a charter was a contract and could not be recalled by the state legislature. New Hampshire had attempted to change the original charter founding Dartmouth, but its trustees, counseled by Webster, sued to retain it. The decision was a great stimulus to the growth of corporations; it brought to the side of nationalism the loyalty of powerful business forces in the country. Creditors found Marshall's opinion in *Sturges* v. *Crowninshield* gratifying. In that case Marshall declared unconstitutional a New York State bankruptcy act easing the plight of the debtor, charging that it impaired the obligations of a contract.

In later cases, *Cohens* v. *Virginia* (1821), and in *Gibbons* v. *Ogden* (1824), Marshall reaffirmed his vigorous nationalism and his encouragement of business enterprise. In the former (where the question of the court's appellate jurisdiction was involved) Marshall was eloquent in his statement of American nationalism and in his demolition of states' rights theories. The United States, he said, "form, for many, and for most important purposes, a single nation . . . In war, we are one people. In making peace, we are one people. In all commercial regulations, we are one and the same people . . . America has chosen to be, in many respects, and to many purposes, a nation; and for all these purposes her government is complete; to all these objects, it is competent. The people have declared, that in the exercise of all powers given for these objects it is supreme. It can, then, in effecting these objects, legitimately control all individuals or governments within the American territory. The Constitution and laws of a state, so far as they are repugnant to the Constitution and laws of the United States, are absolutely void."

In *Gibbons* v. *Ogden* (relating to Hudson River navigation), Marshall freed transportation from the danger of local monopoly and fixed the power of Congress to regulate commerce between the states. The power over commerce, which included navigation, said Marshall, "was one of the primary objects for which the people of America adopted their government." The decision destroyed a shipping monopoly on the Hudson. Thus, on all of America's rivers, the threat of monopolistic control of steamboat navigation was removed. "The navigable waters of this state and of the United States, are again free," declared a New Jersey paper. Transportation all over America (including railroads soon to be built), was to receive a powerful impetus from this decision.

By this series of historic opinions Marshall gave coherence to the doctrine of nationalism. In his thirty-four years of service as Chief Justice, the court overruled state laws thirteen times. His views were to survive the attacks of states' rights theorists and furnish the foundation for imperishable national sentiments of later days. Daniel Webster, who had served as counsel before Marshall in several cases, on the winning side, was a proper heir to the nationalistic tradition of the great Chief Justice.

★ "OLD AMERICA SEEMS TO BE BREAKING UP"

Some of the most strident voices proclaiming American nationalism came out of the West. Here was a region growing with remarkable rapidity, outstripping older eastern communities, and extremely conscious of its expanding strength. "Old America seems to be breaking up, and moving westward," wrote a traveler passing through Pennsylvania on the National Road in 1817. "We are seldom out of sight, as we travel on this grand track, towards the Ohio, of family groups, behind and before us." Many traveled in small, light but strong wagons, drawn by two small horses. Aboard the wagon were loaded bedding, utensils, provisions, and a swarm of children. The more prosperous might go along with a cow or two. The family were on or off the vehicle, depending on the road or the weather, "or perhaps the spirits of the party." The travelers often carried with them a little hard-earned cash with which to buy a homestead. Frequently the westbound traveler used a cart and a single horse. A still poorer pilgrim was reduced to carrying on his back his belongings, while his wife followed "naked footed, bending under the hopes of the family."

An Englishman, George Flower, who settled on the prairie of Illinois at this time and was conscious of Old World contrasts, understood much of the region's spirit. "A real liberty is found in the country, apart from all its political theories," he said. "The practical liberty of America is found in its great space and small population. Good land, dog-cheap everywhere, and for nothing, if you will go for it, gives as much elbow room to every man as he chooses to take. Poor laborers, from every country in Europe, hear of this cheap land, are attracted to it, perhaps without any political opinions. They come, they toil, they prosper. This," said Flower, "is the real liberty of America." The successful pioneers trumpeted their success; the defeated (and there were many) though sometimes loudly complaining, were generally mute, for who cared to confess himself a failure?

The western region filled quickly. Between 1810 and 1820 the population north of the Ohio River more than doubled, and within the next decade Ohio's numbers (nearly a million) were greater than those of Massachusetts and Connecticut together. Southwest, as well as Northwest, people were moving in numbers large enough to bring thinly settled communities into the Union as new states. Louisiana had been admitted into the Union in 1812; within six years of the war's end five more commonwealths were added to the United States; Indiana (1816), Mississippi (1817), Illinois (1818), Alabama (1819), and Missouri (1821). If the totals of these new states were added to those of the older western areas of Kentucky, Tennessee, and Ohio, the region's population at the end of the 1820's was about 3,700,000, over a quarter of the entire nation. In addition to these numbers in the "Western World" (as the settlers called it) there were nearly a million people with a similar outlook in the western portions of New York, Pennsylvania, Virginia, and Georgia.

In a single generation a new section had emerged, stamped in the North by a vigorous democratic pattern and loudly insistent in the expression of its economic interests and its political ideals. This section's eighteen votes in the Senate, which exceeded that of any other region, gave it a powerful voice in the affairs of the nation.

To settle and exploit the West at a faster pace, and to market its agricultural surplus, required steady advances in transportation. "Internal improvements" was therefore a popular subject of everyday conversation and a solid plank in the platform of western politicians. Transportation companies, operating four-horse freight wagons, ran between the eastern and western states, carrying a constantly increasing cargo. In 1820 more than 3,000 wagons shuttled between Philadelphia and Pittsburgh, carrying goods worth $18,000,000 annually. Nevertheless excessive freight charges hampered the region's growth. In 1817 the rate from Philadelphia to Pittsburgh frequently ran to seven dollars or more a hundredweight; in a few years the cost was cut in half. Even eastern states, in their inland communities, were badly handicapped by cumbersome transportation. One observer in Virginia (1818) noted that at a distance of eighty miles from tidewater it cost a farmer one bushel of wheat to pay the expense of carrying two to the coast.

★ ON INLAND WATERS

While building better roads eased the problems of transport, improved water communications seemed the best answer to the country's needs. England, France, and other countries had solved many problems by building canals. Why not the United States? Americans had already built some short waterways, but it was the Erie Canal which focussed the nation's eyes on the value of such projects. The great task, by far the most formidable yet undertaken by Americans, was begun on July 4, 1817. Ingenious Yankees developed new devices to speed the large construction jobs, while Irish immigrants supplied the manual labor to get them done. In the marshes of upstate New York, where part of the canal ran, Irishmen, wearing only long flannel shirts and slouch caps, were set to work up to their knees in the muck. After eight years the work was done. In late October, 1825, gay celebrants made the trip through the new waterway and then down the Hudson, cheered on by crowds along the banks, the firing of guns, and merrymakers in escorting steamboats. Thousands of visitors waited in New York City to watch the "wedding of the waters" as Governor De Witt Clinton poured out the contents of the kegs brought all the way from the great inland sea; Lake Erie had been joined to the Atlantic.

Swiftly the fruits of immense toil and expense were harvested. The canal cost over $7,000,000 to build, but its earnings were $700,000 annually. It helped insure New York City's primacy as a port (a leadership she had already won), but its effects on the Great Lakes region and the Ohio Valley were correspondingly great. Goods moved from the Ohio Valley to New York City in two-thirds of the former time and at one-half the cost. From Buffalo to New York the time and money saved in transporting freight was even more spectacular; the time was cut from twenty days to six days, and the cost from $100 to $10 a ton.

Along the canal route itself, where there had once been wilderness or forlorn, isolated villages, boom towns sprang up—Rochester, Syracuse, Utica. Elsewhere in America rival ports—Boston, Philadelphia, and Baltimore—spurred by New York's success, undertook similar canal ventures to tap the interior markets, but none benefited to the same extent as did New York City. The craze for canals lasted for some years before they were outmoded by a superior form of transportation, railroads.

The greatest advance in inland water transportation came with the wider use of the steamboat. Fulton's paddle wheel "Clermont" had clanked its way up the Hudson in 1807, belching smoke and sparks from her smokestack. Within a few years steamboats appeared on the western rivers and immediately proved their great value. Keel boats took more than thirty days to go down river from Louisville to New Orleans, and near ninety days to move against the current for 1,500 miles. By 1822 steamboats had cut the downstream trip to seven days and the lengthy, discouraging upstream journey to sixteen days. This improvement in transport, wrote an enthusiast, was "of more momentous consequences to the West than the issues of a thousand battles."

The whole of life on the "western waters" was affected by the steamboats, whose competition for traffic forced them to ever greater speeds and luxury in accommodations. An exuberant western journalist said that easterners, who called "us . . . backwoodsmen, would not believe that such fancy structures of oriental gorgeousness and splendor as the 'Washington' . . . the 'Walk in the Water,' the 'Lady of the Lake' . . . had ever existed in the imaginative brain of a romancer, much less that they were actually in existence, rushing down the Mississippi . . . or plowing up between the forests, and walking against the mighty current . . . bearing speculators, merchants, dandies, fine ladies, every thing real and every thing affected, in the form of humanity," all playing cards, throwing dice, drinking, flirting, and making love. On the deck were the tough young men, "who have seen alligators, and neither fear whiskey, nor gun-powder." A steamboat coming up from New Orleans, said the writer, "brings to the remotest villages . . . and the very doors of the cabins, a little of Paris, a section of Broadway, or a slice of Philadelphia to ferment in the minds of our young people the innate propensity for fashions and finery." Everyone could see that the speed of America's transformation was being accelerated.

★ PURCHASE OF FLORIDA

Calhoun, in 1817, had urged internal improvements to knit the country in greater unity. "Let us . . . bind the Republic together with a perfect system of roads and canals," he urged. "Let us conquer space. It is thus that the most distant parts of the Republic will be brought within a few days travel of the center." The entire country would then be as a web, "in which the slightest impression made on the most remote parts is communicated to the whole system; and the more perfect the means of transportation, the more rapid and true the vibration."

In these years the country vibrated to other developments which expressed strong national sentiments. The expansionist drive of earlier years was curbed along the Canadian boundary by the Rush-Bagot Agreement, but it was still strong on the southeastern frontier. There on the Florida border, American-Spanish relations were in their usual state of instability. The region offered sanctuary for runaway slaves from the South and was a hideaway for nests of smugglers. Spain's feeble garrison was inadequate to cope with the outlaw bands that made the colony their home. Raiding parties, from either side of the border, crossed into the opposite territory in defiance of governmental authority.

American pressure to acquire the colony never relaxed. The Secretary of State at the moment was John Quincy Adams, one of the most ardent nationalists of his day. Here was a situation that challenged his fervid nationalism, and he exploited it to the utmost. He told his fellow cabinet members that the world "must be familiarized with the idea of considering our proper dominion to be the *continent* of North America." All friction between Spain and the United States, he suggested, could be removed by the cession of Florida. Luis de Onis, the Spanish minister, was not yet ready for the step.

Events beyond his control hurried his hand. General Andrew Jackson crashed into Florida, in 1818, in pursuit of offending Seminole Indians. The Indians vanished in the Florida wilderness, but Jackson captured St. Marks and Pensacola, overthrowing Spanish authority. Though the flag of Spain was soon restored to these communities, it was clear that her rule of three centuries was nearing its end. Cede by sale, or lose by seizure, these were the obvious alternatives. On Washington's birthday, 1819, the Spanish minister and Secretary Adams, after protracted negotiations, signed the treaty transferring Florida to the United States for $5,000,000. The treaty also expanded the northwest boundary of the United States to the Pacific. It was truly a triumph for the continentalism of John Quincy Adams. "It was near one in the morning," wrote Adams in his diary, "when I closed the day with ejaculations of fervent gratitude to the Giver of all good. It was, perhaps, the most important day of my life." For his country, he thought, it marked a great epoch in her history. Various complications, however, held up ratification of the treaty until exactly two more years had elapsed.

★ THE MONROE DOCTRINE

The continuing disintegration of the once fabulous Spanish Empire was the occasion for another step in the growth of American nationalism— the issuance of the Monroe Doctrine. Spain's colonies in America were in revolt against the motherland, and there were many in the United States who cheered this further blow at European domination in the New World. It was, said one, "the greatest event of the age for the whole Atlantic world." Clay exulted over the revolutions in Latin America. Jefferson wrote to his friend Alexander von Humboldt that, whatever the political evolution of Latin America, the governments there "will be American governments, no longer to be involved in the never ceasing broils of Europe . . . America has a hemisphere to itself. It must have its separate system of interests, which must not be subordinated to those of Europe."

North Americans had cultivated limited economic and cultural contacts with South America for many years, and a number of prophets had foretold the day when the colonies of Spain and Portugal would emulate the revolution of the colonies of England. That day had arrived. One Latin American community after another proclaimed its independence, until by the fall of 1822 only a small fraction of the Western Hemisphere (Canada excepted), remained part of a European empire. The American government had already recognized the independence of several Latin American states and, despite Spanish protests, established diplomatic relations with them.

Influential Americans had been urging the United States to be the first to recognize the new states in order to gain commercial and ideological advantage over rivals. A variety of motives brought recognition of the independence of Spain's former colonies—a real desire to encourage the growth of republican institutions, the desire for territorial expansion of the United States, and the expectations of businessmen that enlarged markets would be opened in an independent South America freed of Spain's mercantile restrictions.

It was one thing for these colonies to proclaim independence; it was another to maintain it. In the twistings and turnings of European history, Spain's power, once struck down by a revolutionary France, was now upheld by a reactionary France. A Franco-Spanish expeditionary force to reconquer the lost colonies was being organized. In the overheated imagination of Americans, the Holy Alliance, crushing revolt in Europe, was stretching forth its smothering cloak to America as well. A revived French Empire, to which Spain would be an adjunct, spelled danger to England, as well as a dire threat to republican institutions in the New World.

England had built up her commercial interests in Latin America to impressive proportions and she had no wish to see them diminished by a restored Spanish control. She had been reluctant to follow America's lead in recognizing the independence of the liberated colonies; the very conservative political atmosphere of official England, fearful at the moment of radicalism at home, could hardly be benevolent toward revolution abroad. And yet, to delay further might yield commercial pre-eminence and a dominating political leadership to the United States in Latin America. "It is obviously the policy of the United States," said the British Foreign Secretary, George Canning, "to connect itself with all the powers of America in a general Transatlantic League, of which it would have the sole direction. I need only say, how inconvenient such an ascendancy may be in time of peace, and how formidable in case of war."

In the summer of 1823 Canning suggested that a joint Anglo-American warning be sent to France against intervention in South America. Here was the offer of the Anglo-American marine alliance, which a shrewd observer forty years before had predicted would come some day. Monroe was inclined to accept, but first sought the advice of his old friends, Madison and Jefferson. They both responded with enthusiasm. Jefferson thought the proposal of Anglo-American cooperation the most important event in United States history since 1776. He believed, like Bolívar, who was a leader in the South American revolutions, that America, North and South, had "a set of interests distinct from those of Europe . . . She should, therefore, have a system of her own, distinct from that of Europe . . ." Only England, Jefferson said, "could disturb us in this pursuit; she now offers to lead, aid and accompany us in it." England's great weight would be brought "into the scale of free government," and a continent would be emancipated at one stroke.

Secretary Adams distrusted Canning's proposal, preferring that the United States act independently; she should not, he said, "come in as a cock-boat in the wake of the British men-of-war." A few years earlier Adams had written: "For the repose of Europe as well as of America, the European and American political systems should be kept as separate and distinct from each other as possible."

The United States had been gradually leading up to the position which Adams thought was now the ripe moment for its explicit unfolding. He was concerned not only with threats of European intervention in South America. Russia, whose expansion eastward across Asia had carried her to Alaska, was pressing down the Pacific coast into Oregon. American fur traders had no wish for Russian competition. After considerable discussion in the cabinet, it was agreed that President Monroe would include in his annual message to Congress, in December, 1823, a statement on foreign policy; this was the famous Monroe Doctrine.

The Western Hemisphere was henceforth not to be considered an area "for future colonization by any European powers." "The political system of the allied powers is essentially different . . . from that of America . . ." Monroe went on to say that "we should consider any attempt on their part to extend their system to any portion of this hemisphere as dangerous to our peace and safety." The United States had no intention of interfering with "the existing colonies and dependencies of any European power." But "any interposition for the purpose of oppressing" the new Latin American states or "controlling in any other manner their destiny," would be "the manifestation of an unfriendly disposition toward the United States."

Here was a declaration of foreign policy which was to be fundamental in America's future history, though in time it was to undergo strange transformations. For the moment it achieved its purpose of proclaiming to the world American republican principles and warning Europe of the dangers in meddling with the New World. Actually, as Professor Dexter Perkins made clear in his authoritative study of the Monroe Doctrine, the Holy Alliance had no intention at the time of warring upon American liberties. George Dangerfield has recently written that the Doctrine was more of a challenge to England "whose fleet sustained it, than it was to Holy Alliance" or France "against whom it was ostensibly directed."

Within a few weeks Richard Rush, the American minister to Britain, was writing from London to Adams: "The most decisive blow to all despotick interference with the new States is that which it has received in the President's message . . . the question of the final and complete safety of the new States from all European coercion is now considered as at rest." Latin America, said Adams, had been emancipated from "colonial thraldom."

Prince Metternich, the central European statesman whose name has symbolized the reaction of this era, perceived the significance of Monroe's message. "These United States of America which we have seen arise and grow," he said, "have suddenly left a sphere too narrow for their ambition, and have astonished Europe by a new act of revolt, more unprovoked, fully as audacious, and no less dangerous than the former. They have distinctly and clearly announced their intention to set power against power . . . They have cast blame and scorn on the institutions of Europe most worthy of respect . . ." In fostering revolutions the Americans "lend new strength to the apostles of sedition, and reanimate the courage of every conspirator. If this flood of evil doctrines and pernicious examples should extend over the whole of America what would become of our institutions," asked Metternich, and of Europe's "conservative system?"

★ JOHN QUINCY ADAMS

The overwhelming majority of Americans would have answered Metternich by expressing a hope that Europe's "conservative system" be destroyed and a democratic one be set up in its place. They had an affinity for revolutions, whether they were in Latin America or in Greece, where the banner of independence had been hoisted against Turkey.

It was, however, domestic politics that more deeply engrossed Americans. In the "Era of Good Feelings" Monroe had been re-elected, without opposition, in 1820, getting every electoral vote but one. Four years later, in 1824, no single candidate dominated the field; four aspirants, all from the Republican party, and three of them strong nationalists, elbowed one another for the presidency.

William H. Crawford, Secretary of the Treasury, had the blessing of Monroe and the aged Jefferson, but a paralytic stroke hampered his campaign. Henry Clay, "The Western Star," Speaker of the House and author of the "American System," had an immense following that was thrilled by his oratory and charmed by his person. His program was to join together the interests of the West with the industrial East; he spoke of himself as a man of the West with northern principles. He proposed a protective tariff (it would help Kentucky's hemp industry), federal support for internal improvements, and a central banking system. General Jackson, the "Old Hero," crystallized the aggressive nationalism and the strengthening equalitarianism of the country. John Quincy Adams, the fourth candidate, was not only heir to the second president's name and fame, but in his own long career of public service he had won great distinction by his achievements.

Adams had been taken to Europe as a youngster of eleven, and there he learned to speak French and Dutch. When he was only fourteen he went to Russia as secretary to the American minister. His formal diplomatic career, begun at the age of twenty-seven, included missions to half a dozen countries of Europe. He served as a Senator from Massachusetts, 1803–8, was a member of the peace commission which ended the War of 1812, and was named Secretary of State in Monroe's cabinet. The initiated knew of his valued services to his country, but his stern personality was not of the type to win the devotion of the masses. Adams, however, as the candidate of the North had a significant advantage over the others who were expected to split among themselves the votes of the South and West.

Jackson, who was not counted as an important contender by many politicians, picked up strength as the campaign wore on. His opponents complained that the Jackson supporters only needed to shout "8th of January and battle of New Orleans!" As the election tallies came in his followers felt he had been the popular choice, with 153,000 votes; Adams, the second man, had 108,000. In the electoral college the vote was divided, Jackson with 99, Adams 84, Crawford 41, and Clay 37. Luck, often kind to Clay, deserted him at this critical moment. A light carriage, carrying two of his supporters to the legislature in Louisiana overturned, injuring them so badly they could not attend. Their absence, plus the loss of votes of two others who arrived late, largely destroyed "Harry of the West's" chances for the run-off in the House of Representatives. There he may well have won.

Since no candidate had a majority, the House of Representatives was called upon to decide the election from among the top three. In reality it was the top two, for Crawford's crippling ailment had practically removed him from consideration. In the House, Speaker Clay's influence was decisive, and he threw it to the side of Adams with whom he felt in closer ideological kinship than with Jackson. The popular soldier's elevation to the presidency, said Clay, would be dangerous to democratic institutions, for it would glorify the military spirit. "I cannot believe," said the disappointed Clay, "that killing two thousand five hundred Englishmen at New Orleans qualifies [a person] for the various, difficult and complicated duties of the chief magistracy."

President Adams' immediate choice of Clay as Secretary of State, which was a logical appointment, stirred talk of an "unholy alliance" between them, and political campaigns for years thereafter were to ring with denunciations of their alleged "corrupt bargain." The friends of Jackson, said Clay, turned upon him and called him "a deserter from democracy, a giant at intrigue; [I] have sold the West—have sold myself." Though no certain proof has ever turned up of a "bargain" between Adams and Clay, friends of the latter let it be known that the West would be pleased at his appointment to the cabinet. Adams made no promises but, says Professor Clement Eaton, "he virtually told them that if he were elected by the votes of the West he would appoint a Western man to his cabinet. Despite his New England conscience Adams made not one but several implicit bargains with influential congressmen from crucial states." *

Adams was wholly committed to a strong nationalistic tradition. His father had written during the Revolution, "I never was . . . much of John Bull. I was John Yankee and such I shall live and die." The son's sentiments on this point were, if anything, stronger. "I have lived for my country and for her alone," he wrote three years before his election; "every faculty of my soul and every desire of my heart has been devoted to her interest and to the promotion of her welfare."

Adams espoused a Hamiltonian theory of government, though he himself had abandoned the Federalists for the Republicans years before. "The great object of the institution of civil government," he said, "is the improvement of the condition of those who are parties to the social compact . . ." He therefore urged that the federal government

* Clement Eaton, *Henry Clay and the Art of American Politics* (Boston: Little, Brown, 1957), pp. 52–53.

sponsor scientific expeditions and build educational and research institutions to learn how best to exploit the rich resources of the country. He
asked Congress especially to embark on a large program of internal
improvements. From the latter, said Adams, "I am convinced that the
unborn millions of our posterity who are in future ages to people this
continent will derive their most fervent gratitude."

However grateful posterity may have been to Adams for his nationalist program his immediate contemporaries in Congress looked at it
with jaundiced eye. The manner of his election antagonized many, especially Jackson's supporters, who under other circumstances might have
been favorably disposed. A deeper reason for the growing hostility to
nationalism lay in an awakened suspicion of too much federal power,
and in the resurgence of sectional feeling.

★ ECONOMICS AND SECTIONALISM

The nationalism of the postwar years could not conceal an underlying
hostility to a strong central government. Marshall's judicial decisions
had stirred the latent anger of Jeffersonians and they roused the old
patriarch himself to denounce the court. "That body," he said, "like
gravity, ever acting, with noiseless foot and unalarming advance, gaining
ground step by step and holding what it gains, is engulfing insidiously
the special governments."

Jefferson was speaking for more than the political power of state
governments. He was spokesman of an agricultural way of life which
felt itself endangered by the Hamilton-Marshall philosophy of government. An incisive, comprehensive attack on that philosophy was made
by John Taylor of Caroline County, Virginia. His writings, *Construction
Construed and Constitutions Vindicated* (1820) and *New Views of the
Constitution of the United States* (1823), as well as previous works,
justly earned him the title, "philosopher and statesman of agrarianism."
Taylor started with a familiar assumption, that the only truly productive element in the community was the farmer, and for the sake of
society his safety needed to be guarded. The Virginian warned that the
agrarian was at the mercy of a newly risen capitalistic class, exploiting
him through inflated public paper, bank stock, and a protective tariff.
Hamilton's economic and financial policies built up this class; Marshall's decisions were solidifying its hold on the whole structure of
American life.

One of Marshall's decisions, *McCulloch* v. *Maryland,* had favored
the Bank of the United States. The bank, a national institution whose
stockholders were nevertheless mainly in the East, was charged with
deepening the panic of 1819. All banks were to blame. Hundreds of

state and private banks had issued, by 1817, $100,000,000 in paper money with inadequate collateral behind so vast a sum. Everybody was buying land from the government: 1,000,000 acres a year in 1815, then 2,000,000 a year, and by 1819 over 5,000,000 acres in one year.

A country-wide orgy of land speculation, in which men hoped to benefit from the inflated prices of cattle, grain, and cotton (thirty-two cents a pound in 1818), had ended in the usual way—deflation (cotton in 1820 was eighteen cents a pound) and bankruptcy for thousands of people and many state banks, especially in the South and West. The national bank, angrily called "The Monster," was accused of pressing its debtors hard. "All the flourishing cities of the West," cried Benton of Missouri, "are mortgaged to this money power. They may be devoured by it at any moment. They are in the jaws of the monster!"

One of the effects of the panic was to force a reconsideration of the public land policy. For years there had been a running fight between those, like John Quincy Adams, who thought of the western lands primarily as a source of federal revenue, and opponents who believed these lands should be placed in the hands of settlers regardless of national finances. "The public lands," said Benton, "belong to the People and not to the Federal Government." Payments for public lands were over $22,000,000 in arrears, for installments were hard to meet, and political expediency, as well as common humanity, would not permit eviction of delinquent debtors from their homes. In 1820 a new act was passed, abolishing credit but reducing the price of land from two dollars an acre to one dollar and a quarter; the smallest unit of sale was now to be eighty acres. The next year, another measure, the Relief Act, was passed to aid the debt-burdened. Easier payments were provided for, or return to the government of that fraction of the purchase still unpaid for.

Social discontent, however, was not quieted. Calhoun and Adams agreed in 1820 that in the previous two years "an immense revolution of fortunes in every part of the Union" had occurred. Many had been ruined or were in "deep distress." Out of this convulsion had come "a general mass of disaffection to the Government not concentrated in any particular direction," they agreed, "but ready to seize upon any event and looking out anywhere for a leader." Within a few years that leader was found. He was the hero Andrew Jackson.

★ "A FIRE BELL IN THE NIGHT"

Serious as were differences of opinion about judicial decisions and the effects of economic setbacks, a more significant portent of weakened nationalism was the bitter fight over Missouri's request for admission to the Union. Starkly the question of slavery was thrust to the forefront of everyone's consciousness.

The hopes of older Southerners, like Washington, Jefferson, and Monroe, that slavery might gradually disappear were vain. Eli Whitney's cotton gin, invented a quarter of a century earlier, had boosted greatly the profits of cotton culture; other profitable crops of the South, especially sugar in Louisiana, made more illusory the prospect of emancipation, because slaves were now considered indispensable by Southern planters.

The extension westward of plantation culture had brought slavery to Missouri and other parts of the Louisiana Purchase. In 1819 Missouri's application to enter the Union suddenly precipitated a crisis. At that time there were twenty-two states, evenly divided between slave and free. Missouri's entrance would tip the balance in favor of the South.

Northerners, fretful over alleged Southern aggressiveness and genuinely fearful of the spread of slavery, determined to place reservations on Missouri's application. Congressman James Tallmadge of New York amended the bill permitting the entry of Missouri by forbidding further importation of slaves into that state. It provided, too, for emancipation at the age of twenty-five of resident slaves born after the state's admission to the Union. The amended bill passed the House where Northern votes outnumbered Southern, but was defeated in the Senate, where an infuriated South was in control.

The whole country was quickly in an uproar. A Georgia politician warned that a fire had been kindled "which all the waters of the ocean cannot put out, which seas of blood can only extinguish." For months, in the press and public assembly, the debate over Missouri went on. Each side threatened secession if it failed to win its point. National leaders worked toward a compromise. In March, 1820, a compromise measure was carried through Congress by a close vote after days of stormy debate. When Missouri was admitted to the Union she entered as a slave state, but she was balanced by Maine (formerly part of Massachusetts) as a free state. Slavery was to be excluded from the remaining territory of the Louisiana Purchase north of the line 36°30'. The South thus conceded federal control over slavery in the territories.

Missouri's entrance was delayed by a new issue, which Clay's moderation settled. His reputation as a "compromiser" was not made in connection with drawing the line of 36°30'. His contribution was a second compromise when Missouri's constitution had to be passed on, a requirement in keeping with the process of admission. The constitution of the new state prohibited free Negroes from entering the state, a clear violation of the federal Constitution. Sectional conflict was renewed. Clay offered a solution. Missouri's constitution should never deprive any citizens, entering it from other states, of their rights and privileges guaranteed under the Constitution of the United States. Missouri accepting the proposal then became a new state, August 10, 1821.

The solution was generally satisfactory, and a surface calm returned to politics. But thoughtful contemporaries shuddered at the revelation of the deep abyss. Jefferson said it was "like a fire bell in the night"; "I considered it at once as the knell of the Union. It is hushed, indeed, for the moment. But this is a reprieve only, not a final sentence." And John Quincy Adams confided to his diary: "Much am I mistaken if [this question] is not destined to survive [Monroe's] political and individual life and mine . . . I take it for granted that the present question is a mere preamble—a titlepage to a great tragic volume."

★ FRUSTRATED JOHN QUINCY ADAMS

The debate over Missouri had lit up for all the South to see the ties that knit the communities below the Mason and Dixon line. "The discussion of this Missouri question," wrote the hostile John Quincy Adams, "has betrayed the secret of their souls." In these years the South moved toward a solidarity that hardened with the passing decades. Southerners feared potential injury if existing political trends were to continue strengthening the national government. Within the decade of the 1820's it was estimated that over 90 per cent of the citizens of South Carolina had shifted from approval to disapproval of loose construction of the Constitution because they foresaw danger in a strong federal power.

In the debates on Clay's protective tariff of 1824 the South, for the first time, placed considerable stress on its alleged unconstitutionality. Her representatives argued that Congress had power to impose a tariff for raising revenue, but not for purposes of protection. It was unjust to the South, whose cotton market in England would be endangered if the United States shut out British manufactured goods. When the vote was taken, the result, a close one, showed a tendency toward a North-South cleavage, similar to that in the fight over Missouri.

It is not surprising, therefore, that the administration of President Adams should have been relatively barren of positive achievement. His strong national lead in domestic politics did result, it is true, in his gaining larger appropriations for internal improvements, over $2,330,000 compared to $1,000,000 for all his predecessors combined. But the individual states, though always eager for federal appropriations, were preferring to control their own roads and canals.

In foreign affairs, where Adams was expert, his administration recorded no marked success. He failed, as had others before him, in the effort to win for America satisfactory conditions for direct trade with the British West Indies. Even in Latin America, where the prestige of the United States was presumably high, Adams was checkmated by Great Britain and the Senate. The latter had not been consulted in the original agreement to send United States delegates to a congress of Latin American republics in Panama, where problems of common interest were to be discussed. The Senate held up funds for necessary expenses, and in its debate showed its hostility to Adams and its contempt for Latin Americans.

The truth is the rift between Adams and Congress on many matters was too great. Even his own supporters were impatient with him. He had no skill in building a political machine, and he was unaware of the changes in American life that caused a turning away from candidates of his type to those with a greater mass appeal. Popular pressure was bringing about greater democracy in the choice of presidential candidates, as well as members of the electoral college. The Republican caucus that had named Crawford for the presidency had been ignored by the other aspirants who were nominated by their own state legislatures. Members of the electoral college, formerly chosen by state legislatures, were popularly elected everywhere except in Delaware and South Carolina by 1828. Two years later, the device of nominating candidates through a national party convention began to be used.

The removal of property qualifications for voting, which extended the franchise, had resulted in a greater proportion of voters in the population. In the 1830's there was an even greater expansion in the size of the electorate. Political leaders skilled in the art of public relations, like Martin Van Buren of New York, were better able than Adams to adjust themselves to the pressures of the new democracy. The political preeminence of the patrician, in the North at least, was drawing to a close.

★ ELECTION OF JACKSON

One of the main reasons for the relative stalemate of Adams' administration was that in those four years most politicians were thinking of the next presidential election. A political opponent, watching the inauguration of Adams in 1825, had predicted "he will stand worse in four years than his father did." In the intervening period party alignments were forming which were to dominate the national political scene for a generation. The Adams-Clay group became the National Republicans (later the Whigs), while the Jackson-Calhoun followers created the long-lived Democratic party.

Jackson's popularity, dramatically shown in 1824, made him the obvious figure around whom all anti-Adams men could rally in 1828. He was the great military hero, and he was presented as the symbol of the rising democracy in the growing towns and the spreading farms. Adams was associated with the aristocracy, with the discredited Federalists, and with the "corrupt bargain" of 1824. Jackson, whose political ideas were not broadly circulated, was publicized as the friend of all sections and the enemy only of privilege. The bitter campaign, in which supporters of each candidate freely accused the opposition of every imagined evil, had all the aspects of a barroom brawl.

Voters turned out in great numbers, and the election was a striking victory for Jackson. His popular vote was 647,000, while Adams got 508,000; in the electoral college Jackson won by a large majority. The South and the West went for Jackson, as did the majority in the important eastern states, Pennsylvania and New York. Benton, a fervent Jacksonian, hailed the election as a "triumph of democratic principle, and an assertion of the people's right to govern themselves."

Adams was overwhelmed by his defeat. "It seemed," he said, "as if I was deserted by all Mankind." The foundations of his life appeared to be slipping away. Two years earlier the death of his father, John Adams, and Thomas Jefferson on the same day, July 4, 1826, had ended an era. Jefferson's life ebbed away while the Liberty Bell sounded its Independence Day message in Philadelphia. Adams, on his death bed in Quincy, Massachusetts, not knowing that the holiday had been clouded by the death of his friend, said: "It is a great day"; and with his last breath, "Thomas Jefferson survives."

The world of patrician leadership had closed with the death of the aged revolutionaries and the election of Jackson. It was to be succeeded by something different, something which was alien to John Quincy Adams. Fortunately for the nation his power was still unspent, and his great moral strength was to serve his country well in the years that lay before him.

BOOK 5

THE GROWTH OF DEMOCRACY

IN EUROPE and America the period from 1830 to 1850 was filled with dramatic changes—changes that cut more of the ground from under the feet of the nobility and autocratic monarchs. Kings and ministers who had attempted to turn the clock back after Napoleon's defeat lived to see much of their own work undone. In France the revolution of 1830 exalted the middle class whose symbol was the bourgeois monarch, Louis Philippe. In Central Europe Metternich held on, but with gradually diminishing power. Belgium and Holland, which had been united, went their separate ways in 1830. In Italy discontent boiled over into revolution. On the other side of the Adriatic, in Serbia and Greece, the flames of revolt burned away Turkish rule that had lain heavily on the region for centuries. The light of revolution in Greece kindled the ardent hopes not only of Lord Byron but young men of good will everywhere.

In England the rigid stance of reaction had relaxed, and though it gave ground reluctantly, and only under great pressure, give it did—in the famous Reform Bill of 1832. This was a first, long step in the democratization of England. The pace, however, was too slow for England's liberals and radicals.

Chief among those who would hurry the march of progress were the Chartists, so-called because of a charter they had drawn up asking for radical political and social changes in England. The people who were Chartists found in Jacksonian Democracy ideals worthy of support and emulation. The Anglo-American world was immensely stimulated in these years by crosscurrents of social reform—in education, in politics, in the emancipation of women, in the agitation against Negro slavery.

The English journalist, William Cobbett, with an audience on both sides of the Atlantic, lit the pages of his paper with flaming denunciation of the new financial aristocracy, whose wealth had come from the smoking mills of Manchester and the other murky towns of the British Midlands. In America the Jacksonians caught the spirit of Cobbett, for it was kin to their own. "The merchants and the lawyers, that is, the moneyed interest broke up feudalism," said Bancroft, the American historian. "The day for the multitude has now dawned." "It is now for the yeomanry and the mechanics to march at the head of civilization."

Americans, whose genius for popular government was recognized everywhere, would spearhead an international fellowship of democratic peoples. The mass of mankind, cried the English firebrand, Fanny Wright, "have but one Cause." And a Jacksonian radical, Theophilus Fisk, asked that Americans be co-workers "with the friends of freedom throughout the world."

In America, with the election of Jackson, the common man believed that his day had dawned. He had been grateful enough to Thomas Jefferson, whose patrician democracy was essentially eighteenth century in spirit—the liberal aristocrat ruling wisely and well, but not really a man of the people. Jackson, so it seemed, had been thrust up from the mass of humanity—his temper the crowd's temper, his mind the crowd's unsubtle mind, his righteous wrath, the blazing fury of an angered crowd. The noted liberal clergyman, William Ellery Channing, caught the times' prevailing spirit in one of his contemporary essays (1829). This, he said, was one of those "seasons in human affairs of inward and outward revolution, when new depths seem to be broken up in the soul, when new wants are unfolded in multitudes, and a new and undefined good is thirsted for."

The released energies of this generation won many a battle to enlarge the area of man's freedom—through better schooling, through abolition of imprisonment for debt, through curbs on business monopolies. The ideal—that careers should be opened to talents, that quality of birth was less important than the quality of man—had apparently become reality in Jacksonian America. "Ours is a country," said a proud American, "where men start from an humble origin . . . and where they can attain to the most elevated positions, or acquire a large amount of wealth, according to the pursuits they elect for themselves. No exclusive privileges of birth . . . no civil or political disqualifications, stand in their path; but one has as good a chance as another, according to his talents, prudence, and personal exertions. This is a country of self-made men, than which nothing better could be said of any state of society."

These self-made men, within two decades of Jackson's inauguration, had taken a vast new western region from Mexico and added it to the United States. Some of these same men were washing gold from California hillsides. Farther north, in the Oregon country, settlers reached journey's end after the long months' pull over the trail that led up from Missouri across the Rocky Mountains. From Pacific shores American ships were making voyages to the Hawaiian Islands, and beyond to distant China.

Not all Americans were moving west. Great numbers of them were moving into the fast growing eastern cities, where they were joined by newly arrived European immigrants. Thus town and country kept pace with each other in this period of accelerated growth.

Growth was the most obvious fact in American life—growth of the country's size, the number of its people, or their wealth. Even in phases of their life less apparent to the casual eye—their intellectual and artistic interests—growth was real. The prospect ahead seemed rosier than that faced by contemporary peoples anywhere else in the world.

Yet the glowing promise in the United States was seen only in the northern and western sky. The South was clouded with omens of impending crisis; slavery was the evil shadow. Young men growing up in Jackson's time lived to see the dark thunderheads crash in a fierce roar over a smitten country.

CHAPTER XV

Jackson—a People's President

★ "THEIR OWN PRESIDENT"

The nation's capital waited with nervous expectancy the day of Jackson's inauguration. Daniel Webster, writing to his Boston friends, said: "Nobody knows what he will do when he [arrives] . . . My opinion is that when he comes he will bring a breeze with him . . . which way it will blow, I cannot tell . . . My *fear* is stronger than my *hope*." The doubts and fears of men like Webster were of small moment to the surging crowds of Jackson's followers who filled the capital on March 4, 1829.

"It was like the inundation of northern barbarians into Rome," wrote a critical contemporary. "Strange faces filled every public place and every face seemed to bear defiance on its brow." "I never saw anything like it before," said Webster. "They really seem to think the country is [to be] rescued from some dreadful danger." The general, sixty-one years old, was a tall, gaunt man with a thick shock of whitening hair. Dressed in a black suit, his erect, magnetic figure dominated the crowd gathered to hear his inaugural address. "It was a proud day for the people," one of his supporters wrote; "General Jackson is *their own* president."

Without question he was their president, but it is doubtful that the people knew much of Jackson's political ideas. He seemed to incline toward Clay's American System, though he upheld Jeffersonian economics in opposing a national debt. He thought the latter a "curse to a republic, inasmuch as it is calculated to raise . . . a moneyed aristocracy dangerous to the liberties of the country." On the other hand, in his Tennessee community, where he lived on a prosperous plantation near Nashville, his associations were with well-to-do landholders who disliked eastern moneyed men but at the same time distrusted inflationary proposals of debt-ridden poor farmers.

While Jackson's economic and political views were little known, his personal history was everyone's property. It had grown to legendary proportions, beginning with the incident of the saber cut by an English officer during the Revolution when the boy refused to clean the Briton's boots. He had been born in a log cabin on the Carolina frontier, in 1767, and knew the poverty of the backwoods in the Revolutionary era. He moved on to Tennessee, where he rose to distinction in political life, becoming a United States Senator.

In middle life his Olympian rage often choked his words, but advancing years brought greater calm and control. Like many Americans of his day he chewed tobacco and spat, or smoked a long-stemmed pipe and blew billowing white clouds which filled the room to suffocation. Men of learning and of great experience in worldly affairs felt the power of his dominating presence. He asked and heard their counsel, but he said, "[I] always take the responsibility of deciding for myself." Once he had decided on a course of action nothing could change him; "I care nothing about clamors . . . I do precisely what I think just and right." Cultivated and thoughtful friends were amazed at the working of Jackson's unlearned mind, devoid of sophisticated subtlety. "He saw intuitively into everything," wrote a close observer, and he "reached a conclusion by a short cut while others were beating the bush for the game."

Leadership came naturally to this backwoods idol, who had become the national folk hero of an adoring people. And he responded in kind to their abiding faith. It was his close friend and Secretary of State, Martin Van Buren, who sensed this affinity between the president and the people. Jackson he said, believed that "to labour for the good of the masses was a special mission, assigned to him by his Creator and no man was ever better disposed to work in his vocation in season and out of season."

★ JACKSON'S POLICY

Jackson's belief in equality was expressed in his message to Congress in 1829: "The duties of all public offices are, or at least admit of being made, so plain and simple that men of intelligence may readily qualify themselves for their performance." Clearly then, officeholding should not be the exclusive possession of a privileged class. This presidential statement was of course congenial to the views of Jacksonian party managers who wished to share the spoils of victory with their importunate followers. Jackson removed about 10 per cent of the officeholders to make room for his own appointees. Though his record of removals was no worse than Jefferson's, and much better than that of many successors, it was in his administration that the spoils system was more firmly fixed in Washington.

Satisfying the demands of the party machine was only one of Jackson's tasks. In the field of international relations where his impetuosity might have been dangerous, he was markedly successful. His administration finally worked out a settlement (1830) with Great Britain which permitted American shippers to trade freely with her West Indian islands. Another long standing controversy, one with France over "spoliation claims" arising out of her interference with American ships during the Napoleonic wars, came to its rasping end (1831) with a promise of compensation to United States citizens.

Almost at the outset of Jackson's administration he was faced with challenging economic and political problems. He handled them in accordance with his basic policy—the federal Constitution must be obeyed, the national debt must be paid, unnecessary expenditures were to be avoided, the Union must be preserved. These, said Jackson, "are the objects I have in view, and regardless of all consequences, will carry into effect."

Curbing expenditures meant watching over reckless outlays for internal improvements. In a masterly veto message (the Maysville veto) which owed much to Van Buren, Jackson turned down a request for funds to build a road in Kentucky from Maysville to Lexington. Though within a single state, the road was to be a link in an existing system of interstate communications. The president reminded his petitioners that he stood "committed before the Country to pay off the National Debt." He doubted its constitutionality, particularly as it was to be constructed within the state. Clay, remembering that it had taken him four days to cover the sixty-four miles between Maysville and Lexington, was furious with Jackson. Other Westerners, though disappointed, were not embittered, and Old Hickory's hold on their affections was scarcely diminished.

Whatever support Jackson may have lost over this issue was more than regained by his Indian policy, which favored removal of the redmen from regions coveted by the whites. Unlike President Adams, who had attempted to protect the treaty rights of Creeks and Cherokees in Georgia, Jackson encouraged the state to expel the Indians. In the case of *Worcester* v. *Georgia,* the Supreme Court sought to protect the Indians but Georgia paid no heed to it, and Jackson left the decision unenforced. Not long before this case was decided, Marshall had written to Justice Story, "I often think, with indignation, on our disreputable conduct . . . in the affair of the Creeks of Georgia." In the opinion he wrote, Marshall spoke sadly of the Cherokees, "a people once numerous, powerful, and truly independent, found by our ancestors in the quiet and uncontrolled possession of an ample domain, gradually sinking beneath our superior policy, our arts, and our arms." The trek westward of these displaced persons was one of the most tragic episodes in the history of Indian-white relationships.

Though Jackson had the typical frontiersman's disregard for legal niceties where Indians were concerned, he exacted obedience to the Constitution from his fellow white men. His forceful views were made known to South Carolina whose hotspurs were threatening nullification of the federal tariff laws.

★ NULLIFICATION

Jackson supporters before the election of 1828 had worked out what they thought was an ingenious scheme to present their candidate to the North as favoring a high tariff, and to the South as an opponent of this policy. Such high rates were to be placed on raw materials that Northern manufacturers were expected to join shippers and Southern planters in opposing the measure. Amendments making the tariff more palatable to manufacturers were to be defeated, thus Jacksonians could pose in the North as friendly to a high tariff, and in the South as its adversary. The bill, said the acid-tongued John Randolph, "referred to manufactures of no sort . . . but the manufacture of a President of the United States." To the surprise of its initiators (though not to Van Buren, who really favored it), "The Tariff of Abominations," as its critics called it, secured enough votes to be passed.* Webster, who had been converted to a protectionist view as New England's economic interests shifted from commerce to manufactures, was a strong supporter of the measure. "Its enemies," he said, "spiced it with whatever they thought would render it distasteful; its friends took it, drugged as it was."

Other states besides South Carolina had denounced the tariff of 1828 as damaging to Southern interests, but it was her leaders who were most rabid. The difficulties facing the South were probably due less to the tariff than they were to other factors. With the steady western expansion of cotton producing areas, especially in the rich soil of Alabama and Mississippi, production increased enormously, from 80,000,000 pounds in 1811 to 330,000,000 in 1826. But the markets failed to keep pace with the crop. Cotton fell from near thirty cents a pound in 1816 to nine cents in 1827. South Carolina, with worn-out lands, and falling behind in the race for economic and political power, thought it time to weigh the value of the Union.

* George Dangerfield analyzes a dispute among scholars as to whether Van Buren really wanted the tariff to pass. See his *The Awakening of American Nationalism 1815–1828* (New York, 1965), pp. 281–82.

Calhoun, then vice-president of the United States, had been striving to restrain South Carolina's extremists, but the pressure was too great and he was swept along with the tide. As an alternative to the secession urged by firebrands, he proposed nullification. He was enough of a nationalist to wish the Union's preservation, and his hopes for the presidency would be permanently blasted if the extremists had their way. He drew up a statement, the *South Carolina Exposition* (though his authorship was not public knowledge), indicting the protective tariff as unconstitutional, for it benefited only the North, he claimed.

The tax on imports, said Calhoun, in reality fell on the South, because the North compensated itself by the increased profits secured to its manufactures by protection. The South was a heavy exporter (it supplied two-thirds of America's exports), but its products faced obstacles in Europe, higher tariffs imposed in retaliation against the United States. Calhoun had abandoned former beliefs in the value of tariffs and was conscious now only of their burden. Southerners spoke of being exploited by Northern middlemen, who allegedly exacted large profits in shipping to the South imports from Europe. Calhoun suggested that if the South had its own customhouse it would have available for its own use a revenue of over $16,000,000 from foreign trade alone, without counting the millions that might be accumulated in taxing imports from the North.

Since the states, Calhoun argued, had created the federal government in 1787, they were superior to it, and each could therefore nullify any federal law hostile to its interests. Here was a proposal designed to protect the minority views of South Carolina, and of other states in the South, no matter how powerful an opposing majority might become. For the time being, however, the matter rested with angry words of denunciation, and with hopes that Jackson would favor a reduction in the tariff.

★ "OUR UNION: IT MUST BE PRESERVED"

Southerners realized that they could strengthen their position in national political councils only by support from the West. If the Southerners threw their weight behind a more liberal program for distribution of the federal lands the chances for a political alliance between South and West seemed bright. The West's perennial cry was for lower land prices, or even free gifts, as well as federal funds for roads and canals. Senator Benton of Missouri proposed a scheme of graduated reductions in the price of unsold federal land from $1.25 an acre to 75 cents, then to 50 cents, and if there were still no buyers it was to be given away. The West held the balance of power between the high tariff North and the low tariff South. The Northwest itself favored a tariff, but was using its voting strength to bargain with the East. The government's revenues at this time were largely derived from taxes on imports and from sales of federal lands. As the receipts piled up, paying off the national debt, there was fear in the Northeast that a chief argument for high tariffs (that they were needed to increase national funds) would be destroyed. Proposals had been made to distribute among the states funds received from public land sales.

The alignment between West and South seemed natural in view of grievances shared in common against the Northeast. A particular Western grievance at the moment was a proposal made by Senator Foot of Connecticut, which favored a conservative policy in disposing of the public lands. Foot represented a New England view which feared continuing westward migration as damaging to her economy. In particular, her manufacturers were charged with opposing Western settlements in order to keep at home a large labor supply to hold wage rates down.

Senator Foot's resolution touched off a spectacular debate in the winter of 1829–30. The Southeast, by backing the West, saw its opportunity to destroy the East-West alliance. For weeks the argument raged. Manufacturers, thundered Senator Benton, "want poor people to do the work for small wages; these poor people wish to go to the West and get land . . . and to start their children on a theatre where they can contend with equal chances with other peoples' children for the honors and dignities of the country." As one speech followed another the emphasis was less and less on the land question, and more and more on the nature of the Constitution. Senator Hayne of South Carolina, an eloquent supporter of Calhoun's doctrine of nullification, was locked in combat with Webster from Massachusetts. As long as Hayne had sided with the West on the land issue his support was welcome to Jacksonians, but when he branched off to endorse the theory of nullification he alienated them.

Toward the end of January, 1830, Webster arose in the small, crowded Senate chamber to make his historic reply to Hayne. Webster was an imposing figure, thick-set, dark-skinned, with a massive head of jet-black hair and smoldering eyes. His great, deep voice and the rhythm of his speech carried his audience along with him in hypnotic trance. Like a "great cannon loaded to the lips" (this was Emerson's description of Webster), the Massachusetts Senator thundered away at South Carolina's doctrine of nullification. "The Constitution," he said, "is not the creature of the State government. The very chief end, the main design for which the whole Constitution was framed and adopted was to establish a government that should not . . . depend on State opinion and State discretion." The Constitution and the government, he said in words that burned deep in the memory of Abraham Lincoln, were "made for the people; made by the people, and answerable to the people." Webster ridiculed the "words of delusion and folly, 'Liberty first and Union afterwards,'" and he closed with the memorable phrase "Liberty *and* Union, now and forever, one and inseparable."

The country read the speeches of Hayne and Webster in tens of thousands of copies; enraptured schoolboys were soon to declaim Webster's words in countless classrooms. What everyone wanted to know was where Jackson stood, with Webster or with Hayne? A few intimates knew Jackson's views and soon the whole country learned them.

The answer came with dramatic suddenness at a memorial dinner to Thomas Jefferson on April 13, 1830, the anniversary of his birth. The scheduled speeches and toasts, prepared by South Carolinians, built up support for that state's doctrine of nullification. Jackson sat immobile through the twenty-four toasts. Time came for the volunteer toasts. The President of the United States arose, and looking hard at Calhoun proposed:

"Our Union: It must be preserved."

Calhoun, though stunned, offered the next toast:

"The Union—next to our liberty, most dear."

The gulf between Vice-President Calhoun and Jackson was now wide. It widened still further when Jackson found out that, years before in 1818, when Calhoun was Secretary of War, the South Carolinian had joined those anxious to censure him for his actions during the Seminole War.

Secretary of State Van Buren and Calhoun were rivals for the succession to the presidency, and the former did everything possible to make the gulf unbridgeable between Jackson and the vice-president. A matter of social relationships, the Eaton affair, played into his hands. Jackson's Secretary of War, John H. Eaton, had married Peggy O'Neale, sociable daughter of a tavern keeper. Wives of cabinet members ostracised her, for her reputation was the stuff gossip feeds on. Jackson defended her, while Van Buren, a widower, was gallant in her behalf. Social tension was so great that Van Buren offered to resign, followed by Eaton. Jackson asked for the remaining cabinet resignations. In reorganizing the cabinet Van Buren, who became minister to England, was successful in having all the Calhoun men kept out. The challenge was thus flung into the face of South Carolina nullifiers, and Calhoun's presidential ambitions muzzled.

The next year, 1832, a new tariff bill with lower schedules was passed. It still retained sections objectionable to South Carolina. Calhoun and his followers thereupon raised the banner of nullification higher than before. In November, a convention in South Carolina denounced the tariffs of 1828 and 1832 as unconstitutional and not binding on its citizens. Federal customs officials were to be forbidden in the state, and any attempt at coercion by the national government would be met by immediate secession. Jackson countered by encouraging Unionist elements in the state, and by a vigorous proclamation to her people (drafted by Edward Livingston, Secretary of State), denying the right of nullification. "To say that any State may at pleasure secede from the Union," Jackson announced, "is to say that the United States is not a nation." "I consider the power to annul a law of the United States assumed by one State, incompatible with the existence of the Union, contradicted expressly by the letter of the Constitution, unauthorized by its spirit, inconsistent with every principle on which it was founded, and destructive of the great object for which it was formed." To a South Carolina Unionist Jackson wrote, "Nullification . . . means insurrection and war; and other states have a right to put it down." A "Force Bill" was passed authorizing the president to use national troops if South Carolina obstructed federal customs officers.

The president was cheered by the loyal support of states North and South, and it appeared that South Carolina was belligerent in splendid isolation. Though he would have been glad to lead an army to overawe the secessionists, calm heads proposed compromise. At length common ground was found. On March 1, 1833, both parties agreed to a gradual reduction in the tariff while South Carolina was to revoke her ordinance of nullification.

Clay's instinct for compromise had found the way out of the impasse. It was he who had proposed lowering the tariff duties, though he did so at the risk of sacrificing his "American System." In reality he had taken the practical politician's view of saving part of his program lest the whole of it be lost. His bill, he believed, "would protect the manufacturers for the present and gain time . . . for them." It would "preserve the Union, prevent Civil War, and save us the danger of entrusting to Jackson large armies." It was in these trying times that Clay won the affectionate tribute, the "Great Pacificator."

A great crisis had passed, to the immense relief of the country. New England, which had not been too friendly to Jackson as a presidential candidate, liked his show of executive strength. "No nullification here," said a companion to Jackson on a trip through the region. "General," he continued, "Mr. Calhoun would stand no more chance down east than a stump-tail bull in fly time." Nationalism had triumphed, and

Jackson wrote privately, "Nullification and secession are for the present, I think, effectively, and I hope forever put down." But a close observer in South Carolina saw the episode with different eyes: "Nullification," he said, "is not dead but sleepeth; the grand object is disunion, and it will be attempted again."

Though South Carolina had stood alone she had many sympathizers throughout the South who believed in the right of secession. The whole nullification episode had left them with a sense of oppression, and in much of their thought and actions thereafter was an emotional tension which precluded calm analysis of national questions.

★ THE "MONSTER"

The nullification issue challenged Jackson's powers of command and called forth all his fire. In truth his reaction was not unlike that of a military commander faced by a mutinous unit; and mutiny was unlikely to succeed with General Jackson in charge. The outcome of the episode revealed his mastery of the situation and won him the gratitude of most of the country. It is improbable, however, that the issues involved in this contest, ominous as they were to thoughtful individuals, touched very deeply the emotions of great masses of the people. Issues involving constitutional theory, however important, are generally too abstract for the average man. His emotions are more likely to be kindled by a deeply felt moral issue, which may possibly be bound up with economic questions. It was in handling just such a problem—rechartering of the Bank of the United States—that Jackson gained his greatest fame as the people's president.

The Bank, B.U.S. it was called, since the panic of 1819 had been doing a useful job. It handled government funds efficiently, it stabilized the currency, and well-to-do men found it an invaluable instrument of business enterprise. But it could not live down the charge of monopoly; the label "Monster" clung to it like the can tied to the tail of an ill-favored dog. The spirit of Jackson's age, though friendly to capitalism, was anti-monopolistic and anti-aristocratic. The Bank seemed the most glaring symbol of the twin evils Jackson opposed. There were other symbols. Amos Kendall, a strong Jacksonian, spoke of "Nobility Systems" that had been built up in many countries by a "few rich and intelligent men," who "are enabled to live upon the labor of the many." The United States also had its "Nobility System," said Kendall. "Its head is the Bank of the United States, its right arm, a protecting tariff and Manufacturing Monopolies; its left, growing State debts and states incorporations."

Nicholas Biddle, head of the bank, was as imperious as the president of the United States. Biddle's point of view was that he presided over an independent entity, scarcely inferior in power to the state which created it. It almost seemed, as he surveyed the scene, that he and Jackson were heads of rival powers. Certainly Biddle did nothing to quiet fears of the bank's great power. When asked once if the bank had at any time oppressed any of the state banks, he replied, "Never. There are very few banks which might not have been destroyed by an exertion of the powers of the Bank. None have ever been injured." The implication remained that Biddle's bank, though up to that moment forbearing, might at any time turn its strength against weaker state banks. It was a realization of this power that frightened competing bankers, small-businessmen and workingmen, as well as western farmers.

Roger B. Taney, a strong Democrat, expressed the sentiment of Jackson's circle when he spoke of "this power concentrated in the hands of a few individuals—exercised in secret and unseen although constantly felt—irresponsible and above the control of the people or the Government for the 20 years of its charter," which "would awaken any man in the country if the danger is brought distinctly to his view."

The time was at hand when the danger was brought to every man's view. The bank had applied for a recharter in 1832 though the old charter had four years to run. The question was brought up in that presidential year because Henry Clay, expecting to be Jackson's opponent, thought that a fight on the bank issue would result in victory for himself. After a sharp debate the bill to recharter passed both houses of Congress and was sent to the president on July 3. He awaited it grimly. "The Bank," he said to Van Buren, "is trying to kill me, *but I will kill it*."

Jackson's veto message castigated the bank as unconstitutional and a monopoly. He put his party on record as champion of the unprivileged. "It is to be regretted," he said, "that the rich and powerful too often bend the acts of government to their selfish purposes"; "when the laws undertake . . . to make the rich richer and the potent more powerful, the humble members of society—the farmers, mechanics and laborers—who have neither the time nor the means of securing like favors to themselves, have a right to complain of the injustice of their Government."

Conservative interests reacted instantly. Senator Webster, a director of the Bank, its chief counsel and large debtor, denounced the veto: "It manifestly seeks to influence the poor against the rich. It wantonly attacks whole classes of the people for the purpose of turning against them the prejudices and resentments of other classes." The battle lines were being drawn between those who, like Webster, believed that property had a prior stake in the state, and those like Jackson, who refused to grant any privileged position to wealth. Jackson's veto was sustained.

★ BREAKING THE BANK

The election campaign in 1832 was bitterly fought. Clay was the candidate of the National Republicans (predecessors of the Whigs), while Jackson was his Democratic opponent. An unusual entry in the presidential sweepstakes was the Anti-Masonic party, originating in western New York. Masons and other secret organizations had come under attack when a former Mason, who had disclosed its inner workings, disappeared without trace. By blaming Masonry for his assumed murder, much support, in and outside New York, was rallied against secret societies. Anti-Masonry borrowed some of the features of Clay's American System, adding to it a tinge of prejudice against Catholic immigration. William Wirt, noted Southern attorney, was named for the presidency in 1831 by the Anti-Masonic party, which was the first group to call a national convention for the express purpose of nominating a presidential candidate.

Despite the Anti-Masons and the familiar accent on personalities that characterize political campaigns, the bank was the central issue. "The present contest," said the worried Edward Everett, "is nothing less than a war of Numbers against Property." Clay, the National Republicans' choice, was backed by all the resources of the bank. About two-thirds of the press, much of it indebted to the bank for loans or advertisements, supported its cause. Conservative lawyers, merchants, and intellectuals rallied to the side of Henry Clay, "leader of the aristocratic party." Wealth, the press and other agencies of public information nearly all favored Clay against Jackson. A widely circulated picture showed Jackson, Van Buren, Benton, and others as burglars attempting to smash the impregnable bank. As a later president, Franklin D. Roosevelt, expressed it, it seemed almost that all were against Jackson —"all but the people of the United States."

The people spoke out with torchlight parades in city streets, singing campaign songs, marching with hickory poles, or noisily gathering around great bonfires where they shouted their praises of Jackson. In a New York parade marchers carried portraits of Jackson as general and as Tennessee farmer, holding his famous hickory cane in his hand. Pictures of Washington and Jefferson were mingled with various emblems glorifying the Democrats. A husky sailor marched along under a pole, to the top of which was tied a live eagle.

Election day came, and the news, said a doleful supporter of Clay, "blows over us like a great cold storm." Jackson's popular vote was 687,000 topping the combined opposition by over 150,000. The president had an electoral vote of 217 to Clay's 49. Wirt got Vermont's seven votes. The nullificationists who dominated South Carolina's legislature gave that state's eleven electoral votes to John Floyd, of Virginia.

The bank's doom was sealed though Biddle did not yield easily. "The Bank of the United States," he cried, "shall not break." But break it did, despite Biddle's forceful countermeasures to wring a new charter from the government. The bank brought such great pressure on debtors as to suggest a deliberate attempt on its part to start a panic. Jackson was equally direct in his strategy. He decided, in 1833, to remove government deposits from the B.U.S. and place them in local banks—"pet banks" they were called by the president's critics. The B.U.S. was thus shorn of much of its strength though it continued to function until the expiration of its charter. After 1836 it operated for a few years under a charter from the state of Pennsylvania, but its great days had passed.

Nicholas Biddle was undoubtedly an autocrat, to whom the spirit of Jacksonian democracy was alien and contemptible. It crushed him, but in the process it also did the country grave harm. If a strong B.U.S. had been functioning it is quite possible that the panic which hit the Americans in 1837 might have been cushioned. It was the strongest rein the country had against excessive speculation. The B.U.S., when handled properly, was the best stabilizer of currency and of business in the nation, better than anything which the country had until the twentieth century.

A vast increase in land speculation and an easing of credit restrictions followed Jackson's war on Biddle. Government sales of its lands jumped from 4,000,000 acres in 1834 to 20,000,000 in 1836, with a corresponding increase in treasury receipts. "Pet banks" then made loans to borrowers to speculate on more land. Much of the best land being gobbled up was being paid for in financial paper of doubtful value. Many Jackson supporters were outraged by this turn of events. "I did not join in putting down the Bank of the United States," said Benton, "to put up a wilderness of local banks. I did not join in putting down the paper currency of a national bank to put up a paper currency of a thousand local banks."

The administration issued the "Specie Circular" in July, 1836, requiring that government land bought in the future had to be paid for in gold or silver. Extravagant expenditures in the states for various enterprises, particularly internal improvements, fed the speculative fever. Distribution among the states of the surplus in the federal Treasury, to start January 1, 1837, expanded plans for spending. On top of it all British investors were bullish on America's economic future. Their attitude changed when the United States trade balance grew more unfavorable. English credits dried up, and settlement of old accounts was requested. Crop failures aggravated the financial stringency. Banks failed in Britain and tumbled like ninepins in America. The boom was over, to be followed by years of depression.

★ SOCIAL REFORMS

The panic of 1837, which really came after Jackson's term was over, was not identified in most men's minds with him though his policies helped bring it on. He was the kind of president whose successes were remembered and his failures forgotten. His triumph over the bank was counted by supporters his most spectacular success for democracy. Less dramatic, but of high importance, was his appointment in 1836 of Roger B. Taney as Marshall's successor as Chief Justice. Marshall had died the year before, one of "the greatest men of his age," Jackson conceded, though he quickly added that he dissented "from some of his expositions of our constitutional law." Taney and other Jackson appointees brought to the court something of that liberal social spirit characteristic of these years. "New men and new opinions have succeeded," wrote Justice Story with pained regret.

The strategy of Jackson's campaign for democracy included other objectives, in particular, the promotion of direct action by the people in political affairs. One proposal that enlisted his support was an amendment to the Constitution providing for the election of the president and vice-president by popular vote. Other amendments to the Constitution, suggested in this period, included the right to overturn a presidential veto by a majority of Congress, rather than by a two-thirds vote, and the election of Senators by the people rather than by state legislatures. It is true that none of these proposals were favorably received, but it was Jackson's leadership that provided the friendly climate in which such ideas could be born and nurtured. His unconquerable will gave strength to timid men to transform the pattern of their lives.

It was in the states, however, rather than in the national government, that Jacksonian democracy registered many of its most notable advances. Workingmen's parties developed considerable force in large northern cities, where they brought pressure against laws that weighed on them unjustly. One of these laws threw into jail men who were unable to pay even trifling debts. In Philadelphia, during an eight-month period, over 250 people were jailed for individual debts of less than $5, including 30 for less than $1. Workingmen agitated for mechanics lien laws which gave them prior right over any creditor to the assets of their employer.

Workers complained bitterly of inadequate education for their children. Children of the prosperous had private schools; children of ordinary workingmen went to despised charity schools. There was also a large group of craftsmen and small shopkeepers who were unable to afford the private schools, and at the same time were ineligible to send their children to charity schools. A vigorous campaign for free, tax-supported schools was undertaken by workingmen, in association with many businessmen and intellectuals. Without education, it was argued, there could be no social and political equality; "Lack of education deprives the poor from representation in government," said the *Mechanic's Free Press* in 1829.

The temper of the times had vented its anger against aristocracy in politics, and monopoly in business and finance. It expressed itself similarly in demanding a broad program of public education. "The original element of despotism," said a workers' committee in Pennsylvania, "is a monopoly of talent, which consigns the multitude to comparative ignorance, and secures the balance of knowledge on the side of the rich and the rulers—this monopoly should be broken up, and . . . the means of equal knowledge (the only security for equal liberty), should be rendered, by legal provision, the common property of all classes."

Workingmen and their liberal, middle-class allies also denounced the evils of the long workday, from dawn to dark, which had been carried over into industry from agriculture. The issue of shorter hours was to be a principal one in the program of American labor for many years after the Jacksonian era. It did win a limited success in the ten-hour day established by Van Buren's administration for labor on federal projects. The reforms sought by workingmen were many, not the least of them was a demand for a less expensive legal system.

In order to win adoption of their program, workers organized political parties which gained temporary successes in Philadelphia and New York. These political organizations distrusted both major parties, though before Jackson's second term had run out many workingmen were convinced that he was their champion. Though the workingmen's parties quickly disappeared, their programs generally were taken over by other groups. These parties had really never been true labor parties to begin with. Many of their members, and the candidates endorsed by them, were well-to-do merchants or lawyers with democratic inclinations. The parties were temporary political coalitions, formed by men interested in achieving together humanitarian objectives.

★ VAN BUREN

In the fall of 1831 Jackson had written to Van Buren: "I hope circumstances will occur to enable me to retire to the Hermitage [his Tennessee home] in due season . . . to open the door" for "employment" by the country of others—*"you will understand me."* Not only Van Buren but the whole country understood who would be the successor of Jackson when the latter finished his second term.

Van Buren was in striking physical contrast to the tall, thin president. The former, of Dutch stock from the Hudson Valley of New York, had the short, roundish figure of an Amsterdam burgher. There was nothing dull about him; his lively eyes and keen mind warned his opponents that he was an able foe. He was one of New York's most prominent and liberal politicians before he joined Jackson in Washington. His rise to national distinction came from his ability to think in terms that transcended local boundaries. In his native state he had evolved improved techniques of appealing to the masses of voters and bringing them to his side. "Those who have wrought great changes in the world," he once wrote, "never succeeded by gaining over chiefs; but always by exciting the multitude. The first is the resource of intrigue and produces only secondary results, the second is the resort of genius and transforms the face of the universe."

Van Buren, who usually worked quietly (a caustic critic said he "rowed to his objective with muffled oars"), did not, as a person, excite the multitude, but he apparently understood their needs and hopes. He certainly knew how best to further his own career, which Jackson did everything to advance. Though Van Buren ran as the candidate of the Democrats in 1836, people went to the polls in a mood of voting a third term for Jackson. Four years earlier an experienced politician had written after the election of 1832 that Jackson might be president for life if he so chose.

The opposition, known now as Whigs (recalling ancient hostility to royal despotism in Stuart England) fixed on no single candidate. Their strategy was to have several candidates in the field in the hope that the voting might be so split as to throw the presidential contest into the House of Representatives. But the plan failed, and Van Buren, the "little magician," benefiting from the magic of Jackson's name, carried his party to victory in the presidency and in Congress.

On March 4, 1837, Jackson, pale and pain-wracked from long illness, watched while his successor was sworn in. The crowd's eyes and heart were with the retiring president. For once, said Benton, "the rising was eclipsed by the setting sun." A few days after the inauguration

Jackson left Washington for the Hermitage and the journey home was a triumphal procession. His place in history was secure, his controversial personality a source of vital strength to much that is best in the American democratic tradition.

From his Tennessee plantation he watched the national political scene, keeping a close eye on the Van Buren administration. That administration quickly found itself in hot water when the panic of 1837 burst upon the country. Van Buren sought to solve the nation's ills by the creation of an "Independent Treasury" in the capital and sub-treasuries elsewhere in the country, freed from the control of men like Biddle as well as from manipulation by wildcat state banks. Van Buren's plan, not adopted till 1840, was in keeping with the Jacksonian tradition and won him great popularity with radical elements in the Democratic party.

The most radical wing of the party was in New York, the Locofoco group, so-called after the new matches they used to relight a meeting after conservative opponents had turned off the gas lights. Their financial program was Jackson's; they asked for popular election of judges, and for free grants of public lands to the landless. Though not numerous, the Locofocos cast a pivotal vote and thus had an influence beyond their apparent strength. The ideas and political techniques used by this group were the precedents for radical movements in after years.

The mantle of Jackson had fallen on lesser shoulders. Van Buren's political skill, which had won him many victories in former days, was strangely wanting in his own administration. His party was split on the question of financial policy, many Democrats believing the president's plan harmful to the interests of state banks. Nor did his political appointments promote harmony among the Democrats. Van Buren had not the hold on southern and western voters that Jackson had. Party lines were not rigidly drawn, voters finding it easy to shift allegiance in this period. The accent was on personality, not principle—anything to excite the multitude, as Van Buren himself had urged. Whigs had learned from him how to influence friends and win elections. "We have taught them how to conquer us!" cried a Democratic publication.

★ "TIPPECANOE AND TYLER TOO"

The Whigs had learned their lesson well. They nominated General William Henry Harrison, famed hero of Tippecanoe, as Jackson had predicted they would. The Whigs, he argued, "have got to take up a soldier; they have tried orators enough." Poor Henry Clay moaned: "I am the most unfortunate man in the history of parties: always run by my friends when sure to be defeated, and now betrayed when I, or any one, would be sure of election." Clay's expectations for the nomination had received a severe jolt in the summer of 1839. On his swing through the North seeking support he was urged to withdraw by the powerful New York Whig boss, Thurlow Weed. Weed told him that several influential factors in the North were operating strongly against his candidacy. They included abolitionism, antibank sentiment, and the still lingering anti-Masonic bias. John Tyler of Virginia was named as Harrison's running mate to conciliate the backers of the disappointed Clay.

The Democrats, who had renominated Van Buren, were faced with the kind of campaign they themselves had formerly waged for Jackson. The Whigs ran on no platform, avoiding association with the bank issue, which might have defeated them. "Every man is a patriot, and guns and hurrahs are splitting the air in all directions," said Prescott, the conservative historian. A log cabin and hard cider, he agreed, were "indifferent qualifications for the presidency. But these," he said, "are words to gull the many, who love to be gulled." Slogans, songs, torchlight parades, cider—these were the ingredients of the campaign of 1840. "Tippecanoe and Tyler too" carried the Whigs on to victory. "Sung down, lied down, drunk down," cried a frustrated Democrat.

A Democratic paper had sneered that General Harrison needed nothing more than a barrel of hard cider and a pension and "he will sit the remainder of his days in a log cabin." The Whigs turned the sneer into a boast: yes, their candidate was a democrat living on little. Van Buren, they said scornfully, lived in the White House in aristocratic luxury, dining with gold spoons and aping European royalty. The Whigs, the party of gentlemen and wealth (which was spent lavishly in the campaign), successfully created the illusion that theirs was the people's party. From the West came the roundelay:

> Ole Tip he wears a homespun suit,
>   He has no ruffled shirt—*wirt-wirt*
> [*wirt-wirt* simulated by spitting through the teeth.]
> But Mat he has the golden plate,
>   And he's a little squirt—*wirt-wirt*.

Log cabins appeared at Harrison rallies and cider flowed endlessly down the voters' thirsty throats, while they yelled with glee, "Van Van is a used-up man."

In September, Whig hopes reached a new high when Maine's returns came in. Joyous Whigs sang a new song:

> And have you heard the news from Maine,
>   And what old Maine can do?
> She went hell-bent for Governor Kent,
>   And Tippecanoe and Tyler too,
>   And Tippecanoe and Tyler too.

A vast outpouring of citizens voted that year, far greater than ever before. Nearly 2,500,000 votes were tallied, Harrison winning by almost 146,000. The electoral vote of 234 for the Whigs against 60 for Van Buren was not an accurate index of the strength of the Democrats. It was a severe blow to the old, retired warrior in the Hermitage, but the iron-willed Jackson was not despondent. *"Beaten,"* he said, *"but I trust not conquered . . .* I do not yet despair of the Republick." Rally round Van Buren, he urged his followers, and elect him "by a triumphant majority" in 1844.

Jackson's party was not "conquered." It did eventually return to power, but it was not then the same party he had once headed. Its name, the Democratic party, was the same, but the democrats in it were overshadowed by the conservative plantation owners of the South, who thenceforward to the Civil War supplied its leadership and dictated its policy. The liberal spirit of Jacksonian democracy lived on in northern urban centers and in agrarian communities scattered over the land. It lived on in the hearts of men and women who grieved when news came from the Hermitage, in June, 1845, that the Old Hero had died. Michael Shiner, a free Negro in a government shipyard, expressed the people's sorrow: "the Hon Major General andrew Jackson is gone and his voice are heared no moore on earth. But his name still lives in the heart of the American people . . ."

CHAPTER XVI

As the Country Matured

It had been one thing for the Founding Fathers to proclaim the birth of a brave new world and to lay its firm foundation. It was quite another matter for their successors to construct the edifice envisaged in the eighteenth century. Jefferson, by his own example, sought to inspire his countrymen, who in turn were to prove to the world "that a free government is of all others the most energetic," and would "ameliorate the condition of man over a great portion of the globe." The citizens of the Republic must be enlightened men and women whose moral force would be decisive in the affairs of the world.

To prepare American citizens for their great role in renovating society universal public education would need to be established. The plan of education was to be such as would provide opportunities for the best minds to place their talents at the service of the community. Intellectual activity must be unhampered. Ecclesiastical systems which, through partnership with states had often blocked the growth of science, should be shorn of their power through separation of Church and State. The generations that followed Jefferson turned to him again and again to refresh their spirits.

Jefferson, who lived on to the dawn of the Jacksonian era, had set an example for succeeding generations; the learned should not hold themselves aloof from leadership. His amazing versatility and explorations in varied fields of knowledge were characterized by their purposefulness. Each activity was to contribute its share to make a complete life. His example was not lost on Jacksonians, for many of them were intellectuals and artists. Intellectuals were not divorced from the political turmoil of their day. They shared in the formulation of democratic ideas and took their part in seeing that these were translated into legislative acts.

Among the ardent Jacksonians were such talented men as Hawthorne, the young Whitman, William Cullen Bryant, the sculptors Horatio Greenough and Hiram Powers, and the historian George Bancroft. Emerson, too, though less inclined to participate in the rough and tumble of politics, lent his voice to the support of Jacksonian ideas. "The philosopher, the poet, or the religious man, will, of course," he said, "wish to cast his vote with the democrat . . . for wide suffrage, for the abolition of legal cruelties in the penal code, and for facilitating in every manner the access of the young and the poor to the sources of wealth and power." Emerson's strong attachment to Webster, however, placed him more frequently on the side of the Whigs.

The Whigs, in turn, had their articulate spokesmen—cultivated men who, in their writing as in their politics, presented a conservative view of life. They had a strong sense of solidarity and were embittered when a fellow intellectual betrayed, as they thought it, his own class. Thus Edward Everett denounced Hawthorne, asking why was he "on the side of barbarism & vandalism against order, law & constitutional liberty?" The fastidious aristocrat who recoiled from the turbulence and excitement of democracy was answered by Whitman. "All the noisy tempestuous scenes of politics witnessed in this country . . . are *good* to behold," he wrote. "They evince that the *people act;* they are the discipline of the young giant, getting his maturer strength."

★ EDUCATION

It was clear that an accelerated growth of American culture was occurring in the Jacksonian era. The flowering of art and learning was not sudden—the seeds had been planted years before—but the slow fruition began to be apparent only after 1815. However maturation then came rapidly, attaining such heights of achievement as to warrant speaking of the 1840's and 1850's as the American Renaissance.

Several factors help to explain the rising standards of American accomplishment. One was the example of excellence created by German scholarship in history and philology. The whole level of American cultural standards was raised by familiarity with superior models abroad. When George Ticknor, the noted historian of Spanish literature, was a student at Harvard he thought that the university possessed a large library. On his return from Europe, where he saw large collections, Harvard's "seemed a closetful of books." "Every day I feel anew," wrote Ticknor in 1815, "what a mortifying distance there is between a European and an American scholar. We do not yet know what a Greek scholar is; we do not even know the process by which a man is to be made one." Ticknor knew that many years must elapse before much improvement in scholarship could occur, but through the efforts of individuals like himself a beginning was made.

The colleges of 1830 were modest institutions, usually associated with a particular religious denomination. Some sixty colleges were staffed by 400 instructors, teaching 5,000 students. Thus, in the country at large there was one undergraduate for about 2,500 people. The proportion in the eastern part of the country, where the majority of the colleges were situated, was higher than in the West. By the eve of the Civil War many more colleges had been established. Congregationalist institutions followed the Yale pattern, and Presbyterian the Princeton example. The schools were usually small, with less than a dozen professors, and rarely more than 300 students, pursuing the traditional liberal arts course. Women also had an opportunity for higher education when Oberlin, in 1833, initiated coeducation. A few years later Mount Holyoke was established specifically for women's higher education.

Americans having freed themselves from European political domination were anxious to show the same independence in their arts. Emerson, in a famous address delivered in 1837, said with unwarranted confidence, "Our day of dependence, our long apprenticeship to the learning of other lands, draws to a close . . ." While there was a proper pride in native achievement, Americans gradually became less belligerent in proclaiming their accomplishments. Artists went about their work regardless of European praise or censure, though it pleased Americans much to hear commendation from abroad.

Due to the momentum gained in this period by the Industrial Revolution, technological improvements in printing, publishing, and art reproduction made possible rapid inexpensive diffusion of knowledge. Increased wealth permitted greater patronage of arts and letters. Writers, especially historians and biographers, fared very well indeed. Bancroft, Prescott, Motley, and Washington Irving enjoyed wide popularity, and many of their works have an enduring quality. As always, some of the brightest lights of the generation were not adequately esteemed in their own time, among them Hawthorne, Melville and Thoreau. The *International Magazine,* published in New York, did, however, acclaim Hawthorne as "the greatest living American writer," and asserted correctly that *"The Scarlet Letter* will challenge consideration in the name of Art, in the best audience which in any age receives Cervantes, Le Sage or Scott." *The Scarlet Letter* and *Moby Dick* are justification enough for calling this era a golden age.

Among intellectuals the steady weakening of religious orthodoxy was apparent. Science and other secular influences promoted the growth of

Unitarianism to which Congregationalists steadily drifted. From German philosophers Americans derived much of the inspiration for the creation of a school of thought called Transcendentalism. In Emerson's phraseology it emphasized a belief in the divine goodness of human nature, opposing the Calvinistic preoccupation with sin and eternal damnation; it was a belief in the excellence of human instincts. The accent among Transcendentalists was on the intuitive power of the mind to know the truth and to live by it. The Transcendentalist, said a friendly observer, "treads the earth as though he were a god, who calls upon men to become gods, and from the beauty of his demeanor and his character we are induced to think more highly of human nature."

Transcendentalism, in its practical manifestation, sought a reform of society's ills through humanitarian movements, especially in education. Its followers also hoped, by founding co-operative enterprises like Brook Farm, to moderate the fiercely competitive spirit of men and turn their energies into channels for mutual good. Most of these idealists were much too strongly individualistic to stay long together in their planned Utopias, but the educational experiments they tried had permanent influence in American life. The real achievement of the Transcendentalists and allied reformers was to pinpoint the evils in the social scene and prick the community's conscience. It was Melville who noted the darker side of industrialism in New England, where "machinery—that vaunted slave of humanity—stood menially served by human beings." Influential ministers, William Ellery Channing among them, were deeply troubled over the growing inequalities in wealth which showed up sharply in an industrial era.

The low level at which mass education remained was an evil vigorously denounced by the reformers. The old Puritan ideal of free public schools had lost its strength; the district schools of the early nineteenth century were impoverished and staffed by teachers who knew little more than their pupils. One critic observed, in 1835, that New England's school system "had degenerated into routine, it was starved by parsimony. Any hovel would answer for a school house, any primer would do for a text-book, any farmer's apprentice was competent to 'keep school.'" In Massachusetts, for example, the sum spent to educate a child in a public school was a mere pittance compared to what was spent on the child in private school.

It was at this time that an aroused citizen of Massachusetts determined to reform the educational system. Horace Mann studied the best that Europe, especially Prussia, had to offer, and he adapted foreign educational methods to the American scene. He insisted on freeing schools from sectarian influences, he increased salaries for teachers, improved the existing school buildings and opened many new ones, and established a school year of at least six months. One of his most important achievements was the creation of the first state normal school in the country, in 1839, to prepare teachers properly for their profession.

While Horace Mann was revolutionizing the educational system of Massachusetts, Henry Barnard was leading a similar movement in Connecticut. Possibly Barnard's greatest accomplishment was his editing of *The American Journal of Education*. The *Journal* did more than any other publication to familiarize the English-speaking world with the latest educational treatises and practices of continental Europe. Barnard's periodical spread New England's educational ideas all over the United States.

Throughout the country educational reformers prompted their states to strengthen the common school system. The struggle was often hard: these programs were generally opposed by wealthy taxpayers and by religious groups who disliked the secular character of the public schools. Soon after the middle of the century, however, the struggle for compulsory elementary education in free public schools was well on the way to complete victory.

In these years the United States probably provided more educational opportunities than had hitherto been available to the mass of men anywhere in the world. Conservative opponents of a public education system were gradually won over when they were reminded that, in a democracy, education of the common people was a crucial matter. Since in that form of government the masses choose the rulers of society they should be instructed so as to learn how to choose wisely.

In the elementary schools of America the minds of countless children were being molded by a few widely adopted books. Chief among them were the McGuffey Readers, compiled by William H. McGuffey, who had been active in establishing the public school system of Ohio. Along with much information, his books inculcated moral precepts and a strong sense of nationalism, which took its cue from Daniel Webster. So popular were the McGuffey Readers that publishers scattered through the country were licensed to print them; 2,000,000 copies a year were being sold by 1860. Westward-bound emigrants carried them in their caravans; freight wagons found room for them; cow town and mining camp had their supply of readers. Their pages pictured a vigorous people building a strong society. From McGuffey millions of Americans first made acquaintance with choice literature—Scott, Byron, and Wordsworth. The first taste of Shakespeare for many youngsters came from selections in the readers.

Americans, said Tocqueville, had "a lively faith in the perfectibility of man; they are of opinion that the effects of the diffusion of knowledge must necessarily be advantageous, and the consequences of ignorance fatal; they all consider society as a body in a state of improvement, humanity as a changing scene, in which nothing is, or ought to be, permanent; and they admit that what appears to them to be good today may be superseded by something better tomorrow."

★ ADULT EDUCATION

Education was the lever by which the masses, not just a few favored individuals, were to be raised steadily higher in the scale of civilization. Such was the optimistic faith of the Jacksonian generation, and it carried over into fields outside the formal classroom. Expanded programs of adult education were inaugurated throughout the country. Mechanics' institutes, libraries, lyceums, and innumerable lectures attracted large numbers of adults anxious to be informed. The cult of self-improvement spread through northern and western towns and villages almost with the power of a new religious faith. While people often attended meetings for vocational purposes alone, lecturers also carried their audiences far beyond their work-a-day world. Noted speakers, such as Wendell Phillips and Emerson, attracted large audiences, who rewarded them generously.

From platforms in large cities and small towns scientists, perfectionists, itinerant healers, and advocates of every manner of personal and social regeneration informed and exhorted their rapt listeners. For an intense period phrenology was all the rage, and exotic foreign professors were glad to read, for a fee, an American client's "chart of bumps."

In addition to organizations set up by community enterprise to further education, individual philanthropists, like Lowell in Massachusetts and Astor and Peter Cooper in New York, established institutes and libraries to assist in the advancement of learning. Many prosperous Americans subscribed to the doctrine of the stewardship of wealth, which recognized that riches had been placed in their hands for the well-being of society at large. The practice of generosity in philanthropy had already reached such proportions as to prompt one American observer to say that the sums contributed in his country by private individuals for schools, colleges, churches, hospitals, and scientific institutions "put to shame the official liberality of the oldest and wealthiest governments in Europe."

Americans were especially proud of the fact that their country had gone far beyond Europe in the attempt to bridge the gap between the learned few and the uncultured many. Europeans warned the Old World that it must follow the American example in popularizing knowledge if it wished to avoid despotism and revolution. The American ideal, democratization of learning, had firm support in the period from Jackson to Lincoln. "We must reach the minds and hearts of the masses," said Robert Dale Owen. "We must not deal it [*i.e.,* knowledge] out to scholars and students alone, but even to Tom, Dick and Harry, and then," said Owen, quoting a wit, "they will become Mr. Thomas, and Mr. Richard and Mr. Henry."

★ THE PRESS

A powerful agent of mass communication was the "penny press" which emerged in the 1830's. The papers were little dailies, generally four pages in length, written for the mass taste. They differed from the staid, formal presentation of the conservative press, with its emphasis on political and literary topics. The new papers were brief and cheap, emphasizing sensational reports of police courts and juicy scandals as well as "human interest" stories. Twentieth-century journalism was already foreshadowed in the "penny press" of the 1830's.

The *New York Sun,* founded in 1833, was the first successful penny paper, and it was followed two years later by the *New York Herald,* published by James Gordon Bennett. Not long after, Horace Greeley issued the *New York Tribune,* which was destined to become the most influential paper in America. Greeley gave space to the issues that deeply touched the American people before the Civil War—abolitionism, temperance, free homesteads, Utopian co-operative settlements, and the problems of labor. The weekly edition of the *Tribune,* with 100,000 subscribers, had a remarkable influence in rural areas, especially in Western communities. "The *Tribune,*" said a qualified contemporary, "came next to the Bible in the West."

Americans were reputed to be the most avid readers of periodicals in the world. An English observer enviously calculated that, in 1829, the number of newspapers circulated in Great Britain were enough to reach only one out of every thirty-six inhabitants weekly; Pennsylvania in that same year had a newspaper circulation which reached one out of every four inhabitants weekly. Statistics seemed to justify the common belief that Americans were devoted to periodicals; newspapers in the United States increased from 1,200 in 1833 to 3,000 on the eve of the Civil War, which far exceeded the number and circulation of newspapers in England or France.

Many magazines, catering to varied interests, were issued in these years, but their life was usually short. Competition from cheap reprints of pirated English novels was severe, and subscribers were lax in maintaining payments. Despite their handicaps some of the magazines survived long enough to make an impression on the cultural scene. To the older *North American Review* with its New England flavor were added *The Knickerbocker Magazine* in New York and *The Southern Literary Messenger* in Richmond. The most widely circulated magazine of the period was *Godey's Lady's Book,* whose literary editor was Sarah J. Hale. By the late 1840's, as a result of her intelligent choice of literary contributions, plus the skill of the magazine's staff in catering to women, the periodical's circulation reached 40,000 and jumped to 150,000 by 1860. It was in the 1850's that magazines of a general appeal, and with high standards, were successfully launched. Their number included the *Atlantic Monthly* and *Harper's.* Expanding outlets were making the literary life somewhat more attractive for Americans.

New editorial personalities brought fresh vigor to periodical publication. James Russell Lowell headed the brilliant *Atlantic,* the business-like Robert Bonner made the *New York Ledger* a huge financial success, Frank Leslie with his *Illustrated Newspaper,* a weekly, set new standards in news illustration, and J. D. B. De Bow made his New Orleans *Review* chief spokesman of the South. Its material on the economic life of that region before the Civil War is invaluable to scholars. *Putnam's Monthly,* with contributions from Longfellow, Thoreau, Melville, and others equally distinguished, was "resolutely American." Frank L. Mott, in his history of American magazines, says that "its stand for original and American contributions was intended and received as a stinging rebuke to the disgracefully successful *Harper's* with its 'borrowed' English serials." All religious groups had their own publications which exercised great influence in their respective spheres. New York on the eve of the Civil War had become the publishing center of the country but the quality of Boston's *Atlantic* and the prestige of New England's writers won for Massachusetts the homage of all America. Americans prided themselves on their vast number of intelligent readers. *Putnam's Monthly,* while admitting the superior quality of English writing, claimed that neither England nor France could compare with America in the size of its reading public.

The audience for magazines and books in the United States was constantly growing. Technological advances in printing made larger production of papers, magazines, and books possible, and low prices opened up a mass market. Histories, travel accounts, religious works, biographies, manuals of useful information, and encyclopedias of popular knowledge were issued in vast numbers. American publishers, in the absence of copyright laws, pirated the best English authors. A favorite was Dickens, who fumed at the loss of royalties. English publishers, in return, performed the same disservice for American authors, notably Longfellow, who was as popular in Britain as he was in his own country.

The fame of Longfellow was astonishing on both sides of the Atlantic. The *Times* of London spoke of him as a "household word to the English people. No poet of our own or of any other land is so widely known and appreciated by strangely various classes of society . . . He is not less the poet of the people than a chosen companion of the cultured and refined." British students gladly conceded that Longfellow had taught more people to love poetry than any other writer of English.

The whole era was one of mass movements, for it seemed as though all mankind could be pushed forward into the millennium by teaching, by preaching, or by the power of some new religious faith. "Madmen, and women . . . Dunkers, Muggletonians, Come-outers, Groaners, Agrarians, Seventh-Day Baptists, Quakers, Abolitionists, Unitarians, and Philosophers"—these, said Emerson, all promised assurance for the future.

Emerson himself expressed more accurately than anyone else the spirit of his time, its optimism and self-reliance, its love of speed and delight in the superlative. Stagecoaches traveled too slow for him. While he extolled the "dreamlike travelling on the railroad," he regretted that his day was not "quite yet fit for Flying Machines." Like his fellow Yankees Emerson was completely alive to everyday things; the characteristic American interest in practical science was never more active than in his time. Something of this same temper appeared in a letter of Theodore Parker, written from Rome, in which he confessed that the fine arts interested him less than "the coarse arts which feed, clothe, house and comfort a people." "Mechanics fairs, and ploughs and harrows and sawmills," appealed to Parker, who took "more interest in a cattle show than in a picture-show" and who asserted he would "rather be such a great man as Franklin than a Michael Angelo."

★ AMERICA IS "YET UNSUNG"

It should not be inferred from the remarks of Emerson and Parker that they or their fellow Americans were insensitive to things of the spirit. But they wanted an art and literature that would express the native soil, its people and their dreams. "We do not, with sufficient plainness, or sufficient profoundness, address ourselves to life," said Emerson, "nor dare we chant our own times and social circumstance . . . We have yet had no genius in America, [who] knew the value of our incomparable materials . . . Banks and tariffs, the newspaper and caucus, Methodism and Unitarianism, are flat and dull to dull people, but rest on the same foundations of wonder as the town of Troy and the temple of Delphos. Our log-rolling, our stumps and their politics, our fisheries, our Negroes, and Indians, our boats . . . the Northern trade, the Southern planting, the Western clearing, Oregon and Texas are yet unsung."

Emerson, who needed no urging, was pressed by Thomas Carlyle to carve an American hero out of the contemporary scene. Carlyle himself had constructed a possible myth of the American frontier, he wrote Emerson. "How beautiful to think of lean tough Yankee settlers, tough as gutta-percha, with most occult unsubduable fire in their belly steering over the western Mountains to annihilate the jungle, and bring bacon and corn out of it for the Posterity of Adam. There is no *Myth* of Athene or Herakles equal to this *fact*."

Even as Emerson was regretting the failure of American artists to exploit the wealth of their own materials, poets and novelists, painters and sculptors were discovering the riches that lay at their hands. Emerson, in his missionary zeal, was ignoring the fact that some artists had early depicted important events in the nation's history. They had celebrated the maritime achievements of the War of 1812 with paintings of victorious ships. Naval heroes and other personalities of the time were also perpetuated on canvas; a favorite subject, because of his personality and his distinguishing sharp features, was Andrew Jackson.

Painters roamed through the country penetrating remote western regions to capture the native scene before it was altered by the pressure of the white man's civilization. The glorious colors of birds in their natural setting were preserved for an entranced posterity in the magnificent folios of John James Audubon. With infinite patience and determination this sharp-eyed man, whose home for years was the American woods and swamplands, painted with great delicacy the wilderness creatures. George Catlin painted the western Indian while other artists recorded scenes of the wildest regions of the unsettled West. "The future spirit of our art," said an American critic, "must be inherently vast like our western plains, majestic like our forests, generous like our rivers."

In the settled area of the East, the Catskills and the Hudson River were irresistibly attractive to the artistic imagination. Washington Irving, in the *Sketch Book,* made the region forever memorable in prose, while Thomas Cole and Asher Durand preserved its romantic beauty in their paintings. Cole and Thomas Doughty loved to paint the White Mountains, whose cloud forms and shining crags fed the romantic imagination. William Cullen Bryant, describing Cole's pictures, said they "carried the eye over scenes of wild Grandeur peculiar to our country, over our aerial mountain tops with their mighty growth of forests never touched by the axe, along the bank of streams never deformed by culture and into the depth of skies bright with the lines of our own climate."

More intimate scenes of American folk life, natural and unpretentious, were painted by George C. Bingham and William S. Mount. While Bingham was depicting the familiar in political campaigning and Mount was painting everyday life on Long Island, John Rogers, using a different medium, also recorded popular aspects of the passing scene. Rogers fashioned plaster groups, "Checker Players," "Village Schoolmaster," and the like, which were reproduced in his New York workshop for many thousands of buyers.

Rogers, Mount, and many of their contemporaries echoed Emerson's affirmation: "I embrace the common . . . and sit at the feet of the familiar." Mount himself had stated his credo: "Paint pictures that will take with the public—never paint for the few, but the many." Horatio Greenough, the sculptor, was not discouraged with the relatively slow growth of American art. He thought that the art of an immature people should develop slowly and not by forced stimulation in a hothouse atmosphere. In the long run, he said, "the monuments, the pictures, the statues of the Republic will represent what the people love and wish for —not what they can be made to accept."

★ "SEEDS OF NATIVE TALENT"

There were some artists—painters, sculptors, architects—whose work the Americans apparently embraced with a strong devotion. In the earlier years of the Republic hundreds of portraits by Gilbert Stuart were commissioned, and many of them hung in the fashionable houses designed by Charles Bulfinch. Other artists, Thomas Sully and Samuel F. B. Morse, to mention two of a large number, maintained the well-established tradition of excellence in American portrait painting. While men were generally painted with realism, conventional idealization of women suffused female portraits with a misty languor.

Prosperous Americans, who had made money from trade, real estate, or industry, had become discriminating collectors. Patrons sent their protégés to Europe to study, but they also encouraged them to depict the native scene in their painting. Morse faced the problem that has always confronted the artist in America—whether to nourish one's talent in the friendlier environment of Europe, and then hopefully transplant the matured art to a less congenial America, or develop at home, facing initial discouragement in the belief that ultimately artist and public would meet on common ground. Morse observed that the expatriate artists returning to their American home would find themselves out of touch with native taste, but he was not discouraged. "Our own soil," said Morse, "must warm into life the seeds of native talent." In offering advice to young artists at the National Academy of the Arts of Design in New York, Morse used language similar to that of Horatio Greenough. A sound public taste, said Morse, must grow gradually, "urged onward by the constant action and reaction of the artists and the public upon each other."

In Morse's time artists had begun to overcome certain handicaps that had hampered them, in particular the conventional prudery which had prevented them from studying the nude. Although continuing to learn techniques from foreign masters, Americans were successfully challenging the prevailing attitude which valued the European over the native artist.

Many of the Americans who did study abroad—Italy was a favorite haunt for sculptors—gave to their work a pseudo classicism which, while fashionable for the moment, meant that it would not endure. An outstanding example of such art was Hiram Powers' sculptured figure, the Greek Slave, a female nude, which was enormously popular throughout the country. "People sit before it," said one reporter, "as silent as devotees at a religious ceremony." Spiritual in conception, it was, unfortunately, spiritless in execution. Another statue of this period, Greenough's George Washington, made the father of his country appear a Greek god. Greenough's conception was grandiose, but his contemporaries, though applauding a sculptured Greek Slave, found it difficult to accept their own Washington seated on a marble throne, part nude, legs covered by drapery, and sandals on his feet. What Greenough himself had said in criticism of American copies of Roman architecture might have served as a warning to his own practice in sculpture: "The want of an illustrious ancestry may be compensated, but the purloining of a coat of arms of a defunct family is intolerable."

★ A HOUSE OF ONE'S OWN

American architects in adapting classic models were less slavish than sculptors. Throughout the country, architects and plain carpenters, guided by builders' manuals, erected homes and public buildings incorporating characteristic Greek or Roman features, while at the same time revealing considerable originality. Banks, it is true, were imitations of the Parthenon, but luxurious plantation homes of the South displayed a freer adaptation of the Greek style. Their rich furnishings showing varied foreign influences—green and red Italian stone mantel pieces, French wallpaper, large gilded mirrors—made the wealthy planter's home a setting of luxury.

The Americans were not attached, however, to any one architectural style for long. In time the desire for Gothic design succeeded the passion for Greek. In an age when the medieval historical romances of Sir Walter Scott were part of everyone's reading it was natural that feudal castles and Gothic cathedrals should inspire architectural design for homes, churches, and public buildings. Gothic was followed by Tuscan and Norman styles, ending in what has been called the "Indescribable." The massive Smithsonian Institution in Washington looked like a twelfth-century feudal stronghold. Perhaps the most successful structures in Gothic design were the attractive churches planned by James Renwick and Richard Upjohn. Renwick's Grace Church and Upjohn's Trinity, built in New York in 1846, were harmonious and impressive.

James Fenimore Cooper, as well as other Americans, conceded that their country was not widely supplied with fine art, meaning beautiful pictures. But these observers claimed for their countrymen an artistic instinct in fashioning objects of utility. America's ploughs and axes and her graceful sailing vessels, they said, were more beautiful than anything of their kind in Europe.

The esthetic taste of the Jacksonian era, as expressed in its folk art, was inadequately appreciated by the generations that came soon after, but the twentieth century has learned to admire its charm again. A sense of beauty was not limited to an exclusive minority, but was shared by a far larger number of people than historians had formerly imagined.

★ SCIENCE

The characteristic emphasis on utilitarian values explains the willingness of state legislatures to appropriate funds for geologic surveys and studies of local mineral resources. The need for engineers and other trained personnel in America's expanding industry and transportation accounts for the establishment of the Rensselaer Polytechnic Institute at Troy, New York, in 1824. Its training in engineering was on a very high level, and its innovation in the use of laboratories for students set a model for later schools. Franklin Institute was founded in Philadelphia the same year as the Troy school. Slowly other institutions of higher learning adopted courses of study to prepare young men to become engineers.

In medicine the contribution of Americans to the alleviation of human ills was substantial. The most spectacular advance, the use of anesthesia in surgery, was hit upon by several Americans at about the same time, during the 1840's. It was then, too, that Dr. Oliver Wendell Holmes, more familiarly known as an essayist, proudly announced the control of puerperal fever.

A new generation of scientists, with a greater degree of specialization than their predecessors, devoted themselves to the advancement of knowledge. They were often professors, or other skilled men retained by the federal or state governments which subsidized their researches. "We believe," said Horace Greeley, "that the government, like every other intelligent agency, is bound to do good to the extent of its ability —that it ought actively to promote and increase the general well-being— that it should encourage and foster Industry, Science, Invention, Social, and physical Progress . . . Such is our idea of the sphere of Government."

The most famous example of federal support for scientific investigation was the United States Exploring Expedition. It was commanded by Lieutenant Charles Wilkes, and in the four years 1838–42 it surveyed hundreds of miles of Pacific coast line in North and South America, nearly 300 islands in the southern hemisphere, and established proof of an antarctic continent. Civilian scientists who accompanied Wilkes accumulated vast masses of data in mineralogy, geology, biology, and ethnology, which eventually were published. James Dwight Dana's contributions in geology were of special importance.

In the American environment no great theorist of the quality of Lyell, Darwin, or Faraday appeared. Tocqueville, the astute French observer of the American scene, noted that Americans had not contributed much to basic science (their spirit was "averse to general ideas"), though they had been quick to apply the findings of others to practical ends. "These very Americans," he said, "who have not discovered one of the general laws of mechanics have introduced into navigation an engine that changes the aspect of the world . . . If the democratic principle does not on the one hand induce men to cultivate science for its own sake, on the other it does enormously increase the number of those who do cultivate it . . . Permanent inequality of conditions leads men to confine themselves to the arrogant and sterile researches of abstract truths, whilst the social condition and institutions of democracy prepare them to seek the immediate and useful practical results of the sciences."

★ "THE LAND OF EXPERIMENT"

No one did more in these years than Benjamin Silliman to promote an interest in science among students and laymen. His career had started long before with his appointment, in his early twenties, to Yale's new chair of chemistry and natural history. In 1818 he brought out *The American Journal of Science and Arts,* and his editing made it an important scientific periodical. Through his journal, by textbook writing, and by lectures delivered throughout the country, he brought to many thousands of people knowledge of the latest discoveries in science. Silliman, along with other students of geology, especially the peer of them all, Sir Charles Lyell, was gradually weakening the prevailing belief in the story of creation as recorded in the Bible. While Silliman had not really an original mind he helped create an environment in which such minds might find sustenance and flourish.

Scientists of a superior order were soon to appear in the United States. Louis Agassiz, who had come from Switzerland in 1846, joined the Harvard faculty where he stayed for many years. During that time he made contributions of first importance to geology and zoology. He also succeeded in arousing the interest of laymen and scholars in many branches of natural science. The reputation of Agassiz has been unduly diminished because of his refusal to accept the Darwinian theory of evolution. It was a colleague of Agassiz at Harvard, Asa Gray, himself the most distinguished American botanist, who became the outstanding champion of Darwin in the United States when the latter's *Origin of the Species* was published just before the Civil War.

Scientists in southern states, notably the Le Conte brothers, John and Joseph, added to the rapidly accumulating studies in geology. A Virginian, Matthew F. Maury, was one of the world's most eminent oceanographers, and mariners remembered with gratitude his charts of winds and currents in the Atlantic. Maury, in fact, was credited with the creation of oceanography as a new science.

Perhaps the most original scientific mind of the time was Joseph Henry, the son of a laborer in Albany. Henry managed to get an education, and his genius showed itself in his experiments with the magnet. His early work, pursued independently of the researches of the great British scientist, Michael Faraday, led to the discovery of magneto-electricity. Soon Henry's countryman, the versatile Morse, was applying this knowledge in his development of the telegraph. Henry taught for a while at Princeton, and then, in 1846, went to Washington to head the newly established Smithsonian Institution.

James Smithson, a British citizen, had left a legacy of over £100,000 for the founding of an institution in Washington to increase and widely diffuse the sum of man's knowledge. Henry administered the bequest in a way that made the Smithsonian one of the most important centers in the country for the promotion of scientific researches. At the same time that Henry was named director of the Smithsonian, the Harvard Astronomical Observatory was enabled to make great strides in its work with its newly acquired giant telescope. Scientists all over the country felt the need for a national organization to promote higher standards in teaching and to stimulate further research. In 1847 the American Association for the Advancement of Science was founded to attain those objectives.

It was because of developments like these in the 1840's and in the next few years that George Ticknor was able to write with enthusiasm about educational progress in his country. In a letter to his friend Sir Charles Lyell, he told the British scientist of the establishment of the Museum of Comparative Zoology at Harvard: "I think such an institution will tend . . . to lay the foundation for a real university among us, where all the great divisions of human knowledge shall be duly represented and taught. I had a vision of such an establishment forty years ago," said Ticknor, "when I came fresh from . . . Göttingen; but that was too soon. Nobody listened to me. Now, however, when we have the best law school in the country, one of the best observatories in the world, a good medical school, and a good botanical garden, I think the Lawrence Scientific School, with the Zoological and Paleontological Museum, may push through a true university and bring up the Greek, Latin, mathematics, history, philosophy, etc. to their proper level. At least I hope so, and mean to work for it." Ticknor's optimism was, after many years of disappointment, finally justified. Daniel C. Gilman and Andrew D. White, his young contemporaries, were likewise making plans for raising the whole level of American university training. Their dreams were realized not long after the Civil War.

America "is the land of experiment," said Fredrika Bremer, the Swedish traveler; "its commencement in the field of experimental humanity reveals a boundless prospect as to what it may yet bring forth. In electricity, in steam navigation, in the discovery of anesthesia, America has pioneered." And all this, she said, "has been done in the early morning of the country's life, for . . . two centuries existence is merely as the morning hour; the day lies before it as its future. What will not this people accomplish during the day? Of a verity, greater things than these."

★ "UNTO US A MAN IS BORN"

It was with pride that Americans watched the maturing of their cultural life. This awareness reached a climax in Emerson's acclaim at the appearance of Whitman's *Leaves of Grass,* which owed much to the Concord sage himself. "I find it the most extraordinary piece of wit and wisdom that America has yet contributed," said Emerson to the author. "I give you joy of your free and brave thought. I have great joy in it. I find incomparable things said incomparably well." And to a friend, when sending a copy of *Leaves of Grass,* Emerson wrote proudly,

"Americans who are abroad can now return; unto us a man is born."

Whitman, with a joyous faith in democracy, chanted his devotion to his native soil, and called upon his fellow poets to join with him. "These states," he said, "conceal an enormous beauty, which native bards . . . should justify by their songs, tallying themselves to the immensity of the continent, to the fecundity of its people, to the appetite of a proud race, fluent and free."

While Whitman's faith in his countrymen seemed unclouded, many of his literary contemporaries looked at the social scene with foreboding. They were particularly wrought up over the dark blot of slavery. James Russell Lowell, in his *Biglow Papers,* indicted the Mexican War as a conspiracy on the part of slaveholders to expand the area of slavery. Whittier, with a deep religious intensity that upheld the tradition of Quaker hostility to slavery, made himself the poet of abolitionism. The mounting literary pressure against slavery reached the high point with Harriet Beecher Stowe's *Uncle Tom's Cabin,* in 1852. The Beecher branch of her family was strongly abolitionist, and in her home in Cincinnati she had learned something of the character of the slave system from Negro fugitives. Her novel was a great success, selling several hundred thousand copies in the United States.

In England Mrs. Stowe's book, with its deeply emotional appeal, had an even greater hold on the public mind. There, 1,500,000 copies were reported to have been sold within a year of British publication. *Uncle Tom's Cabin* was the greatest best-seller England had yet experienced, surpassing the initial success of the famed works of Scott or Dickens. The enormous appeal in England of Mrs. Stowe and Longfellow (the latter was also opposed to slavery) helps to explain the prevailing friendliness of the mass of Englishmen to the Northern side when the Civil War came.

★ THE AMERICAN RELIGION

The theme of equal membership in a common humanity, explicit in the politics of Jacksonian democracy, and implicit in the art and literature of that generation, also found expression in contemporary programs to organize world society. When Henry Wheaton, the distinguished writer on international law, returned to America after long service abroad, a leading periodical hailed him and his work: "It is . . . striking that the last great commentary on International Law is the work of an American. This is as it should be; for to our country and its principles is given the mission to reconstruct the mutual relations of all nations in the future, and to one of our republican creed, therefore, doth it especially belong to give new interpretation to the true law of nations."

The American Peace Society was another instrument of reformers anxious about world relationships. Its leading spirit was William Ladd, a retired shipowner in New England. The Society condemned all wars, and to further its program backed Ladd's proposal for a congress of nations and an international court of arbitration.

Even more insistent than Ladd, in his advocacy of international action to eliminate war, was Connecticut's "learned blacksmith" Elihu Burritt. The latter was a remarkable character who had taught himself to read many foreign languages, and whose learning comprehended a wide understanding of history and geography. Burritt, in his enthusiasm, called together the first world peace congress, in 1848, at Brussels. He organized the League of Universal Brotherhood, on an international basis, to renounce war. Articles written by him were placed in forty of Europe's important newspapers, reaching over a million readers. Probably no American had ever had so large a European audience. To him is given chief credit for creating a mass sentiment for peace.

Burritt always kept his eye on a scene larger than that of his native land. When some of his contemporaries were engaged in the movement to have the American Congress establish cheap, uniform postage rates in order to facilitate the diffusion of knowledge, Burritt immediately saw in the proposal an instrument of international action. He wanted the original plan enlarged so that immigrants could correspond more cheaply with their European homelands, and thus advance good will among nations. But he was also thinking that "ocean penny postage" would spread more generally knowledge of America's free political institutions among "the misruled multitudes of the Old World."

Burritt was ahead of his time in his plans for international co-operation, but in his belief that America had a mission to convert the world to its own superior way of life, he was at one with his generation. European visitors who traveled in the United States felt this sentiment running through the country like an electric shock. If they were sympathetic to American democracy they reacted favorably to it, and themselves became the channel through which the invigorating current flowed homeward.

More than any other idea in American life, this belief in the superiority of democracy cut across barriers of class and religion. It was *the* religion in the United States which transcended all sectarianism. Americans, said Tocqueville, "are separated from all other nations by a common feeling of pride. For the last fifty years no pains have been spared to convince the inhabitants of the United States that they constitute the only religious, enlightened, and free people. They perceive that, for the present, their own democratic institutions succeed, while those of other countries fail; hence they conceive an overweening opinion of their superiority. . ." Americans, to a man, subscribed to the confident statement of Oliver Wendell Holmes: "Not by aggression," he said, "but by the naked fact of existence we are an eternal danger and an unsleeping threat to every government that founds itself on anything but the will of the governed."

CHAPTER XVII

The North and the Cotton Kingdom

The quest for wider horizons was more energetic, and more successful, in the North than in the South. Northerners were more venturesome in their *doing,* as well as in their *thinking.* While idealists in Northern towns and villages planned new societies, restless business promoters built factory towns and fleets of ships to carry America's produce across the oceans of the world. On the wide land mass of the United States the first slight threads of the railroad web were expanding outward and filling in, like ribs on a lengthy skeleton. The whole country seemed to be on the move, from New England farm to factory or to western farm, from Virginia and Carolina to the southwest plantations.

From Europe came a flood of excited, eager immigrants to add their strength to the young nation. Herman Melville, watching the tide of emigrants swarming over the docks at Liverpool, exclaimed, "We are not a narrow tribe of men . . . whose blood has been debased in the attempt to ennoble it, by maintaining an exclusive succession among ourselves. No; our blood is as the flood of the Amazon, made up of a thousand noble currents all pouring into one. We are not a nation, so much as a world." Immigrants settled in the poorer quarters of fast growing cities, or they pushed out to join other land-hungry settlers on the still fresh plains and slopes and valleys of the north central states. The North and the West believed they had a firm grip not only on today but on tomorrow as well. The South's way of life seemed committed to an outmoded past.

★ MEN AT WORK

The rate of increase in the American population never ceased to inspire wonder at home and abroad. When Jackson became president about 12,500,000 people lived in the United States; in 1850 the numbers reached 23,000,000, and a decade later there were 31,000,000.

Immigrants had been swelling the population rapidly in the same period, rising from 2,800,000 by 1850 to almost double that over the next ten years. In the large cities the proportion of foreign born was striking. In New York in 1850, 45 per cent of its population was foreign born, with Ireland and Germany having furnished most of the immigrants. In Philadelphia about one in every four residents had come from Europe. The middle Atlantic states, with their large cities, and the Northwest with its farms and towns, were the two fastest growing regions in the country.

The wealth that New England, New York, and Pennsylvania had accumulated from their seagoing trade went into manufactures and improved land communications. The increasing power of industry and banking in the East, and the promise of greater wealth to come, drew the able and ambitious to the cities. In the earlier years of the Industrial Revolution in the United States labor was recruited from nearby native farm families. In later decades immigrant workers supplanted many of the native hands. Factory wages varied widely, ranging up to six dollars a week. Though wages in America were usually higher than in Europe, living costs in cities were proportionately high and housing conditions unsatisfactory. Sometimes a whole family lived crowded in a single room, which could offer little relaxation after a day of twelve or fourteen hours in the mill.

The product of the growing swarms of textile and iron-mill operatives had multiplied six times in the period from Jackson to Lincoln, reaching a figure of $330,000,000 in 1860. Ship tonnage, very profitable in these years, kept pace with the expansion of mill and agricultural productivity; the 500,000 tons of shipping in 1830 had increased to 5,000,000 in 1860. New York, which had long since become the chief port in the United States, shipped manufactures to the South and West, as well as to foreign countries. The Hudson and East River docks were "studded like a forest, with the lofty and graceful spars of the finest and fastest sailing ships that the world ever saw." Of the eastern manufactures, worth over $800,000,000 annually in the early 1850's, some went to the South and were exchanged for bills on London or Liverpool; and some went to the West which paid with its grain and cattle.

The concentration of industry and finance in the East could only be supported by a more intensive cultivation of the interior. The expansion of the railroad network was the answer. John Murray Forbes of Boston, and Commodore Vanderbilt of New York, were two of the spectacular business leaders of the time who built new railroads or consolidated existing routes. In the 1850's railway building took a phenomenal spurt; 4,000 miles were built east of Pittsburgh, 7,500 miles were built in the grain-rich Northwest, and 5,000 miles in the South. The promoters had, in addition to their own capital, government support. It was both federal and local, given in the form of grants of millions of acres of public lands. Money for United States railroads also came from Europe, $450,000,000 of it.

The economic picture throughout the country was generally bright in the period after the mid 1840's. Several good-crop years, the low tariff of the United States, and England's policy of free trade all contributed to America's unprecedented economic growth. The productive capacity of the United States, in industry and agriculture, was already large enough to meet the country's obligations to foreign capitalists and leave a supply adequate to meet most domestic needs. Thus the United States avoided the onerous weight placed on many newly opened areas in the world, which had the burden of surrendering a disproportionately large fraction of their output to meet the claims of foreign creditors. Residents of the United States enjoyed relative economic independence, along with political independence. Although other regions of the world, formerly in a colonial status like the United States, have won their political independence, they remained much longer in a condition of economic subservience to alien control.

★ FAREWELL TO EUROPE

It was the aliens themselves who, pouring into the country as immigrants, did much to build up America's economy so that it became less dependent on investments from Europeans. Immigration in the eighteenth century had been really slight, although an average of 4,000 a year looked large to contemporaries. In the period shortly before the Revolution the figures were sometimes double or triple that. After the Napoleonic wars the totals quickly mounted, and when 20,000 aliens arrived in 1818, it was clear that a new era had begun in American life. Germans, Irish, English, Scottish, and Scandinavians comprised the bulk of immigration in this period, with the Irish topping them all. A million Irish men, women, and children left for America in the period between 1815 and 1845. At first it was a relatively orderly transfer; within a few years it became a mass flight.

Everywhere in Europe it was becoming more and more difficult to earn a livelihood in field and factory. Irish farmers were being forced off the land because fields were given over to pasturage; German farmers were discouraged by crop failures and by their inability to compete with large landowners. In Britain and in Germany, due to the expansion of the factory system, handicraftsmen found their pay diminishing while their workday lengthened. Irritating religious and social discrimination (which was especially true in Norway and Sweden) added to the general discontent. There were revolutions on the continent in 1830 and 1848, but they failed to improve matters, and disillusionment was a final spur to thousands to abandon the Old World.

Where to go? was a question easily answered for the vast majority. It was the United States which had been widely publicized. Gazetteers, emigrant guidebooks, travel accounts, and newspapers informed Europeans of New World conditions. Workingmen's clubs discussed the pros and cons of emigration. Emigrant letters, "America letters," they were called, and the visits of migrants returned from America were the most powerful forces influencing the decision of Old World families.

Pressure was exerted even in the remotest European villages by shipping companies and their agents whose interest was in profiting from the passenger traffic. Inn-keepers, labor contractors, and land speculators joined in the profitable business of rounding up emigrants for America. Posters, handbills, and other forms of emigrant literature advertised the special attractions of Wisconsin or Iowa or Michigan. The pull from America was always stronger than the push from Europe, and the pull from the New World was naturally more powerful in times of American prosperity. Fluctuations in the rate of capital investment in Europe, which affected the job situation there, also determined the volume of emigration to America. The heavier the investment at home the more numerous were the jobs; a fall in local capital outlay in Europe lessened economic activity and impelled emigration.

Dispirited men in many a European village were shaken from their dull apathy by news from the world overseas. English villagers, bitter and frustrated, experienced a remarkable transformation when a letter came from one of their former neighbors praising his new home in Iowa, and urging his old friends to join him. "The letter was read in almost every cottage," a sympathetic observer noted. "It was read at the village inn and at the Methodist Chapel every Sunday until it was nearly worn out. The Lord had now opened a door of escape. Special prayer-meetings were held to know the Lord's will, which was that they should go. For several weeks nothing was thought or talked about but going to America. The whole village was at work in packing and mending clothes. A farewell service was held in the Methodist Chapel . . . and the services lasted through night till daybreak. The following evening, in the glorious springtime of May, some thirty-three men, women, and children knelt down in the street and, after a short prayer-meeting, marched through the village singing hymns. The whole village turned out, and many accompanied them for miles. 'Goodbye: God bless you!' rang from every cottage door . . . Prayers . . . were regularly offered up for the exiles until news came of their safe arrival and settlement. This induced others in batches of threes and fours, to follow for several years."

Edwin Bottomley was one of the emigrant Englishmen in 1842. He had left to save his children from following the path of their elders as factory workers. Ultimately reaching Wisconsin, he acquired his eighty acres. After hard but satisfying work, the future he desired for his family seemed assured. "Thank God," he wrote back to England, "I have not to rouse my children at the sound of a bell from their beds and Drag them through the pelting storm of a Dark winters morning to earn a small pitance at a factory."

Individuals, families, parts of villages, and sometimes almost the entire local community abandoned the ancient homesteads. High wages and easily acquired lands were irresistible magnets. When it was reported in Norway, in the 1830's, that wages in America were up to a dollar a day in winter, and twice the amount in summer, and that servant girls earned up to two dollars a week, Norwegians were startled by the contrast with their own low wages. A servant girl in Telemarken then received a maximum of one dollar a month, a laborer about thirty cents a day, and a skilled workman not quite forty cents a day.

Migration to America shook up the whole Atlantic world, causing a re-examination of the structure of life in the Old World. Scandinavian reformers frankly acknowledged that they used the issue as a "vehicle for social legislation." In Sweden one writer observed that "to discuss Swedish emigration is the same as to discuss 'Sweden': there is hardly a single political, social or economic problem in our country, which has not been conditioned, directly or indirectly, by the phenomenon of emigration." Leaders of workingmen hoped that large scale emigration would compel the upper classes to more thoughtful realization of the value of labor.

Emigrants from Europe's interior, most of them Germans, found their way out by freight wagon or by boat down the Rhine to North Sea ports. Wagons that trucked American cotton southward from Le Havre returned from Basel and Strasbourg loaded with brightly clad emigrants for vessels bound for New Orleans. From this Gulf port the newcomers spread up the Mississippi Valley. In the main, however, Germans and others entered the United States by way of New York, arriving from Bremen and Hamburg.

Some went by way of Liverpool, where Herman Melville watched them fascinated. "Old men, tottering with age, and little infants in arms; laughing girls in bright-buttoned bodices, and astute, middle-aged men [smoking pipes] would be seen mingling together in crowds of five, six and seven or eight hundred in one ship." In the evening they "gathered on the forecastle to sing and pray. And it was exalting to listen to their fine ringing anthems, reverberating among the crowded shipping, and rebounding from the lofty walls of the docks. Shut your eyes, and you would think you were in a cathedral."

These sober Germans, said Melville, were counted among America's "most orderly and valuable" additions from a foreign population. They settled in the Old Northwest, making Wisconsin a "colony" of Germany. They settled in the cities of the Middle West and along the Atlantic seaboard. Revolution in Germany in 1848 sent a group of intellectuals to the United States, where they strove to maintain their familiar cultural vitality. These refugees of revolution created "a little German world" in St. Louis, and introduced Hegel to the Middle West. Carl Schurz best typified the group, reminding fellow Germans to retain the best of their Old World heritage, yet urging them to partake freely of the New.

Mixed with anticipation over the promise of the New World were regret and justification for leaving the Old. One Norwegian poem expressed these mingled feelings:

> Farewell, Norway, and God bless thee.
> Stern and severe wert thou always, but as
> A mother I honor thee, though thou
> Skimped my bread.

Irishmen had been migrating to America in larger numbers after the War of 1812. Fares fluctuated; in the 1830's the rate from England (most embarked at Liverpool) was £5 or less. Irishmen found cheaper passage aboard returning Canadian lumber vessels which took them to Quebec for £2 10s. For even less, $5, an Irishman was able to reach Newfoundland if he slept on deck of a fishing boat and ate salt cod. Irish emigrants normally did not remain in Canada; jobs were more plentiful in the United States. An Irish emigrant song told of the American land where:

> They say there's bread and work for all,
> And the sun shines always there.

The majority who were leaving were Protestants, from the north of Ireland. By the middle 1830's, however, larger numbers of Catholic Irish were leaving for the New World. This emigration had none of the frantic quality that marked later flight. The emigrants had some money and, in general, were a group superior to their famine-driven countrymen of the late 1840's.

Fleeing from starvation when potato crops failed, Irishmen now filled the westbound ships. Government, private philanthropy, and landlords anxious to be freed of the weight of human misery which bore heavily on local taxation all contributed to send Irishmen by the thousands to America. Funds for passage money after 1850 for the most part were remittances sent home by emigrants already established in the New World. By 1863 £20,000,000 had been sent home by these emigrants who had scrimped and saved this large sum from their earnings.

Reports from overseas were optimistic. Wages were high, often two or three times what they were in Ireland; famine was unknown in the United States; and disease even in the city slums was less widespread than in stricken Ireland. A laborer, and most Irishmen became laborers, lived longer in America. Even when the pot of gold at the end of the New World rainbow turned out to be a delusion there was still justification enough for the journey; hope was given to millions whose vocabulary had lost the word.

★ THE NEW WORLD

The leading British emigrant port was Liverpool, though many Irish left from Cork and Galway and many Scots boarded ship at Glasgow or Greenock. On crowded freighters, of less that 400 tons generally, emigrants were herded into cramped steerage quarters. Conditions on sailing vessels were not much different from those in the eighteenth century, the ships were foul smelling and vermin-ridden; passage usually required six weeks or more. The sight of land was welcome indeed! By 1850, 75 per cent of the immigrants were entering through the great port of New York.

Adventure and misadventure lay before the new arrivals in the Empire City. Sharp-eyed "runners" for hotels and boarding houses, and agents for inland transportation companies badgered the bewildered immigrant, who was at the mercy of fellow countrymen fattening on the ignorance of the "greenhorn." The flood of immigrants in the 1840's, and after, overwhelmed the slight resources of churches and immigrant societies that had tried to give some aid to newcomers. By the middle of the century, however, some of the worst abuses in immigrant boarding houses and among transportation agents had come under the ban of New York.

From the port city immigrants scattered to the West or to other urban centers. Irish immigrants, most of whom had just enough money to pay for the ocean voyage, rarely left the cities; only about 10 per cent became farmers. Rapidly expanding industries absorbed thousands of immigrants who went to work in the garment trade, and in construction work of all kinds—new city streets, water supply systems, house-building, canals, railroads, and shipyards. The miles of wharves in New York bustled with activity. Here the many tongues of the earth mingled in noisy babel.

The living quarters of most laborers, skilled and unskilled, were ramshackle tenements or remodeled private homes into which they were crowded at high rentals. Backyard privies were a menace to health, and were responsible for the rapid spread of epidemics that cut a grim reaper's swath through congested cities. Thousands of Irish and German workingmen lived in "shanty towns" on the outskirts of more thickly settled areas. In these semirural surroundings squatters, paying neither rent nor taxes, kept cows, pigs, goats, and chickens. The line of demarcation between town and country in the middle of the nineteenth century was not yet very sharp. Even in cities water was still taken from a well or from a nearby street pump.

★ "GO AHEAD"

The great influx of aliens, while bringing strength to America, also added strains on the social structure. The Irish immigration came more and more from Catholic Ireland, and many of the Germans were also Catholic. The United States was overwhelmingly Protestant, and the traditional tension between the two faiths was reflected in many controversies. Their mutual adjustment was often difficult, and differing social customs aggravated their relations. When frolicking German picnickers upset the sober calm of a Puritan Sunday with their banging of glasses and their constant calls for beer, native Americans felt that their way of life was deliberately insulted.

Raspiness in social relations slowly wore away when the old residents and the new learned to tolerate each other's differences. Foreign language newspapers helped ease the aliens' transition to American life. The immigrant, from his first day, was torn between the different cultures of the Old World and the New. Foreign languages were Americanized and English was yoked to alien tongues; "freier lunch" and "stumpf-speeches" were familiar expressions to German-Americans. Children of immigrant parents shared the cultural inheritance of the Old and the New World, and in time, abandoning the Old, they were merged with the native population.

Aliens and native workmen were rivals for jobs but they were allies, too, in the labor organizations which were beginning to show strength in the pre-Civil War days. Workingmen were more successful in improving their status through social reforms than by changes in their working conditions. Mechanics lien laws and abolition of imprisonment for debt marked great progress for workingmen. The length of the usual work day was, however, little altered, and wages were more likely to be affected by general business conditions than by union pressure. For several years after the panic of 1837, for example, unemployment was widespread and wages were deeply cut, 30 per cent or more. From 1843 on to the end of the decade, wages were stabilized, but the estimated cost of living in New York rose almost 50 per cent. Wages continued to lag behind prices well into the Civil War period.

The realities of life in the United States often bruised the unprepared immigrant who was more vulnerable precisely because he believed in American ideals. Evidences of class distinction in Brahmin Boston or Knickerbocker New York bewildered and angered him. One disillusioned worker from England thought social distinctions were more rigidly enforced in the United States than elsewhere. "Money is the be-all and the end-all in the States," he said. "With it you are everything, without it nothing. The working man is as much hemmed in the iron circle of his class as with us [in England]; the petty store-keeper even looks down on him, and the 'dignity of labor' is both disbelieved in and ridiculed." This disappointed worker was obviously one of a minority, for Europeans continued to throng with confidence to the New World.

Sprawling cities and farms carved from the wilderness and the midwest plain pulsed with nervous energy. Tocqueville thought that Americans were more deeply interested in commerce than in politics: "When I contemplate the ardour with which Americans prosecute commercial enterprise, the advantages which befriend them, and the success of their undertakings, I cannot refrain from believing that they will one day become the first maritime power of the globe. They are born to rule the seas as the Romans were to conquer the world."

"Go ahead" was a national slogan, and the Yankee best typified its drive. The Yankee, said an admiring foreigner, "is a young man (no matter if he be old) who makes his own way in the world in full reliance on his own power, stops at nothing, shrinks from nothing, finds nothing impossible, tries everything . . . hopes everything . . . and comes out of everything . . . ever the same . . . If he is unsuccessful, he says 'Try again!' 'Go ahead!' and he begins over again." His energy was apparently endless, "always working, building, starting afresh or beginning something new, always developing, extending himself or his country."

The restlessness, the teeming urban life, the ambition, the endless planning of new enterprises, the dissatisfaction that motivated many in the North seemed to make of that region an unstable community. But its kind of instability was proof of its growth, both material and spiritual, for the alien and the native had this in common—the quest for tomorrow was in their eyes.

★ THE COTTON KINGDOM

The South seemed less unquiet than the North, though its plantation owners were as active as Northerners in expanding their enterprises. Outside of the older areas of Virginia and the Carolinas, where class stratification was well developed, ambitious men in newer Southern communities moved up the social ladder as readily as their Northern contemporaries. Nevertheless the impression left with observers was that the mass of Southerners, in contrast with Northerners, seemed to accept their allotted station in life with patient resignation. Society in the South was apparently far less fluid than it was in the North.

The surface orderliness of Southern life was less the sign of social health than it was of upper-class resistance to change. Inquiry was not encouraged in Southern society. It disturbed the status quo, and Southerners, committed to a way of life based on slavery, were guided by a sure instinct in resisting any social change. In the region that had been Jefferson's home democratic principles had lost their strength, and he himself had become a dim memory.

In a perceptive comparison of Northern and Southern characteristics Olmsted remarked that Southern aristocrats "are invariably politicians, and they generally rule in all political conventions and caucuses. They are brave, in the sense that they are reckless of life, and they are exceedingly fond of the excitement of the hazard of life. They are as careless of the life of others as of themselves. They are especially ambitious of military renown. . . ." The Southerner, said the New York journalist, was "passionate, and labors passionately, fitfully, with the energy and strength of anger, rather than of resolute will. He fights rather than works to carry his purpose. He has the intensity of character which belongs to Americans in general. . . . But he has much less curiosity than the Northerner; less originating genius, less inventive talent, less patient and persevering energy. And I think this all comes from his want of aptitude for close observation and his dislike for application to small details. And this, I think, may be reasonably supposed to be mainly the result of habitually leaving all matters not either of grand and exciting importance, or of immediate consequence to his comfort, to his slaves, and of being accustomed to see them slighted or neglected as much as he will, in his indolence, allow them to be by him."

The Cotton Kingdom stretched a thousand miles from South Carolina to Texas. From south to north it averaged some 200 miles in Carolina and over 600 in the Mississippi Valley. The region was heavily wooded, supplying vast quantities of lumber, and its numerous rivers provided easy transportation of bulky crops. The lower South had easy access to ports on the Atlantic or the Gulf, and the river wharves were solid with tightly packed bales of cotton.

Great quantities of corn, wheat, and livestock, as well as cotton, were raised in the South. The lengthy growing season permitted two or even three crops of vegetables a year. New arable lands were secured by clearing away brambles and heavy undergrowth, and "deadening" trees by girdling the trunk. The dead trees, standing tall and naked, with brittle branches broken and scattered everywhere by the wind, gave the scene a lonely look. Southerners, like Northerners, ravaged the land in their hurry for quick profits. Isolated voices warned of the dangers of careless agricultural practices and urged conservation, but they were literally crying in the wilderness.

The relentless pressure for more land on which to grow cotton crowded the Indians off their preserves and sent them, despoiled and displaced, to the area west of the Red River. In the vast domain of the Cotton Kingdom the labor force was chiefly made up of Negro slaves. The lower South recruited its slave labor from the surplus in Virginia, Maryland, and the southeastern states. It was not surplus Negroes exclusively who made the journey southwestward; thousands of whites, with or without slaves, left the older, worn-out lands of the East for the glittering El Dorado. Throughout the lower South the impact of men and ideas, nurtured in South Carolina, was a dominant fact.

A large number of whites with limited means forsook the environment of the older South to settle across the Ohio in the Northwest where the future looked brighter. Though they were then out of the South, the South was not out of them, and these hundreds of thousands (a half million by 1850) gave to the parts of Ohio, Indiana, and Illinois where they settled a distinctly Southern flavor.

The character of the white population in the South had not changed much since colonial days. British stock predominated, though there were sizable elements of Germans in the back country who, by merging with the majority, had lost everything of their identity save their names. The French in South Carolina preserved their accent and their names, which alone reminded them of an ancient homeland. Of the flood of immigrants who inundated the North, not more than a trickle reached the South; only one out of nine immigrants went to the Southern states, where most of them settled in cities. Good land was not cheap in the South, industries to absorb workers had scarcely developed, and the system of slavery alienated them, for they quickly learned that all manual labor was thus degraded.

Only in New Orleans was there something of the polyglot atmosphere found in Northern cities. People of Spanish, French, and British descent had mingled their blood, and to this mixture was added that of newcomers—Germans, Irish, and Italians. Free Negroes, themselves owners of slaves, joined white gentlemen in directing the affairs of the community. The flavor of the city's life—its manners, its music, its theater, its cosmopolitanism—gave it a European aspect. Charles Lyell, the famous English geologist, was in New Orleans in 1846. "We might indeed have fancied that we were approaching Paris," he wrote, "but for the Negroes and mulattoes, and the large verandahs reminding us that the windows required protection from the sun's heat." Within the next few years Northerners came into the city in greater numbers and the Yankees gave to New Orleans a different tone.

★ THE SOUTHERN ARISTOCRACY

Economic power and community leadership in the South had become vested in about 4,000 families, who possessed the choice lands. At the top of the social pyramid a thousand families, in 1850, had a total income of $50,000,000 annually, which was not much less than the total income of all the remaining families in the Cotton Kingdom. The practice of cotton magnates was to divide their great landholdings into units; a thousand acres worked by a hundred slaves was judged an efficient arrangement. The Hairston family had 1,700 slaves on plantations scattered in Virginia, Alabama, and Mississippi.

In the vicinity of Natchez the inquiring Olmsted was being informed of the locality's wealth by one of the less prosperous inhabitants. "I asked how rich the sort of men were of whom he spoke."

"Why, sir, from a hundred thousand to ten million."

"Do you mean that between here and Natchez there are none worth less than a hundred thousand dollars?"

"No, sir. . . . Why, any sort of plantation is worth a hundred thousand dollars." The slaves alone, he said, would sell for that.

"How many negroes are there on these plantations?"

"From fifty to a hundred."

"Never over one hundred?"

"No; when they've increased to a hundred they always divide them; stock another plantation. There are sometimes three or four plantations adjoining one another, with an overseer for each, belonging to the same man. But that isn't general. In general, they have to strike off for new land."

"How many acres will a hand tend here?"

"About fifteen—ten of cotton, and five of corn; some pretend to make them tend twenty."

"And what is the usual crop?"

"A bale and a half to the acre on fresh land and in the bottom. From four to eight bales to a hand they generally get; sometimes ten and better, when they are lucky."

"A bale and a half on fresh land? How much on old?"

"Well you can't tell. Depends on how much it's worn and what the season is so much. Old land, after a while, isn't worth bothering with."

"Do most of these large planters who live so freely, anticipate their crops as the sugar planters are said to—spend the money, I mean, before the crop is sold?"

"Yes, sir, and three and four crops ahead generally."

"Are most of them the sons of rich men? are they old estates?"

"No, sir; lots of them were overseers once."

"Have you noticed whether it is a fact that these large properties seldom continue long in the same family? Do the grandsons of wealthy planters often become poor men?"

"Generally the sons do. Almost always their sons are fools, and soon go through with it." "They drink hard and gamble, and of course that brings them into fights."

Acreage and slaves were the measure of wealth in the South, and cotton was the money crop which enabled the planter to get more of each. In 1850 the cotton crop was 2,500,000 bales, and thereafter for the next decade it rapidly increased until it had doubled within ten years. The value of slaves had steadily mounted; in the late 1850's a healthy young Negro sold for $1,500 or more. In these circumstances planters were complacently rich. But they grieved over injustices, real as well as fancied.

Southern planters felt they were being exploited by Northern shippers and merchants who handled most of the South's exports. The North supplied the South with its manufactured goods, and thus was able to reap an additional profit from trade with the Southern states. Sales of cotton, rice, and sugar reached almost $120,000,000, in 1850, but bank deposits in the southern region totaled only about $20,000,000. It is true that much of the South's profits was ploughed back into additional acreage and the purchase of more slaves. Southerners were, nevertheless, increasingly conscious of the disparity between the great value of commodities they shipped out and the little that remained for the growers. Planters complained that tariffs, freight, commissions and other charges by Northern merchants took a huge slice out of the earnings of Southern agriculture.

The towns of the South, even busy New Orleans, seemed scarcely more than transfer points for outgoing crops and incoming goods. The increased wealth of the South thus appeared an illusion, and disconsolate planters began to speak of themselves as mere custodians of their own crop returns for the Northerners who ultimately were the chief beneficiaries of the work of the Cotton Kingdom. The Kingdom had shrunk to a colony in a large commercial empire whose capital was New York.

★ THE PLAIN FOLK

In the Southern back country and in the hilly regions where land was cheaper were hundreds of thousands of the plain folk whose way of life was remote from that of the wealthy planter or the sophisticated townsmen of Charleston or New Orleans. But wherever located, on rich soil in Mississippi, or on thin, eroded slopes, or in coastal ports and inland towns, the white population of the South was committed to slavery as a way of life. The owner of many slaves wanted more; the owner of a few wanted many; the owner of none hoped for some, or at least consoled himself with the belief that Negro slavery guaranteed his own superiority as a white human being. Only in isolated mountain areas was there a small number of whites who knew little of slavery and cared less for the prosperous planter. Hunting and fishing were what they preferred; they raised some corn which was often distilled into strong drink. On the sandy soils of the piney woods, and in the rugged highlands, herdsmen and hunters lived a life apart from the slave economy. Their language and practice were democratic and their idol was still Thomas Jefferson.

Some two-thirds of Southern whites, in 1850, had no direct association with slavery, and their share of the community's wealth was very slight. The small farmer, either owner or tenant, and the squatter in the piney woods, consumed most of what they produced. From their limited surplus they might send to market a bale of cotton, some pork, poultry, and eggs. Oxcarts or creaking wagons jouncing behind dispirited nags over rutted roads hauled to market the produce which was exchanged for Yankee clothes and notions, or some coffee or molasses.

"Crackers" or "hill-billies" in northern Georgia or northern Alabama might own a few slaves, and by joint labor of whites and blacks a few bales of cotton were raised and shipped to market along with some wheat and corn. Southern agriculture actually produced more than its

famous staples; it raised enough food to feed itself and even had a surplus. But as the price of cotton advanced in the 1850's large planters
raised less food and more of their chief cash crop.

A familiar impression of the old South remains with most of us. It
pictures a region divided into aristocrats and slaves, the first living in
placid, tree-shaded mansions, the graceful women in crinolines pos-
ing on curving staircases, while the Negroes sing at their work in the
cotton fields. For the few dominant whites life was almost as pleasant
as romantic memories have recorded. "Willow Dale," for example, a
Mississippi plantation on the Yazoo River, did have a fine residence
shaded by beautiful trees; and the honeysuckle did climb over the lat-
tice-work on the well-house close by. Here the planter made eating a
ceremony; he did not bolt his food as so many Northerners did. "Leisure
and ease," said a Yankee visitor, "are inmates of his roof." Here young
men and women played at being medieval knights and ladies, and their
literary god was Sir Walter Scott.

The picture of the South as a whole, however, was that of a region
of small, independent farmers, several millions of them. They cultivated
their 200 acres or less themselves or with the help of a few slaves, working with them side by side. This class of yeomen for the most part owned
their lands; tenantry was infrequent. But in the decade of the 1850's
the extension of the large plantation economy made life much more
difficult for the independent yeomen. They moved away to Arkansas
and Texas, their covered wagons, filled with women, children, and old
folks, and "household plunder," stirring up the dust on the roads that
led westward.

A Southerner from an older region in Alabama grieved over the desolation in Madison County, his birthplace. "In traversing that county," he
said, "one will discover numerous farm-houses, once the abode of industrious and intelligent freemen, now occupied by slaves, or tenantless,
deserted, and dilapidated; he will observe fields, once fertile, now unfenced, abandoned, and covered with those evil harbingers—foxtail and
broom-sedge; he will see the moss growing on the mouldering walls of
once thrifty villages; and will find 'one only master grasps the whole
domain' that once furnished happy homes for a dozen white families.
Indeed, a country in its infancy, where, fifty years ago, scarce a forest
tree had been felled by the axe of the pioneer, is already exhibiting the
painful signs of senility and decay, apparent in Virginia and the Carolinas;
the freshness of its agricultural glory is gone; the vigour of its youth is
extinct, and the spirit of desolation seems brooding over it."

An important element in the South was the large group of semi-
nomadic herdsmen who pastured their cattle on unsettled land out to

the edge of the Indian frontier. Their homes were the rudest of huts, and they tilled the soil for a few vegetables and just enough corn to make their bread and whiskey. On the lowest level of white society in the South a class of "poor whites" lived a shiftless life on barren ground, demoralized by aristocratic contempt and ravaged by hookworm and malaria.

Most yeomen lived in log houses, "dog-run" cabins, made up of two rooms separated by a "breezeway," all under a single roof. The crude door creaked on its hinges as it scraped across the floor. Cooking was done at a large fireplace, with pots hung on cranes. Furniture and soap were homemade in these simple residences, and luxuries unknown.

In rural districts the church, whether small log house or elaborate building, was the community's center. Outside the large cities where Episcopalians and Catholics were numerous, most Southerners were members of Methodist, Presbyterian, Baptist, and Church of Christ congregations, whose preachers were powerful evangelists. Revivals and annual camp meetings were the great events in the community. Hymn singing and long sermons whipped up the vast crowd into hysterical tension. This was their release in a daily life of great toil and little return. In their normal relationships the plain folk were kindly and friendly, practicing a generous hospitality. "There was this great advantage," wrote one who had grown up among them, "that while none were very wealthy few were poor enough to suffer actual want."

Even relatively large landowners generally lived in unpretentious homes. A Georgian, in a retrospective view, described his grandfather's plantation, which had over eighty slaves. "The mansion in which we lived was a very modest affair," he said. "It did not, in the least, resemble a Grecian Temple which had been sent into exile, and which was striving, unsuccessfully, to look at ease among corn-cribs, cow-pens, horse-stables, pig-styes, chicken-houses, negro cabins, and worm-fenced cotton fields. It did not perch upon the top of the highest hill for miles around and browbeat the whole community with its arrogant self-assertion. No; ours was just a plain house and none too large . . . built out of . . . timbers torn from the heart of the long-leaf Georgian pine." In his religion, said the affectionate grandson, the old man "was a non-combatant, which is saying a good deal, for in those days most men were either rampant Methodists or militant Baptists."

In Olmsted's travels through Louisiana he met a transplanted Northerner who had formerly lived in western New York, in the Genesee Valley. "I asked him if he thought, among the intelligent class of farmers and planters, people of equal property lived more happily in New York or Louisiana. He replied immediately, as if he had carefully considered the topic, that, with some rare exceptions, farmers worth forty thousand dollars lived in far greater comfort, and enjoyed more refined and elegant leisure, than planters worth three hundred thousand, and that farmers of the ordinary class, who laboured with their own hands, and were worth some six thousand dollars, in the Genesee Valley, lived in far greater comfort, and in all respects more enviably, than planters worth forty thousand dollars in Louisiana. The contrast was especially favourable to the New York farmer, in respect to books and newspapers. He might travel several days, and call on a hundred planters, and hardly see in their houses more than a single newspaper apiece, in most cases; perhaps none at all: nor any books, except a Bible, and some government publications, that had been franked to them through the post-office, and perhaps a few religious tracts or school-books."

Despite the revised picture we now have of the class structure of the old South, the fact remains that a few thousand families dominated the region's life, for by their monopoly of the richest soil they garnered the major share of the money crops. It was this relatively small group which held political office, dictated the affairs of the local community, and spoke for the South in national councils. "There are great individuals in the Southern States," said a visitor from Europe, "but no great community, no united aspiring people."

★ THE SLAVE

Though cotton was king in the South (it was worth $102,000,000 in 1850), the value of other cash crops was not negligible. In that same year sugar, mainly from Louisiana's plantations, sold for nearly $15,-000,000 and rice for $2,600,000. The money crop of Virginia, North Carolina, and Kentucky was tobacco, worth $10,000,000 in 1850. Much of it went to the lower South; Southerners, both "quality" and the masses, chewed tobacco or "dipped" snuff to excess. Caravans of covered wagons trucked the manufactured tobacco south from Richmond to reach an eager market.

A cash crop which men preferred not to talk about was the surplus of slaves sold from the upper South or the older eastern states to the labor hungry plantations of the Southwest. In the thirty years after 1830 Virginia sent out some 300,000 slaves, Maryland and Kentucky about 75,000 each. In that same period, South Carolina exported about 170,000, North Carolina about 100,000. Missouri and Tennessee sent out smaller numbers. All told these states were exporting annually about 25,000 slaves. Traders, with expert eye, appraised the Negroes offered for sale, making sure their hands were quick and strong for picking cotton. "Prime field hands," men and women in their early twenties,

were the first pick. They were sent to the lower South by boat or overland, in slave coffles, the men manacled, the women and children un-
chained.

The ache of broken family ties found echo in Whittier's "Farewell of
a Virginia Slave Mother":

> Gone, gone,—sold and gone
> To the rice-swamps dank and lone,
> From Virginia's hill and waters:
> Woe is me, my stolen daughters!

A noted Virginian who had heard the greatest orators of his time once
remarked that no speech had ever so moved him as that of a slave; "She
was a mother, and her rostrum was the auction-block."

Negroes were the most important labor force in the South. Their
work was not confined to agriculture. To a large extent theirs was the
brawn that built the railroads of the South. They worked too in urban
communities, at almost every occupation, skilled and unskilled. The
overwhelming mass of Negroes were slaves, though in 1850 almost
240,000 in Southern states were free. A number, nearly as large, lived
in the North, mainly in the big cities. In the cotton region the Negro
population almost equaled the white, but the slaves were distributed
very unevenly. By 1860 more than half the slaves were living on plantations with more than twenty Negroes; one-fourth of them were on
units with over fifty slaves.

Large plantations, with numerous slaves, were more generally the
rule in the cotton states than in the upper South. In the lower South
about two-fifths of the Negroes belonged to lesser slaveowners (those
possessing less than twenty slaves); in the upper South the figures were
reversed, three-fifths of the Negroes there were owned by the lesser
slaveowners. In general where farms and plantations were smaller, and
contact with the master more direct, the conditions of slavery were less
harsh than on the larger units where the overseer exacted the fullest
expenditure of slave energy. A Negro "driver" with a big blacksnake
whip cracked it over dark, sweaty backs of the men to see that they
kept up the steady pace of work. An overseer was judged by the production he could show at the season's end, and the health of slaves
was of little concern to him. Excessive labor, particularly in hot weather,
took a heavy toll of slaves who fainted or died of exhaustion in the
fields. For the most dangerous and unhealthy work white laborers,
usually Irishmen hired by the day, were occasionally substituted for
valuable Negro field hands. For the most part, however, planters depended upon their own labor force for every type of task.

The slave was not without defense against excessive pressure. Passive resistance took the form of slowed pace; and planters ordinarily bowed to this aggravating, but uncontrollable, stratagem. Negroes feigned illness to lessen the work load or escape it entirely. Frederick Law Olmsted, a Northern journalist in the South, believed that the average slave did only half as much work as a farm hand in the North, though other evidence suggests that the unfree worked as well as the free. Cruel masters, inflamed by anger, sometimes destroyed their valuable slave property by beating or shooting, but such extreme behavior was rare. Whipping was very common, however, and the scars it left on the minds of Negroes lasted longer than the marks on their bodies. Theft and arson were much feared weapons in slave hands. On a number of occasions slaves organized revolts (which brought swift retribution) or ran away from the South, but the overwhelming majority of them lived out their lives in resigned or grudging acceptance of an old, established way of life. In their plaintive songs they expressed the sorrow that lay heavy upon them. The master's power was absolute over his chattels and seemed unchallengeable.

The routine and conditions of life for the Negro, in some respects, did not differ greatly from those of the neighboring white farmer, always excepting the priceless element of freedom. Many white farmers lived in log cabins no better than the quarters of slaves. Their food was often similar, though the diet of Negroes was probably more monotonous. Forbidden to have firearms, with which they could kill wild game, they were generally unable to supplement their regular diet of corn meal and salt pork or bacon. Blacks and whites usually went barefoot in the summer.

Vital statistics, though kept carelessly, showed a heavier incidence of disease among Negroes than among whites. More burdensome labor, greater exposure, and poorer medical care all contributed to shorten the life expectancy of Negroes as compared with whites. Infant mortality was heavy for both races, but among Negroes it was frequently twice that of whites. Despite the grievous Negro mortality rates, the slave population of the South grew, by natural increase, about 23 per cent each decade between 1830 and 1860. Earlier marriages of slaves and more numerous children per marriage accounted for that fact. As Professor Kenneth M. Stampp observed, "a slave mother gave birth to two or three babies in order that one might grow to be a 'prime hand' for her master." *

Whether slavery was profitable or not has been debated by many historians. Louisiana sugar planters, who were among the most prosperous

* Kenneth M. Stampp, *The Peculiar Institution* (New York: Alfred A. Knopf, 1956), p. 321.

of all plantation owners, said their cost for food and clothing for each slave was as little as $30 a year. And yet it could be argued that slave labor, though unpaid, was expensive. Many Negroes, because of age or illness, were unfit for hard work; a disproportionate number of slaves were taken from field work and assigned to tasks as domestics. Taking all factors into account, however, slave labor on well-managed plantations was efficient and profitable.

It has been maintained that slavery had beneficial aspects as a transitional status between barbarism and civilization. The Negro slave learned something of the technology of western society. In exchange he made contributions of his own to the culture of the western world through his music and humor. House slaves and the mechanically apt did have better opportunities than their fellows to rise above the level of brute existence. But for the overwhelming majority of slaves there was little promise of moving on to "civilization." The South had abandoned early beliefs in the transitional status of slavery. Slavery in fact had become for Southerners a permanent institution, the very keystone of their civilization.

★ SOUTHERN INDUSTRY AND COMMERCE

Owners of slaves often hired them out for a fixed fee to other farmers or to employers in city shops and factories. Enterprising Southerners, notably William Gregg of South Carolina, saw great advantages for their region in industrialization. Cotton mills, they said, should be brought to the South; planters "have been paying toll to the English mill long enough." "Spindles and looms must be brought to the cotton fields. This is the true location of this powerful assistant of the grower." Despite the strenuous efforts of a few men, the South made little progress in manufactures; Lowell, Massachusetts, alone had more spindles than the entire South. The total manufactures of every kind in the South accounted for less than 10 per cent, in value, of the whole American output on the eve of the Civil War.

The South's interest in manufactures belongs to a later date. In pre-Civil War days her main concern was agriculture and the sale of her surplus. Until the crops were sold the needs of farmers were supplied by local merchants who extended long-term credit at high costs. Nearly three-fourths of all merchandise bought by farmers was on a credit basis. In the larger Southern seaports merchants did business on a scale comparable to that in leading Northern cities.

New Orleans, "Queen of the Mississippi," was the region's greatest port. Racing steamboats, spreading smoke and sparks from their wood-burning boilers, were the pride of the city and the whole Mississippi. Stephen Foster sang the praises of the magnificent "Glendy Burk":

> De Glendy Burk is a mighty fast boat
> Wid a mighty fast captain too;
> He sits up thar on de hurricane roof
> And he keeps his eye on de crew.
>
> De Glendy Burk has a funny old crew
> And dey sing de boat-man's song,
> Dey burn de pitch and de pine knot too
> For to shove de boat along.

Each year 4,000 flatboats and 450 steamboats, piled high with cargo from the whole Mississippi Valley, unloaded at the city's busy docks. From the upper part of the valley came flour, grain, bacon, lumber, whiskey, furs and hides; from the lower valley came thousands of bales of cotton and great quantities of sugar from the rich plantations of Louisiana.

The ships that left the Southern coast, with their freight for Europe, did not return to the same harbors with imports. They usually unloaded European goods in New York and Northern ports. The ships which returned direct to Southern ports often had so little cargo that ballast was added to steady them. European cobblestones laid in Charleston's ancient streets are reminders of many a profitless homeward voyage.

The Northerners, who handled most of the South's commerce, took a large portion out of the planter's dollar; forty cents, said Southerners. Each summer merchants from Southern towns went North to New York to buy their annual supply of manufactured goods, for which the Empire City's dealers charged their usual middleman's profit. Additional profits came to Northern businessmen from insurance of cargoes, broker's fees, freight charges, and the current high interest rates.

Southerners thus felt themselves on a financial treadmill, even though it was well-carpeted. Their community in many ways seemed indeed to be standing still while the world was passing them by. The tendency of progressive peoples was in the direction of democracy, and none had made greater strides than the Northern American states. Practice there still fell short of theory, but the gap was slowly closing. In the South both practice and theory were moving in a direction away from democracy. The Declaration of Independence was repudiated by the Southern sons of its signers: belief in the *inequality* of man had become orthodox doctrine. Jefferson's voice had been smothered in his birthplace. It echoed strongly in the western drawl of a lanky lawyer, Abraham Lincoln.

CHAPTER XVIII

The Gift of the Negro *

They came in chains to a New World, whose wealth was to owe much to their sweaty brawn. The human toll was high for whites and blacks alike in the American colonies, but Negroes paid more dearly. It has been estimated that slaves brought to America before 1800 may have equaled in number immigrants from Europe. Yet when the first United States census was taken in 1790 the colored population was but one-fifth of the total.

In America there was a steady, small demand for Negro domestics. In New England and the middle colonies slaves also worked on farms and in various trades. By the middle of the eighteenth century slaves were about 16 per cent of the population of both Newport and the city of New York. Slave insurrections in Long Island, 1708, and in New York City, 1712, badly frightened the community. An alleged plot to revolt in New York in 1741 created such hysteria that eighteen slaves were hanged and thirteen burned alive.

Though colonials were desirous of cheap labor they began to fear that too many slaves would threaten white security and adversely affect white immigration. White workers, hostile to Negro competition, asked colonial assemblies to pass laws preventing the hiring out of black artisans. The assemblies, on occasion, complied, but owners and employers of skilled slaves evaded the prohibition. It was slave labor which contributed greatly to the growth of the economy in the Atlantic community.

The crowded ships that bore the blacks from Africa's west coast carried people who were heirs to an ancient cultural tradition, rich in metal and wood sculpture, carving in ivory and bone, weaving, and the making of jewelry and pottery. Negroes in West Africa lived in established agri-

* I wish to thank my brother, Harry Kraus, of the Queens College (N.Y.) History Department and Professor Joseph A. Boromé, of the City College (N.Y.) History Department for their assistance in writing this chapter.

cultural communities, planting a variety of crops and raising herds of cattle. Africans lived in neat villages, where mothers exercised close supervision of the children who, to the astonishment of Europeans, were rarely punished or made to work. Africans had family and social groupings strange to Europeans. Nor did the latter understand their intricate arrangements of property holding and inheritance.

Captains of slave ships were surprised at the attractive physique and graceful bearing of the young blacks, male and female. Europeans remarked on the beauty of their teeth, the cleanliness of Negroes, and the custom of daily baths in Africa. Recent anthropologists maintain that African Negroes surpassed most other preliterate groups in the fields of government, law, and technology.* Travelers wrote of their firmly established trade patterns and their knowledge of astronomy. Negro merchants, controlling trade in the interior, dealt shrewdly with Europeans. In the nineteenth century troubled abolitionists were unwilling to believe that Negroes played a large part in the slave trade.

In the New World Africa's cultural legacy was, to a large extent, lost. Physical transplantation to a different, often hostile civilization, snapped the Negro's link to much of his past. Whatever artistry lay dormant in a slave found no outlet in the hard labor of America's cotton and rice fields. But no people is a "cultural zero." In song, dance, pantomime, poetic language, Negroes in America found outlets for artistic expression that their African homeland had once provided more widely. Even in the strange environment of America skillful black hands still carved in wood and made cabinets to furnish colonial mansions. Noted Negro blacksmiths in New Orleans relearned their prized art of metal-forging to make hand-wrought iron grilles for the balconies and step-balustrades of the city's distinguished homes.

Negroes in Africa had no tradition of easel painting or sculpture in marble. Hence their achievements in these arts were slight. About 1770 Scipio Moorehead, who had received some training, followed current example in his painting of allegorical landscapes based on classical legends. Three-quarters of a century later, a Boston girl, child of Negro and Indian forebears, grew to become a noted sculptor. Edmonia Lewis made a bust of the valiant Colonel Robert Gould Shaw, commander of the famed Negro Civil War regiment, which brought her praise from the public and from fellow artists. The distinguished Story family (W. W. Story was a sculptor) took her under its wing and sent her to Italy, where she remained for many years. In the post-Civil War

* D. B. Davis, *The Problem of Slavery in Western Culture* (Cornell Univ. Press, 1966), p. 450.

era her sculptured busts of men hostile to slavery—John Brown, Charles Sumner—won her wide recognition.

Pioneers in unfamiliar arts are necessarily few. Robert Duncanson, of Cincinnati, ranks very high among these early gifted Negroes. He benefited from study in Canada, England, and Scotland, where an exhibition of his paintings in Glasgow won him favorable notice. London art circles embraced him, and he enjoyed the patronage of Lord Tennyson and the noted Duchess of Sutherland. In 1866, the *London Art Journal* said that Duncanson ranked with the best landscapists of his time. Murals and figure painting also came from his studio. His work, illustrating life in America's West, struck a responsive chord in Europeans, fascinated by this exotic world, painted by an exotic artist.

The interplay between the culture of Negroes and whites is clearly shown in the dance. The original religious and ritualistic dances of Africa were altered under Christian influences in the New World. However, carried over from their native region, and preserved, were the characteristic hand-clapping, foot-stamping, and jumping and leaping which were part of an ancient ritual now incorporated into a new faith.

The Negro's incomparable sense of rhythm guaranteed him superior achievement in song and dance. A traveler in the West Indies, Richard Ligon, was fascinated by the unusual drum rhythms of the blacks. He began teaching a slave, Macow, a greater variety of tunes. Almost immediately the slave knew the significance of sharps and flats and even invented an instrument like a xylophone. The process of acculturation is never easy. Considering all the handicaps confronting blacks in America they displayed a remarkable adaptive capacity.

Acting the part of society's jester, the Negro comforted the white man's sense of self-proclaimed superiority. Instead of being "children" (as whites always thought) Negroes, said an observant white, "know us better than we know ourselves." The black's comic side added richness to the culture of the South and eventually reached into all corners of the nation. Ragamuffin, grinning slaves danced, jigged, and sang in improvised entertainment for plantation masters. Out of such improvisation blackface minstrelsy was born. In turn came vaudeville. The two forms of entertainment were to be the main staple of theatrical fare for most of the nineteenth century. Black-faced white actors, imitating Negro slave entertainers, established the minstrel tradition. After the Civil War Negroes gave professional minstrel shows which were well stylized by that time.

For many years the Negro on stage was identified with "comic relief," grotesque appearance, and speaking a crude English. More pol-

ished performers, the African Company of Negro Actors, gave perform-
ances in New York in 1821. Its leading player was James Hewlett, who
starred in *Othello* and *Richard the Third*. A particularly gifted student
of the African Free School in New York, which educated Negro children, was Ira Aldridge, stage-struck as a child. He went to the University of Glasgow for higher education, but acting remained his first love.
Skilled in several roles, his favorite was Othello, played opposite illustrious Edmund Kean's Iago. Aldridge, finding America hostile to Negro
actors, became a British subject and his triumphs belong to theatrical
history overseas. Europe, as well as America, was entertained by Negro
minstrels, who were counted among the more popular native-culture exports from the New World.

The gift of song that lay deep in black men found most distinctive
expression in "spirituals." Their true value was little appreciated in pre-
Civil War days, for these religious songs bespoke a dignity which whites
ordinarily refused to accord Negroes. Thomas Wentworth Higginson,
no ordinary man, who led black troops in the war, inspired a fellow
Northerner, William Allen, to record the "peculiar but haunting slave
songs" sung by Negro freedmen in refugee camps. In Georgia slave
songs were sometimes called "ant'ems." Two years after the end of the
war Allen published *Slave Songs of the United States,* melodies he had
transcribed.

In later years it was these "sorrow songs" of former slaves which won
world-wide acclaim as "Negro spirituals" after the Fisk Jubilee Singers
sang them to enraptured audiences. The sadness of earthly existence was
to be followed by a joyous life in a vividly realized heaven. Such spirituals as "My Lord What a Morning," "Nobody Knows the Trouble I've
Seen" express a deeply felt and ennobling piety. Among the most moving of the spirituals are those retelling the Crucifixion, notably "He
Never Said a Mumblin' Word" and "Were You There?"

Included in the black man's heritage is the "gift of spontaneous harmony" which enable choral groups to gain unusual effects. Sharing the
deep religious emotion evoked by spirituals erased, temporarily at least,
the barriers of denominationalism. It should be said that whites, as well
as blacks, were responsible for the creation of spirituals. Even though
they were frequently similar, Negro spirituals possessed a distinctive
flavor of optimism which blanketed a threatening despair. Spirituals
were the escape from slavery.

The noted Negro composer, W. C. Handy, maintained that a continuous sequence of Negro music can be traced from spirituals through
ragtime to jazz. Certainly, as Mrs. Butcher remarks (in *The Negro in*

American Culture), "in the camp-meeting style of jubilation, the dividing line between the spiritual and ragtime almost completely breaks down." *

Not all songs sung by Negroes were sorrowful or of religious inspiration. Many were secular. Like other peoples they had their labor and work songs. "John Henry," said to be "the Negro's greatest folk character," has been immortalized in many versions:

> John Henry said to his captain
> Well-a man ain't nuthin' but a man,
> And before I'll let your steam drill beat me down
> I'll die wid' my hammer in my hand
> I'll die wid' my hammer in my hand.

Laughter at themselves and their smaller trials found vent in:

> Way down yon'er un de Alerbamer way,
> De Niggers goes to wo'k at de peep o' de day.
> De bed's too short, and de high posts rear,
> De Niggers needs a ladder fer to climb up dere.
> De cord's worn out, and de bed tick's gone.
> Niggers' legs hang down fer de chickens t' roost on.

Among the richest contributions of Negro folk culture are the tales of Uncle Remus. James Weldon Johnson spoke of them as "the greatest body of folklore America has produced." Joel Chandler Harris, who gave them to countless enchanted readers, has been criticised for his alleged apology for slavery. The docile black was the "good" Negro; the malcontent the "bad Negro." Harris also fostered belief in the benevolent relationship between masters and slaves, insuring contentment on the plantation. Students of folk lore have traced many American Negro folk tales to earlier African legends which include much more than Uncle Remus stories—proverbs, songs, and saga cycles. By a trick of fate the people most oppressed and burdened with sorrow have through song and story given much joy to fellow Americans.

Southern whites, as well as Northerners, generally preferred to romanticize life in the South. A cover of romance blurred the harsh reality of a society based on slavery and possibly eased a troubled conscience. Stephen Foster's ballads have preserved the traditional romantic image of the happy, irresponsible slave. Nevertheless, he did capture the special flavor of black folk thought and song. "Swanee River," "My Old Kentucky Home," and "Old Black Joe" became the treasured possession of posterity which delighted in their sentiment. It may be no exaggeration

* Margaret J. Butcher, *The Negro in American Culture* (New York: Alfred A. Knopf, 1956).

to say that Foster's songs "did more to crystallize the romance of the plantation tradition than all the Southern colonels and novelists put together." *

An unlettered people, usually lacking encouragement to gain literacy, leave few literary remains, though the situation for Negroes changed by the nineteenth century. While formal literary expression was not common among blacks their speech was often marked by a terse economy. A group of slaves who had been brought to an island off the American mainland preferred death to captivity. They walked into the water saying, "The water brought us here. The water will take us away." †

Before the nineteenth century records of Negro literary accomplishment are few. Some slaves, favored by indulgent owners, were proficient enough to win a modest fame by their writings. In the eighteenth century Jupiter Hammon, from Long Island, and Phyllis Wheatley, in Boston, wrote conventional poetry that usually reflected acceptance of the status quo. The very title of Hammon's "The Kind Master and the Dutiful Slave" indicated the poet's mood. Miss Wheatley was an abler writer, though she, too, like a host of other poets in England and America, became a pale imitator of Alexander Pope. A Negro poet writing acceptable verse was, itself, novelty enough to win Miss Wheatley warm praise in influential circles in England, which she visited in 1773.

Only once did Miss Wheatley write of black men's desolation in America. In after years the note of racial consciousness enters more vigorously into the writing of Negro poets. A Southerner, George Horton, with a "bizarre imagination," wrote poems expressing antislavery sentiments in the first half of the nineteenth century. More intense antislavery verses were written by Charles Reason and Elymas Rogers. The latter's "The Repeal of the Missouri Compromise Considered" (1856) was a very creditable achievement as poetry and history. James Whitefield, barber and poet, touched a modern note in his excoriation of national hypocrisy in *America, and Other Poems:*

> Thou boasted land of liberty
> It is to thee I raise my song
> Thou land of blood, and crime, and wrong.

Longfellow, Whittier, Whitman and Lowell were among Northern poets who joined Negro authors in denunciation of slavery.

White novelists in the early decades of the nineteenth century fixed the stereotype of the loyal, old black servant. William G. Simms, in *The Yemassee* (1835) depicts a resourceful Negro servant, Hector, who is

* *Ibid.,* p. 114.
† Quoted in L. Parrish, *Slave Songs of Georgia Sea Islands* (New York, 1942), p. 37.

an able scout. Offered liberty, he rejects it, thus proving the loyalty of the black man. Simms, though an ardent defender of slavery, does write of Negroes overmastering their rulers. In portraying Negro life more realistically Simms was something of an exception. His contemporaries were generally presenting the stereotype of a loyal, patient, docile black man. Such an idealized being provided psychological comfort to uneasy Southerners.*

Far more important than poetry in creating a revulsion against slavery was the spoken and written prose of whites and blacks alike. The contributions of whites in this crusade are fairly well known to history. Less familiar are the efforts of their Negro contemporaries, with some exceptions, notably Frederick Douglass and Harriet Tubman. Slavery had been denounced by Samuel Sewall, in Massachusetts, as early as 1700. But even enlightened men, Jefferson in Virginia and Ezra Stiles and Moses Brown in New England, who later became opposed to slavery, accepted the institution as a matter of course before the 1770's. In the heady era of the American Revolution, however, many voices, especially those of Quakers, spoke against the slave trade and slavery itself. Most prominent were John Woolman, Thomas Clarkson, Granville Sharp in England and Anthony Benezet and Benjamin Rush in America. Benezet, a tireless propagandist, did more than any one to spark an international movement against slavery.

A generation earlier, in 1739, Scots Highlanders in Georgia, foretelling the future, said that slavery was "shocking to human nature." Some day the blacks will be "our Scourge . . . for our Sins; and as Freedom to them must be as dear as to us, what a Scene of Horror must it bring about! And the longer it is unexecuted, the bloody Scene must be the greater." Rush reminded fellow Americans of the incongruity of denouncing "the servitude to which the Parliament of Great Britain wishes to reduce us, while we continue to keep our fellow creatures in slavery just because their color is different from ours." Supporters of slavery were already using the argument that Christianity was a bar to disloyalty and revolt, for it could be and was used to inculcate submissiveness.

Slaveholders were not always convinced that conversion of blacks to Christianity induced loyalty. Insurrections were attributed to ministers who were said to instill notions of liberty into the minds of slaves. But dedicated missionaries did build schools and taught Negro children to read and recite the Bible. To be received into Christianity did not mean usually reception into churches nor, at death, into an unsegregated grave.

* Tremaine McDowell, "The Negro in the Southern Novel Prior to 1850," in S. L. Gross and J. E. Hardy, eds., *Images of the Negro in American Literature* (Chicago: Univ. of Chicago Press, 1966).

Perpetrators of crimes against slaves had little fear of the judicial process. In a few communities slaves had some of the legal safeguards possessed by freemen. But abolitionists asserted that legal protections granted slaves were only window dressing.

Manumission did gain for some Negroes what uncertain law enforcement failed to secure. For service during the American Revolution the number of free Negroes in Virginia doubled shortly after the war's end. However, within a few years Virginia was requiring that free Negroes and mulattoes register, and an emancipated slave was to lose his freedom if he stayed in the state over twelve months without securing a certificate of good character, indicating a permanent place of residence.

The belief in the Revolutionary era that slavery might be abolished soon vanished. Fear of black rebellion quenched generous hopes, especially in the aftermath of events in Santo Domingo in the 1790's. The whites there were almost entirely wiped out by black revolutionaries; survivors by the thousands fled to the United States. Panic in America was intensified when a black rebellion in Virginia broke out in 1800 led by Gabriel Prosser and Jack Bowler. Some thirty of their followers paid with their lives in the abortive revolt.

It should be noted that when restrictions upon free Negroes were being eased in Brazil and the West Indies, blacks in the southern United States were being subjected to an ever-tightening rein. Free Negroes, who formerly had the right to vote were disfranchised in all the Southern states and in the new communities in the West. In the North some of the states took away the franchise from the blacks. By the 1840's free Northern Negroes had equal voting rights only in Massachusetts, New Hampshire, Vermont, and Maine.

Race prejudice existed in England decades before the first settlers arrived in America. This sentiment had deep roots going back to early travelers' reports from Africa detailing mutilation practices and other usages offensive to Europeans. Familiar words themselves promoted racial antipathy. "White" and "black" suggested contrasting associations: "white" identified with goodness, "black" with something less attractive, ominous. Winthrop D. Jordan, in his recent book, *White Over Black,* states that "from the beginning white Englishmen met black Negroes on a footing of inequality."

In 1789 an anonymous Negro published in Baltimore a striking denunciation of slavery and the slave trade and the action of the Constitutional Convention in dealing with them. His work, *Negro Slavery by Othello: a Free Negro,* reminded Americans that they had revolted from Great Britain on the principle that all men by nature and of right ought to be free. After a victorious struggle can Americans, he asked, "so soon forget the principles that governed their determination?" On the slave trade, "Othello" said that instead of countenancing "that vile traffic in human flesh, the members of the late Constitutional Convention should have seized the opportunity of prohibiting forever this cruel species of reprobated villainy."

"Othello" may have been the remarkable Benjamin Banneker, the almanac maker, whose scientific achievements prompted Jefferson to write about them to the Academy of Sciences in Paris. To Banneker he said, "your accomplishments are a justification against the doubts which have been entertained of them." Banneker chided Jefferson, a slave holder, author of the Declaration of Independence, which declared "that all men are created equal; that they are endowed by their creator with certain unalienable rights . . ." "How pitiable is it to reflect," wrote Banneker, "that although you were so fully convinced of the benevolence of the Father of Mankind . . . that you should at the same time counteract his mercies, in detaining by fraud and violence so numerous a part of my brethren, under groaning captivity, and cruel oppression."

Jefferson, like Patrick Henry, was hostile to slavery, but as Henry said, they were "drawn along by the general inconvenience of living here without them [slaves]." "I will not, I cannot, justify it," wrote Henry. Jefferson was sorely troubled by his own inconsistency, but he felt that public opinion was not ready for emancipation. Yet he felt it would come. "Nothing is more certainly written in the book of fate," he said in 1821, "than that these people are to be free."

Lemuel Haynes, Peter Williams, and David Walker were blacks who indicted slavery in the early years of the nineteenth century, prior to the first Convention of the Free Men of Color in Philadelphia in 1831. Occasionally, discontent among Negroes boiled over into open revolts which were crushed with fearful retribution by terrified whites. Though revolts led by Denmark Vesey and Nat Turner failed, the very act of militancy challenged the cherished assumption of whites that slaves were docile and contented.

Matching the ardor of white abolitionists, who often served as mentors, Negroes vigorously engaged in the crusade against slavery. In 1827 the first Negro newspaper, *Freedom's Journal,* founded by John B. Russwurm and Samuel E. Cornish, initiated a sustained attack which lasted until slavery was overthrown by the Civil War. In the intervening years Martin Delaney, Henry H. Garnet, Samuel Ringgold Ward, and William Wells Brown, all Negroes, played important parts in promoting abolitionist sentiment. Indomitable Sojourner Truth cried from the pulpit: "America owes my people some of the dividends . . . there is a debt to the Negro people which [whites] can never repay. At least they must make amends."

Most abolitionists followed the path of nonviolence, though Garnet urged militancy: "Let your motto be resistance; no oppressed people have secured their liberty without resistance." A remarkable man among Negro abolitionists was wealthy Robert Purvis of Philadelphia. Purvis, often mistaken for a white, gave Garrison money to help found the antislavery newspaper, *The Liberator,* in 1831.

Chief among the Negro spokesmen was Frederick Douglass, onetime slave turned journalist and gifted orator. Douglass' own paper, the *North Star* (later, *Frederick Douglass Paper*), was the most famous of Negro journals. These papers, generally well-edited, were opposed not only to slavery but also to discrimination in the North, advocating full civil liberties.

Negro abolitionists, notably Brown and Douglass, went to the British Isles, where they succeeded in winning hosts of sympathizers for their cause. In stirring the consciences of whites an effective literary weapon were several hundred "slave narratives," some fiction, others edited. The best were genuine autobiographies. Of the latter none was more moving than Josiah Henson's *Truth Stranger than Fiction* and Douglass' own story. It is said that Douglass' life and Henson's conversations with Harriet Beecher Stowe informed and inspired her.

Douglass' humanitarianism placed him with the most distinguished of universal reformers in his advocacy of women's rights, land reform, civil rights legislation, and free public education. His most inspiring eloquence was reserved for the cause of abolitionism. His vision reached beyond the goal he set for his fellow black men. "No people," he wrote, "to whom liberty is given, can hold it as firmly and wear it as grandly as those who wrench their liberty from the iron hand of the tyrant."

The oratory of Douglass unmasked the smugness of fellow Americans, exposed their hypocrisy, and prodded their sleeping conscience. In a famous speech, July 4, 1852, he asked what that day meant to the slave. He answered "a day that reveals to him more than all other days of the year, the gross injustice and cruelty to which he is the constant victim. To him your celebration is a sham; your boasted liberty, an unholy licence . . . . your shouts of liberty and equality, hollow mockery . . ." Americans, he said, in their prideful possession of democracy, denounced Russian and Austrian autocrats, yet themselves consented "to be the mere tools and bodyguards of the tyrants of Virginia and Carolina." Tears were shed over fallen Hungary, but for the "ten thousand wrongs of the American slave" it was demanded that Americans remain mute.

Douglass' words won a more immediate response from blacks living in cities. As he himself once put it, "Slavery dislikes a dense popula-tion." Rural blacks, especially field hands, showed much less of the in-dividuality that often marked the urban Negro. A Louisiana planter re-marked that "Slavery is from its very nature eminently patriarchal and altogether agricultural. It does not thrive with master or slave when transplanted to cities." *

As observant Northerner Frederick Law Olmsted noted, the slaves in cities had improved so greatly in intelligence that they could become dangerous to their masters. "Hundreds of slaves in New Orleans," he wrote, "must be constantly reflecting and saying to one another, 'I am as capable of taking care of myself as this Irish hod-carrier or this German market-gardener; why can't I have the enjoyment of my labor as well as they of theirs; . . . why should I be subject to have [my family] taken from me by those other men who call themselves our owners?' "

When Olmsted was making his tour through the South in the 1850's slaves in the cities were becoming fewer. Some forty years earlier slaves had totaled 20 per cent or more of the population in the South's larger cities; in Charleston they outnumbered whites. Homes could hardly func-tion without slaves; shops and factories employed them; roads, bridges, sewers, and buildings in large measure were the creations of their hands. They served as firemen, and such was their fame in Savannah that they lent special distinction to the city.

By 1840 a marked drop had occurred in the number of urban families holding slaves. In Richmond, for example, where two-thirds of the fam-ilies had slaves in 1820, a score of years later the percentage had fallen to fifty. The ratio of slaves to whites in most Southern cities dropped precipitately in the last two decades before the Civil War.

The dependence of large-scale Southern enterprises on Negro labor was substantial. In Richmond, in the 1840's over fifty-four corporations owned at least ten slaves each, several had seventy-five or more; the Virginia Central Railroad held over 270 slaves. In Richmond's efficient Tredegar Iron Works, which competed profitably with Northern produc-ers, slaves did the skilled work of puddling, heating, and rolling.

Negroes performed well in a New Orleans sugar refinery. That same city's gas works was run by Negro labor, superintended by a very knowl-edgeable black. Railroads were especially delighted to use slaves on con-struction. On one Alabama project it was claimed that they did more work, at one-fourth the cost than twice the number of hired workers. A grim reminder of the reduction of man to the status of property was

* R. C. Wade, *Slavery in the Cities: The South 1820–1860* (New York, 1964), pp. 3–4.

the auction block found in every town as well as in country districts. Buying and selling of blacks was big business, valued at $150,000,000 in the last year of the 1850's.

Throughout the country blacks engaged in a multitude of skilled and unskilled occupations. In the North, in Massachusetts, Paul Cuffe had built ships to engage in oceanic commerce. Boston's 2,000 Negroes in 1860 included engravers and tailors as well as ministers, teachers, lawyers, and dentists. In New York and Philadelphia the story was much the same. Substantial property owners were not uncommon among free Negroes, North and South. In New Orleans affluent Negroes owned a total of over $15,000,000. On the Mississippi, Simon Gray, a highly intelligent slave, became captain of a flatboat, supervising and paying wages to a mixed crew of whites and blacks. He built and ran sawmills as agent for a lumber company. He was given a regular salary, rented a house, where his family lived in privacy, and vacationed in Hot Springs, Arkansas.* The growing hostility of whites, however, restricted Negroes to menial work. In the North, Irish immigrants were displacing blacks in many occupations.

Masters with more slaves than were needed at home or in business hired some of them out to other employers. A Negro might be "hired out" for any length of time up to several years. "Hiring out" became a half-way step to independence for many slaves. Masters told slaves to make their own arrangements for employment, and to hand over a specified sum weekly or monthly. Any profit remaining belonged to the slave. "Hiring their own time" put the Negro into a relationship more akin to that of tenant and landlord rather than one of conventional bondage. This changed relationship was further emphasized when slaves rented quarters away from their masters. Earnings from "hiring out" enabled slaves to purchase a prized freedom.

"Hiring their own time" loosened and even severed the tie between slave and master, as indicated by the census in Richmond in 1860. Over 400 hired slaves were listed by name, each with the note, "owner unknown." Southerners feared the growing rift in a customary relationship, but the need for black labor forced them to blink at the danger. Master and the slave found the arrangement mutually profitable. A Charleston couple paid $670 to hire their own time, yet saved enough to pay for their food, clothing, and separate housing.

"Living out" became fairly common despite official opposition. Living quarters of urban slaves, on or off their master's premises, were as cheerless as slum housing for immigrants in Northern cities. To "live out" was a sign of partial escape from enslavement. A normal family life for

* Davis, *op. cit.*, p. 230, for Simon Gray.

slaves, however, was almost impossible. The law did not recognize a marriage contract for them, and their children were the property of a master. Attachments, of necessity, were often temporary.

In all Southern cities Negroes lived side by side with whites. In this way a divided black society could not easily evolve to threaten white domination. In time, at the edge of towns separate, rundown Negro sections did appear. Segregated communities, North and South, were in evidence before 1860.

The military flavor in Southern society manifested itself in the urban "patrol" which policed slaves who were away from their owner's quarters. The "patrol" functioned well in a stable, rural environment, but in a mobile, urban society difficulties in enforcement constantly arose. Masters complained when their slaves, sent on an errand, ran afoul of the "patrol."

The whole bent of regulatory action was to prevent a sense of community from arising among the blacks. Nevertheless, in their churches, they found a common meeting place where fears could be expressed and hopes nurtured. Harassment of Negro groups was frequent, for whites could not contain a gnawing fear that religious services might spawn revolt.

Another meeting place for blacks was the grog shop. These drinking and gambling places were found in every town, with whites and blacks together, men and women, joining in easy conviviality. Authorities tried to suppress them, newspapers denounced them, and laws were passed to prevent the sale of liquor to slaves. All measures were in vain; grog shops multiplied everywhere. Miscegenation was very common, despite its illegality; in some cities mulattoes comprised half the Negro population.

Living in an urban environment made it easier for slaves to become literate. Here again, fearful whites sought to stifle black attempts to learn reading and writing. Against opposition many Negroes did learn to read and write. Travelers in Richmond and Charleston reported that slave literacy was fairly widespread. Ambitious Frederick Douglass, as a slave, carried Noah Webster's speller in his pocket. "When sent on errands, or when play time was allowed me," he recollected, "I would step, with my young friends, aside, and take a lesson in spelling." In Columbia, South Carolina's capital, about thirty literate Negroes held regular evening classes to teach others for a fee of one dollar a month.

In Northern cities, through their own efforts and also aided by philanthropic whites, Negroes established schools for their children. Philadelphia and New York were especially active in their behalf. In the latter city the well-known African Free School had over 500 Negro children by 1820. Local government support was eventually given to these schools which long remained segregated. By the 1850's some communities had arranged for joint white and black attendance. For two decades Negro leaders, demanding integration, had been denouncing segregated schools as inferior. "Contact on equal terms," said Douglass, "is the best means to abolish caste. *It is caste abolished.*"

Blacks were eager for education as enrollments indicated, especially in Boston. Even in higher education a few Negroes were students at Northern colleges, including Harvard Medical School. Before the Civil War, blacks could go to their own colleges, Lincoln University in Pennsylvania and Wilberforce in Ohio.

To demean the Negro, free and slave, was the constant aim of the dominant white, especially in the South. Authority was maintained by demanding deference to arrogance and instilling a nearly hopeless sense of inferiority. The South Carolina Court of Appeals in 1832 declared that free blacks should "by law be compelled to demean themselves as inferiors, from whom submission and respect to the whites . . . is demanded." What discipline milder forms of restraint failed to secure, the lash exacted. Unlike practice on the plantation, where master or overseer used the lash, in cities stripes were laid on at a workhouse to which the offending slave had been sent with a note and a small sum of money to pay the public whipper.

Urban slaveowners thus evaded the onus of harsh mastery which could more easily be detected in a city than on a plantation. As the ex-slave Douglass said, "He is a desperate slaveholder who will shock the humanity of his non-slaveholding neighbors, by the cries of the lacerated slaves, and very few in the city are willing to incur the odium of being cruel masters."

By a maze of devices white society sought to hem in the Negro. Detailed regulations, "concerning Negroes," were adopted by every Southern city. Yet the urban slave found his way through the maze to a quasi-freedom foreign to his rural brother. "A city slave is almost a free citizen," wrote Douglass who knew town and country. "He enjoys privileges altogether unknown to the whip-driven slave on the plantation." The intent of the master class to keep Negroes from close communication, one with another, was defeated. Urban slaves of different owners were able to meet each other and join with free Negroes in easy friendship. The house of a free black or one "living out" was a common meeting place for Negroes in the vicinity. These gathering places were in every city, surviving despite all attempts to suppress them.

In their churches Negroes found a training ground for organizing their own lives. They had the responsibility for recruiting members, hiring ministers, finding suitable quarters and running Sunday schools. Thousands of Negroes attended church in the larger cities, more than 6,000 in Charleston in the 1840's.

This ability of blacks to administer their own affairs surprised whites. Sir Charles Lyell, the English geologist visiting Savannah, wrote in admiration of Negroes who had "built a church for themselves, who had elected a pastor of their own race and secured him an annual salary, from whom they were listening to a good sermon, scarcely, if at all, below the average of the compositions of white ministers . . ."

On plantations slaves attended church with whites, though segregated. Separate worship became common despite surveillance by whites. A Negro preacher was usually a man of distinction among his fellows. In the North Negro churches did more than minister to religious needs. They were active in the abolitionist movement, serving as "stations" in the "underground railroad." Wholly apart from its religious function the church was for blacks, even more than it was for whites, a social center. As James Weldon Johnson put it, church was "an arena for the exercise of one's capabilities and powers, a world in which one may achieve self-realization and preferment." Baptist and Methodist churches had a greater appeal for Negroes than did other denominations, though prosperous Northern blacks attended Episcopal or Congregationalist churches. Blacks, like whites, wrote Sarah Grimké regretfully, were class conscious: "they have as much caste among themselves as we have."

The ultimate step in an individual challenge to servitude was flight. Port cities, Charleston and Savannah, were convenient exits for runaway slaves, secreted aboard packets from Boston or New York. Often the more highly valued slave ran away. Fear of a concerted challenge to servitude by mass uprisings was never far beneath the outward assurance of whites. The real or fancied plot of Denmark Vesey, 1822, in Charleston, sent a shiver through the master class. In their panic thirty-five blacks were sent to the gallows, most denying guilt, others defiant.

Vesey was a free Negro, a skilled carpenter, a close reader of the Bible, and well thought of by whites. Others, allegedly associated with him, belonged to the select group of urban Negroes. The very fact of large numbers of intelligent slaves living within the city of Charleston seemed to whites a dreaded threat. But under the police state system which characterized Southern society such threats were nullified.

On the eve of the Civil War fears of Negro uprisings in towns had probably greatly abated. Male blacks needed for an expanding agriculture, had become far fewer in Southern cities. In 1860 less than 17 per cent of town residents were Negro; forty years earlier it had been 37 per cent. For blacks remaining in the cities work was plentiful. "As carpenter, as blacksmiths, as shoe-makers, as factory hands they are far more valuable than field-laborers," wrote a newspaper in 1853. Though valuing the services of slaves in the city whites may have breathed easier to see many of them go to plantations. A reverse trend occurred among freed Negroes. They generally left the countryside to seek a new life in the cities.

That life could be thorny. While the free Negro could marry, lead a fairly normal family life, own property, and keep his earnings, genuine freedom was denied him through increasingly coercive legislation. Free, along with bonded, were placed on the same scale of punishment by city ordinances. Uneasy legislators passed laws making emancipation more difficult or forbidding it entirely. Free Negroes, as well as slaves, were banned from taverns, hotels, and restaurants. Segregation was decreed on street cars and in the theater.

In the North and West attitudes toward Negroes underwent a change when their percentage in the population increased. Even in Philadelphia, formerly hospitable to blacks, hostility became violent in the 1830's and 1840's. Riots and burning of Negro homes occurred in Pennsylvania, New York, and Ohio. Unlike the South, however, Northern Negroes could fight for their rights, in which they were often supported by whites. Blacks assembled in conventions to discuss procedures to improve their lot. In powerful statements they spoke their pride in their achievements despite the "relentless prejudice and persecution" that pursued them. For the most part Negroes saw no escape in colonization in Africa or elsewhere. Despite much talk and financial expenditure, fewer than 15,000 free Negroes left the United States.

The example of free Negroes living in close proximity to slaves was a spur to discontent among the unfree. Discontent, bursting into insurrection, did occur in rural surroundings, as Nat Turner's rebellion proved. A less explosive assertion of human dignity developed in urban surroundings. The decline of Negro population in Southern cities, however, handicapped the black man's progress. When freedom did come most blacks were in the countryside. There, says Wade, "accustomed only to routine tasks, imbruted by the severe limitations of plantation existence, and unused to managing their own affairs, they became free under the most difficult of circumstances." Tocqueville had forecast that the abolition of slavery would not end the troubled relationship between whites and blacks. History has fulfilled his doleful prophecy.

CHAPTER XIX

The Eagle Spreads Its Wings

The North and the South had come to look upon each other with accusing eye by 1850. The future of the country, however, was not to be determined by these two sections alone. In the West was a third power whose weight in national affairs grew more impressive as the century advanced to the midpoint. The Mississippi Valley absorbed hundreds of thousands of the sons and daughters of the older eastern regions, and in their new homes in the West they expanded their visions of the country's future. "The destiny of the American people," intoned a prophet, "is to subdue the continent . . . to rush over this vast field to the Pacific Ocean." Nor was the end to be at the water's edge. On the other side of the immense ocean were many hundreds of millions of people, and it was America's task "to agitate these herculean masses . . . to regenerate superannuated nations . . . to unite the world in one social family . . ."

★ BACK OF BEYOND

The westernmost reaches of the nation stretched to the Oregon country which was part of the Louisiana Purchase. Lewis and Clark had been sent by Jefferson to seek out the secrets of the new land. On the Great Plains they met vast herds of the shaggy-maned buffalo and the prong-horned antelope. Across the endless plains led the buffalo trails, worn deep by the millions of hoofs that had trodden them through unnumbered ages. The buffalo provided the plainsman, red or white, with life's necessities: meat, fresh or "jerked" (dried), tents, clothing, skin boats; and fuel (dried dung—"chips") was always plentiful. In the night the ominous baying of wolves mingled with the uncanny wail of the coyotes. It was a land of light rainfall; the shallow rivers, "a mile wide and an inch deep," described great curves through sandy beds, but in spring flood would suddenly fill from bank to bank boiling with muddy turbulence.

The two explorers reached the majestic forests of the northwest coast late in 1805 and wintered there. In March of the next year they started eastward to report to President Jefferson on the marvels they had found. Lewis and Clark had unlocked the door to the Far West. Hunters, trappers, fur traders followed soon after, and in time made way for the ranchers and farmers who came to possess the land. Here was an empire of towering mountains, of big skies, of dry earth, of hostile Indians challenging the oncoming whites. It was a land, too, of hidden mineral wealth, of riches in furs, of succulent pasturage and green valleys whose fertility promised a happy future to the pioneer breed.

In the generation immediately following the expedition of Lewis and Clark, however, most of the region west of the Missouri River was thought of as the Great American Desert. Americans who had grown up in the timbered area east of the Mississippi associated the absence of trees with a barren soil. The explorers had spoken of the sterile, treeless land and, occasionally, the word "desert" appeared in their journals. Zebulon Pike, whose name was given to the famed Colorado peak, was another explorer who found the West a desert. The legend grew that only nomadic Indians could live there; the dry land "back of beyond" yielded only cactus.

River men and mountain men knew the legend to be false, but their knowledge did not correct mistaken judgments. Men like Jedidiah Smith first traced the way westward through the Rockies at South Pass, to be followed in after years by a pioneer host. Smith found a region, beyond the mountains, to be a rich source of beaver. The mountain men, "free trappers," were of the breed of French *voyageurs,* proud of their lonely dominion, leaving it once a year to rendezvous with traders. With them the trappers exchanged their furs for the necessities not found in the wilderness.

The annual meeting place might be along the shores of Bear River; in other years it might be Jackson's Hole, or Pierre's Hole, where quiet water mirrored the lofty peaks of the Grand Tetons. Then again the rendezvous might occur below the red cliffs of the Wind River Mountains. Hundreds of bearded trappers, guiding their fur-laden pack mules, converged at the annual "Rocky Mountain Fair." Their furs underpriced, the items they needed overpriced, their gain gone in gambling and raw alcohol, the trappers felt relief on returning to their seclusion. Fearing neither God nor the devil, they scarce knew restraint of any kind. Half of their white civilization gone, half that of the Indian savage acquired, the mountain men who lived only for the present bequeathed to an orderly future an immense realm.

The men who really knew the distant wildness usually shoved off from St. Louis. The town, which had over 7,000 people in the early 1830's, had long been mistress of the western waters. Washington Irving, a visitor at this time, remarked on its "mixture of French & American character—French billiard room—market place where some are speaking French, some English." From the upper Mississippi and from the far reaches of the Missouri came the Indians and trappers loaded with their furs, adding a splash of barbaric color to the cosmopolitan town. From St. Louis the coveted pelts went out to the great metropolises of the world—New York, London, Canton, Constantinople.

The Americans did not have the field to themselves. Their great rivals were the enterprising men who worked for the Hudson's Bay Company. The company, which was Britain's imperial spearhead in the region, had remarkable leadership, notably in the person of huge Dr. John McLoughlin, an experienced fur trader, "King of the Oregon." He was, said a friendly contemporary, "such a figure as I should not like to meet in a dark Night . . ." He was dressed in clothes once fashionable, "but now covered with a thousand patches of different Colors, his beard would do honor to the chin of a Grizzly Bear, his face and hands evidently shewing that he had not lost much time at his Toilette . . . his own dimensions forming a *tout ensemble* that would convey a good idea of the highway men of former days." The savagery of the country was matched by the wildness of the trapper and trader whose reckless courage tamed the land.

★ THE OREGON TRAIL

The fur traders ranged over an immense area, more than a million square miles of mountain and plain, where no whites had fixed a permanent home. Over half of the region was claimed by alien powers, but boundary arrangements were vague and governmental authority scarce existent. The land was a vast vacuum which sucked in the foot-loose Americans. In time the fur trade declined; it flourished for only a score of years after the 1820's. The colorful traders and trappers shuttling between savagery and civilization gave way to missionaries and patient settlers seeking new homes.

Oregon and California enthusiasts, in Congress, in the press, and in public speeches, urged their fellow Americans to establish themselves permanently on the Pacific coast. Hall Jackson Kelley, a New Englander, produced a constant stream of writings glorifying Oregon. His attempt at settlement there, in 1832, ended in failure. But the torch he lit was carried by a fellow New Englander, Nathaniel J. Wyeth.

Wyeth, a prosperous businessman of Cambridge, Massachusetts, headed a group in 1832 that pioneered the famous route from Missouri to the Northwest which came to be known as the Oregon Trail. Two years later missionaries were in the region; succumbing to the attractions of the Willamette Valley, they established there a nucleus for future American settlement. The alleged yearning of western Indians for Christianity had stirred the missionary fervor of the East to an excited pitch. Dr. McLoughlin, in charge of the Hudson's Bay Company headquarters at Fort Vancouver, eased the path of missionary groups. In the long run his hospitality was a factor in the undoing of British influence in Oregon. Though the missionaries who hurried west saved few Indian souls in Oregon, their constant propaganda kept alive American interest in the Northwest until the trickle of newcomers in the area swelled to large proportions.

Emigrant trains of covered wagons set out from Independence, Missouri, to take the trail to Oregon, 2,000 miles away. The trail crossed the plains, and went along the Platte River to Fort Laramie, over 600 miles from Independence. After passing through the pleasant "tall grass" country, the wagons creaked their way over a matting of short grass. Wagons were overhauled at Fort Laramie and made ready for the rugged trip northwestward through the Rocky Mountains. South Pass, a gap 7,500 feet above sea level, permitted the emigrants to move on to Fort Bridger, west of the continental divide. That old mountain man and guardian angel of newcomers to the West, Jim Bridger, had built the post as a supply station. Farther along, after passage through a gorge-like valley, was Fort Hall, on Snake River; the river ran through a canyon four-fifths of a mile deep. More hard mountain traveling had to be faced before the relatively easy path along the Columbia River was reached. The trail passed Fort Walla Walla and Fort Vancouver, and then led on to its end at Astoria or the fertile Willamette Valley. Most of the pioneers in the early period of Oregon's history staked out their claims in this attractive valley.

Emigrant trains fended off Indians, got mired in quicksands; people and animals thirsted for water—but on they came. Frequent use of the familiar route wore deep ruts in the trail. Hard times in the Mississippi Valley after the panic of 1837 and the glowing accounts of Oregon and California turned the eyes of farmers once again westward. Oregon beckoned with the promise of 640 acres for every settler, plus 160 acres each for the other members of the family. In a land without frost a newcomer, no matter when he arrived (so promoters said) was guaranteed a first year's crop. When permanently settled he could count on two or three crops annually. Oregon may have been a mirage, but the Mississippi Valley was an ugly reality in these depression years. When wheat brought only ten cents a bushel and corn found no buyers, why linger? But the number who left was small at first.

It was not until some degree of prosperity returned, enabling farmers to raise the needed funds from sale of their crops and farms, that larger numbers could leave the Mississippi Valley. In late May of 1843, a large party of 1,000 men, women, and children, with 1,800 oxen and cattle, started from Independence over the famous Oregon Trail. Flour and sugar were carefully stored in double sacks to withstand moisture. Despite the warnings of guide books that wagon loads exceeding one ton could not be carried across the mountains, families found it hard to leave cherished possessions behind. But they soon yielded to necessity.

Emigrants discarded heavy furniture and excess equipment. Oxen were found preferable to horses for pulling the wagons and, besides, the Indians were inclined to ignore oxen where they might steal horses. At night the wagons were drawn up in a tight circle a hundred yards deep, behind which the settlers could barricade themselves against Indian attack. Women cried in the lonely darkness for the comforts of home back East. Colds, fevers, dysentery were their companions on the trail. And always there were the frightening vastness and the relentless sun. But the heavy trials were over when the party reached the Willamette Valley in late November. The success of this large group inspired a mass migration in the following years. The destiny of Oregon as a part of the American Union was assured.

In the eastern parts of the country an image of the West was being fashioned out of missionary reports, travel descriptions, popular fiction, and the paintings of roving artists. George Catlin displayed his famous collection of western pictures in the cities of the East, and then he took them to Europe where enthralled observers shared the thrill of vicarious adventure in the wild West. Catlin was among the first to give Americans a pictorial representation of the Far West. In his pictures of Plains Indians, lumbering buffalo, and western landscapes, Americans saw the region which was then stirring the imagination of the nation. Alfred Miller in 1837 made the first pictures of landmarks that were soon to be known to every traveler on the Oregon Trail—Fort Laramie, Independence Rock, Devil's Gate, the Wind River Mountains, and many others. Cheap prints and popular fiction imbedded in the mind of the people an image of the Far West whose fascination has never faded. In communities of the East, on farms in the Mississippi Valley, the call of Oregon was insistent.

American settlement in Oregon rapidly expanded, and public opinion

The growth of the United States

became increasingly hostile to the arrangement (originally made in 1818) for joint occupancy with Great Britain of the northwest region. The eagle was spreading its wings, and the cry of "Manifest Destiny" sounded through the land. The Democrats demanded the "re-occupation of Oregon," and in 1844 Polk's presidential campaign was enlivened by the slogan "Fifty-four forty or fight." * Fortunately there was no fight with Great Britain; for various reasons she was ready for an accommodation. The pressure of 5,000 aggressive American settlers had endangered the position of the Hudson's Bay Company. Its Fort Vancouver, made of logs and stocked with £100,000 worth of goods, was an inviting target to incendiary Americans. In the face of this threat the company, in 1845, abandoned Fort Vancouver for the more secure Fort Victoria on Vancouver Island. The fur trade along the Columbia was dwindling, and was more lucrative to the north.

English opinion was in a mood for compromise also because the moderate American tariff of 1846 made it easier for British manufacturers to sell their wares in the United States. The Americans, on the other hand, had long been ready to negotiate a settlement on the basis of an extension westward of the 49th parallel, despite the loud talk of "Fifty-four forty or fight." By a treaty, in 1846, the boundary of the United States, the 49th parallel, was run westward almost to the Pacific, leaving Vancouver Island in British hands. The American vision of a republic stretching from ocean to ocean had become a reality.

At the same time that Anglo-American relations were being roiled by a dispute over the northwestern boundary, a similar controversy was erupting at the opposite end of the continent, in Maine. The line dividing Maine from Canada had been vague ever since the close of the Revolutionary War, and on more than one occasion militant borderers of each side had invaded the other's territory. Canada was anxious that, in any boundary settlement, she retain a strategic road for possible future defense of her southeastern region.

Though twisting the lion's tail was already conventional practice in American politics, cool counsel in the United States suggested an amicable solution. Anglo-American negotiations were eased by the discovery of maps made by each side which seemed to substantiate the claim of the other. In a conciliatory mood both made gestures of magnanimity. It should be mentioned, too, that Webster, by subsidizing newspapers in Maine, found it easier to get the citizens of that state to accept the settlement he had negotiated with Lord Ashburton in 1842. Thus the

---

* See E. A. Miles, " 'Fifty-four Forty or Fight'—An American Political Legend," *Mississippi Valley Historical Review,* XLIV (September, 1957): 291–310, for new evidence that denies the importance of the slogan in the campaign.

United States–Canadian boundary was settled; English and American diplomats had surmounted another crisis in the long history of their nations' close relationship.

★ THE SANTA FE TRAIL

"Manifest Destiny" had spurred the actions of Americans in Oregon and Maine, but its greater drive was toward the Southwest, to Texas and then beyond. In that part of the continent Americans found themselves facing the frontier of New Spain. Daring friars and explorers had pushed Spain's northern imperial boundary from eastern Texas across to the shores of San Francisco Bay. Presidios and mission stations had been planted in this vast land. Catholicism had made many converts among the Indians, and the Church had left an indelible impress on the architecture of the region. Spanish example set the pattern for the way of life followed by the farmer, the rancher, and the picturesque cowboy in the Southwest. This enormous territory, a branch of Spain's empire, was insecurely held to the trunk. And when the trunk itself grew steadily weaker in the first quarter of the nineteenth century there was scarce any strength in the extended limbs. "Manifest Destiny" was the rushing wind which sheered off the boughs.

The Mexican Revolution cast off trade restraints imposed by Spain. In 1821 frontiersmen from the United States, with their goods, entered the mart of Santa Fe. Three thousand Mexicans there, and thousands more in the surrounding area, were an eager market for American goods. Within a short time, by 1824, trade with this Mexican outpost was a regular feature of Far West enterprise. In that year eighty men, with 25 wagons, 150 pack horses, and carrying goods worth $30,000, made the hazardous 900-mile trip to Santa Fe, and returned with silver and furs worth $190,000. For a score of years lengthy caravans, totaling 100 wagons or more, hauled their increasingly valuable loads to Santa Fe.

It was the traders on this route who worked out the technique of crossing the plains in wagon trains, protecting themselves from Indian attack by quickly forming a circle or hollow square. Though the trade with the Southwest never reached large proportions, it did bring to the Mississippi Valley needed specie. Chiefly what the traders brought back was the news of Mexico's weak hold on her northern region. Her weakness was a standing invitation to America's westward penetration.

★ THE LONE STAR REPUBLIC

Texas was the province of Mexico which first attracted Americans. Frontiersmen were critical of the 1819 treaty between the United States and Spain which gave to the latter control of the territory from the Sabine to the Rio Grande. They believed that this region rightly belonged to the United States as part of the Louisiana Purchase, and were resentful at its alleged surrender by weak-kneed American diplomats. Filibustering expeditions had sought, unsuccessfully, to detach it from Mexico. The less spectacular method, colonization, ultimately proved more effective.

Not that the earliest organizers of American settlement in Texas necessarily planned eventual independence. The Austins, father Moses and son Stephen, the most prominent promoters of American settlement in Texas, were loyal to the government of Mexico. But slowly the son (who directed the colonizing project after his father's death) became convinced that Texas should raise the flag of independence.

Stephen Austin, after many delays, was finally in 1823 granted the right to form an American colony in Texas. Colonists were given fixed quantities of land depending on the use made of it; farmers were to get 177 acres, while a family engaged in grazing was allotted 4,428 acres. Austin, as *empresario,* sponsoring the migration of many families, was to be rewarded by a very large land grant, over 66,000 acres. The Mexican government stipulated that all immigrants were to be Roman Catholics, though this regulation was easily evaded. From the start the new settlers who had come from Southern states brought with them their slaves.

Mexico did not then see that it was undermining itself by permitting American settlement. From every part of the United States and from every class pilgrims turned their eyes to Texas. Masters of the Cotton Kingdom saw it as a natural extension of their realm; humbler citizens saw it as a land which promised release from a bleak future on the wornout soils back East. In most of the American colonists stirred the sentiment that this foreign land should not long be alien; it should one day soon be theirs. In a sense this rivalry was a repetition of the Anglo-French conflict of the eighteenth century. Added to the struggle for empire was the tension born of mutually antagonistic cultures. Protestant Anglo-Saxons felt superior to allegedly decadent Latins whose way of life preserved an authoritarian society scorned by Americans. An acute Mexican official, in 1827, noted how slight the influence of his government was in East Texas; there the ratio of Mexicans to foreigners in some communities was one in ten. He warned his superiors to take timely measures; Texas, he said, "could throw the whole nation into revolution."

An unsuccessful revolt against Mexican rule by a handful of Americans late in 1826 resulted in a move to forbid further immigration from the United States. The Mexican government also aimed a blow at the Americans by decreeing the abolition of slavery throughout the country, but the influence of Austin and fellow colonists in Texas prevented the decree from taking effect in that province. In the summer of 1830 armed Mexican forces crossed the Nueces River to establish garrisons north of the Rio Grande; the rivalry for Texas had now entered a more militant phase. On summer evenings hot-tempered immigrants from "the United States of the North" talked angrily of the Mexican "invasion," and consoled themselves with the thought that fellow Americans would come to their aid.

Their expectations were realized in full measure. The "Texas fever" ran through the Mississippi Valley, hurrying thousands westward. Before the close of 1835 near 30,000 Anglo-Americans were in the region, outnumbering the Mexicans almost nine to one. Sam Houston, whose name was soon to sound triumphant in Texas, had already written to President Jackson that Texas was ripe for acquisition by the United States.

Mexico had fallen under the control of the dictator Santa Anna. His policy toward Texas became increasingly repressive until it drove even moderate Americans, like Stephen Austin, into open revolt. Only a slight incident was needed to light the flame of revolution. A Mexican colonel at San Antonio sought to take a small cannon from the Americans in Gonzales, a nearby settlement. The settlers hid the gun and called for help from fellow Americans. Like their forebears in 1775 at Lexington and Concord, Texans hurried from the valleys of the Colorado and Brazos to assemble at Gonzales. There, on October 1, 1835, two little forces met in quick combat and the Mexicans were routed. The "battle" of Gonzales was the opening of the Texan war for independence.

A provisional government was set up in November, 1835, and Sam Houston was made commander of the army. Commissioners were dispatched to the United States to seek support for the Texan cause. In Texas itself, an assault led by adventurous Ben Milam was made on San Antonio. "We went through the old adobe and picket houses of the Mexicans, using battering rams made of logs ten or twelve feet long," wrote a participant. "The stout men would take hold of the logs and swing them a while and let drive endwise, punching holes in the walls through which we passed."

Less than three months later, February, 1836, the tables were turned, and the Americans found themselves besieged in the Alamo. Under command of Santa Anna 3,000 Mexicans drew a tight ring around less than 200 Texans. From the doomed garrison came the call for aid, signed by Lieutenant Colonel William B. Travis, and addressed "To the

People of Texas & all Americans in the world": "I shall never surrender or retreat . . . I am determined to sustain myself as long as possible & die like a soldier who never forgets what is due to his own honor & that of his country—VICTORY OR DEATH." To Travis and all his men on Sunday, the 6th of March, came a death whose heroism ultimately spelled victory for their cause. Four days earlier, Texas had been proclaimed an independent republic, its flag a single star.

Volunteer companies were raised in various parts of the United States and sent to the Texas battleground. Cincinnati sent two cannon which played an important part in the final victory. But until that day came, Texans were in retreat before Santa Anna. Thousands of Americans abandoned their homes, which they then set afire. Negro slaves, masters, women, and children all fled pell-mell, on horseback, in carts, or on foot eastward ahead of the vengeful Mexicans. At San Jacinto, the Texans under Houston determined to make their stand. They camped in a live-oak grove, with a bayou at their backs. Oaks, huge magnolias, masses of laurel, and rhododendron concealed the Texans. To the southward stretched the prairie across which the Mexicans must march.

On the 21st of April, after preliminary skirmishing proved inconclusive, the Texans caught Santa Anna's army by surprise. With fierce shouts of "Remember the Alamo" they swept in among the bewildered Mexicans, their deadly rifles picking them off like hunted game. The Texans in their wild assault lost only nine killed and thirty-four wounded. Santa Anna's army of 1,250 was destroyed, with over 600 dead, and several hundred prisoners, including the commander himself. The Alamo had been avenged; Texan independence was assured. In October, 1836, Sam Houston was inaugurated first president of the new republic.

★ ANNEXATION OF TEXAS

The Texan Republic immediately sought recognition by the United States. President Jackson, who, it might have been expected, would ardently espouse the request, moved cautiously. He had no wish to be embroiled with Mexico, which refused to acknowledge Texan independence. Jackson was also concerned lest the introduction of the Texan issue into domestic politics harm the chances of Van Buren in the election of 1836. On this point there was good reason for Jackson to move slowly. Antislavery elements in the country were bitterly opposed to the recognition of Texas; one of their leading spokesmen, John Quincy Adams, now in Congress, denounced the proposal as one inspired by slaveholders. At any rate Jackson's administration waited until November had passed, with Van Buren elected, and did not recognize the Texan Republic until just before its term ended.

The Texans, however, wanted more than recognition. They desired annexation to the United States. The road to such a consummation was to be long and tortuous. Mexico still did not relinquish her claim to her lost province, and forces from each side continued to raid the other's territory. The Whigs were hostile to annexation. Indeed, the more extreme among them threatened secession if Texas were annexed. Besides, there were international complications in which France and England played significant roles.

France, as well as England, objected to annexation lest it lose Texas as a market. France was also concerned that a war between the United States and Mexico, with the latter vanquished, might hurt the cause of Catholicism and diminish the prestige of Spain, ally of the French. In addition to meddling in Texan affairs, both France and England were believed to have designs on California, in compensation, they said, for unpaid debts owed their nationals by Mexico.

Though Texas pushed her courtship of the United States, her suit made slow progress. Perhaps an ostentatious wooing of another might cause the United States to respond more quickly! England was logically cast for the role. It was expected that she would be interested in the creation of a buffer state between Mexico and the United States. English support of Texas might mean the founding of a large cotton area, rivaling that of the United States, whose government would favor free trade, and with whom Britain could have profitable commerce. English abolitionists were all in favor of a strong, independent Texas, with slavery prohibited, enlisted on the side of freedom. Lord Aberdeen, British Foreign Secretary, was reported in the American press to incline to this view. For a brief moment Aberdeen even considered a joint Anglo-French commitment guaranteeing Texan independence of the United States.

Annexationists in the United States, especially Southerners, were alarmed. A free Texas close to Southern states, offering asylum to runaway slaves, was an unpleasant prospect. The chances for annexation brightened, however, with the departure from Tyler's cabinet of Webster, and the appointment as Secretary of State of Abel P. Upshur. Upshur, a slaveholder and an avowed annexationist, was deeply suspicious of English intentions in Texas. He would "infinitely prefer to see Texas again in possession of the Mexicans," he said, "than under the influence of the British government." Upshur went so far as to talk war with Britain if she were to persist in efforts to control the newly established republic. Secretary Upshur was not long in office when an accident aboard a warship ended his life. His successor, Calhoun, was every bit as ardent an annexationist, and in April, 1844, a treaty of annexation was signed between Texas and the United States.

The fight now was carried to the floor of the Senate, where the Whigs were strong enough to hold up the treaty. Annexation, they said, meant war with Mexico, and the whole project, they maintained, was a conspiracy to extend the power of slaveholders. At this same time the political parties were making preparations for the presidential campaign of 1844. Clay, the perennial Whig candidate, first opposed annexation and then later wrote an equivocal letter which straddled the issue. It was evident that the Whigs had misjudged the temper of the American people. Whig leadership had believed that only militant slaveholders wished Texan annexation. Too late they awoke to the realization that practically the whole country wanted Texas and expansion to the Pacific.

Immigration into Texas continued at a high rate; in one year, 1844, 5,000 passed through Arkansas on the way to the new republic. Immigrants crowded one another on the long lines that waited before land offices for "certificates" entitling them to free land. Whole colonies were settled by Europeans, especially Germans and Frenchmen. The population of Texas increased from 30,000 to 142,000 within ten years of independence. Galveston, San Antonio, Austin, and Houston, though small towns, were alive with activity and the promise of future growth.

The general expansionist mood of the country was also supported by groups of people with particular objects in view. Speculators in Texan lands, sometimes holding dubious titles granted by Mexico, realized that only in an independent Texas could their ownership be made secure. Holders of Texas bonds also had good reason for urging annexation. In 1845 her debt was over $7,000,000, and her 8 per cent bonds sold for three cents on the dollar. These bonds were widely held in the United States, and owners of them saw that annexation was almost certain to result in a rapid rise in their value.

The Democrats, under the leadership of their candidate, James K. Polk, had a keener understanding of their fellow citizens than the Whigs; annexation was their chief doctrine. The election in November, 1844, endorsed the Democratic view, though not overwhelmingly. Without waiting for the new administration to take office the champions of annexation sought once more to achieve their aim. In place of annexation by treaty (which had been defeated in the Senate) the same object could be won by joint resolution of both Houses. Some Whigs, bowing to public pressure, joined Democrats in voting for the resolution inviting

Texas to become a state of the Union, and President Tyler signed it on March 1, 1845. The Mexican minister at Washington then demanded his passports, leaving with a threat of war in the air.

★ SETTLING THE MISSISSIPPI VALLEY

The pioneer settlers who had gone to the Oregon region and to Texas came mainly from the Mississippi Valley. There they had applied the lessons of adjustment to a new environment that generations of pioneering had taught them. There were no better colonizers in the country than these tough frontiersmen and farmers in the valley of the great river. From this region came the men who, with their families, were pushing into Texas, patiently seeking Oregon's virgin land, or arrogantly staking claims in California. The future had been foretold by a resident in the Mississippi Valley in 1817: "The centre of population and wealth is rapidly inclining *westward, and within a very* [few] *years hence* it will cross the mountains." "Towns, villages and settlements are rising where, a few months ago, there was nothing but a trackless forest." He foresaw the time "at no great distance," when there would be "great and flourishing ports on the lakes and great western rivers! These 'notions' may to many seem extravagant, but I verily believe that the event will justify them."

This was no ordinary breed of men who went beyond the rim of settlement. In their own eyes they built a legend of themselves as supermen before whom all the world would stand in awe. They could outshoot, outdrink, or outfight any two-legged "critter" in creation. They were "ring-tailed roarers, half-horse and half alligator"; and they lived on "whiskey and bear's meat salted in a hailstorm, peppered with buckshot, and broiled in a flash of forked lightning." The reality was little short of the legend. In the great valley pioneers accomplished deeds thought beyond the power of mortal men.

In the old Northwest, men tamed the stubborn land with ax and rifle. The gun of the pioneer was more than a weapon. It had guarded his home and supplied his wants; it was a symbol of life and liberty. It was often cared for more tenderly than the children of the pioneer himself. The ax was almost as precious. Its creation was an art, and the reputation of an expert spread far and wide; men would ride a hundred miles on horseback to buy an ax from a famed maker and gladly give $5 for it from their little store of cash. An English farmer and traveler paid his tribute to the Yankee ax which he thought was twice as efficient as any British ax. The American instrument with its handle, he said, "is a scientific implement—much more so, indeed, than many who use it are aware of—and it is most beautifully made of the very best materials, cast steel of the finest quality being used."

The man who had "larned the sling o' the axe" could perform prodigious feats with it. Singlehanded he assaulted trees 10 feet in diameter and 80 feet to the lowest limbs, and felled them within a yard of the line laid out. These towering trees came crashing down with a roar that shook the forest. Often the larger specimens were girdled and, in the winter following, the dead trees were fired. A several-acre "deadnin'," sending flames sky high at night, was an awesome sight. It was hard work clearing fields for planting, and only a few acres were cleared at a time. For many years the pungent smoke from burning piles of wood hung over the western settlements. Months and even years of toil with brush hooks and mattocks were needed to rid the soil of roots and underbrush and briars.

Breaking new land was as wearisome as clearing it of trees and thickets. Plows, though improved over those of colonial days, were still unsatisfactory. The newcomer who thought prairie land would be easy to break was soon corrected. The heavy prairie grass, taller than a man on horseback, with roots a half inch thick and a foot long, formed a tough sod for a plow pulled by five or more yoke of oxen. By 1837 a satisfactory prairie plow was finally designed to handle the sticky, black soil. The cost of breaking and fencing prairie land, bought at $1.25 an acre, was usually triple the purchase price. A span of horses, a yoke of oxen, a double wagon, one cow, a plow, and various tools—all considered necessary for a new settler—would, in 1840, cost some $250.

Corn, as usual, was the first crop, for it prospered even on land only partially cleared. It wasn't long before rich prairie lands were raising over 100 bushels of corn to the acre, the stalks reaching a height of over twelve feet. The preparation of the soil for wheat was another matter; seven years or more had to pass before a good flour grain could be produced. Crops of corn, rye, and buckwheat had to be harvested before edible wheat could be grown. To protect the crop from the birds, the deer, and the squirrels, the women and the children patrolled the fields several times a day. Fencing, which was expensive in regions without timber, was required to control livestock.

All observers noted the leveling effects of a frontier environment. Equality in social relationships was part of the natural order of things. Yet, even in the pioneer stage, a community after a few years often showed striking contrasts between its citizens of wealth, living in brick homes, luxuriously furnished, and the lesser folk dwelling nearby in rude log cabins. Many settlers in their first year lived in an open-faced camp. Bear skins or wolf pelts lined the walls, and were used also as mattresses and blankets. Before the open side, which usually faced south, burned a log fire for winter warmth and protection against prowling animals at night. It was in this kind of a home that Lincoln's family spent their first winter in southern Indiana.

The wearing apparel that settlers brought with them did not last long in the rough frontier environment, and the newcomers often reverted to the more primitive dress of the hunter or Indian. Buckskin moccasins, dressed skin breeches and shirts, and coonskin caps satisfied the forest dweller or the farmer. Youngsters continued to wear moccasins, long after shoes were readily available. Ready-made clothing could be purchased in larger western towns by the 1830's and, within a short time, even in smaller communities. The habits of settled areas were so quickly re-established that when a lanky pioneer appeared in public in hunting dress and long rifle he seemed conspicuous.

Game and fish were plentiful in the earlier days of settlement; a few hours hunting would supply a family's needs for a week. Pigeons, flying in flocks sometimes thirty miles long, shook the air with hurricane force. But such plenty could not last. The bear and deer, especially prized for their hides, grease, and sinews, as well as for food, were first to become scarce. But even when the housewife had to go to market to buy venison she found the price low. Sweetening for the table came from the honey of the wild bee which had migrated from domestic hives and had preceded man in his westward march. The forest offered no greater treasure than the precious honey, and wooded areas close to prairie lands were particularly rich in it because of the proximity of a colorful variety of wild flowers. With cattle and bees and crops in plenty the region for many was truly one of milk and honey.

★ "COME ALL YE YANKEE FARMERS"

The settlers who streamed into this region, south of the Great Lakes, were of no one type. They were hunters and squatters from earlier frontiers; they were men from eastern settled areas with some capital, prepared to make a fresh start; or they were young lawyers, craftsmen, and storekeepers planning new enterprises. They came from New England, the middle states, Ohio, Kentucky, and Tennessee. They came in thousands directly from Europe, especially Germany. In 1850, the population in the old Northwest totaled 4,500,000, one-eighth of whom were foreign born.

People in the Mississippi Valley were youthful, and travelers in the region were struck by the absence of old men or even "a gray hair." In one group of over 300 from Vermont more than half were under twenty-five years of age. Throughout New England, wrote a regretful contemporary (1835), "you will not find one in twenty who lives where his fathers lived or does as his fathers have done." When Western land could be bought for $1.25 an acre, New England prices were as high as $30 an acre. When it cost the New England farmer 50 cents to produce a bushel of corn, in Illinois it could be done for less than 15 cents. Abandoned farms in New England blighted the countryside as the young people fled from rural decay. They were hurried on their way by the challenge in the popular song:

> Come all ye Yankee farmers who wish to change your lot,
> Who've spunk enough to travel beyond your native spot,
> And leave behind the village where Ma and Pa do stay,
> Come follow me and settle in Michigania,
> Yea, Yea, Yea, in Michigania.

New Englanders were said to have the sharpest nose for opportunities in the western settlements. "Of all the emigrants to the West," said James Hall, the observant journalist, "Brother Jonathan alone knows where he is going to—the cheapest mode of travel, and what he is going to do when he gets there." He knew his rights under the land laws, and in every respect was an alert citizen ready to take his place in the new community. Southerners who settled in this area differed greatly from their New England neighbors—in speech, in manners, in economic enterprise. Easygoing Southerners disdained the thrift and money-grubbing which they associated with New Englanders. The latter, in turn, thought emigrants from the South lazy, ignorant, and lawless.

The language of the westerner was a blend, though the strongest influence came from the southern Appalachians, where the speech of Elizabethan England had survived. The southern highlander "blowed," "ketched," "knowed," and was "borned"; he "heered" or "hearn say." The laws of grammar were treated as casually as other laws. The voice had a nasal tone, the delivery ordinarily deliberate, and like his colonial ancestors the nineteenth-century American was very imaginative in coining descriptive words and phrases; "shootin'-iron," "lackbrain," "clutchfist" were some of his lively inventions. The westerner liked practical jokes and a special kind of humor. To the question, "Where does this road go?" came the stock reply, "Don't go nowheres, mister; stays right there."

Though tensions existed between Southerners and New Englanders in the West they agreed on the fundamentals—they co-operated in important social affairs and generally saw eye to eye in politics. Whatever each thought of the other, together they believed that the land should belong to him who cultivated it—even if the occupant were only a squatter. The squatter was found everywhere in the newer areas; one official said that four entire counties of northwestern Indiana in 1838 were occupied by squatters. In any new region it was normal for more than half of the settlers to be squatters on government land. Pressure for easier land ownership helped pass a national bill, in 1841, which gave adult males the right to pre-empt 160 acres. Under the bill squatters could buy their claims at the minimum price, $1.25 an acre.

★ THE FRONTIER WORLD

Travelers over roads in prairie country often found them more impassable than forest paths. In the fall dried prairie grass caught fire with frightening speed, burnt grass and blinding smoke blackened everything in their path—animals, homes, and sometimes men were caught in the enveloping flames. At an early date settlers on the prairie learned to build backfires or plow wide furrows to protect buildings and crops against lesser fires. The traveler in the villages and small towns of the West found life little different from that in the country. Houses, which were closer together, were lined irregularly along a road filled with stumps and holes, dusty or muddy, depending on the season. Paralleling the road were cow paths, and in the "business section," comprising a store, post office, blacksmith shop, shoemaker, and tavern, were hitching racks and perhaps a short span of wooden sidewalks. Churches, a schoolhouse, and possibly offices of a doctor and lawyer completed the establishments in a country town. Residents cultivated vegetable patches and usually a nearby field. They kept pigs, chickens, and often a cow which was led out to pasture. The transition from country to town or vice versa required no radical readjustment in this period of American history.

The relative simplicity of social organization was apparent also in the ease with which an ambitious young man prepared for a professional career. A few months as clerk in a lawyer's office and "reading law" were frequently the sole preparation for bar and bench. Pill-rolling often qualified an apprentice for medicine; the call to preach was usually enough to meet the standards for the ministry in most denominations. Even though many westerners did not boast the formal training of their eastern contemporaries, a number of them did achieve distinction in the professions. Several noted surgeons performed daring operations which, in more tradition-bound communities, might not have been considered at all. A highly respected profession in new settlements was that of surveyor; "surveyin' and bookkeepin' " were what barefoot Indiana schoolboys wanted, but their teacher gave them Latin and Greek instead.

The education that young boys and girls received came less from their short term at school than from the woods, the animals, and all the things that grew. Children had their many pets—goats, lambs, dogs, cats, and even ponies and 'coons. In their frontier world, unfenced and filled with the promise of endless adventure, was a school of experience which bred men and women who were fiercely proud of their way of life, and who carried the nation's boundaries to the far Pacific.

James Hall, in the *Western Monthly Magazine,* spoke the mind of his region: "We live under Republican institutions, where the whole power of the government is in the hands of the people, and where every act of sovereignty is but an emanation of the public will. No mighty monarch graciously assumes the burthen of conducting our affairs; no hereditary parliament kindly relieves us from the difficult task of enacting our laws, no established church in charitable consideration of our weakness deigns to accept the tithe of the produce of our labors, in return for the amiable office of directing our consciences in the world, and selling us the right of admission to a better existence. In government, in religion, in social life, we think our own thoughts, and act at our own pleasure."

★ IN THE HALLS OF MONTEZUMA

Two days after Polk had been inaugurated, the Mexican Minister, General Almonte, had protested against the annexation of Texas as "the most unjust aggression in the annals of modern history," and "the spoliation of a friendly power." Before the end of March, 1845, diplomatic relations between Mexico and the United States were severed.

The American president was not disturbed by this course of events. "Little Jimmy Polk," as a political rival described him, was in many ways a small man, but with a big ambition for his country—its expansion to the Pacific. It was in his administration that the thorny question of Oregon was settled. There was also a vast area under Mexican control that Polk meant to have—California, New Mexico, and the boundary of the Rio Grande. He worked at his task with single-minded devotion, rarely leaving Washington during his four years of office. His long hours, chronic illness, and intense preoccupation with his labors exhausted him, and he died a few months after his term had ended—but not until he had seen the triumph of his expansionist program.

In fact, Polk came into power with four great objects in view, which he announced to his Secretary of the Navy, George Bancroft. They were, first, a reduction of the tariff; second, the establishment of an independent treasury system to regulate the national finances; third, the peaceful settlement of the Oregon question; and fourth, the acquisition of California. All four objects were attained before he left office. The Democrats carried what was called the Walker Tariff, after Robert J. Walker, the Secretary of the Treasury; a measure fixing duties at a very low level. When this was done, after a severe struggle, Polk rejoiced. "The capitalists and monopolists," he wrote in his diary, "have not surrendered the immense advantages which they possessed, and the enormous profits which they derived under the tariff of 1842, until after a fierce and mighty struggle. This city has swarmed with them for weeks . . . but all has proved to be unavailing, and they have been at length vanquished." The Democrats also reestablished the subtreasury system introduced by Van Buren in 1840; and they thus divorced the Federal Government completely from all connection with the private banking apparatus of the country. But above all else, Polk intended to enlarge the United States.

Americans had been on Pacific shores from the end of the eighteenth century in search of sea-otter skins. Opportunities for expanded trade were opened up in California when, with Mexico's independence in 1821, the ports of that new republic were freed to international commerce. Rich California ranches annually supplied thousands of hides and tons of tallow. Tallow for candles in South American mines and leather for shoe manufacturers back East were the basis for the lucrative "hide and tallow trade" that drew many shippers to the west coast. Around Cape Horn came ships from the Atlantic ports loaded with coffee, sugar, molasses, hardware, clothing, boots and shoes, combs for the women, furniture for the home—almost anything imaginable to trade for hides and tallow. In harbor the ship became a department store displaying its goods to wide-eyed men, women, and children. After a year or more spent in trading along the coast the vessel began its long homeward voyage. For better organization of trade, agents of American shippers began to reside in California, to become the first permanent United States citizens there.

In addition to trade the lure of California lay in the large grants of land, a minimum of six square miles, given to prospective citizens. All the swelling emotions that had pulsed through Americans for generations when they thrust themselves westward were crystallized in John L. O'Sullivan's phrase, "manifest destiny," first used in 1845. "Our manifest destiny," said this New York newspaper editor, was "to overspread and possess the whole of the continent which Providence has given us for the development of the great experiment of liberty and federated self-government entrusted to us."

Polk was no coiner of the magic phrase, but he believed in O'Sullivan's words as fervently as his fellow Americans. He had no wish to fight if the desired territory could be secured by other means. Mexico at this time owed American nationals about $4,500,000 in claims. In November, 1845, Polk sent John Slidell to Mexico with an offer that the United States should take over the claims of its citizens, in exchange for Mexican recognition of the Rio Grande as the American boundary instead of the Nueces River. In addition $5,000,000 was offered for New Mexico, and if California were also to be ceded, Mexico could almost name her own price.

Polk seemed to be obsessed with thoughts of acquiring California, and England's rumored interest in the region hurried his hand. A month before Slidell had been sent on his mission, a message had gone out to the American consul at Monterey, California: "Whilst the President will make no effort and use no influence to induce California to become one of the free and independent States of the Union, yet if the people should desire to unite their destiny with ours, they would be received as brethren, whenever this can be done without affording Mexico just cause of complaint." Slidell cooled his heels while the Mexican government refused to receive him. Charges by an opposition group that the existing Mexican government was ready to barter away its land resulted in an overthrow of the regime, and the installation of a militant administration, truculent in its denunciation of the United States.

When Polk learned of the Mexican refusal to receive Slidell, the president, in January, 1846, ordered General Zachary Taylor to move the American troops across the Nueces River to the Rio Grande. Tension increased between the two countries, and after news arrived in Washington of a skirmish between the opposing forces along the Rio Grande, Congress, spurred on by the president, declared on May 13, 1846, that a state of war existed with Mexico.

In the United States most of the country, in particular, the Mississippi Valley, seemed to share the war fever of Congress. An army of 50,000 men was authorized, and volunteers rushed to enroll. But enthusiasm for "Mr. Polk's War" was uneven. The nearer people were to the scene of hostilities the greater was the president's support. To the opponents of slavery, however, especially in New England, the war was initiated by "Land-Jobbers and Slave-Jobbers." Residents in the country's interior felt differently. Tennessee had 30,000 volunteers for 3,000 places, while other western states raised three or four times the numbers requested. In California, where United States citizens, about 7,000 in number, equaled the population of the local Mexicans, the Americans were well prepared for the expected conflict. Within a few months all of California was in their hands. New Mexico, too, had fallen away from Mexico's feeble grasp, when Brigadier General Stephen Kearny accepted the willing surrender of Santa Fe.

Elsewhere the conflict was more uncertain and much more bitter. Inefficient transport, inadequate supplies, lack of training, desertion, and sickness among the American soldiers greatly weakened their fighting strength. Disease cost military units 50 per cent or more of their effectives. Political rivalry also dulled the edge of fighting power. The Democratic administration had no wish that a Whig general gain such luster from battle that the presidency would be his reward in 1848. In northern Mexico, the Whig, "Old Rough and Ready" General Zachary Taylor, won the battles of Monterey and Buena Vista, though the latter was almost lost through faulty generalship. The regiment of Mississippi Rifles, under command of Jefferson Davis, distinguished itself in snatching victory from defeat in this action.

It became apparent, however, that the war could not be brought to a decisive end by invasion of Mexico from the north. A new plan was therefore adopted, which was expected to bring victory more quickly to the Americans. It involved the capture of Vera Cruz, and then a march over rugged country to Mexico City. While Taylor was kept in command in northern Mexico, General Winfield Scott was assigned the formidable task of capturing Mexico's capital.

Scott, a vain, military dandy, "Old Fuss and Feathers," was nevertheless an able general. He got his men ashore without loss on a beach south of Vera Cruz, and promptly laid siege to the city. After a bombardment lasting several days, it surrendered. Scott hurried away from the coast, where yellow fever was more dangerous than the Mexicans, and struck inland for the capital, following the road that Cortés had taken over three centuries earlier.

Now began one of the most difficult campaigns in American military history. Illness, increased opposition (Santa Anna stomping about on a wooden leg had again risen to the top in Mexico), and always the terrain were hard obstacles. Scott was ably assisted by junior officers, Captain George B. McClellan, Lieutenant U. S. Grant, and especially Captain Robert E. Lee. It was the latter who made possible the movement outflanking the Mexicans at Cerro Gordo. This was a very skilful operation, which involved the transport by hand of artillery up and down slopes too sharp for animals to climb.

Scott's army went on to Puebla, where it stayed for three months. Volunteers, whose one-year terms of enlistment were up, were replaced. Scott waited impatiently for replacements and, to add to his irritation, a peace emissary, Nicholas P. Trist, sent by President Polk appeared at Puebla. After an abortive attempt at peace-making Scott left Puebla to lead his army of 10,000 on to Mexico City. The Americans moved over towering heights until, on August 10, 1847, the beautiful valley of Mexico lay before them. Hard fighting won Churubusco, and the capital's outer defenses were shattered. The Molino del Rey, massive stone structures at the foot of Chapultepec, was successfully assaulted, but at frightful cost to the Americans. The steep, fortified hill of Chapultepec was itself stormed, and in furious hand-to-hand fighting the Mexican defenders were overcome. Scott's army then crashed into Mexico City, and by the morning of September 14 was in possession of the capital. The plumed general, in full dress, clattered into the city on a big bay horse, while tough marines took over the halls of the Montezumas.

Not until several months later, February 2, 1848, was the war formally ended with the Treaty of Guadelupe Hidalgo. By it Mexico finally recognized the independence of Texas, with the Rio Grande as the boundary, and gave up New Mexico (which included Arizona), and also Upper California. The United States agreed to pay the claims of its nationals against Mexico and $15,000,000 in addition. Thus, with the acquisition of this immense area, the United States had almost reached the continental boundaries it holds today. Between February, 1845 (before the annexation of Texas), and 1848 the United States had added 1,200,000 square miles to its domain and had extended it to the Pacific. In 1853 one further addition of a relatively small territory in southern Arizona was made: the Gadsden Purchase, bought from Mexico for $10,000,000.

On the day that President Polk sent the Treaty of Guadelupe Hidalgo to the Senate, February 21, 1848, John Quincy Adams slumped in his seat in the House, felled by a paralytic stroke. The voice of the "Old Roman" was forever stilled, but his warnings against the spreading power of slavery had echoed throughout the country. Quarrels over organizing the spoil stripped from Mexico hardened the sectional and political divisions in the United States. Disunion was one of the sour fruits of victory.

★ WILMOT PROVISO

The note of disharmony had been sounded in the early months of the Mexican War. One humid evening in the summer of 1846, a Pennsylvania Representative in Congress, David Wilmot, a strong Jacksonian Democrat, moved that an appropriation bill be amended to bar slavery from any lands won during the war. Wilmot had copied his proposal from the Northwest Ordinance of 1787. Immediately a storm broke over the country; every Northern state with but a single exception passed resolutions approving the proviso, while in the South there was belligerent denunciation. President Polk and others thought the whole controversy needless, for slavery, they said, was not likely to flourish in the unpromising soil of New Mexico or in California's mountain wilderness. But antislavery forces hailed the Wilmot Proviso as a battle cry.

Walt Whitman, in the Brooklyn *Eagle,* said that the issue was clear: the interests of the great body of millions of white workingmen and farmers versus the ambitions of a few thousand aristocratic slaveowners. Northern Whigs and Democrats joined in supporting the argument that "the presence of the slave will exclude the laboring white man."

Advocates of slavery extension, led by Calhoun, introduced resolutions in Congress denying federal power to restrict slavery in the Territories. Thus Congress was denied the right to do what it had been doing for sixty years. Furthermore, said Calhoun, if slavery had been forbidden in Territories north of 36°30′ by the Missouri Compromise that act was therefore unconstitutional. Neither the Wilmot Proviso nor the Calhoun resolutions were adopted, but they widened the distance between extremists on both sides.

Militant Northerners opposed the creation of any new slave Territories; equally fiery Southerners, threatening secession, demanded the right to take slaves into all Territories. A third view, advanced by Lewis Cass of Michigan, and supported by Douglas, favored the doctrine of popular sovereignty—the people of each Territory should themselves decide the issue of slavery or freedom. As yet moderates outnumbered extremists, but the "firebell" that had once alarmed Jefferson during the debates over Missouri's admission to the Union had now a more insistent, ominous ring.

★ TAYLOR AND 1848

The sad-faced Polk was worn out by the summer of 1848. "My . . . great labor has exceedingly exhausted me," he wrote in his diary. His administration ran its course without reaching any decision about slavery in the newly acquired Territories; Oregon alone, after much debate, was finally organized as a Territory without slavery. Polk himself had believed that extension to the Pacific of the Missouri Compromise line was a fair solution. A new president, however, was called upon to face the problem as a result of the election of 1848.

The successor to Polk was the military hero Zachary Taylor, who had captured the imagination of the whole country. As a Southern Whig and slaveowner it was expected that his election would moderate political tensions. Discerning men in the Whig party agreed that General Scott's services to the nation were far greater, but they conceded that Taylor's popularity and democratic manners had an irresistible appeal. The Whigs, guided now by younger men and anxious for a winning candidate, had picked Taylor, elbowing aside the still magnetic Clay.

The Democrats nominated Lewis Cass, an old party regular, who had held public office since the days of Jefferson's presidency. Both parties evaded a stand on the controversial question of slavery in the Territories. The action of the Democratic convention infuriated the New York partisans of Van Buren, who sought revenge for his failure to get the nomination in 1844, and who also pressed for a strong position on slavery. The "Barnburner" faction of Democrats in New York (the name recalled the farmer who burned down his barn to get rid of the rats) joined with antislavery Whigs and the tiny abolitionist Liberty party to form the Free Soil party. With Van Buren as their standard bearer, and their slogan "free soil, free speech, free labor, and free men," they took an uncompromising stand against the extension of slavery. In a bid for Western votes the Free Soilers also asked for free lands to actual settlers.

The campaign was carried on with little enthusiasm, except among the Free Soilers, who had no chance though they elected nine men to Congress. Taylor won both the popular and the electoral vote, but the election results showed disquieting trends. Sectional feeling was sharpened, many Northerners were more deeply confirmed in their hostility to slavery expansion, while angry Southerners were more militant than ever in upholding their rights to take their slaves to any of the Territories.

In the carriage which Polk shared with the incoming president on a sleety inauguration day, Taylor said that Oregon and California were too remote to become states of the Union. But the headlong rush to California was already on, and it quickly swelled her population who were soon clamoring for admission to the Union.

★ "FORTY-NINERS"

In January, 1848, a mechanic discovered gold in the mill-race of John Sutter, the spectacular overlord of Sacramento Valley. News of the find spread to San Francisco and other Pacific areas and, more slowly, to the East and to Europe. For a moment the East was skeptical of reports of gold finds, writing them off as part of a long line of speculators' deceptions to lure people west. But the proofs grew more convincing, particularly when a Californian showed up in Washington, in December, 1848, with 230 ounces of pure gold. Thereafter no one seemed immune to the bite of the gold bug.

The whole world seemed to go crazy in the rush to California. Farmers left their plows, preachers their pulpits, sailors their ships, workers their tools, as they dashed off for the West. By ship via the Horn, or through the fever-ridden Isthmus of Panama, or directly across the continent by the covered wagon route went the hopeful "Forty-niners," singing new words to the gay tune of "Oh! Susanna":

> Oh! California,
>   That's the land for me;
> I'm off for Sacramento
>   With my washbowl on my knee.

In mid-May, 1849, the slow-turning wheels of 5,000 wagons rutted the California Trail. In another few weeks 40,000 men started from Missouri for the new El Dorado. Thousands never reached it, dying of hunger and disease or freezing in snow-covered mountain passes.

On the overland trail west a favorite stopping place was the Mormon settlement at Great Salt Lake. The Mormons, after many trials in an unfriendly East, had gone to a remote desert wilderness in the hope they would be free of hostile neighbors, who disliked especially their practice of polygamy. Under the commanding leadership of Brigham Young, the Mormons built a powerful community in Utah which drew converts from European countries as well as from the several states. The Mormons profited from sales of supplies to the westbound gold seekers, and some of the "Latter-day Saints" themselves joined the throng.

Within a year California had drawn many thousands from the ends of the earth, though Americans naturally predominated. By the close of 1849, 100,000 people were living in California. Tough men fought over claims and gambled away in a night the gold they had won by days of sweat. Porters charged $2 for carrying a bag; truckmen made $25 a day. Though the average individual won no great fortune, washing out about an ounce of gold daily (worth $16 in 1849), the total output was impressive. Within five years half a billion dollars worth was taken from the gold fields. Crude communities were given choice names: Last Chance, Blue-Belly Ravine, Grub Gulch, Poker Flat, and Hangtown. Yankees mixed with "Limies" from London, "Coolies" from China, "Paddies" from Ireland and "Keskydees" from France, the name coming from the Frenchman's frequent question, "Qu'est-ce qu'il dit?"

In six months Sacramento grew from four houses to a city of 10,000 inhabitants. San Francisco, formerly a village, became an exciting city of over 20,000. The law was often a mob's rope or the vigilante's pistol shot. Gradually a more stable order was provided for with the drafting of "mining codes," protecting mining claims. Though continuing to be a society in which justice was handed out unevenly, the bases of civilized existence were at length constructed in this wilder West.

Despite the growth of California, Congress still failed to give it a territorial government. Impatient Californians, under President Taylor's instigation, decided to organize into a state and skip the territorial phase entirely. They adopted a constitution which, by an overwhelming majority, forbade slavery. With an elected governor and legislature California formally launched itself as a state in 1850. It had already asked to be admitted to the Union. What seemed a simple request turned into an angry quarrel which almost wrecked that Union.

★ "HEAR ME FOR MY CAUSE"

Through the winter of 1849–50 tension mounted in the country. The national legislative machinery stood still while the House battled through sixty-three ballots before a Speaker was chosen. Publicists in both North and South struck hard blows for their respective sections, William Gilmore Simms with secessionist talk in the *Southern Quarterly Review,* Horace Greeley in the New York *Tribune* with warnings against compromise in the Territories. Orators whipped up the crowd's fierce emotions. Wendell Phillips, with two fugitive slaves on the platform of famed Faneuil Hall, told his cheering audience that Congress might pass its petty laws in Washington, but "Faneuil Hall repeals them in the name of the humanity of Massachusetts."

Ill feeling in the South was intensified by the collapse of cotton prices, from sixteen cents a pound in 1845 to four and a half cents in 1849. Southern disunionists were planning a convention in Nashville. President Taylor sternly warned against secession, at the same time favoring California's entry into the Union as a free state and the organization of New Mexico and Utah as territories without mention of slavery.

Into this feverish atmosphere the calming presence of popular Henry Clay came as a cooling breeze. Though now seventy-two, and not strong, his mind was sharp; his silvery voice still held his audience captive. In the crowded, red-carpeted Senate chamber, Clay spoke impressively for his beloved Union, urging the North to be magnanimous, and the South to banish thoughts of disunion. Secession would mean war and that war, he prophesied correctly, would be "furious, bloody, implacable, exterminating." Clay urged that a group of separate measures, originally sponsored by Douglas, be joined together for action by Congress: (1) admission of California as a free state; (2) establishment of Territorial governments in New Mexico and Utah without reference to slavery; (3) adjustment of the Texas–New Mexico boundary; (4) assumption by the national government of the public debt of Texas; (5) prohibition of the domestic slave trade in the District of Columbia; (6) enactment of a new and more binding fugitive slave law. The nation was in great danger, said Clay, noting that he had never spoken to an assembly "so oppressed, so appalled, so anxious."

Calhoun, the South's chief spokesman, prepared to answer, though as he told Rhett, a worshipful disciple, "My career is nearly done. The great battle must be fought by you younger men." The ghost-like, worn

Calhoun (dead within a few weeks) sat with his cloak wrapped around him while his friend, Senator Mason, of Virginia, read the Southern oracle's address. Responsibility for preserving the Union lay with the North, said Calhoun. The North must permit the South to take its slaves to California and the Territories; Northern states must arrest fugitive slaves; because of an alleged imbalance of power between the sections a constitutional amendment should be adopted to restore the former equality (the proposal seemed to involve a dual executive, each having a veto); and finally, the North must "cease the agitation of the slave question." If the North refused to meet his ultimatum Calhoun urged secession, preferably peaceful, but if need be at the cost of civil war.

As the debate grew hotter Webster entered the fray, but his heart was heavy. "I am nearly broken down with labor and anxiety," he wrote his son. "I know not how to meet the present emergency, or with what weapons to beat down the Northern and Southern follies now raging in equal extremes." But Webster's tired spirit and eloquent voice rose to the occasion on the seventh of March with one of the greatest speeches in his life. "I wish to speak today," he began, "not as a Massachusetts man, not as a Northern man, but as an American . . . I speak today for the preservation of the Union. 'Hear me for my cause.' " He fairly weighed the complaints of each section against the other, but he scorned the possibility of secession without strife. "Sir, your eyes and mine are never destined to see that miracle! . . . There can be no such thing as a peaceable secession." The burden of his speech supported Clay's compromise, though Webster looked upon a stronger fugitive slave law with some misgivings.

Senator Seward of New York, speaking for the strong antislavery elements opposed to compromise, recognized the right of Congress to permit or prohibit slavery in the Territories. But, he went on in a husky, monotonous voice, "there is a higher law than the Constitution." He was against any concessions to the slave interests, and he looked forward expectantly to the ultimate extinction of slavery everywhere. Southerners were enraged by Seward's speech, and unsympathetic Northerners, including Webster, ridiculed the appeal to the "higher law."

Though Webster was assailed by abolitionists and Free Soilers, and the North writhed at the thought of being impressed to hunt fugitive slaves, his masterly speech insured victory for the compromise. Disunion sentiment gradually diminished. The Nashville convention, called by Southern extremists, fell under the control of moderates. In commercial centers, both North and South, mass meetings endorsed a compromise solution of the crisis. In the Senate the vigorous Douglas spoke strongly for the compromise, urging the doctrine of popular sovereignty in the Territories, though he was sure that slavery would never flourish in the trans-Mississippi region.

In the midst of the stormy debate, which ran on during the hot summer of 1850, President Taylor was stricken with typhoid fever, and died on July 9. Vice-President Millard Fillmore, who succeeded, was friendlier to compromise than the inflexible Taylor had been. Before summer ended the compromise had won—California admitted to the Union under its own constitution prohibiting slavery; New Mexico and Utah Territories organized on the principle of popular sovereignty; no slave trade in the national capital; the Texas–New Mexico boundary established, and the debt of Texas assumed by the federal government. "I can now sleep of nights," Webster wrote to a friend. "We have now gone through the most important crisis that has occurred since the foundation of this government . . . the Union stands firm. Disunion . . . [is] put under, at least for the present, and I hope for a long time."

In the South secessionists spoke sullenly about the compromise, and though they showed considerable strength when the issue was tested in state elections the following year, they were beaten everywhere by the Unionists. But the price was high. The Whig party in the South which, more readily than the Democrats there, could be counted on to take a national view of controversial questions, was on the way to extinction. The Southern Unionists themselves, though favoring compromise, laid down conditions. "It is our deliberate opinion," they said, "that upon the faithful execution of the Fugitive Slave Law, by the proper authorities, depends the preservation of our much-loved Union."

It was that very law, however, which could not be executed in the North. Mild individuals joined fanatical abolitionists in hurling defiance at it. The conservative Edward Everett admitted the South's right to an efficient extradition law; but it is a right, he said, "that cannot be enforced." Emerson wrote with unaccustomed violence, "I will not obey it, by God!"

President Fillmore had uttered the fervent hope that Americans would support the compromise as "a final settlement." The "final settlement" had a life of just ten years.

BOOK 6

THE UNION PLUNGES TOWARD DESTRUCTION

CHAMPIONS of the compromise of 1850 did not need to wait a decade to foresee its impermanence. Webster and Clay, though living but two years beyond the compromise, came in that short time to fear for the nation's unity. As the debate between the forces for and against slavery grew shriller, a middle ground became more difficult to maintain. Just when it seemed that the question was put to rest by some new political accommodation, its insistent voice would break the surface quiet. In the period between the close of the conflict with Mexico and 1860, nearly all national problems became enmeshed with the intrusive issue of slavery.

There were also other questions that competed for the attention of Americans in the 1850's. "Manifest Destiny" still exerted its seductive appeal, and its objective now was Cuba and Central America. O'Sullivan, the journalist who had coined the expressive phrase, himself supported the actions of filibusters against Cuba. The unsatiated Polk tried, vainly, to buy the island. A few years later, in a blustering "Ostend Manifesto," American ministers stationed abroad maintained that their country was justified in seizing Cuba if an obstinate Spain refused to sell it. Southerners, anxious to enlarge the area of slavery, were especially prominent in the aggressive moves against the "Pearl of the Antilles." Young scions of noted families gave their lives in quixotic attempts to add the lush island to America's domain.

In the Caribbean area American expansionism met the counterthrust of British imperialism. Involved in the rivalry were the hopes of each to control an interoceanic canal to be built through Nicaragua. But once again Anglo-American diplomacy solved a troublesome problem—this time in the Clayton-Bulwer Treaty of 1850. Both parties agreed to encourage the building of a canal, but neither would be allowed to fortify it nor possess sole control over it. The treaty was a recognition by Britain of America's expanding imperial interests. Remembering that United States maritime strength was then inferior to England's, this was a solid advance for American diplomacy. Rabid expansionists in the United States saw it in a different light, and they denounced the alleged weakness of American diplomacy in bowing to British pressure.

The gleaming sails of American vessels which disturbed the British in the Caribbean were found on every sea. They had been in Chinese waters since the end of the eighteenth century, when Salem ships had gone to Canton. In the 1840's, when expansion to the Oregon region brought the Pacific more vividly into the consciousness of Americans, the tie between the west coast and Asia seemed direct. Calhoun spoke of the advantages of America's Pacific coast in trading with China and Japan, and prophesied that increased markets would be opened there for the trade of the United States. In 1844, the year after Calhoun's prophecy, Caleb Cushing, United States minister to China, gained access for American ships to the treaty ports and established the foundations for Chinese-American diplomacy which lasted until well into the twentieth century. Ten years after Cushing's treaty with China, Americans, as a result of Commodore Perry's famous expedition to Japan, forced open the doors of that hermit kingdom to United States trade.

National glory, it was clear, was not to be won only in the restricted area of an oceanbound republic. The voice of America, said Senator Cass, must be heard in every land. "The man is now living," he said in 1852, "who will live to see one hundred and fifty millions of people, free, prosperous, and intelligent, swaying the destinies of their country, and exerting a mighty influence upon those of the world. And why not . . . ? Is it not likely to be more beneficially exerted, than the influence now exercised by the despotic Powers of the earth?"

The self-imposed mission of Americans to nurture the flickering flame of liberty wherever it had been kindled found full expression in the mid-nineteenth century. As one after another of the subject peoples in Europe rose in revolt, American sympathies were quickly extended to the revolutionaries. Chief among them were the Hungarians, whose leader, Louis Kossuth, won supporters everywhere by his flaming eloquence. On a December morning in 1851, Kossuth was given a welcome in New York which was unmatched for popular enthusiasm. Later, at a large dinner attended by Congressmen, cabinet members, and Supreme Court judges, Webster, then Secretary of State, said, "we shall rejoice to see an American model upon the lower Danube and on the mountains of Hungary."

The United States was prepared to recognize the independence of a strong revolutionary Hungary, Webster told the protesting Austrian representative, Chevalier Hülsemann. America's interest, said the Secretary of State, was in spreading liberty and democratic self-government all over the world. "The power of this republic," said Webster, in a mood of chauvinism, "is spread over a region one of the richest and most fertile on the globe, and of an extent in comparison with which the possessions of the House of Hapsburg are but as a patch on the earth's surface."

Rebels had need of more than words but, apart from financial contributions from private sources, the disillusioned Kossuth gained nothing from the excitement he stirred up on his tour through the country. Americans felt, however, that they had thrown another challenge at despotism. "I'll not advocate going to war," said Cass, "but the time is coming when the voice of this nation will be potential throughout the world. I trust the time will soon come when not a hostile drum shall roll, and not a hostile cannon be fired, throughout the world, if we say, 'your cause is not a just and right one.' And a glorious consummation that will be for true democratic principles."

Cass spoke the sentiments of many Americans, though some conservatives at home had no wish to encourage revolution abroad. It was the "Young America" movement which best symbolized the aggressiveness of the country and its domineering way of dealing with other nations. The political hero of the Young Americans was Douglas, whose brashness and drive caught their imagination. When the Illinois Senator proposed that American commerce on the Great Lakes gain access to the St. Lawrence River, and when he urged a treaty of reciprocity with Canada, Douglas was looking toward ultimate annexation of our northern neighbor. The entire continent was to owe fealty to the Stars and Stripes. Such was the dream of most Americans, young and old.

At the very time that Americans were most vigorous in pushing their claims in various parts of the world, and generally meeting with success, they were, in handling domestic political affairs, at a low point in their history. The larger vision of earlier political figures was succeeded by the parochialism of lesser men, who risked their country's future in the push for local gain. The presidency, from Taylor through Buchanan, was in the weakest hands since the country's founding. This succession of presidents drifted from crisis to crisis and, in the absence of strong executive leadership, the real direction of public affairs fell into the hands of a small group of presidential advisers contending for power among themselves.

Intelligent statesmanship might have utilized existing factors promoting integration to counterbalance the forces tending toward disunion. Of first importance in tying together the far-flung nation was the rapid growth in communications—an improved postal service, the telegraph, and above all the railways. Before the end of the decade of the 1850's the United States railway system had become the greatest in the world; along with the superb facilities of rivers, canals, and the Great Lakes, the railroads, though still technically deficient in many ways, brought to a vast national market the products of American farms and factories.

All elements in the nation took pride in the great growth of the country, even though it was evident that the industrial Northeast, and the agricultural Midwest centering in Chicago, were the chief beneficiaries. In politics, too, despite disruptive tendencies, there were unifying elements. The Democratic party, though now largely under Southern domination, was a national body which marshaled beneath a single banner men of divergent views. In their cultural interests, likewise, there was more that bound than divided the varied sections of the country.

It was a race, then, between integration and disintegration. Clear-eyed men saw the two paths that stretched before their country. But there were too few with clear eyes and cool heads. As the sectional struggle grew more embittered, rage pre-empted reason, blurred vision concealed the road to compromise, and the nation stumbled into the dread abyss.

CHAPTER XX

A House Dividing

★ "I WILL BE HEARD"

The Fugitive Slave Law, enacted as part of the Compromise of 1850, was for the South a symbol of the North's desire to prolong the Union; for the North it was a pact with evil. It had taken more than twenty years to stir deep emotion on this issue among people in the Northern states, but the agitation and self-sacrifice of antislavery advocates were now reaping their reward.

Antislavery sentiment had strong eighteenth-century roots in America, in the South as well as in the North. In the former, hopes of gradual emancipation faded when the cotton gin tied the South more firmly to an economy based on slavery. In the North the ideals of the Declaration of Independence were a constant reminder of the incongruity of slavery in a free society. Northerners resented also the political advantage the South possessed by counting slaves for apportioning representation in Congress through the three-fifths clause.

Religious revivalists, notably Charles G. Finney, stirred their audiences to undertake reforming the world, and the most urgent reform to many was the abolition of slavery. The temperate abolitionism of Benjamin Lundy, in the 1820's, gave way to the stronger stand of Theodore Weld, James G. Birney, and the New York merchants, Arthur and Lewis Tappan. The most uncompromising position of all was taken by William Lloyd Garrison, who scorned the thought of gradual emancipation. His thunder broke the conspiracy of silence which often smothered the North's troubled conscience.

Garrison, son of a Massachusetts sea captain, called for "immediate enfranchisement of our slave population." In his fiery weekly, the *Liberator,* which he began on January 1, 1831, Garrison wrote his famous words: "On this subject I do not wish to think, or speak, or write, with moderation . . . I will be as harsh as truth and as uncompromising as justice . . . I am in earnest—I will not equivocate—I will not excuse—I will not retreat a single inch. AND I WILL BE HEARD."

Even in the North, however, only a few heard Garrison with sympathy; the rest were either apathetic or actively hostile. The South kept abolitionist literature out of the local mails and proposed a gag on antislavery petitions in Congress. Former President John Quincy Adams, now in Congress, was no abolitionist, but the "gag rule" angered him and thereafter he was a chief spokesman for the antislavery cause. The skill of Theodore Weld, "eloquent as an angel and powerful as thunder," the energy of Birney, the devotion of the Grimké sisters, Angelina and Sarah, former slaveowners themselves, and the money and enthusiasm of the Tappan brothers built up a large organization of abolition societies whose membership by 1840 totaled over 150,000. Though leadership was concentrated in the Northeast, newly established Oberlin College, in Ohio, became an important center for the abolitionist movement. Its dedicated students went out to preach the word. Indeed most of the abolition leaders were young, from middle-class, conservative, rural families.

Pulpit and press were enlisted, and escaped slaves, Frederick Douglass in particular, added their eloquent voices to the great cause. The blood of martyred abolitionists brought new conversions to the crusade. British example in freeing the slaves in their West Indian possessions in 1834 further served to inspire Americans. The fight against slavery in the Atlantic world was one of the shining examples of Anglo-American co-operation in a day when the two countries were often at odds on other questions.

The old fugitive slave law of 1793 gave the owner the right to recapture his property in a free state after appearance before a local magistrate. Southerners were in the habit of making no distinction between their own escaped slaves and free Negroes, and the latter were often kidnapped by slaveowners. Hostile Northerners began to harass slave catchers, and even to take the fugitives forcibly from their captors. State legislatures in the North passed "personal liberty laws," which placed a protective net around their own free colored citizens, and at the same time threw additional obstacles in the path of the man hunters.

Abolitionists organized an "Underground Railroad" which carried daring slaves from bondage to the freedom of the Northern states or Canada. Abolitionists passed the huddled fugitives from one farmhouse to another, hiding them by day and moving them warily by night. Only a very tiny proportion of slaves escaped to freedom (the annual loss was less than a thousand out of nearly 4,000,000), but the South was enraged by the mere existence of the Underground. The success of the "U.G." was not to be measured by the numbers it rescued. Its achievement lay in a continual dramatization of the struggle against slavery; never again would the public conscience be allowed the comfort of apathy.

Nor must the significance of the abolitionists be judged by their slim success in standing for political office. Their Liberty party in 1844 polled only 65,000 votes out of a total of 2,500,000. The few Congressmen who were committed to their cause, notably Adams and Joshua R. Giddings of Ohio, however, were a host in themselves, taunting with stinging invective their Southern adversaries. Small as was the political strength of antislavery elements, they held the balance of power in some elections, and cautious Northern politicians were forced to trim their sails to the winds of abolitionist doctrine.

The latent antislavery feelings of the inarticulate mass were displayed for all the world to see in the sensational sales of Harriet Beecher Stowe's *Uncle Tom's Cabin,* in 1852. Poets opposed to slavery, Whittier and Lowell, for example, had readers by the thousands, but no writer of fiction dealing with this theme had had much success. Then came Mrs. Stowe's book. It appeared when the North was still denouncing the Fugitive Slave Law, and when its feelings were lacerated with highly charged newspaper descriptions of runaway blacks frozen to death as they attempted to reach Canada through the deep snow. "Hattie," Mrs. Stowe's sister-in-law had written to her, "If I could use a pen as you can, I would write something which would make this whole nation feel what an accursed thing slavery is." Mrs. Stowe, who had long ago acquired an abiding hatred of slavery, vowed, "I will write something. I will if I live."

Uncle Tom's Cabin was an instant success when it originally appeared serially in a magazine. Deeply moved, impatient readers awaited each new installment. In book form the response was sensational. In less than a year 300,000 copies had been sold and eight presses were working day and night to satisfy the intense demand. It became as treasured as the Bible, and in many translations it bound the world together in a common revulsion against slavery. In Britain 500,000 women signed a petition against slavery. Plays based on the novel added another vast audience to the millions who read the book. That it gave a distorted view of life in the South, idealizing the Negro while painting the Southern white unfairly, made no difference to the readers of *Uncle Tom.* Their emotions were caught up in the fortunes of Uncle Tom and Little Eva, and no Southern refutations, not even thirty anti-Tom books, could change Northern opinion. *Uncle Tom's Cabin* deepened, for millions, the horror of slavery.

★ SLAVERY "A NATIONAL BENEFIT"

While hostility to slavery was gaining in the North, grim determination to defend it was growing in the South. In an earlier day Southerners had been apologetic about slavery, but by the late 1820's they had become committed to the institution as a beneficial way of life. The Governor of South Carolina in 1829 denied that slavery was a national evil; "on the contrary," he said, "it is a national benefit." Southerners argued that the glory of ancient civilizations had rested on slavery, and that the Bible surely sanctioned it. In an age when most people accepted the Bible as the revealed word of God, scriptural support for any argument could be very powerful.

George Fitzhugh and James Henry Hammond moved from the defensive to the offensive when they maintained that the Negro slave was better off than the Northern wage worker. The wage slave, they insisted, was worse off because the factory owner had no concern for his employee and gave him hardly enough to live on. "What avail is it," Hammond asked an abolitionist correspondent, "when you go through the form of paying them a pittance of what you call 'wages,' when you do not, in return for their services, allow them what alone they ask— and have a just right to demand—enough to feed, clothe and lodge them, in health and sickness, with reasonable comfort. Though we do not give 'wages' in *money,* we do this for *our slaves* and they are therefore better rewarded than *yours.*" The whole collective mind of the South, in journalism, in politics, in sermons, in literary discussions, and even in scientific studies, was absorbed in the defense of slavery. Everywhere men sought safeguards for the South's "peculiar institution."

In the same month that Mrs. Stowe's book was published, the abolitionist editor, Edmund Quincy, had predicted "that a house divided against itself cannot stand." Either slavery must be abolished or its mounting pressure, he said, would "at last make a fissure that will shatter into heaps the proud structure upon the heads of those that put their trust into it." He anticipated the growing strength of Southern secessionists and a desperate bid to break their ties with the Union: "It is not unlikely; for men's passions, in revolutionary times, overpower their cooler reason. And these are such times."

★ PIERCE, "THE CANDIDATE OF THE SOUTH"

Whatever frustration Southerners may have had in fighting the literary battle over slavery, they had none for the moment in politics. The

Democratic candidate for president in 1852, Franklin Pierce, was very acceptable to the South. Buchanan had been their first choice, but when the dark horse, Pierce, won the prize, they had no regrets. Though Pierce was a Northern man, said Herschel Johnson of Georgia, he was "in truth, the candidate of the South."

The Whigs, whose only successes had been with military men as standard bearers, turned to General Scott, though with little enthusiasm. "I suppose we must run Scott for President, and I hate it," wrote Horace Greeley. The Whigs were torn by factional strife and had little hope for victory. The great Whig leaders of former days, Clay and Webster, now had little strength in the party. "Harry of the West" lay dying in Washington in the summer of 1852; a disappointed Webster, failing to win the nomination himself, repudiated Scott as the party leader.

The Democrats on the other hand smoothed over their differences on the slavery issue for the time being and were confident of success. The result justified their expectations. Pierce carried twenty-seven of the thirty-one states in the electoral count, and he had a large lead in the popular vote as well. "The Whig Party seems almost annihilated by the recent elections," mourned one of its leaders. And another prominent Whig, Thurlow Weed, confessed, "There may be no political future for us." Even the most experienced of politicians could not guess how quickly Weed's forecast would be verified.

Southerners had good reason to call Pierce their man. He was a kindly, convivial person (hero of many a well-fought *bottle,* sneered the Whigs), but very weak. Without real convictions, he was the instrument of stronger wills, and it so happened that these were possessed by cabinet members with a proslavery bias. The administration and its head were held in such low esteem, even among its Southern supporters, that one of the latter wrote: "It has not vitality enough in both houses of Congress to lift it above the sneers and scoffs and ridicule of the veriest dolt that chooses to assail it . . . Bye and bye . . . [unless the administration gains popularity by annexing Cuba] the whole country will be ready to write *to let* on the door of the White House."

★ "THE HELL OF A STORM"

There was no more anxious prospective tenant for the anticipated White House vacancy than Senator Stephen A. Douglas of Illinois. Now that the brilliant stars of former years were gone—Calhoun, Clay, Webster— Douglas' light shone more brightly. He was hailed by his followers as opening "the way to the dynasty of a new generation." His popularity was great with Democrats everywhere, but his chief strength lay in leadership of the Old Northwest. "The N.W. is powerful in numbers and wealth and becoming more so. The N.W. has never had a President," wrote a Douglas enthusiast. She has *"insuperable claims* to the Presidency next term," and Douglas, as the region's candidate, was assured of the nomination.

Douglas sought to discourage a premature presidential boom, in 1853, and called attention rather to several questions before Congress. The tariff should be lowered, he said, rivers and harbors improved, and a railroad built to the Pacific with the aid of land grants from the federal government. Fast-growing Chicago, where Douglas himself had large holdings of real estate, was the natural center for the railroad web which was expected to spin out to San Francisco. But competing plans for other routes to the Pacific, including one from New Orleans, made for sectional discord.

To build a railroad to the Pacific required organizing into a territory the intervening land—the region of Nebraska—and also the cession of millions of acres of land from the Plains Indians, who were to be placed on reservations. Settlers were once again pressing toward the western lands, and establishment of orderly government was becoming imperative. Douglas, who was chairman of the Senate Committee on Territories, prepared a bill in January, 1854, which would win Southern votes for his railroad project by opening the Territory to the possibility of slavery. This latter could be done under the principle of "popular sovereignty," whereby local residents could decide for or against slavery. The proposal was made despite the fact that the Nebraska region was north of the Missouri Compromise line of 36°30′, and hence supposedly "forever" closed to slavery. The huge area was to be divided into Kansas and Nebraska, with the expectation that Southerners might control the former, while Northerners predominated in the latter.

Southerners, led by Senators Atchison of Missouri and Dixon of Kentucky, were not satisfied with Douglas' implicit scuttling of the Missouri Compromise. They insisted on its outright repeal. Douglas was hesitant, but finally bowing to their pressure, he agreed, though with misgivings; "it will raise the hell of a storm," he predicted. The storm did break and before it subsided it was overtaken by the greater cataclysm of 1861.

★ THE KANSAS-NEBRASKA ACT

Douglas was inspired by several motives in bringing out the Kansas-Nebraska bill. He thought it would revitalize his party, for it possessed attractive elements for Democrats, North and South. He was doubtless thinking, too, of his presidential aspirations, and support from the South would guarantee success. The Northwest wanted a Pacific railroad and Douglas was its champion. A number of observers thought the Senator from Illinois, often impulsive, was prompted by the desire "to get up some counter excitement to call off the public attention from the [weak] conduct of the Administration." The "excitement" came—much more of it than Douglas or anyone else wanted.

This challenge to the revered Compromise of 1820 rallied the South and enraged the North. Flung into the Illinois Senator's teeth were his own words, of five years earlier, when he had praised the Missouri Compromise as a "sacred thing, which no ruthless hand would ever be reckless enough to disturb." Douglas had no aversion to slavery; if it paid it was good, and if it did not it should be abandoned.

His blindness to principle left him unprepared for the fury of the North which felt a sense of betrayal with the opening of fresh lands to slavery. As the moderate Robert Winthrop of Massachusetts put it: "We are guardians of the infant commonwealths which lie cradled in these new Territories. We must do to them as we would be done by. If I thank God that Massachusetts is not a slave state, how then can I turn around and let Nebraska or Kansas become one by refusing to interpose for their protection." The usually restrained *New York Times* declared that enactment of the bill would destroy the last remains of Northern confidence in the supporters of slavery, and create an "ineradicable hatred of the institution which will crush its political power . . . at any cost."

For four months the country engaged in passionate debate. "We are on the eve of a great national transaction," said Seward, "a transaction that will close a cycle in the history of our country." Conservative businessmen, many of them formerly very friendly to the South, free soil editors, and clergy of all denominations joined in condemning the Kansas-Nebraska bill. Recent immigrants, frequently Democrats, also attacked the measure as blocking free settlement of the West.

In the Senate, party pressure forced the Democrats into line, but Sam Houston of Texas made a last appeal. As the vote was taken he pleaded: *"Maintain the Missouri Compromise . . . Give us peace!"* Possibly not even Clay and Webster could have wakened a spirit of compromise where all was rancor. By May 25 the bill was also driven through the House, but the vote was fairly close, 113 to 100. Northern Democrats were split almost evenly, 44 in favor, 42 against. All 59 Southern Democrats voted aye, except two. Northern Whigs, 45 of them, voted to a man against the measure; Southern Whigs divided, 12 for, 7 against. The Whigs had become almost entirely a sectional party, and the division among Democrats was ominous. "We accept the gauntlet thus thrown down to the free states," cried a free soiler. "I am ready for the fight between slavery and freedom."

★ "KIDNAPPERS! KIDNAPPERS!"

Even as Congress was preparing to take its final vote a spectacular episode in the fight between slavery and freedom flared up in Boston. Anthony Burns, a fugitive slave, had been imprisoned and a mob, inflamed by the eloquence of Theodore Parker and Wendell Phillips, made a daring, if futile, attempt to rescue him. It required a formidable display of military strength—artillery, marines, and infantry—to get the lone, trembling Negro to the ship which was to carry him back to slavery in Virginia. Fifty thousand people lined the way, cursing the soldiers with cries of "Kidnappers! Kidnappers!" Buildings were hung in black crepe, while church bells tolled. Conservatives and abolitionists alike joined in the angry demonstration.

Throughout the North the Fugitive Slave Law was defied; its violation became almost a sacred duty. Douglas had made more converts to antislavery in a few months than abolitionists had in twenty years. What had once been the opinion of extremists in the North had now become accepted by the soberest members of the community. Therein lay the foundation of great social change.

★ "BLEEDING KANSAS"

The Kansas-Nebraska Act, with its provision for "popular sovereignty," was an open invitation to North and South to fight it out in the Territories. "Come on, then, gentlemen of the slave States," cried Seward, "since there is no escaping your challenge, I accept it on behalf of the cause of freedom. We will engage in competition for the virgin soil of Kansas, and God give the victory to the side that is stronger in numbers as it is in right." And Douglas replied: "I accept your challenge; . . . call up your forces; preach your war on the Constitution, as you have threatened it here. We will be ready to meet all your allied forces."

Even before the Kansas-Nebraska bill had become law pro-Southern groups had moved in from Missouri, and Northerners were preparing to send antislavery colonists to the disputed region. An Emigrant Aid Society sent militant settlers from the North to Lawrence, Kansas, where they pitched their tents. Southern Aid societies assisted a counteremigration. Slaveowners were reluctant to risk their valuable property in these dangerous surroundings, trusting "border ruffians" from Missouri to uphold the Southern cause. On the day in November, 1854, set aside to elect a delegate to Congress, 1,700 Missourians crossed over to Kansas to cast a fraudulent vote, which helped send a proslavery representative to Washington. A Free State Party thereupon sent a rival delegate to Congress. Both sides were building up their strength in Kansas, though the Northerners had much the larger number of permanent settlers. Most of them were typical of the older frontier stock from the Ohio Valley, looking for new homes, and while not abolitionist in temper, they were anxious to keep the new land free from slavery.

In March, 1855, armed invaders from Missouri forced the election of a proslavery legislature. They terrorized the community and destroyed hostile newspapers. The weak President Pierce gave tacit support to Southerners in the fight for Kansas, being constantly pressed by the firebrand Senator Atchison. Killings and pillage marked this test of "popular sovereignty." Each side drew up its own constitution and awaited admission to the Union. What Kansas needed, said the *New York Tribune,* was "the spirit of martyrdom and Sharpe's rifles." A proslavery paper in Kansas countered with the call to Southerners to come armed with rifle, knife, and revolver to destroy the abolitionists. Lawrence was sacked by a Southern mob, with the connivance of federal officials.

In Washington itself, where the Senate's partisanship favored proslavery elements in Kansas, a Massachusetts Senator, Charles Sumner, cruelly indicted the South in his sensational speech, "The Crime Against Kansas." Eloquent, erudite, self-righteous, intemperate in speech, and personally offensive to many of his colleagues, he was one of the most disliked men in the upper Chamber. He spoke of the "Slave Power" as "heartless, grasping, and tyrannical," and his language was filled with direct insults to Senator Butler of South Carolina and Senator Douglas. Several days later, Butler's nephew, Congressman Preston Brooks, walked up to Sumner in the Senate Chamber and beat him senseless with a heavy cane.

While the South acclaimed Brooks the North was deeply aroused by his attack. Mass meetings and resolutions of state legislatures denounced the assault as a brutal display of Southern arrogance. Coming together with news of the horrors in Kansas, Northern feeling was at a dangerous pitch, while a South Carolinian in Washington said, "Everybody here feels as if we are upon a volcano."

In Kansas the volcano erupted when fanatical John Brown, seeking vengeance for Northern lives lost, slaughtered five innocent, proslavery settlers on Pottawatomie Creek. The infrequent, isolated murders of previous months were now succeeded by organized attacks of large groups of men. Civil war raged in the Territory; "bleeding Kansas" was the prelude to more tragic bloodletting five years later.

★ NEW POLITICAL ALIGNMENTS

Senator Chase of Ohio, defying Douglas in debate on the Kansas-Nebraska Act, had predicted the formation of a new political party to undo it. His prediction was not remarkable, for great numbers of people had been wavering for several years in their political allegiance. The Kansas-Nebraska Act gave a firm sense of direction to the hesitant. Northern Democrats and Whigs now called for the creation of a Fusion or Anti-Nebraska party. Douglas, once so popular in the North, was booed even in his home territory of Chicago.

In the fall elections of 1854 the Democratic party suffered a disastrous defeat. In New York, of 31 Congressmen chosen, 29 were anti-Nebraska men. New England was almost solid for free soil. In Ohio and Indiana, of 30 Congressmen chosen, 28 were against the Kansas-Nebraska bill. Only two years before, both states had gone heavily Democratic. The Whig party, grievously hurt in 1852, was given a mortal blow, disappearing entirely in some states, while its Southern wing flapped helplessly. An aged Negro wittily summed up the history of the Pierce administration; it "came in wid *little* opposition, and is going out wid *none.*"

In the overthrow of traditional party alignments a new group made its appearance, the Native Americans or Know Nothing party (its members replied "I know nothing," when queried about its principles). Its basis was hostility to immigrants, especially Catholic, whose growing strength in eastern cities frightened native Protestants who felt their institutions were endangered. Democratic politicians, in particular, were assailed for wooing the immigrant voter. Whigs joined the Know Nothings in droves. For almost two years after 1854 the movement had great power, carrying most of New England, just failing in New York, and showing significant strength in the Ohio Valley.

The Know Nothings, who boasted they had elected in 1854 nine governors and over 100 members of Congress, began to decline the next year. At a national convention in 1855, the members divided on the slavery issue, and when Southerners won out, adopting proslavery resolutions, Northerners withdrew. Its collapse thereafter was rapid. Lincoln ridiculed the whole movement of intolerance. We began our nation, he said, by declaring that "all men are created equal. We now practically read it, 'all men are created equal except Negroes.' When the Know Nothings obtain control it will read: 'All men are created equal except Negroes, foreigners and Catholics.' "

★ POLITICAL SENTIMENT IN THE OLD NORTHWEST

It was in the Old Northwest particularly that great numbers of people were ready for a new political allegiance. The revulsion against the extension of slavery was as strong there as anywhere else. But the moral consideration was re-enforced by other factors. Southerners were opposed to increased expenditures for internal improvements sought by the Northwest. This region chafed particularly under repeated obstacles raised by the South to the enactment of a Homestead Bill, which would grant 160 acres of land to actual settlers.

Farmers and businessmen of the upper Mississippi Valley knew they were engaged in a struggle with the South for the unsettled West. Southerners knew it, too, for they saw that free grants of land would benefit them much less than it would the North. One Senator from the South expressed it very clearly. Lands in his section, he said, were generally poorer than those in the North and West. "Poor men, dependent on their manual labor for support, [would] go north to the best lands. We would thus lose in population and the North would gain what we lost." The South, he claimed, also paid much more in taxes than the North, and would have to make up the deficit in the federal treasury caused by giving away land. "Thus the South would lose by the free farm policy in land, money, and population." Besides, he concluded, "it would provide a most efficient ally for Abolition by encouraging and stimulating the settlement of free farms with Yankees and foreigners pre-committed to resist the participancy of slaveholders in the public domain. The 'Emigrant Aid Societies' now organizing in the North will flourish and multiply under the fostering aid of such federal legislation."

★ THE REPUBLICAN PARTY

The former commercial ties between the upper Mississippi Valley and the South, which the great river had woven, were being superseded by steel bands of a railroad net which joined the West with the North Atlantic ports. Between 1849 and 1857 almost 17,000 miles of road were built in the country, with the largest share going to the north central states. By 1852 a passenger could travel from Chicago to the East on a through line, though the lack of a standard gauge seriously diminished railroad efficiency. Chicago, which had not a mile of railroad in 1850, ten years later was the center of eleven main lines, as well as many branch lines, the whole adding up to some 5,000 miles. The booming city on Lake Michigan had already become the chief distribution center of the West.

The West's foodstuffs, which had once been floated down the river to New Orleans, now went to eastern cities. British demand for American grain increased the advantages of North Atlantic ports over the more distant New Orleans. The economic prospects of the north central group of states were so dazzling that in the decade of the 1850's their population more than doubled, to over nine millions. The rapid growth of Western agriculture was threatening the reign of King Cotton. The economy of the West was further joined to the East when the great piles of copper and iron ore on the shores of Lake Superior were carried through newly built Sault Ste Marie Canal (the Soo), onward to eastern mills.

The economic alliance that was cementing the Northeast and Northwest made a political understanding between them easier. Out of common interests and a common antipathy to the handling of national problems by the two older parties a new party was formed. The name of Jefferson's old organization was borrowed for the new, and it was launched as the Republican party. The name recalled the equality of Jeffersonianism and, said a practical politician, "it is the cherished name with our foreign population of every nationality." In the spring of 1854 preliminary meetings were held in various places.

In a grove of oaks at Jackson, Michigan, a great mass meeting on July 6, 1854, formally organized the new party. Whigs, Free Soilers, and anti-Nebraska Democrats flocked to the new standard. The following winter Congress assembled with new faces representing the Republican viewpoint, even if they did not all call themselves as yet by that name. Republicans claimed 108 in a House of 234 members, making them the largest single group. They achieved a great victory in the new Congress by electing one of their own members, Nathaniel P. Banks of Massachusetts, Speaker of the House. In the Senate, Lyman Trumbull, foe of Douglas, was a new face from Illinois. Henry Wilson, the "cobbler of Natick," self-educated, risen from the lowly, and never forgetful of that fact, was the new Senator from Massachusetts.

A face not present in Washington, but which had made an impression in Illinois, was Abraham Lincoln's. In a refutation of Douglas' defense of the Kansas-Nebraska Act, Lincoln lifted the whole debate to a high moral plane. He stated that the worst aspect of the Act was not its repudiation of the Missouri Compromise; it was the betrayal of principles imbedded in the Declaration of Independence. "I particularly object to the new position which the avowed principle of this Nebraska law gives to slavery in the body politic. I object to it because it assumes that there can be moral right in the enslaving of one man by another. I object to it as a dangerous dalliance for free people—a sad evidence that feeling over-prosperity, we forget right; that liberty, as a principle, we have ceased to revere." This was a voice that recalled Americans to their own first principles and, in a short time, it was to be heard beyond the Illinois prairie and over the entire land.

★ ELECTION OF 1856

An electric excitement filled the air in anticipation of the presidential election in 1856. The Democrats had to stand on the platform Douglas had built for them in the Kansas-Nebraska Act. But they thought it politically unwise to have such an obvious target head the ticket. A Democratic candidate was needed who could appeal to the North as well as to the South. James Buchanan from the important state of Pennsylvania, minister to England, friend of Southerners, and not prominently involved in the Kansas-Nebraska debate, was chosen by the Democrats.

The Republican convention gathered in Philadelphia, filled with the zealous belief that a new day was dawning in America. No Southern state sent delegates, and only a few came from border states. Wilmot, author of the noted Proviso which had sharpened the controversy over slavery, read out the platform in a strong, defiant voice. It called for opposition to slavery extension, denunciation of the "Ostend Manifesto," admission of Kansas to the Union as a free state, and construction of a railroad to the Pacific. John C. Frémont, an adventurer in the West with many valuable political connections in the East, won the nomination for president with relative ease. The Know Nothings chose the colorless former President Fillmore, of New York. Fillmore could only take votes from Frémont.

The campaign was fought in the North, for the South was solid for Buchanan. Frémont's votes must all come from the free states, which had 176 electoral votes to the South's 120. Practiced politicians and inflamed citizens joined hands in one of the greatest political crusades in American history. The glamorous Frémont and his romantic wife, Jessie Benton, were pictured as an ideal couple to grace the White House. Hesitant Whigs, including Lincoln, moved over into the Republican ranks. News of continued outrages in Kansas strengthened Republican convictions. Their overwhelming victory in Maine's state elections in September stirred them to even greater efforts—but it also warned the Democrats of their danger.

Democratic managers, capitalizing on their party's role as the conservative party, collected large sums in Wall Street for distribution in the doubtful states of Pennsylvania and Indiana. Democratic campaigners in the North said Buchanan, if elected, would not intervene against free-soil elements in Kansas. Democrats claimed theirs was the party of union; the "Black Republicans" were disunionists. Southern Democrats said a victory for Frémont would mean secession, and extremists were already planning a Southern confederacy. Against the Republican slogan, "Free Speech, Free Press, Free Soil, Free Men, Frémont and Victory," an angry Virginia editor roared: "We have got to hating everything with the prefix free—from free negroes up and down through the whole catalogue—*free farms, free labor, free society* . . . and *free schools*—all belonging to the same brood of damnable *isms.*"

The Republicans, with a new, inexperienced organization, and short of funds, were beaten by the well-oiled machine of the Democrats. The latter's appeal to moderates was convincing to thousands, especially in Northern regions close to the Mason-Dixon line. Buchanan won, but a significant portent of the election lay in the figures of the popular vote. Frémont and Fillmore together polled far more than Buchanan. Pennsylvania, along with Illinois and Indiana, had given the Democrats victory, but by small margins. The drift was steadily toward the Republicans. The signposts for experienced politicians were well marked; the North threatened to go solidly Republican in the next election, and could then win the presidency regardless of the South. No wonder Republican politicians congratulated one another on their "victorious defeat."

CHAPTER XXI

The Deep Abyss

The Virginia editor who hated "everything with the prefix free" expressed an extreme opinion, but undoubtedly many in the South agreed with his denunciation of Northern democratic principles. It was also true that most Northerners were convinced that the editor spoke the mind of the majority of Southern whites. This was the tragic pass to which Americans had come. Though they had begun their national existence together speaking a common ideological language, changing economic and social circumstances had created sharply contrasting approaches to the preferred way of life. A growing chasm yawned between the members of the "house dividing." Perhaps not even the wisest statesmanship could prevent the plunge into the deep abyss.

★ SOUTHERN NATIONALISM

Hundreds of thousands of Southerners had reached the conviction that the United States had become two distinct nations. The possibility of Frémont's election had only sharpened the awareness of these diverging developments. One Virginia newspaper urged the establishment of a separate nation should the Republican candidate win election, arguing that it would promote Southern manufactures and commerce, local educational institutions, a new set of fashions, a new dialect, and a vigorous literature. In short, the whole life of the South, allegedly then under Northern domination, would be greatly stimulated by the creation of an independent nation. A struggle for economic and cultural independence preceded the test in the grimmer field of military conflict.

As Southerners looked at the national, and even world, economy they firmly believed that their region held the key to the prosperity of the Atlantic peoples. The real foundation of American wealth, they said, lay in Southern agriculture. The North, like a parasite, depended for its existence on the very institution of slavery she so violently indicted. Merchants, mechanics, farmers, lawyers, and doctors in the North all directly or indirectly "derive profit from that source," a Southern paper asserted. Imposing cities—Boston, New York, and Philadelphia—all depended on economic ties with the South. Were they to lose these benefits "their huge proportions would fall to decay, and scenes of wretchedness more absolute than words could depict mark their ruin." As for Great Britain (which depended for 70 per cent of its vast cotton imports on the South), were she to be deprived "of the fruits of her commerce in our great staples," gloated the same writer, "she would be almost stricken from the list of independent states; without them she could not clothe and give employment to her thronging masses, nor long stagger under the oppressive weight of her accumulating debt." Northerners and Britons alike were the despised middlemen who took the profits that would remain to enrich an exploited South were she economically independent.

To achieve that economic independence a number of Southern commercial conventions were called. Strong statements were made calling for the establishment of locally owned shipping lines to carry Southern products; a Southern route for the projected railroad to the Pacific (the Gadsden Purchase had been made with that intention); Southerners to patronize their own manufactures; school children to use books written by Southerners; and adults to encourage Southern literature by reading their own authors. Little of this program ever materialized, though Southerners did send a larger percentage of their youngsters to college than did Northerners. Southern capital continued to flow into agriculture, Southern writers starved for want of patronage, and Charleston gained the unenviable distinction of becoming the graveyard of magazines.

Despite failure to achieve economic and cultural autonomy, Southerners remained certain of the superiority of their way of life over that of the North. The fact that the South withstood the panic of 1857 much better than did the North re-enforced belief in its superior advantages. "When thousands of the strongest commercial houses in the world were coming down and hundreds of millions of dollars of supposed property evaporating in thin air; when you came to a deadlock and revolutions were threatened what brought you up?" Senator Hammond challenged the North. "Fortunately for you it was the commencement of the cotton season, and we have poured upon you 1,600,000 bales of cotton just at the crisis to save you from destruction." The Southerners boasted that their slave economy was more stable than the money-mad free society of the North.

In the year of the panic the *Southern Literary Messenger,* upholding the superiority of slave society, spoke of it as one in which the employer and employed had an identity of interest throughout life. "This union of labor and capital," it asserted, "counteracts . . . all those social, moral, material, and political evils which afflict the North." Southern society, William L. Yancey proudly maintained, was happier and more cultivated than the materialistic North, where "the masses are day-laborers, confined closely . . . to the work shop, the factory and the field."

Free society, said a Virginia paper, was "immoral," "unnatural," and must give way to slavery, "a social system as old as the world, universal as man." An Alabama journal asserted that workers and farmers in the North were not even fit to sit with the servant of a Southern gentle-man. Free society, it said with contempt, "was nothing but a conglom-eration of greasy mechanics, filthy operatives, small fisted farmers, and moonstruck theorists."

★ HELPER'S "IMPENDING CRISIS"

Not all Southerners were sure that they had found the right answers to life's problems. The continuing migration from the South across the Ohio to the Old Northwest was evidence enough of a deep-running dissatisfaction. Southerners regretted the stigma that attached to working at a trade or engaging in unskilled labor. Slave labor was always a threat to the wages of whites. Northern textile workers earned $205 annually in 1860; for Southerners it was $145. "The poor white man," com-plained a Southern Senator, "will endure the evils of pinching poverty rather than engage in servile labor under the existing state of things." Another Southern observer said regretfully, "I never knew a slaveholder permit his son to learn a trade. They seem to think it disgraceful to work at mechanical vocations. They must all be preachers, merchants, lawyers or gentlemen blackguards. True, there are white mechanics and excellent men here, but they acknowledge that there is a coldness shown towards them by the slave holders unless the working man owns negroes."

The class division in the South was most widely publicized by a book of Hinton Rowan Helper, *The Impending Crisis,* in 1857. Helper, a roving Southern journalist sprung from the yeoman class, was unin-terested in the fate of Negroes; the slaves, he said, should be emancipated and resettled in Africa. His concern was with nonslaveholding whites who, he believed, were victimized by the institution of slavery. "Non-slaveholders of the South," he called out to farmers, mechanics and workingmen, "we take this occasion to assure you that the slaveholders . . . have hoodwinked you, trifled with you, and used you as mere tools for the consummation of their wicked designs. They have purposely kept you in ignorance, and have, by moulding your passions to suit themselves, induced you to act in direct opposition to your dearest rights and interests."

Helper assembled data to show how far the free North had outstripped the slave South in wealth, productive power, and cultural institutions. Southerners generally ignored or suppressed Helper's book, but Northern papers were delighted with it. Many printings of *The Impending Crisis* were exhausted, public addresses and editorials were based upon it. A condensed, inexpensive version was published in an edition of 100,000 copies by Republicans, who hailed the book as an invaluable ally in the fight on the slave South.

★ "DIFFERENT IDEALS"

The steady drifting apart of North and South affected all levels of both populations. With the rising tide of nationalism in the South large numbers of her children left colleges and academies of the North to enroll in their own institutions. It became more and more difficult for Southerners to travel in the North without constraint, while Northerners in the South felt oppressed by the growing hostility.

Religious bonds between the two sections were also snapping. Baptists and Methodists divided into Northern and Southern churches in the controversy over slavery. Other religious groups, in particular the Presbyterians, were torn by dissension. Southerners maintained that North and South were, in origin, settled by two different peoples. They cultivated the myth that the plantation aristocracy was descended from Cavalier England, while inferior Yankees were sprung from the plebeian class in the Old World. Believing themselves sons of ancient Cavaliers, Southerners revived the cult of chivalry and organized medieval tournaments. Young men dressed as knights and tilted with lances, while adoring belles waved handkerchiefs in encouragement.

Allied with the tendency to differentiate North and South on the basis of supposed contrasting social origins were the ethnological studies of Southern scientists. Some of these studies revealed careful scholarship, but they were vitiated by the need of their authors to prove the innate inferiority of Negroes to whites. Mingled with the pride of the South was a defensiveness that betrayed a deep unease.

Thus in fundamental interests—political, economic, educational, religious—North and South followed diverging paths. "We were all of us Americans—intense, self-satisfied, self-glorying Americans," wrote George Cary Eggleston in retrospect, "but we had little else in common . . . We had different ideals . . . different traditions and different aspirations."

★ THE WAY OF LIFE IN THE NORTH

And what were the ideals, traditions and aspirations of the North? Northerners ridiculed the myth Southerners had created of their own superiority. The former were ready to acknowledge serious flaws in their own society, but contended that the good far outweighed the bad and that their civilization, inspired by democratic, humane ideals, was the most progressive on earth. Southerners, they said, lived in a dream world; they were the dupes of their own myth which shielded them from a harsh reality.

As for the North the realities of life had their depressing as well as cheering aspects. The Industrial Revolution was making great headway, and with its marvels came evils. Merchant princes, whose wealth came from commerce, were looking to their laurels as larger fortunes began to pile up from transportation and manufacturing. The capital invested in manufactures almost doubled in one decade, reaching a figure of over $1,000,000,000 in 1860. American technology, in toolmaking and in manufacturing firearms, locomotives, and farm implements, was equal, if not superior, to Europe's best.

The Patent Office in Washington was a perfect mirror of the ceaseless energy of American inventors whose products—the Howe sewing machine, Goodyear's vulcanized rubber, the Colt revolver, the Hoe printing press, the McCormick reaper—had a revolutionary effect on society. Mass production, based on division of labor and interchangeable parts, was already a striking characteristic of American enterprise, in making shoes, guns, watches, furniture, and other products.

Despite the phenomenal growth of American industry, however, the United States was still surpassed by the industrial might of Great Britain. The two countries were each other's best customers; the British exchanging manufactured goods for grain, cotton, and California's gold.

Almost half of all the United States corporations established between 1800 and 1860 were founded in the one decade of the 1850's. They greatly expanded business enterprise, but they also made it more impersonal. There was much truth in Southern charges that Northern employers treated workmen like a commodity. It was also noted that concentration of economic power in the North, while not as marked as in the South, was already significant. Fifteen of Boston's prominent families combined, in the "Boston Associates," to control one-fifth of the country's cotton spindles, about a third of the Massachusetts railways, two-fifths of their city's banking capital, and the same proportion of their state's insurance capital. In New York a directory of wealthy local residents listed many with large fortunes, topped by John

Jacob Astor's $25,000,000. In state capitals rich corporations were exerting a corrupting influence in politics.

Big business had few restraints in dealing with labor. Unions were weak and, while skilled labor was generally independent, a vast pool of unskilled workers was generally available among the mass of immigrants from Europe and from American farms. In depression days employers were wont to demand extra-long hours of work, and "difficult" workers found themselves on a blacklist which circulated among employing groups. Sweatshops sometimes paid women needleworkers as little as twelve cents a day. The use of child labor, as everywhere else in the world, was common throughout the country. The inadequate income of the father often made the need for additional earnings mandatory. On his annual wages of less than $300 (the usual figure in the 1850's), a workman could not support even a moderate-sized family.

Absentee owners were more common now than formerly, and they ruled their industrial baronies with little regard for human personality. Even the model mills in Lowell, with their intelligent and ambitious young women operatives, once the pride of Massachusetts, had degenerated into grimy factory communities with a dispirited labor class. In these same years when wages were often low and hours always long, profits were frequently high.

Unlike the South, however, where no criticism of slave society was condoned, the North faced the constant barbs of homegrown critics. Despite all talk of regiments of factory workers doing the bidding of captains of industry, Northerners did not live in a regimented society. Workmen, reformers, clergy, and enlightened employers combined to bring pressure on state legislatures to reform the worst abuses of child labor, long hours, and unsafe factories. Strikes, though often failures, did win concessions from employers. The evils long remained, but they were not sanctioned, as was slavery, as a blessed way of life.

★ "WE ARE A PEOPLE, A NATION"

Northern business identified its needs of tariffs, rail and ship subsidies, internal improvements, and a more efficient banking system with the national good. A more centralized nation, with increased Congressional power to foster business enterprise, was in the making. Cultural factors, which made themselves felt more strongly in the North than in the South, likewise contributed to a strengthened sense of nationalism. Northern publishers circulated millions of copies of books throughout the country. Magazines and journals of national circulation, such as the *New York Ledger,* with 400,000 copies a week, or *Harper's Monthly,* with 200,000, promoted a common response in a mass audience. National scientific societies made their members conscious of belonging to a larger political entity than that represented by a section or state.

American art lent its aid in stimulating nationalism. Emanuel Leutze's historical paintings were ardently patriotic, and portraits by other artists of famous national figures helped create an American folklore. The Revolution was celebrated in painting, historical narratives, biographies, and poetry. In dozens of plays the theater commemorated historic events of the Revolution, the War of 1812, and the Mexican War, stirring audiences in a common patriotic emotion. Anthems, such as "America," with its praise of the "sweet land of liberty" and its exhortation, "Let freedom ring," awakened powerful national sentiments.

The North was confident that its free society would ultimately triumph in the United States. As Senator Sumner expressed it, in the debate on the Kansas-Nebraska bill: "It annuls all past compromises with slavery, and makes all future compromises impossible. Thus it puts freedom and slavery face to face, and bids them grapple. Who can doubt the result?"

Southerners, on the other hand, believing themselves threatened by the increasing pressures of an industrialized North hostile to slavery, developed the concept that two nations had evolved in the United States. While all the tendencies in the North—political, economic, cultural— were toward a more intensified nationalism for the entire country, the South was moving in the opposite direction, cultivating the idea of Southern independence. The North, said William Gilmore Simms, seeks to dictate to the South on the question of slavery. "But we are a people, a nation," he cried, "with arms in our hands, and in sufficient numbers to compel the respect of other nations; and we shall never submit the case to the judgment of another people, until they show themselves of superior virtue and intellect."

Alienation of the South and North from each other had thus grown so great that each might be said to be only within *shouting* distance of the other. In an atmosphere of angry shouting calm words were likely to die on the wind.

★ DRED SCOTT

The wind reached hurricane force early in March, 1857, when the Supreme Court announced its famous decision in the case of Dred Scott. Buchanan was anxious for a judgment of the Court which he hoped would finally quiet the shrill debate over slavery. He feared secession and, dominated as he was by a Southern cabal, he was constantly yielding to their intimidation. Not that he needed undue pressure to champion the Southern view on slavery. He had long believed that the South had reason enough to secede if agitation against slavery continued. Even toward his own fellow Northern Democrats like Douglas (whom he despised as a person) he felt loathing for their principle of "squatter sovereignty." He lacked statesmanship himself, and, to the country's misfortune, he was surrounded by men strong only in their pugnacious assertion of the slaveowner's views. Jacob Thompson, Secretary of the Interior and a vindictive politician, was a man whose vision was bounded by the lower South. The president's chief adviser and boon companion was Howell Cobb of Georgia, Secretary of the Treasury, and master of a thousand slaves.

Buchanan, in his inaugural address, denounced the agitation over slavery and hoped that the forthcoming decision of the court would end it. The president was aware of the nature of the decision, for he had directly intervened with the court to make a sweeping statement on slavery in the Territories. Widespread speculation had anticipated a majority decision voiding the Missouri Compromise, and accurate predictions were made as to the division of the vote among the Justices. The verdict was tensely awaited, for the debate as to who should control slavery in the Territories—the local residents, or Congress, or neither—had reached a high pitch while the case of Dred Scott was being considered.

Dred Scott, a Negro slave, had been taken from Missouri by his master to Illinois and Minnnesota Territory, where he had resided for two years, and then returned. Some time later he sued for his liberty in Missouri courts on the ground that residence in a free state and in territory north of the Missouri Compromise line had automatically conferred freedom upon him. Under the guidance of free-soil adherents the case ultimately was carried to the Supreme Court.

When aged Chief Justice Taney rose to read the decision, in his high-pitched, thin voice, the Washington courtroom was packed. Despite foreknowledge of the nature of the decision, Taney's words came with the force of a thunderclap. Dred Scott's claim was denied on three grounds: (1) Negroes could not be United States citizens, therefore they could not sue in federal courts (2) Illinois laws could not affect his situation in Missouri, where he now resided (3) Residence in Minnesota Territory, which was north of 36°30', did not confer freedom as the Missouri Compromise itself was unconstitutional.

Northern papers blazed with the inflammatory news—"The Missouri Compromise Unconstitutional—The Triumph of Slavery Complete." It was plain to everyone that the court was heavily biased in favor of the South, seven of the nine Justices were Democrats, and five of the seven were Southerners. Their decision meant that slavery followed the flag; squatter sovereignty seemed dead. The voice of Calhoun, stilled these five years, was never more alive.

Without hesitation the North spurned the verdict. The prestige of the court, overweighted as it was in the South's favor, had been declining for some years in Northern opinion and now it almost vanished. Northern legislatures condemned the decision; New York announced that any slave brought to that state would be immediately freed, and an individual even passing through the state with a slave risked a prison term of up to ten years. Press and pulpit denounced the court, and people everywhere in the North felt that the decision was not binding upon them.

People in the North and West were strengthened in their convictions by the opinions of the two dissenting Justices, Curtis and McLean. The minority view, citing theory and fact, refuted Taney's judgment that Negroes could not be citizens, and that Congress had no right over slavery in the Territories. Republican journals looked forward to a reversal of the court when their party came to power and appointed new judges. "The remedy is union and action; the ballot box," said the *Chicago Tribune*. "Let free States be a unit in Congress on the side of freedom. Let the next President be Republican, and 1860 mark an era kindred with that of 1776."

★ DISUNITY AMONG DEMOCRATS

Republican hostility to the Dred Scott decision was to be expected, but the greater danger to national unity came from the split in the Democratic party which soon followed. Triumphant Southerners were now demanding that the party go beyond the older principle—that Congress could not force slavery *out* of the Territories—to the more radical position that it was obligated to defend slavery *in* them. This was the ultimatum of the South to the Northern wing of the Democratic party which had put its faith in the doctrine of popular sovereignty.

The depressed Chief Justice, smarting under the savage attacks of his critics, told a visitor "that the unity and power of the Democratic Party have alone saved the Union from being torn in pieces by two conflicting factions—North and South—and that the growing dissolutions in that Party must end in arraying North and South in actual hostility against each other." The imperious Jefferson Davis was writing a friend at about the same time: "In the next four years is . . . locked up the fate of the Union. If the issues are boldly and properly met my hope is that the Constitution will prevail; if the attempt is made to postpone them the next Presidential election will probably bring us to the alternative of resistance to oppressive usurpation or the tame surrender of our birthright."

The history of the next four years showed how often the issues were improperly met and how seldom boldly faced.

★ "KANSAS IS TO BE A FREE STATE"

In the same year that Dred Scott lost his chance for freedom Southern extremists made a desperate effort to force slavery on Kansas, despite the overwhelming sentiment against it (only some 200 slaves were there). In the spring of 1857 free-soil emigrants to Kansas outnumbered those from the slave states, ten to one. A proslavery constitution was drawn up at Lecompton that fall and sent to Congress for admission of Kansas to the Union. At this point Douglas, staunch believer in political democracy and the principle of popular sovereignty, flung out a challenge to the "rule or ruin" Southern element in his party. He insisted that the people of Kansas, who obviously wanted a free-soil state, be permitted to vote on the Lecompton Constitution. "Any attempt," he said, "to force a proslavery constitution upon the people without an opportunity of voting it down at the polls will be regarded . . . as so decidedly unjust, oppressive and unworthy of a free people, that the people of the United States will not sanction it." And with an eye to the fortunes of his party, he wrote, "it would add thousands to the vote of the Republican party in every State of the Union."

The fight was transferred to Washington where a titanic battle began over Kansas and the Lecompton Constitution. The division between Northern and Southern Democrats was greater than ever. Buchanan, notably weak, was whipped by his Southern tamers, and he fell into step with them in support of the Lecompton Constitution. Douglas, rising now to great heights of statesmanship, aiming to save the Union, fought with tigerish energy against this betrayal of democratic principles. He hurled his words against his opponents with the crash and roar of a cannonade. He even entered into a temporary alliance with the Republicans to frustrate the Southern Democrats.

The administration struck back through the power of patronage and every other pressure available to it. The only test now was: were you for or against Lecompton? Despite administration coercion Northern Democrats knew that a vote for the proslavery Kansas constitution would be political suicide. In the end Douglas won, a compromise measure was adopted, and Kansas was given its right to vote on the hated constitution. When her citizens did, in August, 1858, they buried it by the overwhelming margin of six to one. Some months before,

Douglas had written, "Kansas is to be a free State." There was no doubt about it.

★ "PIKE'S PEAK OR BUST"

Not everyone in the country, not even in Kansas, was thinking only of the fight over slavery in the climactic years 1857 and 1858. Men's eyes were fixed on western lands where lay hidden fabulous wealth in precious metals, where cattle freely roamed, and where great stands of timber promised riches to lusty lumbermen. Oregon already boasted 50,000 people, while in golden California factories were springing up, and the infant state instead of importing was exporting foodstuffs. Speculation in land was universal. A German traveler on a steamboat from Dubuque to St. Paul thought his fellow passengers might care to watch the beautiful landscape. But no, everyone was busy talking of the price of farms and the profits in quick sales of town lots.

Toward the end of summer, in 1858, a prospector brought news to Leavenworth of gold finds in the Pike's Peak region. The word spread fast, tall tales inflated the value of the discoveries. The panic of 1857 had impoverished farmers and left many workmen unemployed. They furnished willing recruits for the gold fields. A young man who had gladly caught the fever to escape from his dull round of clerking wrote, "Never have a great boom, a fabulously wealthy mining district, and a new civilization been started on slimmer realities. It was all talk and dream, and yet in Iowa we were hotter about it than a prairie fire." Within a few months hundreds of cabins and tents were strung out on Cherry Creek, where Denver was laid out.

Thousands started for the diggings, their covered wagons flaunting the message "Pike's Peak or Bust." Most of them took the homeward trail "busted," for the lone miner soon found that with his inadequate pick, shovel, and "washing pan" he faced the prospect of diminishing returns. The riches that still lay entombed in the Rockies could only be extracted by expensive machinery and professional engineers—in short, corporate enterprise. Soon mine superintendents and bands of wage workers, all subject to absentee owners, began to supplant the colorful prospector whose eye had first seen the signs of wealth.

It was shiftless Henry Comstock who gave his name to fantastic Comstock Lode in Nevada in 1859. The lazy Comstock with a glib tongue had talked his way into sharing the find made by others. Shortly he and his partners were extracting thousands of dollars a day in gold and silver from one of the richest mines ever discovered. A new rush was on. To house the thousands of newcomers in the first months the crazy quilt town, Virginia City, was constructed of brush, potato sacks, blankets, and anything else that came to hand. Within a year the city had a theater, hotels, stores, and numerous saloons, all charging prices that rapidly depleted most miners' earnings. Despite the fabulous rewards of the few, "pay dirt" was hard to come by for the many. Most of the gold and silver buried in the Comstock Lode could only be unlocked after the investment of considerable capital.

Indeed big business quickly invaded other forms of enterprise in the West. Transportation, lumbering, large ranches, and huge wheat farms all required outlays of capital far beyond men with small means, who had often prospered in the more compact East. Even so, the lands across the Mississippi held promise for the farmer, the small cattleman, and the always hopeful prospector. But they also held great rewards for the men who laid out new towns, gained control of vast timber tracts, built the railroads, and organized mining companies.

★ STAGE COACH AND PONY EXPRESS

As the Far West began filling up, the need for better communications with the East grew more insistent. The slow pace and high cost of mails via the Isthmus of Panama hurried demands from the Pacific coast for overland service. Hunger for contact with folks back home and desire for merchandise unobtainable locally forced quick satisfaction of these needs. With government aid transportation companies were organized to carry goods, passengers, and mail over the vast stretches from Missouri to California. The largest freighting firm in this western region before the Civil War was Russell, Majors & Waddell. Headquarters was Leavenworth, Kansas, where mountains of merchandise were sorted out to fill the acres of wagons making ready for the westward pull. In 1858 it had 4,000 men in its employ, and needed 40,000 oxen to pull its 3,500 covered wagons. It supplied army posts and mining camps; indeed much of the trans-Mississippi West depended on it for existence.

To speed the mails and provide fast passenger service two experienced expressmen—John Butterfield and William Fargo—organized the Overland Mail Company. It followed a route southward from Tipton, Missouri (where the railroad from St. Louis ended) across Texas, through southern New Mexico and Arizona, and thence into California. The first stages left, with great fanfare from eastern and western terminals, on September 15, 1858. Before twenty-four days were up each wagon had rolled to a stop, almost 2,800 miles from the start.

For several years the well-built Concord Coaches, painted a bright green or red, raced over the plains and deserts behind their galloping horses. They stuck close to schedule, two each week in each direction, though coaches were sometimes caught in the snows of mountain passes or riddled with bullets of marauding Apache and Comanche. Dissatisfaction with the long southern trail led Kansans and Californians to back a shorter central route. With their encouragement, Russell, Majors & Waddell launched the famed Pony Express on April 3, 1860, to rush the mails across the continent. From St. Joseph, Missouri (the western end of the railroad system) to San Francisco, "home stations" were built every thirty miles and "swing stations" every ten miles, where riders changed their fleet Indian ponies. Each of the carefully selected light-weight riders (less than 135 pounds) covered his stage from one "home station" to the next, where he passed the mailbag on to a fresh rider, who was off within two minutes. In less than eleven days the mails had gone through, halving the time of the fastest stagecoach. The Pony Express, though glamorous, was a financial failure. In any event, it was soon outmoded by the telegraph, but for the eighteen months it lasted it thrilled the country with its example of grit and courage.

Farther east, along the Atlantic ports, great interest was shown in another step to speed up communications. In August of 1858 the Atlantic cable was laid between Newfoundland and Ireland. Anglo-American co-operation, spurred by the organizing genius of Cyrus Field of New York, made possible this achievement. The cable snapped after a few weeks, but the persevering Field ultimately laid a stronger one which, in terms of communications at least, reduced the dimensions of the Atlantic to a pond.

★ LINCOLN

Men might think of an ocean telegraph, a pony express, mines of gold and silver, or the wealth of farm acreage or town lots, but they were not allowed to forget for long the cancer of slavery. In that same August, 1858, when the Atlantic cable was first laid, Kansans had repudiated the attempt to force a slave constitution upon them. Two months before, the Republicans of Illinois had nominated Abraham Lincoln for Senator to run against the redoubtable Douglas. Lincoln's platform demanded that slavery be kept out of the Territories; it denounced the Dred Scott decision and the Lecompton Constitution. It asked that public lands, which had been gobbled up by speculators, be put into the hands of actual settlers.

Lincoln, leader of the Illinois Republicans, was almost fifty when his party conferred upon him this high honor. Not until the debate over the Kansas-Nebraska Act did he show much of that moral magnificence forever associated with his name. Some years before, he had served in Congress for one term as a Whig without attracting much attention.

Like many of his neighbors he had struggled upward from poverty, working the family farm, and studying with intense concentration his few books. The gangling young man worked on a flatboat carrying produce to New Orleans, played his part in the Black Hawk War, was surveyor and storekeeper, and, after mastering the required lawbooks, was admitted to the bar.

There was no special distinction to his political career until the mid 1850's. He had, however, a wide acquaintance among Illinois politicians, and his legal practice, which made him relatively prosperous after 1850, had taken him to all corners of the state. Nobody could mistake Lincoln for anyone else. His bony frame of six feet four and his expressive, homely face made him stand out among his fellows. People responded warmly to his character, his humanity, his wisdom, his will to know the truth, and his saving humor.

Lincoln's first prominent speech was the Peoria address, in October, 1854, against Douglas and the Kansas-Nebraska Act. Though he had long been a free soiler, he was no abolitionist, and he knew the immensity of the problem in ridding the country of slavery. Nevertheless he touched a deep chord with his words: "Slavery is founded on the selfishness of man's nature—opposition to it in his love of justice. These principles are in eternal antagonism, and when brought into collision so fiercely as slavery extension brings them, shocks and throes and convulsions must ceaselessly follow."

Lincoln, in a widely publicized speech at Springfield, June, 1857, strongly attacked the Dred Scott decision. Again he appealed to the principles of the Declaration of Independence as the platform on which people everywhere could ultimately stand in the dignity of free men. Jefferson, he said, "meant to set up a standard maxim for free society, which should be familiar to all, and revered by all, constantly looked to, constantly labored for, and even though never perfectly attained, constantly approximated, and thereby constantly spreading and deepening its influence, and augmenting the happiness and value of life to all peoples of all colors everywhere."

★ LINCOLN-DOUGLAS DEBATES

Douglas, though now restored to public favor because of his stand against Lecompton, realized that he had a fight on his hands to save his place in the Senate. Lincoln, he knew, was the ablest opponent the Republicans could have chosen. In the first speech of the campaign Lincoln sounded the theme on which his future talks played variations: "We are now far into the fifth year since a policy was initiated with the avowed object and confident promise of putting an end to slavery agitation. Under the operation of that policy, that agitation not only has not ceased, but has constantly augmented. In my opinion, it will not cease until a crisis shall have been reached and passed. 'A house divided against itself cannot stand.' I believe this government cannot endure permanently half slave and half free. I do not expect the Union to be dissolved—I do not expect the house to fall—but I do expect it will cease to be divided. It will become all one thing, or all the other. Either the opponents of slavery will arrest the further spread of it and place it where the public mind shall rest in the belief that it is in the course of ultimate extinction; or its advocates will push it forward until it shall become alike lawful in all the States, old as well as new, North as well as South."

Douglas and Lincoln agreed to discuss the issues in a series of joint debates throughout the state. Everywhere they were greeted by intensely interested crowds, and throughout the nation an unseen audience of millions was kept informed by excellent newspaper coverage. Thousands of listeners thronged to each meeting place. Clouds of dust were thrown up by the carriages, wagons, and horsemen hurrying to the scene of debate. Town dignitaries accompanied the candidates to the wooden platform set in the sun-baked public square.

The two debaters presented startling physical contrasts. Douglas, five feet tall, solidly built, became all fire and frenzy in his speech—"a steam engine in britches," someone called him. His dark face had a fierce bulldog quality, and his voice a powerful bark that had brought many an opponent to heel. Lincoln, said a reporter, was "built on the Kentucky type," very tall, angular, awkward, with big feet, and clothes much too short for his long arms and legs. His deep-set eyes reflected quickly his mirth or sorrow. When he was stirred he became truly impressive—"his eye glows and sparkles, every lineament, now so ill-formed, grows brilliant and expressive, and you have before you a man of rare power and of strong magnetic influence. He *takes* the people every time, and there is no getting away from his sturdy good sense, his unaffected sincerity, and the unceasing play of his good humor, which accompanies his clear logic and smoothes the way to conviction." His shrill, penetrating voice carried to the farthest edges of the patient crowds who stood for hours to listen to America's most famous debate.

The outstanding meeting was at Freeport, where 15,000 people heard the two men. Here they asked and answered questions each had given the other. Lincoln asked Douglas how he could square his doctrine of popular sovereignty, which gave residents of a Territory the right to keep slavery out of it, with the Dred Scot decision? Douglas' answer, the "Freeport Doctrine," said that residents of a Territory, in practice, could admit or exclude slavery by the exercise of local police regulations. Local legislatures had the right to establish regulations, "and if the people are opposed to slavery they will elect representatives to that body who will by unfriendly legislation effectually prevent the introduction of it into their midst." Thus the Dred Scott decision stood, but so, too, did the principle of popular sovereignty.

Douglas gave as good as he received, but Lincoln fixed the country's eyes on slavery as a great moral wrong. To Douglas' statement that the nation could exist "forever divided into free and slave states," Lincoln replied that "ultimate extinction" of slavery was the end that all good men sought. Slavery, contained in the South, and with no possibility of expansion, would gradually disappear, he thought, without war or violence.

Douglas won in a very close election, though the price was high. His victory made him the chief figure in Democratic plans for the presidency in 1860, but it also brought renewed dislike from the South. The Buchanan faction, which had worked against him, was even more malignant than before. Douglas was deposed from his important post as chairman of the Senate committee on Territories. The radical, proslavery wing of the Democrats declared a war to the death on the "Freeport Doctrine" and its author, who was almost as obnoxious as a "Black Republican." Southern extremists meant to rule *and* ruin the Democratic party.

★ THE "IRREPRESSIBLE CONFLICT"

The elections in 1858 in the North were a disaster for the administration. The states were swept by Republicans or Douglas Democrats. Hostility to Buchanan's support of proslavery elements in Kansas brought out a torrent of votes to submerge the president. In New England and the middle states winning candidates emphasized tariff and homestead issues. In New York, Seward spoke of the systems of free and slave labor in America coming into collision: "It is an irrepressible conflict between opposing and enduring forces." The omens for 1860 were unmistakable.

Southern radicals like Yancey, Rhett, and Edmund Ruffin, seeing the engulfing tide rise about them, became even more aggressive. Congress, far from permitting a Territory to act on slavery, must itself adopt a code to protect the "peculiar institution" in the Territories. Even more, the clandestine slave trade which had been bringing Africans over to the United States in increasing numbers, must now be legalized. Prices for Negroes were mounting and pressure from smaller landowners for a greater supply was becoming more insistent. Now is the time to strike for independence, cried Yancey. Three millions had won their freedom from England; could not eight million win it from the North? Everywhere in the South extremists were whipping up sentiment for disunion. The moderates far outnumbered them, but counteraggression from the North was playing into their hands.

When the North indicted the South for violating the law by running in slaves from Africa, the tables were turned by Southerners who asked why the Fugitive Slave Act was not enforced? It was almost impossible now to recover fugitive slaves in most Northern states, and the Wisconsin legislature, in 1859, declared the Dred Scott decision null and void. Thus nullification in the North matched secession in the South.

Into this inflammable situation John Brown charged with a fiery sword. He had come East from his scourge of Kansas with plans to invade the South and free the slaves. Fanatical, and bordering on the insane when his rigid mind fixed on slavery, Brown had gained the support of Northern abolitionists for his mission. Together with him they believed the slaves would rise en masse at freedom's signal and strike for their own liberty. Even should this first objective not be achieved, however, the hope was that Brown's blow would be the opening gun in a civil war which would destroy slavery.

Brown collected, in great secrecy, a small force of twenty-one men, including his sons, for his projected attack. He planned to take Harper's Ferry, with its supplies of arms in the federal arsenal, and move southward stirring up slave revolts. On the night of October 16, 1859, moving in gloomy silence under an overcast sky, Brown's little group rushed into the town, seized the arsenal, and took some prisoners.

The Negroes he expected to flock to his side did not come. Instead, the alarm which spread through Virginia and Maryland during the night brought hundreds of militia to Harper's Ferry where they cut off Brown's escape routes. He took refuge in a small engine-house, built of brick. Most of his men were dead or dying but the iron-willed leader would not surrender. Col. Robert E. Lee, commanding a company of marines, finally forced the heavy doors and overwhelmed Brown and the few still fighting by his side. Brown was taken alive but unconscious.

Within a short time Brown was brought to trial in Virginia on charges of insurrection, murder, and treason. The accused refused to plead insanity. The jury on October 31 returned with the expected verdict of guilty. Allowed by the judge to make a statement, Brown spoke to the millions beyond the courtroom's walls. "Now, if it is deemed necessary that I should forfeit my life for the furtherance of the ends of justice, and mingle my blood further with the blood of my children and with the blood of millions in this slave country whose rights are disregarded by wicked, cruel, and unjust enactments, I say, let it be done." He was content, he told his children, "to die for God's eternal truth on the scaffold as in any other way." He was hung on December 2.

During the trial Brown had written his family "that *posterity* at least will do me justice." Northerners did not wait that long. The trial and long period between his sentence and death made him martyr to millions. They did not know the full extent of his plans to spread death and destruction throughout the South. All they saw was a heroic figure in the courtroom whose spirit, if not his body, remained unconquered. Bells tolled in Northern towns and villages on execution day and flags were lowered to half staff. Before John Brown's body was cold the legend of a sacrificial figure was swiftly spreading through the land.

It was granted that his act was lawless, yet nobly inspired. Moderates, however, were alarmed by John Brown's deed and denounced it. Inflamed Southerners heard only the praise and not the North's revulsion. The South was now convinced that even the sober citizenry in the North were behind John Brown and were plotting its destruction. A wave of terror ran through the South, fearful of further insurrection. As the white man's fears increased, the lot of the black was worsened. John Brown's raid toughened the North against slavery, but the South was hardened even more against the Yankees whose hatred, it was thought, craved the blood of peaceful men and women.

★ POLITICS, 1859

All the signs pointed to crisis in 1860. Douglas, the only figure who might have transcended sectional differences, was ruled out by the implacable hostility of Buchanan and Southern extremists. Their intrigue and pressure were unending in building obstacles to the Democrats' nomination of Douglas in 1860.

The state elections in the fall of 1859 offered further proof of Democratic demoralization. Republicans carried Ohio, Iowa, Minnesota, and, most significantly, Pennsylvania. It was clear that free-soil Democrats would have no more of Buchanan. In Pennsylvania, the victors placed heavy emphasis on the need to raise the tariff. In the West resentment, which was strong enough over the Kansas issue, had mounted against the administration's policy of favoring land speculators rather than legitimate settlers. The Panic of 1857 had hit the West harder than any other part of the country. "Old Buck" was blamed by a Kansas paper for men being in rags, "women and children barefooted, with starvation staring them in the face—many of them could not raise ten dollars to save their souls from perdition." The final blow was Buchanan's veto of the Homestead Bill. Champions of land reform had nowhere to turn except the Republican party.

Confidence among Republicans had increased with every election since 1856. The presidential prize now seemed within their grasp, but with which candidate? It was really Seward against the field. Seward, abetted by his fellow New Yorker, Thurlow Weed, had built one of the strongest political machines in the country's history. But his words, more reckless than were his real beliefs, had alienated influential people who distrusted his leadership.

A number of Republicans aspired to lead the party; one of the less prominent among them was Lincoln. Quietly he built up his strength in the Old Northwest by speeches, conferences, and correspondence with fellow politicians. He gained control of the party machine in Illinois. Lincoln was no innocent in the rough and tumble of politics. One who had known him closely for many years observed that he "handled and moved men remotely as we do pieces upon a chess-board." * His pre-convention campaign in 1859 emphasized the conservatism of the Republican party, while it also re-enforced his earlier condemnation of slavery as a base institution. In his home territory of Illinois his name was being boomed for the presidency, but in the East it scarcely counted among the possibilities.

Lincoln soon gave the East a chance to measure him in an important address delivered at Cooper Union, New York, February 27, 1860. One of the city's most distinguished audiences greeted with skepticism the prairie giant with ill-tailored clothes. But it soon warmed to his own warmth, his sincerity, and his moderation. Before he was through he had taken captive this critical audience as he had done often before with western crowds. An enthusiastic reporter wrote that "no man ever before made such an impression in his first appeal to a New York audience." Seward now had a formidable rival for the Republican nomination.

★ DEMOCRATIC CONVENTION, 1860

Meanwhile the Democrats were making preparations for their convention in Charleston in April, where a "stop Douglas" movement came to a climax. Under Yancey's leadership seven states of the lower South agreed to leave the convention unless the party platform favored Congressional protection of slavery in the Territories. Against this demand Northern Democrats were adamant. Must the party be harnessed to the

* David Donald, *Lincoln Reconsidered* (New York: Alfred A. Knopf, 1956), p. 67.

chariot of 300,000 slave masters? asked **Senator Pugh of Ohio**. "Gentlemen of the South," he cried, "you mistake us—you mistake us! We will not do it." The delegates from the Cotton Kingdom were outvoted and, by prearrangement, they walked out of the convention. The Democratic party was split, a Republican victory guaranteed, and secession made almost certain.

The Charleston convention broke up without naming a candidate. In June another gathering met, this time in Baltimore, with the forces of Douglas in control. He easily won the nomination. But the anti-Douglasites still hounded him. They organized another meeting and named for president John C. Breckenridge of Kentucky, to run on a platform protecting slavery in the Territories. In May, a Constitutional Union party, made up of old-time Whigs who hoped to attract all moderates to their side, also met in Baltimore. It nominated Senator John Bell of Tennessee, but neither he nor his party had much spirit. Opponents laughed at it as the "Old Gentlemen's Party."

★ LINCOLN NOMINATED

The Republican convention met in Chicago in the latter part of May, 1860. The whole gathering radiated victory. The most influential newspapers in the country were on their side and the trend of the elections had been uniformly in their favor. Seward was absolutely sure of the nomination—and yet there was Lincoln. Astute managers of Lincoln's campaign won support from doubtful states by the usual job promises and other maneuvers. They coined for him the homey nickname of "Rail-Splitter," and the fence rail was as important a political symbol for him as the hickory pole had been for Jackson. Lincoln backers swamped the convention hall with his supporters, while judicious seating of delegates on the convention floor helped create a psychology favorable to him. Seward led on the first ballot; the second showed Seward 184½, Lincoln 181. On the third, amid a tremendous roar, Lincoln was named Republican candidate for president.

Before the candidate was picked the platform had been laid down. In it the western farmers got a free-homestead plank. "This Homestead measure," said a delegate from Minnesota, "overshadows everything with us, and throughout the West." Internal improvements and a Pacific railroad were also endorsed. And Pennsylvania got its protective tariff plank, though not as strong a statement as it wished. The campaign money that had once gone to Democrats now flowed to Republicans.

★ LINCOLN ELECTED

Lincoln's election was taken for granted, in view of the divided opposition of the Democrats. Douglas himself was certain of it. He knew much better than disbelieving Republicans that the Southerners this time intended to carry out their threats to secede, and he engaged in a remarkable campaign to save the Union. Carrying his gallant fight into the South, he warned seceders that the president of the United States, "whoever he may be, should treat all attempts to break up the Union . . . as Old Hickory treated the Nullifiers in 1832."

The early fall elections in the states, with sweeping victories for the Republicans, prefigured the November vote. As the returns came in at night on November 6, and on into the next morning, the electoral total showed a clear majority for Lincoln. The final count was Lincoln 180, Breckenridge 72, Bell 39. Douglas got only 12 electoral votes, but his popular vote was an impressive 1,376,957, second to Lincoln's 1,866,452. Springfield, Illinois, was a rollicking mass of humanity, singing and yelling throughout the night, repeating over and over the party song:

> Ain't you glad you joined the Republicans?
> Joined the Republicans—Joined the Republicans!

★ SECESSION

Southern secessionists had already made plans to leave the Union, waiting only for the election results to be official. South Carolina led the way, on December 20, to be followed in the next few weeks by Mississippi, Alabama, Georgia, Florida, Louisiana, and Texas. In all these states considerable Union sentiment existed, but it was unorganized and terrorized by the domineering tactics of secessionists. A demand for loyalty to the state and to the South made all other loyalties suspect. On February 8, 1861, delegates from the seven seceded states met in Montgomery, Alabama, to form the Confederate States of America. Jefferson Davis was named President, and Alexander Stephens, Vice-President, of the Confederacy.

Meanwhile Northern opinion, still discounting Southern threats until South Carolina acted, floundered without leadership. Some, including Greeley, thought secession permissible if majority opinion in a state so willed. William Cullen Bryant, editor of the New York *Evening Post,* raised the standard of Jackson: "If a state secedes it is revolution, and the seceders are traitors. Those who are charged with the executive branch of the government are recreant to their oaths if they fail to use all lawful means to put down such rebellion."

Around the head of President Buchanan himself raged a tremendous storm ever since Lincoln's election. His own wish was to preserve peace until the spirit of compromise might come into play. But the frightening speed of hurrying events left little time for negotiation. The circle of Southerners who had been Buchanan's intimates—Cobb, Thompson, and the tireless intriguer Slidell—exerted enormous pressure to force him to agree with secessionist aims. Southern states were to be allowed to depart peacefully, taking with them control over federal forts and other United States property in their region.

At first Buchanan leaned toward the view that he could do nothing to stop secession; then under Northern pressure the vacillating president reorganized his cabinet, took the advice of strong Unionists, and finally arrived at the position that it was his duty to uphold the flag of the United States over federal property in the South (including forts) even at the risk of civil war.

To the demand of South Carolina that federal troops be withdrawn from the fortifications in Charleston harbor, Buchanan now replied in accents Jacksonian: "This I cannot do; this I will not do"; Fort Sumter would be defended "against hostile attacks from whatever quarter they may come." Here was a policy, tragically late it is true, of strong nationalism that all Unionists hailed. In its last moments the administration saved its good name and lifted the gloom from Northern hearts.

Beneath the dangling swords the dove of peace fluttered helplessly. Men hoped that compromise, as in other years, might stave off the holocaust. Several plans were brought forward, the most important by Senator John J. Crittenden, fittingly from Clay's state of Kentucky. Crittenden's proposal involved amending the Constitution to extend the Missouri Compromise line of 36°30′ to California; Congress was not to interfere with slavery in slave states; nor was it to abolish slavery in the District of Columbia without the consent of its residents; Congress was to recompense owners of fugitive slaves rescued forcibly, the money to come from the locality failing to uphold the law.

There was strong support for Crittenden's plan in many parts of the country. But President-elect Lincoln set his face sternly against the extension of slavery. "Let there be no compromise on the question of extending slavery," he wrote a fellow Republican. "If there be, all our labor is lost, and ere long, must be done again . . . The tug has to come, and better now than at any time hereafter." The possibility that either side might yield was never more than slim; Southern intransigence could not give ground, and neither could Lincoln abandon principle.

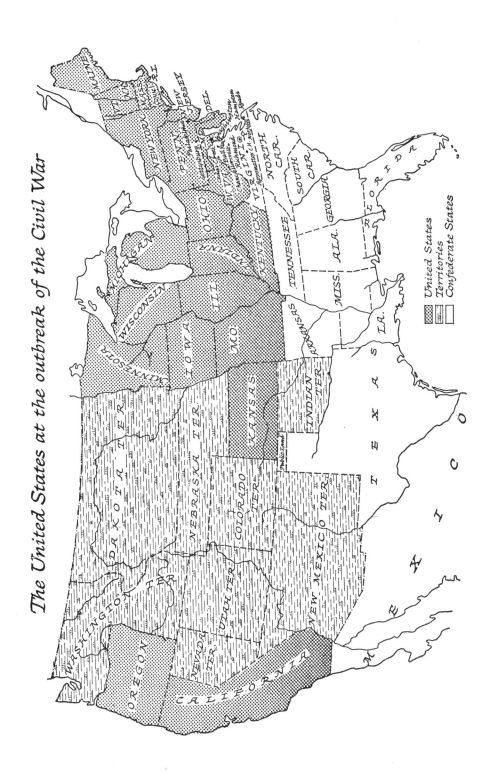

The United States at the outbreak of the Civil War

United States
Territories
Confederate States

The catastrophe, prophesied by Alexander Stephens of Georgia at the Charleston Convention almost a year earlier, seemed to be arriving on schedule. "What do you think of matters now?" he was asked at that time. "Why," he replied, "men will be cutting one another's throats in a little while. In less than twelve months we shall be in a war, and that the bloodiest in history."

CHAPTER XXII

The Union Forged in Fire

Lincoln left his neighbors in Springfield to go to Washington on February 11, 1861. Many came to say goodby despite the early hour and stormy weather. From the rear platform of the train Lincoln spoke his sensitive words of parting:

"My friends: No one, not in my situation, can appreciate my feeling of sadness at this parting. To this place, and the kindness of these people, I owe everything. Here I have lived a quarter of a century, and have passed from a young to an old man. Here my children have been born, and one is buried. I now leave, not knowing when or whether ever I may return, with a task before me greater than that which rested upon Washington. Without the assistance of that Divine Being, who ever attended him, I cannot succeed. With that assistance, I cannot fail. Trusting in Him who can go with me, and remain with you, and be everywhere for good, let us confidently hope that all will yet be well. To His care commending you, as I hope in your prayers you will commend me, I bid you an affectionate farewell."

★ LINCOLN INAUGURATED

The president-elect moved along toward the national capital by easy stages. He maintained a steady, outward calm, and to the anxious people who came to hail him he made many brief speeches on the need to preserve the Union. Rumors of plots and sabotage swirled through February's leaden days. The air was so thickly hostile in Baltimore, through which he was obliged to pass on the way to Washington, that Lincoln went through the city secretly at night.

The days before inauguration were filled with public appearances, meeting office seekers (all those Democrats to throw out!), consultations with close advisers, and finally settlement of the cabinet slate. Seward, already named Secretary of State, gave notice at the last moment he would not serve in the same cabinet with the radical Salmon P. Chase of Ohio, whose post was to be the Treasury. But Lincoln, anxious for a variety of opinion in his cabinet, finally prevailed on Seward to serve with Chase. Simon Cameron, the hard-bitten, very practical politician of Pennsylvania, was named Secretary of War. Gideon Welles of Connecticut, the New England representative in the cabinet, proved a splendid choice for Secretary of the Navy. A contemporary observer, with a gift for prophecy, believed that Lincoln himself would run the ship of state, and that his officers, soon learning who was captain, would "obey orders."

March 4, 1861, arrived; there still was neither peace nor war. Under a cheerful sun the inaugural parade got under way. Washington was heavily guarded against violence to the incoming president but no incident marred the day. Senator Douglas sat close to Lincoln and looked with kindly eyes upon the man who had won the place he sought. The inaugural address had been carefully prepared in consultation with Seward and other advisers. Strong phrases were toned down; but Lincoln emphasized his duty to uphold governmental authority. "I . . . consider that . . . the Union is unbroken; and to the extent of my ability I shall take care . . . that the laws of the Union be faithfully executed in all the States. Doing this I deem to be only a simple duty on my part . . . In doing this there needs to be no bloodshed or violence; and there shall be none, unless it be forced upon the national authority."

Lincoln then made a direct appeal to the people of the South. "In your hands, my dissatisfied fellow-countrymen, and not in mine, is the momentous issue of civil war. The government will not assail you. You can have no conflict without being yourselves the aggressors." His attentive audience listened hushed as he concluded with hopes of reconciliation:

"I am loath to close; we are not enemies, but friends. We must not be enemies. Though passion may have strained, it must not break our bonds of affection. The mystic chords of memory, stretching from every battlefield and patriot grave to every living heart and hearthstone all over this broad land, will yet swell the chorus of the Union when again touched, as surely they will be, by the better angels of our nature."

★ MAJOR ANDERSON ASKS FOR SUPPLIES

Northern opinion was heartened by Lincoln's address; "there's a clank of metal in it," wrote a New Yorker. It "seems to introduce one to a *man,* and to dispose one to like him." In the South it was denounced as a war message. From Montgomery, Alabama, capital of the Confederacy, came dispatches which spoke of public belief that war was now inevitable.

Behind the scenes, on inauguration day, a fateful drama unknown to the public was moving toward a climax. Word had just come to Washington from Major Robert Anderson, in command at Fort Sumter, that his supplies were running low, and could last not more than six weeks. Thus April 15 was the deadline by which the Federal garrison must either get food or be withdrawn. Lincoln consulted with his cabinet; all except one advised evacuation of the fort. At a second cabinet meeting, three of the seven members favored sending relief for Sumter. The president, after a period of hesitation, decided not to surrender the fort.

Lincoln weighed his decision with great care. At stake were war or peace. But also in the balance were the loyalties of the upper South, whose decision would determine whether that war, if it came, would be short or long. As yet the key state in the group, Virginia, had not joined the Confederacy. Indeed, in a test of public opinion in February, 1861, the people of Virginia voted against secession and for the Union. But the situation was precarious; it was realized that Unionists in Virginia could continue to hold their state in the Union only if peace prevailed. If war broke out between the North and the lower South, Virginia would throw in her lot with her Southern sister states. Through sleepless nights Lincoln wrestled with the problem, but by the end of March he had made his momentous decision.

★ FORT SUMTER

The ships sent to Fort Sumter were to land provisions, and only in the event of attack were they to re-enforce the garrison. Anderson, it was hoped, would hold out till the supplies arrived and, if attacked, was to resist long enough to satisfy the code of military honor and then surrender. Lincoln aimed to do his duty to uphold Federal authority, but in the most inoffensive manner possible. The president notified Governor Pickens, of South Carolina, of his intention to send provisions to Major Anderson. But the South's fire-eaters meant to have Fort Sumter before the supply ships arrived.

Anderson was called upon to surrender. He replied that military honor forbade, but he would not fire the first shot. Even if not attacked, he said, he would soon have to surrender or starve. When Anderson refused to give up the fort immediately a signal mortar was discharged at 4.30 in the morning of April 12, 1861. The red ball described a semicircle and exploded directly over Fort Sumter. The war, so often prophesied, and so widely feared, had now burst upon the country. For over thirty hours the small Federal garrison defended the fort, but in the afternoon of April 13 Anderson surrendered. The next day his troops marched out of Fort Sumter to the tune of "Yankee Doodle," "with colors flying and drums beating . . . and saluting [the] flag with fifty guns."

★ "BEAT! BEAT! DRUMS!"

An uncertain North, divided by conflicting counsels, now closed ranks behind the president. On April 15, not many hours after Fort Sumter fell, Lincoln issued a proclamation calling on the states to supply 75,000 militia for three months to deal with "combinations too powerful to be suppressed by the ordinary course of judicial proceedings."

Everywhere in the North—in mass meetings, special legislative sessions, governors' proclamations, and parades—pledges were taken in support of the Union. Volunteers started to drill, camps were formed, arsenals ransacked, pro-Confederates attacked, and money generously subscribed. Wherever men met, whatever their political beliefs, they rallied to the flag. Walt Whitman felt the fevered day:

Beat! beat! drums!—blow! bugles! blow!
Through the windows—through doors—burst like a ruthless force,
Into the solemn church, and scatter the congregation,
Into the school where the scholar is studying;
Leave not the bridegroom quiet—no happiness must he have now with his
    bride,
Nor the peaceful farmer any peace, ploughing his field or gathering his grain,
So fierce you whirr and pound you drums—so shrill you bugles blow.

In this dangerous period Senator Douglas was a pillar of strength to Lincoln. Though reserving the right to differ with the administration on political issues he defended the president and praised men who "love their country more than their party." The day before Lincoln issued his proclamation Douglas called on him. The Senator told the president he agreed with "every word" of the document, except that he would have asked for 200,000 men instead of 75,000. Together the two men looked at a map and Douglas offered suggestions for comprehensive military strategy. Douglas nobly gave these last months of his life (he died in June, 1861) to the cause of Union. He denounced the Confederacy's "war of aggression," and he reminded fellow Americans that their duty was to bequeath the legacy of a united people to posterity "and to the friends of . . . self-government throughout the world."

Such appeals went unheeded in Virginia which was swept along by secessionist sentiment after the attack on Fort Sumter. On April 17 she adopted an ordinance of secession. The lead of the Old Dominion was followed in three weeks by Arkansas and Tennessee, though in the latter sentiment for the Union was very powerful. North Carolina, which had held back for weeks, finally joined the Confederacy on May 20. The upper South was now leagued with the lower South in the struggle to establish an independent republic.

That republic had drawn up a constitution at Montgomery even before the attack on Fort Sumter. In its main outlines the document copied the federal Constitution, though Lincoln noted how far Southerners had moved from Jefferson's ideals. Their declarations of independence, "unlike the good old one, penned by Jefferson," he said, "omit the words 'all men are created equal.' " The Confederate Constitution emphasized, as one would expect, states' rights, and it also guaranteed slavery. It included some interesting variations from its model. The president was to be restricted to one term of office, for six years. No bounties were to be paid out of the Confederate treasury, nor could a protective tariff be passed. A praiseworthy innovation permitted cabinet members to sit in Congress to discuss departmental matters. When Jefferson Davis arrived in Montgomery to take charge of the new government he told the cheering crowd, "Our separation from the old Union is complete, no compromise . . . can now be entertained." The issue was now to be settled on the battlefield.

★ THE BORDER STATES REMAIN LOYAL

At the very outset Lincoln won a struggle which, in the long run, probably won the war. The border slave states stayed in the Union, though as many of their men fought for the South as for the North. Maryland's decision permitted Washington to remain the Federal capital, while Kentucky's insured the safety of the Ohio Valley for the Union. To lose Kentucky, said Lincoln, "is nearly . . . to lose the whole game. Kentucky gone, we cannot hold Missouri, nor, as I think Maryland. These all against us, and the job on our hands is too large for us." The Union cause was further strengthened when the western counties of Virginia, opposed as they were to a slave society, refused to follow the rest of the state into the Confederacy. This region later formed the state of West Virginia.

Lincoln knew that the battle for men's minds generally preceded a resort to open warfare, and that success in the first was needful to gain victory in the second. "This," he said, "is essentially a people's contest. On the side of the Union it is a struggle . . . to elevate the condition of men—to lift artificial weights from all shoulders; . . . to afford all an unfettered start, and a fair chance in the race of life." More than the future of the United States was at stake; the great experiment in democracy, as an example to the whole world, hung in the balance. The issue presented "to the whole family of man the question whether a constitutional republic or democracy—a government of the people by the same people—can or cannot maintain its territorial integrity against its own domestic foes." Failure here would doom the world to prolonged delay in the march to freedom.

★ THE CONFEDERACY AGAINST THE UNION

It was easy enough for the president to send out a call for 75,000 men; it was another matter to shape untrained soldiers into an army. Scarcely anything had been done in Washington to prepare for the crisis; in fact because of the inadequate preparations made to receive the soldiers some of the states were told to reduce the numbers offered to the federal government. It was all improvisation in the early months of the conflict, with governors and private citizens taking the initiative which the federal government lacked. The regular army in April was a small force of 13,000, most of it scattered over the country in various posts. It had no one in service, except two aged officers, who had commanded a unit as large as a brigade. The top-ranking general, Winfield Scott, was an old man, unable now to sit a horse. His military sense was still keen, however, for almost alone he spoke of a war of long duration, two or three years, and an army of 300,000 before the North could win. His strategy for victory, a comprehensive blockade combined with encirclement—"Scott's anaconda"—was laughed aside. Men, North and South, counted on a short war. Northerners believed the South all bluff and bluster; Confederates thought the Yankees would not stand and fight.

Certain obvious advantages seemed to lie with the North. Its pool of men on which to draw was vaster than the South's. The census of 1860 indicated a population of over 21,000,000 in the free states and border region combined. Over 200,000 Negro civilians worked for Northern armies as cooks, laborers, blacksmiths, teamsters, servants, etc. "Whenever a Negro appeared with a shovel in his hands," wrote a black veteran, "a white soldier took his gun and returned to the ranks." As spies mingling easily with local blacks they were invaluable. The legendary Harriet Tubman continued to bedevil the South in war as she had in peace. As soldiers the black contribution was substantial, and in the Union navy before the war's end Negroes comprised a quarter of the crews. The North gained added strength from immigration during the war. Its financial and industrial power greatly exceeded that of the South. The latter fought the war mainly with fiat money; during the four years it had at its disposal only about $27,000,000 in hard cash.

Communications in the North, with some 22,000 miles of railroad, were much better than in the South, where only 9,000 miles had been built. For the greater part of the conflict the North was able to supply nearly all its war needs from domestic sources. The South, on the other hand, had to run the blockade for many indispensable items.

The South's 9,000,000 people, 3,500,000 of whom were slaves, seemed definitely overmatched. And yet the odds were not nearly so overwhelming as they seemed on paper. The whole South was convinced it was the victim of Northern military aggression. A French Lieutenant-Colonel, Camille F. Pisani, traveling in the United States with Prince Napoleon, visited the Southern camp immediately after Bull Run. Writing to a friend, he said the Southerners dismissed as "secondary problems . . . questions concerning slavery, tariffs, territories, Lincoln's election, even the constitutionality of secession. They raise the debate to a plane where they feel there can be neither discussion nor controversy: they are waging an implacable war because the North invaded, by force, their territory, their native land . . . from the general down to the last private, everyone speaks the same language." The Frenchman was impressed with their gallantry. "On the whole, nothing is as picturesque as the Southern cavalry. They wear the most impossible outfits: mostly rags . . . boots without soles. Yet, they could make Don B— jealous for their martial bearing and countenance . . . the boldness of their riding technique make[s] it impossible not to admire these ragged riders . . ." *

The South's military leadership at the war's outset would have done credit to any nation. Robert E. Lee, J. E. B. Stuart, "Stonewall" Jackson, Beauregard, Albert Sidney Johnston, and Joseph E. Johnston were commanders of unusual ability. Their task was to keep an army and government in being, and to hold off the North until such time as she should tire of war. Southerners believed that Northern devotion to the idea of Union was less passionate than their own consecration to a separate Confederacy. In this they were mistaken. The genius of Lincoln kept before the tired eyes of Northern men and women the ideal of Union which triumphed in the end.

Until that ultimate triumph four years passed, filled with death and destruction, humiliation and heroism. Of Northern lives over 359,000 were lost; Southern deaths were over 250,000. Wealth and blood had been poured into the crushing struggle; when all was over the South's impoverishment darkened the future of a whole generation. Out of the gore and sorrow of defeat, however, the South built the legend of a

* G. J. Joyaux, ed., "The Tour of Prince Napoleon," *American Heritage,* VIII (August, 1957): 75, 76.

"lost cause," which eased the heartbreak. The North, by its hard-won victory, passed on to all future Americans a legacy of Union and freedom; and to the world it gave the glory of Abraham Lincoln.

★ BULL RUN

The explosion at Fort Sumter was not followed immediately by any important military engagements. Lincoln asked for an additional 42,000 men in May, and two months later, he requested another 400,000 men and $400,000,000. It took time to train the recruits, but a friendly English observer was deeply impressed by the character of the men. "I have seen the armies of most European countries," he said, "and I have no hesitation in saying that, as far as the average raw material of the rank and file is concerned, the American army is the finest."

The observer, Edward Dicey, an English journalist, went on to say that the officers were "undoubtedly, the weak point of the system." But he was full of praise for the adaptability of men unused to war. "It was remarkable to me how rapidly the new recruits fell into the habits of military service. I have seen a Pennsylvania regiment, raised chiefly from the mechanics of Philadelphia, which, six weeks after its formation, was, in my eyes, equal to the average of our best-trained volunteer corps, as far as marching and drill exercise went . . . the American volunteers looked to me more business-like than our own. . . . From every part of the North; from the ports of New York and Boston; from the homesteads of New England; from the mines of Pennsylvania and the factories of Pittsburgh; from the shores of the Great Lakes; from the Mississippi valley; and from the far-away Texan prairies these men had come to fight for the Union. It is idle to talk of their being attracted by the pay alone. Large as it is, the pay of thirteen dollars a month is only two dollars more than the ordinary pay of privates in the Federal pay during peace times." Dicey did point out that "wherever there is an army, the scum of the population will always be gathered together; but the average *morale* and character of the couple of hundred thousand troops collected around Washington was extremely good. . . . The number of papers purchased daily by the common soldiers and the amount of letters which they send through the military post was astonishing to a foreigner, though less strange when you considered that every man in that army, with the exception of . . . recent immigrants, could both read and write."

Civilian pressure on the president for immediate military action became insistent, though the army was far from ready. The cry of "On to Richmond" (to which the Confederates had moved their capital) was taken up by politicians (Radicals) who thought Lincoln not ag-

gressive enough. More than three months had passed since Sumter—
and the war was still continuing its nonviolent course.

The lull was broken on Sunday, July 21; Union troops crossed Bull
Run (the little stream about twenty miles southwest of Washington)
close to Manassas. After four hours of fighting the Confederates seemed
smashed, and rumors even flew to Richmond of a Southern debacle. But
Southern soldiers rallied; fresh men were thrown in, and a counterattack
launched against tired and overextended Federal troops. The Union
line was broken, part of its army became a fleeing mob jumbled together
with a crowd of spectators and Congressmen, who had come from the
capital to the field of battle to cheer an expected Northern victory.
Because some of the Federal troops held firm, covering an orderly retreat of their units, the Confederates were blocked in their pursuit.
Southerners immediately criticized their commander, General Johnston,
for not pushing on to Washington. But he knew better than civilians how
strong the Federal troops were, and then he added the significant comment that the Confederate army "was more disorganized by victory than
that of the United States by defeat." The South had won a resounding
victory, and the press of the North and of Europe was filled with lurid
tales of Northern disaster.

A miasma of despair settled over the North. Commanders were distrusted, McDowell was immediately succeeded by McClellan. No confidence was felt in the administration (a few months later contentious
Edwin M. Stanton replaced Cameron in the War Department). An attack on Washington was momentarily expected; cries for peace filled the
air. Lincoln was stunned, but with characteristic fortitude rallied himself
and his people. In the sleepless night that followed Bull Run he drew
up a memorandum of military policy suggested by the defeat. The plan
included strengthening the blockade, increased aggressiveness in the
West, discharge of militia who refused to serve longer than three
months, addition of new volunteers, capture of key points in Virginia,
then a drive forward in a movement co-ordinated with an advance on
the western fronts. Here was a comprehensive strategy which, though
destined for many changes, was to furnish a basis for eventual victory.

★ ENGLAND AND THE CIVIL WAR

While General McClellan was forming an army out of raw material during the next few months, the Northern navy captured a number of
islands off Southern ports to tighten the blockade. A more spectacular
achievement was the interception of the British steamer "Trent," in
November, 1861, by the U.S.S. "San Jacinto," under Captain Charles
Wilkes. Wilkes removed two Confederate diplomats, Mason and Slidell,

from the vessel which then was permitted to go on its way. When England heard of Wilkes' audacious action the press and the government rang with denunciations of the United States. War between the two countries seemed very close. Americans made a hero of Wilkes, while England was infuriated by his aggression and alleged violation of her neutral rights.

Influential elements in English life, particularly among the aristocracy, were sympathetic to the South. They disliked American democracy and were happy to see it threatened with disruption. They would have been glad to throw in their strength to help smash the United States to pieces. Fortunately, after a few weeks, excitement in England moderated and conciliatory talk could be heard above the din. Outstanding liberals in England, Richard Cobden and John Bright, urged a peaceful settlement of the dispute. Their views were communicated to Senator Sumner, who then laid them before the president and his cabinet.

A full discussion resulted in agreement to yield Mason and Slidell to the British. After all, as Lincoln remarked, he had no wish to have "two wars on his hands at a time." The British, having been satisfied by the recognition of their claims to the Confederate statesmen, dropped their belligerent talk. The American minister to London, Charles Francis Adams, thought that the "Trent" affair had cleared up Anglo-American misunderstanding. It dispelled the belief, he said, that "we were intending to pick a quarrel." Other tensions remained, however, to keep relations between the two countries inflamed for some time.

★ MC CLELLAN

The months of nerve-wracking inactivity dragged on into the winter of 1861 and McClellan's Army of the Potomac still made no move. Again impatient civilians called for action, while militant politicians spoke their warlike pieces in Congress. Lincoln's aim to carry on the struggle with a minimum of vindictiveness, so as to make the eventual reconstruction of the Union easier, was no part of the program of the Radicals in his party. Their hatred of the South was greater than their love of the Union, and they meant to use the war for partisan advantage. Under their leadership a "Joint Committee on the Conduct of the War" was organized in December, 1861, its chief personalities being Ben Wade of Ohio and Zach Chandler of Michigan. Though not one of its members had had military experience the committee interfered in the running of the war. They made grave difficulties for Lincoln; their inquisitional committees weakened morale; and they persecuted Democratic generals, especially McClellan. However, others besides Radicals were critical of McClellan. The favorites of the Radicals were Frémont,

Butler, Burnside, Pope, and Hooker, to whom they gave every advantage.

McClellan, who bore himself, said an observer, with "an indescribable air of success," believed himself a "man of destiny." He really did achieve great success, but his enemies deprived him of its fruits. The men who served under him held him in high regard; so long as he was in command the Union army did not suffer a major defeat. Only when the Army of the Potomac was handed over to other generals did it suffer its worst disasters. The best measure of McClellan's ability is that Grant in 1864, with a more experienced army and whole-hearted support behind the lines could make no more progress toward Richmond than did "Little Mac" in 1862.

★ "UNCONDITIONAL SURRENDER" GRANT

While McClellan was biding his time, a dejected North was cheered by reports of victories from the West. Ulysses S. Grant, whose star had fallen since the days when it had shone so brightly in the war with Mexico, headed a regiment of Illinois volunteers in the spring of 1861. In the summer he was given a brigadier's commission, and stationed at Cairo, Illinois, where the Ohio joins the Mississippi. Some fifty miles from Cairo, on the Ohio, the Tennessee and Cumberland rivers afforded relatively easy access to the center of the Confederacy. Guarding the

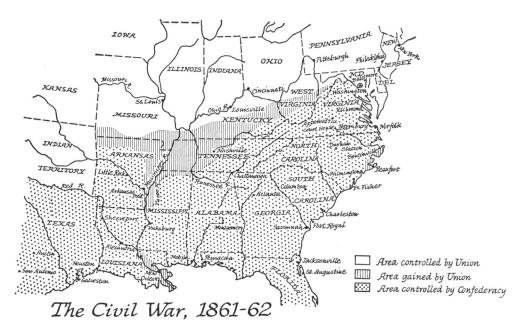

The Civil War, 1861-62

river routes were Fort Henry and Fort Donelson. On February 7 gunboats reduced the former, its garrison taking safety in Fort Donelson, fifteen miles away. The latter was a harder nut to crack, but after a seesaw battle Grant forced an unconditional surrender, on February 15, 1862. "Unconditional Surrender" Grant was quickly known throughout the country. His victories practically detached Tennessee from the Confederacy and forced an enemy retreat southward. Much of his military success was due, says Professor David Donald, to his lack of familiarity with the standard military manuals. Other generals fought according to the prescribed rules; Grant made his own.

Three weeks later, a reorganized Confederate force under Albert Sidney Johnston, catching Grant at a disadvantage at Pittsburg Landing, initiated the tremendous battle of Shiloh. Through April 6, and on into the next day, the fierce fighting raged. The battlefield was strewn with thousands of dead; among the dying was the Confederate leader, General Johnston. The Unionists, perilously near defeat, finally held firm and the Confederates withdrew to Corinth.

General Halleck, Grant's superior, then took direct command of the army in the western sector, but did nothing with it for the remainder of 1862. The main action in this theater was borne by the Union river gunboats which tried to keep the Mississippi free of Confederate craft. By July 1 the gunboats moving south linked up with Farragut's ships near Vicksburg.

Captain Farragut had performed a remarkable feat in forcing his way up the Mississippi. His ships, on April 24, had crashed through a boom guarding the passage up-river, faced the fire of protecting forts and enemy boats, and the next day anchored off the once gay city of New Orleans. The city, which lived by trade, had been made lifeless by the blockade, and no fight was made for it. On April 26 the Union troops took possession. Farragut's ships then moved upstream, capturing Baton Rouge and Natchez, eventually joining the river gunboats. Vicksburg was the obvious next objective but Halleck was unwilling to challenge its strong fortifications. It remained in Confederate hands for another year, enabling the South to retain contact with friendly forces across the Mississippi.

★ "ON TO RICHMOND"

While the North was winning significant victories in the West, the eastern theater was filled with disappointment. McClellan's inaction stood in glaring contrast to the aggressiveness of Grant. Even Lincoln, who had shielded McClellan against the mounting criticism, finally ordered him to launch an attack. At the same time McClellan's troops were subdivided among other commands, leaving him the troops of the Army of the Potomac, a splendid force of 100,000 men. Much of the military planning thereafter was taken out of McClellan's hands by Lincoln and Secretary of War Stanton.

McClellan decided to outflank Richmond by an attack leading inland from the York peninsula. Confederate strength had been bolstered at sea by the appearance of the iron clad "Virginia" (formerly the "Merrimac"), which frightened the wits out of Washington officialdom when she sank Union warships almost at will. She met her match, in Hampton Roads, on March 8, 1862, when she was engaged in battle by the "Monitor," a low slung vessel with guns mounted in a revolving turret. Though neither vessel succeeded in crippling the other, the "Virginia" was no longer an offensive threat. Southern Negroes, especially the skilled Isaac Tatnall and the daring Robert Smalls, were indispensable as pilots for Northern war vessels plying the coastal waters of Georgia and South Carolina.

McClellan believed he would win a crushing victory within a few months, by taking Richmond, and end the rebellion before the close of summer, 1862. Confederate testimony, of later date, seemed to justify his optimism. A Southern officer remarked that if McClellan's subordinates had been equal to their task, "and there had been no interference from Washington, it is probable the Confederate army would have been driven out of Virginia and Richmond captured by midsummer, 1862." But the rate at which McClellan moved belied his hopes. For a month, through April, his troops were stalled before the Confederate line stretching across the peninsula from Yorktown. McClellan's deliberateness gave the outnumbered Southerners an opportunity to engage in bold strokes which neutralized much of the Union's superior strength.

General Robert E. Lee, military adviser to President Davis and directing genius of the South's strategy, had drawn up a comprehensive plan. It called for defensive operations against the Federals in the peninsula, while a striking force was to harass Northern troops near Washington and thus draw off soldiers intended for McClellan, whom they were supposed to join in a concerted attack on Richmond. Lee's plan worked brilliantly. Stonewall Jackson, a quiet, granite-like man, very devout (he avoided war on the Sabbath) toppled one Union commander after another in the battles of the Shenandoah Valley, and frightened panic-stricken Washington into withholding troops scheduled to assist McClellan.

The Confederates, with great confidence, now took the offensive against McClellan. But the Battle of Fair Oaks did not go according to plan, and the Southern commander, Joseph E. Johnston, was badly wounded. McClellan strengthened his own lines and waited the favorable moment to advance, hoping to win by "artillery and engineering."

Lee, now in command of the Army of Northern Virginia, anticipated McClellan by initiating, on June 26, the sanguinary Seven Days' Battles. Under extreme pressure McClellan fought off one Confederate force after another eager for the kill, and by superb leadership kept his army, guns, and supplies intact. He lost 16,000 men to the Confederates' 20,000. The South could ill afford so great a drain. Richmond, it is true, had been saved, but there stood the Union army, its confidence unbroken.

McClellan wished to advance once more on Richmond, but he was overruled from Washington. Politicians bedeviled him, and civilians were aghast at the sacrifice of so many men, without any apparent result having been achieved. The Army of the Potomac was then ordered out of the peninsula, its gains completely nullified.

★ "MY PARAMOUNT OBJECT IS TO SAVE THE UNION"

The summer of 1862 saw an apparent stalemate. Certain developments, however, were operating against the Union. European governments, notably England and France, were showing open favor toward the South and appeared to be on the verge of recognizing the Confederacy. Commercial raiders, built in England for the South, were roaming the seas and sending Northern vessels to the bottom. At home enlistments were slowing up, and Lincoln was assailed for an alleged lack of policy in carrying on the war. Abolitionist pressure was especially strong on him to do something about slavery. Sumner, the "moral terrorist," was insistent on emancipation.

Horace Greeley's *Tribune,* August 20, 1862, carried an editorial, "Prayer of Twenty Millions," saying that Lincoln must take strong antislavery measures. Lincoln's famous reply, two days later, made clear his fundamental policy. "My paramount object in this struggle," said the president, "is to save the Union, and is not either to save or destroy slavery. If I could save the Union without freeing any slave, I would do it; and if I could save it by freeing all the slaves, I would do it, and if I could save it by freeing some and leaving others alone, I would also do that. What I do about slavery and the colored race, I do because I believe it helps to save the Union; and what I forbear, I forbear because I do not believe it would help to save the Union . . .

"I have here stated my purpose according to my view of official duty; and I intend no modification of my oft-expressed personal wish that all men everywhere could be free." Negroes intended to be free—in America. Replying to proposals that black men emigrate to Liberia or Haiti, the distinguished Robert Purvis answered: "The children of the black man have enriched the soil by their tears, and sweat, and blood. We were born here, and here we choose to remain."

Congress had already moved some little distance to meet abolitionist demands. Slavery was abolished in the territories and in the District of Columbia, where owners were compensated by a Congressional fund of a million dollars. Even before Greeley's prodding editorial had been published, Lincoln had quietly decided to issue a proclamation freeing all slaves under rebel control by the following January 1. Seward advised, however, that the proclamation wait, to be timed with the next victory, and Lincoln then laid it aside, in full agreement with his Secretary of State.

★ "THENCEFORWARD, AND FOREVER FREE"

Instead of the victory Lincoln waited for so hopefully the North, under General John Pope, was given a heavy defeat at the second battle of Bull Run, on August 29–30. Again, as in May, Washington was fearful of imminent Confederate attack. Lee was making a bold bid for Maryland and planning an invasion of Pennsylvania to capture Harrisburg where rail connections with the West could be severed. In this crisis Lincoln gave McClellan full charge of the Northern forces. Within a few days McClellan, adored by his soldiers, reinvigorated a dispirited army and set out to meet the Confederates. In the battle of Antietam (September 17), the bloodiest engagement thus far, troops of McClellan and Lee met. With greater aggressiveness on McClellan's part the Confederate army might have been destroyed that day. As it was, Lee, though suffering severe losses, was able to get back to Virginia with his army intact.

McClellan had averted a grave danger to the North. For Lincoln it was a good enough victory to warrant his announcing the preliminary Emancipation Proclamation. "Things had gone . . . from bad to worse," said Lincoln in retrospect, "until I felt that we had reached the end of our rope in the plan . . . we had been pursuing; that we . . . must change our tactics, or lose the game. I now determined upon the adoption of the emancipation policy; and without consultation with or the knowledge of the Cabinet, I prepared the original draft of the proclamation, and after much anxious thought, called a Cabinet meeting upon the subject."

Five days after Antietam, on September 22, Lincoln began his historic cabinet meeting by reading a humorous piece from Artemus Ward. Though Chase and Stanton sat glum the others relished the fun. Then Lincoln, assuming a graver tone, told the cabinet he had made up his mind and had promised his Maker to issue a Proclamation of Emancipation as soon as the enemy had been driven out of Maryland. Gently he explained to his Secretaries that he was not seeking their advice; he said, "I must do the best I can, and bear the responsibility of taking the course which I feel I ought to take."

In the proclamation, Lincoln reverted to favorite proposals of colonization for Negroes overseas and compensated emancipation in slave states under Union control. The heart of the document read that on the first day of 1863 "all persons held as slaves" in areas "in rebellion against the United States" were to be "then, thenceforward, and forever free." The great statement was born, as so many famous state papers have been, out of mixed motives—practical and idealistic. As Lincoln told Sumner, he needed men wherever he could find them, including slaves "in the rear of the Rebels." The vast majority of the slaves were not immediately affected by the proclamation. They performed their usual tasks in the South or did manual work in battle areas. In regions under Northern control a further impetus was given to enrolling Negroes in Union fighting units. Some 186,000 colored troops served in Northern armies before the war was over. They were in the infantry, artillery, the engineers, and the cavalry. Whenever a Northern raiding party returned from a slave region it was accompanied by "an outlandish tatterdemalion parade of refugees, men and women and helpless children, people jubilant and bewildered and wholly defenseless, their eyes on the North Star." Thousands of blacks in Georgia fled to the Atlantic coast. In the West they escaped from Missouri to Kansas. A "stampede from the patriarchal relation" is on, said a contemporary. As the conflict wore on Negroes became openly hostile to their masters who, fearful of insurrection, sought protection from Union troops.

The struggle was now, more clearly than ever, identified with the eternal fight for human freedom. European radicals and liberals hailed the proclamation, and thereafter the expectations of the South for English and French intervention began to fade. Southern hopes for European assistance had been jolted in the early months of the war by W. L. Yancey, home from a disillusioning trip abroad. "You have no friends in Europe," he told an audience in New Orleans. "The sentiment of Europe is anti-slavery." The governments of Europe, he said, "will never recognize our independence until our conquering sword hangs dripping over the prostrate heads of the North. . . . It is an error to say, 'Cotton is King.' It is not. It is a great and influential factor in commerce, but not its dictator. The nations of Europe will never raise the blockade until it suits their interests." For the moment it suited the interests of the governments of Europe to await events in America, though to Northerners it seemed that officialdom overseas was hostile.

Lincoln was hopeful that the sympathy of European workingmen for the Union cause would offset governmental unfriendliness. Great mass meetings all over England adopted resolutions of support for the Union. Ten thousand citizens of Birmingham signed a long scroll, assuring Lincoln of the "good wishes of all Men who love liberty." Charles Francis Adams said the proclamation "has rallied all the sympathies of the working classes," in meetings almost unprecedented for size and enthusiasm. Manchester, whose textile industry suffered severely from the Union's blockade of cotton shipments, praised the name of Lincoln for wiping out "that foul blot upon civilization and Christianity—chattel slavery."

European liberals were aware of the meaning to themselves of victory for the North. "The success of free institutions in America," said one English group, "was a political question of deep consequence in England" and "they would not tolerate any interference unfavorable to the North." Henry Adams, who was present at a pro-Union meeting at Manchester wrote, "I never quite appreciated the moral influence of American democracy, nor the cause that the privileged classes in Europe have to fear us, until I saw directly how it works."

Danger of European intervention did not disappear for several months. French and Spanish dreams of empire in America were again stirred by United States weakness—France in Mexico, where Napoleon set up a puppet empire, and Spain in the Caribbean, intriguing to enlarge her possessions. In England armored vessels were being built for the Confederacy to break the Union blockade. But in April, 1863, the English government took command of the ships intended for the Confederacy. The chances for aid to the South through English intervention had now almost vanished.

The decision of England to maintain neutrality was finally determined by several factors: a common bond of humanitarianism, especially antislavery, knitting the North and England; ties between workingmen; the influence of English liberals, particularly Cobden and Bright; wheat from Western farms, more important to England than cotton from Southern plantations; and finally the realization of English businessmen of the danger to their shipping from American raiders and the damage to their export trade by the closing of Northern markets. In the end the English government decided that neutrality was the better part of wisdom.

★ "WE BURIED THEM DARKLY, AT DEAD OF NIGHT"

The battle of Antietam had momentous consequences for the Union, for the slaves, and for the North's relations with Europe. As for McClellan it only won him caustic criticism for allowing Lee to escape. Lincoln, though recognizing his merits, became impatient with him. The president was less deferential to miltary men than he had formerly been. On October 6 (1862), he told McClellan to "cross the Potomac and give battle to the enemy, or drive him South." When the general did not move, Lincoln sent him a letter a week later, urging aggressiveness. "Are you not overcautious when you assume that you cannot do what the enemy is constantly doing? . . . Change positions with the enemy, and think you not he would break your communication with Richmond within the next twenty-four hours?"

Lincoln could stand McClellan's delay no longer. On November 7, late at night, while McClellan was sitting in his tent writing to his wife, he heard a knock on his tent pole. Two generals entered, one of them Burnside, with Lincoln's order that McClellan had been relieved of command, Burnside succeeding. Thus ended the military career of Mc-Clellan, whom Lee thought the ablest of all his Federal opponents. A little more presidential patience and the war might soon have been over, for McClellan had rebuilt the Army of the Potomac into a powerful striking force. But he was no longer its head when next it struck.

The incompetent Burnside, on December 13, in the battle of Fredericksburg, threw the Union troops against the Confederate soldiers who were well protected on wooded heights. Time after time the lines of blue surged across an open field under constant artillery blasts and withering rifle fire to fall before the stone wall below Marye's Heights, a useless sacrifice. Over 6,000 dead and wounded lay in tumbled masses when evening ended the slaughter. Northern bravery made "your soldier's heart almost [stand] still," wrote Confederate General Pickett to his wife. "The brilliant assault . . . of their Irish brigade was beyond description. Why, my darling, we forgot they were fighting us, and cheer after cheer at their fearlessness went up all along our lines."

The North buried its dead where they fell, "committing their story," said a proud comrade, "to their country's keeping."

> We buried them darkly, at dead of night,
> The sod with our bayonets turning.

★ BEHIND THE LINES

Along with the glory went the shoddy—profiteering and "politicking." Northern industry expanded during the war, aided by generous government expenditures. The protective tariff (the Morrill Act of 1861) passed when the Southerners left Congress; the issuance of paper money (greenbacks) and the loosening of credit, generally, resulted in a rapid rise in prices which benefited a new "shoddy aristocracy" and victimized the mass of people.

After two years of war, prices for life's necessities had risen from 60 to 100 per cent, while wage increases lagged behind, less than one-half the rise in food. The most pitiable victims were the seamstresses making army clothing; contractors paid them as little as $1.50 a week. By 1864, however, labor generally had considerably improved its wage position.

Women in towns and on farms supplanted men gone off to war. A visitor to Iowa said he saw "more women driving teams and . . . at work in the fields than men. They seem to have said to their husbands in the language of a favorite song,

> "Just take your gun and go;
> For Ruth can drive the oxen, John,
> And I can use the hoe!"

Immigrants who poured in from Europe, 800,000 of them during the war years, added their strength to the North's war-making power, as soldiers and laborers. Tens of thousands hurried from New York's docks to Illinois, Wisconsin, and other western states where they swelled the North's output in agriculture, mining, and lumbering. The economy and, even more, perhaps, the spirit of the people were bolstered by the long-sought Homestead Act (1862). For a nominal payment settlers could acquire 160 acres of the public domain. During the war more than 15,000 such farms were established.

The North's expanding economy was knit more tightly at the same time. A new railroad trunk line, with a single gauge all the way, linked New York and St. Louis. Chicago, which in 1850 celebrated its first train arrival, fourteen years later was host to over ninety trains daily. Long-standing proposals for railway extension westward, to be assisted by large grants of public land, were enacted into law by Congress in the Pacific Railway Acts. A central transcontinental railroad, Chicago to San Francisco, was authorized in 1862. The next year a southern route, along the 35th parallel, was marked out by Congress for the Atchison, Topeka and Santa Fe. The northern route, from Lake Superior to Portland, Oregon, was to be traversed by the Northern Pacific Railroad, chartered in 1864. While the legislation was passed in the war period actual railroad building generally waited on peace. During the war itself few new lines were constructed but many improvements were introduced. The whole transportation system, though handicapped by need for frequent transshipment, performed a remarkable achievement in sustaining a war and civilian economy.

The one major exception to the general Northern industrial prosperity was shipbuilding and foreign commerce. Even before the war Americans, proud of their preeminence in the day of sail, were laggard in converting to steam. When war came Confederate cruisers, notably the *Alabama,* accounted for more than 250 Northern merchantmen; other hundreds registered under foreign flags to avoid capture. Great Britain was the chief beneficiary of the decline of America's merchant marine.

Labor-saving machinery on farm and in factory was now used in far greater measure than in peacetime. American-built reapers and threshers were the best in the world; the name of Cyrus H. McCormick became internationally famous. Elias Howe's sewing machine made it possible to quickly clothe an army of a million men who were shod too, with the aid of machinery—Gordon McKay's. The latter sewed uppers to soles so fast that shoemaking was now speeded up a hundred times. In nearly every phase of activity the inventive faculty was constantly exercised. New machinery and the need for larger capital outlays hurried along the process of business combination, though this was more characteristic of the postwar era.

The government failed to enact a program of rigorous taxation until near the end of the war. An income tax was imposed and other taxes were increased, making it possible in the last year of the conflict to raise one-third of the costs of war from current income. Fiat money, greenbacks, and bonds paid for most of the costs. Greenbacks were added to the currency in a program of controlled inflation. There were times when it looked as if it had gone out of control; greenbacks at one point fell to less than forty cents in relation to the gold dollar. To facilitate war finance, and at the same time strengthen the banking structure of the country, a National Bank Act was adopted in 1863. Its provisions for uniformity, with a more satisfactory national currency, facilitated interstate financial transactions, and eventually drove out of circulation the state bank notes.

The vast increase in government expenditures and private capital expansion established a new dimension for American finance. Some four billion dollars were spent by the Lincoln administration, to which should be added disbursements by the separate states. Larger sums than had hitherto been known were available for business investment and the flotation of government loans. The latter, up to the war, had scarcely involved the general public. Now, however, with the government's great need of funds, popular loans of a size previously unknown to any nation, were floated. In about twelve months a $500,000,000 loan of five-twenties (payable in five to twenty years) was taken up. People on all levels of income subscribed for government bonds; in central Ohio nearly every farmer and mechanic possessed some. To sell these bonds required skilled salesmanship and organizing ability of a high order; these were supplied in abundant measure by Jay Cooke, a Philadelphia banker. During periods of military setbacks bond sales faltered, but on the whole these, and other Northern financial expedients, eventually achieved respectable success. Indeed, when the government's tax program in 1864 brought in one-third of its expenditures the result astonished financially sophisticated Europeans.

As in most wars fought by Americans easy money meant easy living. "Who at the North would ever think of war, if he had not a friend in the army, or did not read the newspapers?" asked the *New York Independent* in June, 1864. "Ask Tiffany what kind of diamonds and pearls are called for. He will answer 'the prodigious,' 'as near hen's egg size as possible,' 'price no object.' What kind of carpetings are now wanted? None but 'extra.' Brussels and velvets are now used from basement to garret." And yet private indulgence and the pursuit of pleasure were matched by characteristic philanthropy that nursed the war's wounded, sheltered its orphans, and housed the warriors in soldiers' homes. Perhaps the most effective national organization was the United States Sanitary Commission which cared for the needy and incapacitated soldiers.

The heavy demands upon the public purse for war loans and gifts to ease the battle's impact did not exhaust the philanthropic impulse. Funds were supplied for new colleges—Vassar, the Massachusetts Institute of Technology, Cornell University, Swarthmore, and others. Existing schools —Yale, Harvard, Amherst among them—added to their endowments with donations of unprecedented size. Of singular importance for higher education was the passage by Congress of the Morrill Act (1862) which gave huge grants of land to the states to endow local colleges. This beneficent measure was the foundation for higher education in the Middle West and Far West.

The largess that spilled over into educational philanthropy came from Northern pockets. Southern pockets emptied themselves mainly for military objectives. In the South inflationary currency paid for most of the war's costs. The Confederate dollar held up fairly well in the first two years of the conflict but then it fell rapidly, becoming almost worthless at the war's end. In the Confederacy women rioted against high prices, speculators exploited everyone, and price-fixing regulations were generally evaded. Southerners, however, gave more profusely than Northerners of their treasure as of their blood.

Enthusiasm for the war in the North had declined so alarmingly that Congress passed the first American Conscription Act, in March, 1863. The law was poorly drawn, the burden of military service being unfairly distributed to favor wealth. A man subject to the draft could commute his term of service by paying $300; he could, in fact, avoid serving entirely by getting a substitute to enlist for three years. Volunteers were paid bounties, by a locality, to enlist in order to reduce the obligations to service by the residents of that community. "Bounty jumpers" collected their fee and then deserted, many of them repeating the process a number of times.

In New York in July, 1863, when the first call was made for soldiers under the act, bloody riots occurred. Resentment over the drawing, which workingmen charged showed their names always heading the lists, and hostility by white laborers to Negroes, awakened mob fury. For three days New York City was ravaged by roving groups of men and women sacking, burning, looting—and lynching Negroes. Hundreds of lives, black and white, were lost and millions of dollars of property damaged. Order was not restored to the city until Federal troops were sent in to quell the rioters.

The South was also forced to adopt conscription. There, too, the authorities met with difficulties in enforcing the law. Like Northern workingmen Southern poor whites had the feeling that it was "a rich man's war and a poor man's fight." Indeed, in many Southern mountain areas there were as many enlistments on the Union side as there were on the Confederate. Upholders of states' rights, opposing conscription, resented this assumption of authority by the government of Jefferson Davis. South Carolina again asserted the right of nullification. Deserters and draft evaders were very numerous, North and South, and the Confederacy frequently had to detach troops from regular service to round up her reluctant rebels.

Both President Davis and President Lincoln assumed extraordinary powers during the war, which Americans would not normally sanction in peace time. Both suspended, on occasion, the writ of habeas corpus. Civil liberties were curbed by the two executives, and soldiers frequently usurped civilian authority. The North, and to a lesser extent the South, all through the war had to face persistent opposition to the continuance of the conflict. "Copperheads" (as the war's opponents in the North were called) were so numerous and powerful that their challenge to Lincoln's administration has rightly been called "the hidden Civil War." The large number of people of Southern birth living in Ohio, Indiana, and Illinois made those states hotbeds of discontent which often bordered on treason. Disloyalty and patriotism lived side by side in the same community.

★ "A BACKWOODS JUPITER"

The difficulties confronting Lincoln were not created entirely by the ordinary citizen who disliked the war, or whose Democratic affiliation made him antagonistic to all Republicans including the president. From his own party in Congress and in the cabinet Lincoln faced great danger.

Chase was hand in glove with the Radicals whose policy of harshness to the South was contrary to Lincoln's. In December, 1862, the Radicals tried direct dictation to the president, insisting on dismissal of Seward whose moderation was distasteful to them. Congress, under Radical domination, was in effect attempting to usurp presidential authority in formulating policy and organizing a cabinet.

Lincoln triumphed over them, retaining Seward and guiding policy with a firm hand. From now on to the close of his presidency, though he had frequent brushes with the Radicals, not all of whom were opposed to him, he was more than ever the master of the government. Perhaps it was his understanding of politics, his skill in running the political machine and dispensing patronage, that insured his domination. His admiring private secretary, John Hay, testified to Lincoln's mastery. In his diary, in 1863, Hay writes: "The Tycoon is in fine whack. I have rarely seen him more serene and busy. He is managing this war, the draft, foreign relations and planning a reconstruction of the Union, all at once. I never knew with what a tyrannous authority he rules the Cabinet, until now. The most important things he decides and there is no cavil. I am growing more convinced that the good of the country demands that he should be kept where he is till this thing is over. There is no man in the country so wise, so gentle, and so firm." And at another time Hay wrote: "The old man sits here and wields, like a backwoods Jupiter, the bolts of war and the machinery of government with a hand especially steady and equally firm. I do not know whether the nation is worthy of him for another term. I know the people want him. There is no mistaking that fact. But the politicians are strong yet, and he is not their 'kind of a cat.' "

As time went on military men of all ranks learned to respect his judgment and to be uplifted by his presence. "None of us to our dying day can forget that countenance," wrote an infantryman after Lincoln's visit to the army. "Concentrated in that one great, strong, yet tender face the agony of the life and death struggle of the hour was revealed as we had never seen it before. With a new understanding, we knew why we were soldiers."

Lincoln's confidence that he had complete control of the situation was nowhere better indicated than in his famous letter to popular "Fighting Joe" Hooker, when the latter was named to succeed Burnside after the horror of Fredericksburg. "General," wrote Lincoln, "I have placed you at the head of the army of the Potomac. Of course I have done this upon what appear to me to be sufficient reasons, and yet I think it best for you to know that there are some things in regard to which I am not quite satisfied with you. I believe you to be a brave and skilful soldier, which of course I like. I also believe you do not mix politics with your profession, in which you are right. You have confidence in yourself, which is a valuable, if not an indispensable quality. You are ambitious, which within reasonable bounds, does good rather than harm; but I think that during General Burnside's command of the army you have taken counsel of your ambition and thwarted him as much as you could, in which you did a great wrong to the country and to a most meritorious and honorable brother officer. I have heard in such a way as to believe it, of your recently saying that both the army and the government needed a dictator. Of course it was not for this, but in spite of it, that I have given you the command. Only those generals who gain successes can set up dictators. What I now ask you is military success, and I will risk the dictatorship . . . ; and now beware of rashness. Beware of rashness, but with energy and sleepless vigilance go forward and give us victories."

★ GETTYSBURG AND VICKSBURG

Hooker did not bring victories despite the odds in his favor. Against his force of 130,000 men Lee could oppose only 60,000; but Lee and his right hand, Stonewall Jackson, were real generals. Hooker's ineptness resulted in bloody defeat at Chancellorsville, in the first days of May, 1863. A disheartened Northern colonel wrote, "I doubt if ever in the history of this war, another chance will be given us to fight the enemy with such odds in our favor as we had . . . and that chance has been worse than lost to us."

Few Civil War victories came cheaply; Confederate casualties were over 13,000. Most costly to the South was the loss of her great Stonewall Jackson, accidentally killed by his own men. Soon after Chancellorsville Lee prepared to carry the war into Northern territory, and in June his troops moved into Pennsylvania. The climactic battle of the war was now at hand.

Almost by accident at Gettysburg, neither side having planned for it in that place, the great battle began on July 1. Fortunately for the North, a few days earlier command had been turned over to methodical George Gordon Meade. On the second day of July the Confederates swarmed up famed Cemetery Ridge where the Union forces had strong defenses but, while the Southern troops made important gains, they could not hold their advantage. Soon after midday, on July 3, the Confederates made their supreme bid for victory. Against the Union center the flower of Lee's army threw themselves in brave sacrifice. Their battle colors waving, their bayonets "a sloping forest of flashing steel," they came on with almost irresistible force. Pickett's division crowded forward through blasting artillery fire. When the unflinching gray masses of Confederates came near enough for their grim faces to be seen by the defenders, the Union infantry opened fire, aiming low and steady. The momentum of the Southerners carried a few of them over the stone wall on the top of Cemetery Ridge where, for a fleeting instant, the Confederate flag was hoisted. But the few were quickly captured or cut down; the many lay below the Ridge in broken splendor. The roar of Union troops gave the welcome message—the crest was safe.

Meade had won a great victory for the North, but his overcautiousness allowed Lee to escape. Lee himself, taking sole responsibility for the defeat, offered to resign. In reply President Davis, refusing the resignation, extolled Lee's achievements "which will make you and your army the subject of history and object of the world's admiration for generations to come."

The North celebrated the Fourth of July, 1863, with hysterical joy, for along with Gettysburg came the news of Grant's capture of Vicksburg. That Confederate fortress, high on a bluff on the Mississippi, was protected by the river, swamps, and dense woods. Grant, after several vain attempts, decided to launch his Army of the Tennessee against the stronghold from the rear. It was a magnificent campaign, co-ordinated with the action of the river gunboats. Grant's troops crossed the Mississippi from the west shore below Vicksburg, near Grand Gulf. Then

The Civil War, 1863

with 20,000 men, living off the country, fighting as he marched 200 miles in eighteen days, he won five pitched battles, took 8,000 prisoners, and penned the Southern army in Vicksburg.

Grant first attempted direct assault, but failed. He then prepared to wear down the defenders, and at the same time increased his own attacking forces to 70,000 men, with over 200 guns. Toward the end of May the siege of the "Confederate Gibraltar" began. For forty-seven days the beleaguered city was hammered by land and by river. On July 3, when the city was near starvation and the troops mutinous, General Pemberton asked for terms of surrender. The following day 30,000 dejected Confederates marched out of the doomed city, between lines of quiet Union soldiers. Five days later, July 9, Port Hudson, the last Confederate fort on the Mississippi, fell to General Banks. The entire river was now open to Union vessels. In this campaign on the Mississippi, black soldiers won especial distinction. "No body of troops—Western—Eastern or rebel—have fought better in the war," wrote *The New York Times*. Their bravery, said a high official in the War Department, "completely revolutionized the sentiment of the army with regard to the employment of Negro troops." In the East, in July, 1863, blacks added to their laurels and a lengthened casualty list in a futile assault on Fort Wagner, guarding Charleston. Skeptical whites were now convinced that Negroes were the equal of fighting men anywhere.

The year had witnessed great Northern triumphs, but the Union counted its dead in the many thousands. On the battlefield of Gettysburg Lincoln dedicated a national cemetery with words that cannot die:

Four score and seven years ago our fathers brought forth on this continent, a new nation, conceived in Liberty, and dedicated to the proposition that all men are created equal.

Now we are engaged in a great civil war, testing whether that nation, or any nation so conceived and so dedicated, can long endure. We are met on a great battle-field of that war. We have come to dedicate a portion of that field, as a final resting place for those who here gave their lives that that nation might live. It is altogether fitting and proper that we should do this.

But, in a larger sense, we can not dedicate—we can not consecrate—we can not hallow—this ground. The brave men, living and dead, who struggled here, have consecrated it, far above our poor power to add or detract. The world will little note, nor long remember what we say here, but it can never forget what they did here. It is for us the living, rather, to be dedicated here to the unfinished work which they who fought here have thus far so nobly advanced. It is rather for us to be here dedicated to the great task remaining before us—that from these honored dead we take increased devotion to that cause for which they gave the last full measure of devotion—that we here highly resolve that these dead shall not have died in vain—that this nation, under God, shall have a new birth of freedom—and that government of the people, by the people, for the people, shall not perish from the earth.

★ SHERMAN AND GRANT

After the fall of Vicksburg Federal troops moved on Chattanooga, an important railroad junction and a key point in the western sector. In Southern hands it was a base for offensive action in Tennessee and Kentucky; in Northern hands it was a gateway to Georgia. The Union commander, General Rosecrans, on September 9, 1863, entered Chattanooga unopposed, after the Confederate General Bragg had been out-maneuvered. Ten days later the Confederates gave battle at Chicka-mauga and almost broke the whole Union line. Only the steadfastness of General George H. Thomas, "the Rock of Chickamauga," saved the Union army from complete disaster. The Northern army was withdrawn to Chattanooga where it was laid under siege. Rosecrans was succeeded by Thomas who made a brave defense of the city, though his army was on scanty rations. Large forces under Grant, now supreme commander in the western theater, then converged on Chattanooga. In a spectacular campaign, topped by the dashing capture of Missionary Ridge, the Federals won the battle of Chattanooga at the end of November. The road was now open to split the Confederacy in two by invading Georgia and the Carolinas.

With Grant in supreme command of all the Union armies and Sherman in charge of the West, the two elaborated a strategic plan to crush the South in a giant pincers. Great numbers of troops were to

The Civil War, 1864

bear down on Virginia while Sherman and his men were to march south-eastward into the heart of the Confederacy. Sherman's experienced army of 100,000 had as its objective Atlanta, 100 miles away over mountainous country crossed by deep valleys and swift-running streams. In between was a Confederate force of 65,000 under Joseph E. Johnston. On May 7, 1864, the Union army, traveling light, started its campaign. Engineers building bridges and hauling supplies over the single-track railroad did a remarkable job keeping communications open as Sherman marched to Georgia. Johnston's outmatched force fell back slowly before the relentless drive of Northern troops who reached Atlanta's outer defenses before the end of July.

Johnston, though he had fought a skilful retreat, was replaced by the one-legged, impetuous Hood. The latter quickly took the offensive, but his army suffered defeat. Georgia's capital was evacuated on September 1. "Atlanta is ours and fairly won," wired the exultant Sherman to Lincoln. Hood then attempted to cut Sherman's communications with Tennessee, but in December the dependable Union commander, General Thomas, won the most overwhelming victory of the war when he cut the Confederates to pieces at Nashville.

Meanwhile Sherman had destroyed Atlanta to weaken the Confederacy's will to fight. Then, on November 16, 1864, the Union commander turned his horse eastward and began his historic march to the sea. A band struck up "John Brown's Body" and the men joined lustily in the "Glory, glory, hallelujah!" The Northern army, following a "scorched earth" policy, left a trail of desolation sixty miles wide through central Georgia. The lanky, wrinkle-faced Sherman gained the hated reputation of the "Vandal Chief," and his hulking, bearded soldiers the modern Goths. For more than a month Sherman's army went forward against little opposition, entering Savannah on December 21. The Union troops then turned northward.

The northern half of the pincers, directed by Grant, did not move so smoothly. Grant's attack on Lee in Virginia in the spring of 1864 was timed with Sherman's in the West. Lee's army was half the size of Grant's but, fighting on the defensive, the brilliant Southern leader used every advantage the terrain offered to make Grant pay heavily for each yard gained. The Union commander's main task was to destroy Lee's army, and this he proposed to do by attrition, if quick victory eluded him. Lee's purpose was to stave off final capitulation until the North might grow weary of the war and then, perhaps under a new president in 1864, recognize Southern independence. Lee's gamble almost won.

In early May Grant crossed the Rapidan and was quickly entangled in the heavy undergrowth of the Wilderness. For weeks hard fighting between the two armies resulted in no conclusive result. Undismayed, the stubborn, square-jawed Grant made his celebrated statement: "I . . . propose to fight it out on this line if it takes all summer." The conflict bloodied once again the ground where McClellan's men had fought. Northern troops, in the first days of June, flung themselves vainly against Confederate entrenchments at Cold Harbor. One who took part in the battle said "the dead covered more than five acres of ground about as thickly as they could be laid."

In a month of fighting Lee's army lost 30,000, Grant's 55,000—but the North had more to lose. By the middle of June, 1864, Grant was south of Richmond, before Petersburg, whose capture would almost isolate the capital from the rest of the Confederacy. Failing to take Petersburg by direct assault Grant then resorted to siege operations. For the following nine months the two armies waged trench warfare, each unable to dislodge the other.

★ ELECTION, 1864

The strain of soaring prices, endless war, and apparent stalemate resulted in loss of confidence in Lincoln's administration, defeatist talk, and pressure for a negotiated peace. The president was ready to end the war if the South returned to the Union and abolished slavery. This, President Davis was unwilling to accept, still believing in his star of victory.

The Republicans, in June, 1864, named Lincoln again for the presidency. Everybody at the Baltimore convention was so excited that apparently no one thought of telegraphing the President word of his renomination. He first heard of it by chance when the superintendent of the military bureau of telegraphs congratulated him. Powerful radical and other elements in the party attempted to have the nomination reconsidered. The President had defied them by his pocket-veto of the Wade-Davis bill (July 4, 1864), which proposed a more stringent policy than his of dealing with the South. To their malignity he opposed magnanimity. So great was the split in the Republican party (along with the adverse war news) that Lincoln, in the summer of 1864, was ready to admit defeat in the coming November election. Most of the prominent Republican leaders were unfriendly to Lincoln's candidacy.

The Democrats, deeply infected with "Copperhead" sentiment (C. C. Vallandigham, the most prominent "Copperhead," drew up the convention's resolution urging a negotiated peace), nominated General McClellan. Though McClellan opposed the Democratic peace plank, his whole party was nevertheless tarred with accusations of disloyalty to the Union. Defeatist talk was quickly overwhelmed by the timely victories of Sherman in Georgia and Sheridan in the devastated Shenandoah Valley. Republican Radicals fell in line with renewed enthusiasm for Lincoln's administration; and by late October the President's re-election seemed assured. On election night, Lincoln waited quietly for the returns to come in. He won with the overwhelming margin of 212 electors to McClellan's 21, though the popular vote was close.

★ APPOMATTOX—"WITH MALICE TOWARD NONE"

In a speech during midsummer, 1864, strongly supporting Grant's strategy, Lincoln had said: "This war has taken three years; it was begun or accepted upon the line of restoring the national authority over the whole national domain, and for the American people . . . I say we are going through on this line if it takes three years more." Fortunately the end was not so far off. It was in sight in the winter of 1864–65.

The siege of Petersburg was stretching to the utmost the resources that Lee still commanded. Sickness, desertion, and falling food supplies weakened his beleaguered army. Wherever Federal troops approached, field slaves showed their hostility to slavery by slack work, by running away, or even by violence against masters. The South's morale was nearly spent, but her leaders were still not prepared to yield. A peace conference on a ship in Hampton Roads, on February 3, 1865, between Lincoln and Vice-President Stephens of the Confederacy was fruitless, making it certain that the war would continue until the Southern armies collapsed.

Only two Confederate armies were still intact as important fighting forces, Lee's in Virginia and Johnston's in the Carolinas. The pincers was finally closing in on them with Sherman coming up from the South. Sherman's army built corduroy roads and bridges to traverse the swamps of the Carolinas. The march from Savannah northward was a far more difficult achievement than the march from Atlanta to the sea. The Southern commander, General Johnston, thought Sherman's army the greatest "since the days of Julius Caesar." Grant's enlarged army was threatening to swamp Lee's inferior forces. The latter's hope was to escape from the Petersburg-Richmond area westward and link up with the remaining troops of General Johnston. Johnston's men had fought a blistering battle at Bentonville, North Carolina on March 19, but the day ended with his defeat.

At Petersburg Grant was making ready for a final assault the morning of April 3, but during the night Lee's army had abandoned their lines. Union troops then took the long sought objective, Richmond. Tramping horses, exploding cannon, fife and drum, and the roar of conquering Yankees made the burning Confederate capital a nightmare to the crushed Southerners. Only the Negroes welcomed the Northern soldiers. Northerners went wild over the victory. In an upstate New York village a school girl wrote in her diary: "The streets were thronged with men, women and children all acting crazy as if they had not the remotest idea where they were or what they were doing . . . The band was playing . . . On the square they fired guns, and bonfires were lighted in the streets." Her grandmother, she added, preferred to "pray for the poor suffering, wounded soldiers, who are so apt to be forgotten in the hour of victory."

Grant wasted no time in celebration. Working in close collaboration with General Sheridan, he sent his forces hurrying after the fleeing Confederates, and in a few days closed all avenues of escape for Lee. After a last desperate attempt to break through the enclosing iron ring, the great Southern commander agreed to surrender his worn and starving troops on April 9 at the little village of Appomattox Court House. Lee and Grant who remembered each other from happier days during the Mexican war spoke together in friendly fashion. Lee suggested that his opponent write out the conditions of surrender; Grant did so immediately, and his terms were generous. The end had come, simply and without flourish. Within a few weeks the shattered remnants of other Confederate armies laid down their arms. Lee said goodbye to his adoring men, who mingled sobs and roaring acclaim in affectionate tribute. Astride his famous horse, Traveller, he turned homeward to

The Civil War, 1865

engage in another struggle, the restoration of peace to his beloved state. Virginia, he said, "has need for all her sons."

Lee was hopeful that time would heal the South's scars, and that a victorious North would be magnanimous. The signs were auspicious. Lincoln had closed his second inaugural address, in March, 1865, with the noble words: "With malice toward none, with charity for all, with firmness in the right as God gives us to see the right, let us strive on to finish the work we are in, to bind up the nation's wounds, to care for him who shall have borne the battle and for his widow and his orphan, to do all which may achieve and cherish a just and lasting peace among ourselves and with all nations."

The president's mind was filled these April days with plans for a reconstructed Union. In this spring of 1865, when the lilacs opened early and the dogwood spread its pure white blossoms in profusion, Lincoln was hoping that the nation's second birth would be free of complications. When his term of office was up he and his family were to return to Illinois where he planned to practice law. The promise of unembittered reconstruction was not to be fulfilled. The task would have been difficult enough even with Lincoln directing policy; without him it was virtually impossible.

On the night of April 14 the President went to Ford's Theatre, where *Our American Cousin* was being performed. About ten o'clock, while the audience was enjoying the play, a shot rang out above the laughter. A woman's cry fixed the scene at the presidential box; Lincoln had been shot. Lincoln's assassin, an actor, John Wilkes Booth, escaped across the stage. Seward was also a victim in his home, that night, of bullets fired by conspirators who hoped to wipe out the chief officers of the government and yet save the South's independence. The president was taken from the theater to a home nearby, and laid diagonally across a bed too small for his giant, suffering frame. The bullet had entered the brain; he never regained consciousness. In the gloom of a cold, rainy morning Lincoln's worn features settled into "a look of unspeakable peace," and death came soon after seven o'clock on April 15.

Gideon Welles left the death chamber to return to the White House. In front of it he saw "several hundred colored people, mostly women and children, weeping and wailing their loss. This crowd did not appear to diminish through the whole of that cold, wet day; they seemed not to know what was to be their fate since their great benefactor was dead, and their hopeless grief," said Welles, "affected me more than almost anything else, though strong and brave men wept when I met them."

The country was stunned by the tragic news. "All seem to feel as though they had lost a personal friend, and tears flow plenteously," wrote a humble citizen. "One week ago we were celebrating our victories with loud acclamations of mirth and good cheer. Now every one is silent and sad and the earth and heavens seem clothed in sack-cloth." All over the world millions of people gathered in churches to weep over the death of the martyred president. In his own country millions of his fellow citizens stood in grieving silence while the funeral train, passing through cities draped in black, carried his body back to Springfield. There among his friends and neighbors he was laid to rest.

Lincoln had lifted Americans to great efforts which saved their nation, "the last, best hope of earth." From the dangers of a divided land he delivered them to face the coming years with renewed confidence. A people who had braved the perils of pioneering the wilderness in the seventeenth century, who had brought forth a new nation in the eighteenth, and who were able to produce a Lincoln in the nineteenth century were endowed with a rich heritage to face the future.

SUGGESTED READINGS

CHAPTER I—EUROPE DISCOVERS AN UNKNOWN LAND

For the Norse voyages see Edward Reman, *The Norse Discoveries and Explorations in America* (Berkeley: University of California Press, 1949); also J. F. Jameson, ed., "Original Narratives of Early American History," *The Northmen, Columbus and Cabot* (New York, 1906). E. P. Cheyney, *The European Background of American History* (New York, 1904) as well as his *The Dawn of a New Era, 1250–1453* (New York: Harper and Brothers, 1936) are helpful for the Old World scene. L. B. Packard, *The Commercial Revolution, 1400–1776* (New York, 1927), is a good summary. J. B. Brebner, *The Explorers of North America, 1492–1806* (Garden City, N.Y.: Doubleday, 1955) is excellent. S. E. Morison's biography of Columbus, *Admiral of the Ocean Sea* (2 vols.; Boston: Little, Brown, 1942), is splendid.

On the expansion of Spain, see R. B. Merriman, *The Rise of the Spanish Empire in the Old World and the New* (4 vols.; New York: Macmillan, 1918–34); E. G. Bourne, *Spain in America 1450–1580* (New York, 1904); F. A. Kirkpatrick, *The Spanish Conquistadors* (London: A. C. Black, 1946); B. W. Diffie, *Latin America Civilization: Colonial Period* (Harrisburg, Pa.: Stackpole Sons, 1945). W. H. Prescott's classic *The Conquest of Mexico* (many editions) is still fascinating. For a general account see H. I. Priestley, *The Coming of the White Man, 1492–1848* (New York, 1929).

CHAPTER II—THE OLD WORLD IN THE NEW

For background, see Wallace Notestein, *The English People on the Eve of Colonization, 1603–1660* (New York: Harper and Brothers, 1954), and L. B. Wright, *Middle-Class Culture in Elizabethan England* (Chapel Hill: University of North Carolina Press, 1935). G. B. Parks, *Richard Hakluyt and the English Voyages* (New York, 1928), reveals Hakluyt's role in arousing interest in building an empire. Allen French, *Charles I and the Puritan Upheaval* (London: Allen and Unwin, 1955), discusses the reasons for the Puritan migration.

A detailed, authoritative treatment of a long span of colonial history is to be found in C. M. Andrews, *The Colonial Period of American History* (4 vols.; New Haven, Conn.: Yale University Press, 1934–38). H. L. Osgood, *The American Colonies in the Seventeenth Century* (3 vols.; New York, 1904–7), was the first modern treatment of the colonial period. W. F. Craven, *The Southern Colonies in the Seventeenth Century* (Baton Rouge: Louisiana State University Press, 1949), is excellent also on the background of colonization. L. B. Wright, *The Atlantic Frontier* (New York: Alfred A. Knopf, 1947) is an able interpretation of the English background and the evolution of colonial civilization. W. C. Macleod, *The American Indian Frontier* (New York, 1928) is good on relations between the whites and Indians.

Garrett Mattingly, *Armada* (Boston: Houghton Mifflin, 1959), is an artistic and scholarly triumph; Carl Bridenbaugh, *Vexed and Troubled Englishmen 1590–1642* (New York, 1968), the latest study of the causes for English migration in the seventeenth century.

CHAPTER III—FOUNDING THE SETTLEMENTS

Edward Channing's *History of the United States* (6 vols.; New York, 1905–25) is an authoritative treatment by one of the ablest scholars of a former generation; see volume I for this period. Craven's *Southern Colonies in the Seventeenth Century* is a distinguished representation of present-day scholarship. On Puritanism, see M. M. Knappen, *Tudor Puritanism* (Chicago: University of Chicago Press, 1939). A valuable, short treatment is Alan Simpson's *Puritanism in Old and New England* (Chicago: University of Chicago Press, 1955). All readers of American history should know William Bradford's *History of Plimoth Plantation*. On New England, see S. E. Morison, *Builders of the Bay Colony* (Boston: Houghton Mifflin Co., 1930), J. T. Adams, *The Founding of New England* (Boston, 1921), and T. J. Wertenbaker, *The Puritan Oligarchy* (New York: C. Scribner's Sons, 1947). Perry Miller and T. H. Johnson's anthology, *The Puritans* (New York: American Book Company, 1938) is very useful. Morison's *Intellectual Life of Colonial New England* (New York: New York University Press, 1956) is one of his many valuable contributions to American history. K. M. Murdock, *Literature and Theology in Colonial New England* (Cambridge, Mass.: Harvard University Press, 1949) is a fine, short study by a discriminating scholar. For John Winthrop see E. S. Morgan, *The Puritan Dilemma: The Story of John Winthrop* (Boston: Little, Brown, 1958). On Roger Williams, see S. H. Brockunier, *The Irrepressible Democrat: Roger Williams* (New York: Ronald, 1940), and O. E. Winslow, *Master Roger Williams* (New York: Macmillan, 1957). On the Dutch, see T. J. Wertenbaker, *The Founding of American Civilization: The Middle Colonies* (New York: C. Scribner's Sons, 1938), and volumes I and II of *The History of the State of New York* (New York: Columbia University Press, 1933), A. C. Flick, ed.

Richard S. Dunn, *Puritans and Yankees: The Winthrop Dynasty of New England 1630–1717* (Princeton: Princeton University Press, 1962) is an able study of an outstanding family; D. B. Rutman, *Winthrop's Boston: Portrait of a Puritan Town, 1630–1649* (Chapel Hill: University of North Carolina Press, 1963); Perry Miller, *Roger Williams: His Contribution to the American Tradition* (New York: Atheneum Publishers, 1962), is a thoughtful, frequently unorthodox treatment by one of America's best historians.

CHAPTER IV—THE COLONIES SPREAD WHILE ENGLAND TIGHTENS CONTROLS

On Virginia in the seventeenth century see the works of P. A. Bruce: *Economic History of Virginia in the Seventeenth Century* (2 vols.; New York, 1907), *Institutional History of Virginia in the Seventeenth Century* (2 vols.; New York, 1910) and *Social Life in the Seventeenth Century* (Lynchburg, Va., 1927). The volumes by Wertenbaker offer a somewhat different interpretation of Virginia's history in this period, notably *The Planters of Colonial Virginia* (Princeton, N.J., 1922). See also Wertenbaker's *Virginia under the Stuarts* (Princeton, N.J., 1914) and his study of Bacon's Rebellion in *Torchbearer of the Revolution* (Princeton, N.J.: Princeton University Press, 1940).

For an interpretation friendlier to Governor Berkeley, see W. E. Washburn, *The Governor and the Rebel: A History of Bacon's Rebellion in Virginia* (Chapel Hill: University of North Carolina Press, 1957).

D. D. Wallace, *The History of South Carolina* (3 vols.; New York: American Historical Society, 1934) is a detailed study. For Pennsylvania, S. G. Fisher, *The Making of Pennsylvania* (Philadelphia: Lippincott, 1932) is helpful as is W. F. Dunaway, *A History of Pennsylvania* (New York: Prentice-Hall, 1948). William Penn has been the subject of a number of biographies; a recent, dependable one is W. W. Comfort, *William Penn* (Philadelphia: University of Pennsylvania Press, 1944).

A good, short treatment of Britain's administration of the colonies is to be found in C. P. Nettels, *The Roots of American Civilization* (New York: Crofts, 1938). L. A. Harper's *The English Navigation Laws: A Seventeenth Century Experiment in Social Engineering* (New York: Columbia University Press, 1939) is an able study of a difficult subject. C. M. Andrews in the fourth volume of his study of the colonies, *England's Commercial and Colonial Policy* (New Haven, Conn.: Yale University Press, 1938) made the most important modern contribution to this field of study. A pioneer work was that of G. L. Beer, *The Old Colonial System 1660–1688* (2 vols.; New York, 1912). T. J. Wertenbaker, *The First Americans 1607–1690* (New York, 1927) clearly depicts the progress made by the colonists before the end of the seventeenth century.

D. E. Leach, *Flintlock and Tomahawk: New England in King Philip's War* (New York: Macmillan, 1958) is a splendid account of that struggle.

Alden Vaughan, *New England Frontier* (Boston: Little, Brown & Co., 1965); M. M. Dunn, *William Penn: Politics and Conscience* (Princeton: Princeton University Press, 1967); R. A. Billington, ed., *The Reinterpretation of Early American History: Essays in Honor of John E. Pomfret* (San Marino, Calif.: Huntington Library, 1966); W. F. Craven, *The Colonies in Transition 1660–1713* (New York, 1967), product of the most recent scholarship.

CHAPTER V—BEGINNING THE WORLD AGAIN

For colonial migration see Carl Wittke, *We Who Built America: The Saga of the Immigrant* (New York: Prentice-Hall, 1939) and M. L. Hansen, *The Atlantic Migration 1607–1860* (Cambridge, Mass.: Harvard University Press, 1940). More specialized studies are those by W. A. Knittle, *Early Eighteenth Century Palatine Immigration* (Philadelphia: Dorrance, 1936), H. J. Ford, *The Scotch-Irish in America* (Princeton, N.J., 1915), I. C. C. Graham, *Colonists from Scotland: Emigration to North America 1707–1783* (Ithaca, N.Y.: Cornell University Press, 1956), A. H. Hirsch, *The Huguenots of Colonial South*

Carolina (Durham, N.C., 1928). A. E. Smith, *Colonists in Bondage* (Chapel Hill: University of North Carolina Press, 1947) and R. B. Morris, *Government and Labor in Early America* (New York: Columbia University Press, 1946) are important studies of white people at work. J. H. Franklin's *From Slavery to Freedom* (New York: Knopf, 1947) is an able study of Negroes at work.

The most recent contribution to the study of colonial commerce is Richard Pares, *Yankees and Creoles* (Cambridge, Mass.: Harvard University Press, 1956), important for its statistical demonstration of the place of the West Indies in the economy of the continental colonies. See also Virginia Harrington, *The New York Merchant on the Eve of the Revolution* (New York: Columbia University Press, 1935), F. B. Tolles, *Meeting House and Counting House, the Quaker Merchants of Colonial Philadelphia* (Chapel Hill: University of North Carolina Press, 1948). Southern trade with the interior is referred to in V. W. Crane's distinguished book, *The Southern Frontier 1670–1732* (Ann Arbor, Mich., 1928).

CHAPTER VI—STRIVING FOR GREATER FREEDOM

L. W. Labaree, *Royal Government in America* (New Haven, Conn.: Yale University Press, 1930) is a detailed study which notes the increasing difficulties confronting governors. His *Conservatism in Early American History* (New York: New York University Press, 1948) is a stimulating interpretation. Perry Miller's *The New England Mind: From Colony to Province* (Cambridge, Mass.: Harvard University Press, 1953) has important material on political conflicts, as well as on other phases of colonial life. Irving Mark in *Agrarian Conflicts in Colonial New York* (New York: Columbia University Press, 1942) points up an aspect of colonial life common to almost all the colonies. On Zenger, see L. Rutherford, *John Peter Zenger* (New York: Peter Smith, 1941), and Chapter III in R. B. Morris, *Fair Trial* (New York: Knopf, 1952); also *The Trial of John Peter Zenger,* Vincent Buranelli, ed. (New York: New York University Press, 1957). H. L. Osgood, *The American Colonies in the Eighteenth Century* (New York, 1924) is a detailed treatment by one of our ablest scholars.

Recent studies have revised older interpretations of the extent of political democracy in the colonies. Among them are R. E. Brown, *Middle-Class Democracy and the Revolution in Massachusetts 1691–1780* (Ithaca, N.Y.: Cornell University Press, 1955), R. P. McCormick, *The History of Voting in New Jersey* (New Brunswick, N.J.: Rutgers University Press, 1953) and Theodore Thayer, *Pennsylvania Politics and the Growth of Democracy 1740–1776* (Harrisburg, Pa.: Historical and Museum Commission, 1953).

Religion, as well as other aspects of colonial life, is treated in J. T. Adams, *Provincial Society 1690–1763* (New York, 1927). The Great Awakening has been studied by several scholars, the most recent, E. S. Gaustad, *The Great Awakening in New England* (New York: Harper and Brothers, 1957). In Oscar Zeichner's *Connecticut's Years of Controversy 1750–1776* (Chapel Hill: University of North Carolina Press,

1949) is an enlightening discussion of the interrelationship of religious, political, and economic questions.

Alan Heimert, *Religion and the American Mind: From the Great Awakening to the Revolution* (Cambridge, Mass.: Harvard University Press, 1966) is a fresh interpretation of a complex theme; Beverly McAnear, *The Income of the Colonial Governors of British North America* (New York: Pageant Press, 1967) corrects Labaree on governor's salaries, says disputes were serious.

CHAPTER VII—PUSHING WESTWARD—THE STRUGGLE FOR INLAND AMERICA

The classic work on this theme is Francis Parkman's masterpiece, recently abridged in S. E. Morison, *The Parkman Reader* (Boston: Little, Brown, 1955). A later treatment than Parkman's is that of G. M. Wrong, *The Rise and Fall of New France* (2 vols.; New York, 1928). Wrong's brief account, *The Conquest of New France,* Chronicles of America Series, vol. 10 (New Haven, 1918) is excellent. An impressive achievement is L. H. Gipson, *The British Empire before the American Revolution* (9 vols.; New York: Knopf, 1936–56). In D. S. Freeman, *Young Washington* (New York: C. Scribner's Sons, 1948) is a lively description of the Anglo-French conflict. H. H. Peckham, *Pontiac and the Indian Uprising* (Princeton, N.J.: Princeton University Press, 1947) is a scholarly account of the conspiracy. Arthur Pound and R. E. Day, *Johnson of the Mohawks: a Biography of Sir William Johnson* (New York: Macmillan, 1930) is a study of an important personality who held the Indians to the British side. See also A. T. Volwiler, *George Croghan and the Westward Movement 1741–1782* (Cleveland, O., 1926). C. W. Alvord, *The Mississippi Valley in British Politics* (2 vols.; Cleveland, O., 1917) is especially good on land speculation. Channing's second volume (New York, 1908) in his *History of the United States* is still useful for the theme of this chapter.

R. A. Billington, *America's Frontier Heritage* (New York: Holt, Rinehart & Winston, 1966) is a balanced view by a superior student of the subject; C. S. Grant, *Democracy on the Connecticut Frontier Town of Kent* (New York: Columbia University Press, 1961), asserts that original proprietors were not absentees, almost universal male suffrage existed.

CHAPTER VIII—A NATIVE CULTURE EMERGES

The volumes of Carl Bridenbaugh are important for this chapter, especially his *Cities in the Wilderness: The First Century of Urban Life in America 1625–1742* (New York: Ronald, 1938) and *Cities in Revolt: Urban Life in America 1743–1776* (New York: Knopf, 1955). Max Savelle, *Seeds of Liberty* (New York: Knopf, 1948) is a stimulating study of the "parents" of the Revolutionary generation. Two volumes by Michael Kraus contain materials for this chapter; *Intercolonial Aspects of American Culture on the Eve of the Revolution* (New York, 1928) and *The Atlantic Civilization: Eighteenth Century Origins* (Ithaca, N.Y.: Cornell University Press, 1949). Brooke Hindle,

The Pursuit of Science in Revolutionary America 1735–1789 (Chapel Hill: University of North Carolina Press, 1956) is an excellent study. I. B. Cohen, a learned historian of science, is the author of several important publications in colonial science, including *Franklin and Newton* (Philadelphia: American Philosophical Society, 1956). Carl Van Doren, *Benjamin Franklin* (New York: Viking, 1938) is erudite and comprehensive. F. B. Tolles, *James Logan and the Culture of Provincial America* (Boston: Little, Brown, 1957) deals with a man who helped fashion the Philadelphia where Franklin felt at home.

On witchcraft see the dramatic account in M. L. Starkey, *The Devil in Massachusetts* (New York: Knopf, 1949). Merle Curti, *The Growth of American Thought* (New York: Harper and Brothers, 1943) is excellent for this, as well as other periods. V. L. Parrington, *The Colonial Mind 1620–1800,* vol. I of *Main Currents in American Thought* (New York, 1927), is invigorating reading. Oliver Larkin, *Art and Life in America* (New York: Rinehart, 1949) is very good. L. B. Wright in *The Cultural Life of the American Colonies 1607–1763* (New York: Harper and Brothers, 1956) has given us an authoritative and lively synthesis of the whole field. D. J. Boorstin, *The Americans: The Colonial Experience* (New York, Random House, 1958), a stimulating book, appeared while my own was going to press.

E. S. Morgan, *The Gentle Puritan: A Life of Ezra Stiles, 1727–1795* (New Haven: Yale University Press, 1962) is a fine study by one of our ablest scholars.

CHAPTER IX—THE GATHERING STORM

C. L. Becker, *The Eve of the Revolution* (New Haven, Conn., 1921) is a short, stimulating interpretation of these years. J. C. Miller, *Origins of the American Revolution* (Boston: Little, Brown, 1943) is well-written. A. M. Schlesinger, *The Colonial Merchants and the American Revolution 1763–1776* (New York, 1918) was a brilliant, pioneer study. Clinton Rossiter, *Seedtime of the Republic* (New York: Harcourt, Brace, 1953) along with E. S. and H. M. Morgan, *The Stamp Act Crisis: Prologue to Revolution* (Chapel Hill: University of North Carolina, 1953) is excellent.

Biographies of leading Revolutionary figures include J. C. Miller, *Sam Adams: Pioneer in Propaganda* (Boston: Little, Brown, 1936), D. S. Freeman, *George Washington: A Biography* (6 vols.; New York: C. Scribner's Sons, 1948–54); C. P. Nettels, *George Washington and American Independence* (Boston: Little, Brown, 1951); C. J. Stillé, *The Life and Times of John Dickinson 1732–1808* (Philadelphia, 1891); the delightful book by Esther Forbes, *Paul Revere and the World He Lived In* (Boston: Houghton Mifflin, 1942), and the authoritative *Jefferson the Virginian* (Boston: Little, Brown, 1948) by Dumas Malone.

English interpretations are found in L. B. Namier, *England in the Age of the American Revolution* (New York: Macmillan, 1930) and Eric Robson, *The American Revolution 1763–1783* (New York: Oxford University Press, 1955). An American scholar, D. M. Clark, has written a valuable study on the British reaction to the events of this era in *British Opinion and the American Revolution* (New Haven, Conn.: Yale University Press, 1930). The "war of the quill" is discussed by C. L. Becker in *The Declaration of Independence* (New York, 1922) and by M. C. Tyler in *The Literary History of the American Revolution 1763–1783* (2 vols.; New York, 1897). Philip Davidson, *Propaganda and the American Revolution 1763–1783* (Chapel Hill: University of North Carolina Press, 1941) is important in this connection. For the role of newspapers in these years see A. M. Schlesinger, *Prelude to Independence: The Newspaper War on Britain, 1764–1776* (New York: Alfred A. Knopf, 1958). Recent summaries by two very able scholars are to be found in L. H. Gipson, *The Coming of the Revolution, 1763–1775* (New York: Harper and Brothers, 1954), and in the shorter volume of E. S. Morgan, *The Birth of the Republic 1763–1789* (Chicago: University of Chicago Press, 1956).

Bernard Bailyn, *The Ideological Origins of the American Revolution* (Cambridge, Mass.: Harvard University Press, 1967) is a stimulating analysis emphasizing, among other matters, that throughout the English-speaking world there existed a fear of a conspiracy against liberty. Carl Bridenbaugh, *Mitre and Sceptre* (New York: Oxford University Press, 1962) emphasizes that religious disputes were a fundamental cause of the American Revolution.

CHAPTER X—INDEPENDENCE

The Continental Congress is given sympathetic, scholarly coverage in E. C. Burnett, *The Continental Congress* (New York: Macmillan, 1941), and in more lively fashion in *The Reluctant Rebels* (New York: Harper and Brothers, 1950), by Lynn Montross. Richard Pares, *King George III and the Politicians* (Oxford, Eng.: Clarendon Press, 1953) is good on the king's ideas and personality. More inclusive treatments of these years are to be found in C. H. Van Tyne, *The War of Independence* (Boston, 1929), and J. C. Miller, *The Triumph of Freedom* (Boston: Little, Brown, 1948). A recent and dependable work on the military side of the Revolution is J. R. Alden, *The American Revolution 1775–1783* (New York: Harper and Brothers, 1954). Foreign relations are covered in S. F. Bemis, *The Diplomacy of the American Revolution* (New York: Appleton-Century, 1935) and E. S. Corwin, *French Policy and the American Alliance* (Princeton, N.J., 1916). Frank Monaghan, *John Jay, Defender of Liberty* (New York: Bobbs-Merrill, 1935) is valuable for this, as well as later, periods of American history. Volume III of Channing's *History of the United States* is still useful for the whole period from 1763 to 1789.

Benjamin Quarles, *The Negro in the American Revolution* (Chapel Hill: University of North Carolina Press, 1961), an excellent scholar reveals little known aspects of the period; two recent books by R. B. Morris present the results of notable scholarship: *The Peacemakers: The Great Powers and American Independence* (New York: Harper & Row, 1965), and *The American Revolution Reconsidered* (New York: Harper & Row, 1966).

CHAPTER XI—THE REVOLUTION COMPLETED

E. B. Greene, *The Revolutionary Generation 1763–1790* (New York: Macmillan, 1943) gives comprehensive coverage to the materials discussed in this chapter. J. F. Jameson, *The American Revolution Considered as a Social Movement* (Princeton, N.J., 1926) though possibly exaggerating the changes occurring in this era, is still valuable. Merrill Jensen, *The New Nation* (New York: Knopf, 1950) emphasizes the virtues of the government under the Articles of Confederation. Allan Nevins has written a full survey of this period in *The American States During and After the Revolution 1775–1789* (New York, 1924). C. S. Sydnor, *Gentlemen Freeholders: Political Practices in Washington's Virginia* (Chapel Hill: University of North Carolina Press, 1952) reminds us of the continuing influence of the traditional ruling class in Virginia after the Revolution.

C. A. Beard, *An Economic Interpretation of the Constitution of the United States* (New York, 1913) was a landmark in historical writing. A recent work, R. E. Brown, *Charles Beard and the Constitution* (Princeton, N.J.: Princeton University Press, 1956) is severely critical. Excellent general studies are those by R. L. Schuyler, *The Constitution of the United States* (New York, 1923) and Carl Van Doren, *The Great Rehearsal* (New York: Viking, 1948). The first two volumes of Irving Brant's biography of James Madison are valuable for this section, as is Nathan Schachner, *Alexander Hamilton* (New York: Appleton-Century, 1946). Max Farrand, the most learned student of the federal convention, wrote two succinct volumes, *Framing of the Constitution* (New Haven, Conn., 1913) and *The Fathers of the Constitution* (New Haven, Conn., 1921). All students should know *The Federalist,* the famous commentary on the Constitution, written by Hamilton, Madison, and Jay, available in many editions.

Another reconsideration of Beard's work is found in Forrest McDonald, *We the People: The Economic Origins of the Constitution* (Chicago: University of Chicago Press, 1958); J. T. Main, *The Antifederalists: Critics of the Constitution, 1781–1788* (Chapel Hill: University of North Carolina Press, 1961). Main's "Federalists" were commercial classes—noncommercial elements were "Antifederalists"; also by Main, *The Social Structure of Revolutionary America 1763–1783* (Princeton: Princeton University Press, 1965) stresses the mobility and fluidity of American society; Staughton Lynd, *Class Conflict, Slavery and the United States Constitution* (Indianapolis: Bobbs-Merrill, 1968) further modifies Beard's interpretation; Chilton Williamson, *American Suffrage from Property to Democracy 1760–1800* (Princeton: Princeton University Press, 1960) is a careful study of a much debated subject.

CHAPTER XII—THE NEW ROOF

J. B. McMaster, *A History of the People of the United States from the Revolution to the Civil War* (8 vols.; New York, 1883–1913); vols. I and II are good on social conditions in these years. J. S. Bassett, *The Federalist System* (New York, 1906) and H. J. Ford, *Washington and His Colleagues* (1921) are summaries. C. G. Bowers, *Jefferson and*

Hamilton (Boston, 1925), anti-Federalist in tone, is spirited. Relevant portions of biographies of Washington, Jay, Hamilton, and Madison are important for this section; to them should be added Gilbert Chinard, *Honest John Adams* (Boston: Little, Brown, 1933). Significant revisions in interpretation are offered in Joseph Charles, *The Origins of the American Party System* (Williamsburg, Va.: Institute for Early American Culture, 1956) and in M. J. Dauer, *The Adams Federalists* (Baltimore, Md.: Johns Hopkins Press, 1953). C. A. Beard, *Economic Origins of Jeffersonian Democracy* (New York, 1915) was a pathbreaking work. On the Alien and Sedition Acts, see J. M. Smith, *Freedom's Fetters: The Alien and Sedition Laws and American Civil Liberties* (Ithaca, N.Y.: Cornell University Press, 1956). E. P. Link, *Democratic Republican Societies* (New York: Columbia University Press, 1942) deals with the impact of the French Revolution in America. Diplomatic questions are treated in S. F. Bemis, *Jay's Treaty* (New York, 1923), his *Pinckney's Treaty* (Baltimore, 1926), and A. P. Whitaker, *The Mississippi Question, 1795–1803* (New York: Appleton-Century, 1934); also Alexander DeConde, *Entangling Alliance: Politics & Diplomacy under George Washington* (Durham, N.C.: Duke University Press, 1958.)

N. E. Cunningham, Jr., *The Jeffersonian Republicans: The Formation of Party Organization 1789–1801* (Chapel Hill: University of North Carolina Press, 1958). The author maintains there is no evidence that Hamilton influenced Jefferson's election to the presidency in 1801. The real leader of the Republicans, 1793–96, was Madison. S. G. Kurtz, *The Presidency of John Adams: The Collapse of Federalism* (Philadelphia: University of Pennsylvania Press, 1957), a sympathetic study of Adams' administration, downgrades Alien-Sedition laws as a factor in Federalist decline.

CHAPTER XIII—JEFFERSON GUIDES THE REPUBLIC

The great work on this period is Henry Adams, *History of the United States During the Administrations of Thomas Jefferson and James Madison* (9 vols.; New York, 1889–91). Irving Brant's *Madison* (5 vols.; New York: Bobbs-Merrill, 1941–56) differs with Adams on numerous points. Raymond Walters, Jr., *Albert Gallatin: Jeffersonian Financier and Diplomat* (New York: Macmillan, 1957) does justice to an inadequately appreciated figure. L. M. Sears, *Jefferson and the Embargo* (Durham, N.C., 1927) discusses a thorny issue. A. L. Burt, *The United States, Great Britain and British North America* (New Haven, Conn.: Yale University Press, 1940) is a significant study of a triangular relationship. Bradford Perkins, *The First Rapprochement: England and the United States 1795–1805* (Philadelphia: University of Pennsylvania Press, 1955) offers a suggestive interpretation. Vol. IV of Channing's *History of the United States* is an authoritative work by a scholar especially interested in the Jeffersonian era.

N. E. Cunningham, Jr., *The Jeffersonian Republicans in Power: Party Operations 1801–1809* (Chapel Hill: University of North Carolina Press, 1963)—half the federal posts were held by Republicans after two years of Jefferson's administration; H. L. Coles, *The War of 1812*

(Chicago: University of Chicago Press, 1965)—the war was caused by the need to vindicate "national honor"; Bradford Perkins, *Prologue to War: England and the United States, 1805–1812* (Berkeley: University of California Press, 1961) is a detailed, scholarly study.

CHAPTER XIV—END OF AN ERA

George Dangerfield, *Era of Good Feelings* (New York: Harcourt, Brace, 1952) is excellent. So, too, is F. J. Turner, *Rise of the New West 1819–1829* (New York, 1906). The third and fourth volumes of Beveridge's *John Marshall* are important for this section. E. S. Corwin, *John Marshall and the Constitution* (New York, 1919) is a good, short treatment. Glover Moore, *The Missouri Controversy* (Lexington: University of Kentucky Press, 1953) is a recent discussion of this issue. C. S. Sydnor, *The Development of Southern Sectionalism 1819–1848* (Baton Rouge: Louisiana State University Press, 1948) is an important work. On the Monroe Doctrine see the leading authority, Dexter Perkins, *A History of the Monroe Doctrine* (Boston: Little, Brown, 1955). Biographies important for this section are W. P. Cresson, *James Monroe* (Chapel Hill: University of North Carolina Press, 1946), S. F. Bemis, *John Quincy Adams and the Foundations of American Foreign Policy* (New York: Knopf, 1949), Marquis James, *The Life of Andrew Jackson* (Indianapolis, Ind.: Bobbs-Merrill, 1938).

George Dangerfield, *The Awakening of American Nationalism 1815–1828* (New York: Harper & Row, 1965), an original interpretation by a gifted historian, stresses the continentalism of J. Q. Adams and says the Monroe Doctrine was more of a challenge to industrial England than it was to the Holy Alliance or France "against whom it was ostensibly directed"; Bradford Perkins, *Castlereagh and Adams: England and the United States, 1812–1823* (Berkeley: University of California Press, 1964) is the last of the trilogy detailing Anglo-American diplomatic relations. Britain finally recognized diplomatic equality for the United States.

CHAPTER XV—JACKSON—A PEOPLE'S PRESIDENT

The biography by Marquis James cited above is spirited and based on wide research. A. M. Schlesinger, Jr., *The Age of Jackson* (Boston: Little, Brown, 1945) is a brilliant interpretation of this era. Bray Hammond, *Banks and Politics in America from the Revolution to the Civil War* (Princeton, N.J.: Princeton University Press, 1957) offers a more critical appraisal of Jackson's policies. An important reappraisal of these years is found in G. G. Van Deusen, *The Jacksonian Era 1828–1848* (New York: Harper & Bros., 1958). See also T. P. Abernethy, *From Frontier to Plantation in Tennessee* (Chapel Hill: University of North Carolina, 1932). J. W. Ward, *Andrew Jackson, Symbol for an Age* (New York: Oxford University Press, 1953) explains his great popularity. F. J. Turner's *The United States, 1830–1850* (New York: Holt, 1935) was the last work by one of America's most stimulating historians. L. D. White has written several volumes on the federal administrative organization, including one on the Jacksonian period. W. E.

Binkley, *American Political Parties: Their Natural History* (New York: Knopf, 1943) is helpful in unraveling developments in politics.

Outstanding personalities of this era are treated in biographies of Calhoun by C. M. Wiltse (3 vols.; Indianapolis, Ind.: Bobbs-Merrill, 1944–51), of Webster by C. M. Fuess (2 vols.; Boston: Little, Brown, 1930), of Henry Clay by G. G. Van Deusen (Boston: Little, Brown, 1937) and a shorter book by Clement Eaton, *Henry Clay and the Art of American Politics* (Boston: Little, Brown, 1957). Holmes Alexander is the author of *The American Talleyrand . . . Martin Van Buren* (New York: Harper and Brothers, 1935); excellent recent studies of the colorful Thomas Hart Benton are those by W. N. Chambers, *Old Bullion Benton, Senator from the New West* (Boston: Little, Brown, 1956) and E. B. Smith, *Magnificent Missourian: The Life of Thomas Hart Benton* (Philadelphia: Lippincott, 1958). Harrison was the subject of a biography by Freeman Cleaves, *Old Tippecanoe: William Henry Harrison* (New York: C. Scribner's Sons, 1939); O. P. Chitwood was the careful biographer of Tyler (New York: Appleton-Century, 1939).

Lee Benson, *The Concept of Jacksonian Democracy: New York as a Test Case* (Princeton: Princeton University Press, 1961); C. G. Sellers, *James K. Polk, Jacksonian 1795–1843* (Princeton: Princeton University Press, 1957), by the ablest student of Polk; T. P. Govan, *Nicholas Biddle: Nationalist and Public Banker 1786–1844* (Chicago: University of Chicago Press, 1959), a strong defense of Biddle and bitterly anti-Jackson; Walter Hugins, *Jacksonian Democracy and the Working Class: A Study of the New York Workingmen's Movement 1829–1837* (Stanford: Stanford University Press, 1960); W. A. Sullivan, *The Industrial Worker in Pennsylvania 1800–1840* (Harrisburg: Pennsylvania Historical and Museum Commission, 1955), maintains that workingmen's parties were not really representative of wage earners. Edward Pessen, *Most Uncommon Jacksonians: The Radical Leaders of the Early Labor Movement* (Albany: State University of New York Press, 1968), treats little known figures; P. S. Foner, *History of the Labor Movement in the United States* (New York: International Publishers, 1947), vol. I—adds to Commons and differs in interpretation; W. B. Smith, *Economic Aspects of the Second Bank of the United States* (Cambridge, Mass.: Harvard University Press, 1953), emphasizes the role of the Bank in maintaining a stable currency.

CHAPTER XVI—AS THE COUNTRY MATURED

Relevant chapters in Curti's *Growth of American Thought* (cited above) and his *Social Ideas of American Educators* (New York: C. Scribner's Sons, 1935) are important for this section. Lewis Mumford's *The Golden Day* (New York, 1926), and Van Wyck Brooks' *The Flowering of New England* (New York: Dutton, 1936) are well-written studies of this era; F. O. Mathiessen, *American Renaissance: Art and Expression in the Age of Emerson and Whitman* (New York: Oxford University Press, 1941) was a brilliant achievement. Larkin's *Art and Life in America,* already mentioned, is especially good on this period. A wealth of material is in F. L. Mott, *American Journalism: A History of Newspapers in the United States* (rev. ed.; New York:

Macmillan, 1950), and his *A History of American Magazines 1741–1850* (New York: Appleton, 1930). C. R. Fish, *The Rise of the Common Man 1830–1850* (New York, 1927) contains much of value for this chapter. The relevant chapters in C. A. Beard and M. R. Beard, *The Rise of American Civilization* (2 vols.; New York, 1927) are refreshing.

Carl Bode, *Anatomy of American Popular Culture 1840–1861* (Berkeley: University of California Press, 1959), treats the less familiar aspects; R. B. Nye, *The Cultural Life of the New Nation 1776–1830* (New York: Harper and Row, 1960), a comprehensive study.

CHAPTER XVII—THE NORTH AND THE COTTON KINGDOM

An excellent study of the whole field is G. R. Taylor, *The Transportation Revolution 1815–1860* (New York: Rinehart, 1951). S. E. Morison, *The Maritime History of Massachusetts 1783–1860* (Boston, 1921) is lively prose. R. G. Albion, *The Rise of New York Port 1815–1860* (New York: C. Scribner's Sons, 1939) shows how the city achieved primacy in trade. *The World of Eli Whitney* (New York: Macmillan, 1952) by Jeannette Mirsky and Allan Nevins has much of value for this chapter. L. C. Hunter, *Steamboats on the Western Rivers* (Cambridge, Mass.: Harvard University Press, 1949) is the most comprehensive and authoritative work in its field. Volume I of V. S. Clark, *History of Manufactures in the United States* (3 vols.; Washington, D.C., 1928) contains a vast fund of information on industrial growth to 1860. J. R. Commons and others gave us in vol. I of the *History of Labor in the United States* (4 vols.; New York: Macmillan, 1918–35) the standard work, though in need now of revision.

Clement Eaton, in *A History of the Old South* (New York: Macmillan, 1949) presents a good summary. F. L. Owsley, *Plain Folk of the Old South* (Baton Rouge: Louisiana State University Press, 1949) stresses the role of the yeomanry. J. H. Franklin, *The Militant South 1800–1861* (Cambridge, Mass.: Harvard University Press, 1956) notes the evidence of lawlessness in the region. F. L. Olmsted's accounts of his travels through the South, used by all students of this period, have recently been reissued, A. M. Schlesinger, ed., *The Cotton Kingdom* (New York: Knopf, 1953). L. C. Gray, *History of Agriculture in the Southern United States to 1860* (2 vols.; Washington, D.C.: Carnegie Institution, 1933) is a masterpiece of scholarship. A short work, but the result of much thinking on this theme, is that of W. E. Dodd, *The Cotton Kingdom* (New Haven, Conn., 1921). U. B. Phillips, *Life and Labor in the Old South* (Boston, 1929) is the culmination of long, though not always critical, study. Frederic Bancroft, *Slave-Trading in the Old South* (Baltimore, Md.: T. H. Furst Co., 1931) is good. K. M. Stampp, *The Peculiar Institution* (New York: Knopf, 1956) is a splendid re-examination of slave society.

M. A. Jones, *American Immigration* (Chicago: University of Chicago Press, 1960), chaps. iv–vi; Michael Kraus, *Immigration: The American Mosaic* (Princeton: Princeton University Press, 1966), chaps. 3–4.

CHAPTER XVIII—THE GIFT OF THE NEGRO

Richard Bardolph, *The Negro Vanguard* (New York: Vintage, 1959), good biographical sketches of pioneer activists; M. J. Butcher, *The Negro in American Culture,* based on materials left by Alain L. Locke (New York: A. A. Knopf, 1956), excellent, containing materials not easily found elsewhere; S. L. Gross, J. E. Hardy, eds., *Images of the Negro in American Literature* (Chicago: University of Chicago Press, 1966), especially chapter by Milton Cantor, "The Image of the Negro in Colonial Literature" and one by Tremaine McDowell, "The Negro in the Southern Novel Prior to 1850"; D. B. Davis, *The Problem of Slavery in Western Culture* (Ithaca: Cornell University Press, 1966), particularly illuminating for its comparative studies; R. C. Wade, *Slavery in the Cities: The South 1820–1860* (New York: Oxford University Press, 1964), important treatment of a neglected area; L. Parrish, *Slave Songs of Georgia Sea Islands* (New York, 1942); W. D. Jordan, *White Over Black: American Attitudes Toward the Negro, 1550–1812* (Chapel Hill: University of North Carolina Press, 1968), a work of considerable originality; Gunnar Myrdal, *An American Dilemma* (New York: McGraw-Hill Book Co., 1962), deservedly a classic; Henrietta Buckmaster, *Let My People Go,* the story of the Underground Railroad and the growth of the abolition movement (Boston: Beacon Press, 1959), a dramatic retelling of a famed activity; J. H. Franklin, *From Slavery to Freedom* (New York: A. A. Knopf, 1947), a comprehensive work by the leading scholar in the field; J. S. Redding, *They Came in Chains* (New York, 1950), written with literary distinction; C. H. Wesley, *Neglected History: Essays in Negro-American History* (Wilberforce, Ohio, 1965), little-known material presented by a first-rate scholar; Vernon Loggins, *The Negro Author* (New York: Kennikat Press, 1931), a pioneer study, not adequately appreciated; P. S. Foner, *Frederick Douglass* (New York: Citadel Press, 1964); Herbert Aptheker, *American Negro Slave Revolts* (New York: International Publishers, 1943); the writings of W. E. B. Du Bois are of great importance. The literature on the Negro in America has flourished recently; only a small portion can be listed here. One of the great repositories of Negro culture is the Schomburg collection in the Harlem branch of the New York Public Library.

CHAPTER XIX—THE EAGLE SPREADS ITS WINGS

R. A. Billington's two books, *Westward Expansion* (New York: Macmillan, 1949) and *The Far Western Frontier 1830–1860* (New York: Harper and Brothers, 1956) are excellent. H. N. Smith's *Virgin Land* (Cambridge, Mass.: Harvard University Press, 1950) is a critical study of the influence of the West upon the American imagination. N. A. Graebner, *Empire on the Pacific* (New York, Ronald, 1955) is suggestive for its emphasis on America's desire for trade in the Pacific. A. K. Weinberg, *Manifest Destiny* (Baltimore, Md.: Johns Hopkins Press, 1935) is a lengthy analysis of the idea of expansion. R. C. Buley, *The Old Northwest: Pioneer Period, 1815–1840* (2 vols.; Indianapolis, Ind.: Indiana Historical Society, 1950) is a comprehensive survey of the life of this region. On Oregon and California, see J. W. Caughey, *History of the Pacific Coast* (Los Angeles, Calif.: privately printed, 1933) and O. O. Winther, *The Great Northwest* (New York: Knopf, 1947). D. Lavender, *Land of Giants, The Drive to the Pacific Northwest* (New York: Doubleday, 1958) is very well written. Allan Nevins, *Frémont: Pathmarker of the West* (New York: Appleton-Century, 1955) deals with an important figure of the period. Francis Parkman's *The Oregon Trail* is a contemporary description by a great historian.

Bernard De Voto, *The Year of Decision* (Boston: Little, Brown, 1943) is a spirited narrative of the decisive months in 1846. For Texas and the war with Mexico, see R. N. Richardson, *Texas, the Lone Star State* (New York: Prentice-Hall, 1943) and J. H. Smith, *The War with Mexico* (2 vols.; New York, 1919). A. H. Bill, *Rehearsal for Conflict* (New York: Knopf, 1947) is good reading. N. W. Stephenson, an able scholar, wrote a short account in *Texas and the Mexican War* (New Haven, Conn., 1921).

Winfield Scott is the subject of *Old Fuss and Feathers* (New York: Greystone, 1937) by A. D. H. Smith, while Zachary Taylor is the theme of Brainerd Dyer's biography (Baton Rouge: Louisiana State University Press, 1946). C. B. Going, *David Wilmot Free Soiler* (New York, 1924) is useful for this section. In biographies of Webster, Clay, Calhoun, and Douglas are discussions of the Compromise of 1850. Volume II of A. J. Beveridge, *Abraham Lincoln, 1809–1858* (2 vols.; Boston, 1928) has a lengthy treatment of the Compromise. In addition see G. F. Milton, *The Eve of Conflict: Stephen A. Douglas and the Needless War* (New York: Houghton Mifflin, 1934) and J. T. Carpenter, *The South as a Conscious Minority* (New York: New York University Press, 1930). Allan Nevins in Volume I of *Ordeal of the Union* (2 vols.; New York: C. Scribner's Sons, 1947) presents a recent interpretation based on a close examination of the sources and the available scholarship to date.

P. W. Gates, *The Farmer's Age: Agriculture 1815–1860* (New York: Holt, Rinehart & Winston, 1960), a study by the leading student of American agriculture; C. G. Sellers, *James K. Polk, Continentalist, 1843–1848* (Princeton: Princeton University Press, 1966), the best study of Polk's presidency.

CHAPTER XX—A HOUSE DIVIDING

R. F. Nichols, *The Disruption of American Democracy* (New York: Macmillan, 1948), H. H. Simms, *A Decade of Sectional Controversy* (Chapel Hill: University of North Carolina Press, 1942), A. O. Craven, *The Coming of the Civil War* (New York: C. Scribner's Sons, 1942), and Nevins, *Ordeal of the Union* (cited above) are all important for this section, though their interpretations differ. D. L. Dumond, *Antislavery Origins of the Civil War* (Ann Arbor: University of Michigan Press, 1939) is stimulating. A comprehensive biography of a leading abolitionist is to be found in *Prophet of Liberty: The Life and Times of Wendell Phillips,* by Oscar Sherwin (New York: Bookman Associates, 1958). W. S. Jenkins, *Proslavery Thought in the Old South* (Chapel Hill: University of North Carolina Press, 1935) is a good study of changes in the South's thinking. R. B. Nye, *Fettered Freedom* (East Lansing:

Michigan State College Press, 1945) is lively reading. P. S. Foner, *Business and Slavery: The New York Merchants and the Irrepressible Conflict* (Chapel Hill: University of North Carolina Press, 1941) is an excellent study of the attitude of businessmen during the crisis. R. A. Billington, *The Protestant Crusade 1800–1860* (New York: Macmillan, 1938) is valuable for anti-Catholicism and the Know Nothing party. For the Republicans see A. W. Crandall, *The Early History of the Republican Party 1854–1856* (Boston: R. G. Badger, 1930). For Kansas, see J. C. Malin, *John Brown and the Legend of Fifty-Six* (Philadelphia: American Philosophical Society, 1942) and P. W. Gates, *Fifty Million Acres: Conflicts Over Kansas Land Policy 1854–1890* (Ithaca, N.Y.: Cornell University Press, 1954). A. C. Cole, *The Irrepressible Conflict 1850–1865* (New York: Macmillan, 1934) covers many of the topics treated in this chapter.

CHAPTER XXI—THE DEEP ABYSS

Allan Nevins, *The Emergence of Lincoln* (2 vols.; New York: C. Scribner's Sons, 1950) is splendid. A. O. Craven, *The Growth of Southern Nationalism 1848–1861* (Baton Rouge: Louisiana State University Press, 1953) is an excellent presentation of the South's viewpoint. R. G. Osterweis, *Romanticism and Nationalism in the Old South* (New Haven, Conn.: Yale University Press, 1949) is suggestive. R. R. Russel, *Economic Aspects of Southern Sectionalism 1840–1861* (Urbana, Ill., 1924) relates economic ambitions to politics. Clement Eaton, *Freedom of Thought in the Old South* (Durham, N.C.: Duke University Press, 1940) is an able analysis of certain aspects of Southern culture. G. W. Van Vleck, *The Panic of 1857* (New York: Columbia University Press, 1943) is useful. In addition to Nevins on the Dred Scott Case see also C. B. Swisher, *Roger B. Taney* (New York: Macmillan, 1935) and Louis Boudin, *Government by Judiciary* (2 vols.; New York: William Godwin, 1932). R. H. Luthin, *The First Lincoln Campaign* (Cambridge, Mass.: Harvard University Press, 1944) and William Baringer, *Lincoln's Rise to Power* (Boston: Little, Brown, 1937) are very good. D. M. Potter, *Lincoln and His Party in the Secession Crisis 1860–1861* (New Haven, Conn.: Yale University Press, 1942), K. M. Stampp, *And the War Came: The North and the Secession Crisis 1860–1861* (Baton Rouge: Louisiana State University Press, 1950) are both important. Ollinger Crenshaw, *The Slave States in the Presidential Election of 1860* (Baltimore, Md.: Johns Hopkins Press, 1945) adds new details to the story.

CHAPTER XXII—THE UNION FORGED IN FIRE

Good general accounts are C. R. Fish, *The American Civil War* (New York: Longmans, Green, 1937) and J. G. Randall, *The Civil War and Reconstruction* (New York: Heath, 1937). Channing's sixth and last volume of his *History of the United States* has much of value. Clement Eaton, *A History of the Southern Confederacy* (New York: Macmillan, 1954) is a sound study. Other works to be consulted are E. M. Coulter, *The Confederate States of America 1861–1865* (Baton Rouge: Louisiana State University Press, 1950) and B. J. Hendrick, *Statesmen of the*

Lost Cause: Jefferson Davis and his Cabinet (Boston: Little, Brown, 1939).

The Lincoln literature is enormous. For an excellent short study, see B. P. Thomas, *Abraham Lincoln* (New York: Knopf, 1952); longer, valuable works are those by Carl Sandburg, *Abraham Lincoln* (6 vols.; New York: Harcourt, Brace, 1926–39) and the scholarly J. G. Randall, *Lincoln the President* (4 vols.; New York: Dodd, 1945–55), vol. IV by Randall and R. N. Current. David Donald, *Lincoln Reconsidered* (New York: Knopf, 1956) is a collection of critical essays on important aspects of the history of this era. Lincoln and his fellow Republicans are the theme of D. M. Potter, *Lincoln and His Party in the Secession Crisis* (cited above), H. J. Carman and R. H. Luthin, *Lincoln and the Patronage* (New York: Columbia University Press, 1943), and T. H. Williams, *Lincoln and the Radicals* (Madison: University of Wisconsin Press, 1941). Wood Gray, *The Hidden Civil War* (New York: Viking, 1942) deals with Copperheadism. W. B. Hesseltine, *Lincoln and the War Governors* (New York: Knopf, 1948) is valuable.

K. P. Williams, *Lincoln Finds a General: A Military History of the Civil War* (4 vols.; New York: Macmillan, 1949–56) and T. H. Williams, *Lincoln and His Generals* (New York: Knopf, 1952) are authoritative. On Fort Sumter see the lively *First Blood: The Story of Fort Sumter* (New York: Charles Scribner's Sons, 1957) by W. A. Swanberg. Jay Monaghan has written on the neglected western theater in *Civil War on the Western Border 1854–1865* (Boston: Little, Brown, 1955). Bruce Catton's volumes on the war are marked by literary distinction and sound scholarship: *Mr. Lincoln's Army* (Garden City, N.Y.: Doubleday, 1951), *Glory Road* (Garden City, N.Y.: Doubleday, 1952), *A Stillness at Appomattox* (Garden City, N.Y.: Doubleday, 1954), and *This Hallowed Ground* (Garden City, N.Y.: Doubleday, 1956). The most brilliant presentation of Southern leadership is D. S. Freeman, *R. E. Lee, A Biography* (4 vols.; New York: C. Scribner's Sons, 1934–35) and his *Lee's Lieutenants* (3 vols.; New York: C. Scribner's Sons, 1942–44). B. I. Wiley concerned himself with the rank and file of the South in *The Life of Johnny Reb* (New York: Bobbs-Merrill, 1943), and of the North in *The Life of Billy Yank* (Indianapolis, Ind.: Bobbs-Merrill, 1952). F. L. Owsley, *States Rights in the Confederacy* (Chicago: University of Chicago Press, 1925) explains much of the South's weakness. Benjamin Quarles, *The Negro in the Civil War* (Boston: Little, Brown, 1953) deals with a neglected aspect of the conflict. For foreign relations during the war see D. Jordan and E. J. Pratt, *Europe and the American Civil War* (Boston: Houghton Mifflin, 1931); also E. D. Adams, *Great Britain and the American Civil War* (2 vols.; London, 1925.

Allan Nevins, *The War for the Union: The Improvised War, 1861–1862* (New York: Charles Scribner's Sons, 1959), vol. 1, and subsequent volumes—the war not only saved the Union but in a real sense created it—Nevins concentrates on nonmilitary aspects of the war; revised edition of *Civil War and Reconstruction* (New York: Heath and Co., 1961), J. G. Randall and David Donald, benefits from the latest scholarship.

INDEX